SECOND EDITION
PUBLIC POLICY AND POLITICS IN AMERICA

JAMES E. ANDERSON   University of Houston

DAVID W. BRADY   Rice University

CHARLES S. BULLOCK III   University of Georgia

JOSEPH STEWART, JR.   West Virginia University

BROOKS/COLE PUBLISHING COMPANY
Monterey, California

The Brooks/Cole Series on Public Policy

Charles O. Jones, *University of Virginia*
General Editor

Brooks/Cole Publishing Company
A Division of Wadsworth, Inc.

Printed in the United States of America

10   9   8   7   6   5   4

Library of Congress Cataloging in Publication Data

Main entry under title:

Public policy and politics in America.

    2nd ed. of: Public policy and politics in America /
James E. Anderson. c1978.
    Includes bibliographical references and index.
    1. United States—Politics and government.   2. United
States—Economic policy.   3. United States—Social pol-
icy.   4. Policy sciences.   I. Anderson, James E.
II. Anderson, James E. Public policy and politics in
America.
JK271.P8   1984   361.6′1′0973   83-21066
ISBN 0-534-03094-7

Sponsoring Editor: Marquita Flemming
Production Editor: Fiorella Ljunggren
Manuscript Editor: Barbara Pitnof
Interior Design: Victoria A. Van Deventer
Cover Design: Debbie Wunsch
Art Coordinator: Rebecca A. Tait
Interior Illustration: John Foster
Photo Editor: Jude K. Blamer
Typesetting: Allservice Phototypesetting Company of Arizona, Phoenix
Printing and Binding: The Maple Press Co., York, Pennsylvania
(*Credits continue on p. 423*)

FOREWORD

Major changes have occurred since the publication of the first edition of *Public Policy and Politics in America* in 1978. Then a Democrat was in the White House, and there were sizeable Democratic majorities in both houses of Congress. The budget presented to Congress that year topped $500 billion for the first time in history. Now, as we approach another presidential election, a Republican is in the White House, the Senate has been in Republican hands for four years, and the Democrats retain a healthy margin in the House of Representatives. The budget, however, rolls merrily along, seemingly impervious to major political shifts. Outlays are projected to approach $850 billion for 1984 and $920 billion for 1985. We will easily have our first $1 trillion budget well before the end of the decade. Deficits now equal what budget outlays were a few short years ago.

The budget crisis focuses attention on public policy issues as never before. A new agenda has emerged—one that places domestic programs in competition with one another and with defense policies. The central issues on this agenda are economic stability, the status of social welfare programs, costs and effects of federal regulations, benefits available to the middle and upper classes, and the sufficiency and use of national resources. These are some of the topics treated in this second edition of *Public Policy and Politics in America*. James E. Anderson, David W. Brady, Charles S. Bullock III, and Joseph Stewart, Jr., have selected the major domestic issues of our time. They have distilled mountains of information so as to provide succinct and readable analyses of the problems, programs, and prospects concerning each issue. They provide a basis for understanding the present debate on the proper role for government in the social life of the nation—a debate that will dominate the 1984 presidential election. They inform us on what is being done now, how problems get to government in the first place, how programs develop support and momentum, and which alternatives are offered for resolving basic domestic issues. The analysis includes recent policy struggles between President Reagan and Congress.

What government does has come to be every bit as important as how it is organized to do it. Size of government alone makes it imperative that we study the details of how it got that way. The authors of this text provide the building blocks for this analysis. More than that, however, the consistency of their framework offers the basis for understanding what has to change. Thus, students will be better prepared to understand what is and to estimate what will be.

Charles O. Jones
University of Virginia

PREFACE

This book analyzes the making and content of American public policies. By dealing with the major contemporary policy concerns, we acquaint the reader with issues (such as energy usage and economic stabilization) that have attracted great attention from public decision makers in recent years and will undoubtedly continue to be debated, both among private citizens and in policymaking centers.

Throughout this volume we describe the status of current policy and indicate the roles played by individuals and groups in shaping the rules and regulations that the American people live by. Thus, readers will be introduced not only to the requirements of major laws, court decisions, and executive department rules but also to the controversies that had to be resolved before new policies were embarked upon.

The public policy focus helps to bring together many topics that are generally considered part of American politics. Discussions of policy formation require, of course, the presentation of materials showing what part has been played by each of the four major institutions of American government. Thus, descriptions of the development of current policy usually involve an account of what one or more presidents proposed, how Congress responded to the proposals, how the courts interpreted the legislation passed by Congress, and what actions were taken by the bureaucracy to implement the policy.

The policy approach used here also enables us to show the influence of such elements as public opinion, interest groups, political parties, the Constitution, and the socioeconomic system in the realm of policymaking. In the course of this book (although not in every chapter), we show how each of these elements has been important in shaping some component of public policy. For example, interest groups have played significant roles in determining the content of business, labor, and agricultural policies. Party differences have been important in the area of economic stabilization, where Democrats have been more willing to accept higher rates of inflation in order to reduce unemployment whereas Republicans have generally opted for the other side of the prices–employment tradeoff. The Constitution—or, more precisely, new interpretations of the Constitution—may be the stimulus for changes in policy direction. Perhaps one of the clearest examples of this is the Supreme Court ruling in *Brown* v. *Board of Education*, which reinterpreted the Constitution so as to make separate but equal educational systems illegal. Public opinion can also serve as an impetus for change. In the wake of Earth Day 1970 and interest in the environment, stringent new regulations were passed concerning air pollution. The Arab oil embargo and the energy crunch caused a significant change in public opinion, so that there is less interest in rigorous enforcement to achieve the objectives of the 1970 amendments to the Clean Air Act.

The Constitution, public opinion, and the socioeconomic system help structure the range of alternatives that are considered when policy direction is established. Thus, no serious consideration is being given to the idea that the major means of production should be nationalized. Although this alternative has been adopted elsewhere, it is not in keeping with our economic history and is contrary to public preferences.

While the different factors that have been significant in shaping the policy areas dealt with in this book are acknowledged and discussed, a common conceptual framework underlies the various chapters. The sequential approach, described in chapter 1, traces the development of policy from the formative stage, through inclusion on the policy agenda, adoption by a policymaking unit, and on to implementation. The final stage, evaluation, is also considered in sections that discuss the consequences of various programs.

There is no single correct way to view policy results. Whether one evaluates a particular program as wise or foolish, as beneficial or harmful, depends on the individual's values. We have tried, therefore, to leash our own preferences and values. In describing events leading up to and including policy implementation, we try to stick strictly to the facts. In the sections on evaluation and policy alternatives for the future, we present pros and cons but leave it up to the reader to decide whether a program has succeeded or which alternative is preferable.

Not only does our approach refrain from policy advocacy; it also does not preempt the views or the approach preferred by the instructor. The instructor can argue a particular line in assessing programs or advocating changes. Instructors can also fit the materials presented here into whatever analytic model they prefer.

Heaviest emphasis in most chapters is placed on the policy initiatives of the national government. The topics covered are ones in which the role of the national government has grown significantly during this century. Indeed, with the exception of some aspects of education, the policies considered here are those in which federal dollars provide most of the financing and federal rules and regulations provide most of the direction for what is or is not permissible. Although our emphasis is on federal programs, state and local governments are not wholly ignored. State involvement in implementing some types of programs, particularly environmental regulation and Aid to Families with Dependent Children, is noted. Less attention is devoted to the policies of local governments, although their role in education is discussed in chapter 7.

This book may fill the needs of instructors of at least two types of courses. Faculty members teaching an introductory American government course may find that the treatment of policies is an effective way to cover the material generally included in such courses. Presenting this material in the context of policy areas may make the subject more interesting to students. The volume is also appropriate for public policy courses. The instructor using the book in this context may want to augment it with paperback books that go into greater detail on topics of particular interest.

Substantial changes have been made in this edition of the book. We have added new chapters on civil rights and foreign policy. The chapter on social welfare policies in the first edition has been expanded to two chapters for this edition. One of these deals with social welfare policies for the poor; the other treats social programs that are especially beneficial to the middle class (for example, some health care and retirement programs). Material on the budgetary process has been incorporated in the chapter on economic stability policies. All of the chapters have been updated to take into account recent policy developments and the activities of the Reagan administration.

We would like to acknowledge the assistance of several persons who were especially helpful in preparing the second edition. These include Charles O. Jones, Charles S. Bullock II, Bruce I. Oppenheimer, and Richard J. Stoll. Joe Stewart wishes to acknowledge the assistance of the Charles E. Culpepper Foundation through the School of Social Sciences at Rice University. We are also grateful to the reviewers who examined the manuscript for this edition and offered valuable criticisms and suggestions. They are Steve Ballard of the University of Oklahoma at Norman, John W. Books of North Texas State University, Michael F. Digby of Georgia College, Larry Gerston of San Jose State University, Justin Green of Virginia Polytechnic Institute and State University, John E. Monzingo of North Dakota State University, Eric Moskowitz of the University of Illinois at Chicago Circle, and Neale J. Pearson of Texas Tech University. Finally, we would be remiss were we not to express our gratitude to Marquita Flemming and Fiorella Ljunggren of Brooks/Cole Publishing Company for their assistance and encouragement in this revision.

James E. Anderson
David W. Brady
Charles S. Bullock III
Joseph Stewart, Jr.

CONTENTS

ELEVEN   ## Agricultural Policy   341

TWELVE   ## Foreign Policy   371

EPILOGUE   ## Some Final Considerations   401

SECOND EDITION

PUBLIC POLICY AND POLITICS IN AMERICA

ONE

Introduction to Policy Study

People often think of public policy as something that happens only in Washington, D.C., or in other far-away places, and only to someone other than themselves. However, as the following cases illustrate, all of us are deeply affected by public policies in our daily lives.

For example, during the last few decades American civil rights policy regarding racial integration has been dramatically reversed by legislative and judicial action. As a consequence of this policy reversal, thousands of black Americans eat in restaurants, sleep in motels and hotels, and work in places where blacks had never been. Courts ordered busing plans to integrate schools, and neighborhoods previously all white became integrated because of laws prohibiting discrimination by realtors and owners. These changes in policy were accompanied by protests or demonstrations by both blacks and whites in the North and South. Riots in urban areas; busing and desegregation protests in several states; white backlash and black revolutionary action—all were claimed to be effects of America's "new" civil rights policies. It is almost impossible to estimate the impact that civil rights questions and the policy responses to them have had and will continue to have on the United States and its citizens.

Today most people would probably agree that the present rate of inflation in the United States is too high and that it should be reduced, perhaps through governmental action. No one likes to see the purchasing power of one's paycheck or pension eroded by rapidly rising prices; all but the richest or luckiest among us feel the pinch. There is, however, a lack of agreement on what policies, if any, should be used to reduce inflation. Is the present inflation caused by excess demand, administered wages and prices, or inflationary expectations? To what extent is it caused by public policies such as deficit spending or excessive regulation? Will the movement to pass a constitutional amendment for a balanced budget gain momentum? Should the Reagan administration use traditional fiscal and monetary policies or should it follow the precepts of supply-side economics? What part do balance of trade and gross national product play? Would a return to the gold standard help in controlling inflation? Will Reagan's administration be more successful than Carter's in combating inflation? The answer will be reflected in the consumer price index and our pocketbooks.

These are two fairly spectacular illustrations of the social impact of policymaking. However, public policies also determine more mundane events, such as whether our garbage is picked up and our mail delivered. These things do not just happen; rather, they are the results of the actions of public officials taken in response to demands upon them.

Our purpose in this book is to systematically examine some American public policies and the political processes that produce them. To facilitate effective communication of our analysis, we need to develop a precise concept, or definition, of public policy.

CONCEPT OF PUBLIC POLICY

The term *public policy* may be used quite broadly, as in "American economic policy," "Saudi Arabia's petroleum policy," or "Western Europe's agricultural policy"; or it may be used much more specifically, as in "the nuclear regulatory commission's policy toward nuclear energy as a power source," "the policy of the city of Chicago on pollution in Lake Michigan from Milwaukee, Wisconsin," or "the policy of the state of Texas on advertising on highway rights of way." Sections of textbooks devoted to defining *public policy* traditionally give three or four definitions, which are then shown to be inadequate. After showing the inadequacy of other definitions, the author's own definition is then put forward. Rather than use this approach, we will discuss the ideas or elements that an adequate definition of public policy should have and then present the definition to be used in this book.

If a definition of public policy is to indicate the essential characteristics of public policy, it must distinguish between what governments intend to do and what in fact they actually do. We cannot be content to say, for example, that the government's decision in 1964 to eliminate poverty in America fully represented public policy on the topic. Along these same lines, a useful definition must embody the idea that public policy is a course or pattern of activity and not simply a decision to act in some particular way; that is, public policy is a process and not merely a single decision in one place at a particular moment. Public policy may be viewed as a set of decisions directed toward the accomplishment of some goal. Although the goal of governmental actions is not always easy to discern, the assumption that public policy involves purposive governmental action is essential to the study of public policy. In sum, a useful definition of public policy will indicate that policy is a pattern of governmental activity on some topic or matter which has a purpose or goal.[1] Further, it will not equate decision making with policy or confuse the *stated* goal of action with what is *actually* done.

For example, concerning policy on educational facilities for black and white students, if one looks only at what the laws said prior to 1954, the policy would appear to be one of providing separate but equal facilities. However, if one inquires whether the separate facilities were really equal, one would find that the policy was in fact one of separate but unequal facilities, because neither the federal government nor the state governments enforced the requirement of equalness. Following the Supreme Court's 1954 and 1955 decisions in *Brown* v. *Board of Education,* if one views policy as a single decision (or a pair of decisions), one would have to conclude that the goal of integrated and thus equal facilities had actually been achieved. Moreover, with the enactment of the Civil Rights Act of 1964 the Congress joined the Supreme Court in deciding that public school integration should be public policy. Nevertheless, it was not until after 1969, when the federal government really began to exert pressure in support of integration, that public schools in the South were integrated in a meaningful way. Thus, it is important to note that public policy involves what is actually done in the way of governmental action to accomplish a goal. It is a purposive pattern of activity, not a single decision made at a given time by some person or group. Any definition of policy that neglects these matters will lead the reader astray in the search for policy. Obviously, public policy involves more than such formal policy statements as statutes, administrative rules, and judicial opinions.

In view of the above discussion, we offer the following basic definition of policy: "A purposive course of action followed by an actor or a set of actors in dealing with a problem or matter of concern."[2] This definition focuses on what is done, as distinct from what is intended, and it distinguishes policy from decisions. Public policies are developed by *governmental institutions* and officials through the political process (or politics). They are distinct from other kinds of policies because they result from the actions of the *legitimate* authorities in a political system. David Easton designates the authorities in a political system as the "elders, paramount chiefs, executives, legislators, judges, administrators, councilors, monarchs, and the like, [who] engage in the daily affairs of a political system."[3] Moreover, these people are "recognized by most members of the system as having responsibility for these matters, and take actions which are accepted as binding most of the time by most of the members so long as they act within the limits of their roles."[4]

A summary of the implications of this concept of public policy is in order. First of all, public policy is purposive, goal-oriented behavior rather than random or chance behavior. Public policies are not acts that just happen, even though not all of their consequences or effects are anticipated. Second, policy consists of *courses of action*—rather than separate, discrete decisions or actions—performed by government officials. Policy involves not only the decision to enact a law but also the subsequent acts regarding implementing, interpreting, and enforcing the law. Third, policy is what governments *do* in controlling inflation, cleaning up the environment, or redistributing income—not what they say they will do or what they intend to do. Food distribution policy, for instance, involves what is actually done to provide food to the hungry and needy. America's poor cannot eat the government's good intentions. It is nonsense to consider an intention a policy without regard for what subsequently follows. Fourth, public policy may be either negative or positive. Positive policy is involved when the government takes action to affect a particular problem; negative policy occurs when the government decides not to act in an area where government action is sought. Governments, in other words, can decide not to act, thus following a hands-off, or laissez faire, policy. Fifth, public policy is based on law and is authoritative. For example, those who evade taxes or disobey campaign finance laws do so at the risk of fines and jail sentences. Public policy thus has an implied threat of legitimate coercion, which is usually lacking in the policies of private organizations. Finally, public policies are often determined by the politics of public policy.

AN APPROACH TO POLICY STUDY

The study of public policy, or the actions of governments, can be approached in a number of ways. The theoretical approaches developed by political scientists to explain what governments do were not, in general, developed for the analysis of policy formation and administration. However, they can be converted—and have been—to that purpose with little difficulty. Major theoretical approaches to the study of public policy include (1) institutionalism, (2) elite theory, (3) group theory, (4) input-output models, and (5) systems theory. Each of these approaches focuses attention on aspects of politics that are more or less relevant to the study of public policy, depending upon what policy or policies are under discussion. Thus, in the study of civil rights policy, elite theory seems to best fit the data, whereas group theory provides the best analysis for the study of government regulation of atomic energy.

Here our focus is on the *policy process*—that is, the various activities by which public policy is actually formed. Since there is no one single process by which policy is formed, variations in the content of public policy produce variations in the manner of policymaking. Welfare policy, natural resource regulation, economic stability policy, and civil rights policy are distinguished by different processes. Policy in these areas is associated with specific governmental institutions, patterns of behavior, and political situations. Social Security as a part of tax policy is closely associated with the Ways and Means Committee of the House of Representatives, while the protection of consumers is closely associated with administrative agencies such as the Federal Trade Commission.

This does not mean that the environment of each policy area is unique in such a way that precludes generalizations about public policy. Rather, it means that there is no one "grand unified theory of public policy." We can make a useful start toward understanding American public policy by considering such matters as these: Who is involved in policy formation, and on what kinds of issues, under what conditions, and to what effect? Just how do policy problems develop?

In our conceptual framework the policy process involves six distinct stages of activity.[5] These categories are summarized in table 1–1.

Stages of the Policy Process

Problem formation.   A problem is, for our purposes, a situation that produces "a human need, deprivation, or dissatisfaction, self-identified or identified by others, for which relief is sought."[6] Pollution, inflation, crime, unemployment, and OPEC oil policy have become problems because they produce sufficient anxiety and dissatisfaction to cause people to seek relief. There are all kinds of needs and wants; only those that move people to action, and are articulated, become problems demanding policy solutions.

TABLE 1–1 The policy process

Policy terminology	1st stage problem formation	2nd stage policy agenda	3rd stage policy formulation	4th stage policy adoption	5th stage policy implementation	6th stage policy evaluation
Formal definition	Relief is sought from a situation that produces a human need, deprivation, or dissatisfaction	Problems, among many, that receive the government's serious attention	Development of pertinent and acceptable proposed courses of action for dealing with public problems	Development of support for a specific proposal such that the policy is legitimized or authorized	Application of the policy by the government's bureaucratic machinery to the problem	Attempt by the government to determine whether or not the policy has been effective
Common sense	Getting the government to see the problem	Getting the government to begin to act on the problem	The government's proposed solution to the problem	Getting the government to accept a particular solution to the problem	Applying the government's policy to the problem	Did the policy work?

Since our concern is with public problems, we need to know what makes a problem public. The most important thing that distinguishes public from private problems is the number of people involved. Thus, public problems have broad-ranging effects, including consequences for persons not directly involved (as in a labor-management dispute). Not all problems dealt with in government are public, since, for example, members of Congress often give private assistance to individual constituents (for example, helping someone to secure a welfare benefit). Such assistance may be important to the person involved, but it has little or no meaning for the broader public. However, the number of people involved does serve to distinguish most governmental or public problems from private problems. It is important to point out that whether a problem becomes public depends upon the number of people who perceive it as one that government should handle, which leads to the question of why some matters gain the attention of the government while others do not.

Policy agenda.   Of the thousands of needs and wants for which people seek governmental action, only a small number receive serious attention. The problems that receive serious attention from the policymakers compose the policy agenda. Why do some problems achieve agenda status while others do not? One obvious reason is that often the interests of an important group are affected adversely and the group seeks redress from the government. Depending upon the power, status, and number of people in the group, the government may be compelled to put the matter on the agenda—that is, give attention to it.

Political leadership is another important factor in agenda setting. For a variety of reasons—its usefulness in winning votes for election, wide citizen interest in the policy area, officials' concern for the public interest, and so on—leaders may take a problem to heart, publicize it, and propose solutions. The president of the United States is an important agenda setter: economic deregulation secured a place on the national agenda in the mid-1970s because of the interest President Ford displayed in it. President Reagan put income tax reduction on the agenda in 1981.

Crisis events, such as wars and depressions, are automatically agenda items. Less cataclysmic events, such as recessions and the Soviet satellite Sputnik, also may trigger agenda status for matters such as inflation and science research. Massive public protests, such as the 1968 Detroit race riots and peace demonstrations during the Vietnam War, are another vehicle for achieving agenda status. But the important point is that not every problem gets the attention of government—and it is crucial to an understanding of the policy process to know how and why certain problems do achieve agenda status.

Policy formulation and adoption.   Policy formulation involves the development of pertinent and acceptable proposed courses of action for dealing with public problems. Policy formulation does not necessarily result in the adoption of a law, order, or rule of some sort. In short, the fact that a problem is on the policy agenda does not mean that the government will act effectively to resolve it. Income tax reform has been on the policy agenda for several decades but little has been achieved.

The president and his advisers are now major sources of policy proposals in the national political system. If we expand our focus to include the various departments and agencies, then clearly most policy originates in the executive branch. Career and appointed administration officials formulate policy ranging from standards of inspection for nuclear power plants to major changes in American foreign policy. Presidential commissions, committees, and advisory groups are also sources of executive policy formulation.

Legislators and interest groups are probably the next most frequent sources of policy formulation. Sen. Edward Kennedy's (D.–Mass.) national health care package is a case of legislative involvement in policy formulation. Interest groups often formulate policy proposals and then have favorably inclined officials, both elected and appointed, formally propose the policy.

Successful policy formulations must deal with the question of selecting courses of action that can actually be adopted. That is, a chief component of policy proposals is formulating a policy that will be acceptable to the people who make policy decisions. Those formulating the policy will be influenced in what they propose and do by the need to win adoption of the policy. Certain provisions will be included and other provisions dropped, depending upon what builds support for the proposed policy.

The question of policy adoption is generally thought of as building majority support for a policy proposal in Congress. Thus, tax policy adoption usually includes getting the House Ways and Means Committee chair to support it, and then getting a majority vote in both the House and the Senate. However, policy adoption does not always entail the familiar pattern of executive proposals, congressional approval, and presidential signature. Certain of President Nixon's administrative rulings on tax policy benefited corporations, and these policies were not approved by Congress or reviewed by the courts; rather, in these cases adoption ended with the president. The point is that adoption strategies and thus policy formulation will differ depending on how many branches of government are involved in the adopting process.

Policy implementation.   Once the adoption stage of the policy process is over, the law, rule, or order that has been adopted can be called public policy. Nonetheless, the content and effect of public policy may be greatly changed during the implementation stage. Thus, the implementation or administrative stage of the policy process is quite important because without application the policy has no effect, and the application of policy proposals sometimes changes the nature of policy itself. Administrative agencies are the primary implementors of public policy; but other actors, such as Congress and the courts, may also be involved.

Congress affects implementation in a number of ways. In some cases Congress passes specific detailed legislation that severely limits the amount of discretion administrators have available to them. Congressional concern with the details of the food stamp program—who should receive benefits and how much—is a good example of how Congress influences implementation.

The courts' relationship to policy implementation is more direct than is the congressional relationship. In many instances the very meaning of a policy results from judicial interpretation of rules or statutes. Antitrust policy, for instance, has been substantially shaped by judicial interpretation and implementation of the Sherman Act. Bankruptcy, naturalization for aliens, and divorce proceedings are other examples of judicial administration of policy. However, the most important way in which courts affect implementation is through interpretation of statutes and administrative rules and regulations.

The major means of policy administration is, of course, the administrative agency. Agricultural policy is administered by various units in the Department of Agriculture while military policy is implemented by the Defense Department and its branches. Administrative agencies, which are numerous, often act in situations where they have a wide range of discretion in the elaboration of policy and its implementation. For a number of reasons, which will be covered in later chapters, Congress often delegates great authority to an agency, which in turn makes many policy decisions during the implementation process.

It is obvious that agencies, courts, and the Congress often can alter policy through its administration. A clear-cut distinction between policymaking and administration may be desirable, but it does not do justice to the realities of the American policy process. Throughout the book there will be examples of the administration of policy altering or changing policy. At this point it will suffice to say that implementation often affects policy content.

Policy evaluation. The last stage of the policy process is policy evaluation. At this stage those who have made and implemented policy, or those who are interested or affected, attempt to determine whether or not the policy has worked. Thus, evaluators are concerned with appraising the content of policy and its effects. Evaluation may in turn lead to additional policy formation, which starts the policy cycle over. In general there are two types of policy evaluation: (1) "seat-of-the-pants" or political evaluation and (2) systematic evaluation. Seat-of-the-pants evaluation is impressionistic in nature. Such judgments are based on fragmentary evidence and are often strongly ideological or biased. To the oil companies freezes on oil prices or windfall profit legislation are ineffective, nonproductive, and so on. In the same way, the former Office of Economic Opportunity could not have been expected to find that the war *it* waged on poverty was lost. In short, political evaluation cannot sort out personal desires and agency interests from what the policy really achieved.

On the other hand, systematic evaluation of policies and programs seeks to objectively measure the societal impact of policies and the extent to which stated objectives are met. Systematic evaluation focuses on the effects a policy has on the problem to which it is directed. Thus, it gives all concerned with the policy process some feeling for the impact of policy.

Advantages of the Sequential Approach

In sum, our approach to the study of public policy is to take a policy area, such as energy, and trace the process from the point where it became a problem through the point where energy policy can be evaluated. Often the policy process is viewed from an institutional perspective, in which, for example, the relationship between the Congress and public policy is explained. Instead, we will follow certain policy areas across institutions wherever they may lead. The sequential approach avoids assigning to the president the formulation function and assigning to the Congress the adoption function. Of course, the president often formulates and Congress often adopts, but not always. The point, however, is that our conceptual framework allows a needed flexibility in capturing the policy process.

This framework has a number of advantages in addition to its flexibility. First of all, policymaking often does chronologically follow the sequence of activities listed above, so that our approach generally coincides with the flow of action in the policy process. Furthermore, various forms of data (for example, legal, quantitative, and normative data) are compatible with the sequential approach. Again, the approach is dynamic rather than static. It emphasizes the relationships among political phenomena rather than simply listing factors or developing classification schemes. Finally, it lends itself to manageable comparisons between policy areas and across political boundaries.

CONTEXT OF THE POLICY PROCESS

The context within which the policy process takes place is crucial to an understanding of how certain policies prevail over others. History, in the form of past policies, is one important part of that context. Other elements are environmental factors and the structural characteristics of the American political system.

Historical Context

Policy changes always take place in a context provided by past policies in the area involved. Thus, for example, changes in consumer policy have taken place within the context of already established agencies, such as the Food and Drug Administration, and a general governmental attitude that regulation rather than market forces should be used to control certain products. Similarly, in most of the other policy areas covered in this book, the problem has been around for some time, and the agencies that deal with these problem areas are often well-established ones, such as the Environmental Protection Agency or the Department of Agriculture. Therefore, in each of the chapters that follow, we give some attention to the history of public policy in the area covered, since the history of public policy in a given situation is an important contextual limit on present policy.

Environmental Factors

One of the lessons of political systems theory is that policymaking cannot be adequately understood apart from the environment in which it occurs. From the environment come demands for policy action, support for the political system, and limitations or constraints upon what can be done by policymakers. Among the components of the environment are such geographical variables as population size, age distribution, ethnic composition, and spatial location; political culture and opinion; social structure, such as the class system; and the economic system. When foreign policy is at issue, other nations become an important part of the policy environment. In this section we consider several environmental factors: political culture, public opinion, the social system, and the economic system. Our concern is not to describe them but rather to give some indication of how they may affect policy formation.

Political culture.   An important factor shaping the behavior of individuals and groups in government decision making, as in other aspects of social life, is the culture of the particular society within which decision making occurs. While all persons are unique, they also have much in common. Those who live in a particular society share in the various common values and beliefs that constitute part of its culture. Culture is transmitted from one generation to another by a socialization process in which, by "thousands of specific experiences with specific persons (parents, friends, school teachers, political leaders, etc.) in specific situations," the individual learns the values, norms, and beliefs of the society.[7] Culture, then, is acquired by the individual, becomes a part of one's psychological makeup, and is manifested in one's behavior.

One segment of the general culture of a society can be designated as political culture. It consists of widely shared values and beliefs relating to the nature and exercise of political power and the purposes for which it is employed. Obviously, because of different patterns of development, environmental conditions, and historical factors, political culture will differ from one national society to another. Variations in public policy and policymaking among countries can be at least partially explained by their political cultures. For example, public medical care programs are more numerous and extensive in Western Europe because there has been greater public expectation and acceptance of such programs as a proper governmental activity. Conversely, in the United States public attitudes have been much stronger in support of mass public education, and these attitudes are reflected in our extensive public educational system.

Values are criteria or standards by which people evaluate the goodness or badness, the desirability or undesirability, of goals and actions. They serve as general motives and guides for behavior. Sociologist Robin Williams has described a number of "major value orientations" in American society, including individual freedom, equality, progress, and efficiency and practicality.[8] These values—and others such as democracy, individualism, humanitarianism, and material achievement and success—clearly have significance for public policymaking. Democracy is held, at a minimum, to require public participation in and control of government along with governmental responsiveness to recognized needs of the population. There is an adage to the effect that people have a right to be heard, officials a duty to hear. Such conditions contribute to the existence in the United States of what has been called a *participant* political culture.[9] The general approach of Americans to public problems has been practical, or pragmatic, concerned with developing solutions to present problems rather than systematic long-range planning or doctrinal purity. Thus, housing programs were established in the 1930s to encourage home ownership and stimulate the economy without much thought as to the effect they might have on urban development in the future. The same was true for the interstate highway system.

Beliefs are statements about what actually exists (or what we believe to exist), which are used to describe our environment. They are "pictures of reality," which we carry in our minds and which help determine our actions. Widely shared beliefs about the actual nature and operation of the economic system, for example, help shape the interests that groups try to protect and promote through governmental action. In the nineteenth century the belief that economy was governed by natural economic laws, and that a policy of laissez faire was therefore both wise and beneficent, certainly slowed the movement toward regulation. Antitrust policy is still handicapped by the belief that big business is always more efficient than small business, while the belief that government is less efficient than private enterprise has contributed to the minimal role of government enterprise in American society. On the other hand, the beliefs that government is subject to popular control and that many social and economic problems can be remedied by governmental action have contributed to expansion of government activity.

Widely shared social values, of course, do not remain constant. As they change, matters once viewed as beyond the power or ability of governments to control may come to be thought of as amenable to governmental action. The nineteenth-century beliefs that the business cycle is beyond governmental control (which continued to influence many, including Herbert Hoover, even in the face of the Great Depression of the 1930s) has given way to the belief that the government can act effectively to maintain economic stability. The latter belief greatly increases the likelihood of some kind of government regulation of economic forces. Indeed, an administration that does nothing to attempt to control inflation or rising unemployment, or that is unsuccessful in that respect, will be in severe political difficulty. President Carter learned this in 1980.

Within the "consensus" of belief that may exist on a given matter, such as the need for public education, Social Security, or action to maintain economic competition, there remains much room for disagreement. Although the widespread belief in the necessity and desirability of social security programs makes their abandonment unlikely, there is continuing controversy on such matters as eligibility requirements and amounts of benefits. Again, the belief that citizen access to the policymaking process is a necessity for democratic government is not accompanied by agreement on the arrangements required to provide access.

In sum, common values and beliefs help determine the demands made upon policymakers and act to inform, guide, and limit their behavior. As Karl Deutsch notes, political culture "is related to the *frequency* and *probability* of various kinds of behavior and not their rigid determination."[10] Also, widely shared values and beliefs serve as the basis for verbal formulations by which the actions of public officials can be explained or rationalized—as being, say, "democratic," "practical," or "in support of individualized freedom"—so as to win greater public acceptance for them.[11]

Public opinion.   Public opinion, as the concept is used here, designates expressions of public attitudes or beliefs about current political issues, such as whether the national government should prohibit discrimination in housing, provide support for the development of a supersonic aircraft, send or withdraw American troops in trouble spots in the world, or enact health care legislation. Political culture, which is more basic and fundamental than public opinion, underlies political opinion and molds it on particular issues. Thus, the political cultural notion that "a public office is a public trust" directs public disapproval toward officials who engage in chicanery in their public positions. Obviously opinion would differ were the use of public office for private gain widely accepted as proper in our society.

In examining the effect of public opinion on policymaking, we should distinguish between decisions that indicate the general direction of policy and the day-to-day, often routine, decisions relating to specific aspects of policy. Public opinion is not likely to be a significant factor in the second category. As V. O. Key has observed: "Many, if not most, policy decisions by legislatures and by other authorities exercising broad discretion are made under circumstances in which extremely small proportions of the general public have any awareness of the particular issue, much less any understanding of the consequences of the decision."[12] The legislator deciding how to vote on an obscure amendment to a statute will probably be unaffected in any direct sense by public opinion. He or she might try to anticipate public reaction but will have considerable room for the exercise of imagination.

A second useful distinction involves the time dimension within which policymaking occurs. In a crisis situation in which policymakers feel the need to act quickly on some problem, there will be less opportunity for public opinion to come to bear than when action extends over a longer period of time. Public opinion appears to have been less influential in the development of atomic energy policy in

1945–1946 and the Cuban missile crisis in 1961 than in the enactment of Social Security legislation in 1935 and air pollution control legislation in 1970.[13]

Generally, public opinion plays a part in mapping the broad boundaries and direction of public policy rather than the specific content of policies. Existing public attitudes make such actions as the nationalization of the steel industry, repeal of the Social Security Act, or abandonment of environmental protection laws unlikely. Conversely, officials may come to believe that public opinion demands some kind of policy action, as was the case with labor reform legislation in 1959, tax reform legislation in 1969, and tax reduction legislation in 1981. These were generalized rather than specific "demands," which left much of the specific content of policy to the discretion of Congress. In other instances public opinion may be "permissive" in nature—that is, acquiescing to but not requiring some action.

The social system.   American society is divided into a wide variety and large number of societal groups—social, ethnic, economic, political, and religious. Many of these groups serve as the basis for voluntary associations, labor unions, civil rights organizations, church associations, business associations, and recreational organizations, which, in turn, seek to influence governmental action on an intermittent or continual basis. When they do this they may be called pressure groups or, a bit more clinically, political interest groups.

In a pluralist society such as the United States, the existence of a multitude of organized groups serves to diffuse and moderate political power. The power of some groups is checked or offset by that of competing groups. Individuals may belong to several groups, which must compete for their loyalty and support. Nonetheless, power is quite unevenly dispersed in American society. Some segments of the population are much better organized, more active, and more effective in politics than are others. Many individuals and many interests are represented imperfectly, if at all, by the system of pressure groups. Schattschneider has remarked, "The flaw in the pluralist heaven is that the heavenly chorus sings with a strong upper-class accent."[14] It is not our intent to argue here the merits and demerits of pluralist or elitist theories of American society; we are simply using the term *pluralist* to indicate the existence of a large number of separate groups in American society. This is a matter of fact.

In the American political system, private (that is, nongovernmental) pressure groups are a major source of demands for public policy, being clearly more important in this respect than the political parties. Private groups who are dissatisfied with their situation or relationships with other groups commonly seek governmental redress for their grievances. Public policy formation, at least on most major issues, can be viewed as involving conflict and struggle among competing groups or alliances thereof. The policy analyst's task then becomes one of explaining why some groups win and others lose in particular instances, or, in other words, how politics shapes policy decisions.

The economic system.   A society's economic system is concerned with the production, distribution, and exchange of goods and services. Some economic systems, such as that of the Republic of Chad, are relatively simple; others, like that of the United States, are highly complex. One of the prime sources of conflict in modern societies is economic activity. Conflicts may develop between the interests of employers and employees, big business and small business, consumers and sellers, creditors and debtors, oil importers and domestic producers, railroads and motor carriers, the various users of the national forests, and so on. Those who are dissatisfied with their existing relationships with other private groups often seek governmental assistance to protect or advance their own interests. Usually it is the weaker or disadvantaged party in a private conflict that seeks governmental involvement in the dispute. The dominant group, which is able to achieve its goals satisfactorily by private action, has no incentive to bring government into the fray. To do so will expand the conflict and thereby change the nature and outcome of the conflict. As an economy develops and becomes more complex, economic groups become more numerous and interdependent, and opportunities for conflict and government involvement multiply. In the United States, legislation on economic matters currently makes up the major portion of the congressional policy agenda.

It is a truism that the level of a society's economic development imposes limits on the provision of public goods and services by government to the community. However, this fact is sometimes overlooked by persons who assume that the failure of government to act on some matters is caused by backwardness or unresponsiveness rather than limited resources. For example, one factor that clearly restricts what governments can spend for welfare programs is available economic resources. Even in the United States, which now has a trillion-dollar economy, government does not have sufficient resources to do everything that everyone wants done, and thus choices among alternatives must be made. Moreover, both economic resources and public problems are unequally distributed among the states and localities.

Those who possess economic power through the control of economic resources often thereby possess political power as well. This is perhaps most starkly revealed in communities where a single company is the dominant source of employment. What the company favors in governmental action is usually what gets done. A threat by company officials to move their plant if some disapproved action is taken is often sufficient to cause local officials to back off. More broadly, there are some who argue that government in the United States is dominated by those who own or manage large corporate enterprises and that public policy generally reflects their interests. From this perspective, the Populist, Progressive, and New Deal reform movements, which occurred between 1890 and 1940, represent efforts "by leading members of the business community to bring order, stability, and predictability to the chaos of the emerging industrial order, to incorporate labor into the business system through conservative unionism, and to prevent social revolution through the distribution of minimal relief benefits to the poor."[15] Although there is obviously much interaction and interrelationship between the political and economic systems in American society, the validity of such sweeping contentions and arguments is open to strong question. Nonetheless, such statements represent an important viewpoint that cannot be ignored. A challenging question to consider is: What should be the relationship between government and the economic system?

Institutional Context

The formal governmental institutions of the American political system significantly affect the formation, implementation, and substance of public policies. Institutions—patterns of regularized, habitual, or stable behavior that have developed with the passage of time—lend continuity and stability, and sometimes rigidity, to the processes of policymaking and administration. If one wants to comprehend these processes, one must pay attention to more than just the motives and interests of particular individuals and groups, movements in public opinion, or socioeconomic variables. One must also consider the institutional context within which such factors act or are acted upon. Heinz Eulau has stated, "Current behavior is necessarily circumscribed and directed by the past patterns we call institutions."[16] Thus, congressional norms supporting committee consideration of legislation and deference to committee recommendations help explain the importance of committees in legislative decision making. Again, the actions of independent regulatory commissions, such as the Federal Trade Commission, are circumscribed by procedural and jurisdictional constraints set by law.

Federalism.   In the American federal system governmental power is constitutionally divided between the national government and several state governments. The basic division can be briefly sketched. The Constitution delegates to the national government (that is, the Congress) such powers as those to regulate interstate and foreign commerce; to tax and spend for the general welfare; to establish post offices and post roads; to coin money and regulate its value; and to raise and support armies and navies. The national government is also given the power "to make all laws which shall be necessary and proper for carrying into execution the foregoing powers." Then, in the words of the Tenth Amendment, "The powers not delegated to the United States by the Constitution, nor prohibited by it to the States, are reserved to the States respectively, or to the people." Although the governmental powers reserved to the states are not specified by the Constitution, they can be grouped into four categories: (1) police power, or power to protect and promote the public health, safety, welfare, and morals; (2) power to tax and spend; (3) eminent domain, or power to take private property for public use upon payment of just compensation; and (4) proprietary power, or power to own and operate economic enterprises. Under the doctrine of national supremacy, the Constitution and congressional enactments in pursuance thereof take precedence over state constitutional provisions and laws when they come into conflict.

The *formal* constitutional division of power between the national and state governments reads much the same today as it did in 1787. The only amendment conferring substantial *positive* policymaking authority is the Sixteenth, which authorizes the national government to levy income taxes. However, much change has occurred in the *real* allocation of power. Within the framework of the rather vague and general language of the Constitution, and in response to changing political pressures and social and economic conditions, the role of the national government in our society and economy has greatly expanded since the latter decades of the nineteenth century. Today, for example, national economic regulatory activity is more important, if not more pervasive, than that of the states.

A number of factors have contributed to the expanded policy role of the national government. In the first place, government is often called upon to deal with problems that are beyond the ability and legal power of the several states. Illustrative are problems in such areas as inflation, unemployment, agricultural prices and surpluses, collective bargaining, consumer protection, industrial monopoly, and environmental pollution control. Generally speaking, to be effective governmental action must be as broad in scope as the problems with which it is concerned. The individual states, for example, certainly cannot deal effectively with rising inflation or unemployment. In the second place, in some cases uniform national action is needed to make policy effective. Laws relating to the grading of commodities, the labeling of products, and standards of quality for drugs are some examples. Moreover, national action is sometimes in order to make state policies effective. For example, the Connally "Hot Oil" Act of 1935, which prohibited the shipment of oil in interstate commerce when produced in violation of state law, was intended to support state regulation of petroleum production. Again, many federal grant-in-aid programs are designed to supplement and strengthen state programs, as in the area of health care. Finally, the failure of the states to act, or to act adequately in the view of some groups, has led to national action in such matters as child labor, natural resources conservation, meat and poultry inspection, mining and industrial safety, civil rights, and public education.

The primary constitutional bases for the expansion of national policy activity have been the powers to regulate interstate and foreign commerce and to tax and spend for the general welfare, which are delegated to the national government by Article I, Section 8, of the Constitution. In the nineteenth and early twentieth centuries, questions of whether the national government had constitutional power to act played an important, and sometimes determining, role in national policymaking. However, given the broad fashion in which these powers have been interpreted by the Supreme Court, Congress now essentially determines the extent of its own power under the Constitution. Nonetheless, despite the absence of formal constitutional limits, there are still some limitations on the exercise of national power. Political opposition, expedience, constitutional habit (for instance, the belief that some matters, such as professional licensing, still are properly dealt with by the states), or other factors may restrict its exercise.

Notwithstanding the vast expansion of national action in the economic and social welfare domains in the twentieth century, the states continue to have a substantial role. If, as some claim, all power is moving to Washington, then the march is being led by a rather slow drummer. The states continue to be the primary policymakers with regard to the rights of property ownership, the regulation of trades and professions, the provision of educational and welfare facilities, the construction and maintenance of highways, law enforcement, and, in the age of the "energy crisis," the regulation of domestic petroleum production. Many areas of activity—pollution control, banking, transportation, welfare—are shared by the national and state governments. Typically, when the national government enters a field in which the states are already involved, national action supplements rather than replaces state action. Indeed, it is difficult to find many governmental activities that do not involve both the national and state governments.

The objective of the Reagan administration's "new federalism" was to change this situation by separating clearly the roles of the national, state, and local governments. In 1981, fifty-seven categorical grant-in-aid programs were consolidated into nine new block grant programs that gave state governments more discretion in the use of funds. In 1982 the administration proposed that the national government should assume full responsibility for Medicaid while turning full responsibility for the aid to families with dependent children (AFDC) and food stamp programs over to the states. The administration also recommended a "turnback" arrangement under which forty-four other grant programs eventually would be given to the states. These proposals, which provided for a major restructuring of the federal system, quickly encountered strong criticism from persons who feared that the programs involved would be diminished or eliminated if left to the states.

Let us look at some of the ways in which federalism may affect the formation and substance of public policy. First, federalism affects the access of groups to government and, consequently, their opportunities to exert influence on the policy process. Some groups may have more influence at the national level, others at the state level. Those opposing the enactment of civil rights legislation often have done so in the name of "states' rights," arguing that the states have the primary responsibility here. They obviously have been motivated by a belief that civil rights policy will be more to their liking if made (or not made) in Richmond, Virginia, or Jackson, Mississippi, rather than Washington, D.C. In contrast, those favoring positive action on civil rights generally have been strong advocates of national action. Labor groups have found the national government more responsive to their interests than the states and thus have tended to favor national action on labor problems, while business groups opposing labor interests generally prefer state action, which is often more likely to be amenable to their viewpoint. In short, the position of most groups on whether policy should be made at the national or state level will be affected more by considerations of relative advantage than by philosophical or theoretical concern for states' rights or national power.

Second, in formulating national policy Congress is often quite sensitive to state and local interests, whether governmental or nongovernmental, and appears reluctant to infringe drastically upon state powers and functions. Writing on American federalism, an English scholar has remarked, "Congress is composed of a number of individuals who are, at one and the same time, national statesmen and local politicians, although perhaps some members rarely achieve the former status even temporarily."[17] When Congress established the unemployment compensation program in 1935, such factors as the nationwide consequences of unemployment, the poor financial and administrative condition of the states, and the powerful support from within the executive branch pointed toward a solely national program. Congress, however, was unwilling to bypass the states, and so a national-state cooperative program was established. In the mid-1960s the Johnson administration, with the support of organized labor, recommended "nationalization" of the program because of the low quality and benefits of many state programs. Such a move, however, was strongly opposed by state officials, and Congress refused to take action. The various state programs continue to vary considerably in eligibility requirements, and duration and amounts of payment.

Third, in the American federal system the states, acting in response to different interests or perceptions of problems, can adopt policies that contradict or are inconsistent with national policy. National efforts to maintain economic competition, for instance, have been hampered by state action in the form of highly permissive incorporation and tax laws, resale price maintenance legislation, and restrictive occupational licensing laws. (National policy in the antitrust area has not, of course, been a picture of consistency.) The efforts of the Federal Reserve Board to control the money supply for economic stabilization purposes have been impeded by the existence and actions of state-chartered banks beyond its control. Problems of this sort, which are unlikely to arise in a unitary system, complicate the policy process and reduce the effectiveness of some policies.

Fourth, the administration of national policies is often importantly affected by federalism. Certain programs, for example (most notably grant-in-aid programs in such fields as welfare, highway construction, agriculture extension, and public housing), are administered by state and local officials in accordance with national policy standards. Cooperation between the national and state agencies concerned with such programs is necessary if national policy is to be effective, and such cooperation may be forthcoming only at a "price." For instance, much latitude may be permitted the states or their local subdivisions in the administration of these programs. Moreover, national officials usually do not make rules, regulations, and program changes without consulting state or local officials. Also, political realities may permit the existence of practices that run counter to the purposes of a national program. Thus, the Elementary and Secondary Education Act provides funds to improve the educational facilities and opportunities for poor children. Local school districts, however, have sometimes used the funds available for more general purposes. Because state and local officials have traditionally dominated public education, and because they have strong political support in this regard, national officials in the Department of Education cannot readily impose directives that conflict with local priorities. They generally have refrained from so doing.

State and local officials and interests also attempt to influence national administrative structure, personnel selections, and policy in most if not all areas of national action. Thus, local livestock interests have a strong impact on the administration of national grazing control programs in the western states. City government officials continued to exert strong support for retention of the community action program initially set up under the Economic Opportunity Act of 1964. They were successful until 1981, when the Reagan administration acted to phase out the program. Much interaction has occurred among national and state officials concerning air and water pollution control. Although the impact of localism on national administration and policy cannot be attributed solely to the existence of "semi-independent" state and local governments, their existence certainly contributes to the political power and influence of local interests.

Separation of powers.   Besides the separation of state and national government powers and interests, a second basic structural feature of our governmental system is the allocation of governmental powers among separate legislative, executive, and judicial branches. Under the corollary principle of checks and balances, each branch is given some means to check, participate in, or interfere with the exercise of power by the other two branches. Thus, although primary power to legislate is vested in Congress, the president can veto legislation, and the Court can rule on its meaning and constitutionality. The system is well described as one of "separated institutions sharing powers."

This institutional arrangement increases the points of access through which groups and individuals can seek to exert influence on policy. A group that fails to realize its goals through congressional action may seek favorable executive or judicial action. If the congressional enactment of a law cannot be prevented, a presidential veto may be sought. If this fails, the law may be challenged in the courts. Although the likelihood of its being declared unconstitutional is not great, it may be interpreted in a way favorable to a group's interests or its impact may be delayed or modified. Even if a group fails here, it can still attempt to influence the agency entrusted with the administration of a law to act in a congenial manner. Indeed, some agencies have been alleged to be the "captives" of particular groups, as in the case of the Interstate Commerce Commission and the railroads, or the Federal Maritime Commission and the shipping companies.

Within Congress, power is further dispersed. Not only is power shared by the House of Representatives and the Senate but within each house it is scattered among a number of points—leaders and influential members, standing committees, and, often, subcommittees thereof. In short, power in Congress is diffused, not concentrated. Some consequences of this fact can be noted. First, it works to the advantage of those seeking to prevent the enactment of legislation. To succeed in this, a group may need to gain the support of only one center of congressional power, such as a committee or subcommittee or perhaps just its chairman. On the other hand, this dispersion of power works to the disadvantage of those supporting the enactment of legislation, because it multiplies the points at which the legislation can be blocked. Even if eventually passed by Congress, a bill may be substantially changed or watered down as a condition of its passage. A classic case of this involves the Employment Act of 1946, discussed in chapter 2. Second, the congressional committee system often contributes to more rational and comprehensive policymaking in such areas as agriculture, taxation, and labor relations, in that bills on these topics are dealt with by committees that have long experience in handling such legislation. The committee system, as is frequently said, provides Congress with policy specialists. A third consequence of power dispersal is that in some instances the committee system may impede effective policy formation. With regard to urban matters, jurisdiction over legislation is shared by several committees in each house, which undoubtedly contributes to the unsettled and fragmented nature of national policy toward urban problems.

The legislative and executive branches frequently come into conflict or disagree on policymaking, even when both branches are controlled by the same political party. Generally, Congress is more responsive to local interests than is the executive branch. The possibility of conflict is further increased by institutional loyalties, which have developed over time. Congress especially is often quite concerned to protect its prerogatives against executive "encroachment." If the two branches are controlled by different parties, as they were during much of the Eisenhower administration and all of the Nixon and Ford administrations, partisanship becomes another basis for interbranch conflict. This set of conditions has significant implications for policymaking, since most important policy decisions require approval or support by both president and Congress. Consequently, in order to avoid stalemate or inaction, bargaining and compromise will be necessary. For example, in 1968 the Democratic-controlled House refused to act on a tax increase to combat inflation requested by the Johnson administration until the administration had agreed to a reduction in spending. Again, the Reagan administration in 1981 bargained with conservative Democrats in the House to pick up votes needed to enact its economic program. Major policies are established only after consideration of a broad range of affected interests and viewpoints. The separation of powers may also contribute to generality in policy content and slowness in policy adoption.

The development of large-scale, complex bureaucracy adds another dimension to the separation of powers at the national level. Whether one wishes to designate the bureaucracy as a "fourth branch of government," as some have done, is a matter of choice. What is important is to recognize that *agencies often act independently* of the chief executive. Moreover, they frequently have been delegated broad discretionary powers by Congress to make rules and implement programs. Agencies then may become the focal points for intense policymaking controversies, as in the instances of the Environmental Protection Agency and pollution control standards or the Federal Energy Regulatory Commission and interstate rates for natural gas. In short, power to make policy is further dispersed by the existence of semiautonomous administrative agencies, which may adopt or pursue contradictory policies or redirect the thrust of congressional and presidential decisions.

The party system.   Together, federalism and the separation of powers have helped discourage the development of political parties able to act with unity at the national level. Federalism has helped to produce a decentralized party system in which the primary bases of strength are in state and local party organizations. The separation of powers has helped prevent the development of party cohesion within Congress or between president and Congress, even when both are controlled by the same party. This situation has resulted from constitutional provisions whereby the president, the House, and the Senate have different powers, different election constituencies, and staggered terms of office. The absence of strong, cohesive, policy-oriented parties has strengthened the position of special interest groups in the making of policy; undoubtedly, these groups have greater impact here than in countries with strong, unified parties. As David Truman has noted, "Because the legislator's tenure in office depends on no overarching party organization, he is accessible to whatever influences are outstanding in his local constituency almost regardless of more inclusive claims."[18] National issues are often viewed and acted on in the context of their meaning for state and local interests. The party system only partially bridges the gap created between president and Congress by the separation of powers. Much room is left for the play of interest groups in policymaking; whether one finds this desirable or undesirable, it does help shape the policy process.

LEVELS OF POLICYMAKING

Not all policymaking situations are cut from the same mold. Rather, they differ on the basis of such characteristics as the range of participants, the scope and urgency of the issue involved, the governmental location (Congress or a federal court, for example), and the visibility of the issue and situation. Thus, some instances of policymaking involve major issues that affect large numbers of people and attract a wide range of policymakers (an example is the 1978 energy legislation), whereas others involve relatively minor issues affecting only a few people and involving only a limited range of policymakers (such as the enactment of a special tax provision). In this section we will briefly sketch three levels of policymaking—namely, micropolitics, subsystem politics, and macropolitics.[19] Although it is not always easy to draw the line between macropolitics and subsystem politics—or, for that matter, subsystem politics and micropolitics—that does not lessen the utility of these concepts in the study of policy formation.

Micropolitics

Micropolitics customarily involves attempts by particular individuals, companies, or communities to secure favorable government action for their own benefit. Individuals may want a favorable ruling by an administrative agency or the enactment of a private immigration bill; companies may want a favorable ruling by the Internal Revenue Service or authorization for a motor carrier route from the Interstate Commerce Commission; a community may want a public works grant from the Economic Development Administration, or it may oppose the location of a public housing project within its boundaries. Usually only a few persons and officials are involved in these situations. However important the government action may be to those seeking it, it is of limited impact and interest to the general populace. Most citizens will be neither interested in it nor affected by it, nor, indeed, aware of it.

The enactment of special tax provisions by Congress is a good illustration of micropolitics. Every year or two Congress enacts amendments to the Internal Revenue Code that relieve a few persons or companies of paying taxes otherwise due. Sponsored by individual members of Congress, and frequently opposed (usually unsuccessfully) by the Treasury Department, these bills are commonly advocated as necessary to correct "inequities" in existing tax laws. These special tax bills attract little attention on their way through the legislative process and are "invisible" as far as the general public is concerned. They are, however, of much interest and value to their beneficiaries.

Subsystem Politics

Subsystem politics are usually focused on a particular policy or functional area, such as commercial air transportation, agricultural extension activity, river and harbor development, management of public grazing lands, or the granting of patents. Normally, a subsystem consists of a pattern of relationships among some congressional committees or subcommittees, an administrative agency or two, and the relevant pressure groups concerned with the policy area in question. For example, the subsystem focused on agricultural extension activity is composed of the Agricultural Extension Service, the House and Senate Agriculture Committees, and the American Farm Bureau Federation. Another subsystem, which is centered around the management of public grazing lands in the western states, is composed of the House Interior and Senate Energy and Natural Resources Committees, the relevant appropriations subcommittees, the Bureau of Land Management, and groups representing western livestock raisers. This subsystem has expanded in recent years to include some environmental groups.

Political subsystems develop and persist because not everyone is concerned with every area of public policy, nor could one be, given limitations of time, information, and interest. Thus, the official or citizen who is keenly interested in maritime shipping policy may have little or no interest in agricultural extension or public land policies, and consequently will leave them to persons with stronger interests. They, in turn, may largely ignore someone else's preferred policy area. Within the government particular congressional committees and administrative agencies are set up for each area of public policy. As the government's specialists in their field, they develop continuing relationships with one another and with the concerned pressure groups.

These subsystems often have considerable independence from other policymakers in the development and implementation of public policy in their field. Within the bounds of existing legislation, they largely shape governmental action in their area. Thus, for forty years a subsystem involving the House Agriculture Committee, the Sugar Division of the Department of Agriculture, and representatives of the sugar industry (especially producers) was primarily responsible for the formation of policy on sugar prices. In 1974 the authorizing legislation for sugar price supports came up for renewal, in a time of sharp inflation. Consumer groups and industrial users, concerned about high prices, opposed the renewal of the legislation and caused its defeat. This illustrates a second point: When new legislation or the renewal of legislation is needed, approval from the larger political system is needed. Often that approval will be forthcoming, as it was for decades in the case of sugar, since there is a tendency to defer to the experts in an area; however, some sort of disruptive event may expand interest in an area and cause defeat for a subsystem or, alternatively, induce control of it by the larger political system. It should be noted that the sugar program was reinstated in 1977. This time, however, sugar interests were willing and able to bargain with other interests to secure the votes needed to pass their legislation.

Macropolitics

Macropolitics involves the community as a whole and the leaders of government generally in the formation of public policy—whether to combat inflation, provide for an adequate supply of energy, or reform the welfare system. Participants in the macropolitical arena include the president, executive departments, congressional leaders, the communications media, group spokespersons, and others. Participation is thus quite wide. Our attention is often drawn to macropolitics because it tends to be quite visible, spectacular, and well reported. Broad public interests are likely to be considered most fully when policymaking occurs in the macropolitical arena.

Policy decisions made in the macropolitical arena may be considerably different from what they would be if made at the subsystem level. Energy policies in the era before the current energy crisis were usually made within subsystems and were especially reflective of producer interests. Now that energy and environmental policies have been moved into the macropolitical arena, the range of participants has expanded and producers no longer enjoy the dominance they once did.

Whereas limited modifications in existing policies will probably be handled by subsystems, proposals for major changes or developments in public policy will usually be dealt with at the macropolitical level. In 1981 such proposals included renewal of agricultural price support legislation, extension of the Clean Air Act, Social Security reform, income tax reform, and the deregulation of natural gas prices. Positive action occurred only on price supports tax reform and reduction. Major changes in public policies are not easy to achieve in most instances.

NOTES

1. For other definitions of public policy see Thomas R. Dye, *Understanding Public Policy,* 4th ed. (Englewood Cliffs, N.J.: Prentice-Hall, 1981); Charles O. Jones, *An Introduction to the Study of Public Policy,* 2nd ed. (North Scituate, Mass.: Duxbury, 1977); and Richard Rose, ed., *Policy Making in Great Britain* (New York: Macmillan, 1969), p. x.
2. James E. Anderson, *Public Policy-Making: Decisions and Their Implementation,* 2nd ed. (New York: Holt, Rinehart and Winston, 1979), p. 3.
3. David Easton, *A Systems Analysis of Political Life* (New York: Wiley, 1965), p. 212.
4. Ibid.
5. Some parts of this framework draw substantially on Anderson, *Public Policy-Making.*
6. Jones, *Introduction to the Study of Public Policy,* 1st ed. (North Scituate, Mass.: 1970), p. 17.
7. Robin M. Williams, Jr., *American Society,* 2nd ed. (New York: Knopf, 1960), pp. 22–25.
8. Ibid., chap. 11.
9. Gabriel A. Almond and Sidney Verba, *The Civic Culture* (Boston: Little, Brown, 1965), pp. 11–26.
10. Karl W. Deutsch, *Politics and Government* (Boston: Houghton Mifflin, 1970), p. 207.
11. More extensive treatments of American political culture can be found in Donald J. Levine, *The Political Culture of the United States* (Boston: Little, Brown, 1972); and Daniel J. Elazar, *American Federalism: A View from the States,* 2nd ed. (New York: Crowell, 1974).
12. V. O. Key, Jr., *Public Opinion and American Democracy* (New York: Knopf, 1961), p. 14. See also James J. Best, *Public Opinion: Micro and Macro* (Homewood, Ill.: Dorsey Press, 1973), chap. 7.
13. Cf. Charles O. Jones, "Speculative Argumentation in Federal Air Pollution Policy-Making," *Journal of Politics* 36 (May 1974): 438–464.
14. E. E. Schattschneider, *The Semi-Sovereign People* (New York: Holt, Rinehart and Winston, 1960), p. 35.
15. Edward S. Greenberg, *Serving the Few: Corporate Capitalism and the Bias of Government Policy* (New York: Wiley, 1974), p. 88.
16. Heinz Eulau, *The Behavioral Persuasion* (New York: Random House, 1963), p. 18.
17. M.J.C. Vile, *The Structure of American Federalism* (London: Oxford University Press, 1961), p. 90.
18. David B. Truman, *The Governmental Process* (New York: Knopf, 1951), p. 325.
19. See Emmette S. Redford, *Democracy in the Administrative State* (New York: Oxford University Press, 1969), chaps. 4–5; Anderson, *Public Policy-Making,* pp. 48–52; and Randall B. Ripley and Grace A. Franklin, *Congress, the Bureaucracy, and Public Policy,* rev. ed. (Homewood, Ill.: Dorsey Press, 1980), chap. 1.

SUGGESTED READINGS

Anderson, James E. *Public Policy-Making: Decisions and Their Implementation.* 3rd ed. New York: Holt, Rinehart and Winston, 1983.
Dye, Thomas R. *Understanding Public Policy.* 4th ed. Englewood Cliffs, N.J.: Prentice-Hall, 1981.
Jones, Charles O. *An Introduction to the Study of Public Policy.* 3rd ed. Monterey, Calif.: Brooks/Cole, 1984.

Lineberry, Robert L. *American Public Policy*. New York: Holt, Rinehart and Winston, 1977.

Ripley, Randall B., and Franklin, Grace A. *Congress, the Bureaucracy, and Public Policy*. Rev. ed. Homewood, Ill.: Dorsey Press, 1980.

Smith, T. Alexander. *The Comparative Policy Process*. Santa Barbara, Calif.: ABC-Clio, 1975.

Wade, Larry L. *The Elements of Public Policy*. Columbus, Ohio: Merrill, 1972.

TWO

Economic Stability
Policies

Government influence on economic activity takes two general forms: the promotion, regulation, and control of particular activities or industries through such means as antitrust policy, minimum wage laws, environmental pollution controls, and employment programs; and the control of overall levels of economic activity through macroeconomic policies. The second form of government control, which is the subject of this chapter, involves the use of fiscal policies (concerning taxation and expenditures) and monetary policies (concerning money supply, level of interest rates, and management of public debt) to promote economic stability.

What do we mean when we talk about economic *stability*? Some economists define it as the absence of fluctuations, of periods of "boom and bust," in the business cycle.[1] Other components that, singly or in combination, may be employed in defining economic stability include stability of prices, such as the government's consumer price index; stable growth in economic output; rising national income; full employment; and a favorable balance of payments (that is, a trade surplus) in the area of international trade. These possibilities, in turn, are subject to varying definitions (for instance, what conditions constitute "full employment"?) and emphases (some are more concerned about inflation, others about employment levels). Conflict over economic stability policy may arise in part because of disagreements about the meaning of economic stability and, consequently, the causes of instability that policy is intended to remedy. Although we recognize the shortcomings of general definitions, economic stability will be viewed here as involving a rising national income under conditions that provide full employment and general price stability.

Economic *instability* takes the forms primarily of inflation, recession, or depression. Inflation involves upward movement of the general price level for goods and services, with a consequent reduction in the purchasing power of the dollar (or some other unit of money). *Demand-pull inflation* occurs when aggregate demand increases more rapidly than the available supply of goods and services. This is the classic case of "too many dollars chasing too few goods," with the result that prices rise as buyers compete for the available supply. *Cost-push inflation*, in contrast, occurs when prices or wages rise faster than productivity or efficiency because large companies or unions have sufficient market power to "administer" the prices or wages they charge. That is, they are able to exercise discretion and push prices or wages above the levels that would be set by the interaction of supply and demand in the marketplace. Some of the inflation that occurred in the 1970s was attributed to cost-push factors. The rate of inflation in the American economy has varied from one period to another; however, the long-range trend in the twentieth century has been for prices to move upward. (See table 2–1.) As a consequence, "the belief is widely held that 'creeping inflation' (which sometimes breaks into a gallop) has become a permanent ingredient of American economic life."[2] A major task of government is to hold inflation within acceptable limits.

A *recession* occurs when aggregate demand for goods and services falls off, investment decreases, and unemployment increases. Prices may also decrease, al-

TABLE 2-1 Performance of the American economy for selected years (1929–1982)

Year	Labor force (000's)	Unemployment (percent)	Consumer price index (1967 = 100)
1929	49,180	3.2	51.3
1933	51,590	24.9	38.8
1939	55,230	17.2	41.6
1945	53,860	1.9	53.9
1950	62,208	5.3	72.1
1955	65,023	4.4	80.2
1960	69,628	5.5	88.7
1965	74,455	4.5	94.5
1966	75,770	3.8	97.2
1967	77,347	3.8	100.0
1968	78,737	3.6	104.2
1969	80,734	3.5	109.8
1970	82,771	4.9	116.3
1971	84,382	5.9	121.3
1972	87,034	5.6	125.3
1973	89,429	4.9	133.1
1974	91,949	5.6	147.7
1975	93,775	8.5	161.2
1976	96,158	7.7	170.5
1977	99,009	7.0	181.5
1978	102,251	6.0	195.4
1979	104,962	5.8	217.4
1980	106,940	7.1	246.8
1981	108,670	7.6	272.4
1982	110,204	9.7	289.1

SOURCE: *Economic Report of the President, 1983* (Washington, D.C.: U.S. Government Printing Office, 1983).

though in recent decades prices, in the phraseology of economists, have tended to become "sticky," moving upward more readily than downward. Before the 1930s, incidentally, economic declines were usually referred to as "panics." This language was then softened to "depression." The experience of the 1930s gave "depression" a bad connotation, with the result that "recession" has become the favored term.

Until the 1970s, those concerned with maintaining economic stability customarily confronted a situation involving either inflation or recession. In the last several years, however, *stagflation* (a high rate of unemployment combined with substantial inflation) and the persistence of high interest rates have compounded the task of policymakers. Action to reduce unemployment may contribute to more inflation and vice versa. There appears to be no easy solution to this problem.

DEVELOPMENT OF GOVERNMENT RESPONSIBILITY FOR ECONOMIC STABILITY

Only in recent decades, and especially since World War II, has the national government assumed explicit and active responsibility for the maintenance of economic stability. This is probably the most important development in public economic policy in the postwar period.

Traditionally it was thought that government could do little to control fluctuations in the business cycle (even though they appeared to be an intrinsic feature of a capitalistic, industrial economy). The operation of the business cycle was supposedly governed by "natural" economic laws that made governmental action unnecessary and undesirable. Depressions, for example, were thought to be self-correcting. Did not Say's Law, a main feature of classical economic theory, state that supply creates its own demand and that continued unemployment or underconsumption is thus impossible? The best thing government could do was to balance the budget, by cutting expenditures and increasing taxes, lest business conditions be worsened by a lack of public confidence in the government's financial condition.

The actions of public officials and public policy reflected such attitudes. In 1921 the national government sponsored a Conference on Unemployment to consider what could be done about the existing depressed economic conditions. President Harding expressed the position of the government in his welcoming remarks: "There has been vast unemployment before and there will be again. There will be depression and inflation just as surely as the tides ebb and flow. I would have little enthusiasm for any proposed remedy which seeks palliation or tonic from the Public Treasury."[3] No government action was forthcoming. In the early 1930s, the Hoover administration called for a large tax increase in order to balance the budget. Congressional opposition centered largely on the form the tax increase should take; its size and desirability were not really issues. The Revenue Act of 1932 took effect in June, near the bottom of the Great Depression.[4] According to what is now accepted theory, a tax increase is just the opposite of what the situation really called for.

Changing Attitudes

Acceptance of governmental responsibility for economic stabilization, and the alteration of public policy, resulted from the combined influence of several factors. The Great Depression, which began in 1929 and was the most severe the nation had ever known, and the persistence of massive unemployment throughout the 1930s contributed to the notion that depressions are not necessarily "self-correcting." Second, new tools of economic measurement and analysis were developed, such as national income accounting. Next, the economic impact of World War II brought a tremendous increase in government spending and the return of high employment and prosperity. Also of great importance were the ideas of the famed English economist John Maynard Keynes. In his *General Theory of Employment, Interest, and Money* (1936) and other writings, Keynes attacked the classical theory that a free-market capitalistic economy is a self-correcting mechanism that tends automatically to produce full employment and prosperity. He argued that deficit spending by government could add to the total demand for goods and services, offsetting a decrease in private demand and investment, and thus help to maintain a high level of demand, output, and employment. His ideas came to be widely accepted and constituted a rationale as well as a set of guidelines for the use of fiscal policy by government to maintain economic stability.

In 1933 Franklin D. Roosevelt came into office committed to fiscal orthodoxy, but was slowly converted to the Keynesian viewpoint. Consequently, his program for improving the economy—the New Deal—used deficit spending in an effort to stimulate the economy and bring recovery. This technique was often referred to as "pump priming" and "compensatory spending." The deficit-spending activities of the New Deal, though at the time they were regarded by many as highly radical, were really quite moderate (at least in retrospect). Indeed, it has been argued that the reason for the persistence of high unemployment throughout the 1930s was that the budget deficits incurred by the Roosevelt administration were insufficient to compensate for the large drop in private spending.[5]

What the deficits of the 1930s had failed to do was accomplished by the huge deficits (over $45 billion annually during 1943–1945) that resulted from the government's spending for the war effort of the 1940s. Stimulated by these large deficits, the economy expanded, production rose, and unemployment almost disappeared. This experience led to a general feeling that if large-scale government activity could expand production and maintain high employment in wartime it could also do so in peacetime. Before moving on, we might note that a charge frequently leveled against Roosevelt was that "he got us into war to get us out of the Depression." What brought economic recovery was not World War II but the *spending* for the war effort. Large deficits could have been run for other purposes, such as public works or health and welfare programs, but such actions were not politically acceptable. Large deficits became acceptable only when they were linked to national defense. The reader may draw his or her own conclusions concerning the nation's priorities.

Employment Act of 1946

The Employment Act of 1946 formally committed the national government to action to maintain economic stability. The act reflected the belief, based on late Depression and wartime experience, that government could act effectively, through the use of its fiscal, monetary, and other powers, to stabilize the economy. Also contributing to the passage of the act was the fear, supported by the predictions of many economists, that the changeover from a wartime to a peacetime economy would be accompanied by a depression.[6] This had happened following World War I.

Much conflict attended the movement of the Employment Act through Congress. Truman administration leaders and labor and liberal groups wanted to commit the government to the full use of fiscal policy to create conditions that would ensure "full employment" (although the legislation's sponsors were not able to agree on a precise definition for the phrase). In opposition, business and conservative groups argued that extensive use of fiscal policy to maintain "full employment" would lead to high labor costs, budget deficits, inflation, and excessive government intervention in the economy. Whether out of maliciousness or naiveté, some opponents interpreted the phrase to mean that people would have to work whether or not they wanted to. Conservatives emphasized the capacity of the private economy to provide jobs. Also, they placed more faith in the ability of monetary policy to stabilize the economy. Monetary policy had not been adequate to deal with the Depression, in the view of many persons, and it had consequently lost favor, especially with liberals and fiscal policy proponents.

The Employment Act in its final form was passed by overwhelming majorities in Congress, largely because anyone who voted against it might seem to be opposed to low unemployment as an important national goal. Since this was not a viable political position, conflict focused, rather, on particular provisions or language in the bill. This was especially the case in the more conservative House, and the final act was much altered from the bill originally introduced by Sen. James Murray (D.–Mont.). For example, the Murray Bill had specifically provided for the use of public works and favorable loans to maintain employment. This provision was replaced by a commitment to use "all practicable means." The goal of "full employment" in the Murray Bill became "maximum employment" in the final version. Such compromises were part of the cost of policy adoption. The Employment Act did not create a new fiscal policy. It did, however, represent a high level of agreement and a general course for public policy to follow. Also, as Stein suggests, "It helped put an end to a futile, tiresome, and largely meaningless debate between extremists and cleared the way for practical work to evolve a program [for stabilizing the economy]."[7]

The declaration of policy, in Section 2 of the act, states:

> It is the continuing policy and responsibility of the federal government to use all practicable means consistent with its needs and obligations and other essential considerations of national policy, with the assistance and cooperation of industry, agriculture, labor, and state and local governments, to coordinate and utilize all of its plans, functions, and resources for the purpose of creating and maintaining, in a manner calculated to foster and promote free competitive enterprise and the general welfare, conditions under which there will be afforded useful employment opportunities, including self-employment, for those able, willing, and seeking to work, and to promote maximum employment, production, and purchasing power.

The act established some governmental machinery to help carry out the declared policy. A Council of Economic Advisers, consisting of three professional economists (usually drawn from big business and the academic world) and a small supporting staff, was created. The council has the duties of collecting and analyzing data on current and future economic trends and preparing them for the president's use. It also advises on how existing and new programs can be used to effectuate the Employment Act's policy statement. The council has become a major actor in the development of economic stability policy proposals. For example, it played a large role in formulating, and persuading President Kennedy to present to Congress, the tax-cut proposals that became the Revenue Act of 1964.

The Employment Act also provides that the president shall deliver an economic report to Congress at the beginning of each session. In it the president analyzes current economic trends and conditions and presents "a program for carrying out the policy declared in Section 2, together with such recommendations for legislation as he may deem necessary or advisable." Within Congress the act established a Joint Economic Committee (as it is now called) to consider the president's economic report and to advise the two Houses concerning the president's recommendations. The committee also holds hearings and commissions studies on economic policy matters. In general, the council and the joint committee have helped focus attention on economic problems and have contributed to understanding of the overall operation of the economy and the relation of public policy thereto.

The adoption of the Employment Act "did not mean that the federal government proceeded, deliberately and continuously, to use the monetary and fiscal instruments at its disposal to maintain employment and control inflation."[8] Differences of opinion as to *when* government should act, *what form* government action should take, and what the particular *goals* of action should be have persisted both inside and outside the government. Within the scope of the act's policy statement, ample room remains for political conflict and struggle over the shape of policy in given situations. The struggle over "Reaganomics" is illustrative.

POLICY INSTRUMENTS

A variety of policy instruments are available to government decision makers in their efforts to maintain economic stability. These include monetary policy, fiscal policy, automatic stabilizers, wage-price guidelines, and direct price and wage controls. In this section they are treated primarily as means for dealing with inflationary and recessionary movements in the economy (that is, as instruments of counter-cyclical policy).

Monetary Policy

Most of the instruments of monetary policy are under the direction of the board of governors of the Federal Reserve System, or Federal Reserve Board (FRB), and involve control of the supply of money, credit, and interest rates. The FRB has primary responsibility for the implementation of monetary policy because of its authority over the credit-creating and lending activities of the nation's banks. Changes in the nation's money supply result largely from changes in the volume of commercial bank credit. The Federal Reserve System was established by Congress in 1913, primarily for the purpose of adjusting the money supply to the fluctuating needs of commerce and industry and reducing the vulnerability of the nation's banking system to financial panics. One analyst has pointed out, "Nothing in the [Federal Reserve] Act relates the monetary authority to the function of national economic stabilization; yet this is its prime task today."[9] Legislation passed in the 1930s did clarify somewhat the FRB's authority in this area.

The Federal Reserve System has been aptly described as "a pyramid having a private base, a mixed middle, and a public apex."[10] At the top is the board of governors, whose seven members are appointed by the president, with senatorial consent, for fourteen-year, overlapping terms. Members are removable by the president for cause, but none ever has been. In the middle of the pyramid is the Federal Open Market Committee, comprised of the seven Federal Reserve Board members and five of the twelve Federal Reserve Bank presidents. At the bottom of the pyramid are the twelve district Federal Reserve Banks. These are "bankers' banks," formally owned by the Federal Reserve System's member banks in each district. All national banks must belong to the system, and state banks may if they meet certain requirements. The banks belonging to the Federal Reserve System account for about 85 percent of the total commercial bank reserves of the country.

Instruments of monetary policy.   The primary instruments of monetary policy employed by the Federal Reserve System in maintaining economic stability are open-market operations, control of the discount rate, and the setting of reserve requirements for member banks. Formally, these three functions are allocated to the Federal Open Market Committee, the Federal Reserve Bank boards of directors, and the Federal Reserve Board, respectively. In actuality, the exercise of all three is controlled by the FRB, which, in turn, at least in recent years, has been dominated by its chairman. Thus, William M. Martin, Arthur F. Burns, and Paul Volcker, the current chairman, have been highly respected, influential policymakers. Since the real substance of monetary policy depends upon the manner in which the various policy instruments are used, the nature of monetary policy at a particular time will be affected by the economic philosophy and conception of the proper role of the FRB held by the board chairman. In recent years there has been considerable cooperation between the FRB and the administration in office. However, the chairman and the board have sometimes acted independently; in late 1965, for instance, the board's action to restrict the money supply was contrary to the wishes of the Johnson administration. When President Nixon in 1970 appointed Arthur F. Burns, then one of his counselors, to the chairmanship of the FRB, some people thought that the "problem" of board independence would be eliminated. Such did not prove to be the case. On the other hand, in 1981 the FRB acted in general accord with the Reagan administration's desire for restraint on the rate of growth of the money supply. A short examination of the FRB's monetary instruments (open-market operations, discount rates, and reserve requirements) follows.

Open-market operations are the principal instrument of monetary policy. The FRB can buy and sell government securities through the Federal Reserve Banks in the open market—that is, the place where securities are bought and sold (usually New York City). When the board buys securities, they are ultimately paid for through the creation of new deposits at the Federal Reserve Banks. These new deposits serve as bank reserves, which can be used by commercial banks as the basis for further loans, investments, and deposits (that is, an increase in the money supply). Conversely, if the FRB wants to reduce the supply of money, it sells government securities, collecting as payment an equivalent amount of banks' reserves and thus reducing the money supply.[11]

The discount rate is the rate of interest charged by the Federal Reserve Banks to member commercial banks desiring to borrow money to finance lending activities. Raising the discount rate is intended to discourage borrowing by banks for the purpose of making loans, and lowering the discount rate has the reverse effect. Changes in the discount rate are usually moderate and are seldom sufficient by themselves to encourage or discourage bank borrowing. But, whatever its other impact, changes in the discount rate are a means by which the FRB can signal its view of the economy to the banks. If they encounter higher discount rates, the banks know that the FRB believes credit is expanding too rapidly and that they can expect further action to contract credit if expansion continues.

The reserve requirement refers to the ratio of reserves to deposits (or loans) that must be maintained by member banks. If the reserve requirement is 20 percent, banks can make $5 in loans for each dollar of reserves they have. By raising or lowering reserve requirements, the FRB can decrease or increase the amount of money that banks have available for loans, thus contracting or expanding the supply of credit. Open-market operations, however, are regarded as a more flexible and effective means of influencing the money supply.

Two other instruments used by the FRB are moral suasion and selective credit controls. Moral suasion refers to the power of the board to influence bank actions by suggestion, exhortation, and informal agreements. Selective credit controls are exercised over particular groups of borrowers. The board now regulates margin requirements for stock purchases—the minimum down payment that must be made by purchasers of stock. If the margin requirement is 80 percent, only 20 percent of the purchase price of stock can be borrowed. During the Korean War the board was empowered to regulate down payments for real estate and consumers' durable goods, but this power ended in 1952.

Another monetary instrument that may be used for economic stabilization purposes is management of the national debt. The national debt was about 1.3 trillion dollars in 1983. The Department of the Treasury, which handles the debt, is constantly refinancing it, even in periods when there are neither budget surpluses nor deficits. Previously issued securities come due and are paid off; new securities are issued to replace them. The way in which the debt is financed will affect credit supply and interest rates. Long-term securities, for example, usually carry higher rates of interest than short-term securities. In either case, the rate of interest paid on government securities will affect private interest rates and, consequently, private borrowing and investment. Again, during periods of recession the supply of credit can be increased if debt financing takes the form of borrowing through sale of short-term securities to commercial banks. This will enlarge their reserves and thus increase their capacity to make loans.

Easy-money versus tight-money policies.   In periods of recession or high unemployment it is expected that the FRB may act to stimulate the economy by following an "easy-money" policy—expanding the supply of money and lowering interest rates to encourage investment and consumption and thereby adding to aggregate demand for goods and services. This policy was adopted by the board during the 1953–1954 and 1970–1971 recessions, when the decline in spending and employment became apparent. Conversely, during an inflationary period the FRB typically acts to contract the money supply and raise interest rates in order to reduce borrowing and, hence, aggregate demand. This is referred to as a tight-money policy and was followed in 1966 and 1969. Collectively, such short-term actions are characterized as "leaning against the wind."

Disadvantages of monetary policy.   Although the FRB occupies the central position in the area of monetary policy, its actions may not be well coordinated with those of agencies concerned with agricultural, housing, and veterans' loan programs, all of which affect the overall supply of credit. They were, after all, set up to serve particular interests and purposes other than economic stabilization. The FRB may also be limited in effectiveness by demands that it facilitate the Treasury Department's debt management task. During the late 1940s the board was prevented from following an anti-inflationary (tight-money) policy by its agreement to help maintain low interest rates on government securities. In 1951 an "accord" was negotiated between the FRB, which had considerable congressional support, and the Treasury, which had presidential support. The "accord" committed the board to maintain an "orderly" market for government securities but otherwise left it free to use monetary policy for countercyclical purposes. Differences of opinion still develop between the two agencies, however, on debt financing. Chairman Burns once stated that he would "go to war with the Treasury" if its desire for help in selling securities conflicted with the board's tighter-money policy.[12] All is not harmonious in the monetary arena.

Advantages of monetary policy.   The proponents of monetary policy argue that it is more useful than fiscal policy for stabilization purposes because it is more rapid and more flexible. Decisions on monetary policy are made by an administrative agency (the FRB), which can respond quickly to changes in level of economic activity. Fiscal policy, in contrast, is often slower in application because of the need for congressional action on taxation and expenditures.

The proponents of monetary policy also argue that it is a "good" policy because it is indirect and impersonal in its working. The government, in using monetary policy, does not directly control or prescribe individual actions and decisions but rather acts to change the environment in which individuals act and make economic decisions. Thus, the proponents conclude, monetary policy involves less government intervention in private economic activity than does fiscal policy.

Fiscal Policy

Fiscal policy involves the deliberate use of the national government's taxing and spending powers to influence the level of income, employment, and growth in the economy—that is, to maintain economic stability. When national spending was at low levels, the opportunity of the national government to influence the economy through fiscal policy was slight. With the national government's greatly increased spending in recent decades, this situation has changed. Cash payments by the national government now amount to over 20 percent of the gross national product (GNP), as shown in table 2-2. This volume of spending gives the national govern-

TABLE 2-2   Federal finances and gross national product for selected years, 1955-1984 (in billions of dollars)

Fiscal year	GNP	Budget outlays	Percent of GNP	National debt	Percent of GNP
1955	$ 381.0	$ 68.5	18.0%	$ 274.4	72.0%
1965	659.5	116.8	18.0	323.2	49.0
1966	724.1	130.9	18.6	329.5	45.0
1967	777.3	148.9	20.3	341.3	43.9
1968	831.3	153.0	21.4	369.8	44.5
1969	910.6	186.9	20.2	367.1	40.3
1970	968.8	192.8	20.2	382.6	39.5
1971	1,031.5	187.1	20.4	409.5	39.7
1972	1,128.8	207.3	20.4	437.3	38.7
1973	1,252.0	230.8	19.6	468.4	37.4
1974	1,379.4	263.2	19.4	486.2	35.3
1975	1,479.9	279.1	21.9	544.1	36.8
1976	1,640.1	298.1	22.2	631.9	38.5
1977	1,862.8	355.6	21.5	709.1	38.1
1978	2,091.3	399.6	21.4	780.4	37.3
1979	2,357.7	463.3	20.8	833.8	35.4
1980	2,573.9	517.1	22.4	914.3	35.5
1981	2,871.8	559.3	22.9	1,003.9	35.0
1982	3,033.0	617.8	24.0	1,147.0	37.8
1983[a]	3,193.7	597.5	25.2	1,383.7	43.3
1984[a]	3,488.7	659.7	24.3	1,606.3	46.0

SOURCE: Office of Management and Budget, *Federal Budget in Brief* (Washington, D.C.: Government Printing Office, 1984 and earlier years).

[a]Estimated figures for 1983-1984.

ment significant ability to affect the overall operation of the economy, depending upon how the money is obtained and expended. Indeed, national spending will have fiscal policy *effects* even if it is not used intentionally to promote economic stability.

Fiscal policy operates to affect the aggregate volume of spending (or demand) for goods and services in the economy. The basic assumption is that at some level of GNP the economy will operate at a "full" employment level. Gross national product is the market value of final goods and services produced by the economy during a year. It is the sum of private consumption spending, private investment spending, and government spending—or, in equation form, $C + I + G = GNP$. According to fiscal theory, if private spending for investment and consumption, plus "normal" government spending, is inadequate to produce full employment, government can act to increase aggregate demand, and hence production and employment, by spending more than it receives in taxes. Conversely, if an excess of aggregate demand for the available supply of goods and services is the cause of inflationary pressures, government can act to reduce aggregate demand by spending less than its tax take. The powerful instruments of fiscal policy are thus budget deficits and surpluses.

Discretionary fiscal policy involves changes by political decision makers (the president and Congress) in taxing and spending policies to achieve budget surpluses or deficits. These changes can be made in a number of ways: (1) Tax rates can be held constant and the volume of spending varied. (2) The volume of spending can be held constant, and taxes may be increased or decreased. (3) Some combination of changes in both tax rates and volume of spending can be used. Which alternative to use, if any, is often a cause of considerable political conflict.

To counter a recession or stimulate the economy, the government could increase spending, reduce taxes, or both, to inject more money into the economy. If tax rates were cut and spending maintained, more money would be left in the hands of consumers. Assuming "normal" consumer behavior, most of this money would be spent, thereby adding to aggregate demand. If tax rates were left alone and government spending increased, aggregate demand again would be increased. One may now ask: What difference does it make whether a budget deficit (or, in the opposite case, a budget surplus) is achieved by changing tax rates or spending volume, as long as it is achieved? The answer is, quite a bit. If a tax cut is used, private individuals determine how the additional funds will be spent, whereas additional government spending would necessarily be for governmentally determined purposes. Viewed from a "free-enterprise" perspective, the tax cut is more conservative, since it involves less direct intervention by government in the economy. It will thus probably be more acceptable to economic conservatives, although some still may oppose it because the resulting deficit would violate their concept of "sound" public finance. Those who see a need for more government spending for public works and facilities will be inclined to favor the increased spending route. Ideological differences may therefore lead to conflict here.

Budget surpluses and deficits come in two major varieties: those in the actual budget and those in the full-employment budget. Some actual budget surpluses and deficits are reported in table 2–3. The reader will note that deficits tend to be the rule and that in recent years their size has been increasing. The concept of the full-

**TABLE 2–3 National budget receipts
and outlays for selected years, 1901–1984
(in millions of dollars)**

Fiscal year	Receipts	Outlays	Surplus or deficit
1901	588	525	+63
1905	544	567	−23
1910	676	694	−18
1915	683	746	−63
1920	6,649	6,358	+291
1925	3,641	2,924	+717
1930	4,058	3,320	+738
1935	3,706	6,497	−2,791
1940	6,361	9,456	−3,095
1945	45,216	92,690	−47,474
1950	39,485	42,597	−3,112
1955	65,469	68,509	−3,041
1960	92,492	92,223	+269
1965	116,833	111,430	−1,596
1966	130,856	134,652	−3,796
1967	149,552	158,254	−8,702
1968	153,671	178,833	−25,161
1969	187,784	184,548	+3,236
1970	193,743	196,588	−2,845
1971	188,392	211,425	−23,033
1972	208,649	231,876	−23,227
1973	232,225	246,526	−14,301
1974	264,932	268,392	−3,604
1975	280,997	324,601	−43,604
1976	300,005	366,418	−66,413
1977	357,762	402,710	−44,948
1978	401,997	450,804	−48,801
1979	465,940	493,635	−27,694
1980	520,050	579,613	−59,563
1981	599,272	657,204	−57,932
1982	617,776	728,375	−110,609
1983[a]	597,494	805,202	−207,708
1984[a]	659,702	848,483	−188,781

SOURCE: Office of Management and Budget, *Federal Budget in Brief* (Washington, D.C.: Government Printing Office, 1983 and earlier years).

[a]Estimated figures for 1983–1984.

employment budget has been used by economists to gauge the impact of fiscal policy on the economy. According to some, this "budget" calculates what the budget surplus or deficit would be, given existing taxing and spending programs, if the economy were operating at a full-employment level (e.g., with 4 percent unemployment). It controls for the effect of economic conditions—inflation or recession—on budget levels. Thus, a budget deficit would not indicate an expansionary fiscal policy if it resulted from low tax receipts caused by a depressed economy rather than a deliberate decision to cut taxes. During the early 1960s the national budget was persistently in deficit; however, had the economy been operating at a full-employment level, there would have been substantial surpluses. Thus, according to the full-employment budget concept, fiscal policy in the early 1960s was actually deflationary, notwithstanding the deficits in the actual budget. The Nixon administration argued in 1971 that the budget deficit of $23 billion was not inflationary because, had the economy been operating at a full-employment level, there would have been a budget surplus.

At the urging of the Kennedy-Johnson administration, Congress passed the Revenue Act of 1964 to stimulate aggregate demand by cutting taxes, thereby creating more jobs and economic growth. The act provided for a $14 billion cut in personal and corporate income taxes over a two-year period. It was designed to overcome the deflationary or restrictive impact of the federal budget on the economy, as measured by the full-employment budget concept; and it did in fact contribute to increased employment and economic expansion. This was the first time that a tax cut had been deliberately used to stimulate the economy. Tax reductions had helped to mitigate recessions in 1948–1949 and 1953–1954; however, these actions were not planned for fiscal policy purposes (but simply to reduce taxes) and their timing was essentially accidental. From this, one can conclude that luck is sometimes a factor that can contribute to economic stabilization.

Since 1964 tax cuts have been used in a few more instances—1965, 1971, 1977, and 1981—to stimulate the economy. In 1968 a tax increase was imposed to restrain inflationary pressures, while in 1982 taxes were increased to reduce prospective budget deficits. Thus, taxes have become a basic instrument of national economic policy, designed to alter the course of economic activity or to keep it on a desired course from which it might otherwise depart.

Automatic Stabilizers

The fiscal and monetary instruments discussed thus far are discretionary in nature; that is, public officials must make decisions to utilize them in chosen ways in particular situations. Given the political pressures and the conflicting policy viewpoints that help shape the actions of officials, decisions to take action may be difficult to secure. In such situations, some automatic stabilizing devices—which have been built, unintentionally or intentionally, into the economy—may help stabilize the economy without positive action by government decision makers. The federal personal and corporate income taxes and Social Security taxes have automatic stabilizing effects. Without any changes in their rates, they bring in more revenue when national income rises and less revenue when national income falls. Moreover, as is well known, personal income tax rates are graduated (ranging from 14 to 50 percent) and consequently rise faster in proportion than does income; conversely, they fall faster than income when the latter declines. With respect to government spending, Social Security, unemployment compensation, and agricultural price supports have tended to increase in times of recession and to decrease in prosperous times. Thus, with growing unemployment in the 1970s, unemployment compensation payments increased from $3.4 billion in 1970 to $19 billion in 1976. This occurred automatically as unemployed workers drew the benefits to which they were entitled under the law. In general, for every dollar the GNP declines in a business cycle, there is about a 30-cent increase in the budget deficit, which helps limit the decline.[13]

The automatic stabilizers played an especially important role in controlling the recession of 1957–1958. While some argued for a vigorous program of government deficit spending to counteract the recession (by adding to aggregate demand), the Eisenhower administration was reluctant to engage in deficit spending and, further, was afraid that such spending would contribute to inflation. A balanced budget for fiscal year 1959 was sent to Congress. However, there was an actual deficit of $12.8 billion in the 1959 budget. This deficit resulted mostly from the automatic drop in tax revenues and the increase in Social Security and unemployment compensation payments caused by declining income. (Stepped-up spending under authorized programs and an expansionary monetary policy also helped alleviate the recession.) The automatic stabilizers clearly contributed to keeping the recession milder than had been predicted by many economists.

Economists generally agree that the automatic stabilizers by themselves are not adequate to maintain full stability. They mitigate but do not eliminate upward and downward fluctuations in the economy. Unemployment compensation benefits, for example, do not fully compensate for the loss of consumer spending caused by unemployment. Thus, automatic stabilizers, although helpful, are not widely regarded as a substitute for effective discretionary action controlling economic fluctuations.

Wage-Price Guidelines

In the early 1960s, to counteract inflation, the Kennedy administration developed a set of wage-price guidelines. These guidelines specified that wage increases should be held to the long-run growth in annual average labor productivity. The guideline for wage increases was eventually set at 3.2 percent. Under the guidelines prices could increase in industries where productivity did not increase as fast as wages; in industries where productivity increased faster than wages, prices should fall.

These guidelines were "informal" in that they had no explicit legal base or force. They were implemented through "jawboning" (verbal persuasion and exhortation) and informal pressures. Perhaps the most dramatic and successful use of jawboning occurred in 1962, when the Kennedy administration caused the major steel companies to rescind an announced price increase that the administration considered inflationary.[14] As inflationary pressures built up in the 1960s, the guideposts were increasingly challenged, and after 1967 the 3.2 percent wage increase guideline was abandoned. The Johnson administration, however, did continue jawboning—for instance, against price increases in the aluminum and copper industries. In 1969 the guidelines were officially jettisoned by the Nixon administration. President Nixon vigorously declared his opposition to such interference with the private economy. (He later instituted a system of direct controls.) President Jimmy Carter also initially indicated an intention to avoid such intervention; however, in 1978 he changed his mind and put into effect voluntary wage and price standards. They were quickly terminated by the Reagan administration when it took office.

Economists disagree about the role that the guidelines played in restraining inflation in the 1960s.[15] Gordon's conclusion, however, seems reasonable: "Perhaps it is not far from the truth to say that the guidelines helped create an environment favorable to wage restraint but that the chief factors at work were the absence of inflationary expectations and a continued high level of unemployment."[16] When these conditions changed, the guidelines began to falter.

Direct Controls

Direct controls over prices and wages differ from guidelines in that they are mandatory in nature. Various kinds of direct controls were imposed on the economy during World War I, World War II, and the Korean War to restrain inflation. Controls were most extensive during World War II, extending to wages, rents, and wholesale and retail prices. For older Americans, the Office of Price Administration (OPA) symbolizes price controls and rationing. The World War II controls were quite effective in holding down prices; the consumer price index rose only 5 points between April 1943 and June 1946, when most of the controls were eliminated. Between June and November 1946, the cost of living rose 14 points before leveling off.

Direct controls usually lack popularity with many groups—for instance, those whose activities are being restrained, political conservatives who dislike the exercise of governmental power involved, and economists who prefer free (i.e., unregulated) markets. In its 1968 report the Council of Economic Advisers expressed opposition to controls in these terms: "Mandatory controls on prices and wages . . . distort resource allocation; they require reliance either on necessarily clumsy and arbitrary rules or the inevitably imperfect decisions of Government officials; they offer countless temptations to evasions or violation; they require a vast administrative apparatus. All these reasons make them repugnant."[17]

The sweeping program of direct controls the Nixon administration imposed on the economy in August 1971 were unprecedented in peacetime. These controls, which were part of the administration's New Economic Policy, and which came as a surprise to most Americans, will be discussed in a later portion of this chapter.

LIMITATIONS OF POLICY INSTRUMENTS

It is generally agreed that the fiscal, monetary, and other instruments discussed in the preceding section can go far in controlling fluctuations in the business cycle and in encouraging economic growth. Nonetheless, they are not without shortcomings of an economic nature. These shortcomings must be taken into account by policymakers in devising solutions for instability problems, since they will affect the impact of policy actions.

A major problem in the formation and implementation of economic stability policy is the difficulty in accurately analyzing and predicting trends in the economy. If stability policy is to be most effective, it must be geared to what is going to happen rather than what has already happened. Although the tools of economic analysis have been greatly improved, economic analysis is still less than an exact science; precise indicators of the flow of national income are still lacking.[18] This is the result of such factors as the complexity of our economic system and shortcomings in statistical data. Some sectors or industries in the economy may be prospering while others are in stagnation or decline. Relationships between elements in the economy (for instance, between the levels of consumer income and spending) may be changing. Some economic data may be available only at quarterly, yearly, or longer intervals. Several months may elapse before analysts can say with certainty that a boom has ended or that recovery is under way. While proper choice and timing of stability policies are necessary if they are to be most effective, such decisions must be made on less than full information, thereby leaving room for error. Too, in the absence of clear-cut indicators of future trends in the economy, there is a tendency on the part of officials to "wait and see," to let matters work themselves out. Uncertainty may encourage inaction here as it often does elsewhere.

A related problem is limited knowledge of the full impact of particular policies. No one knows, for example, how much stabilizing action results from the operation of the automatic stabilizers; therefore, it is difficult to know when to use discretionary stability policies and to what extent. Nor can anyone say with certainty what effect a given fiscal or monetary action will have on, say, consumer spending. Problems of this sort are most important when concern is with moderate economic fluctuations. In the event of severe recession or inflation, there is less immediate need to be precise in the timing and degree of stabilizing action. What is most needed is strong counteraction until a measure of stability has been achieved.

Both fiscal and monetary policies are inadequate for dealing with cost-push inflation. In such a situation prices and wages rise because powerful corporations and unions push them upward. Fiscal and monetary policies, as we have seen, work by producing changes in aggregate demand. However, administered prices and wages may move upward even when supply exceeds demand, or when demand is falling, as was the case with steel prices in the 1950s. To control inflation caused by administered prices (called a price-wage spiral) might require fiscal and monetary actions so restrictive as to touch off a recessionary movement before they affect the groups pushing up prices or wages. In this case, fiscal and monetary policies are too blunt in their impact to be effective. Other courses of action are possible, such as the use of wage and price guidelines by the Kennedy and Johnson administrations in the 1960s. Moreover, the power of corporations to administer prices may reduce the effectiveness of fiscal policy in combating economic decline. During the Great Depression some of the impact of New Deal deficit spending, especially in the later 1930s, was siphoned off into price increases rather than additional employment.

Another dilemma confronted by policymakers is that of the inflation-unemployment trade-off (the Phillips Curve; see figure 2–1). Some economic studies have confirmed the existence of an inverse relationship between inflation and unemployment—so that, for instance, if fiscal and monetary policies are used to reduce unemployment to low levels, one of the costs is likely to be inflation. In Western European countries, where unemployment rates are lower than in the United States, rates of inflation have been higher. Conversely, policy can be used to hold down inflation, but with the consequence of more unemployment. This relationship between unemployment and inflation is shaped by such factors as the structure of the economy, the composition of the labor force, and public policies. It does not seem to be amenable to alteration by fiscal and monetary actions.[19] Policymakers, in their use of fiscal and monetary policy, have the task of trying to achieve an optimum (and politically acceptable) balance between inflation and unemployment. Although recent experience and research have cast doubt on whether the economy is bound to a single Phillips Curve, the concept is still useful as a statement of the basic unemployment-inflation dilemma.

It is useful to keep in mind that stability policy, like all economic policy, is concerned with influencing human behavior. Economic theory holds in effect that, other things being equal, people will be influenced in borrowing and investing by

FIGURE 2–1   Phillips Curve (hypothetical).

the rate of interest. Among the "other things," however, are the psychological attitudes and expectations of people (and these are not always "equal"). If these attitudes and expectations include a pessimistic evaluation of the economic future, they may well outweigh such material factors as lower interest rates in individual decision making. The restraining effect of the 1968 tax increase, sought by the Johnson administration to combat inflation, seems to have been limited by the fact that it was temporary in nature, while consumers geared their spending to long-range income expectations (which, of course, did not include higher taxes). The result was that consumers reduced savings and continued to spend almost as if taxes had not been increased. In economic activity, as elsewhere in social life, individuals do make a difference, and they do not always act in accordance with the precepts of economic theory.

The use of monetary policy to combat inflation may also have some undesired effects. Restrictions on credit may bear down more heavily on small businesses than on large businesses. When the FRB tightens credit, commercial banks are apt to restrict credit first to small businesses because of the larger amount of risk in such lending. Further, large corporations may meet their financial needs out of retained earnings and depreciation reserves; or they may have access to such sources of credit as insurance companies, pension trusts, and investment banks, which are beyond the reach of the FRB. Monetary policy, in its actual impact, is somewhat less impartial than its proponents sometimes contend. The housing construction industry seems to be especially sensitive to restrictions of the money supply.

The use of the budget for fiscal policy purposes is both restricted and made difficult because it is also used to finance the government's various foreign, military, and domestic policies and programs, and because the budgetary process is a highly political process. Nonetheless the budget is still a vital stabilization instrument. The process by which the national budget is formed and executed is sketched out in the following section.

THE BUDGETARY PROCESS

The federal budget is several things at once: a financial statement; an expression of the policy preferences of an administration; a means for executive control of the departments and agencies; and an instrument of fiscal policy. It is the last aspect of the budget, and the budgetary process, that is of special interest to us here.

Submitted to Congress by the president in January of each year, the budget runs for a single fiscal year, extending from October 1 of the year in which it is submitted through September 30 of the following year. It takes its name (e.g., fiscal year 1982) from the calendar year in which it ends. Although the budget is for a twelve-month period, the total budgetary process, from the time work begins on the budget in the executive branch until the end of the fiscal year, covers a span of approximately thirty months.

The national budgetary process can be divided into four stages.

1. *Preparation of the budget.* This is handled by the executive branch under the direction of the president and the Office of Management and Budget.
2. *Authorization of the budget.* This is the responsibility of Congress. The Constitution provides that "no money shall be drawn from the Treasury, except in consequence of appropriations made by law."
3. *Execution of the budget.* This stage involves the actual expenditure by the departments and agencies of appropriated funds.
4. *The audit.* This activity is performed by the General Accounting Office, which is an "arm" of Congress.

Preparation of the Budget

Work on the budget in the executive branch begins in March of the year preceding the time it is submitted to Congress. At this time the agencies begin reviewing their operations and program objectives and make projections as to their budgetary needs. By May or June the president, with the aid of the Office of Management and Budget (OMB), makes decisions on general budget policy (including fiscal policy considerations), major program issues, and budgetary planning targets. By the end of June tentative budget ceilings are formulated and transmitted to the agencies by the OMB, along with a call for agency budget estimates and a policy letter setting forth the president's decisions on governmentwide policies and assumptions. Guided by the tentative ceilings, the agencies develop their budget estimates, which are submitted to the OMB by the middle of September. From then until the end of November agency requests are reviewed by OMB examiners and hearings are held at which agency officials are called on to explain and justify their funding requests, which may exceed the tentative ceilings. On the basis of these reviews and hearings, recommendations are made to the director of the OMB, for approval or modification. Agencies dissatisfied with OMB decisions on their budget requests may appeal them to the president, although they are not very likely to be successful. Indeed, the president may make further reductions in requests when he reviews the OMB recommendations. In December and early January the budget is put in final shape, fiscal policy issues are given final consideration, the budget message is prepared, and, in the middle of January, the budget is officially submitted to Congress for its consideration. This time schedule, it should be noted, is approximate; it may vary somewhat from year to year. Nonetheless, budget preparation is both systematic and extensive in nature, and it also attempts to predict the future.

The ability of the president and top-level executive officials in making budget decisions is limited by the fact that around three-fourths of expenditures are "uncontrollable," at least in the short run, in that they represent continuing obligations and commitments. Illustrative are entitlement programs (such as Social Security,

Medicare, and veterans' pensions), grant-in-aid payments to the states, and interest on the national debt. A large proportion of the funds that are controllable fall in the area of national defense where major budget changes, especially in the form of reductions, are unlikely to occur. Because of factors such as these, even when the budget totals over $700 billion, the executive will have to struggle to secure reductions. (The Reagan administration's efforts to reduce the budget will be discussed in a later section.) The pressures for increased spending to improve programs, to meet new needs, are ever present. Budget reductions do not come easily as a consequence.

Congressional Authorization of the Budget

Until a few years ago, the budgetary process in Congress was rather chaotic and fragmented in nature. For purposes of legislative enactment the president's budget was broken up into a dozen or so separate appropriations. These were considered in committee and passed individually with little concern for the overall size and shape of the budget. Budget surpluses or deficits (much more likely) were "accidental figures" resulting from the sum of the various appropriations bills. Fiscal policy considerations had little direct impact on congressional budgetary action.

The Congressional Budget and Impoundment Control Act of 1974, which was brought about by such factors as dissatisfaction with the way Congress was handling the budget and conflict between Congress and the Nixon administration over the impoundment of appropriations, was intended to make substantial changes in the congressional budgetary process.[20] In the words of the statute:

> The Congress declares that it is essential: to assure effective Congressional control over the budgetary process; to provide for the Congressional determination each year of the appropriate level of federal revenues and expenditures; to provide a system of impoundment control; to establish national budget priorities; and to provide for the furnishing of information by the Executive Branch in a manner that will assist the Congress in discharging its duties.

To accomplish these goals the act did several things: First, budget committees were established in the House and the Senate. They have the task of determining priorities and overall limits on spending and needed increases or decreases in revenues. Second, a Congressional Budget Office was created to appraise the state of the economy and its impact on the budget, to improve the quality and availability of budgetary information, and to analyze the costs and effects of alternative government programs. Next, a timetable for congressional budget action was established (see table 2–4) and the fiscal year was changed from July 1 through June 30 to October 1 through September 30 to give Congress more time to work on the budget. Lastly, procedures to control presidential impoundment of funds were provided, which will be discussed in the next section.

TABLE 2-4   Budget authorization timetable

Action to be taken	Date
Current services budget submitted to Congress by president	November 10
President submits annual budget to Congress	Middle of January
Congressional committees make budget recommendations to budget committee	March 15
Budget committees report first budget resolution	April 15
Congress adopts first budget resolution	May 15
Congressional committees report all authorizing legislation	May 15
Congress begins floor action on all spending and tax bills	After first budget resolution
Congress completes action on all spending and tax bills	7 days after Labor Day
Congress adopts second budget resolution	September 15
Congress passes budget reconciliation bill	September 25
Fiscal year begins	October 1

We will focus here on a few aspects of congressional action on the budget under the new procedure. On the basis of such data as the current services budget (that is, what would be required to fund existing programs at their current levels for another year), the president's budget, and congressional committee recommendations of appropriations needs, the budget committees develop a budget resolution (to be adopted by May 15), which sets targets for appropriations for various functional areas (e.g., foreign aid, agriculture), total spending, and revenues. This is followed by action on the appropriations bills, which includes hearings, consideration, and mark-up by the appropriations committees. Congress is supposed to complete action on all appropriations and revenue bills on or before September 15, at which time a second budget resolution must be adopted to either affirm or revise the targets set in the first resolution. If the spending targets have been exceeded or estimated revenues are inadequate, a reconciliation bill may be needed. This reconciliation bill, put together by the budget committees, can revise appropriations, change expenditure authorizations, raise or lower revenue, or some combination of these in order to ensure conformity with the ceilings set in the second budget resolution. (The use of the reconciliation process in 1981 by the Reagan administration will be discussed in the section on the Reagan economic program.) The reconciliation bill should be adopted and sent to the president by September 25.

All action on the budget is intended to be completed by October 1, when the fiscal year begins. However, Congress has had difficulty in following the new budget timetable. Indeed, fiscal years 1981 and 1982 began before final action had been completed on *any* of the thirteen annual appropriations bills. Continuing resolutions were required to enable agencies to continue operating until their appropriations were enacted.

Budget decisions still tend to be incremental in nature. In other words, appropriations for most agencies and programs for a given year tend to differ only marginally, whether up or down, from those of previous years. Moreover, Congress is most concerned usually with how an agency's budget request in one year differs from the previous year. Drastic changes in agencies' budgets are not unknown, but they are not especially frequent.

Execution of the Budget

The departments and agencies are not free to begin spending as they see fit, within the framework of appropriations legislation, once congressional action is completed. If an agency's original budget differs from the appropriations legislation, the agency's budget must be revised accordingly. Then the agency must seek an apportionment from the OMB, which is an authorization to expend funds at a specified rate (for example, a certain percentage of the agency's appropriation may be spent during each quarter of the fiscal year). This is intended to prevent the agency from running out of funds before the end of the fiscal year. Also, the OMB may require agencies to set aside funds for contingencies or not to expend some funds when changes in needs or increased efficiency permit savings to be effected without detracting from the accomplishment of agency purposes.

The amount of discretion that agency officials have in the expenditure of funds is certainly affected by the nature of appropriations legislation. The more detailed it is, the less leeway agencies have. On the other hand, Congress sometimes provides agencies with "lump sum" or very broad appropriations, as a way of conferring discretionary powers. Clearly, effective management requires some administrative discretion in the expenditure of funds.

Much controversy has been generated by presidential impoundment of funds appropriated by Congress. Presidents have long claimed discretionary authority to prevent the spending of funds for purposes they disagree with on budgetary or policy grounds. In recent decades, for example, various presidents refused to spend funds for military programs of which they did not approve. Impoundment was usually done on a selective and limited basis; while Congress grumbled, major confrontations were usually avoided.

Following his reelection in 1972, however, President Nixon engaged in the extensive impoundment of funds for such programs as water pollution control, mass transit, food stamps, medical research, urban renewal, and highway construction. Various justifications were given including that impoundment was required to prevent the inflationary effects of "reckless" spending.

One outgrowth of the controversy generated by the administration's actions was the inclusion of controls on impoundment in the 1974 budget reform act. The act provides that a *deferral* of expenditures, in which the executive seeks to delay or defer the spending of funds until a future date when they will be needed, may be imposed unless either house of Congress passes a resolution of disapproval. Then the funds must be released at once. A *rescission* of spending, in contrast, cancels existing budget authority and thus eliminates the expenditure of funds for some purpose. Rescissions become effective only if, within forty-five days of the receipt of a presidential request, both houses of Congress pass a rescission bill. It is, in practice, not always easy to distinguish between rescissions and deferrals. The effect of the new impoundment procedures is to give Congress more formal control over budget execution.

President Ford sought to make considerable use of budget deferrals and rescissions in his efforts to hold down government spending. During fiscal years 1975 and 1976 the Ford administration proposed rescissions totaling over $7.5 billion; Congress enacted rescission bills amounting only to approximately $530 million. Most deferrals were not challenged as they involved routine financial transactions. However, thirty-eight deferrals totaling almost $10 billion were disapproved by resolutions. Congress was especially inclined to be negative when policy impoundments were involved—that is, when the president sought to cut appropriations that exceeded his budget requests.[21]

The Audit

Auditing of agency operations is intended to ensure that agencies, in the obligation and expenditure of funds, follow the provisions of authorization and expenditure legislation. The General Accounting Office (GAO) has the primary responsibility for auditing. The GAO is headed by the comptroller general, who is appointed by the president with the consent of the Senate for a fifteen-year term and can be removed from office only by a joint resolution of Congress. These appointment and removal provisions are intended to make the GAO independent of the executive branch.

In recent years the activities of the GAO have been expanded considerably beyond the traditional focus on the legality of expenditures. Now the GAO is also concerned with the efficiency of expenditures and with policy evaluation activities. The latter concerns often lead to the release of GAO reports with titles such as "The Voluntary Pay and Price Standards Have Had No Discernible Effect on Inflation."[22] (This 1980 report dealt with the voluntary standards developed and administered by the Council of Wage and Price Stability during the Carter administration.) The GAO also has responsibility for monitoring executive compliance with the rescission and deferral procedures under the 1974 budget reform legislation.

The Budget and Public Policy

The budget is, among other things, a statement of the various policies that will be pursued by the government during the budget year (and beyond, because funds obligated in one year may not be actually paid out until later years). The budget has been aptly described as "a compilation of public policy decisions of great complexity and of far-reaching effect upon the national welfare in terms of total outlay, in terms of the . . . allocation of that outlay among various activities, and in terms of the amount available for any one particular endeavor."[23] Of course, the importance of public policies cannot be measured solely by the number of dollars expended in their support. However, the nature, effectiveness, and impact of public policies do depend greatly upon the amount of funds appropriated to carry them into effect. This is so whether one is speaking about food stamps, public housing construction, antitrust enforcement, foreign aid, or synthetic fuel development.

The budget, as we have noted, is also an important instrument of fiscal policy. However, the budget is only partially subject to control by fiscal policymakers on the basis of their preferences. Most expenditures are based on past or continuing commitments and cannot easily be modified. Moreover, notions concerning what is necessary or desirable in domestic or defense policies may conflict with the needs of optimal fiscal policy. Expenditures, in short, cannot be simply raised or lowered for fiscal policy purposes. Beyond this, fiscal policy decisions involving expenditures do not go into effect at the time fiscal policy *decisions* are made. Fiscal policy decisions incorporated into the budget the president submits in January of one year may not be reflected in actual budget behavior until ten to twenty months later during the fiscal year for which it was proposed. By then the economic conditions with which the budget was to deal may have changed considerably. Add to such considerations the difficulties in accurately predicting future levels of expenditures, revenues, and GNP, and one can see that the budget is an imperfect albeit necessary instrument of fiscal policy.[24]

POLITICS AND STABILITY POLICY

The formation and implementation of stability policy are not merely "technical" tasks performed in a vacuum, although policy experts and economic analysis seem more influential here than in most areas of public policy. Rather, these tasks occur in a highly political environment populated with individuals and groups, official and private, having conflicting values, interests, and expectations concerning the content of policy. Conflict and struggle take place over what instruments to use, to what extent, and at what time. Is there a need for positive action? Should monetary or fiscal policy be stressed? Should a budget deficit be obtained by increasing spending or cutting taxes? What is an acceptable level of unemployment? Of inflation? These are only some of the questions that may arise. What is done in the way of policy action will be affected by the structure of the governmental system, political processes, and political behavior.

Differences in Policy Systems

To begin with, we should note that fiscal policy and monetary policy are developed within two very different and distinct policy systems. Fiscal policy formation involves the president, Congress, a variety of administrative agencies, pressure groups, the news media, and public opinion and typically occurs in the macropolitical arena. Monetary policy formation, in contrast, is handled primarily by the FRB, acting in response to whatever pressures or influences its members may feel. Whereas fiscal policy formation is characterized by partisan conflict and the need to mobilize legislative majorities, monetary policy formation, given the independence of the board, takes the form of administrative decision making, largely out of sight of the public. As a result, monetary policy actions typically can be taken much more quickly than fiscal policy actions. One consequence of the existence of these two policy systems is the possibility that their actions may come into conflict. Thus, the restraining effect of the Johnson administration's 1968 tax increase was partially offset by an FRB decision to expand the money supply because of its concern about an economic downturn. Usually, however, the FRB works in reasonably close harmony with the administration in office. It is "independent in but not of the government."

Fiscal Policy: President and Congress

In the fiscal policy arena, authority over taxation and expenditures is divided between the president and Congress. The traditional rivalry between the two branches is here intensified by the zealousness of Congress in protecting its financial powers against "executive encroachment," particularly when the executive is from a different party than the majority party in Congress. Even when the majority and the president are of the same party, Congress is eager to maintain its powers over taxation. For example, acting on the assumption that if taxation and expenditures were to be most effective for countercyclical purposes, considerable flexibility in their use would be required, a proposal was made by President Kennedy that the executive be given authority "to make temporary countercyclical adjustments in the first bracket rate of the personal income tax." This proposal, which would have required Congress to yield some of its authority over taxes, was never seriously considered by the Democratic-controlled Congress. While the development of the executive budget has strengthened the ability of the president to plan expenditures for stabilization purposes, the need to gain congressional approval remains.

One consequence of congressional consideration of fiscal policy proposals is delay. More than a year elapsed before the tax cut proposed by President Kennedy was enacted into law as the Revenue Act of 1964. And, as we will see, it took even longer for President Johnson to get a tax increase through Congress. Another consequence of congressional consideration is that the influence of group and sectional pressures, operating through Congress, will be fully felt on stability proposals. Here it should be noted that every fiscal policy proposal, because it involves taxes or expenditures, will have other policy implications. It will affect not only the overall operation of the economy but also the interests and welfare of particular groups and individuals. They can normally be counted upon to resist changes in taxes and expenditures that they consider adverse to their interests, and they are especially likely to consider increased taxes or reduced expenditures in that light.

In general, group pressures and existing policy commitments make it more difficult to counteract inflation than recession. Since Congress finds it easier to spend than to tax, fiscal policy has generally had an inflationary bias. Also, it is difficult to reduce expenditures because a large portion of the national budget outlay is "uncontrollable" (at least in the short run) in that it is required under existing law or represents contractual obligations of the government. On this basis, approximately 75 percent of national expenditures for fiscal years 1980 and 1981 fell in the uncontrollable category. Most "controllable" expenditures are in the area of national defense. But let's assume that taxes are going to be cut, which is usually popular. There remains the question of *whose* taxes are going to be reduced—those of individuals or businesses, or high-income or low-income groups? Or, if expenditures are to be increased, how will they be used? For military, welfare, or general government spending? For public works or for business expansion programs? In any case, various groups and interests will struggle for preferment. Congressional action on stability measures will reflect compromises and adjustments of the demands of conflicting group, sectional, and local interests as well as the requirements of stability policy as such.

Political Parties

The general policy orientations of the political parties also have importance for stability policy. Though it is often said that the parties differ little on policy matters, there is significant evidence to the contrary. In the stability policy area the parties manifest the following tendencies: Republicans are traditionally more concerned with preventing inflation and maintaining a "sound dollar." They favor the use of monetary policy over fiscal policy, customarily oppose the use of direct controls, and express much affection for a balanced budget. Democrats have been more concerned with combating recession and stagnation and with maintaining a high level of employment. They favor the use of fiscal policy over monetary policy, display more support for direct controls and less support for a balanced budget, want stronger presidential control of the FRB, and have more enthusiasm for job creation programs. These tendencies (they are not, it must be emphasized, hard and fast differences) have been manifested in the policy behavior of the various Republican and Democratic administrations during the past two decades.

Budget Concerns

Although balanced budgets have been a rarity in recent years, concern over balanced budgets has still acted as a restraint on fiscal policy. Despite the general acceptance of Keynesian economics and much experience with unbalanced budgets, there is still substantial public and official sentiment for a balanced budget. To conservatives in both political parties, budget deficits symbolize greater government intervention in the economy. Moreover, the belief persists that governments, like families, cannot wisely spend beyond their means. Both Presidents Kennedy and Johnson found it necessary to agree to hold down government spending in order to secure tax legislation from Congress. In the mid 1970s, in order to restrict the size of current budget deficits and move toward a future balanced budget, the Ford administration sought to hold government spending below the levels recommended by various experts as necessary to combat high unemployment; and President Carter stated that he expected to have the budget in balance by the end of his first term. Carter soon began to waver on this, however, and never achieved his goal.

The Politics of Advice

The formulation of fiscal policy proposals rests mainly with the executive branch and, ultimately, with the president. In formulating these proposals, presidents can and do draw upon various sources of advice: executive branch departments and agencies, presidential staff agencies, personal advisers in the White House, some members of Congress, and private economists from the academic and business realms. There exists, then, what can be called "politics of advice," because these sources may provide differing and conflicting recommendations and struggle to secure their acceptance by the chief executive. To illustrate, we can note that different agencies have "institutional biases," which shape their recommendations. Thus, the Treasury and Commerce Departments tend to be especially concerned with price stability and a favorable balance of payments; the Department of Labor favors low unemployment and economic growth; and the Office of Management and Budget wants to hold down spending. During the Kennedy and Johnson administrations the Council of Economic Advisers was most concerned about economic growth and unemployment and urged an activist fiscal policy. Under the Nixon and Ford administrations, however, the council became less activist and more concerned about inflation. In the last couple of decades the council has been very influential in fiscal policy formation, partly because of its competence, partly because it has no organizational loyalty except to the president, and partly because it has been willing to tailor its advice to the president's philosophy and policy goals.

Conflict among economists and economic advisers, however, is based on more than institutional biases or loyalties. There are also ideological and doctrinal differences that divide them. A familiar division is between liberals and conservatives. Liberals tend to be more supportive of government intervention, fiscal policy, and efforts to combat unemployment, whereas conservatives are more likely to advocate the use of monetary policy and anti-inflationary programs. A somewhat different division exists within the economic profession between the New Economists (who are essentially Keynesians) and the monetarists. The New Economists believe in the use of discretionary fiscal, and monetary, policies to stabilize the economy. The monetarists, who take their lead from Milton Friedman of the University of Chicago, contend that a moderate and steady growth in the money supply would solve the problems of both inflation and unemployment while providing the basis for economic expansion. They point to recent experience as proof that discretionary fiscal and monetary policies are not adequate to the task. Although these characterizations oversimplify the differences between liberals and conservatives, New Economists and monetarists, they reveal that economics is not an exact science and that the sort of advice one gets from an economist on stabilizing the economy will depend partly upon ideological and doctrinal perspectives.

STABILIZING THE ECONOMY: 1966–1981

In this section some of the efforts by five presidential administrations to stabilize the economy are surveyed. The discussion is intended to provide a better understanding of the problems involved in stabilizing the economy and the use of the policy instruments examined earlier.

The Johnson Administration and Tax Increase

The 1960s were characterized by sustained economic expansion, which began in 1961 and which, stimulated partly by the 1964 tax cut, continued until the end of the decade. By 1966 unemployment had declined below the 4 percent level widely accepted as a standard of full employment. As the Johnson administration became more deeply committed to the Vietnam War, military spending began to rise and to create inflationary pressures on the economy. The Council of Economic Advisers recommended a tax increase in 1966 to restrain the economy, but President Johnson was not then politically prepared to seek a tax increase from Congress. He later argued that he could not have secured action on such a recommendation. In a speech to the Business Council in late 1968 he stated: "We knew we needed action on taxes in 1966. Many of you in this room will remember what happened when, in the month of March 1966, I asked how much support you would give me. Not a hand went up. And I was told that I could get but four votes in the Tax Committee [House Ways and Means] of the Congress out of 25."[25]

By the summer of 1967, as spending on the Vietnam War continued to intensify inflationary pressures, the president felt compelled to seek a tax increase. In a special message sent to Congress on August 3, 1967, he requested a 10 percent surcharge on personal and corporate income taxes and the continuation of some excise taxes. Without a tax increase, the president stated, the large deficit projected in the national budget would touch off "ruinous inflation." Tax cut legislation of the sort recommended was not passed by Congress until June 1968, and then only after the president agreed to a reduction of $6 billion in government expenditures at the insistence of Rep. Wilbur Mills (D.-Ark.), chairman of the House Ways and Means Committee. This was the price exacted by Mills, who had the support of most of his committee, for reporting the legislation out of his committee and working for its enactment. Most observers agree that the tax increase came too late to have been most effective. Inflation was under way, and it was to plague the economy through the next decade.

Several factors seem to have contributed to the difficulties of the Johnson administration in getting the tax increase adopted. Tax increases are never popular with the public. This one was made more unpopular because many people viewed it as necessitated by the administration's Vietnam policy, which was coming under increasing criticism. Many members of Congress could not see why expenditure reductions would not work as well as a tax increase to restrain the economy. Moreover, within Congress there was not full acceptance of the use of fiscal policy to stabilize the economy. Finally, in 1966 and early in 1967 the "evils" that a tax increase was designed to combat "were forecasts rather than facts."[26] To be most effective, stability policy must be anticipatory; action must be taken *before* a recession or inflation gets under way. To many, however, the economy *seemed* to be operating satisfactorily; so why, they asked, should the government take action that might be unnecessary or even disruptive?

The Nixon Administration and Direct Controls

The Nixon administration came into office determined to quickly suppress the inflation it had inherited from the Johnson administration. Fiscal and monetary restraints were used; these brought the boom of the 1960s to an end and pushed the economy into a recession in late 1969. Even though unemployment rose to the 6 percent level in 1970, prices and wages continued to move upward. In 1971 the Nixon administration shifted to an expansionary fiscal policy to end the recession.

During 1970, as inflation continued, various critics urged the administration to adopt some kind of wage and price controls. Moreover, Congress adopted the Economic Stabilization Act of 1970, which gave the executive branch broad authority to impose price and wage controls to combat inflation. The act was stoutly opposed by the Nixon administration, which contended that it neither wanted nor would use the authority provided. The legislation was passed primarily at the behest of liberal Democrats, who could thus take credit for wanting to do something about inflation and at the same time embarrass the administration.

During the spring and summer of 1971 Nixon administration officials steadily denied any intention to use price and wage controls. Inflation persisted, however, as conventional policy instruments seemed inadequate to bring it under control. On August 15 the president surprised most of the nation with his announcement of his New Economic Policy, which included a ninety-day price-wage freeze. This set off a three-year adventure with direct controls (or what some call an "incomes policy"), the various phases of which will be outlined here.[27]

In Phase I (August 15, 1971, through November 13, 1971), all prices (except for raw agricultural commodities), wages, and rents were frozen. As one would expect, prices and wages rose very little during this time.

In Phase II (November 14, 1971, through January 10, 1973), the freeze was replaced with mandatory price and wage controls, which were administered by a complex administrative structure including a pay board and a price commission. General guidelines were set: 5.5 percent per year for wage increases and 2.5 percent for price increases. (Profit rates were not subject to control.) Large corporations and unions were subject to more stringent controls than smaller ones, and had to obtain prior approval for price and wage increases. Although the effectiveness or impact of the controls are a matter of controversy, the controls did restrain inflation, especially as measured by the upward movement of the consumer price index. The administration's economic policies, including the controls, also contributed to Nixon's landslide reelection in November 1972.

In Phase III (January 13, 1973, through June 13, 1973), which began a few days after the inauguration of his second term, President Nixon unexpectedly ended most mandatory price and wage controls (excepted were three "troublesome" areas: food prices, health costs, and the construction industry). For most of the economy a system of voluntary guidelines was established. These were backed up by the threat that the government would intervene to roll back price or wage increases considered inflationary. There was considerable talk by administration officials concerning the "club in the closet," which would be used to "clobber" offenders, but little clobbering was done. The lifting of controls unleashed inflationary forces; and prices, especially for food, spiraled upward. Many members of Congress and many economists attacked the administration for abandoning controls, while conservatives generally expressed approval.

Why were mandatory controls abandoned in favor of voluntary controls when the former seemed to be working? A reasonable explanation is offered by Robert Lanzillotti and colleagues:

> In retrospect, political considerations appear to have played a more significant role than did pure economic considerations in both the institution of the freeze and the dismantling of the wage-price controls program. Over time, the apparent success of Phase II increasingly became a source of economic embarrassment to administration officials, who had been driven to adopt direct controls out of political pressures but who opposed this approach on ideological grounds as well as from a severe conviction that such measures are inherently counterproductive in efficient economic processes. . . . From an inside perspective . . . it appeared that [with] the presidential elections out of the way, it remained only to prepare a quiet grave for the controls apparatus.[28]

During Phase IV (June 14, 1973, to April 30, 1974), inflation continued to plague the economy. In response to congressional and other pressures for action, on June 13 the president announced a sixty-day freeze on prices. New mandatory controls were developed for prices and wages during the freeze period, and their administration was assigned to the Cost of Living Council, which had been set up during Phase III to replace the Pay Board and the Price Commission. These controls went into effect on August 15. The administration had little enthusiasm for the new controls, however, and in the fall an industry-by-industry decontrol process was started. In the spring of 1974 all controls were ended, except for those on oil prices, which had soared because of the actions of the OPEC cartel (see chapter 3).

In his last months in office, President Nixon returned to action based on his "old-time religion" beliefs and emphasized the need for tight money and budgetary restraint to offset inflation. Along with much of the public, he was disillusioned with direct controls.

The Ford Administration and Stagflation

At the time Gerald Ford became president, in August 1974, prices were rising at an annual rate of nearly 12 percent. One of his early actions as chief executive was to call a "summit conference" on inflation to consider what could be done. Most of the economists at the conference, which met in late September, concluded that inflation was the prime problem, even though the economy appeared to be facing a recession. In October President Ford called for a tax increase as part of his anti-inflationary program. Spending cuts were also contemplated to reduce the budget deficit. The economy, however, descended into a recession, and by May 1975 unemployment rose to the 9.2 percent level. Inflation continued even though, according to standard economy theory, high unemployment and inflation should not occur together. (The term *stagflation* has been used to describe this condition.) As a consequence of the high unemployment, the administration shifted gears, and in January 1975 the president requested a tax cut to stimulate the economy. Congress responded with a $22.8 billion tax reduction in March.

Confronted with the problem of having to deal simultaneously with high rates of inflation and unemployment, the Ford administration subsequently chose to deal most strongly with inflation while moving more slowly to reduce unemployment. Thus, in early 1976 President Ford called for another tax reduction plus action to hold down government spending. This was a part of his "steady-as-you-go policy," intended to produce moderate economic expansion without touching off inflationary expectations. Under this policy substantial unemployment was expected to continue for several years.[29] Public employment legislation to create jobs, which is popular in Democratic circles, was strongly resisted by the president, who preferred to rely on the private sector to produce economic growth. On the whole, the economic stability policy preferences of the Ford administration were about what one would expect from a rather conservative Republican regime. The Ford policies did have some of the intended effect. By January 1977, the inflation rate had temporarily declined to 5 percent while the unemployment rate stood at 7.8 percent.

The Carter Administration's Dilemma

Since his election the previous November, there had been speculation about Carter's specific proposals for dealing with the economic situation. When Carter's administration took office on January 20, 1977, members of Congress, mayors, governors, and business and labor spokesmen all provided the new president with varying and conflicting recommendations on how to stimulate the economy. A basic difference of viewpoint was between the spenders (governors, mayors, union officials, etc.) and the tax cutters (businessmen, many economists, etc.). One commentator described Carter's dilemma in these terms: "So Carter has faced a classic problem of trying to reconcile conflicting goals: to reduce unemployment rapidly without triggering a new burst of inflation; to preserve his flexibility to finance new programs without plunging the budget into massive, perpetual deficits; and to satisfy spending demands from members of Congress, mayors, unions, and governors without irrevocably committing scarce future resources."[30]

Late in January the Carter administration proposed a $31.3 billion package of economic stimulants to cover a two-year period.[31] For fiscal year 1977 the package included $13.8 billion in tax cuts and rebates ($50 per person on a "one-shot" basis) and $1.7 billion in spending for public works, public service jobs, and job training. The tax rebate was intended to give a quick boost to the economy by stimulating consumer spending.

Although the administration's stimulus package, and especially the tax rebate proposal, encountered considerable criticism, it was passed by the House in March; and by the middle of April it was ready for consideration on the Senate floor. Some alterations had been made by the House, but the administration's package was essentially intact. Then, on April 14, in a surprising move, the president announced that he was abandoning the proposed $50 tax rebate, the business tax credit for hiring new employees, and the increase in the investment tax credit. Both economic and political factors contributed to this reversal in policy. In the early months of 1977 unemployment had declined, retail sales had expanded, industrial production had risen, and a threat of increased inflation had appeared. The abandoned proposals thus seemed unnecessary because the economy was expanding and because they might fuel inflation. Business and banking interests had opposed the rebate proposal as inflationary and now applauded its withdrawal; however, they still wanted the increase in the investment tax credit. In the Senate the Carter proposal faced substantial opposition, partly on its merits and partly because the president's proposed elimination of many water projects from the federal budget had offended many senators. Given his view of the lessened need for the rebate, the president apparently was not willing to expend the political capital required to win Senate approval. The president continued to support the remaining portions of his stimulus package as necessary to "guarantee us durable growth." Carter's economic package cleared Congress in May and was signed into law, although Congress did retain the tax credit for hiring new employees. (As mentioned earlier, policies intended to help create jobs are usually popular among the Democrats in Congress.)

The Carter administration continued to be concerned with reducing unemployment more than combating inflation for the remainder of 1977 and most of 1978. A tax cut proposed in early 1978 to stimulate the economy was subsequently scaled back and delayed in order to reduce the size of the budget deficit and counter growing concern about inflation. By the latter part of 1978, however, it had become clear that inflation was the dominant economic issue. To deal with inflation the Carter administration now instituted voluntary wage and price guidelines, to be implemented by the Council on Wage and Price Stability, in October 1978. This action was followed in January 1979 by the submission of a budget to Congress that was described as "lean and austere." Monetary policy was also tightened, and, in 1979, some credit controls were imposed in further efforts to hold down inflationary pressures. None of this worked very well, and the inflation rate continued to move upward to double-digit levels.

In 1980 the administration manifested some more indecision when it first submitted the annual budget (for fiscal year 1981) to Congress calling for a $15.8 billion deficit (proposed receipts and outlays were $600 billion and $615.8 billion, respectively). Criticism of this budget from Congress and the business and financial community led the administration, in unprecedented fashion, to withdraw the budget and announce that it would work with Congress to balance the budget. The forthcoming presidential primaries and general election were also undoubtedly on the minds of administration officials. A few weeks later the president resubmitted the budget. This time, because of reductions in expenditures and proposed tax increases, a surplus of $16.5 billion was projected for fiscal year 1981. Action in Congress, however, fell considerably short of Carter's proposals. This, coupled with higher than expected levels of spending because of inflation, a short but sharp recession, and other factors, resulted in a budget deficit of over $50 billion at the end of fiscal year 1981. By then Carter was no longer in office, having been defeated in his bid for reelection by Ronald Reagan. Dissatisfaction with the state of the economy was a major factor in his rejection by the voters.

The ambivalence and problems of the Carter administration illustrate two characteristics inherent in economic policymaking: the uncertainty that underlies the development of economic stability policies and, second, the blending of politics and economics in policy formation and adoption.

Reaganomics

The economic program proposed by the Reagan administration soon after taking office in January 1981 represented a significant departure from and rejection of the economic policies that had been followed in the post–World War II era. The Reagan program consisted of four interrelated parts:

1. *Tax cuts*. Marginal personal income tax rates (those people pay on additional dollars of income) were to be reduced by 30 percent over a three-year period and depreciation write-offs were to be accelerated for new business investments in buildings, equipment, and vehicles. The administration intended to propose other tax changes at a later time.

2. *Expenditure reductions*. The president proposed reductions of $48.6 billion in the 1982 fiscal year budget, which had been presented by the Carter administration. These were to be focused on domestic programs; at the same time Reagan proposed substantial increases in national defense spending. Budget reductions were to be even larger in subsequent fiscal years, with a balanced budget being projected for fiscal year 1984. A budget deficit of $45 billion was initially estimated for fiscal year 1982. (It later turned out to be $110 billion.)

3. *Regulatory reform.* Excessive government regulation of business was viewed by the administration as a cause of lessened growth and productivity in the economy. Hence, through the increased use of cost-benefit analysis and other means, the amount of regulation was to be reduced.

4. *Monetary policy.* The growth in the money supply was to be held at a slow and steady rate by the Federal Reserve Board in order to bring down the rate of inflation. The administration believed that this would also have the effect of lowering "inflationary expectations."

The Reagan program reflected several strands of thought: a conservative view of the appropriate role of government in economy and society; a monetarist economic policy; and "supply-side economics." Because of its novelty (it came into prominence only in the late 1970s) and its importance as part of the rationale for the Reagan program, some discussion of supply-side economics is in order.[32]

In contrast to Keynesian economics, which emphasizes the use of fiscal policy to influence aggregate demand and thereby stabilize the economy, supply-side economics stresses the need for fiscal policy to take account of the impact of tax rates on the incentives of people to work, save, and invest. If tax rates are too high (and it was contended by supply-siders that they had been for many years), these incentives would be reduced and a fall-off in productivity and economic growth would result. In such circumstances properly constructed tax cuts would not only increase incentives to work, save, and invest, they would increase productivity and economic growth and, in the view of some of the more enthusiastic supply-siders, reduce inflationary pressures in the economy. Most supply-siders did not worry about budget deficits as productive of inflation, since they believed that inflation was a monetary phenomenon and could be effectively dealt with by holding down growth in the money supply. More orthodox conservatives and Republicans, it should be noted, still worried about the effects of budget deficits, and they were not without influence in the Reagan administration.

Once the Reagan program was announced, speculation quickly arose as to how successful the president would be in securing its enactment by Congress. As it turned out, he was very successful. Before turning to the tax and budget cut actions, a few words are in order concerning the monetary and regulatory aspects of the program. The FRB, which had begun to restrain the growth of the money supply during the latter part of the Carter administration, continued on this course during 1981–1982, with the general approval of Reagan administration officials. Reduction of regulatory activity was achieved by budget reductions for regulatory agencies, the requirement that cost-benefit analyses be made of major proposed regulations, and the appointment of many persons to regulatory agency positions who were not inclined to be vigorous regulators. Now we turn to the tax and expenditure cuts.

The expenditure reduction effort was spearheaded by David A. Stockman, Reagan's appointee as director of the OMB. Rather than try to reduce expenditures in piecemeal fashion through the regular appropriations process, Stockman and some Republican congressional leaders decided to use the congressional budget reconciliation process. Reconciliation was used for the first time in 1980 to trim the fiscal year 1981 budget deficit by $8.2 billion through spending cuts and revenue increases. The first budget resolution, adopted in May, directed twenty-nine House and Senate legislative committees to save some $36 billion by making changes (mostly reductions) in many existing domestic program authorizations. The actions of these committees were then combined in a single comprehensive reconciliation bill. Passed handily by the Senate, which, as a consequence of the 1980 elections, was controlled by the Republicans for the first time in a quarter of a century, the reconciliation bill encountered more difficulty in the Democratic-controlled House. Here too, however, the administration prevailed with the support of conservative Democrats and, in early August, the president signed into law the Omnibus Reconciliation Act reducing spending by an estimated $35.1 billion. Although President Reagan did not secure all the expenditure reductions he wanted, he nonetheless had obtained a major change in the direction of government and a slowdown in the rate of increase in federal spending.[33]

The tax cut proposal submitted to Congress by the Reagan administration took the form of a "lean" bill limited largely to reductions in marginal personal income tax rates and accelerated depreciation allowances for business investments. Once this bill was passed the administration indicated that a second bill would be introduced that would make a variety of lesser changes or reforms in the tax laws. By this strategy the administration hoped to prevent its major supply-side bill from being slowed in enactment by controversy generated by a multitude of particular provisions. The administration did not have much difficulty in getting essentially what it wanted from the Senate. In the House, however, a major controversy developed. The Democrats on the Ways and Means Committee proposed an alternative to the administration bill that, while similar in many respects, provided greater tax relief to persons earning less than $50,000 annually. To attract votes of southern conservatives the Democrats included in their bill provisions providing substantial tax breaks for the oil industry. The White House and the Republicans responded with a revised tax package that included larger tax breaks for the oil producers, annual indexation of tax rates to offset inflation, increased charitable deductions, and a variety of other provisions designed to win votes. "Both Republicans and Democrats admitted their bills were more products of a political bidding war than blueprints for sound economic policy."[34] A couple of days before the crucial House vote on the tax measure, President Reagan went on nationwide television to appeal for public support. The administration bill was approved by a 238 to 195 vote when forty-eight Democrats gave their support to the president.

As enacted, the tax reduction legislation, officially titled the Economic Recovery Act, represented another major political victory for the Reagan administration. The act provided for a 25 percent reduction in individual income tax rates to be phased in over 33 months beginning October 1, 1981. Beginning in 1985 tax rates were to be annually adjusted to offset the effects of inflation. Other provisions provided greater depreciation of business investments in new assets, reduced taxes on oil production, exempted most estates from taxation, reduced the top marginal rate on investment or "unearned" income from 70 to 50 percent (this also had the effect of lowering the tax rate on capital gains from 28 to 20 percent), and increased deductions for charitable contributions. It was estimated that taxes would be lowered by about $38 billion for individuals and businesses in fiscal year 1982; for the three-year period 1982–1984 the total reduction was put at $280 billion.

Why was the Reagan administration able to achieve these major tax and expenditure changes? Several factors seem important. One was President Reagan's popularity and political skill. When he needed to bargain or make adjustments to win votes he did not hesitate to do so. Another was unity within the Republican party. Almost without exception all the Republicans in Congress supported the president on major votes. In the House, for example, only one Republican voted against the administration's revised tax bill. A third factor was the support the administration received from a phalanx of conservative House Democrats (mostly from the South and known as the Boll Weevils). Finally, there was the fact that more orthodox economic policies had not been especially effective in dealing with inflation and unemployment. Why not give something different a try?

Thus, in August 1981, the Reagan economic program was in place, substantially as the president intended.[35] The initial reaction to it, however, was adverse. Early predictions were that the budget deficit for fiscal year 1982 would be substantially in excess of the official estimate of a $42.5 billion deficit. In actuality, it was $110.6 billion. Moreover, many were concerned because the prime lending rate (the rate at which banks lend to their best customers) was hovering around the 20 percent level. This was said to reflect expectations of continued inflation along with doubt that the Reagan program would be successful. In late September President Reagan announced that, in order to meet his budget deficit target, the administration would seek $13 billion in additional budget cuts plus $3 billion in increased taxes for fiscal year 1982. In his view these additional proposed savings would keep the economy on the "firm, steady course" that he had charted earlier in the year. Only $2 billion of the proposed cuts were in the national defense area, where members of Congress believed larger cuts should be made. Resistance grew in response to further cuts in social programs and ultimately Congress approved in December 1981 additional reductions of only $4 billion in domestic programs.

In all, economic developments in 1981 did not take the shape hoped for by the Reagan administration. Although the rate of inflation was significantly reduced, interest rates remained high, and in mid-1981 the economy lapsed into a deep recession. Unemployment shot upward and exceeded 10 percent in the fall of 1982. By the end of 1982 predictions were common that budget deficits would run well over $100 billion annually for the next several years.

The proposed budget for fiscal year 1983 presented to Congress in early 1982 by President Reagan called for additional reductions in domestic expenditures, more increases in defense spending, some limited tax increases, and a balanced budget by fiscal year 1984. Although his advisers had urged a major tax increase (or deferral of some of the 1981 income tax cuts) to reduce the deficit in the 1983 budget, their advice was rejected by the president. Consequently, the president's 1983 budget proposed outlays of $758 billion, receipts of $666 billion, and a deficit of $92 billion.

Skepticism quickly arose concerning the realism of this deficit figure. The Congressional Budget Office, for instance, predicted that the deficit would be in the $140 to $150 billion range. (In early 1983 the administration itself estimated that the deficit would exceed $200 billion.) Pressure for action to reduce the budget deficit in 1983 and later years began to build, leading the administration to support a major increase in tax revenues. Support for such action was especially strong among Senate Republicans. A tax bill written by the Republican-controlled Senate Finance Committee and attached to a minor House bill provided for $98 billion in increased tax revenues over a three-year period. The House Democratic leadership chose to go to conference with the Senate on this tax bill without trying to pass a regular House bill. (This produced contentions that the tax bill violated the constitutional requirement that all the legislation must originate in the House.) The conference measure agreed to after lengthy deliberations largely followed the outline of the Senate bill.

A major campaign of pressure and persuasion was undertaken by the administration to secure enactment of the tax legislation. Many members of Congress were reluctant to vote for a major tax increase in an election year. Unhappiness with the tax bill was especially strong among Republicans in the House. Supply-siders argued it ran counter to the administration's mandate to cut taxes. Others opposed particular provisions in the bill. The unity that characterized the House Republicans in 1981 was not to be found. However, the House Democratic leadership gave full support to the bill in the name of fiscal responsibility. In mid-August, with substantial support from moderate and liberal Democrats, the House passed the tax bill by a vote of 226 to 207 (for, 123 Democrats, 103 Republicans; against, 120 Democrats, 87 Republicans). The Senate acted favorably soon afterward by a fairly partisan 52 to 47 vote. Eleven Republicans opposed the bill while nine Democrats supported it. Although viewed as an important legislative victory for the Reagan administration, the bill was signed into law by the president without a public ceremony.

Called the Tax Equity and Fiscal Responsibility Act, the legislation provided for $15 billion in expenditure reductions and an extension of unemployment benefits (which likely won some votes for it) as well as the estimated $98 billion in revenue increases during the period 1983–1985. The revenue increases were to be generated by stricter or more effective enforcement of existing tax laws, the reduction or closing of some tax loopholes (as for medical care expenses and corporate tax leasing), and increased taxes (as on cigarettes, telephone services, and airline tickets). No change was made in the 1981 income tax reductions as this was strongly opposed by the president. However, some of the 1981 business tax reductions were eliminated.

Whether the tax legislation, by reducing prospective budget deficits, would have a beneficial effect on the economy was conjectural. It certainly did constitute a shift away from supply-side economics back toward a more traditional Republican concern with budget deficits, which the president now acknowledged would persist until at least late in the decade. By late 1982 supply-side economics seemed an idea whose time had both come and passed. The president, however, continued to resist efforts to delay or cut back the scheduled reductions in income tax rates. In this he was successful. However, the budget deficit exceeded $195 billion in 1983.

CONCLUDING COMMENTS

In 1966 Walter Heller, then chairman of the Council of Economic Advisers, proclaimed "the Age of the Economist," because economists had been so successful in influencing economic policy formation.[36] He also expressed enthusiasm over the ability of economists to "fine-tune" the economy. A few months earlier Milton Friedman, a leading conservative economist, had announced that "we are all Keynesians now."[37] There was, in short, substantial agreement and confidence concerning the ability of policymakers, with the advice of economists, to use government programs to maintain stable economic conditions.

This confidence and certainty have diminished in the face of the combined inflation and unemployment of the 1970s and early 1980s, and the inability of the government to deal successfully with them. The standard Keynesian approach to the maintenance of economic stability, which dominated thinking for so long, no longer seems adequate to many people. Supply-side economics emerged as an alternative to Keynesianism but seems to have had its day. Economic theorists are in disarray, and many policymakers are in a quandary as they face the problem of how to achieve low inflation and, at the same time, low unemployment—particularly since there is disagreement as to why the economy is experiencing both substantial inflation and high unemployment simultaneously. Uncertainty generally prevails, although given individuals may have their own clear solutions for the economy's problems.

One thing, though, is certain. There exists widespread expectation of and support for government action to attempt to maintain economic stability. The president and party that fail to take effective action to deal with severe economic disturbances are likely to receive harsh treatment at the polls. The election of 1932 was long the prime cited example; it is a lesson that was renewed with the experience of Jimmy Carter in 1980. Given the monetary and fiscal means at the disposal of the government, the chances that either severe depression or runaway inflation will develop seems unlikely, although some would so characterize the "double-digit" inflation and 8 to 10 percent unemployment of the late 1970s and early 1980s. When inflation and recession—especially the former—are mild, there will undoubtedly continue to be controversy as to what discretionary action, if any, should be taken, and when, by the government. What is done will be shaped by both economic and political considerations. The price of inaction, or unsuccessful action, may be paid at the polls.

NOTES

1. A prominent economist in 1969 wrote about the "obsolescence of the business cycle pattern." He seems to have been unduly optimistic, given the later performance of the economy. See Arthur M. Okun, *The Political Economy of Prosperity* (New York: Norton, 1970), pp. 31–36.
2. Robert Aaron Gordon, *Economic Instability and Growth: The American Record* (New York: Harper & Row, 1974), p. 3.
3. Quoted in ibid., p. 22.
4. See Herbert Stein, *The Fiscal Revolution in America* (Chicago: University of Chicago Press, 1969), pp. 31–38.
5. Cf. Francis M. Bator, "Money and Government," *Atlantic* 209 (April 1962): 116–117.
6. An excellent discussion of the enactment of the statute appears in Stephen K. Bailey, *Congress Makes a Law: The Story behind the Employment Act of 1946* (New York: Columbia University Press, 1950).
7. Stein, *Fiscal Revolution*, p. 204.
8. Gordon, *Economic Instability*, p. 106.
9. Michael D. Reagan, "The Political Structure of the Federal Reserve System," *American Political Science Review* 55 (March 1961): 65.
10. Ibid., p. 64.
11. We should note that *money*, as the word is used here, includes both currency and coins, as well as demand deposits at commercial banks. This definition of *money* (there are various others) is referred to as M1 by economists.
12. Quoted in *Wall Street Journal*, July 31, 1970, p. 1.
13. Barry M. Bleckman, Edward M. Gramlick, and Robert W. Hartman, *Setting National Priorities: The 1976 Budget* (Washington, D.C.: Brookings Institution, 1975), p. 21.
14. See the account of this episode in Theodore Sorenson, *Kennedy* (New York: Harper & Row, 1965), pp. 443–459.
15. Cf. George P. Schultz and Robert Z. Aliber, eds., *Guidelines: Informal Controls and the Market Place* (Chicago: University of Chicago Press, 1966); and George L. Perry, "Wages and the Guideposts," *American Economic Review* 57 (September 1967): 897–904.
16. Gordon, *Economic Instability*, p. 146.
17. *Economic Report of the President, Together with the Annual Report of the Council of Economic Advisers, 1968* (Washington, D.C.: U.S. Government Printing Office, 1968), p. 119.
18. On economic forecasting within the government, see Lawrence C. Pierce, *The Politics of Fiscal Policy Formation* (Pacific Palisades, Calif.: Goodyear, 1971), chaps. 3–4.
19. Okun, *Political Economy*, p. 103.
20. For good discussions of the Congressional Budget and Impoundment Control Act, see Joel Havemann, *Congress and the Budget* (Bloomington: Indiana University Press, 1978); and James P. Pfiffner, *The President, the Budget, and Congress: Impoundment and the 1974 Budget Act* (Boulder, Colo.: Westview Press, 1979).
21. Dennis S. Ippolito, *The Budget and National Politics* (San Francisco: W. H. Freeman, 1978), pp. 146–147.

22. GAO (Washington, D.C.: U.S. Government Printing Office, December 1980).

23. John D. Millett, *Government and Public Administration* (New York: McGraw-Hill, 1959), p. 358.

24. This paragraph draws on Aaron Wildavsky, *The Politics of the Budgetary Process,* 3rd ed. (Boston: Little, Brown, 1979), chaps. 7–11.

25. Quoted in Okun, *Political Economy,* p. 71.

26. Ibid.

27. Detailed accounts of various aspects of the controls can be found in the following works: Arnold R. Weber, *In Pursuit of Price Stability: The Price-Wage Freeze of 1971* (Washington, D.C.: Brookings Institution, 1973); Robert F. Lanzillotti, Mary T. Hamilton, and R. Blaine Roberts, *Phase II in Review: The Price Commission Experience* (Washington, D.C.: Brookings Institution, 1975); and *Inflation and Unemployment* (Washington, D.C.: Congressional Quarterly, Inc., 1975).

28. Lanzillotti et al., *Phase II,* p. 196.

29. Leonard Silk, "Ford's 'Steady' Policy," *New York Times,* January 28, 1976, pp. 41, 45.

30. Robert J. Samuelson, "Carter's Early Economic Choices—It's as Simple as $2 + 2 = 5$," *National Journal* 9 (January 8, 1977): 59.

31. The Carter proposal is discussed in *Wall Street Journal,* January 28, 1977, p. 3; and *New York Times,* January 28, 1977, pp. 1, 12.

32. Cf. James R. Barth, "The Reagan Program for Economic Recovery: Economic Rationale," *Economic Review* (Federal Reserve Bank of Atlanta), September 1981, pp. 4–14; and John A. Tatom, "We Are All Supply-Siders Now!" *Review* (Federal Reserve Bank of St. Louis) 63 (May 1981): 18–30.

33. *Congressional Quarterly Weekly Report* 39 (August 1, 1981): 1337.

34. Ibid. (July 25, 1981): 1323.

35. For some useful background on the Reagan program see Joseph A. Pechman, ed., *Setting National Priorities: The 1983 Budget* (Washington, D.C.: Brookings Institution, 1982).

36. Walter W. Heller, *New Dimensions of Political Economy* (Cambridge, Mass.: Harvard University Press, 1966).

37. Quoted in *Time,* December 31, 1965, p. 65.

SUGGESTED READINGS

Bailey, Stephen K. *Congress Makes a Law: The Story behind the Employment Act of 1946.* New York: Columbia University Press, 1950.

Gordon, Robert Aaron. *Economic Instability and Growth: The American Record.* New York: Harper & Row, 1974.

Okun, Arthur M. *The Political Economy of Prosperity.* New York: Norton, 1970.

Pechman, Joseph A., ed. *Setting National Priorities: The 1983 Budget.* Washington, D.C.: Brookings Institution, 1982.

Pierce, Lawrence C. *The Politics of Fiscal Policy Formation.* Pacific Palisades, Calif.: Goodyear, 1971.

Stein, Herbert. *The Fiscal Revolution in America.* Chicago: University of Chicago Press, 1969.

Tufte, Edward R. *Political Control of the Economy.* Princeton, N.J.: Princeton University Press, 1978.

THREE

Energy Policies

THE ENERGY CRISIS

News reports in the 1970s of blackouts, natural gas shortages, and rising prices for gasoline, home heating, and air conditioning have made it clear to even the most politically unaware citizen that energy supply has sweeping ramifications. In the last decade energy policy in the United States has changed to meet the problems generated by the energy crisis. For the first time since the 1930s the rate of growth in energy usage has declined; in early 1982 we used less foreign oil than we did in 1975. In general, America's energy policy has shifted from the traditional policy of unlimited use at cheap prices to restricted use at high prices. The policy changes were the result of a major upheaval in the politics of energy.

The old politics of energy—pre-1974—was an example of subsystem politics in which a narrow range of actors made minor adjustments in policy, and producer-state interests dominated the process. Each of the major energy sources—coal, oil, natural gas, electricity, and nuclear power—was organized differently in order to participate in the political process.

The new politics of energy is characterized by vastly increased participation. Participation, in the words of Charles O. Jones, "has expanded *up* institutional hierarchies, *out* to citizen groups, *over* to other nations, and *across* from one resource subsystem to others."[1] The range of interested parties now includes consumers, environmentalists, representatives, and senators from states other than energy-producing states. The federal government has structured and restructured itself anew in attempts to deal with increased participation. The Reagan administration has proposed to abolish the Department of Energy (which was Carter's organizational effort to deal with increased participation) and redistribute its programs. Thus the political process rolls along in what Jones aptly calls "crisis response politics."[2]

The new politics of energy has changed America's energy policy and energy habits. Whatever else the future holds, dynamic change in energy policy is a certainty during the next decade, and the new policies must grapple with the same question that policymakers faced in the 1970s: how to assure America's energy future without compromising the present.

Neither the energy policy of the 1970s nor future policies can be comprehended or imagined without an understanding of America's traditional energy policies. The central tenet of energy policy in the past was unlimited use of energy by industry, government, and the consumer. In 1920 Americans used 20,000 trillion British thermal units (Btu's) per year; in 1980 that figure exceeded 78,000 trillion Btu's. This figure is all the more remarkable when one considers that Americans comprise 6 percent of the world population but use over 30 percent of its energy. Some experts have predicted that by the year 2000 we will be using two to three times the present energy output. Even the most optimistic forecasters agree that by the year 2000 Americans will use about twice as much energy as they now use. Turning away from the notion of unlimited use proved to be difficult since the major contributors to the use of energy are motor vehicles, air conditioners, refrigerators, freezers, and so on—items considered necessary by the well-off and desirable by the not so well-off in our society.

Governmental policy until the mid-1970s reflected an attitude of profligate use and unlimited growth. Walter Heller, former chairman of the Council of Economic Advisers, said in 1971, "I think of growth as a source of the problem, but also as a solution. We're doing a bad enough job in the face of growth. An absence of growth would be a corrosive factor."[3] According to economist Arthur Okun, America needed a 4 to 4.5 percent per year growth rate in order to absorb the increasing work force, and in order to have a growth economy, energy production and thus consumption must increase.[4] In order to sustain this growth, the federal government has generally refrained from regulating or interfering with the sources of energy production. Even in the area of natural gas, where field prices are regulated, there has been very little restriction on the amount of natural gas produced. In fact, legal decisions and governmental policy have encouraged drilling for oil and gas and strip mining for coal.

The practice of encouraging energy source discovery, or at least not discouraging it, has been maintained even when such policies were extremely wasteful of natural resources. For example, in Texas prior to the mid-1920s, more than a billion cubic feet of natural gas were wasted each day because only the heavy hydrocarbons were retained, and the other gases vented and flared, or burned off. Court decisions on oil rights increased the probability of waste by encouraging production before a neighboring well could be built to drain off the original pool. (That situation is discussed in detail later in the chapter.) Regulation that did occur in this policy area was designed to prevent surpluses and thus stabilize the market. State regulatory commissions prorationed the amount of oil to be produced in each state. That is, the commissions determined how much oil could be produced in a state in a given time period by ascertaining how much oil production was needed for markets and how much oil could safely be taken without harming available oil resources or depressing the market price for crude oil. Thus, prorationing was determined by applications of both market and conservation criteria. It is clear that unchecked growth and unlimited use have characterized our behavior as consumers of energy and our government's policy regarding energy.

In this chapter we begin by examining the present energy situation in the United States. We then examine traditional energy policies, giving special attention to the ways in which past policies affect present policies on coal, oil, natural gas, and nuclear materials. One of the most important points to be illustrated is that America does not have one comprehensive energy policy but rather several energy policies, which vary as the energy area changes (for example, coal, oil, and gas). It can be shown that the energy crisis changed the politics of energy and thus energy policy, as we consider energy policy in the 1973–1981 period.

The current energy situation is essentially the result of a search for an American consensus on issues brought to a focal point during the 1973–1974 Arab oil embargo. These issues included overreliance on foreign oil, rising costs of energy, and the high costs of readjusting lifestyles and politics to the new energy situation. In 1979, 45.6 percent of all the oil used in the United States came from foreign sources. The price per barrel of oil to refiners jumped from $9.07 in 1974 to $27.05 in 1980, and the average price of gasoline at the pump went from 56 cents per gallon to $1.36 over the same time period. The combination of price increases and dependence on foreign oil supplies meant that America's traditional energy policy—"use much, pay little"—had changed and was still in flux. Whether there will be adequate production and a relatively decreased consumption is the central question facing America's energy policymakers.[5]

Fuel Shortages

Natural gas, which is the cleanest fossil fuel, presents one of the most critical energy questions facing the country. Over the last few years and particularly in the winters of 1976–1977 and 1981–1982, reports of schools and factories closing because of natural gas shortages have increased. The federal government reported that curtailments of natural gas from suppliers to customers were increasing—from 350 billion cubic feet in 1971 to over one trillion cubic feet in 1978. Production of natural gas in the United States peaked in 1975 at 24.7 trillion cubic feet, and since 1968 production has exceeded additions to reserves. In short, since 1968 the United States has been dipping into its gas reserves to meet production goals. Thus, in an effort to expand its gas supplies, the United States has been forced to negotiate with the Soviet Union and other countries that are net exporters of natural gas. The severe winters of 1976–1977 and 1981–1982 demonstrated the inadequacy of domestic supplies.

Coal at first glance would appear to be one answer to the energy crisis. It is by far the most abundant of the fossil fuels, with over 500 years of potential supply available in the United States. However, as the Ford Foundation's energy study puts it, "There are two things wrong with coal today. We can't mine it and we can't burn it."[6] The mining of coal, whether by strip or shaft methods, is often objected to because of human hazards and environmental concerns. Burning coal presents another problem, since 80 percent of supplies are high in sulfur content and emit harmful pollutants. Beyond this, coal is expensive and unwieldy to transport. Efforts to reduce the pollutants released from burning coal are being made, but the technology to cleanse coal is not fully developed. The technology to process coal into natural gas and oil is available but is far too expensive to be an economical solution over the next decade.

The technology necessary for using nuclear fuel to solve the energy crisis also is inadequate. America's nuclear trump card is the fast breeder reactor, which theoretically can generate more fuel than it consumes over a twenty-year period. However, the first commercial demonstration unit had not been opened for operation as of late 1982; moreover, the breeder creates radioactive wastes that must be safely disposed of. Even by the most optimistic account it will be the twenty-first century before nuclear energy produces around half of our electrical capacity. Moreover, recent opposition to nuclear energy development has been strong enough to delay plans for new nuclear facilities.

Because of these problems with gas, coal, and nuclear materials, oil—the present mainstay of American energy—will have to suffice in the immediate future. Oil is a versatile fuel capable of running the family car or huge electrical generators. In 1980 oil carried about 50 percent of America's energy burden. Unfortunately, the United States exhausted its known reserve production capacity in 1970 and will, short of a miracle, be unable to meet its oil needs solely from domestic sources. There is a possibility that the increased exploration undertaken in the late 1970s will increase our reserve capacity.

The increased dependence on imported oil has resulted in trade deficits, dollar instability, changing relations with Israel, and a dollar flow to the Middle East. More important, there has been a shift in power from big oil companies, which supplied the United States and Europe, to the oil-producing nations. The vehicle for this shift in power has been the Organization of Petroleum Exporting Countries (OPEC), which controls half the world's oil production and 90 percent of exports.[7] Through coordinated actions these countries have managed to raise by tenfold the price of oil since 1969.

In 1982–1983, however, the OPEC cartel was weakened by internal dissension caused in part by a decline in world usage of petroleum. Even though world reserves are sufficient to see us through to at least the twenty-first century, it is clear that American energy policy cannot be dominated by the doctrine of unlimited growth and unplanned use. Questions concerning the need for new sources of energy, cutbacks in energy use, and energy versus environmental concerns now dominate the energy policy arena.

Proposed Solutions

Possible solutions to the energy crisis fall into three relatively clear-cut patterns: scientific-technological, economic, and political.

The scientific-technological solution is to increase energy supplies through stepped-up research into solar and geothermal energy, synthetic fuels, and new nuclear fission and fusion possibilities. Lawrence Rocks and Richard Runyon have advocated a crash program to develop coal-based synthetic fuels.[8] Richard Post of the Lawrence Radiation Laboratory in Livermore, California, claims, "We've got two really good horses to ride [nuclear fission and fusion], and we ought to ride them both."[9] The crux of the scientific-technological argument is that while America—and, in the long run, the world—cannot count on the supply of fossil fuels, we can count on our technology and science. Thus, solving the energy crisis is a question of renewed funding and support for scientific endeavors to generate additional and more efficient and reliable sources of energy.

The economic solution to the energy crisis is to ensure more rational allocation of energy by the market mechanism or by taxation. For example, if the price of gasoline is allowed to rise, in theory the result is a decrease in the amount of gasoline used, because marginal buyers (that is, those who cannot afford the higher prices or can do without or use other forms of transportation) will conserve gasoline. Variations on this theme are to impose a higher federal tax on gasoline or a heavier import tax on foreign oil, with the federal revenues thereby generated being rebated to the poor and otherwise redistributed to those most affected by the price increases. However one puts it, such a policy allocates energy by increasing prices, which theoretically forces consumers to use energy more wisely. Conservative economists favor using the market mechanism for allocating energy supplies. Liberal economists are likely to express less faith in the market and advocate government actions (even rationing) to improve the performance of the market.

The political answer to the energy crisis is to employ public policy to balance the interests of energy users—consumers as well as producers. Thus, if gasoline for automobiles is a consumer necessity of top priority, the government could act in a number of ways (for instance, by tax incentives to producers or by price controls) to subsidize the consumer's interest and keep the price low. The crux of this argument is that, since a large number of interests are involved in the energy area, a dependence on the market mechanism means that certain interests are not included or represented in the making of energy policy. Certainly until the last few years, energy politics and thus policy were dominated by the producers of energy and the senators and representatives of the major energy-producing states at the expense of various consumer interests. Currently, no representative in Washington can afford to be ignorant of energy policy, because his or her constituents will surely be affected.[10]

TRADITIONAL ENERGY POLICIES

We have seen that the traditional American attitude toward energy use changed because of increasing rates of consumption and decreased domestic production of fossil fuels. We now turn to the more specific question of governmental policy regarding the primary energy sources of coal, oil, gas, and nuclear energy.

Traditional governmental policies on energy have varied from industry to industry. The basic choices available to the government are public utility regulation and antitrust regulation. Public utility regulation favors consumer interests, and the policy is generally to keep supplies available and prices at a reasonable level. Regulation of the industry, from an antitrust perspective, has tended to promote policies favorable to producer and operator interests. In general, oil and coal policies traditionally have favored producer-operators while natural gas policy has favored consumer interests. However, as we shall see, these general categories do not fully describe governmental policy in the energy area.

Coal

Since the 1920s the demand for coal has declined relative to other energy sources, as has total quantity used. The coal industry was not sufficiently organized and controlled to restrict production and keep prices high. Coal mining offers one of the rare examples of an industry characterized by nearly pure competition. From the turn of the century to the present there have been many producers, and no one producer or cartel has been able to affect market prices. Since coal is plentiful, entry into the market is relatively easy, and production can be expanded quickly. The combination of plentiful supplies, many producers, and decreasing demands has made coal "a sick industry" for many decades.

Production in the coal industry expanded rapidly throughout the nineteenth century but began its long decline in the 1920s, when other fuels were easily substituted for coal and when coal consumption became increasingly inefficient. The problem of imbalance between supply and demand flared in World War I. During the war a large number of new mines were opened and old mines reopened in an attempt to increase coal production for the war effort. During this period the government's policy was to fix maximum coal prices, allocate shipments, and adjust labor disputes. The Lever Act of 1917 gave the United States Fuel Administration the right to fix prices and allocate shipments. In 1919 price controls were ended, but, because of increasing labor-management problems, price controls were subsequently temporarily reinstated. Respite from labor disputes in 1922 brought the industry out of the era of shortages and onto the long path toward depression—oversupply and lower prices. For example, from 1923 to 1932, the number of coal mines and miners was reduced by over 40 percent, while the price of coal per ton fell from $2.68 to $1.31. Given the changing economic situation, the government was under mounting pressure to change policies. In other words, governmental policy during the World War I shortage was to protect consumers from high prices and to assure consumers a reasonable supply; when the economic situation shifted from shortages to oversupply, the government's response was to protect producers from "too much competition."[11]

In the period of decline after 1923, the problem for the coal industry was to control the supply of coal, thereby assuring higher prices. The two groups that could control supply were the miners themselves, through the United Mine Workers (UMW), and voluntary organizations of coal operators.[12] That is, if the union had been strong enough to limit (as do bricklayers) the number of hours its members worked or the amount of coal produced, or if the owners had joined together to limit production, then prices could have been maintained. The influence of the UMW was weakened in the South following the 1922 strike settlement. The fact that southern miners worked for less money caused producers to move southward, and by 1927 this movement had severely weakened the UMW in the North. Thus, miners were not strong enough to limit production. Efforts of owners at voluntary cooperation to control production were equally unsuccessful. Antitrust laws ruled out binding agreements, and other organizational forms were too weak to withstand the forces of competition. In short, neither miners nor operators were successful in controlling production. As a result, over the 1923–1932 period, pressure for government action increased.

Government regulation of coal.   The first government attempt to regulate the coal industry was the Bituminous Coal Code, formed under the National Industrial Recovery Act (NIRA) of 1933, which generally authorized the establishment of industry codes of "fair competition." In essence, under the code producers exchanged labor concessions for restrictions on competition. Minimum prices were fixed for coal in each of five geographic regions; the boards that set prices had to have union representation by a fixed time period. Under this code the miners and the owners both benefited. The UMW organized over 90 percent of the industry, child labor in mines was eliminated, and a 35-hour week became standard. Yearly wages rose by one-third, while the number of workers only slightly increased. Prices per ton rose from $1.31 in 1932 to $1.86 in 1935, and in many cases producers were able to show a profit. However, by 1935 there was an increasing dissatisfaction with the system as both small and large producers and northern and southern coal interests battled each other over code provisions. Then, in 1935, in the *Schechter* case, which involved a challenge to the poultry industry code, the Supreme Court declared the NIRA unconstitutional, thus also eliminating the Coal Code.

Later in 1935, however, at the behest of coal interests, Congress passed the Guffey Act. The Guffey Act created a five-member National Bituminous Coal Commission with authority to set minimum prices and to regulate labor conditions. Again the purpose of the bill was to provide stability for both coal miners and mine owners, and unions were allowed to organize freely and to bargain collectively. Because of another Supreme Court decision concerning the labor clauses of the Guffey Act, an amended Bituminous Coal Act was passed in 1937. This statute expanded the commission to seven members and authorized it to set prices. Through an unbelievably complex process, over 400,000 prices were to be established. The commission's attempts to set prices caused immediate controversy. Small operators, large buyers, and certain regions claimed that the commission favored large operators. In 1939 President Roosevelt transferred the commission's functions to the Department of the Interior, thus ending regulation from within the industry. The Guffey Act was extended through 1943 but then allowed to die.

Since 1943 the UMW has effectively controlled the supply of eastern coal. The increased demand for coal in World War II and the willingness of the UMW to use strikes to gain power and high wages resulted in market control. That is, since wages make up over half of the total cost of coal, there is a real limit on price reductions, and some less efficient mines have closed. Since World War II the union has been "ready and willing" to call for work stoppages whenever supply seemed about to cause problems. For example, in 1978 the UMW started a 110-day strike that stopped production during a boom period. In sum, from World War II until the energy crisis the UMW privately sought to regulate the eastern coal industry.

Strip mining.   With the advent of the energy crisis in the 1970s and especially with the Arab oil embargo, coal gained much greater prominence as a source of energy. Coal production amounted to 840 million tons in 1980 and is expected to rise to one billion tons by 1985. Much of this increased production will occur in the western states since 55 percent of the United States' coal reserves, much of which is low in sulfur content, is located west of the Mississippi River. In 1970, for example, Montana produced only 3 million tons of coal; by 1980 its output had risen to 26 million tons. Because the western coal reserves lie close to the surface, strip mining is the most efficient form of production. And under these conditions the United Mine Workers have little effect on productivity because the UMW dominates in underground coal field operations. In areas where coal can be strip-mined by machine the union is ineffective.

While governmental officials generally agree that coal reserves must be developed, they also express concern over the effect that strip mining will have on the environment. Fears that grazing land would be destroyed, that revegetation may take many years, that underground water supplies may be disrupted or polluted, and that power-generating or coal gasification plants will cause air pollution contributed to the passage of the Surface Mining Control and Reclamation Act of 1977. This act was designed to lessen the environmental effect of strip mining, by requiring industry to restore the mined land to a reasonable approximation of its original contours by replacing topsoil and replanting the land with native plants (see chapter 4).

Another concern is over the effect of coal mining on western towns and cities. Gillette, Wyoming, located in a major coal-producing area, had a population of 1,000 in 1970; by 1980 its population had grown to over 20,000 because of employment and business generated by mining. Similar boomtowns, with mobile homes constituting large portions of their dwellings, deficient city services, and alarming social problems, such as crime, alcoholism, divorce, and suicide, have appeared in mining and refining areas of the West. Westerners deplore these effects in other communities that may experience the same boom, disruption, and ugliness patterns.

A third problem concerns transporting the energy represented by coal to distant markets where it is needed. Suggestions include huge "unit trains" consisting of a hundred or more cars; use of generating plants located near mines, which would supply high-voltage transmission lines; coal gasification plants; and use of coal slurry pipelines, which would carry a mixture of powdered coal and water. Each of the alternatives has its advocates and opponents. Congressional legislation to facilitate the construction of coal slurry pipelines, favored by various producer and utility interests and consumer advocates, has been stoutly resisted by the railroads and by westerners concerned about the impact of the pipelines on scarce water supplies.

Oil

Historically, the state governments regulated the petroleum industry in an effort to prevent excessive competition in the market. Specifically, production was controlled both to help maintain the price of crude petroleum and to conserve petroleum as a natural resource. The initial state regulation was requested by the producers and was affected and shaped by legal and physical peculiarities in the production of oil.

The exploration of oil sites requires advanced technology and large capital outlay. Ownership of land overlying oil pools is normally divided into numerous holdings unrelated to the oil pools. Oil is present in a complex physical blending of gas pressure, water pressure, and structural geologic pressure. Maximization of production from oil reservoirs requires that the natural pressures that keep oil's viscosity high be utilized efficiently. Therefore, it is necessary to carefully space the wells in an oil field to maximize recovery of oil below ground.

Early Supreme Court decisions concerning ownership had the effect of encouraging inefficient exploration for oil. Since the land above the oil pool was normally owned by several private individuals, there was a proliferation of wells as individual owners attempted to extract as much oil as possible before neighboring plot owners drilled wells that drained the reservoir. As a result, depending on geological formation, as little as 10 percent of a field potential might be recovered. The Supreme Court decided that oil was like underground water and that owners could "capture" as much oil as possible.[13] These decisions resulted in either highly unstable gluts or market shortages in the 1920s, as well as in a terrible waste of the resource. Thus, oil was an industry susceptible to boom and bust periods in its early stages.

Government regulation of domestic production.   The first attempt at government intervention in the oil industry was concluded in 1911, when under the Sherman Antitrust Act the Rockefeller Standard Oil Company was found guilty of monopolization and restraint of trade, and its component parts were made independent companies. As a result of this action, the companies that had previously refined oil or distributed it now found it desirable to acquire wells and pipelines, which made for more competition but less effective control of the market.

The government's next major policy decisions came during World War I. Because the war had generated tremendous demands on oil production, President Wilson created a Petroleum Advisory Committee to coordinate the industry's war efforts. The committee was dominated by oil producers seeking preference for their companies. In response the United States Fuel Administration was formed in 1917 to pool production, promote conservation, and allocate supplies. Its policies generally followed the interests of the private companies.

Immediately after the war there was a predicted shortage of oil; the head of the United States Geological Survey, for instance, said that we would run out of oil reserves in ten years. It is against the background of predicted oil shortages that the depletion allowance was passed in 1926. The logic was that just as machinery runs down and can therefore be depreciated, oil wells run dry and become worthless; therefore, something similar to a depreciation tax break was necessary. However, it was not easy to determine the life span of a well. The Republican Senate approved a 30 percent allowance while the Republican House passed a 25 percent allowance; a compromise 27.5 percent depletion allowance was made law in 1926. The law permitted an oil company to deduct annually 27.5 percent of its gross income as long as this figure did not exceed 50 percent of net income.[14] The depletion allowance could be taken for as many years as a well remained in production.

The discovery of the Oklahoma and East Texas fields in 1929 and 1930, respectively, flooded the market with oil and drove the price down to as low as 10 cents a barrel.[15] To control excess production and prop up the price of petroleum, producing states such as Texas and Oklahoma resorted to a form of regulation called *prorationing*. This involved control of production, as on a producer-by-producer basis, to bring supply into balance with demand. In Texas, for example, pumping of oil wells was sometimes permitted for only a few days a month in order to restrict production.

Without agreement from the other oil-producing states, Texas and Oklahoma could not effectively maintain national prices by restricting production in their states. The solution to this problem came in 1935 under the New Deal, when the Interstate Compact to Conserve Oil and Gas was formed: the oil-producing states agreed to cooperate to regulate production and to keep oil prices up. Against the backdrop of state-regulated production and producer-state cooperation on production, the federal government's role was to supplement this arrangement by having the Bureau of Mines make monthly forecasts of demands for oil products at current prices and then convert these forecasts to crude oil production equivalents on a state-by-state basis. Another supplemental federal activity involved the Connally "Hot Oil" Act of 1935, which prohibited shipment in interstate commerce of oil produced in violation of state production control laws.

Government regulation of oil imports. Public policy toward importation of oil shifted as America's dependence on imported oil rose. In the first fifteen years after World War II, the problem of restricting imports was handled by voluntary means. That is, imports were held to approximately 15 percent of total oil usage by an informal agreement among the giant international companies, such as Texaco, Gulf, and Standard Oil of New Jersey; they were careful to keep import levels low enough to prevent Congress from legislating restrictions. However, during the mid-1950s, independent oil companies (such as the Getty Oil Company) began to import oil, and the percentage of imported oil used crept higher. This, of course, stimulated domestic producers to ask the president and Congress to restrict import levels, lest domestic prices be depressed by competition from lower-priced foreign oil. In 1955 President Eisenhower and Congress agreed to a government-coordinated program to restrict oil imports. It proved difficult to implement, and by 1958 the program was more mandatory than voluntary. The formal switch to a mandatory program came during the recession of 1958, when oil-field production time in Texas and Oklahoma was reduced to eight days a month. The decrease in production resulted in domestic unemployment and lower profits for domestic oil corporations. The pressure from unemployed workers and from the corporations resulted in mandatory restrictions on imported oil. This mandatory program was continued (with the amounts of imported oil increasing incrementally) as an uneasy balance between cheaper imports and more expensive domestic oil.

However, as the demand for oil increased rapidly during the late 1960s and early 1970s, the amount of imported oil rose dramatically to meet demand from 20.5 percent in 1964 to 29 percent in 1973 to 44 percent in 1978. After the Arab oil embargo, government policy changed to meet the new circumstances. In spite of successive presidents' policies for energy independence, present policy is to ensure a steady supply of oil to meet demand, and the major actors are the multinational companies and the OPEC countries. Of course, policies that were once useful in controlling supply are not now feasible because of the present energy situation. The major difference is that state agencies, oil compact, and federal shipments have much less significance in a situation where America's own production meets less than two-thirds of national demand. (Specific policy changes are discussed later in this chapter.)

Natural Gas

Until the development of high-pressure welded pipelines in the 1920s, natural gas was not an important source of energy. Often discovered in conjunction with oil, large quantities of gas were vented or flared (burned) at the wellhead. After World War II, long-distance transmission pipelines introduced gas into major new markets, especially in the northern and eastern parts of the country, and consumption of natural gas expanded greatly because of such factors as low price, cleanliness, and convenience. The low price of natural gas was essentially the result of government rate regulation, which began in the 1950s, and of an abundant supply.

Government regulation of gas.   The natural gas industry encompasses three basic economic functions: production and gathering of gas in the field; transmission of gas to the market area; and distribution of gas to the ultimate consumers. A series of Supreme Court decisions placed the first and third functions within the scope of state regulatory power. Much of the transmission of gas, however, takes place in interstate commerce and therefore falls under the jurisdiction of the national government.[16] State utility commissions established to protect consumer interests could regulate the prices charged to local consumers but not the wholesale prices at which gas was sold to local distributing companies by interstate pipeline companies. The lack of power to regulate these wholesale rates greatly handicapped the states in their efforts to regulate and hold down the prices charged to ultimate consumers.

This jurisdictional gap was filled when Congress enacted the Natural Gas Act of 1938, partly in response to abuses in the operation of interstate pipeline companies. The act empowered the Federal Power Commission (FPC), which became the Federal Energy Regulatory Commission (FERC) in 1977, to regulate the transportation and sale of natural gas in interstate commerce. The important role that administrative agencies can play in policymaking, and the broad discretion that they may have, is amply illustrated by the commission's natural gas rate setting.

The commission was directed to ensure that all sales of gas within its jurisdiction were at "just and reasonable" prices. Production and gathering of gas, direct sales to industrial users, and the local distribution of gas were exempted from control by the commission. A problem soon arose, however, because the act did not make clear whether field prices of natural gas (the prices charged by producers and gatherers to pipeline companies) were sales in interstate commerce and subject to FPC control or were a part of production and gathering and thus beyond its power.

At first the commission held that it did not have jurisdiction over field (or wellhead) prices charged by "independent" producers. Then, in 1943, the commission reversed itself and claimed such jurisdiction. This decision was quickly challenged by the gas producers, but the Supreme Court upheld the FPC, ruling that all sales to interstate pipeline companies were sales in interstate commerce and thus within the commission's jurisdiction. Efforts were made in Congress at the behest of gas interests to exempt independent producers from FPC regulation. These culminated in the passage of the Kerr Bill in 1950, which was vetoed by President Truman. (The bill was named for its sponsor, Sen. Robert Kerr of Oklahoma, who was an owner of the Kerr-McGee Gas and Oil Company.)

The FPC now became the primary focus of the regulatory struggle. While the Supreme Court had held that the commission was authorized to regulate the prices of independent producers, it had not said that the commission was *required* to do so. In 1954, in the *Phillips Petroleum Company* case, the FPC again changed its mind and held that the exemption of production and gathering included sales by independent producers to pipeline companies.[17] Consumer interests, represented by the state of Wisconsin and several cities, quickly challenged this action. The Supreme Court reversed the FPC's decision and directed it to regulate independent producers' wellhead prices. The effect of the Court's action was to increase substantially the responsibility of a reluctant commission. In 1956 and 1958 the gas industry sought legislation from Congress to exempt independents from regulation, but both attempts failed.

The commission initially sought to discharge its new responsibility by regulating producers' prices on an individual basis.[18] It was, however, swamped by the large volume of cases (nearly eleven thousand rate requests in the first year) generated by this effort. In 1960 the commission ceased trying to set rates on a case-by-case basis and shifted to a system of area pricing under which the country was divided into several producing areas for rate-setting purposes. The first area rate proceedings, involving areas of West Texas and New Mexico, were completed in 1965. A two-tiered system of rates was developed. One set of rates applied to "old" gas from wells in production before 1961. Gas from wells coming into production after January 1961, and also that which was produced in conjunction with oil, was covered by a higher set of "new" gas rates. The higher rates for new gas were intended to encourage production and make more gas available in the interstate market. Rate proceedings for other areas were completed in subsequent years.

Attempts at deregulation.   By the early 1970s a shortage in the supply of natural gas had developed, as evidenced by the inability of many gas users to secure all the gas they wished to use. Two general, and conflicting, explanations for the natural gas shortage have been put forward. To critics of rate regulation, the low rates set for gas by the FPC were the problem. They say these low rates discouraged exploration and production and caused more gas to be sold in intrastate markets, where prices have been considerably higher. The solution, contend the critics, is to "deregulate" the price of natural gas. An opposing explanation holds that the shortage is partly the result of substantially greater demand for natural gas and partly a consequence of the prospect of deregulation and higher prices, which caused producers to produce and sell less gas in the interstate market. Advocates of this position maintain that eliminating uncertainty about the future of regulation would help alleviate the gas shortage.

In 1975 and 1976, a major effort was made in Congress, with the support of the Ford administration, to enact legislation eliminating the FPC's authority to regulate natural gas rates. A bill to accomplish this was passed by the Senate. In the House, however, supporters of regulation were successful in amending the bill so as to continue regulation of large gas producers and extend federal regulation to intrastate sales, while exempting thousands of small producers from controls. This bill was unacceptable to the gas industry and its supporters, who wanted complete deregulation. The bill subsequently died without being brought to conference.

In the summer of 1976, when it became obvious that Congress was not going to act, the FPC took major action on gas rates. Area pricing was abandoned in favor of a nationwide price for natural gas of $1.42 per thousand cubic feet, with annual escalations.[19] This rate was nearly three times as high as the previous maximum rate. The commission majority said that this higher rate was necessary to induce producers to engage in expanded exploration, production, and sale of gas. They did not guarantee, however, that domestic production of natural gas would actually register an increase. Where once the commission had been primarily concerned with protecting consumers, its focus had shifted to the interest of gas production (and gas producers). The commission's new policy thrust, while providing for substantial deregulation by administrative action, did not halt the campaign for legislation that would provide total deregulation. In 1978, after a long fight, the Congress passed the Natural Gas Policy Act. This law extended federal control into intrastate natural gas pricing, which, of course, allowed the government to set uniform natural gas prices across all fifty states. In addition the 1978 act enabled the government to phase out price controls on new gas discoveries and on some interstate gas by 1985. (More specific aspects of natural gas policy will be discussed later in the chapter.)

Atomic Energy

American nuclear policy has had two stages of development. During the first stage, 1946 to 1954, atomic energy was viewed as primarily military in nature, and policy was dominated by military interests. Atomic material was controlled by the government, and research activity was devoted to improving atomic weaponry. A second aspect of military atomic energy policy was to prevent foreign powers from learning the secret of the atomic and hydrogen bombs. The second stage saw a shift from a government monopoly to a combination of public and private control of energy as nuclear power came to be viewed as an important peacetime energy source. At present atomic energy policy emphasizes research for both peaceful and military uses of nuclear materials, and the regulation of special nuclear materials used in private and public production of energy.

The Atomic Energy Act of 1946 created the Atomic Energy Commission (AEC), which continued the government monopoly of atomic energy begun with the development of the atomic bomb. The act of 1946 established civilian rather than military control of the AEC, although, to be sure, the military interests were represented in the AEC. In the 1946–1948 period the AEC was run by the General Advisory Council, composed of scientists who had built the bomb. Policy during this period was to rapidly develop military uses of atomic energy to provide national security.

The Russian explosion of an atomic bomb in 1949 precipitated new congressional interest in the AEC and atomic energy. The long-range effect of growing congressional interest was to expand emphasis on the atom's potential for generating electrical energy. The pressure to find peaceful civilian uses of atomic energy and the need for international cooperation on atomic research led to the passage of the 1954 revision of the AEC's charter. Private energy companies did not want such a high-potential fuel solely under government control, and the military had good reason to believe that international cooperation would allow it to better monitor other nations' atomic progress.

The 1954 legislation opened up the new atomic industry to private enterprise according to a pattern almost identical to that of the electric power industry. That is, private businesses would dominate generation and distribution of nuclear-produced energy while government would have control through licensing, regulating rates, and assured access to AEC experimental plants. The most important difference between nuclear fuel and electrical power was that the AEC would continue to own all fissile materials and would lease to the private utilities what was needed.

Since the passage of the 1954 revisions, some policy disagreements have arisen over whether or not private industry was progressing at a sufficient rate to provide sufficient electrical power to meet future energy needs. Public power advocates have pushed for legislation creating publicly owned nuclear power plants, while private power advocates have insisted that progress in this area was sufficient.

Policy disagreements today are mostly concerned with the safety of nuclear power plants. Early in the 1970s objections to nuclear power began to take shape. A major event occurred on March 28, 1979, when the water pumps used to cool the nuclear fuel rods at the Three Mile Island nuclear plant in Harrisburg, Pennsylvania, broke down and the core melted. While the radioactive materials did not leak into the environment, similar close calls and the resultant public outcry spawned an anti-nuclear power protest movement.

Opposition to nuclear power continues unabated. In September 1981, thousands of antinuclear power protesters converged on Diablo Canyon in California to attempt to block construction of a nuclear plant. Similar events in New Hampshire, Texas, and other states attest to the growing ranks of the antinuclear power protesters. In New York City, in the spring of 1982, a massive demonstration against nuclear power drew the largest crowds ever for an event of this kind. The Reagan administration has pledged to support America's nuclear industry, but few companies are planning to build nuclear plants given the rising costs—both economic and political—associated with nuclear power. Plants scheduled to be completed by 1985 will in all likelihood be constructed, but not without significant opposition.[20] Moreover, the emergence of public pressure groups, seeking either to eliminate nuclear energy sources or at least to curtail their use, is becoming an important concern. In a number of states such groups have succeeded in getting proposals limiting nuclear energy on the ballot as referenda. Thus far, none has been successful, but continued attempts to limit nuclear energy are assured.

One result of the burgeoning opposition to nuclear power in the 1970s was the reorganization of the Atomic Energy Commission. How can safety standards be enforced in nuclear plants, and how can the government safeguard against illegal uses of nuclear materials once nuclear power is a mainstay of energy? The approach has been first to develop nuclear power and then to assure safety in its use. In 1974 the AEC was abolished and two new agencies were created. The first was the Energy Research and Development Administration (ERDA), which consolidated all federal agencies dealing with energy research. The second was the Nuclear Regulatory Commission (NRC), which took over the AEC's regulatory functions. The creation of the NRC was testimony to the impact of nuclear safety as a political issue.

NEW ENERGY POLITICS

This section on new energy politics is organized around two general questions: How does the new energy politics differ from the old energy politics? And how has the new politics changed policy? Our strategy is to present a case study demonstrating how the new politics changed oil policy rather than to review each of the energy areas separately. The primary reason for adopting this approach is that an underlying political phenomenon cuts across all of the energy areas; that is, the "energy crisis" has vastly expanded the numbers of individuals, groups, agencies, and officials who are interested and involved in energy politics and policy. Moreover, as Schattschneider showed, when a conflict is expanded, the nature of politics and policy is changed.[21]

Because of widening participation, new and diverse viewpoints and interests are relevant and must be figured in the policy equation. As a result, the issues in energy politics have shifted dramatically, from limited fuel production to all-out production, from simple energy growth to energy versus the environment, and from providing cheap energy to achieving national energy independence.

The major factor precipitating expanded participation, and thus the changed issues, was the energy crisis. The Arab oil embargo of 1973–1974 forced upon the United States full recognition of its energy dependence. The crisis had been building for a number of years as petroleum consumption had outstripped domestic production. However, it was the oil embargo that clearly brought home the facts of energy dependence to most Americans. At that time such matters as national energy dependence, investment credits, multinational corporations, the depletion allowance, windfall profits, and energy conservation became pressing issues. In short, the problem moved from the shadows of subsystem politics into the spotlight of macropolitics (see chapter 1). No longer were members of Congress from Texas, Oklahoma, and Louisiana the only ones concerned about energy. Consumer-state representatives felt obliged to be informed about these matters as their constituents waited in long lines to pay twice as much for gasoline. In addition, after an extensive oil spill off the coast of Santa Barbara, California, in 1969, and other such disasters since, environmentalists became concerned about the effects of energy production on natural resources. As both environmentalists' and consumers' demands were being incorporated into the policy process, politicians were prevailed upon to respond. As mentioned before, when the number of participants increases, the issues—and, ultimately, the policy—are changed.

New Participants

In the old energy politics specific participants varied depending on the energy area involved, but the general pattern was for the politics to be dominated by a narrow combination of producers' groups, the relevant government department or commission, and a small number of representatives and senators from producing states. There were, to be sure, variations on this theme, but they were minor and usually fuel related. Thus, the politics of coal, for the reasons given earlier, included the United Mine Workers, whereas the politics of natural gas dictated the creation of commissions to regulate prices at the distribution points. Given these variations, the old regulatory politics had essentially the same purpose: to stabilize the energy industry by controlling production—either through labor union control or through state regulatory commissions. Stabilization was often achieved with the aid of congressional committees dominated by representatives and senators from producing states.

Just who participated in the old energy politics can be briefly summarized by energy area. In coal the mine owners and the UMW were the major participating groups. The agencies most directly involved in coal politics were the Department of the Interior (and its Bureau of Mines), the Department of Labor, and, peripherally, the Department of Health, Education, and Welfare. At the congressional level the House and Senate Interior Committees (the Senate committee has been renamed Energy and Natural Resources), as well as the Labor Committees and related subcommittees, were involved. In the politics of natural gas the traditional group participants were the producers and the local utility commissions who regulated prices and distribution points in the consumer's interest; the FPC dominated interstate regulation of the industry, while the Department of the Interior and its Geological Survey were of aid to producers. In Congress the Ways and Means Committee in the House and the Interior Committees in the House and Senate were the main battlegrounds for natural gas. In oil policy the American Petroleum Institute and the major oil corporations long dominated policy. Regulation came primarily from producing-state commissions, which prorationed oil production. The Department of the Interior and its Geological Survey and Division of Oil and Gas were also involved in a supporting role. In Congress the Ways and Means Committee was the major oil policy battleground. Atomic energy was controlled by the combined interests of the major energy-producing corporations (oil companies, General Electric, and Westinghouse)—the Atomic Industrial Forum, the AEC, and the Joint Committee on Atomic Energy.

Although the participants in the old energy politics varied somewhat, one central point stands out. In most cases the most effective participants were the producer interests directly involved in and affected by policy decisions. Participation was limited in scope, and oil policy clearly reflected the dominance of producer groups. In natural gas policy, consumer groups and interests were more prominent than they were in oil politics. However, in the last decade producer interests have gained much more influence over natural gas policy.

Table 3–1 shows how the energy crisis precipitated an increase in participation, the formation of new agencies to deal with the crisis, and a renewed and broadened congressional interest in energy as well as a changed congressional policy stance. Consumer groups and western-state representatives are now heavily involved in energy politics. Numerous federal agencies (and ultimately the Department of Energy) were created to deal with the problems involved and to process the demands placed on the energy system. Furthermore, OPEC now dominates in the international arena, where as late as 1971 the multinational corporation held sway. As the available supply of low-cost energy diminished, the politics of the unlimited-use policy could not remain stable. Accelerating gas and oil prices more than anything else caused the public to become aware of the energy problem. In light of increased public awareness, new consumer group demands, and disputes with oil-producing nations, the old energy politics were displaced.

The New Oil Policy: A Case Study

The purpose of oil policy in the United States traditionally was to ensure the oil industry a stable market for its products, with attention also given to oil conservation. The result of this policy was cheap energy prices to consumers and unlimited use. Close cooperation between government and industry was evident: the oil industry had its major contact with the government through the Department of the Interior and its Geological Survey and Division of Oil and Gas. The staff of the Oil and Gas Division was small. When asked how such a limited staff could do all that was necessary, its director replied, "The secret of our success lies in government and industry cooperation. Each year through advisory committees and personal contacts the federal government obtains thousands of man hours of invaluable assistance from hundreds of outstanding leaders and technical experts in this industry."[22] It is not surprising, under this arrangement, that government policy and industry policy became intertwined.

The Interior Department in the past was advised on oil policy through a number of commissions and advisory groups, which were staffed by industry representatives. The relationship was more than advisory, in that the Oil and Gas Division took the position that it should not have authority to make policy for the industry. In the words of the division's director, "We would lose effectiveness if we had any authority. We are not authorized to establish federal policy with respect to oil and gas."[23]

At the congressional level the oil industry's major contacts were with Interior Committees and the Ways and Means Committee. The Ways and Means Committee was important because tax policy is made in that committee. (The Public Works and Finance Committees have sometimes also been involved in oil matters.)

Prior to the new oil politics, committee decisions were made, with industry cooperation, in a closed situation. In 1950–1951 and in 1962–1963 presidential attempts to decrease the depletion allowance were defeated in the House Ways and Means Committee without public votes by either committee members or the whole House; and, in general, partially because of the closed nature of the policy process, representatives and senators from oil-producing states were able to control legislation in the Congress. That is, in most cases attempts were being made to change existing policy, and preserving the status quo is easier when the number of interests involved is restricted. In oil politics prior to the late 1960s, moreover, the policy process was dominated by the American Petroleum Institute (API), a trade association of oil companies, including both large and small companies. Through its members' service on the advisory boards and commissions of the Interior Department, the API

TABLE 3-1   Congressional and governmental participants in the old and new energy politics

Old politics	
Governmental and Congressional	Department of Health, Education, and Welfare
	Department of the Interior
	Department of Labor
	House Committees:
	Interior
	Labor
	Ways and Means
	Senate Committees:
	Finance
	Interior
	Labor
	Atomic Energy Commission
	Federal Power Commission
	Joint Committee on Atomic Energy
	State and local regulatory commissions
	Members of Congress from oil-producing states
New politics	
Governmental	Agencies and corporations:
	Civil Aeronautics Board
	Environmental Protection Agency
	Federal Maritime Commission
	Federal Trade Commission
	International Development Cooperation Agency
	Interstate Commerce Commission
	National Aeronautics and Space Administration
	National Science Foundation
	National Transportation Safety Board
	Nuclear Regulatory Commission
	Tennessee Valley Authority
	U.S. Railway Association
	Departments:
	Agriculture
	Commerce
	Bureau of the Census
	International Trade Administration
	Bureau of Standards
	Energy
	Energy Regulatory Administration
	Federal Energy Regulatory Commission
	Regional Power Administrations
	Housing and Urban Development
	Interior
	Bureau of Mines
	Office of Surface Mining
	Bureau of Reclamation
	Geological Survey
	Water and Power Resources Administration
	Justice
	State
	Treasury

TABLE 3-1   *(continued)*

	New politics
Governmental	Transportation
	Federal Aviation Administration
	Federal Highway Administration
	Federal Railroad Administration
	National Highway Transportation
	Safety Administration
	Urban Mass Transportation Administration
	Executive Office of the President
	Council on Environmental Quality
	Office of Policy Development
	Office of Management and Budget
	Office of Science and Technology Policy
Congressional	
House:	Agriculture
	2 subcommittees
	Appropriations
	3 subcommittees
	Banking, Finance, and Urban Affairs
	Budget
	Education and Labor
	Goverment Operations
	2 subcommittees
	Interior and Insular Affairs
	4 subcommittees
	Interstate and Foreign Commerce
	3 subcommittees
	Merchant Marine and Fisheries
	2 subcommittees
	Public Works and Transportation
	2 subcommittees
	Science and Technology
	4 subcommittees
	Select Committee on Outer Continental Shelf
	Small Business
	Ways and Means
Senate:	Agriculture, Nutrition, and Forestry
	2 subcommittees
	Appropriations
	2 subcommittees
	Banking, Housing, and Urban Affairs
	Budget
	Commerce, Science, and Transportation
	3 subcommittees
	Energy and Natural Resources
	5 subcommittees
	Environment and Public Works
	4 subcommittees
	Finance
	Governmental Affairs
	Labor and Human Resources

substantially controlled Department of the Interior policy regarding oil. At the congressional level the industry was able to resist policy changes because of public apathy and a lack of organized counterinterests, which allowed decisions to be made in relative obscurity. This closed subsystem form of politics began to change in the later 1960s.

Transformation in the politics of oil began with the rise of environmentalism as a political issue. Such matters as oil spills and pollutants in the air and water became the concern of more than a few individuals in environmental interest groups. National attention focused on the deterioration of the environment. People began to speak of the concept of "spaceship earth," recognizing that the conditions for human life depend on the conservation of natural resources. Environmentalists, western-state officials, concerned biologists, and college students became active participants in energy politics and advocates of strong federal legislation to control the effects of pollution in the environment. Everyone has seen oil-company-sponsored television commercials or read advertisements that promote big-energy interests at the expense of extreme environmentalists. For the first time oil companies have had to appeal to the general public for understanding and support of their situation.

The creation of the Environmental Protection Agency (EPA) in 1970 was partly in response to public pressure for greater protection of the environment. The EPA was empowered to establish standards and penalize corporations and others who violated these standards. In order to dump pollutants the oil companies had to justify such disposal to the EPA as well as demonstrate that pollution abatement methods were being developed and used. Congress demonstrated that it favored a change in environmental policy by passing legislation to strengthen EPA enforcement activity. With the Congress and the executive branches of government favoring new environmental policy, the oil industry was forced to turn to the public for support. The advertising campaigns mentioned above were indicative of the changing politics of oil; under increased public scrutiny and participation, the politics of oil was no longer able to operate within a closed system. The conflict expanded, and the politics changed.

The major factor accounting for the expanded politics of oil was the OPEC oil embargo of 1973, which caused shortages in gasoline and heating oil as well as greatly increased prices for these and other petroleum products. Thus, the average American waited in long gasoline lines, turned down the thermostat at home, and paid more to use less. Public opinion focused on the oil companies and their "windfall" profits (increased profits due to abrupt price increases). Representatives from consumer states were pressed by constituents to explain rising prices and diminishing quantities of fuel. Senate and House investigating committees claimed that the oil shortage was an attempt by the major companies to force independents from the marketplace. Elected representatives never before concerned about oil policy became involved because their constituents were interested. The oil industry now had to justify the depletion allowance and the foreign investments credit tax (a tax break whereby foreign investments are deductible from American income taxes) to the Senate and House committees. First the Federal Energy Office, then the Federal Energy Administration, and finally, under the Carter administration (1977), the Department of Energy became responsible for policy concerning oil (and gas) interests. Production, transmission, and distribution of oil had become a macropolitical issue, no longer dominated by a select group of producers, oil-state officials, and friendly bureaucrats. Differences in approaches to the problem among Democrats and Republicans, industry interests, environmentalists, and consumers, and independent and major producers became prominent. In the 94th Congress (1975–1976) President Ford proposed one oil policy while House Democrats proposed another, and each Democratic presidential hopeful in the Senate sought his own singular solution. The oil industry had to turn to the public in its efforts to justify higher prices, windfall profits and a number of other industry policies. As Bruce Oppenheimer concluded, "The new public stance the industry has taken is not a sign of strength, but a symptom of weakness."[24] We can predict that oil policy formation in the future will not be easily controlled by the industry. Compromise with consumer and environmental interests will be forthcoming, just as consumers and environmentalists will have to compromise and comprehend the oil industry's problems.

The politics and policies of natural gas, coal, and nuclear energy have followed the pattern observed for oil. The increased participation of environmental and consumer groups has not been limited to oil. Coal, natural gas, and nuclear energy also have their fair share of conservation and consumer groups actively involved in the policy process. Today most members of Congress are informed on the problems of strip mining, gas supplies, radioactive pollution, and the like. Members of Congress also tend to be more responsive to the demands of various interest groups. In sum, energy politics in all areas has "gone public," with the result being a change in who gets what.

There is, however, no consensus regarding energy policy. Large portions of the consuming public are not prepared to accept the fact that energy can no longer be both unlimited in supply and cheap in cost. This problem is further compounded by the fact that in mid-1983 gas and oil were readily available; the Arab countries have reopened the pipelines and Americans are using less energy. Producers, oil corporations, and government officials who warn that the crisis has not passed are not accorded a good deal of attention by the American public. In politics wherever there are constituents, there are political representatives; therefore, there are spokespersons for producers, consumers, internationalists, isolationists, regions, and others. There is still no agreement as to how the goals of energy policy should be achieved. Moreover, since energy is an important policy area that has been shifted from subsystem to a macropolitical level, a myriad of groups and interests are involved, which complicates the task of achieving agreements on policy.

ENERGY POLICY GOALS

It is by now obvious that oil will have to bear an increasing share of America's energy burden. Until some time in the twenty-first century, when nuclear or solar power will perhaps be able to replace oil as the main source of American energy, oil will probably continue to account for about 50 percent of all energy used in the United States. The Arab oil embargo in 1973 hit the United States at a time when demand for petroleum products was growing rapidly and domestic supplies remained constant at 1970 levels. The cutback in oil supplies and subsequent price increases thus defined the nature of the problem in the energy crisis. In the context of the energy crisis with its expanded politics, government energy policy is primarily concerned with four problems: (1) protecting consumers and businesses against short-run energy shortages resulting from foreign (essentially OPEC) initiatives; (2) conservation of natural resources—ensuring energy sources for the future; (3) protecting the environment from damage caused by energy production, consumption, and waste disposal; and (4) ensuring a "proper" distribution of income between producers and consumers.[25]

Protection from Foreign Initiatives

There were essentially two strategies available to presidential administrations regarding dependence on imported oil. The first alternative, the self-sufficiency policy, was to institute policies that would assure self-sufficiency by a certain date. The second strategy, the insurance policy, was to continue oil imports as long as they were cheaper than domestic oil but, at the same time, to protect the economy from embargoes and price increases. The self-sufficiency policy meant increased prices while the insurance policy emphasized lower prices. The Nixon-Ford administration policy stressed self-sufficiency and entailed raising oil prices to cut back on energy consumption. For example, President Ford in early 1975 placed a $3 per barrel tax on imported oil and raised taxes on all oil. (The $3 per barrel tax was subsequently removed.) The increased price of foreign oil was to encourage domestic production as well as decrease dependence on imports. However, the policy did not decrease dependence and was subsequently dropped.

Resource Conservation

Although the United States has an estimated 50 to 100 years' supply of natural gas and oil, over 100 years of oil shale, and over 500 years of coal, it is clear that fossil fuel supplies are in finite supply. Given finite supplies, some people have argued that the free-market mechanism encourages present consumption at the expense of the future generations and that, therefore, the government should pursue a policy that limits present production levels. However, the Nixon-Ford policy of trying to ensure domestic self-sufficiency encouraged short-run expansion of United States output even though it depleted reserves for the future.

Protecting the Environment

The process of producing and consuming energy creates effects that are often not reflected in the market price of energy commodities. For instance, coal can be produced quickly and cheaply by strip mining, but unless the strip-mined land is restored, the environment suffers. Likewise, gasoline used in automobiles contributes to heavy air concentrations of carbon monoxide and smog, and offshore oil drilling risks spillage and pollution. Neither the cost of auto-emission damage nor that of offshore spillage is reflected in the market price of oil and gasoline. Economists call these side effects *externalities* because the market price does not include the cost of polluted land, air, and water. Thus, in the area of externalities, or side effects, governmental policy must make sure that these costs are included in energy prices, if energy prices are to reflect all the costs of production.

Government policy can achieve this end by either prohibiting certain activities or utilizing various taxes and other charges so that social costs are included in the energy prices. Outright prohibition of activities emphasizes the incompatibility of preserving the environment and increasing energy consumption, because in order to get more cheap energy, pollution risks are increased. However, in some areas, such as urban mass transit systems, the goals of preserving the environment and of encouraging efficient use of energy are compatible.

Of course, in many areas the two goals of protection and consumption come into open conflict, and in these fields policy has changed rapidly according to circumstances. For example, prior to the 1973 oil embargo the Nixon administration had moved ahead forcefully in protecting the environment through the creation of the Environmental Protection Agency and other actions. With the advent of the oil crisis and the onset of the 1974–1975 recession, the Ford administration's policy shifted to increased energy production and economic stimulation along with reduced environmental controls. In 1975 the EPA's timetable for the installation of pollution-control devices on automobiles was delayed for five years due to economic pressures.

Distribution of Windfall Profits

The size and durability of the market for fuels is so large that disruptive events, such as the OPEC oil embargo or a great increase in world oil prices, can create windfall profits for oil and gas companies. Correspondingly large costs to consumers in all income brackets occur. Government policy will determine who will pay the increased fuel costs. Market solutions place a disproportionate share of the burden on the less well-to-do, while regulatory decisions place a heavier burden on energy companies. Debates over windfall profits, taxes, and deregulation of natural gas prices all testify to the continuing importance of this problem. Government policy that seeks to redistribute cost burdens can follow one of two broad strategies. On one hand it can let energy prices rise and tax away profits. The other avenue is to prevent a price rise through the use of price controls.

POLICY IN THE NIXON-FORD ERA

The Nixon-Ford policy toward income redistribution as a result of large profit taking by energy companies was to allow prices to increase without severely taxing oil and gas companies. A windfall profits tax and a decrease in foreign investment credits were the major tax-increasing proposals in Ford's 1975 State of the Union message. Public policy regarding the redistribution of income from energy profits was in 1975 an important area of disagreement between the Democratic Congress and President Ford.

The Nixon-Ford administration responded to the energy crisis by creating the Federal Energy Administration (FEA) in 1974. The authority of the FEA was to manage the federal response to energy shortages. In addition, the government succeeded in adopting a $20 billion research program concentrating on conservation, solar energy, coal gasification, and other energy resources. The Congress also passed a 55-mile-per-hour speed limit law, a bill extending daylight savings time for the winter months, and an act extending for half a year the Emergency Petroleum Allocation Act of 1973. This last act authorized the president to control supply allocations and pricing of oil. Conflicts between environmentalists, those favoring price ceilings, and free-market advocates characterized the policy debates. Presidents Nixon and Ford vetoed energy legislation that they felt was not in accord with their policies. For example, Nixon vetoed the Energy Emergency Act because of its low oil price ceilings, while Ford pocket-vetoed a strip-mining bill that the coal industry opposed. Both Nixon and Ford backed bills that would have deregulated natural gas, but due to Democratic majorities in the House and Senate, these efforts met with failure.

1975 Energy Act

In 1975 President Ford signed the Energy Policy and Conservation Act. The most important aspect of the bill was the continuation of domestic oil price controls, which had been instituted in 1973. Ford had earlier opposed price controls but signed the bill when Congress agreed to phase out controls over time.

The 1975 energy legislation reflects the diversity of interests in energy policy. Six House committees and nine Senate committees worked on parts of the bill; for example, the Commerce Committee in the House was responsible for the rollback in oil prices, while the Ways and Means Committee worked on taxation measures such as the depletion allowance. In the Senate the Armed Services Committee dealt with energy matters related to defense, while the Interior and Commerce Committees handled consumer-related aspects of the bill. Besides these committees there were alliances of representatives politicking for the interests of their regions, investigating committees, and policy papers by the hundreds. Obviously everyone wanted a say regarding energy. There was no shortage of policy proposals and recommendations.

Sharp differences arose between the Republican president and the Democratic Congress over the direction of energy policy. The Nixon-Ford approach tended to favor a market solution (that is, to let prices rise), along with the goal of seeking energy independence by 1985. Many Democrats favored price rollbacks and more government regulation and control of the oil industry.

The 1975 Energy Act was therefore the product of compromises between President Ford and the Democratic Congress. An omnibus act, it contained provisions for energy conservation, production stimulation, and income distribution and measures to insulate the nation from the impact of a sudden termination of foreign supplies. The energy bill had five parts, which are outlined below.

Coal production was encouraged by allowing the FEA to order major fuel-burning plants to switch to coal and to loan money to develop underground coal mines, which produce fewer pollutants.

Standby power was given to the president for use in energy crises. Specifically, the president could restrict imports and allocate scarce supplies, require gas and oil production increases, and require gas and oil corporations to maintain and distribute certain levels of oil and petroleum products. Moreover, it was specified that the United States shall create a reserve of one billion barrels of oil and petroleum (a three-month supply of imports) by 1980. The United States by late 1983 had not fully met this reserve requirement.

Fuel economy standards were set for automobiles, as were energy efficiency tests and standards for major appliances. Efficiency measures were also established for states, industries, and the federal government. As an example of standard setting, the act specified that automobiles were to average 18 miles per gallon by 1978 and 26 miles per gallon by 1985.

A fourth section rolled back domestic oil prices from $8.75 per barrel in December 1975 to no more than an average of $7.66 a barrel. The president could adjust the price of various categories of domestic oil as long as the average price did not exceed $7.66 per barrel. In this averaging procedure old domestic oil was priced lower than new, recently discovered, oil ($5.25 per barrel for old oil; $11.28 for new oil in 1977). This average price was, of course, far below the price of OPEC oil ($13.50 a barrel in 1977) and was criticized by oil producers as a serious restraint on the free-enterprise system. Proponents argued that the rollback assured the American consumer that oil prices would not double in a two-year period as they did in 1973–1975. These price controls were slated to last forty months.

Finally, the act provided for congressional review of presidential actions and authorized the GAO (the auditing and investigating arm of Congress described in chapter 2) to audit energy producers and distributors.

In sum, the energy policy in the act of 1975 was meant to encourage the substitution of coal for oil, set energy conservation standards, redistribute income by controlling domestic oil prices, and provide for a billion-barrel petroleum reserve.

Natural Gas Deregulation

Further consideration of the struggle over natural gas deregulation helps in understanding energy policy in the Nixon and Ford administrations. As we have seen, interstate natural gas was in short supply and federally regulated. As a consequence the wellhead price for new natural gas consumed by many Texans in 1974 was $2.20 per thousand cubic feet while the pipeline price for gas sent to New Jersey was $1.42 per thousand cubic feet. People in Texas paid more but were usually assured of a continuing supply, while those living on the East Coast paid less but experienced shortages of gas. The problem of equal allocations of both prices and supplies became serious.

In 1975 the Senate passed a natural gas bill dealing with short-term shortages by setting priorities for curtailment in use. When the bill came to the House floor in early 1976, a major amendment was proposed by Rep. Robert Krueger (D.–Tex.). This amendment would have ended price controls immediately for onshore natural gas and after five years for offshore gas. However, opponents of deregulation, mostly northern Democrats, managed to substitute for the Krueger proposal an amendment that deregulated several thousand small independent producers but retained controls on twenty-five to thirty major producers and extended the controls to the intrastate sales of these producers. The amended measure passed the House by a narrow vote of 205 to 201. It was strongly opposed by those who favored deregulation, including President Ford.

Later in 1976, the Senate Commerce Committee approved a compromise bill, which would have permitted gas prices to rise considerably while retaining federal controls. Although the prospects for this bill looked good, no floor action was taken, and the 94th Congress ended without the enactment of any gas price deregulation legislation—partly because proponents of deregulation, such as Representative Krueger, refused to budge from their advocacy of total deregulation. During the 1976 presidential campaign, both Carter and Ford favored deregulation of natural gas prices.

ENERGY POLICY IN THE CARTER ADMINISTRATION

Strategy

On April 20, 1977, President Carter proposed his comprehensive energy policy to a joint session of Congress. As suggested earlier in this chapter, solutions to the energy problem could be either economic, political, or technical in nature. President Carter's proposed policy was essentially political in nature, with some economic and technological components. The president sounded a theme of sacrifice for all Americans—no group or individual would get an unfair advantage. The policy attempted to balance interests among concerned parties. Thus, for example, consumer needs were balanced against producer needs; residents of midwestern and eastern states were more likely to have stable energy sources but would have to pay more. The specific policy theme was conservation of energy. The energy problem, as perceived by Carter and James Schlesinger, his top energy adviser, was that the world was fast running out of traditional fossil fuel energy sources. A Central Intelligence Agency study predicted severe shortages, demand outrunning supply, by 1985—far too early, in Carter's opinion, for either nuclear, solar, or geothermal sources to fill United States energy requirements. Given these perceptions the Carter administration formulated a policy of strict energy conservation, which would reduce energy consumption so that the United States could buy time to move into the nuclear-solar age. The specific provisions were designed to encourage conservation through tax rebates and other incentives and, if necessary, to enforce conservation through higher prices.

Policies: The National Energy Act

In the Carter policy package the major features that encouraged conservation of energy were tax breaks and rebates to individuals who conserved energy, for instance by insulating their homes or installing solar units. Energy would be conserved because the government, through rebates, would reward conservation practices. However, the most controversial segments of the proposed policy were those that sought to enforce conservation—most notably, a proposed federal tax on gasoline at the pump and a tax on "gas-guzzling" cars (those averaging 12 miles per gallon or less). The tax on large cars, which could rise to as much as $600, met immediate opposition from car manufacturers in Detroit. The intention was to encourage Americans to buy smaller and more efficient cars by giving rebates to small-car buyers while taxing big-car buyers. The proposed tax on gasoline at the pump contained an escalator clause allowing the president to increase the tax, thereby ensuring a rise in price, if gasoline consumption was too high. Opposition to this tax was substantial, especially in Congress, because the tax hit consumers in their pocketbooks, and there were millions of voting consumers who demanded lower prices. This part of the policy proposal was quickly rejected by the House Ways and Means Committee.

The economic component of the president's energy policy featured raising the interstate price of natural gas to $1.75 per thousand cubic feet and allowing the prices of both new and hard-to-recover oil to rise to the world price. Although the Carter administration regarded these price increases as inducements to increase exploration, the oil and gas companies did not share that view. (It should be noted that later in his administration Carter no longer supported total deregulation of natural gas, as he had during the 1976 presidential campaign.)

Objections to Carter's natural gas policy were immediate. The major objection was that the $1.75 price for interstate sales represented a price increase, but that $1.75 for previously unregulated intrastate gas represented a decrease in price, so that natural gas companies that had been selling gas at up to $2.25 per thousand cubic feet in producing states (Texas, Louisiana, Oklahoma) would get a lower price. Oil companies objected to Carter's oil policy because it did not, in their view, encourage exploration for new sources. In short, oil and natural gas companies did not get the deregulation policies that they favored. The major objection to the policy from producers was that it did nothing to stimulate exploration and production.

Another part of the president's policy was the conversion of industrial facilities from natural gas and oil to coal. The goal was to more than double coal production and usage by 1985. In combination with the energy conservation measures the conversion to coal would (at least in Carter's view) reduce our dependence on foreign energy sources.

President Carter's energy policy also included a technology component, but it was a surprising one in that the president in effect wrote off breeder reactors. Many nuclear experts have said that the breeder is our best energy hope because it generates more nuclear materials than it uses. However, because of the dangers associated with fabricating and processing plutonium, the Carter policy favored reactors that used uranium. The uranium reactors are safer, but, like fossil fuels, uranium is an exhaustible fuel. Besides favoring uranium over plutonium, Carter promised that licensing and building of uranium reactors would be accelerated. Solar energy production was to be encouraged through a tax rebate to those installing solar units in individual heating units.

There are, of course, other aspects of the detailed proposal not mentioned above, but the major thrust of the proposed policy was clear. President Carter's policy asked Americans to pay more and use less energy. Actually getting a policy that asked for sacrifice and higher prices through Congress proved to be beyond Carter's leadership ability.

To facilitate consideration of the Carter proposal by the House, Speaker O'Neill established a thirty-seven member Energy Committee. It handled the Carter proposal as a single package once the component parts had been considered by the appropriate standing committees. By handling the proposal in this centralized fashion, the leadership restricted "logrolling" on the various taxes, rebates, and price controls and produced a comprehensive, integrated piece of legislation. The special Energy Committee membership represented all regions and special interest groups and was somewhat weighted in favor of consumer interests and against drastic changes, such as total deregulation of oil and gas prices. While the ad hoc committee changed Carter's proposal somewhat, the final package received Carter's stamp of approval.

In the Senate the Carter administration's energy package was divided into a number of separate bills, dealt with in separate committees, and debated individually on the Senate floor. Moreover, the Senate leadership did not give the administration the close support accorded it by the House leadership. As a result, senators from producing states like Russell Long (D.–La.) were able to greatly alter the Carter proposals and make them more in accord with petroleum industry interests. For example, producing-state senators were able to win a narrow vote providing for deregulation of natural gas prices. Generally, more emphasis was placed on incentives for increased production of oil and gas than on conservation in their use.

On the whole, the Senate version of energy legislation was more congruent with producer than consumer interests. Several factors contributed to this. First, the decentralized decision-making process in the Senate gave producing-state senators more opportunity to affect action. Second, the Senate "overrepresents" producing states because of the two-senators-per-state rule. And President Carter did not effectively manage his interests during Senate consideration.

The final energy package was shaped by a House-Senate conference committee. The result was a compromise, giving producer interests more incentives and deregulation than proposed by the Carter administration but less than they wanted, while the administration got some conservation measures but less than it requested. In October 1978 the Congress finally presented the president with an energy bill that, as passed, contained only remnants of Carter's original proposals. The five major areas of the National Energy Act concerned natural gas, coal conversion, utility rates, conservation, and taxes. They are summarized here.

• *Natural Gas Policy Act.* This part of the 1978 statute allowed the prices of newly discovered gas to rise about 10 percent a year until 1985 when the controls would be lifted. In addition special pricing categories were set that made industrial users pay higher prices for gas until a certain cost was reached.

• *Coal Conversion Act.* New plants (industrial and utility) were required to utilize coal or fuels other than gas or oil. Already existing plants were to switch away from oil and gas by 1990, and on an individual basis the Secretary of Energy could order plants to change from gas or oil before 1990.

• *Public Utility Regulatory Policy Act (PURPA) and Utility Rates Act.* State regulatory agencies and utility commissions were to formulate policies to save energy. For example, they could choose to price energy at lower levels during off hours. Further, utility commissions were to cease giving discounted rates to heavy users, and the Secretary of Energy was empowered to intervene in the regulatory process in order to conserve energy.

• *Energy Policy and Conservation Act.* Utility companies were required to disseminate information to customers on ways to conserve energy. However, said utilities were not allowed to sell or install energy-saving devices. Schools and hospitals were to receive $900 million to have energy-saving devices installed. Home appliance industries were required to meet mandatory efficiency standards by the mid-1980s.

• *Energy Tax Act.* Homeowners and businesses would receive tax credits for installing energy-saving devices. New cars that used fuel inefficiently were to be taxed to discourage sales. In 1980 cars getting less than 15 miles per gallon would be taxed $200; by 1986 the taxes and standards would be higher such that a car averaging 12.5 miles per gallon would be taxed almost $4,000. As a result American automobile manufacturers have met these standards by producing lighter, more fuel-efficient cars.

The 1978 legislation was a patchwork of provisions that reflected the bargaining necessary to secure its adoption. The president signed the act rather than vetoing it because he felt that no better bill was possible given the diversity of opinion and policy preferences regarding energy policy in the United States. Regional, sectional, ideological, partisan, and producer-consumer differences were severe and intense. Once again, policy was changed because energy politics now involved macropolitics instead of subsystem politics. The wide representation of all the relevant interests in Congress assured that all parties would have access to and influence on energy legislation. The result could only be a watered-down compromise policy.

If the president did not get what he wanted in the National Energy Act, he fared much better with legislation creating a Department of Energy. The Department of Energy was created in 1977 and brought together over sixty federal agencies and programs. Its purpose was to encourage energy production, efficiency, and conservation. Box 3–1 outlines the organization and powers of the Energy Department.[26]

Other important energy legislation passed during the Carter administration were the 1978 amendments to the Outer Continental Shelf Lands Act (1980), the Windfall Profits Act, and the Synthetic Fuels Act (1980). The amendments to the Outer Shelf Act were designed to increase competition in bidding for oil and gas leases, increase the states' role in determining leases, and protect the environment.

The Crude Oil Windfall Profits Tax Act, which was the largest tax ever levied on industry, was expected to produce revenues of around $227 billion over the next decade. It was levied on the "windfall profits" the oil companies would receive because of President Carter's 1979 decision to gradually remove oil price controls. The windfall profits tax was designed to take from 30 to 70 percent of the difference between the regulated price of oil and the higher selling price after deregulation. The highest rates were levied on oil discovered after 1978 and on the major oil companies. The legislation also provided incentives for energy production and conservation and set up a program for fuel assistance to the poor.

The windfall profits tax was in effect the political price the oil industry paid for the deregulation of domestic oil prices.[27] However, because of the subsequent decline in the market price of oil, the tax has not generated as much revenue as was expected.

The Energy Security Act established a U.S. Synthetic Fuels Corporation to stimulate the development of synthetic fuels (as from oil shale) by private companies. The corporation was authorized to spend up to $88 billion in the next decade on loans, loan guarantees, purchase agreements, or price guarantees for companies producing synthetic fuels. To make this controversial program more politically accept-

---

BOX 3-1   Brief Summary of the Organization and Powers of the Department of Energy

Titles 1 and 2 declared that the energy situation could best be dealt with through a Department of Energy and established such a department. The Department of Energy was given cabinet status and given broad functional responsibility over which the assistant secretaries would have control. These areas include fuel supply, research and development, environment, international energy policy, competition, consumer affairs, and nuclear waste management among others. These titles included the establishment of an Energy Information Administration.

Title 3 transferred to the Secretary of Energy all functions previously the responsibility of the FEA and ERDA. In addition, many of the energy functions held by other government agencies were also transferred to the Department of Energy.

Title 4 created the Federal Energy Regulatory Commission, which was given the right to set rates on natural gas, prices for oil transportation by pipe, and oil prices.

Titles 5, 6, and 7 established the administrative procedures and rules necessary to run the department.

Title 8 required the president to submit to Congress a biennial energy plan summarizing the nation's energy goals for the next five and ten years.

Titles 9 and 10 provided for the initiation and congressional review of the new Department of Energy.

---

able, Congress added provisions to the act for conservation, solar energy, gasohol, and petroleum reserves programs. In its first three years of operation the Synthetic Fuels Corporation accomplished little in synthetic fuels development, partly because lower oil prices reduced the economic feasibility and urgency for such activity.

The Carter presidency was a period in which energy legislation dominated the congressional agenda. Many other energy bills not discussed here passed Congress during these years, for example, the Naval Oil Reserves Act, the Gasoline Rationing Act, and the Utility Rates Act. In addition many energy-related bills were proposed but not enacted into law.

The Carter answer to the energy problem fits into the "political" category of solutions. The main thrust of the policy was deregulation of oil and natural gas *over time,* with safeguards built in to lessen the economic shocks this might produce. Policies such as research, the use of synthetic fuels, and windfall profits tax point to the political nature of the Carter policies. The Carter view emphasized the need for conservation of energy over the remaining two decades of the twentieth century. This would buy time until nuclear, solar, coal, and other alternative sources could be made feasible.

ENERGY POLICY UNDER REAGAN

With the election of Ronald Reagan as president, America's energy policy shifted dramatically. Reagan changed the deregulation timetables by deregulating oil prices a few months ahead of schedule. In September 1981, President Reagan proposed the dismantling of the Department of Energy. (Congress declined to act on this matter.) The basic rationale behind early deregulation and the proposed dismantling of the Department of Energy was that the market mechanism was the best way to conserve energy. Reagan believed that if prices were allowed to rise to meet market conditions then energy companies would invest capital to discover new oil and gas fields. In line with this policy, Interior Secretary James Watt announced the Reagan administration's intentions to make public lands (especially in the West) more accessible to energy companies. This policy would also include more exploration of the continental shelf. Market solutions to energy problems rest heavily on the assumption that there are energy resources available for development if prices are high enough to encourage exploration. (Higher prices, of course, will also reduce demand by pricing many people out of the market.) Drilling deeper and in heretofore unprofitable locations for natural gas and oil, finding new technologies to recover oil from old fields, and gasification of coal and other techniques, would, according to Reagan's reasoning, provide sufficient energy resources for the future.

Given their strategy for coping with energy problems, the Reagan administration's proposals for dismantling the Energy Department, early deregulation of oil prices, and making exploration easier on public lands made sense. It is clear that the Reagan energy policy favors market solutions. One factor that worked in Reagan's favor was the world oil glut: since about March 1981 there has been a glut on the oil market caused by decreased usage by Americans and others and by Saudi Arabia's continued high levels of oil production at lower prices, a policy that many OPEC members do not favor. This combination created an oil surplus that caused world oil prices to decline in the early 1980s. The Reagan solution to energy problems was thus proposed at a most opportune time, namely, during a period of lowered stable prices.

However, the new politics of energy has placed restrictions on pure market solutions. The severe winter of 1981–1982 resulted in increased use of natural gas, which heats 60 percent of American homes. Reagan had originally planned to ask Congress to decontrol natural gas prices before the 1985 Carter phase-out date (about one-half of natural gas would be decontrolled in 1985 under the Carter plan). Decontrol of natural gas would have caused a sharp price rise at a time of high usage and the cost would have been borne across the board by most Americans. This situation was not deemed desirable by northeastern Republicans beginning to campaign for reelection in 1982; thus, in early February, Reagan announced that decontrol would not be pushed by his administration during the 1982 session of Congress. In 1983 the Reagan administration did propose gradual elimination of natural gas price controls. This proposal immediately encountered strong opposition in Congress from consumer-oriented members.

Since American politics does not allow for pure solutions to problems, it is more accurate to say that Reagan tended toward market solutions while Carter favored regulatory ones. Both found it necessary to modify their proposals in accord with political realities.

CONCLUDING COMMENTS

Until the Arab oil embargo of 1973, American energy policy had featured unlimited use at cheap prices. As stated earlier, Americans use about one-third of all the energy generated and pay lower prices than anyone else in the world. Government energy policy was formed during energy crises, and in each case the policies sought to stabilize markets by controlling energy supplies. In the case of natural gas and oil, government policy supported the producers' ability to control supply either directly, as in the case of oil, or indirectly, as in natural gas. In short, government policy traditionally was geared to the anticipation of oversupply. The subsystem politics of energy during the era of oversupply was characterized by few participants and well-established big-business lobbies.

Two major events changed both the nature of energy questions and the politics of energy. The first event was the environmental protection movement touched off by the oil spill in Santa Barbara, California, in 1969. An effect of the environmental protection movement was to increase the number of participants in energy politics and to advance the question of clean energy sources. The more important event was the OPEC oil embargo of 1973–1974. The OPEC policy made it clear that the United States no longer fully controlled its energy future. As long as OPEC was able to keep its policy unanimous, America faced higher energy prices and the spectre of energy shortages. Thus, the new problem in energy became one of how to ensure supply in the face of increasing demands, rather than how to control supply itself.

During the 1970s the politics and policy of energy were in dramatic flux. Both the changed politics and policies were responses to the "crisis" of the Arab oil embargo. Jones has observed that "whereas a perceived crisis often encourages a demand for coordination, comprehensiveness, and rationalism, expanded participation in decision making, so common in crises, ensures that the demand will not be met. Further, just when speedy action is presumed to be required, the normal system is slowed to a crawl by organizational adjustments, new information, citizen involvement, and media attention."[28] In the years since the original oil embargo, America's political process has been characterized by "crisis-response politics" instead of anticipatory actions. Policy solutions that are beyond the government's ability are demanded by all participants.

It appears that oil will remain America's primary energy source until the twenty-first century. Maintaining a steady supply of foreign oil imports looms as a major problem. The largest suppliers of foreign oil are the Middle Eastern nations, an area fraught with constant turmoil. Successive presidents have sought both to maintain a steady flow of Middle Eastern oil to the industrial West and to ensure Israel's continued existence as a nation—policies beset with increasing uncertainty. The relationship between American Jews and Israel, increasing Islamic revolutionary zeal and instability, worries over Soviet influence in the Middle East, the fate of the Camp David peace talks since the death of Anwar Sadat in Egypt, the Iran-Iraq war, the invasion of Lebanon by Israel, the PLO and the Palestinian question—all are pressing policy questions. Maintaining peace in the Middle East is paramount to ensuring stable energy supplies. Policymakers continue to seek to convince Israel to make concessions to Arab and Palestinian interests in order to ensure peace. Shifting Arab alliances and changing sentiments about the United States' relationship with Israel and the Middle East make the situation even more tenuous.

One might logically expect the United States to tap the rich oil resources of our nearest neighbors to the north and south—Canada and Mexico. While there will be some increase in the supply of oil from these nations, neither can be counted on to solve our dilemma. Canada and especially Mexico need sizable energy reserves for their own purposes. Mexico must use its oil wisely in attempting to transform its economy from an underdeveloped economy into a modern one, while the Canadians have serious regional and cultural differences to overcome. Without expanding economies their problems will be exacerbated.

Technological solutions such as solar power, wind power, coal gasification, synthetic fuels, and nuclear energy all have assorted difficulties—both political and technological. Reagan's first Secretary of Energy James Edwards, for example, supported government participation in the development of certain synthetic fuels, whereas David Stockman of the Office of Management and Budget favored letting free-market forces determine energy alternatives. In early 1982, Secretary Edwards won Reagan's support for the Synthetic Fuels Corporation. The development of solar power, coal gasification, and other technological solutions are long-range solutions. Moreover, their development as regular energy sources depends upon their profitability and higher traditional energy prices. Accordingly, technological solutions, while advancing, are not likely to solve America's energy problems in the next decade.

The American political process itself creates problems for solutions to the energy crisis. Kash and his colleagues have described the problem in this fashion: "The energy policy system . . . suffers from all the problems associated with pluralism and fragmentation. Pluralistic politics requires an often difficult process of compromise between competing interests—a process which governmental institutions with fragmented and overlapping responsibilities and ad hoc modes of operation are often ill-equipped to handle."[29] The demand for well-planned long-range solutions is not easily incorporated into a system based on subsystem politics. As we have shown, each energy source generates its own problems, interest groups, and congressional and governmental structures. Thus organization and reorganization (and even dismantling) are features of the government's response to the energy crisis. Since major changes in the structure and process of American politics are not expected, the policy process in the 1980s will continue to be characterized by congressional, presidential, and bureaucratic compromises in a piecemeal fashion. One should not expect a comprehensive, integrated, and well-planned response to continuing energy problems.

In spite of the perplexities outlined above, Americans are now more conscious of energy problems than in the mid-1970s. By 1982 we reduced the amount of imported oil to pre-1975 levels. In general, Americans are aware of the dilemma and are using less energy. Cars are smaller, homes are warmer in summer and cooler in the winter, synthetic and alternative fuels are being developed. The higher cost of energy has in fact caused us to use less while paying more. That such a situation has resulted from the mid-1970s crisis is in itself an encouraging development.

NOTES

1. Charles O. Jones, "American Politics and the Organization of Energy Decision Making," *Annual Review of Energy* 4 (1979): 105.
2. Ibid., p. 101.
3. Quoted in John Noble Wilford, "Nation's Energy Crisis: It Won't Go Away Soon," *New York Times*, July 6, 1971, p. 24.
4. Ibid.
5. In discussing the energy situation, we find it helpful to proceed by considering, in turn, each of the fossil fuel categories. The first authors to use this approach were Merle Fainsod, Lincoln Gordon, and Joseph Palamountain, in their *Government and the American Economy* (New York: Norton, 1959). David Davis, *Energy Politics* (New York: St. Martin's, 1978), also uses this approach. In the next section, we rely on these works, particularly Fainsod et al.
6. *Exploring Energy Choices: A Preliminary Report* (New York: Ford Foundation, 1974), p. 45.
7. OPEC was created in 1960. Member countries are Algeria, Ecuador, Gabon, Indonesia, Iran, Iraq, Kuwait, Libya, Nigeria, Qatar, Saudi Arabia, United Arab Emirates, and Venezuela.
8. Quoted in William D. Smith, "Energy Crisis: Shortages among Plenty," *New York Times*, April 17, 1973, p. 26.
9. Quoted in John Noble Wilford, "Nation's Energy Crisis: A Nuclear Future Looms," *New York Times*, July 7, 1971, p. 24.
10. G. Garvey, *Energy, Ecology, Economy: A Framework for Environmental Policy* (New York: W. W. Norton, 1972); and S. D. Freeman, *Energy, the New Era* (New York: Vintage, 1974), have overviews of this position. J. C. Fischer, *Energy Crisis in Perspective* (New York: Wiley, 1974), offers a balanced summary of energy alternatives.
11. This section relies on Fainsod et al., *Government and the American Economy*, chap. 20.
12. A description of the struggle between workers and owners can be found in Morton Baratz, *The Union and the Coal Industry* (New Haven, Conn.: Yale University Press, 1955); and George S. McGovern and Leonard Cuthridge, *The Great Coalfield War* (Boston: Houghton Mifflin, 1972).
13. The court case that first made use of the "capture" theory was *Medina Oil Development Company* v. *Murphy*, 233 S.W. 333 (1921). The capture theory rests on the assumption that oil percolates below the surface much as wild animals and birds roam upon the surface. Oil belongs, then, to those who can capture it.

14. Davis, *Energy Politics* (1974), pp. 48–51.

15. Fainsod et al., *Government and the American Economy*, chap. 20.

16. For background on natural gas regulation, see the excellent discussion by Ralph K. Huitt, "National Regulation of the Natural-Gas Industry," in *Public Administration and Policy Formation*, ed. Emmette S. Redford (Austin: University of Texas Press, 1958), pp. 53–116.

17. *Phillips Petroleum Company* v. *State of Wisconsin*, 347 U.S. 672 (1954).

18. The following discussion draws on Daniel J. Fiorino, "Regulating the Natural Gas Producing Industry: Two Decades of Experience," in *Economic Regulatory Policies*, ed. James E. Anderson (Lexington, Mass.: Heath, 1976), pp. 89–103.

19. Richard Corrigan, "FPC Boosts Gas Rates to Raise Production," *National Journal* 8 (November 13, 1976): 1626–1631.

20. See A. W. Murphy, ed., *The Nuclear Power Controversy* (Englewood Cliffs, N.J.: Prentice-Hall, 1976).

21. E. E. Schattschneider, *The Semi-Sovereign People* (New York: Holt, Rinehart and Winston, 1960).

22. Quoted in Robert Engler, *The Politics of Oil* (New York: Macmillan, 1961), p. 291.

23. Ibid., p. 290.

24. Bruce Oppenheimer, *Oil and the Congressional Process* (Lexington, Mass.: Heath, 1974), p. 151.

25. See Sam H. Schurr et al., *Energy in America's Future: The Choices before Us* (Baltimore: Johns Hopkins Press, 1979), for a good overview.

26. Bruce Oppenheimer, "Policy Effects of U.S. House Reform: Decentralization and the Capacity to Resolve Energy Issues," *Legislative Studies Quarterly* (February, 1980): 5–30.

27. See Bruce Oppenheimer, "Resolving the Oil Pricing Issue: A Key to National Emergency Policy," in *American Politics and Public Policy*, ed. Allan P. Sindler (Washington, D.C.: CQ Press, 1982), chap. 6.

28. Jones, "American Politics," p. 100.

29. D. E. Kash et al., *Our Energy Future: The Role of Research Development and Demonstration in Reaching a National Consensus on Energy Policy* (Norman: University of Oklahoma Press, 1976), quoted in Jones, "American Politics," p. 100.

SUGGESTED READINGS

Commoner, Barry. *The Poverty of Power, Energy and the Economic Process*. New York: Bantam Books, 1977.

Davis, David. *Energy Politics*. 2nd ed. New York: St. Martin's, 1982.

Engler, Robert. *The Brotherhood of Oil*. Chicago: University of Chicago Press, 1977.

Freeman, S. David. *Energy, the New Era*. New York: Vintage, 1974.

Jones, Charles O. "American Politics and the Organization of Energy Decision Making," *Annual Review of Energy* 4 (1979): 99–121.

Oppenheimer, Bruce. *Oil and the Congressional Process*. Lexington, Mass: Heath, 1974.

Sanders, Elizabeth. *The Regulation of Natural Gas*. Philadelphia: Temple University Press, 1981.

FOUR

Protecting
the Environment

For most of our history, Americans have thought of their land as having unlimited natural resources that were there for the taking. Water was abundant and free and could be used to turn the wheels of industry and to carry away wastes. Wind was also free and would disperse the soot and other emissions belched forth by homes and factories. Timber could be cut without concern about reforestation or erosion. Minerals could be extracted from inexhaustible reserves with no consideration for the consequences for those living downstream from or near slag heaps. Farmland and grazing lands could be exploited with little attention given to using the land so as to retain its productivity. When the minerals or timber had been stripped from the land or the productive capacity leached out, one simply moved to areas that had not been exploited.

Careless disregard for the consequences of exploitative practices remained possible as long as we were a nation of farmers scattered with low density across the map. Now, however, we can no longer ruin the environment in one area and then escape the consequences of our action by moving farther into the wilderness.

During the latter half of the 1960s public concern about environmental conditions became widespread. Large oil spills, dirtier air, the rape of the land by strip miners, and other factors combined to draw attention to problems long ignored. Newspapers printed more stories about environmental conditions, and between 1965 and 1970 the Gallup Poll showed that concern about air and water quality was the fastest-rising item on the public agenda.[1] By 1970 pollution control was the second most frequent problem cited by Americans. It was mentioned by 53 percent of the public, more than three times more frequently than five years earlier.

In response to public concern, the government changed its policies regarding environmental exploitation. After protracted debate, Congress enacted legislation that discouraged the unthinking abuse of our resources. This legislation (which will be discussed later) made it less economical to pollute water and air.

Industry has generally opposed legislation designed to clean up the environment. Industry opponents have argued that compliance with pollution standards will increase costs of production. Thus, if strip miners must heal the scars inflicted by their giant scoops, or steel mills must reduce the smoke from their stacks, or chemical plants must filter their wastes, or automobile manufacturers must purify the gases contained in exhaust, new and often costly technology will be needed. Small, inefficient concerns sometimes warn that they cannot afford to make extensive changes and that therefore stringent pollution control standards will force them out of business.

Critics counter that environmental costs are a component of production costs and therefore should be added to the price of goods. They contend that to act as if there were no costs involved in degrading the environment results in nonusers having to bear a disproportionate share of the burden. Allowing factories to send plumes of smoke into the air may reduce the quality of life for people living in the vicinity. In some instances the emissions from factories may contain deadly substances, such as the Kepone dust that was emitted for several years during the

1970s in Hopewell, Virginia. In many communities pollutants cause diseases and shorten the lives of residents. Allowing toxic wastes or untreated sewage to flow into streams makes life more than simply unpleasant for people living downstream, necessitates more expensive purification systems for downstream communities that take their water from the river, destroys wildlife, and puts some fishermen out of work. Although difficult to calculate in dollars, certainly there is a value in being able to use a stream or lake for boating, fishing, swimming, and water skiing.

Rather than focus on the state of the environment or some of the more serious abuses to nature, this chapter looks at the current state of national public policy in this sphere. The greatest attention will be given to policy initiatives dealing with water and air quality, the National Environmental Policy Act, and the controversy over use of public lands.

CLEAN AIR AND WATER LEGISLATION

As the dangers to health and the ecology have become more widely recognized, removing pollutants from the air and water has become a major objective of environmentalists. Several major pieces of legislation have been passed to improve water and air quality. And as the federal role in environmental regulation broadened, the Environmental Protection Agency (EPA) was created in 1970 to oversee the expanding environmental responsibilities. The EPA was assigned responsibility for both air and water quality programs. This section describes the most significant pieces of legislation on air and water pollution and then discusses the EPA's efforts to enforce the legislation.

Pure Water

Waterborne pollutants are of three main types: waste and sewage, heavy metals, and toxic organic compounds such as pesticides. The extent to which sewage and animal feedlot runoff are degrading water conditions is measured in three dimensions: level of fecal coliform bacteria, dissolved oxygen levels (which determine the capacity of water to sustain fish and other animal life), and phosphorus levels (which produce algae blooms when too abundant). Deadly heavy metals such as mercury work their way into the food chain by accumulating in fish. Some pesticides and other chemicals that wash into streams are carcinogenic.

Efforts to remove pollutants from the nation's streams and lakes have relied chiefly on two techniques. One strategy has been to reduce the amount of pollution emptied into the water by setting effluent controls for the amount of pollution allowed in streams. The second strategy has been to provide grants to communities to encourage them to construct sewage treatment facilities.

Early legislation: Water Pollution Control Act, 1956. Until the mid-1960s, the federal government acted only halfheartedly to reduce water pollution.[2]

Legislation passed in 1956 sought to do little more than alert the public to problems in this sphere. Federal authorities sponsored conferences to discuss problems of pollution. Although these conferences could ultimately lead to a Justice Department suit against a polluter, only one suit was ever filed and it had little effect.[3] The 1956 legislation also launched a federal grant program that made funds available to communities to help finance construction of sewage treatment plants. Federal funds could be used for a maximum of 55 percent of the facilities' cost. For the most part, pollution control was left to the states.

Water Quality Act, 1965.   The 1956 legislation failed to significantly improve water quality; in 1965 the Water Quality Act marked the first step toward establishment of specific standards for water quality. However, rather than mandating nationwide criteria, the legislation left it up to each state to devise its own standards. These were to be submitted to the Department of Health, Education, and Welfare (more recently to the EPA) for approval.

In the absence of vigorous federal guidelines, states displayed little interest in forcing resident polluters to clean up their discharges—largely because state officials worried that setting tight limitations on pollution would make production more costly in their state, perhaps inducing some manufacturers to relocate in less demanding states and discouraging the location of new industries within their borders. Responding to federal urging that water quality not deteriorate further, most states set standards that simply reflected current conditions. However, states with relatively pure water often balked at setting standards higher than those of states with dirty water. Thus, conditions in states with the poorest-quality water became the norm nationwide. Federal authorities did little to force development of more demanding standards.

Water Pollution Control Act, 1972 and 1977 amendments.   Heightened public awareness of pollution problems resulted in passage of amendments to the Water Pollution Control Act, in which the federal government moved to correct the weaknesses of earlier legislation. In place of the state-developed standards called for in 1965, Congress set nationwide objectives. The goals set in the amendments of 1972 were very high: to make all streams safe for fish and swimming by 1983 and to eliminate all discharges of pollution into navigable streams by 1985. To achieve these objectives, all private concerns discharging wastes into streams were to adopt the "best practicable technology" for waste treatment by 1977 and the "best available technology" by 1984. Economic feasibility, or cost, could be considered in meeting the 1977 standard but would not be relevant in determining the adequacy of a corporation's pollution abatement efforts after 1983. Since determinations of economic feasibility include considerations of the expenses relative to the emissions reduction achieved and the age of the machinery included, the EPA would have to make numerous case-by-case determinations of what steps would be necessary for an installation to achieve compliance.[4] Less demanding standards were set for public sewage treatment facilities. There was to be secondary treatment of wastes (that is, removal of 85 percent of the pollutants) by 1977, and the "best practicable technology" was to be in use by 1983.

The 1972 legislation also established a nationwide discharge permit system and empowered the EPA to set water quality standards for interstate streams. Applications for discharge permits specified the amount of effluents allowed to be released by the installation and the steps to be taken to comply with the 1977 deadline. The EPA was to administer the permit system in each state until the state developed an acceptable set of standards and could assume administration of the program under general EPA supervision. The EPA could also establish standards for intrastate waters if states failed to do an adequate job. To correct the problems encountered in earlier legislation, permit standards were to be the same nationwide for each industry, so that states could not use water quality standards as a bargaining device in attempting to lure industry. To help communities meet their obligations, federal aid for the construction of municipal sewage treatment facilities was expanded. The size of the maximum federal contribution was raised from 55 to 75 percent.

Progress in achieving water standards.   While the EPA authorized $33 billion for sewage plant construction between 1972 and 1981, much remains to be done to meet water pollution control standards. Estimates place the additional needed costs at between $90 and $106 billion.[5] The Reagan administration has indicated a desire to reduce federal appropriations by almost 75 percent. The financial implications of this proposal for state and local governments are serious. Unless the deadlines are delayed or the standards for water quality weakened, states and localities will be confronted with a staggering bill for sewage treatment.

Latest evidence indicates that there has not been great progress in making waterways swimmable and fishable. As shown in table 4–1, the frequency with which excessive amounts of the three chief sewage-related forms of pollution are found has remained constant. Moreover, most cities continue to exceed standards for untreated sewage discharge at least occasionally. In part this stems from insufficient treatment capacity and in part from a failure to maintain and operate treatment plants properly. Nonetheless, the president's Council on Environmental Quality

TABLE 4–1   Frequency of violations in river water quality

	1975	1978	1980
Dissolved oxygen	5%	5%	5%
Fecal coliform bacteria	36	35	31
Phosphorus	47	48	48

SOURCE: U.S. Bureau of the Census, *Statistical Abstract of the United States, 1982–1983* (Washington, D.C.: U.S. Government Printing Office, 1982), p. 204.

(CEQ) concluded that "the fact that the nation's surface water has not deteriorated despite a growing population and an increased gross national product is an accomplishment for control efforts."[6]

That conditions have not deteriorated may be due to success in getting 80 percent of the major nonmunicipal dischargers of wastes and 40 percent of municipal dischargers to meet the standards set for 1977.[7] Many of those who failed to comply were sued.

A scarcity of data makes it difficult to assess the adequacy of the EPA's other water-related responsibilities. Although there is some indication that the quality of drinking water supplied by municipal systems is declining slightly, the EPA has done little to establish the national standards that it was directed to set in 1974.[8] The EPA has also paid little heed to legislative directives to ensure the quality of the ground water that most cities rely on.

Clean Air

Much of the justification for imposing pollution standards has been premised on public health concerns. Table 4–2 reports the sources and health-related problems of major air pollutants. Substances that the EPA has banned altogether, such as asbestos, have been shown to have fatal consequences.

Although the items for which the EPA has set primary standards (that is, levels necessary to protect public health) are less lethal than those banned, the former, by contributing to emphysema and other health problems, can reduce life expectancies. It has been estimated, for example, that sulfate pollution plays a role in the premature deaths of one-hundred-fifty thousand Americans annually.[9]

Federal efforts to improve air quality largely paralleled initiatives in the sphere of water pollution. In 1955 Congress made a tentative move, registering largely symbolic concern for air quality by authorizing federal officials to study the problem and to make information available to states wishing to take corrective actions.

Clean Air Act, 1963.   A more promising federal initiative came in the Clean Air Act of 1963, which was modeled on the 1956 Water Pollution Control Act. The 1963 legislation authorized the Secretary of HEW to convene conferences of all interested parties to set standards for airsheds. As with water conferences, the impact of the conference approach to improving air quality was far less than the legislation's proponents had hoped. HEW made modest use of its authority to call conferences, hold public hearings, and file suits, despite the fact that by 1970 no state had fully implemented an air quality plan.

Clean Air Act, 1970 and 1977 amendments.   In 1970 Congress directed the EPA to establish primary and secondary ambient air quality standards. It was then up to the states to propose plans for meeting the standards and to submit these plans to the EPA for approval. States were slow in developing plans; only five were approved by 1979.[10]

TABLE 4-2 **Major air pollutants and their health effects**

Pollutant	Major sources	Characteristics and effects
Carbon monoxide (CO)	Vehicle exhausts	Colorless, odorless, poisonous gas. Replaces oxygen in red blood cells, causing dizziness, unconsciousness, or death.
Hydrocarbons (HC)	Incomplete combustion of gasoline; evaporation of petroleum fuels, solvents, and paints	Although some are poisonous, most are not. React with NO_2 to form ozone, or smog.
Lead (Pb)	Antiknock agents in gasoline	Accumulates in the bone and soft tissues. Affects blood-forming organs, kidneys, and nervous system. Suspected of causing learning disabilities in young children.
Nitrogen dioxide (NO_2)	Industrial processes, vehicle exhausts	Causes structural and chemical changes in the lungs. Lowers resistance to respiratory infections. Reacts in sunlight with hydrocarbons to produce smog. Contributes to acid rain.
Ozone (O_3)	Formed when HC and NO_2 react	Principal constituent of smog. Irritates mucous membranes, causing coughing, choking, impaired lung function. Aggravates chronic asthma and bronchitis.
Total suspended particulates (TSP)	Industrial plants, heating boilers, auto engines, dust	Larger visible types (soot, smoke, or dust) can clog the lung sacs. Smaller invisible particles can pass into the bloodstream. Often carry carcinogens and toxic metals; impair visibility.
Sulfur dioxide (SO_2)	Burning coal and oil, industrial processes	Corrosive, poisonous gas. Associated with coughs, colds, asthma, and bronchitis. Contributes to acid rain.

SOURCE: *Congressional Quarterly Weekly Report,* February 7, 1981, 39, p. 271. Copyright 1981 by Congressional Quarterly, Inc. Reprinted by permission.

Attainment of primary standards (levels necessary to protect public health), originally set for 1975, was postponed until 1982 and may be delayed still further. Compliance with ozone standards in heavily polluted urban areas has been put off until

1987. Thus far the EPA has established primary and secondary standards for levels of carbon monoxide, hydrocarbons, nitrogen oxides, particulate matter (dust and soot), ozone, and sulfur oxides. In addition, the EPA has prohibited emission of five particularly dangerous items (asbestos, beryllium, vinyl chloride, benzene, and mercury) from both new and existing sources. Secondary standards (levels necessary to prevent damage to materials, vegetation, and so on) are to be met within "a reasonable time."

The 1970 amendments also directed the EPA to set emission standards for about twenty categories of new industrial plants. The EPA now requires that the "best feasible technology" be used in new plants for manufacturing cement, sulfuric acid, and nitric acid, and for electric generating plants that use fossil fuels.

The implementation of EPA standards for coal-burning power plants built since 1978 has been particularly controversial. These new plants were to remove 90 percent of the sulfur oxides in the coal they burn, regardless of whether relatively "clean" (low-sulfur) or "dirty" (high-sulfur) coal is being used. To remove the sulfur oxides, "scrubbers," which use a spray of water and limestone to filter out the polluting sulfur, must be installed. This requirement has not been popular with the utility industry, whose representatives say "scrubbers are costly, unreliable, and likely to cause new problems such as excess sludge."[11]

In addition to specifying the percent of sulfur to be removed, the EPA set maximum levels of pollutants per million Btu's of heat produced. The effect of this second provision is to prevent the burning of high-sulfur-content coal at new generating facilities. Some older facilities have been able to comply with state environmental standards by building tall smokestacks that disperse pollution without reducing quantity. Some power companies find it financially advantageous to continue to operate outmoded plants rather than bear the expenses that pollution control devices add to construction costs for new facilities.

The foregoing discussion illustrates the difference in legislative approaches to new and existing facilities. The EPA can regulate the emissions of new operations, but its influence over existing facilities is indirect. The EPA sets the primary air quality standards. In the course of implementing these standards states may put pressure on the operators of existing facilities to clean up their emissions.

Guidelines for air quality. The EPA has developed three classifications for the 247 air quality control regions into which it has divided the nation. Class I areas, which include national parks and wilderness areas, are to be kept pristine with no diminution in air quality permitted. In Class II areas, some increases in pollution are allowed. The quality of air in Class III areas would be allowed to deteriorate until it reached the national primary standard; no areas have yet been transferred into this category from Class II.

In areas where pollution levels have reached the upper limits set by the EPA, new polluting factories can be built only if the present level of pollution in the area is reduced. In order to offset anticipated emissions from the new facility, some businesses have cleaned up or closed down some of their own nearby dirty operations. Others have bought sources of high emissions for the sole purpose of acquiring an offset by closing the operation!

A second alternative allows a factory to treat its operation as if it were surrounded by an invisible "bubble," with the emissions from the whole operation monitored at a single outlet. This approach has allowed the business flexibility in cleaning up the aspects of its operation that can be most easily improved. For example, steel mills may find it cheaper to reduce particulates by paving their parking lots rather than installing a huge vacuum cleaner in the mill.

A third possibility is that local governments or businesses that reduce their emissions can keep the reduction in the form of a negotiable credit. Cities could offer such credits to lure new industry while private operators might develop a market for exchanging pollution reduction credits.

Automobile emissions.   The first federal scrutiny of automobile emissions came in the 1965 Motor Vehicle Air Pollution Control Act. Since the internal-combustion engine produced approximately two-thirds of the country's air pollution, the requirement that new cars meet standards for reducing the emission of hydrocarbons and carbon monoxide by 1968 seemed to hold great promise.[12] However, various weaknesses in the EPA's certification process have dashed many pre-enactment hopes. First, large numbers of cars were approved on the basis of tiny samples; in one instance, 1.2 million cars were approved after only four prototype engines had been tested. Second, even if engines are successful in reducing emissions when the cars roll off the assembly line, tests indicate that cars in use quickly slip below acceptable levels of cleanliness.

When the 1965 legislation failed to substantially reduce the pollution caused by cars, higher auto emission standards were included in the 1970 amendments to the Clean Air Act. This legislation called for a 90 percent reduction in hydrocarbon and carbon monoxide emissions by new cars by 1975. A similar reduction in nitrogen oxides was to be achieved by 1976. Manufacturers could be fined $10,000 for each car not in compliance.

Automobile manufacturers who opposed the 1970 standards on the grounds that insufficient time was allowed for the development of needed technology found the 1973 Arab oil embargo to be a useful bargaining lever in their continuing efforts to modify the standards. In response to Detroit's contention that emission reduction would come only at the price of higher rates of fuel consumption, the EPA has postponed deadlines.

Acid rain and the greenhouse effect.   While the EPA has concentrated on establishing and monitoring air quality standards designed to protect the public's health, two other consequences of pollution are stirring concern. Rain and snow with the acidity of vinegar can result when moisture joins with sulfates and nitrates in the air in a combination called *acid rain*. The phenomenon is widespread in eastern North America; in New England and New York's Adirondack Mountains the acidity levels from polluted precipitation in many lakes is so high that all fish and most other animals and plants have been killed. Acid rain also harms some crops. Burning coal is thought to be the primary source of the pollutants that cause acid rain. Use of tall stacks to disperse emissions has contributed to the scope of areas affected by acid rain, since pollutants from tall stacks travel farther before returning to earth.

Removal of sulfur dioxide from the emissions of coal burners would be expensive. Members of Congress have proposed legislation to gradually reduce the sulfur dioxide from utility plants. Several ways of paying for the cleanup have been suggested. If utilities that burn coal having a high sulfur content are required to absorb the cost, the customers' electric rates may go up 20 to 50 percent.[13] A second approach, which has been endorsed by Senator John Glenn (D–Ohio), would tax utilities in 31 eastern states three-tenths of a cent per kilowatt hour of electricity produced by burning fossil fuel. The broad incidence of this tax would result in less than a seven percent increase in affected customers' electric bills. The revenue raised would be available to install pollution control devices. A third alternative, which would distribute the burden even more widely, would collect a tenth of a cent per kilowatt hour in the 48 continental states.

Clouds of carbon dioxide from vehicles and stationary sources accumulate in the atmosphere and may produce what is called a *greenhouse effect*. Many scientists fear that high concentrations of carbon dioxide may cause the climate on earth to warm slightly, which could change weather patterns and perhaps melt some of the polar icecap, which in turn would flood many coastal cities.

Progress in meeting clean air standards.   Despite frequent industry protests that standards are unreasonable, some progress is being made. Figures compiled in 1979 show that the amount of sulfur dioxide in the air of our cities has decreased by two-thirds since 1964; particulates are down by one-third since 1960; and carbon monoxide has been reduced by one-third since 1972.[14] The president's Council on Environmental Quality reported that "an examination of data from the four or five counties with the poorest air quality in each federal region shows that in most regions, and for most pollutants, the frequency of violations of ambient air quality standards either stayed constant or decreased over the 1974 to 1977 period."[15]

Despite improvements, problems remain with hundreds of areas having concentrations of at least one pollutant in excess of federal standards and with Los Angeles out of compliance on five pollutants.[16] Nonetheless, the National Commission on Air Quality predicts that by the end of the 1980s all but eight urban areas will be in compliance with EPA air quality standards.[17]

As the air in many cities has improved, total amounts of most pollutants emitted nationally have declined. Table 4–3 shows that for carbon monoxide, hydrocarbons, and particulates the amount of pollution has been substantially reduced

TABLE 4-3   Estimated amounts of air pollutants in the United States (in millions of metric tons)

	1970	1980
Carbon monoxide	110.9	85.4
Hydrocarbons	27.1	21.8
Nitrogen oxides	18.5	20.7
Particulates	17.6	7.8
Sulfur oxides	27.9	23.7

SOURCE: U.S. Bureau of the Census, *Statistical Abstract of the United States, 1982–1983* (Washington, D.C.: U.S. Government Printing Office, 1982), p. 205.

TABLE 4-4   Motor vehicle pollution in the United States (in grams per mile)

	1970	1979	Projected for 1981	Goal set by legislation
Carbon monoxide	86.9	65.2	55.5	3.40
Hydrocarbons	12.1	7.3	5.8	0.41
Nitrogen oxides	4.7	3.8	3.4	1.00

SOURCE: U.S. Bureau of the Census, *Statistical Abstract of the United States, 1980* (Washington, D.C.: U.S. Government Printing Office, 1980), p. 217.

across the country. Figures in table 4–4 indicate substantial improvements in cleaning up vehicle emissions. Despite improvements, vehicle emission levels remain higher than the objectives of the 1970 legislation.

When industry-by-industry comparisons are made, there are wide variations in the extent of compliance. For example, industry representatives claim that 96 percent of the members of the Chemical Manufacturers Association meet EPA standards, compared with a quarter of the steel plants.[18] Assessing the impact of legislation designed to reduce air pollution reveals that statistics are often ambiguous. One's conclusion depends on data selected for interpretation; both may be determined by one's values and what one hopes to prove.

PROBLEMS OF ENFORCING LEGISLATION

In carrying out its congressional mandate to reduce water and air pollution, the EPA encountered a number of obstacles. Several of these stemmed from the detailed nature of the environmental legislation enacted by Congress. Although the members of Congress were motivated by the best of intentions (that is, they tried to specify the corrective actions to be taken, because they feared that administrators might not pursue environmental cleanup with sufficient vigor), some of the requirements written into law by Congress appear to be counterproductive.

First, the water and air legislation set specific timetables. For example, Congress directed that 90 percent of several pollutants were to be eliminated from automobile emissions by a certain date. Similarly, it stipulated that the EPA must bring suit against a water polluter who does not take corrective action within thirty days after receiving notification of a violation. By setting such specific objectives for the EPA, Congress has complicated the agency's operation by reducing its latitude of action. The EPA's ability to improve air and water quality through negotiation and compromise is, thus, somewhat restricted.

Second, in attempting to specify in detail what the EPA was to do, Congress caused some confusion because overlapping requirements sometimes created apparent contradictions or made it difficult to determine which provision was more applicable. Observers have pointed out, "By trying to cover all possible situations, and thus having several provisions dealing with closely related situations and functions, it is frequently left to the administrator to determine which section of the law to apply to a particular polluter or state."[19]

A third problem is created by the requirement that the EPA devise environmental cleanup standards on matters about which relatively little is known. In the absence of scientific testing, the EPA may have little evidence with which to justify imposition of a particular standard on the emissions allowable for a factory or plant. In analyzing a series of legal setbacks for the EPA, it can be seen that "in each of the cases, the court found the burden of proof lay on EPA to show that its standards were based on reliable data and that the available technology had been adequately demonstrated. In most of the cases the court found that EPA could not sustain the burden of proof."[20]

A fourth problem area for the EPA has been its relationship with the states. Although polluted streams and dirty air do not respect state boundaries, environmental policy still leaves a fair amount of responsibility to the states. The EPA sets national standards, but it is up to the states to design the programs that should achieve compliance with the air standards. As mentioned earlier, this has meant that differing amounts of pollution are permitted in differing parts of the country. In the case of automobile emissions, for example, California has more rigorous standards than those found in the rest of the nation.

Fifth, while the EPA can draft plans for achievement of air and water standards when state proposals are inadequate, the federal government is less influential when it comes to the construction of sewage treatment plants. Distribution of federal funds for this purpose is left up to the states, and states have rarely devised comprehensive strategies for cleaning up a watershed. Instead, construction funds for sewage treatment facilities have been distributed to municipalities on a first-come, first-served basis. In addition to the inefficiency of this approach, the waste treatment construction program has been further marred by the absence of standards for the facilities that are built or for their subsequent operations.

Finally, Congress has, at times, called on the EPA to achieve a level of pollution control before the requisite technology has been developed. For example, it has been said that the 1972 water legislation "abounds with technical barricades to implementation."[21] It can be argued that this sort of mandate is useful in that it can force those who are being regulated to expedite the development of new technology. An example is automobile emission control; until technological advances are made, implementation is impossible.

Criticism of Standards

In retrospect, it appears that the 1970s may mark the furthest advance achieved by the advocates of pure air and water. The oil embargoes and subsequent price increases created a public climate far different from the one in which the amendments had passed with hardly any dissent.

As the Clean Air and Clean Water acts came up for review in the early 1980s, critics attacked them on several grounds and proposed numerous changes. Most of the efforts to weaken the requirements came from businesses, often those that were most affected by the legislation. Eight specific issues were presented to Congress for resolution.

First, industry charged that EPA standards to prevent significant deterioration in air quality unreasonably curb industrial expansion. In place of the EPA approach, which would allow a constant increment of additional pollution in Class II areas, regardless of the current level of air quality (for example, an additional 20 micrograms of sulfur dioxide per meter per day is permitted in Class II areas), industry prefers to allow air quality to decline until the national primary level is reached. Environmentalists object since such a policy would result in a general deterioration of air quality. The National Commission on Air Quality questions whether clean air requirements have interfered with industrial growth. If the significant deterioration standard is waived, a consequence could be accelerated departure of industry from the North to the Sun Belt where more additional pollution would be permitted.

Second, critics contend that primary standards are too restrictive. A speaker for the Business Roundtable summed up his organization's position: "Nobody wants to jeopardize public health. But the question is, how clean is clean?"[22] Current standards prevent levels that endanger the health of the most vulnerable segment of the population—those with chronic respiratory problems. Critics suggest that a "reasonableness" test be substituted, under which some share of the population would be inconvenienced.

In the third place, business would like to see cost-benefit analyses carried out before the EPA establishes standards. The Clean Air Act prohibits consideration of cost or feasibility of attainment when EPA sets primary standards. This is another facet of industry's claim that environmental regulations contribute to the disadvantages faced by business in competing not only for the world market but even for sales at home. Thus pollution control is cited as one cause of America's unfavorable balance of trade. On the other hand, a Carter administration EPA official charged that "anyone who tells you they want to mandate that benefits outweigh costs wants to gut the act."[23]

Fourth, businesses are critical of the requirement that they provide an offsetting reduction in pollution before building a new facility in a polluted area. They favor an arrangement whereby they could pay a fee in return for the right to build. Environmentalists warn that in the absence of offsets, conditions will continue to deteriorate.

The fifth issue concerns projected expenses. The Business Roundtable places the cost of pollution control to industry at $400 billion for the period 1970–1987, a factor they say is a significant cause of inflation.[24] On the other side, the National Commission on Air Quality estimates that pollution control has added only 0.2 percent to the annual rate of inflation. Moreover, the CEQ estimated the value of cleaner air at $21.4 billion annually during the 1970s, which goes a long way toward balancing the $27 billion it estimates that environmental cleanup cost during each of those years.[25]

In the sixth item presented by industry, utilities continue to oppose the requirement that 90 percent of the sulfur dioxide be removed regardless of the sulfur content of the coal. They would prefer at most a sliding scale for emission reductions, or better yet that they simply be held to a specific level of emissions per million Btu's produced. Utilities argue that the result would be emission levels within the healthful range and perhaps lower than at present, since cleaner coal would be used whenever that was cheaper than expensive scrubbing devices. Legislators from eastern coal-producing states, led by Democratic Senate leader Robert Byrd (W.Va.), have opposed the substitution of western coal with its lower sulfur content since this would cause higher unemployment in eastern coal fields.

Furthermore, there has been criticism of the absolutist terms of control objectives, such as "zero discharge by 1985." A great deal of the impurities could be removed for relatively modest cost; however, as the proportion of the pollution to be removed increases arithmetically, costs rise geometrically. According to analysts:

> Depending upon the industry or pollutant, going from, say, 97 percent to 99 percent removal may cost as much as the entire effort of going from zero to 97 percent. In one analysis, the total ten-year costs of eliminating 85 to 90 percent of water pollution in the United States was estimated at $61 billion. Achieving 95 to 99 percent freedom from pollution would add *another* $58 billion, bringing total costs to $119 billion. . . . A 100 percent objective (zero discharge) would demand an *additional* $200 billion.[26]

The final criticism in the list is that obtaining permits for new construction is too long and costly. Some claim that to negotiate the red tape and carry out the simulations necessary to estimate the amount of pollution that would be generated may take years and hundreds of thousands of dollars. The EPA is trying to streamline this process, while still protecting the environment.

At the heart of many of the above criticisms is the cost of compliance. In initially setting environmental policy, Congress acted with little appreciation of or concern for how expensive implementation would be. The extent to which standards are ultimately weakened will depend on how accurate industry's cost estimates are, the relative credibility of industry and the EPA, and public willingness to pay whatever higher prices result.

Public Attitudes

Public opinion polls continue to find widespread willingness to pay higher prices in order to curb pollution. A 1978 national sample found five times more people preferring environmental protection regardless of cost than believing that cleanup efforts were not cost-effective.[27] A 1981 CBS–*New York Times* poll found that even in the early days of the Reagan administration's rhetoric about budget balancing, 31 percent of a national sample endorsed higher spending to control pollution.[28] Of eight programs considered, support for higher spending for environmental protection was third to national defense and Social Security. Only 18 percent wanted to reduce federal spending to protect the environment, while 46 percent favored funding at current levels.

Environmental protection was seen as one of the nation's two most important problems by only 3 percent of a 1983 sample.[29] Although it is not at the top of the policy agenda, most Americans support continued enforcement of standards. Almost three-fifths of the respondents to a 1983 national survey thought that, when it came to protecting the environment, standards could not be too high. It appears, then, that concern for environmental cleanup has risen since 1980, when only 42 percent of a national sample favored higher standards and additional improvements, regardless of cost.[30]

Alternative Plans

Critics contend that the pollution control strategy being pursued is inefficient. They object to efforts to specify precise standards for the level of emissions to be tolerated, which, according to critics, produce only short-term improvements. Once a city or factory reduces its emissions to the level specified by the EPA, it has little incentive to adopt more efficient control devices. With policies of this type, the air of areas experiencing population and/or industrial growth will, in time, deteriorate until it reaches the maximum tolerated by EPA.

Similarly, couching objectives for reducing water pollution in terms of "best practicable technology" or "best available technology" may actually create disincentives for industry to improve control methods even for new plants, since they fear they might later be ordered to install these devices in all existing facilities. Critics also object to the kinds of penalties assessed for noncompliance. For example, the $10,000 fine for each new automobile that violates emission standards is so large that it will never be imposed, for to do so for even one or two defective models would be an impossible burden for America's already troubled auto industry.

Some economists have recommended that the regulatory approach be replaced by market incentives, which would reward efforts at maximizing pollution reduction. To encourage removal of pollutants, a tax could be levied on each unit of pollution discharged. For example, taxes could be assessed on biodegradable pollutants dumped into waterways on the basis of the pounds of biochemical oxygen demand. Polluters of the air could be taxed on the number of pounds of sulfur oxides, particulates, or other matters they release. Metering devices could be installed on smokestacks and discharge pipes to measure the volume of pollution of each offender. Applying the classical economic formula, polluters would reduce emissions to the level at which costs of further purification exceed the unit tax on pollution. From the beginning, therefore, an emissions tax should substantially reduce discharges, with the extent of reduction being determined by the size of the per unit tax. Emission taxes could be increased in order to create cleaner conditions. Desires by industry to reduce its tax burden create an incentive to develop and install more efficient technology for removing pollutants. Since industries or companies having more thorough pollution control systems will be able to undersell competitors who pay higher effluent taxes, the latter will be encouraged to reduce discharges.

There are additional advantages to the use of effluent charges to encourage pollution cleanup. First of all, a national system of taxes would remove the incentive for industry to relocate to states with more lenient pollution standards. Moreover, effluent charges generate revenue, unlike subsidies for sewage treatment plants, which cost money. By establishing a taxing system, and not simply mandating uniform levels of cleanup to be achieved by all, policymakers acknowledge that some industries and some types of discharge can be more easily cleaned up than can others. In contrast, uniform control standards may prove reasonable for some installations but impossible for others.

Despite its advantages, a system of effluent taxes has not been adopted, partly from a reluctance to make such a major change in approach. Other considerations include the question of whether collection of such a tax would rely on voluntary compliance or be based on a monitoring scheme. A voluntary approach could be easily circumvented, while monitoring may be objectionable as an intrusive form of enforcement. Moreover, it is not clear that the necessary technology for continuous monitoring has been developed.

OTHER TYPES OF POLLUTION

In addition to the more extensive and historically longer legislative concern about the quality of the air and domestic waterways, there have been congressional efforts to reduce other types of pollution, such as noise, ocean pollution, strip-mining effects, toxic materials, and solid waste disposal, each of which is discussed below.

Noise

Amid estimates that 40 million Americans risk hearing impairment because of high noise levels and that the homes of 64 million Americans are disturbed by sounds generated by aircraft, traffic, or construction, Congress passed a Noise Control Act in 1972. The legislation called for the EPA to work with the Federal Aviation Administration in setting noise standards for airplanes. In late 1976 the Department of Transportation unveiled standards for jet noise. The Department of Transportation estimated that by 1985, when the requirements become effective, it will have cost between $5.5 and $7.9 billion to bring the nation's jet fleet into compliance.[31] While most planes can be brought into compliance, some older ones will have to be replaced.

During the 1980 campaign Ronald Reagan promised to eliminate most federal noise controls. As president he scheduled the phasing out of EPA's noise control program, with responsibility shifted to the states. The transportation industry favors a continuation of federal standards, fearing that some states and cities may begin to set their own stricter limits for trucks and trains.

Ocean Pollution

With passage of the 1972 Marine Protection, Research, and Sanctuaries Act, use of the oceans as gigantic cesspools came under regulation. Dumping of radioactive wastes and products manufactured for chemical or biological warfare was prohibited. Ocean disposal of municipal sewage and industrial wastes was regulated by a permit system through 1981. It is unclear whether all ocean dumping will be discontinued in the near future.

Strip Mining

After a struggle of several years, coal strip-mining legislation was enacted in 1977 (the Surface Mining Control and Reclamation Act). Strip miners were ordered to restore future sites to their premining conditions. Restoration involves grading to achieve earlier contours, replacing the topsoil, and replanting the land. Land that cannot be restored is off limits for all types of surface mining. Funds collected through taxes on coal will be used to restore abandoned strip mines. Coal producers seek to amend the legislation to permit state differences in place of national standards.

Hazardous Wastes

Public awareness of the nation's hazardous waste problems was triggered by the discovery of severe health problems in the Love Canal area of Buffalo, New York. This neighborhood, which was built on a chemical dump, was found to have an extraordinarily high incidence of cancer, miscarriages, and birth defects. Although the cause is still being debated, many residents attribute these health problems to the mixture of dozens of chemicals, some of them carcinogenic, which were leaking from the rusted barrels in which they had been buried in the long abandoned canal. In the wake of Love Canal, hundreds of chemical waste sites have been located. A number of these have been abandoned and no one knows what they contain.

In addition to locating dump sites and identifying their contents, the public is concerned with how to clean up existing sites and what to do to prevent future chemical dumps. Congress addressed some of these concerns when it approved what has become known as the 1980 Superfund Bill. A sum of $1.6 billion, most of it coming from the chemical industry, was established to pay for cleaning up dump sites. The Chemical Manufacturers Association claims this is several times over the amount needed while the EPA estimates that the cost may run to between $22 and $44 billion.[32] These funds will be used primarily for detoxifying abandoned dumps, with the government authorized to sue dump operators if their identity is known. The Reagan administration wants to reduce such funding for cleanups. No funds have been provided for helping those who lose their health or homes.

Prevention of creating new dumps was addressed in the 1976 Resources Conservation and Recovery Act. The EPA was directed to set standards for handling dangerous chemicals from the time they are manufactured until they are disposed of. In addition to making sure that situations similar to what happened at Love Canal do not occur, a second consideration in disposal is that wastes not seep into the nation's ground water supply. Despite this legislation, some share of the hazardous wastes are dumped along highways and in vacant lots by "midnight dumpers," who underbid legitimate disposal operations.

In addition to the problems of illegal dumping are the difficulties caused by the slowness with which EPA has implemented its responsibilities. Only two of ten thousand facilities handling dangerous wastes have received final permits. In the face of such delays, congressional committees were considering legislation in 1982 that would require EPA to issue permits within four years or the facilities would have to close. Environmentalists attribute the delays to budget cutting and what they perceive to be unsympathetic appointees of the Reagan administration.

The provision of safe disposal is made more difficult by strident local opposition whenever location of a site is proposed. President Carter's head of the EPA, Douglas Costle, referred to this as "the backyard syndrome," pointing out, "Everyone wants these wastes managed, but not in his backyard. And our entire nation is someone's backyard."[33]

Local opposition is also an obstacle to finding places for storing radioactive wastes, some of which will be deadly for generations. Storage in natural subterranean salt domes has been suggested, but is opposed by legislators representing areas where such domes are found. Some arrangements will have to be made during the 1980s. One possibility would be to store radioactive materials, such as spent fuel rods from nuclear generating plants, on federal lands.

Solid Waste

The size of the problem of solid waste disposal is staggering, since only 8 percent of the 148 million tons of residential and commercial waste is recycled.[34] Most of the recycling involves paper; yet, even there, only 20 percent of discarded paper is reused. In the absence of recycling, most solid wastes are burned—contributing to air pollution—or buried in land fills. Both disposal processes place a heavy burden on our natural resources.

Efforts to handle solid wastes have been limited primarily to locally operated recycling programs, usually for paper or aluminum (see figure 4–1). A more permanent solution of part of the problem was pioneered in Oregon when it prohibited the sale of beverages in disposable containers. This legislation, since passed in about eight states, reduced container litter by two-thirds but some claim there were concomitant job losses among container manufacturers. Still mostly in the planning stage are proposals for making some use of the mountains of garbage generated daily. One idea is to fuel steam plants by burning garbage, while recovering reusable metals.

NATIONAL ENVIRONMENTAL POLICY ACT

Unlike the piecemeal environmental legislation discussed thus far, each of which was aimed at cleaning up one component of the environment, the National Environmental Policy Act (NEPA) was intended to ensure that environmental consequences be considered as a factor in all relevant federal policy decisions. The act was signed into law on January 1, 1970, as the first legislation of the new decade, and environmentalists hoped that it would usher in an era of greater environmental responsibility.

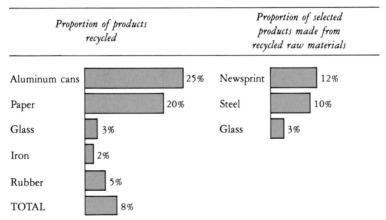

FIGURE 4–1   Levels of recycling in the United States. (*Source: Council on Environmental Quality*, Environmental Quality, 1979. *Washington, D.C.: U.S. Government Printing Office, 1979; chap. 4 and p. 685.*)

Provisions

The most controversial part of the act is the requirement for environmental impact statements (EISs). Such statements—which are required for all proposed federal actions that might affect environmental quality—must address the following items: (1) the environmental impact of the proposed activity; (2) unavoidable negative consequences that would result from the activity; (3) alternatives to the proposed activity; (4) the relationship between the short-term uses to be made of the environment and the maintenance and enhancement of long-term productivity; and (5) any irreversible commitments of resources that would result if the activity were carried out.

Environmental impact statements are supposed to be prepared well in advance of the initiation of the proposed activity, so that concerned citizens have an opportunity to oppose the project on the grounds that the harmful consequences outweigh the benefits. The statements are filed with an office created by NEPA, the three-person Council on Environmental Quality (CEQ).

Implementation

In performing its functions, the CEQ has opted for a relatively low profile. It has chosen to rely heavily on persuasion and therefore has tried to avoid antagonizing other agencies. Moreover, its public role seems to be limited to simply collecting environmental impact statements rather than evaluating their adequacy or the merits of projects in light of the likely environmental consequences. Although there are guidelines specifying when an environmental impact statement should be filed, these are often vague; some federal agencies, for example, require statements when "actions are likely to be highly controversial." Even when statements are presented, they may gloss over matters of great concern to environmentalists. Since the agencies generally prefer to carry out programs rather than to question whether some environmental damage may result, they are ill prepared to undertake the introspection called for by NEPA. Consequently, it is not surprising that the CEQ has concluded, "Too often the environmental impact statement is written to justify decisions already made, rather than to provide a mechanism for critical review."[35]

Environmental groups such as the Wilderness Society have interceded when they believed that CEQ was not sufficiently vigilant. By seeking injunctions when they believe that an agency has failed to file a needed EIS, or that its EIS is inadequate, or that the concerns raised in the EIS have not been considered by policymakers, private groups have delayed some projects and secured additional protection for the environment. During NEPA's first decade, private plaintiffs filed 1,200 suits.

While judges have often agreed with conservationists to the extent of requiring statements when none has been filed, they have shown greater tolerance in deciding what constitutes an adequate study. Thus, if an agency has prepared an impact statement, plaintiffs are unlikely to prevent a project unless they can prove that an official has incorrectly interpreted the law.[36] Since NEPA requires only that environmental consequences be considered and does not specify when environmental protection is to take precedence over project objectives, projects may be carried out despite the environmental harm noted in the impact statements.

Although they may ultimately fail to prevent a project, environmentalists have caused delays in 15 to 20 percent of the energy projects where suits have been filed.[37] These delays occur relatively infrequently. An average of more than 1,200 EISs are filed each year; less than 10 percent of these result in litigation. Plaintiffs win only about one-fifth of the cases they file.

The infrequency with which NEPA has obstructed federal projects has been lost sight of because of a few heavily publicized issues, the best known of these being the Alaska pipeline.[38] The point of the 1970s controversy was the desirability of laying an 800-mile pipeline to transport 2 million gallons of oil daily from Alaska's North Slope to the year-round port of Valdez. Conservationists warned that placing the pipeline above ground might impede migratory patterns of the region's wildlife. Even less desirable, they cautioned, would be the practice of burying the pipeline underground. In the first place, they argued, the high temperature generated by the speed of the oil being pumped southward would cause the surrounding tundra to melt, so that the pipeline might sink and rupture. In the second place, earthquakes in the area also could produce a massive spill. Even with the best technology, if the line should break when it was operating at capacity, at least 165,000 barrels of oil would spurt out before the flow could be stopped.

The EIS on the project pointed out that damage would occur to the flora and that scars inflicted during construction would take as long as 150 years to heal fully. Opponents of the pipeline concluded that the damage to the environment would be so severe that it would be preferable to transport the oil by tanker direct from the North Slope, even though ice floes would curtail such shipment for several months each year.

On the other hand, oil companies involved in tapping Alaska's oil reserves pointed to the chronic need for new domestic oil. These needs became quite real to many Americans during 1973 and 1974 as angry motorists queued up to purchase rationed supplies of gasoline. Oil company arguments had already won over the Department of the Interior, whose secretary authorized construction of the pipeline.

The critical event leading to congressional participation was an environmentalist suit, *Morton* v. *Wilderness Society*, decided by the Supreme Court in 1973. The decision blocked construction of the pipeline because it would require usage of more than the 50-foot-wide right-of-way permitted by the 1920 Mineral Leasing Act. In November 1973 Congress passed legislation prohibiting further delays under NEPA or through litigation raising environmental questions. Thereupon the authorization for the pipeline granted by the Secretary of Interior became effective; and the struggle by environmentalists, which had lasted several years, came to an end. The trans-Alaska pipeline was completed in 1977.

The response by Congress to the environmentalists' challenge to the Alaska pipeline suggests that, given current needs, energy policy will ultimately take precedence over environmental policy when the two policies clash head to head. On the other hand, although they eventually lost the struggle to prevent construction, the environmentalists were able to secure some important modifications in the design of the pipeline.

PUBLIC LANDS: CONSERVATION OR COMMERCIAL DEVELOPMENT

The United States government continues to own vast stretches of land, particularly in the western states: most of Alaska is federally owned; in five other states the federal government holds title to more than half the land; and even California, with its sprawling cities, is 44 percent federal land. Where federal holdings are extensive, the health of the local economy often hinges on the uses made of federal lands. If the lands are left as trackless wilderness, they generate no revenue for the local areas. Making some of the land available for recreational use will bring in some local income from the sale of camping supplies, fishing gear, and so on; however, sometimes the greatest income will accrue to the local community if the land is made available to private concerns. Each year individuals and large corporations are permitted to use millions of acres of public lands to make private profits. Mining companies extract valuable minerals from public lands, ranchers lease grazing rights, and timber rights are sold to logging companies.

Opposing the ranchers, miners, and timber companies are environmentalist groups. They counter the proposals for making money from the exploitation of federal lands by extolling the land's natural beauty, which once sullied cannot be regained. Environmentalists argue that today's increasingly urban population needs to be able to escape to inspiring vistas, wild streams, and quiet forests. Moreover, they urge that some parts of the nation should be left unchanged for the enjoyment of future generations. Environmentalists also point to the biological function of forests, which provide wildlife habitats and convert carbon dioxide into oxygen.

Representatives of a variety of interests eager to make greater use of federal lands, such as James Watt, President Reagan's former Secretary of Interior, charge that the nation is economically handicapped because resources on federal lands cannot be developed. They contend that if we were allowed to extract the petroleum and minerals on federal property it would reduce the balance of payments deficit and reduce our dependence on foreign countries for a number of minerals, such as cobalt, manganese, nickel, and zinc. This dependence, they warn ominously, could become critical in time of war. Timber interests, claiming that timber yields from private lands are approaching the upper limits, want Congress to allow additional logging in national forests. As timber companies are quick to point out, trees are a renewable resource and plastics or metals will be substituted if wood products are unavailable.

Whether to use or conserve national resources has become something of a regional confrontation. Some westerners complain that restrictions on federal lands limit their region's development. They see these restraints as imposed by an eastern-dominated Congress.

Through the 1960s and 1970s the conservationists had the upper hand. Legislation authorizing the protection of wild, free-flowing rivers, designations of wilderness areas in which development was prohibited, and the creation of national seashores was approved (see table 4–5). In addition the amount of land encompassed in national parks and monuments and state parks grew substantially. Passage of the Alaska Lands Act in the waning days of the Carter presidency, which designated 104 million acres as national parks, forests, wildlife refuges, and wild and scenic rivers, may signal the culmination of conservationist efforts.

The Reagan administration is opposed to expanding national park lands. It has also shown itself prepared to tolerate development of the resources on federal lands, including wilderness areas. This suggests that President Reagan's many supporters in the West—the region where he outpolled Jimmy Carter by the largest margins—may have been instrumental in turning the tide in the struggle between users and conservationists.

TABLE 4-5 Major conservation legislation and expansions, 1960–1980

Legislation/Program	Purpose	Extent
New legislation		
Wilderness Act, 1964	Restrictive designation for use of federal lands	94 million acres
Wild and Scenic Rivers Act, 1968	Maintain free-flowing (undammed) rivers	27 rivers, 700,000 acres[a]
National Trails Act, 1968	Trail preservation and maintenance	257 trails
Endangered Species Act, 1973	Promote survival of rare plants and animals	
Alaska Lands Act, 1980	Preserve land in Alaska with limited use	104 million acres
Existing programs		
National Wildlife Refuges	Protect habitats of wild animals and fowl	Enlarged by 25 million acres[a]
National Parks	Preserve natural areas for public enjoyment and recreation	Enlarged by 5 million acres[a]

[a]Figures exclude lands added in Alaska.

THE ENVIRONMENT VERSUS ENERGY: THE TRADE-OFFS

In this chapter we have described the major requirements of legislation designed to protect the environment, with special emphasis on efforts to rid air and streams of pollution and to limit emissions from automobiles. The preceding chapter outlined our nation's current energy policy, including the comprehensive program that President Carter sent to Congress in the spring of 1977. In the course of these two chapters we have sometimes noted in passing that some objectives of environmental protection legislation require greater use of energy, or that achievement of some energy goals may necessitate fouling the environment. In this section we deal more explicitly with the conflicts between the policies of these two areas.

One such conflict concerns the increased use of coal. Each of the last four administrations has emphasized the need to increase coal production and the use of coal as a fuel substitute for petroleum products. President Carter urged that annual coal production be increased from 665 million tons to 1.1 billion tons by 1985. Hiking coal production will require more extensive strip mining. But if strip miners are forced to reclaim the land, coal extraction will become more expensive and possibly slower. Since any additional costs would be passed on to consumers, they will not switch from natural gas or oil to coal until petroleum products become even more expensive, so that the conversion from gas and oil will be delayed. It should be noted that deep-pit mining, while a potential alternative to strip mining, has drawbacks of its own: subsidence of surface land, higher cost, and higher incidence of injury to workers.

Even if coal production goals are met, there remain obstacles to the use of this fuel. Large amounts of the coal reserve contain high levels of sulfur. The strictures of the Clean Air Act and the regulations proposed by the EPA prevent the burning of much of this coal in large sections of the country unless steps are taken to reduce the sulfur oxide that is emitted. In areas where "scrubbers" would have to be installed to clean up emissions, the adaptation would be costly. Moreover, there are problems involved in disposing of the sludge from the scrubbers. Dumping it into a nearby river—a popular solution in some quarters—is prohibited by the 1972 amendments to the Water Pollution Control Act.

In addition to coal, hydroelectric power is an energy alternative to petroleum products. While hydroelectric power cannot provide more than a small share of America's energy needs, some environmental legislation limits the extent to which water power can be used to generate electricity. Rivers protected by the Wild and Scenic Rivers Act cannot be dammed. The construction of several other dams has been held up temporarily because of the 1973 Endangered Species Act, which prohibits actions detrimental to rare animals or plants.

A third potential source of fuel is oil shale, which is found in many parts of the West. At present the costs of extracting oil from shale are too high to make it a feasible alternative. Should recovery of oil from this source become economically feasible, there would probably be objections from environmentalists, since the extraction technology requires vast amounts of water—a quantity in short supply in the arid West. Furthermore, the shale residue left after the oil has been removed would, some environmentalists warn, be blown by the winds, producing great clouds of dust, which would pollute the air and the remaining water.

The requirement for environmental impact statements is seen in some quarters as a serious impediment to various activities that would provide some relief to the energy crisis. Environmentalists have often sued to prevent activities when federal agencies responsible for protecting the environment have no objections to the contemplated private development. (The earlier discussion of the Alaska pipeline is an example.) The construction of power plants, especially those that would use radioactive materials, is often delayed for years as power companies seek to overcome judicial challenges brought by environmentalists. New refineries and offshore docking facilities capable of handling supertankers have also been targets of objections based on their potential harm to the environment. Similar challenges to proposed new offshore drilling for oil have been voiced in some parts of the country. Environmentalists have been particularly fearful that offshore transfer or recovery of oil will produce additional devastating spills. Oil companies argue that they take great care to prevent such accidents, and they admit that they cannot eliminate all risks but insist that the benefits offset the likely costs.

Finally, efforts thus far to reduce auto emissions have resulted in less efficient use of gasoline. Estimates are that pollution control devices have increased gasoline consumption by approximately 10 percent. In a number of instances, then, the objectives of environmental protection and conservation of domestic petroleum supplies are incompatible.

CONCLUDING COMMENTS

Both in his campaign and since his inauguration Ronald Reagan has indicated that he believes that environmental concerns have received too much emphasis. As a candidate he charged that nature in the form of Mount Saint Helens and even trees and other plants caused far more air pollution than does industry. As president, Reagan quickly began cutting back the scope of federal environmental efforts. The staff of the CEQ was chopped and the Reagan budget cut environmental funding levels to 42 percent below what President Carter had proposed. The president's cutbacks affected all aspects of environmental protection. In terms of water pollution, not only were few funds earmarked for sewer construction but funding was to go only to the larger systems, where it would be available for remedying current problems and not for extending sewer mains. There was also less money for rehabilitating strip-mined land and for cleaning up chemical dumps.

Congressional investigators were particularly suspicious of Rita Lavelle, the EPA's assistant administrator responsible for cleaning up toxic dumps under the superfund legislation. Before her EPA appointment, Lavelle worked for a firm charged with dumping wastes at a site now slated for cleanup. While at EPA, she had frequent contacts with firms that were under investigation for creating toxic dumps in violation of EPA rules. Lavelle's sympathy for the preferences of polluters rather than environmentalists became apparent when she indicated an unwillingness to assess financial penalties to discourage the use of landfills to dispose of hazardous wastes.[39] Part of the reason given for her dismissal in February 1983 was a memo that she allegedly wrote criticizing EPA's chief counsel for "systematically alienating the primary constituents of this Administration, the business community."[40]

On the issues considered when legislation designed to improve water and air quality was reviewed in the early 1980s, President Reagan usually sided with business. Reagan and his advisers endorsed plans to reduce the influence of EPA as part of their deregulation effort. They have also gone on record in favor of making federal lands more accessible for energy development.

Another aspect of Reagan administration proposals for reducing federal authority over environmental protection is to decentralize decision making. Shortly before taking office President Reagan urged: "We should return to the states the primary responsibility for environmental regulation in order to increase responsiveness to local conditions."[41]

Environmentalists have found little in President Reagan's program to applaud. They plan to monitor closely the actions of the Reagan administration and to see that the positive legislation of the last two decades is not ignored. As a director of the Sierra Club said, "The old rapist days are over. Even the worst that could happen is not as bad as the worst that could have happened ten years ago. We're all expecting to be in court a lot more."[42] Environmental groups may be able to take advantage of the rapid growth in their membership ranks and contributions after the 1980 Republican victories, as frightened environmentalists rallied to the colors.

NOTES

1. Walter A. Rosenbaum, *The Politics of Environmental Concern*, 1st ed. (New York: Praeger, 1973), p. 14.
2. For a discussion of early federal efforts, see Lettie McSpadden Wenner, *One Environment under Law: A Public-Policy Dilemma* (Pacific Palisades, Calif.: Goodyear, 1976), pp. 71–84.
3. J. Clarence Davies and Barbara S. Davies, *The Politics of Pollution*, 2nd ed. (Indianapolis: Pegasus, 1975), p. 208.
4. Ibid., p. 194.
5. Lawrence Mosher, "Clean Water Requirements Will Remain Even if the Federal Spigot Is Closed," *National Journal* 13 (May 6, 1981): 874–878.
6. Council on Environmental Quality (CEQ), *Environmental Quality, 1980* (Washington, D.C.: U.S. Government Printing Office, 1980), p. 100.
7. CEQ, *Environmental Quality, 1979* (Washington, D.C.: U.S. Government Printing Office, 1979), p. 137.
8. CEQ, *Environmental Quality, 1980*, pp. 86, 87, 119.
9. Kathy Koch, "Dealing with Environmental, Health Effects of Coal Use," *Congressional Quarterly Weekly Report* 38 (May 31, 1980): 1490.

10. Kathy Koch, "Coming Clean Air Debate Will Reflect Traditional Costs vs. Benefits Quandary," *Congressional Quarterly Weekly Report* 39 (February 7, 1981): 268.

11. Prudence Crewdson, "Congress Faces Hard Choices on Clean Air Act," *Congressional Quarterly Weekly Report* 34 (June 7, 1976): 1172.

12. Rosenbaum, *Politics of Environmental Concern,* p. 156.

13. Lawrence Mosher, "Acid Rain Debate May Play a Role in the 1984 Presidential Sweepstakes," *National Journal* 15 (May 14, 1983): 998–999.

14. Koch, "Coming Clean Air Debate," p. 268.

15. CEQ, *Environmental Quality, 1979,* p. 44.

16. Timothy B. Clark, "A Market for Air Pollution," *National Journal* 10 (August 19, 1978): 1332.

17. Kathy Koch, "National Commission Report Starts Congressional Debates on Renewing Clean Air Act," *Congressional Quarterly Weekly Report* 39 (March 7, 1981): 424.

18. H. Barclay Moxley, "Cleaning the Nation's Air," *National Journal* 12 (November 29, 1980): 2054; and Lawrence Mosher, "Big Steel Says It Can't Afford to Make the Nation's Air Pure," *National Journal* 12 (July 5, 1980): 1088.

19. Davies and Davies, *Politics of Pollution,* pp. 196–197.

20. Ibid., p. 93.

21. Walter A. Rosenbaum, *The Politics of Environmental Concern,* 2nd ed. (New York: Praeger, 1977), p. 163.

22. Quoted in Lawrence Mosher, "Clean Air Act an Inviting Target for Industry Critics Next Year," *National Journal* 12 (November 15, 1980): 1928.

23. Quoted in Koch, "Coming Clean Air Debate," p. 270.

24. Ibid., p. 268. The federal OMB estimates that during the 1980s compliance with environmental requirements could cost business half a trillion dollars.

25. CEQ, *Environmental Quality, 1979,* pp. 665–668.

26. Allen V. Kneese and Charles L. Schultze, *Pollution, Prices, and Public Policy* (Washington, D.C.: Brookings Institution, 1975), p. 21.

27. Dick Kirschten, "Something to Cheer About," *National Journal* 10 (December 16, 1978): 2031, quotes poll undertaken by Resources for the Future.

28. CBS News–*New York Times* Poll, released February 2, 1981, p. 13.

29. CBS News–*New York Times* Poll, released April 1983, p. 11.

30. CEQ, *Environmental Quality, 1980,* p. 407.

31. "Federal Officials Announce Efforts to End Half of Jet Noise by 1985," *Houston Chronicle,* November 19, 1976, section 1, p. 11.

32. Kathy Koch, "Cleaning Up Chemical Dumps Posing Problems for Congress," *Congressional Quarterly Weekly Report* 38 (March 22, 1980): 796.

33. Quoted in ibid., p. 802.

34. CEQ, *Environmental Quality, 1979,* p. 262.

35. CEQ, *Environmental Quality, 1971* (Washington, D.C.: U.S. Government Printing Office, 1971), p. 26.

36. Rosenbaum, *Politics of Environmental Concern,* 1st ed., p. 272.

37. CEQ, *Environmental Quality, 1979,* p. 590.

38. The discussion of the Alaska pipeline is drawn from Gerald Garvey, *Energy, Ecology, Economy* (New York: Norton, 1972), pp. 106–107.

39. *National Journal* 14 (May 29, 1982): 956.

40. Steven R. Weisman, "Uproar over Toxic Waste," *New York Times* (February 17, 1983): 15.

41. Lawrence Mosher, "Reagan and Environmental Protection—None of the Laws Will Be Untouchable," *National Journal* 13 (January 3, 1981): 17.

42. Bill Keller, "Environmental Movement Checks Its Pulse and Finds Obituaries Are Premature," *Congressional Quarterly Weekly Report* 39 (January 31, 1981): 214.

SUGGESTED READINGS

Boyle, Robert H., and Alexander, R. *Acid Rain.* New York: Lyons/Schocken, 1983.

Davies, J. Clarence, and Davies, Barbara S. *The Politics of Pollution.* 2nd ed. Indianapolis: Pegasus, 1975.

Jones, Charles O. *Clean Air: The Politics and Policies of Pollution Control.* Pittsburgh: University of Pittsburgh Press, 1975.

Kneese, Allen V., and Schultze, Charles L. *Pollution, Prices, and Public Policy.* Washington, D.C.: Brookings Institution, 1975.

Rosenbaum, Walter A. *The Politics of Environmental Concern.* 2nd ed. New York: Praeger, 1977.

Wenner, Lettie McSpadden. *One Environment under Law: A Public-Policy Dilemma.* Pacific Palisades, Calif.: Goodyear, 1976.

FIVE

Welfare, Medical Care, and the War on Poverty

The roots of welfare run deep in our history, even if the fruit produced is not always bountiful. During the last two generations, welfare became increasingly a responsibility of the federal government. Its benefits have been broadened into new areas and distributed through a growing number of programs, and the cost has spiraled ever upward. This chapter first describes the social and political environment in which welfare programs developed. We will then describe the major programs. Some of these provide cash, as does Supplemental Security Income. Others, such as the housing programs, offer a commodity but no money for the poor. Still other programs help the needy obtain specific benefits, such as food or health care, by paying federal dollars directly to the provider rather than to the person being helped. Through the combination of these programs, the federal government provides, at least in rudimentary fashion, for basic human needs.

This chapter addresses (1) the major welfare programs initiated during the administration of Franklin D. Roosevelt; (2) subsidized housing programs; (3) Medicare and Medicaid programs; (4) programs that emerged as a result of Lyndon B. Johnson's War on Poverty (for instance, Project Head Start, various job-training programs, and community action programs); and (5) the food stamp program. Reforms proposed and implemented by President Reagan for each area will also be noted.

ALLEVIATIVE PROGRAMS: THE WELFARE STATE

Every society has its orphans, widows, aged, and sick—people who cannot fully care for themselves and must depend on others to some degree. Traditionally, care for the unfortunate was provided locally, primarily by the relatives of the poor; the elderly were cared for by their children, and orphans were taken in by aunts and uncles, cousins, or grandparents. Then, at about the same time that English colonization of America began, Parliament passed the first welfare laws. This early legislation provided that poor people who could not be cared for by their families were the responsibility of the local community. This same pattern—of families caring for their less fortunate members, with local authorities providing whatever supplemental assistance was available—was adopted in this country.

This approach evidenced little change until the Great Depression of the 1930s. As the country sank to the nadir of the economic cycle, local and state resources proved insufficient for the massive levels of unemployment and the widespread need for income and essential goods and services. With the unemployment rate exceeding 20 percent, the rudimentary welfare system designed to help widows, orphans, and the elderly was inundated with millions of able-bodied people who would gladly work and support their families but could not find jobs.

The depression placed greater strain on the traditional system of assistance than had previous financial panics, since during earlier depressions most Americans could at least provide bare economic necessities for themselves. Until 1920 most Americans lived on farms, so that even when times were bad many families could raise their food, continue to live in their homes, and help each other. Moreover, an opportunity that in the past had helped large numbers of people begin their economic recovery, namely, cheap land along the frontier, was no longer available.

The lines outside the depression soup kitchens raised doubts in the minds of some Americans about the adequacy of commonly accepted attributes of the nation's approach to poverty. One of the first assumptions to be questioned was the proposition that the federal government bears no responsibility for the care of the poor. As it became increasingly clear that local resources, both private and public, were inadequate to the mammoth tasks confronting them, the federal government emerged as the only possible bulwark for the needy.

Second, some people began to wonder whether—as had long been assumed—the poor really were solely responsible for their plight. A widespread belief (not wholly displaced today) was that poverty is caused by laziness, drunkenness, or some other personal shortcoming. The joblessness and resulting need of the depression affected former factory owners as well as former factory workers, pointing up the fact that poverty could and did touch even those who were most hardworking and conscientious about setting something aside for a rainy day. No longer were the old virtues of thrift and diligence sufficient. Individuals no longer controlled their destinies but instead were dependent on corporations and banks, which succeeded or failed depending on distant fluctuations of the stock market and the international financial community.

Awareness of these societal changes brought about a growing support for programs that would provide some income and services for the poor and unemployed. Although millions of formerly middle-class citizens suffered and came to support the idea of federal welfare assistance, the conservative element in society continued to oppose federal involvement in this new sphere. They clung to the old myths of self-reliance and raised the symbol of states' rights as a barrier to federal intervention. If federal revenues were given to the poor, these people said, they would lose all initiative to care for themselves and would grow lazy as they dined at the federal trough. Conservatives also warned that even if the initial programs were modest, they would, in time, be expanded. Therefore, even a small-scale federal program would be a dangerous precedent.

With the election of Franklin D. Roosevelt as president in 1932, proponents of comprehensive welfare assistance gained ascendance among the federal policymakers. Supported by huge liberal majorities in Congress, the New Deal programs were enacted, ushering in a series of federal programs designed to help those in need.

The relief policies begun during the New Deal were alleviative in nature. Programs, such as Old Age Assistance, were designed to provide small amounts of money to reduce the hardships of poverty for people who for some reason could not work.

The rationale behind alleviative programs is that each citizen is entitled to some minimal level of subsistence; therefore, the federal government will provide a small amount of money or goods with which the recipient is to care for self and family. The money is not, however, simply there for the asking. To get it, one must demonstrate need and also fit into a category that qualifies for aid. The "needs test" is clearly initiated in response to critics who suspect that the indolent and undeserving will try to obtain benefits improperly. Need has been defined in terms of wealth and number of dependents. Thus, a widow with one child must have less income to qualify than would a widow having several dependent children, since the former will have fewer expenses than the latter.

Cash Assistance Programs

The categories of people who qualified for federal relief programs were the elderly, who could receive Old Age Assistance; widows (and other women without husbands) and their dependent children, who could participate in the Aid to Families with Dependent Children (AFDC) program; the blind; and the permanently and totally disabled. Until 1974 all four categoric aid programs were operated in the same way. That is, federal grants constituted part of the benefits, while the states that operated the programs (under a system of matching funds) also provided some of the funding. In 1974 a major change was made in the programs for the aged, blind, and disabled; that is, the more than 1,000 state and local categoric programs that received federal aid were combined, and their funding was taken over by the federal government. The new creation, called Supplemental Security Income (SSI), introduced uniform minimum benefits throughout the country. Increases in benefits are tied to the cost of living. Beneficiaries in poorer states have received more money as a result of the federalization of these programs. In September 1982 federal payments averaged $127.61 for aged recipients but more than $200 per month for each blind or disabled person. In most states, the state makes a payment in addition to the SSI grant. In some states—for instance, California and Massachusetts—the state contribution exceeds the federal. Some other states provide only a token subsidy.[1] The AFDC program continues to be administered under the "matching funds" system, which allows even greater disparities in benefits. AFDC payments in 1981 averaged $29 per month in Mississippi per person, compared with $171 per month per recipient in Alaska.[2] The federal contribution constitutes 50 to 77 percent of the AFDC payments made by states.

The SSI program, unlike most others discussed in this chapter, has not experienced soaring increases. Indeed, from 1975 to 1980 there was a gradual decrease in recipients. This is the only entitlement welfare program (entitlement programs are those in which the federal government guarantees benefits to all who are eligible) for which annual costs have grown at a moderate pace—an average of only 6.2 percent a year.

Of the four categories of cash assistance, three have come to be almost universally accepted. The AFDC program, however, remains very unpopular in some quarters. Some critics insist that the program fosters illegitimacy by paying money to unwed mothers, since the larger the family the greater the amount of benefits received. The size of the program also contributes to its unpopularity. It has many more beneficiaries than the other three, approximately 11 million in recent years. In addition to attracting opposition because of its numbers of participants, increases in the cost of AFDC have contributed to its unpopularity among conservatives. As table 5–1 shows, the cost more than doubled between 1970 and 1976, even though the number of participants has remained between 9.7 and 11.4 million since 1970. Another aspect of AFDC has been the disproportionate number of black participants. Although blacks make up about 12 percent of the population, they comprise more than 40 percent of all AFDC recipients.

In short, conservatives criticize the AFDC program for being expensive and poorly designed. As AFDC rolls began to swell rapidly, conservatives in Congress tried several tactics in hopes of curbing expenses. The first strategy was to increase the number of social workers assigned to AFDC families, in hopes that more intensive counseling and supervision would increase the number of families able to leave welfare by becoming self-sufficient.[3] But as the number of AFDC recipients continued to rise, Congress tried a new tactic. AFDC mothers were first allowed

TABLE 5–1   Aid to Families with Dependent Children (AFDC) program participation and costs

	Participants (in millions)		Cost (in millions)
	Total	Children	
1960	3.1	2.4	$ 1,055
1965	4.5	3.4	1,809
1970	9.7	7.0	4,857
1971	10.7	7.7	5,653
1972	11.1	8.0	6,710
1973	10.8	7.8	7,292
1974	11.0	7.9	7,990
1975	11.4	8.1	9,211
1976	11.2	7.9	10,140
1977	10.8	7.6	10,603
1978	10.3	7.2	10,729
1979	10.4	7.2	11,069
1980	11.1	7.6	11,102
1981	11.1	8.0[a]	12,550[a]
1982	11.0		

SOURCE: U.S. Bureau of the Census, *Statistical Abstract of the United States* (Washington, D.C.: U.S. Government Printing Office, annual issues for the years shown).

[a]Estimated figures.

and then, in 1971, required, to sign up for work-training programs. (There were some exclusions; mothers of preschool children, for instance, were not forced to participate in work training.) The assumption behind this approach was that mothers who wanted to work could be trained for jobs that would pay enough for them to get their families off welfare. To make work training a realistic possibility for mothers of dependent children, day-care centers were to be provided for participants. Defects in the program have been the failure to create enough day-care facilities, the inadequacy of the training provided, and the low salaries offered many mothers who took jobs after completing the training. Often women would be better off continuing to receive welfare and other benefits, rather than taking the available poor-paying jobs and forfeiting public assistance. Beginning in 1967 AFDC recipients lost sixty cents worth of benefits for each dollar earned,[4] but starting in 1982 their benefits are cut by an amount equal to what they earn.

The third attempt by Congress to hold down welfare costs showed the least imagination. The Ways and Means Committee of the House of Representatives put a ceiling on the amount of money available to care for children added to AFDC rolls because of illegitimacy or desertion by their fathers. This placed the burden squarely on the states, since while program registrants would continue to grow, the federal government's contribution to the costs of the program would not. Having exhausted its own supply of remedies, Congress tried to force the states to come up with some ideas. Pressure from the states, which did not want to assume the additional financial burden, quickly forced Congress to relent and remove the ceilings.

On the other side of the political spectrum, AFDC is criticized for providing inadequate benefits. Specifically, critics note that benefits rarely lift families to the federally established poverty level. In 1980 federal officials, using Department of Agriculture estimates of how much income would be needed to inexpensively feed a family (the Orshansky Index), classified a family of four having less than $8,410 yearly income as poor. With the average monthly benefits received by an AFDC family of four being less than $400, this program alone is insufficient to raise most recipients out of poverty. (AFDC critics note that participants in this program typically receive other benefits that, in combination, may suffice to lift a family above the poverty line. We will return to this point shortly.)

Both liberals and conservatives agree that the program is poorly administered. Liberals complain about the red tape and petty rules that may keep some of the eligible from receiving benefits. They deplore the long applications, embarrassing needs tests, and questions about personal matters such as sex life. Some liberal critics charge that some of the regulations are counterproductive. For example, although female-headed households are much more likely to be poor than are those having male heads, some states' AFDC regulations encourage fathers to desert their families. (Although federal matching funds have been available since 1961 to states that extend benefits to families with unemployed fathers, only 25 states have exercised this option.) Where the presence of an unemployed male in the home makes the family ineligible for AFDC, a father may decide that his family will be better off if he leaves. Thus, the family is broken up, and a potential breadwinner and needed role model may be gone forever. On the other hand, some conservatives believe that the eligibility requirements are not stringent enough.

Liberal critics of AFDC have urged the federal government to take over the program as it took over the other categoric aid programs. They point out that there would then be equality of benefits among the states, with increases coming in states that are least generous. Moreover, if all states paid the same benefits, there would no longer be an incentive for AFDC families to move from states offering low benefits to states that are more generous. Financially hard-pressed state and local administrators also urge the federal government to relieve them of their welfare burdens. For example, New York City's brush with bankruptcy was in part caused by the huge sums it pays out in AFDC.

The very costliness of AFDC has caused many congressmen concerned about widening federal budget deficits to oppose increasing federal responsibilities for the program. Instead of incurring greater expense and standardizing benefits nation-wide, recent federal laws have attempted to reduce costs. One technique has been to order states to locate fathers who have deserted their children and to extract support payments from them. The Department of Health and Human Services makes Social Security numbers available to states to help locate fathers who have ceased supporting their families. (President Carter convinced Congress to divide the Department of Health, Education, and Welfare into a Department of Health and Human Services and a Department of Education.)

Many critical policymakers continue to suspect that the welfare rolls contain large numbers of cheats. These suspicions were fueled by recent studies reporting that 16 percent of all AFDC payments involved errors, costing approximately $1 billion annually. To force the states, which are responsible for day-to-day adminis-tration of the program, to tighten eligibility screening, the federal government has threatened them with loss of a share of the federal matching funds.

Reagan proposals.   Liberals charge that President Reagan has tried to balance the federal budget on the backs of poor people. Conservatives respond that "this administration wants welfare to help only people who are down and out."[5] Irrespec-tive of one's value judgment, both sides agree that legislation supported by the Reagan administration has tightened up eligibility standards so as to exclude the working poor. Other changes are designed to force the poor who can work to do so for as many hours as it would take when earning the minimum wage to pay for the benefits received. Many of those who have retained eligibility have lost some benefits.

Changes in the rules made 10 percent of the households that had received AFDC ineligible in late 1981 and cut the benefits of another 7 percent. This was done by reducing the value of assets families can have and still be eligible, as well as the amount a recipient can earn, and cutting the amount of child-care expenses that can be offset against earnings. The impact of cutting back AFDC rolls is magnified since people ineligible for AFDC may also lose Medicaid benefits, a program to be discussed shortly.

The president's budget proposal for fiscal year 1983 called for further belt-tightening in order to scale AFDC costs back to $10.4 billion, a figure below any amount spent during the last half decade, especially if one adjusts for inflation.

A more revolutionary change than that encompassed in the budget-cutting efforts was outlined in President Reagan's 1982 State of the Union address. He proposed that states assume full responsibility for AFDC and food stamps in return for Washington making Medicaid a wholly national program. This is precisely the opposite of what occurred when SSI assigned three other categoric aid programs to the federal government. Those who speak for the poor oppose giving states full control of AFDC since, they argue, many states have never provided adequate funds. Elimination of a federal role would, they fear, result in even less generous funding than is currently found in some states. In February 1982 the nation's governors voted by a 36 to 5 margin not to take on the AFDC and food stamps programs, although not surprisingly they did favor federal operation of Medicaid. Congress has taken no steps to enact the proposed exchange of programs.

IN-KIND PROGRAMS

In-kind programs discussed in this section provide a commodity or service rather than money to the poor. In part this strategy stems from the distrust of the poor that is widespread among policymakers. From the suspicion that the poor are in large part responsible for their plight comes the belief that if they are given money they will spend it foolishly rather than for the commodities that policymakers intended. One way to assure that a program designed to feed the poor does result in food and not "luxuries" being purchased is to give recipients food stamps rather than cash. The creators of the New Deal programs that provide cash believed that beneficiaries would be "deserving" poor who were temporarily down on their luck but could return to self-sufficiency. A more pessimistic view of poor people underlies the programs discussed here.

A second reason for structuring programs so that benefits may only be used for the purpose intended is that poor people are not the sole beneficiaries. Part of the rationale for food programs has been to help farmers by creating additional consumers. Moreover, housing programs have helped the construction industry whose health is vital to the nation's economy.

Housing Programs

For more than forty years there have been programs to subsidize the housing costs of some low-income families. Federal housing programs have been motivated by two considerations. First, poor housing conditions have been linked to a number of pathologies, particularly sickness and crime. It was hoped that new housing, by eliminating filth and vermin and by providing more pleasant surroundings, would make the poor healthier. Second, because the construction industry is such an important component of the economy, federal aid that spurs new building has wide-ranging economic consequences.

In this section we will discuss the range of housing programs for the poor. We will then evaluate the federal housing efforts and briefly note some of the recent proposals for redirecting efforts to provide decent shelter.

Public housing.   For many years the only form of housing assistance was public housing. In this program federal funds are given to local communities for the purpose of building or buying inexpensive rental units. Public housing projects have generally lacked amenities but have been structurally sound. The appeal of public housing has been that units rent for less than what private landlords would charge for comparable shelter. Thus, it allows families who would otherwise be forced to live in rat-infested, dilapidated tenements or shacks to rent a unit with a good roof, airtight walls and floors, central heat, and, in some new projects, air conditioning. Rents in housing projects are based on the tenants' income and the size of the family. The program was designed for the less affluent working poor. Some income is needed to qualify; however, growing income or declining family size could make one ineligible, forcing a move to privately owned housing.

Since its beginning in 1937, public housing has been erected in hundreds of towns and cities. In smaller communities projects are often composed of duplexes or two-story apartments with only four to eight units per building. Projects often have extensive public grounds, and tenants are allowed to have flower and vegetable gardens. Within a project may be units of various sizes—from efficiency apartments for the elderly to single-family, detached houses with as many as four bedrooms. In some small cities housing projects compare favorably, visually, with private developments designed for moderate-income families. In large central cities, however, public housing has followed a very different design. Exorbitant land costs have prompted erection of high-rise buildings by public housing authorities. Since the main objective was to house a maximum number of people on a minimum of land, little space was left for recreation.

The population density of high-rise projects has drawn a great deal of criticism. The impersonal nature of these developments is blamed in part for the high crime rates found in some of them. In describing high-rise public housing projects, one observer charged, "They spawn teen-age gangs. They incubate crime. They are fiendishly contrived institutions for the debasing of family and community life to the lowest common mean."[6] A study of two adjoining public housing projects in New York City found that the high-rise one had four times as many robberies as did the low-rise one.[7] In the Pruitt-Igoe Project in Saint Louis—a multibuilding, high-rise project that upon completion had been hailed as the way of the future for urban public housing—crime and vandalism became so rife that people refused to live in the development. Vacant units had windows smashed and plumbing fixtures ripped out. After several unsuccessful efforts to attract residents, Saint Louis authorities gave up on their dream-turned-nightmare and dynamited the buildings.

The high incidence of various forms of antisocial behavior in projects like Pruitt-Igoe has been a factor in making public housing an unattractive program in many circles. The high proportion of black residents (70 percent) in public housing is a second factor in its unpopularity. Further contributing to the relatively low levels of support for public housing has been middle-class distaste for programs to help the poor. While those attitudes have become modified with time, they seem to remain fairly strong where public housing is concerned.

Not only has the public housing program failed to develop a strong clientele who could achieve its expansion in Congress; it has also faced a powerful coalition of opponents. Conservative groups like chambers of commerce have opposed the program on ideological grounds. Some real estate interests, such as the National Association of Home Builders and the National Association of Real Estate Boards, have opposed public housing on economic grounds. They prefer alternatives in which the federal government does not compete with the private sector in building and renting apartments.

Subsidies and supplements: 1960s.   The unpopularity of public housing led to the development of alternative programs, which allowed a larger role for private industry. Congress authorized participation of profit-making components of the housing industry in the task of sheltering the poor. In two programs launched in 1968, low- and moderate-income families paid a specified proportion of their income for shelter, and the federal government made up the deficit between what the family could afford and the market price of the unit. The rent supplement program (Section 236) required that tenants pay 25 percent of their income toward rent. The government approved apartment developments for participation in the program and regulated the rent that landlords could charge.

In theory at least, all participants benefited from this program. The rent supplement program was less expensive for the federal government than public housing, since private entrepreneurs bore the costs of initial construction as well as management expenses. Tenants escaped the stigma attached to public housing projects, and they would not be forced to move if their earnings rose—as they would in public housing; instead, the size of the federal rent contribution would be gradually phased out as tenant incomes increased. Finally, rent supplements were attractive to private investors, who received tax breaks by depreciating the value of their apartments. Moreover, the federal supplements made it economically feasible to rent to a less affluent clientele, thereby opening a new market to the rental industry.

The other housing innovation of 1968 was the Section 235 mortgage subsidy program. The intent of this legislation was to permit families earning between $3,000 and $7,000 annually to buy homes. Eligible families were to pay 20 percent of their incomes in mortgage payments on houses selling for $15,000 to $20,000.

The federal contribution would be paid to the lending institution and would be used to reduce the purchaser's interest rate to as little as 1 percent (at the time of the legislation, housing interest rates varied from 6.5 to 7 percent). Loans made to participants were guaranteed by the Federal Housing Administration (FHA), which had extensive experience in guaranteeing the home loans of millions of middle-income Americans.

The rationale behind mortgage subsidies was based on the concept of pride of ownership. People working in real estate had long recognized that home owners tended to take better care of their dwellings than did renters. Owner-occupied homes are more likely to have well-kept yards and better-maintained dwellings than are rented premises. Program supporters hoped that mortgage subsidies would not only allow low- and moderate-income families to build up equity but would also stem the deterioration of many urban neighborhoods where the housing stock was structurally sound. Realtors and builders, who saw a whole new market opening before them, were strong supporters of the program. Chester Hartman says that the 1968 rent and mortgage subsidy programs "were largely the work of the most powerful Washington lobbying group in the housing and urban development field, the National Association of Home Builders, and a broadly based organization of large and small home builders, mortgage bankers, and some land speculators and realtors."[8]

Both the rent and mortgage subsidy programs developed serious problems. While they functioned successfully in some communities, elsewhere they became tainted by scandals, which received wide publicity. In retrospect, the programs relied too heavily on good intentions, with insufficient attention given to drafting precautions to prevent abuses by the unscrupulous and to screen applicants. Section 235 housing proved to be particularly susceptible to exploitation. Dishonest developers bought old houses needing extensive work, but they made only cosmetic improvements—for example, a paint job, a new ceiling, or stop-gap repairs on the furnace. They would then bribe the FHA appraiser whose job it was to establish the fair market price of the house. In this way, a developer might pay $9,000 for a house, spend $1,000 to make it more attractive, pay a $100 bribe, and then have the house appraised at $20,000. The developer would make a huge profit, and the house would be sold to an unsuspecting family that relied on the validity of the FHA's appraisal. After moving in and discovering that the roof leaked, or that rotted walls were crumbling under cheap wallpaper, or that the plumbing or furnace needed to be replaced, many new home owners decided that the joys of buying were vastly overrated. Unable to pay for costly repairs in addition to the mortgage, many buyers allowed lenders to foreclose. The down payment required was so small—a minimum of $200—that many purchasers had little incentive not to abandon their homes when they encountered difficulties. Since the loans are guaranteed by the FHA, the lender suffered no loss if the purchaser stopped making payments; the federal government simply paid off the balance of the loan and acquired the property. By mid-1975 the Department of Housing and Urban Development

(HUD) had more than 200,000 foreclosed units worth $2.7 billion on its hands. Vandals quickly broke into the foreclosed units, stripping them of copper pipes and plumbing fixtures. Losses to HUD mounted into the hundreds of millions of dollars as vandalized units deteriorated to the point at which they had to be razed.

Overpricing was not the only defect in the mortgage subsidy program. Too little care was exercised in screening loan applicants. Since loans were guaranteed by the FHA, the lender had less incentive to thoroughly check out the credit of applicants. Even reasonable diligence by lenders might have been unavailing in some circumstances, since some realtors doctored the credit records of applicants to make them appear to be good credit risks. Thus, even in the absence of fraudulent pricing, many Section 235 purchasers proved unable to make their payments.

Another cost created by the mismanagement of the mortgage subsidy program is less easily calculable although no less real. The presence of vacant houses owned by HUD provided a haven for transient alcoholics and drug addicts. By attracting undesirables to a neighborhood, Congress's well-intentioned but poorly conceived effort accelerated the deterioration of some of the very neighborhoods it was designed to save.

Poor families who sank their savings into decrepit wrecks and the American taxpayers were the big losers. Some dishonest realtors, developers, and appraisers were the only winners. Not surprisingly, HUD substantially altered the Section 235 program.

Subsidies: 1974.   The failure of the earlier subsidy programs led to refocusing. Requirements for participation in the 1974 revision of Section 235 are designed to exclude many who could have purchased homes under the earlier version. Interest rates are reduced to as low as 4 percent rather than 1 percent, minimum down payments are pegged to the price of the house but are at least 3 percent of the sale price, and minimal annual earnings for participation are much higher. Where the first Section 235 program's emphasis was on including a new segment of the population in the ranks of the prospective home owners, the post-1974 objective is less ambitious: "The program's focus is on low- and moderate-income families who traditionally have been buyers of new single-family homes but who are priced out of the market."[9] In 1981 families earning up to 130 percent of the median income in the area could qualify for mortgages of up to $40,000. If a participating family's economic condition improves, the size of the subsidy is reduced.

The Brooke-Cranston program, which is available only during recessions in order to stimulate the construction industry, is aimed at more expensive homes. Mortgages for houses costing as much as $60,000 are available at 3 percentage points below the prevailing rate.

Alternatives to the mortgage subsidy program were introduced by the Nixon administration. Section 8 of the 1974 housing legislation provides cash housing supplements not tied to a particular apartment complex. Under this program, families must be approved for participation and then locate an apartment that qualifies for the subsidy. As devised, the program is available to a broader economic range of tenants than is public housing. The 1974 legislation extended eligibility to families earning up to 80 percent of the local median income. Most participants have much lower incomes and Congress has considered lowering eligibility to those earning 50 to 60 percent of the median income.

Participants pay between 15 and 25 percent of their income for rent, depending on family size. While participants can look throughout a metropolitan area for an apartment, there are upper limits on the total cost for rent and utilities. Income eligibility is tied to rent costs; that is, families are ineligible if their earnings are more than four times the amount of the rent plus utilities.

In theory, the rent assistance program allows participants a much wider selection of apartments. In reality, the program as implemented in some cities has unrealistically low limits on the amount of rent that can be paid. In these cities decent units—particularly larger ones—simply are not available for the amount specified by HUD.

Some 40 percent of the units covered by Section 8 have involved rent assistance to families in existing buildings. In new units built under this program, HUD guarantees the developer a subsidized tenant population for 20 years. Because of high construction costs, new units cost almost as much as private single-family residences to build.

Urban homesteading.   Initially tried by a few cities, an experimental urban homesteading program was authorized by Congress in 1974. In this program abandoned houses are sold for a nominal price—sometimes as little as $1—to purchasers who agree to make whatever repairs are necessary to bring the dwellings into compliance with local housing code requirements. For do-it-yourselfers, urban homesteading provides an opportunity to acquire a house for very little money. The city also benefits to the extent that abandoned property goes back on the tax rolls and neighborhood decay is halted.

Evaluation of housing programs.   In 1949 Congress went on record as favoring the idea that all Americans should be able to have a decent home. To achieve this objective, the construction of 810,000 new housing units was authorized. Completion of the task was contingent on Congress's actually appropriating funds for construction, and it was at this point that commitment faltered. Because of the factors noted earlier, which made public housing so unattractive to a large segment of Congress, appropriations were consistently far below levels needed to provide enough housing. During the next decades, only about 80 percent of the new units authorized in 1949 were actually constructed.

The urban riots of the mid-1960s alerted Congress to the unfinished task of providing low-income housing, since inadequate housing may well have been a contributing cause of the riots.[10] In 1968, therefore, Congress reasserted its intention of providing adequate housing. Since urban renewal projects, highway building, and abandonment by landlords had substantially reduced the supply of inexpensive housing, Congress set a goal of six million new low-income units by 1980.

This ambitious goal was not met. As earlier, Congress was less willing to follow through with needed appropriations than it has been to simply set objectives. The president has, at times, been even less interested in meeting housing goals than has Congress. In 1973–1975, President Nixon showed his disapproval for existing programs by refusing to spend money appropriated for new housing projects. Commitments already made were kept, but no new projects were begun. In general, support for low-income housing has been eroded by the Section 235 scandals and the record federal budget deficits.

Moreover, inflation has caused costs for land and construction to increase, so that each dollar appropriated for housing programs purchases less. Inflation, unemployment, and the acceptance of higher proportions of welfare families have resulted in higher subsidies being needed to operate public housing. In 1980, average annual subsidies were estimated at $4,200 per existing unit and $6,200 per newly constructed unit.[11] By the time the federal obligation is satisfied, a total of $59,000 may have been spent on an existing apartment and a whopping $710,000 on a new unit. The cost of constructing each new unit of Section 8 housing was a hefty $57,000 in 1980.[12]

The price tag attached to public housing causes some to question the efficiency of the approaches currently used. A former deputy assistant secretary of HUD offered this provocative observation: "If [the annual subsidy] amount were provided directly to public housing tenants, it would enable them to rent almost any new apartment now being built privately. . . . If the subsidy were given in cash directly to tenants, it would be enough to lift virtually all of them out of poverty."[13]

Although all options have a sizable price tag, placing the poor in existing units is substantially cheaper than new construction. Greater emphasis is not placed on rehabilitating and leasing existing structures partially because the construction industry—whose lobbying is critical for passage of housing legislation—derives greater profits from building new units. Moreover, apartment vacancy rates have been very low for several years and numerous structures that could be rehabilitated are in undesirable neighborhoods. Consequently housing subsidy programs reach only 5 to 10 percent of those who are eligible. In recent years, a disproportionate share of the new units have been built for the elderly while large, poor families encounter growing difficulties in locating housing. Waiting lists for subsidized housing in some cities contain hundreds of names. Obviously the programs rate poorly in terms of equity.

Despite problems in adopting new legislation and the shortcomings of some recent programs, the use of housing codes in urban areas, urban renewal projects, and federal housing assistance programs have contributed to a general improvement in housing conditions. In 1979, less than 3 percent of the nation's housing lacked some or all plumbing, down from 34 percent in 1950 and 15 percent in 1960. The proportion living in overcrowded conditions (more than 1.5 persons per room) was just under 1 percent in 1977.[14]

Reagan proposals.   President Reagan has proposed major changes in the federal approach to helping the poor with their housing needs. These changes would cause rents to rise, eligibility to become more restrictive, and alter the way in which aid is distributed.

In 1981, Congress approved the administration request that families receiving a federal housing subsidy be required to pay 30 rather than 25 percent of their income in rent. Of even greater significance was the president's suggestion, which had not been approved as of 1983, that food stamps be counted as income. Since poorer families receive more food stamps, counting the stamps as income would cause the rents charged the very poor to more than double.[15]

President Reagan has also proposed eliminating most of the funds for new construction and using the money for a voucher system. The president explained in his 1983 budget proposal, "The housing construction programs are being terminated because they are very costly, provide too large a subsidy for too few people and do not address the nation's current housing problem."[16] Another reason for discontinuing the construction program is the reduction in the number of substandard housing units. A system of vouchers would give the poor an average of $2,000 per year that they could use to rent privately owned units. Adoption of this change is problematic because of opposition from the building industry. In the meantime, funding for new low-income housing projects has plummeted from $30 billion in fiscal 1981 to a proposed $515 million three years later.

Food Stamps

Launched as a limited experiment in 1961, the food stamp program was gradually expanded until by 1973 it became the predominant program for providing nutritional assistance. The food stamp program gives poor people stamps that can be redeemed at stores, for food only. In 1983 the average food stamp participant received a subsidy of about $43 per month.

The history of food stamps has been marked by rapid growth in recent years and has been tinkered with as Congress has tried to find a balance between reasonable support and spiraling costs. As shown in figure 5–1, participation in the food stamp program increased tenfold during the first five years after passage of the Food Stamp Act of 1964. This growth occurred during a period in which counties had a choice of offering food stamps, surplus food, or no food program at all. By 1974, when food stamps were made available nationwide, participation had risen to almost 13 million. As unemployment soared during the mid-1970s, so did food stamp enrollments. Elimination in 1977 of the requirement that stamps be purchased resulted in millions of new participants, during another period of high un-

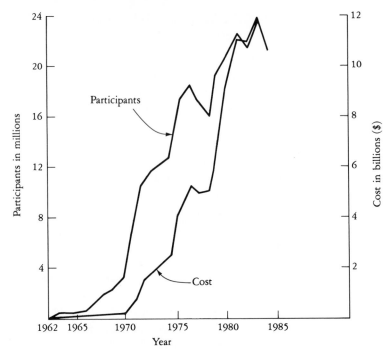

FIGURE 5-1   Food stamp program participation and costs. (*Source: U.S. Bureau of the Census,* Statistical Abstract of the United States. *Washington, D.C.: U.S. Government Printing Office, annual issues.*)

employment. (A 1 percentage point increase in unemployment translates into a million more food stamp recipients.)[17] These factors have more than offset reductions caused by stricter definitions of eligibility so that by 1979, 7.5 percent of the nation's families participated in the program. There were millions of others who were eligible but did not receive stamps.

Spreading participation, coupled with provisions that pegged increases in benefits to changes in the consumer price index, have caused program costs to explode. From a minor initial appropriation of $13 million, the costs of the program have doubled repeatedly until the expenses for fiscal 1983 were estimated at $12 billion.

Spiraling costs have generated increasingly vocal opposition to the food stamp program, which has resulted in tighter eligibility standards and closer monitoring. While acknowledging that many beneficiaries are deserving, program critics complain that under some conditions families earning more than $12,000 a year may qualify for food stamps. It was particularly galling to critics when thousands of voluntary poor—such as students, strikers, and those who had chosen not to work, including at one time the son of a United States senator—received stamps.

In trying to reduce costs, conservatives in Congress reduced the amount of deductions applicants could claim, made it more difficult for students to qualify, eliminated the eligibility of most strikers, reduced the frequency of cost-of-living adjustments from twice to once a year, and strove to reduce overpayments due to fraud or error. It was estimated that reforms passed in 1981 would eliminate one million recipients.

In addition to manipulating eligibility standards and sizes of benefits, since 1977 Congress has tried to cap expenditures for food stamps. In that year Congress limited appropriations to $6.2 billion per year. In setting appropriations limits, Congress relies on certain assumptions about the rate of inflation and the rate of unemployment for future years. These assumptions have been off target and Congress, rather than allowing benefits to lapse, has come to the rescue with additional funds. For example, Congress assumed a 5.5 percent rate of inflation and 4.9 percent unemployment for 1980. Thus it was predicted that there would be 15 million food stamp recipients in fiscal year 1981 at a cost of $5.55 billion.[18] In actuality, inflation and unemployment galloped along well above the predicted levels and 23 million people received food stamps, which cost about $11 billion (see figure 5–1). With this kind of track record, it is understandable why one congressman referred to the assumptions as "a matrix of fantasy."[19]

The tightening up of eligibility standards in 1981 did not go as far as conservatives, led by Sen. Jesse Helms (R.–N.C.), had hoped. Should the spending caps imposed for fiscal years 1982–1984 (between $11 and $12 billion annually) prove inadequate, conservatives will probably reintroduce some of their proposals that were rejected in the past. These include reducing benefits by an amount equal to what children receive through the school lunch program and reinstating a provision for selling stamps rather than giving them away.[20] Although it would probably have little impact on program cost, Senator Helms would like to see able-bodied recipients participate in public work programs in return for food stamps.

Liberals consider the caps in the 1981 legislation unrealistic. Not simply do they view the 1981 cuts as unjustified, they predict that cutbacks in federal funding for jobs and welfare will force millions more to turn to food stamps, which could push costs above the caps.[21] Liberals also cite nutritionists who say that food stamp benefits (currently a maximum of $233 for a family of four) provide only the barest essentials. "For example, one sample menu [devised by the Department of Agriculture] provides one-half pound of hamburger, two-thirds of a pound of liver, a small ham, a chicken, a can of tuna and some bologna as the meat for a family of four for a week."[22]

The biggest ally of the poor in congressional battles over food stamps are food producers and sellers. Enlarging the purchasing power of the poor for groceries generates millions of dollars of additional sales for farmers, processors, and retailers. This linkage is made explicit in the House of Representatives where food stamp legislation is paired with legislation to help farmers. Thus far others who stood to benefit from sales generated by food stamps have been able to protect the program from the more severe cuts that critics would like to impose.

Reagan proposals.   The impact of the 1981 budget reconciliation act, which cut a million people out of the food stamp program and reduced the value of the stamps given most others, was exceeded by the president's recommendations for fiscal year 1983. The president sought to reduce costs by one-fifth by counting a larger share of the earnings of the working poor so that they would qualify for fewer benefits.

The president asked that states assume responsibility for the food stamp program, along with AFDC, in return for the federal government taking responsibility for all of Medicaid. Opponents distrust relying on the states to handle food stamps and AFDC. They point out that the federal government launched these programs because states failed to address these needs. Moreover, while federal welfare benefits are pegged to increases in the cost of living, in only two states have welfare payments kept pace with inflation.[23] Also, unless stringent standards are imposed by Congress, there is concern that states would allow the adequacy of food programs to deteriorate or even dispense with them altogether. If responsibility were given to the states with no strings attached, there would certainly be disparity among the states in the level of benefits as there currently are in AFDC and Medicaid, two programs for which states have partial responsibility.

MEDICAL CARE

Beginning in the 1920s some congressmen urged that federal dollars be used to assure minimal health care for the indigent, and in 1945 President Truman became the first chief executive to lend his influence to this cause. His efforts were unsuccessful, however; and the notion of federally supported health care continued to generate much controversy and little legislation for the next twenty years. Leading the opposition to compulsory health care proposals were the American Medical Association (AMA) and the insurance industry. To rally backers, the AMA tarred the proposals with the "socialized medicine" label. Doctors warned that compulsory health insurance would be the first step toward destroying the existing health care system. Pointing to what happened following nationalization of medical care in Great Britain, the AMA cautioned that Americans were being threatened with loss of the right to select a personal physician, assembly-line treatment at clinics, long delays in waiting rooms, and a decline in the quality of medical practices.

The insurance industry, like the medical profession, feared financial loss if the federal government assumed responsibility for guaranteeing health care. Should the government establish a health care insurance program and require all citizens to participate, private insurers would lose substantial revenues.

Conservatives in the House Ways and Means Committee were a powerful ally of the AMA and the insurance industry. For years Republicans and conservative southern Democrats constituted a majority of this committee, which would have to approve any health insurance program. The conservatives' distrust of social welfare programs and unwillingness to use federal authority on behalf of the poor—preferring to leave such matters to individuals or to the states—provided the dominant rationale for blocking health care proposals.

Finally, in 1965 the 89th Congress, boasting the largest liberal membership in a generation, responded to President Johnson's urgings and enacted two health care programs. The Johnson landslide had replaced so many conservative Republicans with liberal Democrats that even traditional foes of health insurance saw the inevitability of what they had dreaded. Wilbur Mills (D.–Ark.), chairman of the Ways and Means Committee, changed his position on federal medical insurance and assumed direction of the legislative effort in the House. Even the AMA, seeing that opposition was futile, proposed a voluntary plan dubbed "eldercare," which would be optional for the states. The forces of change had become too strong, and the AMA's proposal was rejected for a more comprehensive program.

Medicare

One of the health care programs enacted in 1965 was Medicare.[24] This legislation, which was assigned top priority by President Johnson, provided up to 90 days of hospitalization, 100 days in a nursing home, and 100 posthospital visits by a nurse or therapist. While Medicare benefits cover most of the expenses, the patient must pay part of the cost of extended treatment. Medicare is funded from additional payroll taxes collected along with Social Security taxes. In addition to the hospitalization and related benefits, Congress incorporated one provision from the AMA's "eldercare" alternative and made it possible for the elderly to get federal aid for paying doctors' bills. People over 65 years old can participate in a voluntary program that pays 80 percent of "reasonable" fees for doctors after the patient pays the first $60 each year. Some medical services, such as X rays and electrocardiograms, were included among the benefits provided by the supplementary plan. Participants in the supplemental program paid $13.50 per month in 1983, an amount that will doubtless increase.

Medicaid

The second medical program instituted by the 89th Congress provided free care to people receiving categoric aid such as AFDC. Called Medicaid, this is a welfare program in which states can obtain up to 78 percent of the costs of medical treatment for the poor. Although not required to, most states also extend coverage to the "medically indigent"—people who would be self-sufficient except for the high cost of health care. In fiscal year 1984 the total cost for Medicaid was estimated at more than $38 billlion, with the states paying 45 percent of the total cost.

Evaluation of health care programs.   On the positive side, no one denies that many poor Americans are now receiving health care, which until the mid-1960s they could not afford. Many of the elderly and those receiving welfare, who once had to forgo even critically needed medical attention, now receive treatment, including care from costly specialists. Between 1966 and 1976 hospital admissions among the elderly rose by almost one-third while nursing home usage doubled between 1963 and 1973.[25] Moreover, life expectancy among the elderly rose while infant mortality rates declined. These changes cannot be wholly attributed to Medicare and Medicaid but the presence of these programs doubtless played some role.

Despite the needs being met by Medicare and Medicaid, many policymakers believe that major restructuring of the programs is urgently needed. While a number of shortcomings are pointed out, the underlying cause is rapidly escalating costs. As figure 5–2 shows, the costs of the two programs have doubled repeatedly. By 1983 Medicare cost approximately $57 billion, four times greater than Congress had thought the program would cost in 1990 when it was originally approved.[26] With 30 million elderly signed up for Medicare and another 23 million receiving Medicaid, one-fifth of the nation's population benefits from one of these programs. A number of factors contribute to the cost increases of the health programs.

First, certain inefficiencies are built into Medicare and Medicaid. For example, some expenses will be reimbursed by the federal government only if they are incurred in a hospital. A patient is therefore encouraged to go into the hospital for treatment rather than have the work done on a less expensive out-patient basis, although this is now changing. The program standards also fail to encourage a preventive approach. In addition, since hospitals are reimbursed for all their expenses, there is less incentive to be frugal. Former Secretary of Health, Education, and Welfare Caspar Weinberger told the House Ways and Means Subcommittee on Health: "I . . . firmly believe that the faulty design of Medicare and Medicaid is the principal culprit responsible for this super inflation in health care costs. [With the] guaranteed government payment of health care costs in virtually any amount submitted by the provider, and with normal market factors absent in the health care area, inflation was bound to happen, and it did."[27]

Second, expenses for Medicare and Medicaid indicate that the program may be overused. The poor, who in the past would have chosen to spend their limited resources for needs other than health care, are less often forced to make a choice, since the health care is subsidized or in some cases free. A lucrative new industry servicing the health care needs of the poor has developed. One governor has estimated that overuse of the programs costs three times as much as fraud.[28]

Third, the cost of medical care, whether it is for the wealthy or the poor, has risen substantially. The causes of rising costs will be explored in somewhat more detail in the next chapter. Here we will simply provide one illustration. Between 1972 and 1976, Medicaid expenses in Idaho tripled, although there was *no increase* in the number of people enrolled in the program.[29]

Fourth, there has been inadequate monitoring of the operation of Medicare and Medicaid, so that fraud has contributed to rising costs. Critics claim that doctors sometimes submit bills when they have done little more than walk through a ward

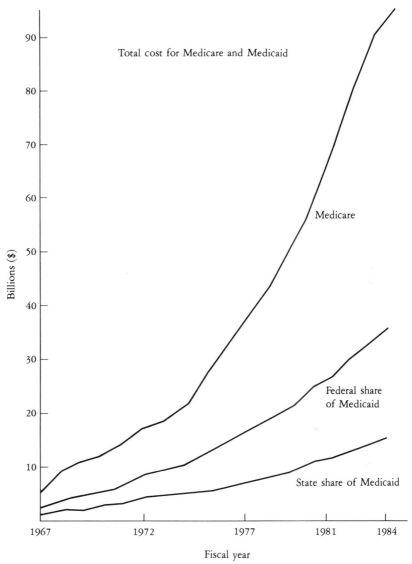

FIGURE 5-2 Expenses for Medicare and Medicaid, fiscal years 1967–1984. Figures for 1982–1984 are estimates. (*Source:* President's Budget Appendices *for appropriate years. Washington, D.C.: U.S. Government Printing Office.*)

of Medicare patients. Former Sen. Frank Moss (D.–Utah) has charged that, partly because of poor monitoring and light punishment for those who are caught, Medicare has been defrauded of as much as $1.5 billion annually.[30] In Illinois approximately 20 percent of the payments made for Medicare and Medicaid laboratory services were tainted by fraud.[31] A New York official, who found that nursing home operators were billing Medicaid for mink coats and stereos, testified before a Senate committee: "The conspiracies to defraud the public in the health care field are enormous in scope and complexity and pervasive through every area of our nation."[32]

Inadequate monitoring has also created conditions under which hospitals can "maximize reimbursements."[33] Indeed, the professional organizations for hospitals inform their members how to go about collecting all the money that they legally can from the federal government, which at times runs to more than 100 percent of the cost. Governor George Busbee of Georgia, who chaired the National Governors' Conference task force on Medicaid, asserted that this health program is "the most complex, confusing, duplicative, and administratively wasteful system ever conceived—one that will surely bankrupt the states and the federal Treasury unless substantial reforms are undertaken, both at the state and federal levels."[34]

Recent changes.   Following disclosures of extensive fraud, Congress created the position of the inspector general in the Department of Health and Human Services. This new office is responsible for catching those who try to cheat on Medicare and Medicaid. Another effort to curb unreasonable expenses involved setting up professional standards review organizations (PSROs) made up of doctors who determine the standard treatment in a locale and whether the charges are in line. The federal government has recovered some Medicaid and Medicare money as a result of PSRO reviews, although the Congressional Budget Office judged it a losing proposition with each dollar spent on PSROs producing only seventy cents in savings.[35]

A more direct way to limit hospital costs, which are a major component of the federal health care budget, was approved by Congress in 1983. Beginning in October of that year, the Department of Health and Human Services will set the rates at which hospitals will be reimbursed for 467 types of treatment ranging from setting broken bones to heart bypass operations. Setting rates in advance of treatment, known as prospective reimbursement, has also been instituted by some states in their Medicaid programs. Prospective reimbursement rates for Medicare can be altered annually and will reflect regional and urban/rural differences in costs. In California, hospitals whose costs are below the figures set by the government are allowed to keep the difference. Those whose charges exceed standards will have to absorb the costs themselves, pass them on to patients not covered by Medicare or Medicaid, or try to collect the difference from the person receiving treatment.

President Reagan's budget cuts necessitated a scaling back in federal health care funding. Cutbacks resulted in higher charges for the optional insurance to cover Medicare patients, higher physicians' charges, increased payments by beneficiaries before the federal government picks up the tab, and lower reimbursements for some health care providers.

As federal funds dried up, many states reduced Medicaid coverage. In this jointly funded state-federal program, economizing took different forms from state to state.

Some of the changes included:

1. Charging a nominal fee for services that had been free.
2. Reducing the rates of reimbursement paid to hospitals, physicians, and pharmacists who cared for Medicaid patients.
3. Limiting the number of physicians' visits and the length of hospital coverage for most patients.
4. Limiting the rate at which health care providers could raise their charges.
5. Limiting the rate at which federal reimbursements given to states will increase, so that if states do not constrain cost increases, they must be prepared to shoulder a larger share of the total cost.
6. Threatening to reduce the federal funds given states that do not eliminate all errors in payments.
7. Limiting patients' choices in selecting physicians or hospitals.
8. Paying for outpatient treatment for some procedures that would have required hospitalization in order to collect reimbursement.

These proposals drew opposition from several quarters. Representatives of beneficiaries objected to charging for what had been free. Some health care providers complained that new limits on reimbursement eliminated profits and therefore they quit serving Medicaid patients. Thus one likely consequence was to reduce the availability of health care, turning the clock back toward pre-1965 conditions. A second potential result was that those who continued to treat people with Medicaid cards would increase what they charged other people in order to make up for expenses that they could not collect from Medicaid.

Reagan proposals.   President Reagan has been toying with the idea of replacing Medicare with a system of vouchers. These vouchers would be used to purchase medical insurance from private companies or to contract for health care from health maintenance organizations (which will be discussed in the next chapter).

For some elderly people, the vouchers would probably not buy coverage sufficient to pay for all of the health care they need, meaning that they would have to pay out of pocket for some expenses. Another concern is that private insurance companies would refuse to enroll people from high-risk categories. The elderly, as well as organized labor and insurance companies, have opposed a shift to a voucher system. This opposition might be partially allayed by a guarantee that the value of the voucher would keep pace with inflation.

As part of the budget proposal for fiscal 1984, President Reagan has urged a major redesign of Medicare. His recommendations would reorient Medicare from being primarily concerned with relatively short-term needs to catastrophic coverage. Under the Reagan plan, Medicare patients would pay $28 a day for the second through the fifteenth day of a hospital stay and a slightly lesser amount for each of the next forty-five days; there would be no charges for stays longer than sixty days.

Under current regulations, Medicare patients pay nothing from the second to the sixtieth day, $87.50 per day for the next thirty days, and $175 per day for up to sixty additional days. If the changes proposed by President Reagan are adopted, patients hospitalized less than seventy-four days will pay more, whereas the few patients who are hospitalized for extended periods will benefit. The average hospital visit for Medicare patients lasts eleven days, and this would cost an extra $280 under the Reagan plan. The proposed changes would save Medicare about $700 million in fiscal 1984.

President Reagan has recommended increasing the premiums for the optional Medicare insurance that pays doctor bills. Premiums would be placed at 35 percent of the cost of the program, up from the 25 percent of the cost that they now provide but below the 50 percent that they initially provided. The president has also asked Congress to raise the amount of the doctor's bill that Medicare users must pay. Representatives of the elderly are incensed by proposals to make the elderly pay for a larger share of the doctor's bills. They note that about half of all doctors' charges exceed what federal authorities consider to be reasonable costs,[36] and these excess charges are the responsibility of the patient. Some patients have "medigap" insurance, which pays the difference between what physicians charge and what Medicare pays.

The possible bankruptcy of Medicare that some analysts predict before the end of the 1980s would necessitate still further changes. If program costs continue to run ahead of revenues, it will be necessary to increase taxes or sharply reduce the scope of the program. The latter could be achieved by requiring that participants pay a larger share of their health expenses or by changing the program to one based on need.

CURATIVE PROGRAMS: THE WAR ON POVERTY

In his 1964 State of the Union message President Johnson announced, "This administration today, here and now, declares unconditional war on poverty in America." A few months later, after the Congress had responded to Johnson's forceful leadership with remarkable speed, the president boasted at the signing of the Economic Opportunity Act: "Today for the first time in the history of the human race, a great nation is able to make and is willing to make a commitment to eradicate poverty among its people."[37] Confidence among poverty warriors was so boundless that some of them predicted that poverty would be eliminated in America by the mid-1970s.

In setting out to eliminate poverty, the Johnson administration was accepting no small challenge. While the poor of the 1960s were far better off than the poor of the depression had been, there were still some 36 million Americans whose incomes were below the poverty level in 1964. In light of the magnitude of the task, and also the fact that the percentage of the population that was poor had been approximately halved since the depression, why did President Johnson fix on this as a major goal of his administration? Writers who have tried to explain the motivation behind President Johnson's War on Poverty cite a set of circumstances that coincided to produce the spark needed for a major policy initiative. The first impetus for a new look at poverty predated Johnson's occupancy of the White House. Official concern about the plight of the poor seems to have been spurred by John F. Kennedy's glimpses of the sagging shacks and ravaged bodies in the forgotten hollows of West Virginia during his 1960 primary campaign in that state.

Kennedy's concern became intensified when he read Michael Harrington's book *The Other America*.[38] The president, like many other Americans, was made aware of the extent of poverty in this country, a nation that most middle-class citizens thought of as a land of plenty. Toward the end of his second year, President Kennedy told Walter Heller, chairman of the Council of Economic Advisers: "I want to go beyond the things that have already been accomplished. . . . For example, what about the poverty problem in the United States?"[39] During the remainder of the Kennedy presidency, groundwork proceeded although no new programs with a nationwide scope were launched.

Upon ascending to the presidency, Lyndon B. Johnson turned his considerable legislative skills to getting the Kennedy program enacted.[40] Johnson's attack on poverty, launched in the 1960s, aimed at a quite different target than had the effort of thirty years earlier. In the first place, whereas the depression-era programs were alleviative, the new ones were supposed to be curative. That is, the War on Poverty was supposed to break the cycle of poverty and to provide escape routes by which millions of people could move into the working class and perhaps ultimately into the middle class. The theme of the War on Poverty was "rehabilitation, not relief." In sending the War on Poverty legislation to Congress, President Johnson said: "The act does not merely expand old programs or improve what is already being done. It charts a new course. It strikes at the causes, not just the consequences of poverty."[41]

A second difference was that the new program consciously recognized a different clientele. That is, the program designers recognized that the New Deal programs, which had been intended to help middle-class people who found themselves temporarily suffering deprivation, were not adequate for the second- and third-generation poor whom they were now serving.

Third, an important component of the War on Poverty rested on the premise that the poor may be better judges of what needs to be done than are planners, bureaucrats, or legislators. Consequently, unlike other programs, which made funds available for meeting narrowly defined needs, some War on Poverty money was set aside for poor people to use to improve conditions in their communities as *they* saw fit.

To oversee the multifaceted War on Poverty a new agency, the Office of Economic Opportunity (OEO), was created. Sargent Shriver, whose reputation as an administrator was at its peak after a stint as director of the Peace Corps, was tapped to head the OEO. Establishment of a new agency and appointment of a famous and talented director were in keeping with the emphasis placed on the War on Poverty during its early days. Setting up the OEO, rather than parceling out programs to existing offices, was supposed to ensure that the new federal programs moved toward their objective in a coordinated manner. Creation of a new agency would help focus attention on poverty elimination as a goal. Also, giving the programs to a new agency should mean that attainment of objectives would not be subordinated to other organizational goals.

Most portions of the War on Poverty that were intended to be curative were aimed at either young adults or youth. For the former there were programs to improve their employability by giving them basic skills. Youngsters were to be encouraged to stay in school where it was hoped they would be adequately prepared so that they could become self-sufficient adults. The specific programs are discussed in the following sections.

Educational Programs

In trying to improve educational achievement, designers of the War on Poverty accepted the premise of many educators that by the time a child is old enough to enter public school, he or she may already be past the prime age for learning. Moreover, the child from a culturally deprived background, because of fewer intellectual stimuli in the environment, may begin public school substantially behind middle-class children who have attended preschool, played with educational toys, and had greater exposure to the books and ideas that are associated with success in school. To offset the disadvantages of growing up in a low-income home, Project Head Start was established to provide poor children with the basic knowledge that most middle-class children have by the time they reach school. In Head Start children were prepared to compete with their more fortunate peers by being taught the alphabet, numbers, colors, and so on. Initially the program operated during the summer and was attended by lower-income children just before they entered school. Because the program became popular with members of Congress, the number of projects was increased and the duration of enrollment broadened, so that younger children could participate and children in school could continue to attend after school, on Saturdays, and during the summer.

Although some early evaluations raised doubts about the effectiveness of Head Start, more recent research indicates that it is a valuable experience. A survey conducted of young people a decade after they were in Head Start found that those who had been through this program differed from those who had not in several ways. Former Head Start students (1) were less likely to be placed in special education; (2) were less likely to fail a grade or drop out; (3) were less likely to run afoul of the law; and (4) did better in math courses.[42]

Other programs of the War on Poverty were aimed at encouraging older students to pursue further education. These programs offered opportunities for youngsters from poor families to earn money while staying in school, so that the choice between going to school or to work did not have to be made. The largest of these programs was the Neighborhood Youth Corps (NYC), which provided money for public service employment for young people. In addition to creating jobs, the NYC offered counseling services in an effort to encourage participants currently in school to remain there, and to convince dropouts to go back and earn diplomas.

The Work-Study program sought to facilitate college attendance among the poor. Under Work-Study, federal funds provide 80 percent of the cost of hiring students to work part time on campus or in the community. Since the students can arrange their work around their class schedules, Work-Study has helped a number of low-income students to continue to pursue degrees on a full-time basis.

A program aimed primarily at dropouts is the Job Corps, which is still in effect. Originally modeled on the New Deal's Civilian Conservation Corps, it initially provided work experiences in rural areas. Pressures from people unhappy with camps in their communities, combined with high dropout rates among disoriented urban corps members and the high cost of maintaining each member, led to congressional demands for reform.[43] In response to these demands, the Job Corps has become increasingly urban in its orientation. The rural camps, with their emphasis on conservation, have been replaced by urban training centers, which are meant to prepare enrollees for productive work in the cities.

Job Programs

The primary emphasis of War on Poverty efforts on behalf of adults was to make welfare recipients self-sufficient. There were several aspects to these efforts, although manpower training received the greatest emphasis. With the call to arms of the War on Poverty, the recent and relatively small manpower efforts of the federal government were increased.

In time a smorgasbord of programs was devised (see table 5–2), so that different types of experiences were available to a wide range of needy. Some of these programs actually provided little structured training, for example the Work Incentive Program (for welfare mothers), and simply placed workers in entry-level, low-paying jobs. These programs rarely included opportunities for participants to get training that would enable them to win promotions. However, providing federal money to state and local governments enabled them to hire people to perform public service work that otherwise would not have been done. Participants in these programs were frequently put to work on conservation projects or as recreation aides, social work aides, or hospital aides.

A second type of program was intended to provide structured job training. The largest of these was the Manpower Development and Training Act (MDTA). Although not initially designed to help the poor, by 1974 almost two-thirds of the new participants in the classroom component were at the poverty level, as were almost 40 percent of the enrollees in on-the-job training. Even larger numbers of

TABLE 5-2   Major jobs programs

Title	Target	Activity	Present status
Manpower Development and Training Act	Unemployed	Classroom and on-the-job training	Superseded by the 1973 Comprehensive Employment and Training Act; substantially reduced under President Reagan
Neighborhood Youth Corps	16–21-year-old students, and those who might return to school	Public service jobs during summers and after school	
Operation Mainstream	Unemployed heads of households	Public service jobs	
JOBS	Unemployed	On-the-job training cosponsored by businesses	
Work Incentive Program	Welfare mothers	Public service jobs	Elimination proposed in 1983 budget
Job Corps	16–21-year-old school dropouts	Work experience and job training	Still functioning
Public Employment Programs	Areas of high unemployment	Public service jobs	Eliminated in 1981
Youth Conservation Corps	Summer jobs for 15–18-year-olds	Federal land improvement projects	Eliminated in 1981

participants, while still above the poverty level, were out of work at the time that they joined MDTA programs.

Another structured training program was JOBS (Job Opportunities in the Business Sector). This program was jointly sponsored by the Department of Labor and the National Association of Business. JOBS was the product of Lyndon Johnson's effort to get the private sector involved in the War on Poverty. Corporations that participated in JOBS were reimbursed for the additional costs entailed in training disadvantaged workers. Thus, if low-income recruits required one more week of training than did nondisadvantaged workers, the federal government would pay for the extra week's training.

As the final column in table 5-2 shows, President Reagan launched a full-scale attack on the existing jobs programs. All of them have experienced cuts in funding if not outright elimination. Opponents charge that these cuts are shortsighted, particularly during a recession, since people who lost these jobs will have to be taken care of with welfare.

Community Action Programs

The most innovative feature of the War on Poverty was to allow the poor to participate in designing programs and in allocating the funds that were supposed to help them. The program designers felt that the poor would know what their needs were, whereas policymakers with middle-class backgrounds might ignore some of these needs. In addition, some felt that such participation, by giving poor people experience in making decisions and spending money, would help to break the cycle of poverty.[44]

Finally, by building participation of the poor into the poverty programs, some of the policy professionals who created the War on Poverty hoped to redistribute power to the poor. If they were given control over some financial resources, these professionals believed, the poor would become a force to be reckoned with, so that, in time, they might have enough influence to refashion the institutions that serviced them.

To achieve these objectives, two-thirds of the new funds for the first year's poverty effort were given to the community action programs (CAPs).[45] These locally run programs, designed to meet local needs, were to be carried out with "maximum feasible participation" of the poor. With the federal government contributing 90 percent of the funding for CAPs, a wide range of activities was initiated. Among the more common CAP endeavors were family-planning clinics, legal aid offices, consumer education courses, day-care centers, and recreation centers for the elderly. CAP personnel helped poor people challenge unfair credit practices of local merchants, use rent strikes and other pressures to force landlords to improve living conditions, and organize to seek political concessions from local public decision makers.

This sort of boat rocking was most irritating to local interests confronted by an organization of poor people who were able to use the law as well as electoral muscle in the pursuit of their objectives. Mayors, merchants, and landlords were particularly distressed by the fact that CAP funds came directly from the federal government and therefore were largely independent of the local power structure. Indeed, as some exponents of the CAP concept had hoped, the federal funding enabled some ambitious community organizations to find their way into the chambers of the decision makers.

Demise of the War on Poverty

The War on Poverty proved to be generally unpopular. There was much interdepartmental infighting and resentment. By 1974 support for OEO had declined so much that Congress abolished it, giving its remaining programs to other departments eager to regain control.

A number of explanations have been offered for the demise of the War on Poverty. As with most important social phenomena, the causes are too numerous and tangled to permit much more than a listing of what appear to be the eight important ones. Undoubtedly a major problem was that the initial goals were unrealistically high. A former OEO administrator has written, "The Johnson War on Poverty was conceived in a mood of political optimism which bordered on naiveté."[46]

In the second place, as the country became more deeply immersed in the quicksand of war in Vietnam, winning the War on Poverty receded in significance. The dilution of presidential resolve contributed to a third reason for the failure of the War on Poverty, lack of money. Writing in 1967, well before the extent of the ultimate collapse of the poverty effort was clear, Donovan observed, "Most of the programs of the Economic Opportunity Act, with the possible exception of the Neighborhood Youth Corps and Project Head Start, have never been budgeted at anything more than a pilot-project level."[47] A fourth factor lay in the decision concerning the distribution of poverty programs. In an effort to develop political support by placing programs in a large number of communities, Shriver diminished the likelihood that projects could substantially improve the conditions of any given community's poor. Thus, instead of concentrating the limited funds in a few communities and trying to maximize impact, the program's administrators passed out the money in small dollops to hundreds of communities.

Fifth, a number of big-city mayors accused the community action programs of meddling in their cities. They preferred to have the money pass through their hands rather than go directly from Washington to local poverty groups.

Sixth, since Congress had played a small role in the creation of the War on Poverty, neither its leaders nor rank-and-file members felt great responsibility for rescuing the program when it began to be buffeted by swirling political pressures. The ranks of the program's supporters were ravaged in 1966, when forty Democratic members of Congress, most of whom were liberal, lost their seats. The remaining Democrats were generally less committed to OEO's objectives and more responsive to the demands of local political figures that less latitude be allowed in the expenditure of poverty funds.

Seventh, congressional critics leveled charges of mismanagement and misguided objectives by pointing out, for instance, that in Chicago some OEO funds were turned over to the Blackstone Rangers, a street gang; that the costs of training Job Corps members were extremely high; and that some Job Corps camps were marked by high dropout rates and antisocial behavior.

Finally, even under the best of conditions, the design of the War on Poverty was such that it could not have eliminated poverty within the time scheduled. Programs emphasizing manpower training had the potential of helping many poor families but offered little immediate help to the millions of poor who were too young, too old, or too infirm to work. The old and the weak could probably not be made self-sufficient by any of OEO's programs. Although the young might be able to use education and job training to escape the centripetal force of the cycle of poverty, even under the best of conditions this would take at least a generation.

IDENTIFYING THE POOR

When the War on Poverty was declared, administration speakers optimistically predicted victory within the foreseeable future. A quick look around us provides sufficient evidence that promises to eliminate poverty have not been fulfilled. Government statistics indicate that in 1980 there were still approximately 29.3 million Americans, or 13 percent of the population, having base incomes below the poverty level of $8,410 for an urban family of four.

Some groups in society are more likely to have low incomes than are others. As table 5–3 shows, people of Hispanic origin are more than twice as likely to have low incomes as whites are. Blacks are the poorest racial group; almost one-third of all blacks are in the low-income set. However, although a larger segment of blacks and people of Hispanic origin are poor, two-thirds of all low-income people are white. Other data in table 5–3 show that only 6 percent of all families with a male as head of household are poor. In contrast, almost one-third of all Americans in families headed by a female are poor. Age and location also appear to be related to the incidence of poverty. Young people and the elderly are more likely to be poor than is the total population. Poor people are disproportionately represented in rural areas, large cities, and in the South.

Figure 5–3 shows that the number of poor Americans declined sharply in the years immediately after passage of Lyndon Johnson's package of antipoverty programs. The number of poor people, which totaled almost 40 million in 1960, fell below 30 million in 1966 and reached its lowest point of just under 23 million in 1973. The number of poor remained fairly stable through most of the 1970s but rose rapidly beginning in 1979. By 1982, there were more than 34 million poor

TABLE 5–3 **Selected characteristics of Americans below the low-income level**

	Percent of all poor people		Percent of group	
	1981	*1974*	*1981*	*1974*
White	67.7	67.1	11.1	8.9
Black	28.8	29.8	34.2	31.2
Hispanic	11.7	10.7	26.5	23.2
In families with male head[a]	48.8	56.0	6.1	6.5
In families with female head[a]	51.2	44.0	32.7	36.8
Under 18 years of age	37.6	45.1	19.5	15.8
Over 65 years of age	12.0	13.6	15.3	15.7
Central cities	35.3	36.3	18.0	14.4
Suburbs	25.7	23.9	8.9	7.1
Outside metropolitan areas	39.2	39.9	17.0	14.4
North and West[a]	58.3	55.6	12.3	9.5
South[a]	41.6	44.4	17.4	16.1

SOURCE: U.S. Bureau of the Census, *Current Population Reports, Characteristics of the Population below the Poverty Level: 1974 and 1981,* Series P-60, Nos. 102 and 138 (Washington, D.C.: U.S. Government Printing Office, 1976 and 1983). *Money, Income and Poverty Status of Families and Persons in the United States: 1980,* Series P-60, No. 127 (Washington, D.C.: U.S. Government Printing Office, 1981).

[a]1980 data.

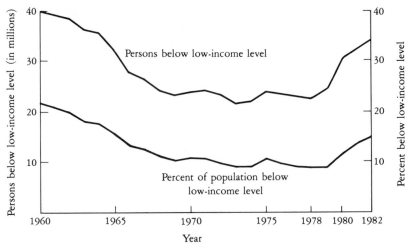

FIGURE 5-3 Numbers and proportions of the population below the poverty level, 1960–1982. (*Sources: U.S. Bureau of the Census, Current Population Reports,* Characteristics of the Population below the Poverty Level: 1981, *Series P-60, No. 138. Washington, D.C.: U.S. Government Printing Office, 1983,* p. 7. Money, Income and Poverty Status of Families and Persons in the United States: 1980, *Series P-60, No. 127. Washington, D.C.: U.S. Government Printing Office, 1981. Robert Pear, "Poverty Rates Rose to 15% in '82, Highest Level since Mid-1960's,"* New York Times, *August 3, 1983, p. 1.*)

people, the largest number since 1965, when the War on Poverty was in its infancy. The high levels of unemployment and cutbacks in social programs had left their mark. Because of the increase in the size of the nation's population since 1960, the increase in the proportion of those below the low-income level (which is the lower line in figure 5–3) was not as sharp as that in the actual number of poor people (the upper line in figure 5–3). Nonetheless the percent of the population that fell below the poverty level increased from 11.7 in 1979 to 15 in 1982.

There is, however, another perspective from which to view the conditions of the poor. Two economists at the Brookings Institution contend that figures such as those presented in figure 5–3 give an inflated picture of the actual number of poor people.[48] While acknowledging that poverty remains a condition of millions of Americans, they argue that a sizable proportion of the poor (44 percent in 1972) received sufficient amounts of in-kind transfers—for instance, food stamps, housing assistance, or Medicaid—to lift them above the low-income line. A survey by the Bureau of the Census found that more than 27 million households (or almost 35 percent of all American households) received some form of in-kind benefit from the federal government in 1979.[49] President Reagan's chief domestic adviser estimates that if these benefits are added to the recipients' income, then there were only 8 million poor Americans.[50]

A third perspective suggests that even inclusion of transfer payments still overlooks an important consideration: that $8,410 is an unrealistically low figure for the poverty level. The Census Bureau seems to acknowledge the possible inadequacy of this figure by also including statistics on the number and characteristics of those earning less than 125 percent of the poverty figure, or over $10,500. If this figure is used, then there would be an additional 10 million poor people in 1979.

Characteristics of participants in three types of federal welfare programs are presented in table 5–4. In all three, beneficiaries are disproportionately minority members, exist below the poverty level, and live in central cities.

TABLE 5–4   Selected characteristics of families participating in three welfare programs in 1979

	Total population	*Food stamps*	*Subsidized housing*	*Medicaid*
Number of families (in thousands)	79,108	5,911	2,511	7,993
Race:				
White	88%	63%	59%	68%
Black	11	35	39	30
Hispanic	5	10	8	9
Head of household:				
Male	89%	58%	34%	64%
Female	11	42	66	36
Median income	$16,533	$5,300	$6,747	$5,990
Below poverty level	12%	61%	47%	48%
Households with members:				
Over age 65	20%	17%	34%	33%
Under age 19	43	66	NA[a]	51
Live in central city	30%	42%	55%	41%
Region:				
Northeast	22%	23%	32%	24%
North Central	26	21	21	24
South	32	41	32	31
West	19	15	15	21

SOURCE: U.S. Bureau of the Census, Current Population Reports, *Characteristics of House-holds and Persons Receiving Noncash Benefits: 1979* (*Preliminary Data from the March 1980 Current Population Survey*), Series P-23, No. 110 (Washington, D.C.: U.S. Government Printing Office, 1981).

[a]Not available.

PROPOSED REFORMS

Calls for new approaches to welfare stem from the ever-rising cost of the nation's welfare budget and the realization that past programs have left millions of poor people untouched. A review of some of the proposals that have been set forth follows.

Full Employment

Like the goal of decent housing for all, full employment has been listed among our nation's policy goals for more than a generation. In 1946 Congress passed legislation proclaiming: "All Americans able to work and seeking to work have the right to useful, remunerative, regular, and full-time employment, and it is the policy of the United States to assure the existence at all times of sufficient employment opportunities to enable all Americans to freely exercise this right."

During the recession of the 1970s, when unemployment rates reached a high of 8.9 percent nationwide and stood above 10 percent for months in some areas, the failure of employment policy to live up to the 1946 rhetoric was brought home to many people. In 1971 the federal government took a tiny step toward assuming the role of employer of last resort. The Emergency Employment Act of that year funded a Public Employment Program (PEP), which created more than 200,000 jobs in state and local governments. Under this program and its successors, federal dollars were used to underwrite the bulk of the costs of hiring people to perform public service work for state and local governments.

A second strategy—designed as a countercyclical, short-term measure to reduce unemployment—has been to increase the funding for federal public works projects, such as the construction of sewage treatment plants, thereby creating additional jobs for construction workers.

A third approach would make the federal government the employer of last resort. The Humphrey-Hawkins Act of 1978 reiterated the 1946 pledge of full employment, defined as 3 percent unemployment of the labor force 20 years of age and older. This legislation was the top priority of the AFL-CIO in 1976 and was strongly endorsed by blacks and liberals. The Humphrey-Hawkins Act called for coordinated efforts among the president, Congress, and the Federal Reserve Board to use monetary and fiscal policy to achieve 3 percent adult unemployment within five years. The legislation has been exclusively symbolic, so far, and seems destined to remain so.

Supporters of the Humphrey-Hawkins Act and other legislation intended to curb unemployment argue that such programs are necessary because of the dignity associated with working to pay one's way. The availability of job opportunities, it is contended, will counter the despair that often leads to drug dependency, crime, and family disintegration in areas of high unemployment. They also note that the cost of the program will be offset by reductions in the number of recipients of unemployment compensation and welfare benefits and by increased tax collections. Therefore, according to the Congressional Budget Office, the expenditure of an additional $1 billion on public service employment will actually have a net cost of approximately $615 to $754 million, depending on how many new jobs are created.[51]

Opponents contend that job creation programs are too expensive. They also question whether they are effective. Public works efforts are criticized for being too slow in actually putting people to work, since a planning period is required before unemployed construction workers are given jobs. Public service programs are criticized because they simply allow state or local government units to charge personnel costs, which would otherwise be borne locally, to the federal government and thus fail to create new jobs.[52]

The Reagan administration, while displaying little interest in having the government guarantee jobs for all workers, nonetheless heartily endorses the concept of full employment. The proposals described in chapter 2, which set forth Reagan's economic policy, are expected by the administration to reduce unemployment levels. This would be done by stimulating the private sector, not by having the government create jobs.

Reagan Welfare Proposals

President Reagan has sought to reduce spending for most welfare programs. The president has claimed, however, that the belt-tightening will not harm the truly needy. Instead, Reagan has spoken of a "safety net" that will save the "deserving poor" from want.

To successfully cut the budget without shredding the safety net, there seem to be several assumptions. One is that a sizable share of current expenditures are due to fraud or error. President Reagan has recommended that after 1986, states not be reimbursed for erroneously made welfare payments.

One observer claims that improper payments constitute a negligible share of the cost of food stamps. The observations concerning food stamps may be apropos to other welfare programs.

> The fact is that less than 5 percent of total spending goes to ineligible recipients or is overissued. The rate of fraud is much lower than with income tax returns. Incidentally, the major frauds generally have been perpetrated not by poor recipients, but by crooked caseworkers in collusion with disreputable retailers and hard-core criminals.[53]

This observer goes on to warn that turning programs over to the states is unlikely to reduce erroneous payments: "There is far more corruption, waste and favoritism at the 'grass-roots' level than in the federal establishment."

A second assumption that guides the Reagan administration is that the coverage of welfare programs has become too encompassing. President Reagan disagrees with the efforts of some of his predecessors who sought to extend benefits to the working poor. The idea behind this effort was that by gradually phasing out welfare benefits as recipients' incomes rose, there would be greater incentives for people to work even at low-paying jobs. In cutting back programs, the Reagan administration and its conservative allies in Congress have opted to reserve the available benefits for the poorest. Thus they have reduced the maximum income at which one can qualify for housing assistance and food stamps. Reducing eligibility standards for federal day-care subsidies has been counterproductive, however, since some mothers have had to stop working and go on welfare in order to care for their children.

A third assumption behind the Reagan approach to welfare is that able-bodied recipients should work for their benefits. The president favors "workfare," a program he instituted while governor of California and that may now be tried in other states. As approved by Congress, people on the welfare rolls who are physically able—except for the mothers of small children—can be required to work on public or private jobs at the minimum wage to repay the amount of aid they receive. This idea appeals to those who believe that working enhances one's skill, habits, and self-esteem as well as to those who suspect that some welfare recipients are malingerers. It is attractive also to those who believe that our welfare system provides the wrong kind of incentives. Black columnist William Raspberry writes that the black mainstream probably agrees with the idea behind workfare since "You can work hard on a bad job and try to impress somebody so you get a promotion, or you can go find yourself something else. But welfare just traps you. And the more generous the benefits, the stronger the trap."[54] A similar rationale underlies proposals to see that disability benefits do not exceed what one could earn by working.

Reagan critics claim that workfare had little impact in California. A report released in 1975 by the California Employment Development Department concluded that fewer than 10,000 of the state's 2 million welfare recipients were put to work and that it did not dissuade new welfare applicants.[55]

A number of people who have been active in poverty programs also oppose workfare. They see welfare as an entitlement for which one should not be forced to work on public projects. Others believe that forcing people to work on public projects is demeaning, while some unions fear that minimum wage welfare recipients may be substituted for union members who would otherwise be hired.

Negative income tax.   The idea of a negative income tax has at times drawn support in Congress and the White House but never enough to secure enactment. A negative income tax would provide cash assistance to people earning less than a specified amount regardless of whether they have children or whether there is an adult male in the household. All people having no earnings would receive money. As incomes rise, the negative income tax benefit would be gradually diminished. To illustrate, if Congress were to decide that each person was entitled to a negative income tax of $1,000 a year, a family of four having no earnings would receive $4,000 from the United States Treasury. Supporters of a negative income tax usually suggest that benefits be reduced by 50 cents for each dollar earned. Thus, a family of four that earned $2,000 would receive $3,000 in negative income tax benefits, while a family earning $4,000 would receive an additional $2,000. Four-person families earning less than $8,000 would get some benefits in this example.

Advocates of a negative income tax point to a number of advantages. First, the program encourages recipients to work. Unlike some programs, such as AFDC, which terminate all benefits once participants' incomes reach a certain level, negative income tax benefits are phased out gradually; therefore, the more a family earns, the greater its total income. Second, administrative expenses for a negative income tax would be much lower than for AFDC. Negative income tax payment could be made on the basis of federal income tax returns, thereby eliminating the need for many of the expenses of investigations and the red tape of need documentation that are found in many current programs. Third, a negative income tax would standardize benefits nationwide and would increase the level of benefits paid in a number of poorer states.

A fourth consideration is that a negative income tax would be a step toward elimination of inequities that sometimes exist between welfare recipients and the working poor. Under current conditions, it has been estimated that a family of four in which the breadwinner earned the minimum wage would end up poorer than would a four-member family in which no one worked but that received Medicaid, AFDC, housing assistance, and a food stamp subsidy.

The mood of the Reagan administration makes it unlikely that a negative income tax will become law during this presidency. However, should such a policy eventually be adopted, two important disputes will have to be resolved. First is the question of the level of benefits. Second is the question of the extent to which the negative income tax should replace current aid programs. Would the negative income tax benefit replace some or all of the current aid programs, or would it provide a layer of benefits above the programs providing food, housing, health care, and money?

CONCLUDING COMMENTS

Public support for, or at least acceptance of, welfare initiatives is probably keyed to economic conditions. Major expansions in American welfare policy have come during what one might call "the best of times and the worst of times." During the depression of the 1930s poverty was so widespread that even southern Democrats who have traditionally been opposed to welfare were generally supportive of the relief programs launched by the Roosevelt administration. Then during the optimistic afterglow of the Kennedy years, Congress rubber-stamped Lyndon Johnson's War on Poverty. Under Ronald Reagan, who ran a campaign that questioned the competence of the federal government to resolve the issues of the eighties, the federal welfare role has shrunk. Unless the rate of inflation falls to levels of a generation ago, the amount spent on welfare will increase, but new programs will not be added and existing ones will be pruned.

Reagan's thumping defeat of Jimmy Carter was one indication that the challenger was in step with most of the electorate. Polls conducted since the election provide evidence that Reagan's approach to welfare is popular. More than 60 percent of a sample of registered voters believed that the Johnson poverty programs either had no effect on the poor or actually made things worse.[56] A bare majority in the same survey showed their suspicions by telling polltakers that they thought that most welfare recipients could get along without these programs. By a margin of almost 3 to 2, Americans were unwilling in June 1981 to pay more state taxes to make up for cuts in social programs caused by President Reagan's efforts to balance the budget.[57]

These poll results indicate that a majority of the public supports Reagan's efforts to reduce welfare expenditures and apparently believes the president when he says that the cuts will not harm the truly needy. Although Congress may not cut welfare programs as deeply as President Reagan would like, it appears that the public backs his plan to cap Medicaid expenses, remove a million people from food stamp eligibility lists, disqualify hundreds of thousands of AFDC recipients, slow increases in housing assistance programs, and end the emergency employment program. Many have faith that all of this can be done with no trauma being suffered by the poor.

Some economists and many who have worked with poverty programs vehemently disagree. They charge that Reagan's safety net protects the elderly and the middle class but misses many poor people.[58] Moreover, they fear that Reagan budget cuts—particularly of things like public service jobs—will push even more families below the poverty line.

NOTES

1. Joel Havemann and Linda E. Demkovich, "Making Some Sense out of the Welfare 'Mess,'" *National Journal* 9 (January 8, 1977): 51.
2. *Quarterly Public Assistance Statistics* (December 1982).
3. Gilbert Y. Steiner, *The State of Welfare* (Washington, D.C.: Brookings Institution, 1971), pp. 35–40.
4. Harrison Donnelly, "What Reagan Budget Cuts Would Do to Poor," *Congressional Quarterly Weekly Report* 39 (April 18, 1981): 668.
5. Acting director for policy in the Department of Health and Human Services Office of Family Assistance quoted in Harrison Donnelly, "Millions of Poor Face Losses Oct. 1 as Reconciliation Bill Spending Cuts Go into Effect," *Congressional Quarterly Weekly Report* 39 (September 26, 1981): 1836.
6. Harrison E. Salisbury, *The Shook-Up Generation* (New York: Harper & Row, 1958), p. 75.
7. Robert E. Forman, "Housing and Racial Segregation," in *Racism and Inequality*, ed. Harrell R. Rodgers, Jr. (San Francisco: Freeman, 1975), p. 55.
8. Chester W. Hartman, *Housing and Social Policy* (Englewood Cliffs, N.J.: Prentice-Hall, 1975), p. 137.
9. President Ford's Secretary for Housing Carla Hill, quoted in Charles Evans, "500,000 Housing Units Will Get U.S. Backing in '77 Budget, Hill Says," *Houston Chronicle*, January 19, 1976, section 1, p. 15.
10. Hartman, *Housing and Social Policy*, p. 3.
11. Laura B. Weiss, "New Middle-Income Housing Plan Passed by Committees," *Congressional Quarterly Weekly Report* 38 (June 7, 1980): 1576.
12. John C. Weicher, *Housing: Federal Policies and Programs* (Washington, D.C.: American Enterprise Institute for Public Policy Research, 1980), p. 55.
13. Ibid., p. 60.
14. Ibid., p. 14.

15. Diane Granat, "Subsidized Housing Cut Sharply for FY '84," *National Journal* 15 (February 5, 1983), p. 283.

16. Quoted in *Congressional Quarterly Weekly Report* 40 (February 13, 1982): 277.

17. Estimate of the Congressional Budget Office reported in Linda E. Demkovich, "The Food Stamp Cap Again," *National Journal* 13 (September 21, 1981): 1643.

18. Congressional Budget Office, *The Food Stamp Program: Income or Food Supplementation* (Washington, D.C.: U.S. Government Printing Office, 1977), pp. 61–63.

19. Rep. Thomas Foley (D.–Wash.) quoted in *Congressional Quarterly Weekly Report* 39 (May 16, 1981): 872.

20. Prior to 1977 all but the poorest food stamp program participants had to buy their stamps. The subsidy, which was keyed to income, resources, and family size, was conveyed by providing recipients with stamps having a cash value in excess of what they paid.

21. Harrison Donnelly and Peg O'Hara, "House Panel Makes Cuts in Food Stamp Program, but Not All Reagan Wants," *Congressional Quarterly Weekly Report* 39 (May 2, 1981): 771.

22. "What Recipients Eat," *Congressional Quarterly Weekly Report* 39 (February 7, 1981): 278.

23. Jean Mayer, "The Food Stamp Dilemma," *Washington Post*, February 19, 1982, p. E3.

24. In terms of its mode of being financed and the extensiveness of its coverage, Medicare is not a welfare program but instead shares characteristics with Social Security, which is discussed in the next chapter. We have chosen to discuss Medicare in conjunction with Medicaid because evaluations and proposed reforms frequently take the two in tandem and a single agency, the Health Care Financing Administration, has responsibility for both programs.

25. Louise B. Russell, "Medical Care," in *Setting National Priorities: Agenda for the 1980s*, ed. Joseph A. Pechman (Washington, D.C.: Brookings Institution, 1980), p. 179.

26. Linda E. Demkovich, "Reagan Takes On the Elderly Again as He Seeks to Slow Medicare's Growth," *National Journal* 13 (September 12, 1981): 1616.

27. Quoted in John K. Iglehart, "Government Searching for a More Cost-Efficient Way to Pay Hospitals," *National Journal* 3 (December 25, 1976): 1822.

28. Elizabeth Bowman, "Hearings Held on Ways to Cut Soaring Costs of Medicaid, Medicare," *Congressional Quarterly Weekly Report* 34 (August 7, 1976): 2127.

29. John K. Iglehart, "The Rising Costs of Health Care—Something Must Be Done, but What?" *National Journal* 8 (October 16, 1976): 1462.

30. William Hines, "Medicare, Medicaid Said Virtual License to Steal," *Houston Chronicle*, July 29, 1976, section 1, p. 7.

31. "Medicaid Lab Fraud, Kickback Found," *Congressional Quarterly Weekly Report* 34 (February 21, 1976): 454.

32. Quoted in "Medicaid Called 'Greatest Rip-off,'" *Houston Chronicle*, November 18, 1976, section 1, p. 1.

33. This draws on Linda E. Demkovich, "The Touchy Business of Hospital Reporting," *National Journal* 11 (November 17, 1979): 1940–1942.

34. Quoted in Iglehart, "The Rising Costs of Health Care," p. 1462.

35. Russell, "Medical Care," p. 185.

36. Elizabeth Wehr, "Lobbyists Fight Federal Regulation of 'Medigap' Health Insurance Abuses," *Congressional Quarterly Weekly Report* 38 (February 16, 1980): 403.

37. Quoted in Daniel P. Moynihan, *Maximum Feasible Misunderstanding* (New York: Free Press, 1969), pp. 3–4.

38. Michael Harrington, *The Other America* (Baltimore: Penguin, 1962).

39. Quoted in James L. Sundquist, *Politics and Policy: The Eisenhower, Kennedy, and Johnson Years* (Washington, D.C.: Brookings Institution, 1968), p. 112.

40. For an analysis that disputes the myth that Lyndon Johnson came from an impoverished background (a myth perpetuated by Johnson), see Larry L. King, "Bringing Up Lyndon," *Texas Monthly* 4 (January 1976): 78 *ff.*

41. Quoted in *Congressional Record*, 88th Congress, 2nd Session (1964), 110, p. 5287.

42. Gil Sewall et al., "A High Grade for Head Start," *Time*, October 8, 1979, p. 102; and Spencer Rich, "Lasting Gains Are Found from Preschool Start," *Washington Post*, November 30, 1979, p. 23-A.

43. Edward R. Fried; Alice M. Rivlin; Charles L. Schultze; and Nancy H. Teeters, *Setting National Priorities: The 1974 Budget* (Washington, D.C.: Brookings Institution, 1973), p. 220.

44. John C. Donovan, *The Politics of Poverty*, 2nd ed. (Indianapolis: Pegasus, 1973), pp. 35–43.

45. Moynihan, *Maximum Feasible Misunderstanding*, p. 94.

46. Donovan, *Politics of Poverty*, p. 113.

47. John C. Donovan, *The Politics of Poverty*, 1st ed. (Indianapolis: Pegasus, 1967), p. 122.

48. John L. Palmer and Joseph J. Minarik, "Income Security Policy," in *Setting National Priorities: The Next Ten Years*, eds. Henry Owen and Charles L. Schultze (Washington, D.C.: Brookings Institution, 1976), pp. 519–526.

49. U.S. Bureau of the Census, *Characteristics of Households and Persons Receiving Noncash Benefits: 1979*, Current Population Reports, Series P-23, No. 110 (Washington, D.C.: U.S. Government Printing Office, 1981), p. 8.

50. "Experts Differ on How Many Are Poor," *Congressional Quarterly Weekly Report* 39 (April 18, 1981): 669.

51. Cited in Mary E. Eccles, "Jobs Programs: How Well Do They Work," *Congressional Quarterly Weekly Report* 35 (February 19, 1977): 303.

52. U.S. Department of Labor, *Manpower Report of the President* (Washington, D.C.: U.S. Government Printing Office, 1975), p. 46.

53. Mayer, "The Food Stamp Dilemma," p. E3.

54. William Raspberry, "More Welfare Is Just a Stronger Trap," *Washington Post*, June 1980.

55. "Workfare Failed for Reagan in '70s, Study Says," *Atlanta Journal*, March 30, 1981, p. 6-A; also see Linda E. Demkovich, "Workfare—Punishment for Being Poor or an End to the Welfare Stigma," *National Journal* 13 (July 4, 1981): 1201–1205.

56. CBS News–*New York Times* Poll, released November 15, 1980.

57. CBS News–*New York Times* Poll, released June 30, 1981.

58. See the discussion in Donnelly, "What Reagan Budget Cuts Would Do to Poor," pp. 665–668.

SUGGESTED READINGS

Donovan, John C. *The Politics of Poverty*. 2nd ed. Indianapolis: Pegasus, 1973.

Harrington, Michael. *The Other America*. Baltimore: Penguin, 1962.

Hartman, Chester W. *Housing and Social Policy*. Englewood Cliffs, N.J.: Prentice-Hall, 1975.

Moynihan, Daniel P. *Maximum Feasible Misunderstanding*. New York: Free Press, 1969.

Rodgers, Harrell R., Jr. *Poverty and Plenty*. Reading, Mass.: Addison-Wesley, 1979.

Sundquist, James L. *Politics and Policy: The Eisenhower, Kennedy, and Johnson Years*. Washington, D.C.: Brookings Institution, 1968.

Weicher, John C. *Housing: Federal Policies and Programs*. Washington, D.C.: American Enterprise Institute for Public Policy Research, 1980.

SIX

Economic Benefits for the Many

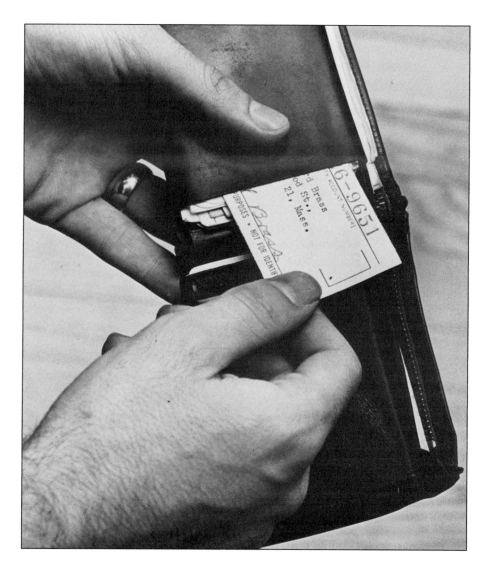

In the previous chapter we discussed a variety of programs designed to provide benefits to the poor or to help them rise out of poverty. Those who succeed in entering the great American middle class will find that in their new economic situation the federal government extends to them a different set of benefits. Although the nature of the benefits available to the middle class is unlike those provided to the poor, they are directed at meeting some of the same basic human needs that poverty programs address.

Programs for the middle class have different basic objectives than do those for lower-income groups. The latter seek to provide what the majority in society judge to be minimal levels for a Spartan existence. Middle-class programs seek either to reduce risk or to relieve financial burdens. These objectives are achieved by having the federal government—and through it society in general—play the role of insurer or regulator. Proposals for national health insurance, FHA home loan guarantees, and Social Security minimize financial risks to the middle-class family by distributing those risks broadly across the population. Tax policies that allow people to deduct payments for health insurance, for interest on home mortgages, or for retirement accounts make it easier for the middle class to obtain these goods and services. Again, these policies, by reducing tax revenues, have the effect of distributing the cost to society at large.

The programs discussed in this chapter do not benefit the middle class exclusively. Containing the cost of health care would benefit all classes. Although there have been proposals to deny Social Security benefits to the affluent, everyone who has paid into the system for a specified amount of time is entitled to benefits. We treat these topics here because the middle class is the largest group of beneficiaries and because the middle class has relatively few alternatives. The wealthy can, if necessary, get along by relying on their own resources; the poor have various welfare programs that help them meet some of their needs.

The first issue we examine is federal policy as it affects health care costs. We review proposals for moderating rising health care expenses for people who are not covered by Medicaid and Medicare (discussed in chapter 5), and discuss proposals for national health insurance. A second policy area is housing. We look at federal initiatives to help the middle class become home owners, with particular emphasis on recent innovations adopted in the face of high interest rates. Finally, we consider retirement, the Social Security system, and federal regulation of private pension plans.

HEALTH CARE

One of the most pervasive fears confronting the middle class is that the expense of a serious illness will cause financial devastation. That fear is far from irrational. Hospital costs rose by 12 to 17 percent a year between 1977 and 1980, doctors' charges have been increasing at only a slightly slower rate, and the number of days of treatment in hospitals or as out-patients and the number of costly laboratory tests have all been surging upward.[1] Because of these trends, the nation's health care budget trebled during the 1960s and trebled again during the 1970s, reaching about a quarter of a trillion dollars in 1980. In the absence of some kind of yet undevised constraint, the rate of increase observed for the last two decades is projected to continue through the 1980s (see table 6–1).

Although we live in inflationary times, the growth in health care costs has far outstripped the rate of inflation, as shown in figure 6–1. As a consequence, the share of the GNP spent on health care has risen from 5.3 percent in 1960 to 9.8 percent in 1981.

The federal government pays more than $74 billion for health care, but the great bulk of federal medical aid goes for either Medicaid or Medicare. Middle-class families, particularly those who are in the costly child-rearing years, receive little direct federal assistance in paying medical expenses.

To help with medical costs, an estimated 90 percent of the American public has coverage from some form of health insurance or federal program. The private insurance programs in which middle-income Americans participate are typically paid for through some combination of contributions from employers and employees. The benefits provided vary greatly, with some covering virtually everything while others have a short list of basic benefits, and still others require the beneficiary to shoulder a share of the cost for the items covered by the policy. To illustrate differences in the extensiveness of coverage for differing kinds of health costs, patients pay for a tenth of all hospital expenses, a third of all physicians' bills and almost half of the expenses of nursing homes.[2]

During the last decade two major thrusts have characterized policy proposals to change the burden of health care expenses. One is to relieve anxieties by instituting a national, comprehensive health insurance program. The other is to develop techniques for retarding the rate of increase in health care costs.

TABLE 6-1   Health care costs for selected years, 1965–1990 (in billions of dollars)

	1965	*1970*	*1975*	*1978*	*1980*	*1985*[a]	*1990*[a]
Hospital care	13.9	27.8	52.1	76.0	97.3	182.8	334.6
Physicians' services	8.5	14.3	24.9	35.3	45.0	78.2	128.8
Dentists' services	2.8	4.8	8.2	13.3	17.9	33.9	59.4
Nursing homes	2.1	4.7	9.9	15.8	21.6	42.0	75.6

SOURCE: *Health Care Financing Review* (Winter 1980), reprinted in Margaret C. Thompson, ed., *Health Policy: The Legislative Agenda* (Washington, D.C.: *Congressional Quarterly,* 1980), p. 12. Copyright 1980 by Congressional Quarterly, Inc. Reprinted by permission.

[a]Estimates.

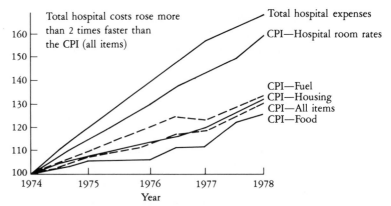

FIGURE 6-1   Relative increases in hospital expenses and several basic needs. To dramatize his argument for hospital cost control, Health, Education, and Welfare (HEW) Secretary Joseph A. Califano, Jr., presented this chart during congressional hearings. It showed hospital costs increasing far more rapidly than other elements of the consumer price index (CPI) in the 1974–1978 period. Califano said federal hospital spending alone would exceed $60 billion by 1984, nearly double the 1979 level, if Congress didn't pass the legislation. (*Source: Margaret C. Thompson, ed.,* Health Policy: The Legislative Agenda. *Washington, D.C.:* Congressional Quarterly, *1980, p. 22. Copyright 1980 by Congressional Quarterly, Inc. Reprinted by permission.*)

National Health Insurance

Some consider the lack of national health insurance (NHI) to be a major omission in federal programs to meet basic human needs. From this perspective, some form of national health insurance, the merits of which have been debated since the New Deal, is generations overdue. Even in the aftermath of the swing to the Right in 1980, NHI was favored by a 52 to 37 percent majority of those who had an opinion on the issue.[3]

During the 1970s the most active proponent of NHI was Sen. Edward Kennedy (D.–Mass.). Although Kennedy's plan has varied from year to year, its essential elements have remained the same. He advocates a compulsory program that would cover the entire population. Funding would come from a combination of taxes on employees and employers along with a contribution from the federal treasury. Funding would be sufficient to cover individuals and families lacking a wage-earner. All hospital and medical expenses—with some exceptions for nursing homes, mental health, and dental care—would be provided for. Kennedy's proposals have been the most comprehensive and, obviously, the most expensive of the alternatives considered by Congress.

Proposals less comprehensive than Kennedy's have suggested voluntary participation and upper limits on the benefits provided. For example, a proposal endorsed in the mid-1970s by the American Hospital Association would have paid for a maximum of ninety days of hospitalization and nursing home care a year, and twelve doctor visits annually. Like Kennedy's proposal, this alternative called for workers to be covered through their place of employment. Some, but not all, proposals have included provisions for handling the needy. Certain plans have called for the federal government to run the programs, while others—not surprisingly those endorsed by a number of insurance companies—would have coverage provided under private insurance policies.

The most limited programs would offer only catastrophic coverage. These have stipulated that benefits would begin only after a family has absorbed a certain level of expense, say $2,500. Participants in these programs could have insurance policies to help with those expenses below the threshold for catastrophic coverage. The rationale behind catastrophic coverage is that since most Americans participate in some program to defray health care expenses, the major need is to protect against the costs few middle-income families are able to save for. At the opposite end of the spectrum, Senator Kennedy sees health care as an entitlement that should be all-encompassing, not conditioned by one's bank balance.

Cost Containment

During the Carter administration a growing number of congressional and administration leaders began to support policy proposals directed toward a far different set of goals than those embraced in previous discussions of national health insurance. Kennedy-style comprehensive health care coverage seems to be an idea whose time has come and gone. It was a product of an era when the emphasis of federal programs focused on higher and higher benefits.

The breezes of change felt during the Carter presidency became a stiff gale under President Reagan. Interest in fuller benefits was supplanted by a concern for limiting the rise in the cost of health care. Two basic avenues for achieving this objective have been suggested. One, which initially enjoyed greater popularity, is the regulatory approach. Its antithesis, which David Stockman (Reagan's director of the Office of Management and Budget) sponsored while a member of Congress, encourages freer competition among health care providers.

The regulatory approach.   Two early, limited attempts to restrain health care cost inflation sought to eliminate needless duplication of facilities and to prevent unnecessary treatment. This effort at planning was adopted by Congress in 1974, terminating the Hill-Burton Act, which had encouraged new hospital construction. Congress endorsed planning when it became apparent that there were at least 100,000 surplus hospital beds, which cost a total of between $1 million and $2 million annually to maintain.[4] Not only was it hoped that planning by federally subsidized state and local agencies would prevent further unneeded hospital expansion; it was also intended to discourage nearby hospitals from acquiring costly new technology where demand was low enough so that physicians in the area could share a single unit. The local health service agencies that were responsible for overseeing the development of local plans have not been popular, can document little in the way of savings, and have been slated for extinction by the Reagan administration.

Attempts at cost containment by having local physicans review the quality and necessity of procedures (PSROs, discussed in chapter 5) have also drawn criticism. Moreover, it has been estimated that the PSROs saved only seventy cents for every dollar it cost to operate them.[5]

More drastic steps for cost containment have been proposed but not adopted. President Carter suggested that a lid be placed on the annual rate at which hospital expenses would be allowed to rise. With hospital charges increasing by 15 percent a year, the American Hospital Association violently opposed the idea that it should be restricted to a 9 or 10 percent increase. The association pointed out that in the absence of across-the-board price controls like those imposed by President Nixon, it would be unfair to single out health care facilities. Hospitals, unlike many industries, are both labor and technology intensive, meaning that they must cope with costly new equipment as well as rising salary demands.

Congress rejected President Carter's approach to capping health care costs. The Reagan administration, whose leading members are far more attracted to the concept of free-market economy, has shown more interest in enhancing competition than in regulating costs.

The competitive approach.   Ronald Reagan ran for president saying, "What ails American medicine is government meddling and the straitjacket of federal programs."[6] The Reagan approach, then, is to stress competition and to turn more toward private insurers than to federal agencies for protection against excessive health care costs. In the same vein, the administration would have individuals bear a larger share of the costs, turning away from the efforts of liberals to provide maximum services.

One type of participant in the more competitive arena would probably be the health maintenance organization (HMO). HMOs have played a role in providing health care on the West Coast since World War II, when the Kaiser-Permanente program was created to meet the health needs of workers in the Kaiser shipyards. The assumptions underlying HMOs are quite distinct from—indeed one might say the polar opposite of—those behind traditional health care. As its name implies, an HMO takes a preventive approach, trying to maintain the good health of its participants. In contrast, most doctors, hospitals, and clinics are oriented primarily toward curing the ill.

The financial arrangements create a situation in which the physicians affiliated with an HMO have an incentive to keep their patients well. Members of an HMO pay an annual fee that entitles them to treatment by the staff of the organization's physicians at no additional cost, much like student health services arrangements on many campuses. The staff of an HMO includes both those who concentrate on family practice as well as a number of specialists. If a patient's illness requires consultation with one or more specialists, it usually involves nothing more than seeing additional doctors at the same facility, often with no need for a separate appointment. This is in contrast with the procedure in most doctors' offices, where the patient pays separately for each visit. If one's physician feels that the services of a specialist are needed, then the patient is referred to another doctor, in another office, at another time, for which another fee is charged. Each visit and each test produce additional revenues for the provider.

An HMO director commenting on the difference between HMOs and the traditional fee-for-service arrangement said: "It has always been a paradox that doctors and hospitals are dedicated to keeping people well and healthy, yet generally derive most of their income from sickness. By contrast, when prepayment is made directly to providers of care, both the hospitals and doctors are better off if the patient remains well."[7] Moreover, since the annual fee is set, there is no incentive for doctors to prescribe unnecessary tests or treatments, or for hospitals to place patients in more expensive surroundings (such as intensive care units) than they need.

By 1982 it was estimated that 11 million Americans were enrolled in HMOs. Many of these were on the West Coast, where approximately 10 percent of the California population receives health care from an HMO. The number of HMO participants rose by 74 percent between 1973 and 1979, even though federal programs have not been as supportive as HMO advocates would like.[8] There have been relatively few federal dollars appropriated to help HMOs get started or expand.

Although federal assistance has been welcome, the initial legislation in 1973 came wrapped in so much red tape that HMOs complained it was often impossible to provide services for less than the traditional fee-for-service physicians. Subsequent amendments have relaxed the range of services HMOs were initially required to provide to be eligible for federal assistance, allowing them to charge extra for preventive dental care for children and other special services. These charges should make the facilities more competitive.

The federal health planning procedures discussed earlier have been another obstacle to HMOs. In a situation in which the left hand seemed to be unaware of the right hand's activities, planning requirements sometimes thwarted development of an HMO alternative in areas where current capacity was judged to be sufficient. These judgments were made by people closely attached to the traditional health care structure, who do not encourage HMOs because they offer a cheaper alternative to that structure.

Stanford economist Alain Enthoven, a major proponent of the concept of increased competition, has developed a proposal that relies heavily on a network of HMOs. Under Enthoven's proposal, each family would receive a voucher with which to purchase health care. Workers would get theirs through their jobs, the elderly would receive theirs from Medicare, and the poor would be issued vouchers through the Medicaid apparatus. These vouchers, which would be uniform per capita, would be used to prepay health care on a yearly basis. HMOs and other providers would compete for consumers' vouchers by offering a basic set of benefits that consumers could easily compare across competing programs. The competitive situation, Enthoven predicts, would bring down costs. Not surprisingly, doctors, insurance companies, and, to a lesser degree, hospitals have shown little enthusiasm for increasing competition.[9]

Another proposal for reducing costs by promoting competition, which could be operated in conjunction with HMOs, would be to make patients more aware of health care costs. Since the vast majority of Americans receive some assistance in paying for health care, particularly for hospital treatment, two consequences emerge, both of which contribute to higher costs. First, because consumers do not pay directly for treatment—instead third-party payment is made by the insurer or the government—they have less incentive to try to minimize costs. Second, because the insurer may pay for treatment administered in a hospital but not on an out-patient basis, there is an inducement to go to the hospital even though that treatment is more costly.

To make the public more aware of costs, some have recommended that the extent of third-party payments be reduced. In an experiment launched in 1973, families with comparable incomes were grouped on the basis of personal liability for medical care.[10] The four groups of families paid 0, 25, 50, or 95 percent of their health care costs up to the point (under $1,000) beyond which their insurance paid the full amount. Families who had to pay a larger share of those costs made fewer visits to physicians and hospitals than did families who could shift the full cost to a third party.

Another technique to make the costs of health care more visible is to alter the tax laws that allow employers and employees to deduct expenditures for health insurance. The current tax laws encourage employees to bargain for more generous health coverage—a tax-free benefit that reduces federal revenue (in 1983 that revenue loss amounted to about $18 billion). In the fall of 1982 Congress considered, but did not approve, a proposal to limit the size of tax-free medical benefits. Bowing to pressure from organized labor, the House and Senate approved a more modest reform, one that reduced the deductions individuals can take for health insurance and medical costs.

Evaluating the alternatives.   Although backers of all of the proposals discussed here argue that these innovations will at least slow the rate at which costs increase, if not actually push costs down, change remains problematic. There are three major obstacles to the adoption and implementation of proposals for promoting competition. First, there is not strong public support for competitive health care programs. For example, in one situation in which a set of federal employees could opt for different levels of coverage, each with a commensurate price tag, most of the young families opted for a high level of coverage even though they had to pay a part of the premium themselves.[11] The limited available research, then, suggests that consumers want high levels of coverage and, within reason, will pay more to obtain them. When their insurance forces them to pay a share of the cost, however, they do restrict usage and may actually shop around for medical care.

Second, the network of HMOs needed to promote competition does not exist. In fact, ten states have no HMOs at all. This obstacle rests in part on the first—lack of public support. Undermining that support is the warning by critics that HMOs will lead to assembly-line treatment and to long delays for routine checkups. Since an HMO's profit margin is reduced if additional treatment is provided, there is some fear that HMO doctors will not give expensive but needed care.

All of this helps explain why Americans have not adopted a cost-benefit approach to health care as some economists would have us do. The premise behind NHI, Medicare, and Medicaid, and a major component of cost increases has been the belief that income should not determine the availability or quality of health care. New equipment (neonatal or cardiac units, CAT scanners) is terribly expensive. Dialysis for victims of kidney failure is a costly procedure. Furthermore, doctors and hospitals have learned, as a result of million-dollar malpractice suits, that it is risky not to prescribe the full range of diagnostic and treatment procedures, irrespective of cost. Americans have rejected the idea that health care is a scarce commodity, the distribution of which is determined by family resources.

Another major obstacle to competition in this sphere is powerful political opposition. Insurance companies and many doctors and hospitals oppose proposals that would alter their current relationships with customers and patients. Since these groups are generous contributors to the campaign coffers of congressional candidates, they are being heard. Indeed, their campaign work has won them well-positioned allies in Congress.

If we continue and perhaps expand on the availability of third-party payment of health care, the trends noted at the beginning of this section seem destined to persist. If payment for a larger share of the cost of health care is made a public responsibility, then it is likely that reallocation will occur within the federal budget as additional resources for health are taken from other programs.

Alternatively, if the burden of paying this growing tab is judged to be too great, some form of rationing will emerge. If people are left to their own resources, the treatment they receive will once again depend on their financial status. If public authorities, perhaps in consultation with doctors, make the determination of who gets extraordinarily expensive treatment, some form of triage may be instituted. Perhaps extraordinary procedures will be reserved for those who show the greatest promise of recovery, or for the young, or for those whose skills are most valuable to society. Scarce treatment may be distributed through use of a waiting list (as is done with public housing) or through random selection (as was once done with kidney dialysis). About all that can safely be predicted for the 1980s is that some shift in responsibility for payment of health care costs seems inevitable.

HOUSING

A dream of middle-class youth is that one day they will own their own home, complete with shade trees, two-car garage, and central air-conditioning. Since the New Deal, federal programs have turned this dream into reality for millions. But is the dream viable for a new generation? The inflation of the 1970s, which relentlessly pushed prices and interest rates to unheard-of heights, has so changed the world of home financing that observers see home ownership slipping beyond the grasp of a growing share of the young middle class. Obviously that group sees this as a serious problem; some economists believe that a redirection of financial resources from homes to industry is actually good for the nation's economic well-being.

In this section we review federal policies that have facilitated the purchase of homes. Then we describe recent changes in home financing, the tax benefits of home ownership, and the consequences of federal housing policies for prospective purchasers and sellers.

Making Home Ownership Easier

During the 1930s the federal government initiated programs that brought the purchase of a home within the reach of the middle class. As with so many New Deal programs, these home-financing initiatives were intended to stimulate the economy by increasing demand through the creation of a new set of consumers.

Prior to the creation of the Federal Housing Administration (FHA) in 1934, the purchase of a home required a substantial down payment, frequently as much as half the purchase price. The terms of the loan would call for repayment within five to ten years. Each year the borrower would pay the interest that had accrued on the note; then, at the end of the period, the entire principal would come due. If the borrower could not make the "balloon" payment (that is, the repayment of the principal in one installment) or get the lender to renew the loan, the bank could foreclose.

The FHA induced banks and savings and loan associations to make loans for longer periods (twenty to forty years) to people who made smaller down payments (as little as 5 percent). Repayment came in a series of equal monthly installments, with an increasing share applied to the principal and a declining share to the interest. The interest rate was fixed for the duration of the loan, regardless of subsequent fluctuations in the money market. Lending institutions accepted these terms because the FHA absorbed the risk by guaranteeing the loan. If the buyer defaulted, the agency repaid the principal, took title to the house, and sustained any loss. To maintain a supply of mortgage money, the Federal National Mortgage Association would buy mortgages from lending institutions, thereby providing funds for loans to new home buyers.

After World War II, FHA activities were augmented by an aspect of the GI bill. The Veterans' Administration (VA) guarantees the home loans of former servicemen and servicewomen under even more advantageous terms than are offered by the FHA. (VA loans require no down payment.)

Of course both the VA and FHA require that an applicant have an income sufficient to indicate a strong likelihood of repayment. So although not everyone qualified for a loan, the opportunity to spread the cost over a generation or more greatly enlarged the pool of potential purchasers. The success of the federally backed programs led thrift institutions and mortgage companies to offer similar terms on loans that were not secured by government promise of repayment. Thanks to the availability of mortgage money, the proportion of home owners in the country grew from 40 percent in 1940 to 65 percent in 1980.[12]

Changes in Financing Arrangements

For many years, mortgages based on the terms introduced by the FHA worked well. Homes were affordable for a growing number of families. This demand kept a major component of the economy, the housing industry, healthy. Savings and loan institutions and other lenders made profits because they could charge a few percentage points more in interest than they paid to their depositors. This set of happy arrangements was spoiled by inflation that produced unprecedented interest rates in the 1970s.

Until the 1970s the upper limit for interest charges was prescribed by state usury laws. During that inflation-riddled decade, however, investors refused to make money available for mortgages if they could obtain higher returns on other investments. As mortgage money dried up, builders, realtors, and savings and loan banks prevailed on state legislatures to raise usury ceilings. Once the lid was removed, the rates for housing loans rose and (occasionally) fell, keeping pace with the cost of borrowing money for other pursuits.

With the trend in interest rates being primarily upward, savings and loan institutions found themselves holding portfolios full of mortgages paying less than 10 percent interest—a lower rate of interest than they were having to pay out to recent investors. Lenders became reluctant to commit money for a fixed return for thirty years. In order to attract depositors, it became necessary to pay substantially higher rates, thus severely cutting into the earnings of lending institutions, forcing some toward bankruptcy.

To compete for investors' dollars, mortgage institutions have asked for and been granted flexibility in adjusting the interest rates charged for home loans. An early deviation from the fixed-rate mortgage was the graduated-payment mortgage, which allowed the lender to increase the rate by an amount agreed upon by the lender and the borrower at the time that the loan was made. The timing of the increases was also set out in the mortgage contract. Interest on these loans was initially below the rate for fixed loans, but would rise above the fixed-loan rate during the life of the mortgage.

The graduated-payment mortgage helped buyers purchase homes they otherwise would be unable to afford until their earnings increased. Because the graduated-payment loan established an upper limit for interest charges, however, it failed to keep up with the amounts investors could earn in other spheres.

Greater flexibility is allowed the lender by renegotiable-rate and variable-rate mortgages (VRMs). The first provides a loan on which the interest rate may fluctuate by half a point a year, but only for a few years—too few to pay off the principal. At the end of the period (usually three to five years), the loan is renegotiated for another five years or less. Over the course of thirty years, the interest rate may go up by no more than 5 percentage points. A VRM is made for the full life of the loan. The interest rate can vary by half a percent a year, with a maximum increase of 2.5 points. Maximum increases of 5 or 2.5 points, although preferable from the lenders' standpoint to fixed-rate loans, have not allowed enough of an increase to keep up with changes in interest rates.

In 1981 the Federal Home Loan Bank Board took yet another step toward flexibility, approving the adjustable-rate mortgage (ARM). Interest rates on ARMs can be adjusted monthly and, unlike other flexible-rate loans, are not limited. Rates are pegged to an established index, such as the yield on Treasury bills, or what savings and loan institutions pay for funds, or the national average for interest rates on houses that are resold. Although lenders could adjust rates monthly, most alter them less frequently.

The ARMs clearly go further than other available options in reducing the lenders' risk that they will have their funds committed to a portfolio paying less than could be earned by other investments. Not surprisingly, lenders like the ARM, while borrowers approach it hesitantly. As can be calculated from table 6–2, an increase of a few percentage points in the interest rate can result in significantly higher monthly payments. For example, on a loan of $50,000, if the interest rate increases from 12 to 15 percent, the monthly payments go from $514 to $632.

TABLE 6–2 Monthly payments for principal and interest depending on amount borrowed and interest rate (principal repaid over thirty years)

Interest rate	Amount borrowed					
	$40,000	$50,000	$60,000	$70,000	$80,000	$90,000
10%	$351.03	$438.79	$ 526.54	$ 614.30	$ 702.06	$ 789.82
11	380.93	476.16	571.39	666.62	761.85	857.08
12	411.45	514.31	617.17	720.03	822.89	925.75
13	442.48	553.10	663.72	774.34	884.96	995.58
14	473.95	592.44	710.92	829.41	947.90	1,066.38
15	505.78	632.22	758.67	885.11	1,011.56	1,138.00
16	537.90	672.38	806.85	941.33	1,075.81	1,210.28
17	570.27	712.84	855.41	997.97	1,140.54	1,283.11
18	602.83	753.54	904.25	1,054.96	1,205.67	1,356.38
19	635.56	794.45	953.34	1,112.22	1,271.11	1,430.00
20	668.41	835.51	1,002.61	1,169.71	1,336.81	1,503.92

SOURCE: Calculated by Jeffry Howard.

Although an ARM, like a VRM or renegotiable rate, drops when interest rates fall, increases have outnumbered declines. If rates go up, higher payments may actually force those whose incomes have grown at a slower rate to default. This has led a critic to complain that "the American people are being robbed of the opportunity to own their own homes and the opportunity to a future of stable housing and stable communities."[13]

Another way to look at the figures in table 6–2 is to see how much one can purchase for a given monthly payment. For example, if a family's budget calls for $720 a month for principal and interest, they can afford a $70,000 mortgage at 12 percent interest. If interest rates go to 14 percent, they lose about $10,000 in purchasing power. At 17 percent interest, $720 a month will be adequate for a mortgage of about $50,000. At 22 percent (not shown), this family could not afford even a $40,000 mortgage. At the other end of the scale, a family that could afford $411.45 for a mortgage of $40,000 at 12 percent would be able to borrow only $28,959 at 17 percent interest and have the same monthly payment.

Tax Incentives

Allowing home owners to deduct their interest and property taxes when computing their income tax liability is a major incentive to buy rather than rent. Since during the initial years of a mortgage the bulk of each monthly payment goes for interest charges, home buyers are charging off a sizable share of their housing costs to the federal government. The progressive nature of the federal income tax means that the size of the benefit a family receives through tax deductions increases with income. For most middle-income families, the largest deduction is for interest paid on their homes. Home owners' interest deductions in 1981 totaled an estimated $39 billion, and might reach $82 billion by 1986.[14]

The tax laws also help home owners when they sell their residences. No capital gains taxes are collected if the profit on the sale is reinvested within eighteen months in a residence costing as much or more. If, after age 55, a home owner decides to move to a less expensive dwelling, no taxes are levied on as much as $100,000 in capital gains realized from the sale of a home.

The Consequences of Federal Policies

The encouragement federal policy has provided for home ownership has been a major factor in shaping America's urban landscape. Tax policy has made it more advantageous economically for the middle class to be owners rather than renters.[15] It has also encouraged the ownership of large homes. Until the high interest rates of the late 1970s, federal policy made it relatively easy to buy homes.

These conditions, coupled with the demand for new homes by returning World War II GIs, touched off the suburbanization of America. Among the consequences of this phenomenon were the decline of most central-city shopping districts, a drop in quality of many city school systems, a smaller population in most central cities, and a decline in their political influence. Urban sprawl has necessitated the development of vast new road networks. Indeed, the population is so far-flung in cities like Houston and Los Angeles that for most residents there is no satisfactory alternative to the automobile. So this spatial distribution also contributes to energy shortages and pollution.

Some economists have pointed out other consequences of federal support for home ownership. Encouraging millions of families and thousands of lending institutions to tie their funds up in residences deprives the economy of capital that could be used to refurbish the nation's aging factories, make them better able to compete in the world market, and create jobs. One critic said, "Housing does not beget more jobs. If you build a factory, it will produce something and employ people, but that isn't true of a house."[16] Housing specialists Steinlieb and Hughes write that "reindustrialization versus housing, the current version of 'guns and butter,' is the major unfolding issue" of the 1980s.[17]

There is nothing to suggest that the tax advantages that accrue to home owners will be eliminated in the near future. The pressures from home owners, realtors, and builders are sufficient to block any such proposal. If there are changes, it is more likely that a maximum annual amount of deductible interest—perhaps $5,000 to $10,000—will be set.

Instead of flowing from new policy directions, the changes occurring in housing are due to broader changes in the economy. Interest rates of 15 percent or higher, coupled with the 146 percent increase in the cost of the median-priced home during the 1970s, make it impossible for a growing number of families to buy the traditional single-family, detached home. To illustrate, "In 1978, according to the National Association of Realtors, the monthly payments on a median-priced home exclusive of taxes averaged $383, or 22.8 percent of average family income. At today's [1981] interest rates, the monthly payment on the median home has risen to $810, or about 37 percent of estimated average family income."[18] In order to buy a home today, purchasers must forgo a greater range of other goods and services.

If adjustable-rate mortgages become the norm, prospective buyers will need to have some uncommitted income in order to meet possible higher interest rates. This will produce several results. First, some share of the population will no longer be able to purchase homes. In 1981, it was estimated that only 3 percent of the population earned enough to buy an average-priced home, which cost $88,400.[19] Second, another segment of the population will have to settle for small homes, row houses instead of detached dwellings, or condominiums. Third, some people who bought their homes when interest rates were relatively low will be unwilling to move. Even a sizable salary increase will not offset the increased house payments caused by higher interest rates, nor will it relieve the anxieties caused by an adjustable mortgage.

Fourth, because high interest rates force people to lower their housing aspirations, the pool of purchasers for any but inexpensive dwellings is reduced. This makes it harder for a person to sell a home. To make a sale, the owner may have to reduce the price and/or participate in what realtors call "creative financing." This means the seller has to give the buyer a second mortgage so that the seller has less for a down payment when buying new shelter. Fifth, the future demand for housing may be reduced. Steinlieb and Hughes go so far as to speculate that "the largest single reservoir of housing for the 1980s, therefore, may well be secured through the partitioning of extant one-family units."[20] A further consequence would be to make earning a living more difficult for millions of construction workers. It could also mean that young people may have to reside longer with their parents and, perhaps, put off marrying.

Since the changes in the financing and selling of homes have serious consequences for so many, it is not surprising that those who are being hurt are turning to the federal government for relief. If restraining budget deficits and reducing federal involvement in the economy remain high-priority items with our national leaders, those pleas for assistance may fall on deaf ears. A return to the "good old days" of home financing is unlikely.

One proposal that has drawn little support so far, but which might be embraced by families desperate to buy a home, would give lenders a share of the equity. If consumer opposition could be overcome, the Federal Home Loan Bank Board might authorize loans in which the lender would be entitled to a share of the increase in the value of the property. Thus, if one bought a residence for $75,000 and sold it five years later for $100,000, the lender would receive not only the balance of the principal but also a predetermined percentage of the $25,000 increase in value. If lenders knew they would get some of the appreciation in the property's value, they would probably lend funds at a lower rate.

This idea may seem farfetched today, but today's interest rates and adjustable mortgages seemed improbable just a few years ago. The housing market and federal policy have undergone cataclysmic changes. Continued change should characterize the 1980s.

RETIREMENT

There are probably very few readers of this book for whom retirement is a major concern. Even though retirement may be decades away, federal policy in this sphere has some very immediate consequences. The funding available for the retirement sometime during the next century of today's college student will be determined, in part, by decisions made in the next few years. If plans are not made now to finance the retirements of those who are part of the post-World War II baby boom, millions of people who were middle class during their working years will live out their old age in poverty. In addition, the magnitude of the Social Security benefits paid to earlier generations of retirees depends upon the willingness of today's workers to tax themselves.

In this section we examine federal policy as it relates to two types of retirement programs. First, we analyze the current state of the Social Security system and review proposals to restore it to health. Second, we discuss federal policies designed to protect workers' contributions to retirement plans operated by their employers.

Social Security

The Social Security system, established in 1935, has become the largest and fastest growing federal program. Approximately 115 million workers pay into the system, and more than $150 billion is paid out to 36 million beneficiaries. Expenditures may almost double by the mid-1980s.

Social Security, or more formally, Old Age, Survivors, and Disability Insurance (OASDI), provides benefits to the retired and their dependents and, under some conditions, to survivors of deceased contributors. OASDI benefits are available to retirees until they die. For dependents of deceased contributors, eligibility depends on age; most children stop receiving benefits at eighteen.

Social Security is seemingly a well-established component of our domestic public policy. Its greatest supporters are the people who receive monthly Social Security checks. Payments are pegged to the level of earnings recipients enjoyed while working, with the maximum benefit being $789 a month in 1982.

Although few political leaders seriously suggest dismantling Social Security, the program has its critics. One charge is that the program is not actuarially sound. With our population aging and the number of people receiving benefits increasing, while the ratio of workers to beneficiaries is decreasing, money is being paid out at a faster rate than new revenue is being collected. After peaking at $48 billion in fiscal year 1975, the Social Security trust fund declined precipitously until the portion designated to pay retirement benefits was exhausted in 1982. More frightening yet was the projection that the fund might come up more than $150 billion short during the 1980s. Since it is inconceivable that Social Security administrators would simply close their offices and declare bankruptcy, substantial reforms were required.

In fashioning a response to the funding crisis, Congress and the president had to resolve conflicting demands. Retirees—who are the largest set of beneficiaries—are a potent political force. More than one-tenth of the population is now over age 65, and, thanks to early-retirement inducements, the number of retirees and their spouses is even greater. Retirees have a valuable ally in organized labor. The elderly and their labor allies not only oppose any talk of reducing or delaying benefits, they want to see benefits increased.

In the past, Congress has responded to the pleas of beneficiaries that they are unable to survive on what Social Security pays. There have been periodic increases in benefits, which, since 1973, have been adjusted annually to keep pace with the Department of Labor's consumer price index. By one measure it appears that Social Security benefits have outpaced inflation. In 1973 the average benefit equaled 39 percent of what the typical retiree had been earning when working; eight years later that figure stood at 55 percent.[21]

Opposing demands for a more liberally funded Social Security program are contributors to the system. Current contributors' opposition is, at least in part, traceable to their uncertainty over whether they will benefit from the program and, in part, to the growing unwillingness of Americans to pay more taxes.

OASDI is funded by payroll taxes levied on earnings. In 1984 both employees and employers will pay a tax of 7.0 percent on all earnings up to $38,100. Since the upper wage limit on which Social Security is collected now rises as incomes rise, data for the last years in figure 6–2 are estimates. Some have projected that by 1990,

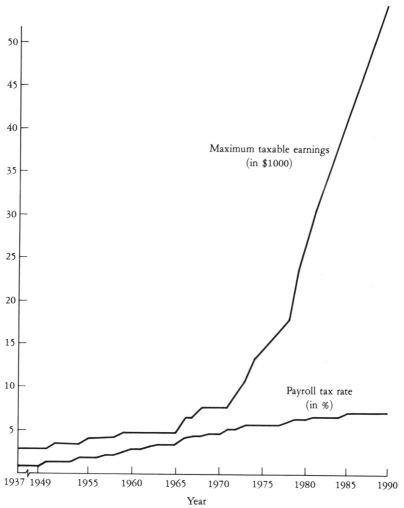

FIGURE 6–2 Earnings and payroll tax rate for Social Security, 1937–1990. (*Sources:* Congressional Quarterly Weekly Report, *March 17, 1979, 37, 447. Copyright 1979 by Congressional Quarterly, Inc.* Congressional Quarterly Weekly Report, *December 20, 1980, 38, 3627. Copyright 1980 by Congressional Quarterly, Inc. Reprinted by permission. As adjusted by legislation.*)

a tax rate of 7.65 percent may be levied on as much as $66,000 in earnings. Or, to put it in another perspective, "The maximum Social Security tax paid by an individual, $374.30 in 1970, was $1,403.77 [in 1980] and [was] $1,975.05 [in 1981]. It is likely to exceed $3,000 in 1985 and could top $10,000 in 1990."[22] The estimates in figure 6–2 are substantially lower.

Even though the size of the Social Security tax bite and the amount on which it is levied are projected to increase, analysts predict that an additional 0.7 percent tax rate above the rates approved in 1983 will be needed to pay benefits to today's young workers, if the system is not changed. In part this is because as our population ages there are fewer workers contributing to pay for each beneficiary. In 1982 there were about 3.3 workers per beneficiary, down from a ratio of 16.5 workers per beneficiary in 1950. By the year 2050 the ratio may be as low as 1.4 to 1.[23] If demographic trends, Social Security tax rates, and payments continue along the paths they now follow, OASDI could be $1.5 trillion short between now and the middle of the next century.[24]

These gloomy projections stand in sharp contrast with the expectations that accompanied the adoption of the 1977 tax program to fund Social Security. At the time, the largest peacetime tax increase in our history was supposed to ensure the system's fiscal integrity into the next century. However, high rates of unemployment reduced contributions and high inflation resulted in higher payouts.

Reforms in 1983.   During the Reagan administration, it became clear that Social Security faced both short- and long-term funding problems. Projections for the 1980s indicate that the retirement fund, which had to borrow from the Medicare and disability funds in 1982 to pay out benefits, will need more than $100 billion. For the twenty years beginning in 1990, the combination of a larger work force (the product of the post-World War II baby boom) and a smaller number of retirees (the product of low fertility rates during the depression era) is projected to keep the retirement fund solvent. Once the baby boom generation begins retiring, another wave of financial problems is anticipated.

In 1983, Congress, acting on recommendations made by the bipartisan National Commission on Social Security Reform, passed legislation to alleviate the immediate problems and to partially resolve the funding crisis expected during the early part of the next century. In order to replenish the Social Security treasury, several steps were taken to raise new revenues:

- The timetable for increasing payroll taxes set in 1977 was moved forward, raising the tax rate for employees and employers from 6.7 to 7.0 percent in 1984, and from 7.15 to 7.51 percent in 1988.
- Tax rates paid by the self-employed were raised to equal the combined levels paid by employees and employers.
- Federal employees hired after January 1, 1984, must join Social Security rather than the separate retirement program to which federal workers have traditionally belonged.

- Single Social Security beneficiaries with incomes above $25,000, and married recipients with incomes above $32,000, must pay taxes on half of what they receive from Social Security.
- State and local governmental units can no longer withdraw from the Social Security system.

Other reforms were designed to reduce payments:

- The timing of the cost-of-living adjustment was delayed from July to January.
- When reserves are low, the cost-of-living increment can be based on the rise in the wage index if it is lower than the consumer price index, as it often is during an inflationary period.
- The benefits paid to "double-dippers" (retired military personnel who also draw Social Security) were reduced.

The combined effects of the savings and the new sources of revenue are expected to pump an additional $165 billion into the retirement fund during the remainder of the 1980s.

In anticipation of the onslaught of retirees expected to begin early in the twenty-first century, the 1983 reforms tinkered with benefits and retirement age. The benefits paid workers who retire at age 62 will be reduced from 80 percent of the full benefits to 75 percent in 2009, and down to 70 percent in 2027. The age for receipt of full benefits will be raised from 65 to 66 in 2009, and to 67 in 2027.

The degree to which these reforms will offset projected deficits cannot be determined precisely. In estimating future revenues and expenses for Social Security, economists consider age distributions in the population (numbers of workers and retirees), fertility rates, rates of inflation, unemployment rates, and levels of economic growth. As these projections are extended a generation or more into the future, they take on the aura of guesswork.

When Congress and the president turn their attention to alleviating the long-term funding problem—which they may not do for a generation—they will probably consider increasing the rate of the Social Security tax and the amount of income on which it is levied, or tapping general revenues. Organized labor favors the latter, arguing that the Social Security payroll tax is regressive because it is collected on all of a low- or middle-income worker's wages but on only a fraction of the earnings of the wealthy.

Values in conflict.   In setting Social Security benefits, the interests of the 36 million recipients are at odds with those of the 115 million workers who pay into the system. Many elderly subscribe wholeheartedly to the notion that Social Security is a social insurance program that should provide for *all* their basic needs. But that objective, while certainly desirable for retirees, bears little similarity to the initial goals of the program. It was never intended that Social Security do more than augment other resources—savings, annuities, private pensions, or family support.

The insurance analogy is another misconception. Unlike an insurance policy, Social Security does not guarantee a precise return on the occurrence of a specific event. If a retiree dies but does not leave a widow or minor children, his or her heirs are not entitled to the amount the deceased paid into Social Security. On the other hand, the benefits a retiree can draw are not limited to the amount the individual paid into the system. The maximum a person could have paid into Social Security from its inception through 1980 was $12,791. Many retirees receive this amount back in benefits within three years. Ironically, only 15 percent of a 1981 national sample thought they would get back more than they had contributed.[25]

Obviously today's workers pay for yesterday's workers' retirement, while looking to the contributions of the next generation to secure their own retirement. And there is the heart of the problem. Many workers would rather keep as discretionary income the money taken from their paychecks to pay for someone else's retirement. This, of course, is partially due to the fact that most young people now doubt that the Social Security fund will have money in it by the time they retire. Among workers ages 18 to 29, 79 percent question whether there will be funds available.[26] Younger workers contend that their retirement would be more secure if they could invest the money they and their employers pay to Social Security. Although this may be accurate, one wonders how many people would prepare adequately for their retirement if not compelled to pay into Social Security. Those who failed to create a nest egg would ultimately have to be supported by taxpayers.

Hints of what may become an intergenerational battle are already visible in responses to a CBS News–*New York Times* Poll. For example, the idea that participation in the Social Security system be voluntary is approved by more than 60 percent of those under age 44 but by only a third of those over age 64. Cutting the benefits of those retiring before age 65 is most strongly supported by young adults and most opposed by those nearing retirement age.

Pensions

Pension plans cover virtually all federal employees, 85 percent of those employed by state and local governments, and half the workers in private industry.[27] Still, there are millions of workers whose employers have no pension program. Moreover, millions of contributors to pension plans have found, on retirement, that they have built up few benefits. Therefore, even those who do not plan to rely exclusively on Social Security may find their meager pensions put them below the poverty line. Even worse off are those whose contributions to a pension fund pay no return because of poor management of the fund or because the workers failed to meet the terms for receiving benefits.

For a century after American Express launched the first pension plan in 1875, pensions were a matter for workers to arrange with their employers. Not until 1974 did federal law establish standards for the operation of retirement programs. The Employee Retirement Income Security Act (ERISA) was supposed to curb a number of abuses that kept retirees from receiving benefits from programs to which they had contributed. The legislation did not mandate pension programs; but it did set federal standards for their operation.

Regulations.   One section of the 1974 act establishes terms under which an employee's rights to benefits become vested. The legislation allows employers three alternatives, but common practice entitles most workers to some benefits after working for an employer for a decade. Thus, even if a person changes jobs or is fired before retiring, he or she will receive some return from the pension program. This law ended the unscrupulous practice of firing longtime workers just before they reached retirement age, to avoid paying them pensions.

A second section of the legislation guards against mismanagement of pension funds. The nation's 500,000 pension funds have millions of contributors, and their resources total about $300 billion.[28] A few funds—notably the one to which many teamsters contribute—have been used by their trustees as sources of unsecured, low-interest loans for investment in risky enterprises. ERISA set standards for pension trust fund fiduciaries.

A third section of the act provides for bankrupt funds. In an attempt to ward off this possibility, the act sets minimum standards for funding. Where these precautions prove inadequate, people who have paid into the plan receive benefits from a federally run insurance program paid for by employers.

Although regulations have improved the situation, they have failed to come to grips with at least two major problems. Given our high job mobility, many workers are never with one employer long enough for their pension rights to vest. Fewer than two in five of the nation's full-time workers have vested rights in their pension plans.[29] To fill this gap, it has been proposed that workers take their pension contributions with them when they accept a new job (this is known as *portability*). That is, their former employers would have to transfer contributions to the pension fund at the new place of employment. Other possibilities for meeting the problem of job mobility include integrating pension plans with Social Security, in a government-run program, and shortening the vesting period.

A second problem is the adequacy of payments. Very few retirement programs, other than those for federal employees and Social Security, increase their benefits to keep up with inflation. It is unlikely that a cost-of-living adjustment will become law. However, without that provision, the purchasing power of pensions will drop by almost two-thirds over ten years of 10 percent inflation. Millions who thought they had provided for their old age will see the purchasing power of their fixed incomes shrink to inadequate levels.

Tax benefits.   In addition to regulating pension plans, federal law creates incentives for private employers to establish those plans and for individuals to save for retirement. Within limits, employers, the self-employed, and many employees can set aside funds for retirement and pay no federal income tax on that money until they draw it out after retirement. Although individuals must ultimately pay taxes on income sheltered in an annuity or an independent retirement account (IRA), they do not have to do so until they retire. At that time, when their income is substantially less, the tax bite is smaller.

It has been estimated that this aspect of the tax laws cost the federal government $12.9 billion in 1980.[30] That cost is going up. Beginning in 1982, IRAs were made available to a much larger share of the work force. Early projections were that between fiscal years 1982 and 1986, $49 billion would be placed in IRAs.[31] The effect of these revenue losses is that all taxpayers help, in a small way, to subsidize these retirement programs.

Retirement in the Twenty-First Century

Although fluctuations in the fertility rate may change projections somewhat, demographers can already predict with a degree of certainty what the population of the United States is going to look like well into the next century. Their vision is not reassuring. Low birthrates in recent years, combined with longer life expectancies for those in the post-World War II baby boom generation, mean that our nation's average age is rising. By 2030, more than 50 million Americans, or approximately one-sixth of the population, will be over sixty-five years old—a figure double that of today. Even increasing the retirement age, as was done in 1983, will leave vast numbers of people who have withdrawn from the labor force and who will need to be cared for.

Plans for meeting that need should be laid now. Instead, no serious steps toward correction are being taken. The primary obstacle is that the options—increasing Social Security funding, eliminating the unfunded liability of pension plans (i.e., many plans are not designed to take in sufficient funds to pay the participants), adding cost-of-living escalators to private plans, requiring portability, or establishing a comprehensive retirement program—each costs money. Taxpayers object to proposals that would require additional taxes, and employers claim they cannot afford to make plans portable or to substantially increase benefits.

As the costs of funding retirees increase, the conflict between retirees and the workers and taxpayers who pay their benefits increases. Delays in resolving the crisis simply make the trade-offs more explicit. Will we pay taxes for Social Security or for defense? Will state and local governments honor the commitments they have made to their workers and ante up the money needed to offset the deficit in their pension programs, an amount now in excess of $8 billion? Doing so will require substantial increases in taxes or decreases in services. What are the consequences of increased funding for private pensions so that they can pay higher benefits to offset the ravages of inflation? Will this bankrupt some firms, forcing the federal government to care for their pensioners, to say nothing of throwing their employees out of work? To what extent would passing the costs for larger pensions on to consumers fuel inflation that would wipe out any gains in retirement benefits? These questions have no easy answers. Despite the inevitability of the fact that they must be met, only a few Americans perceive the problem, and even fewer are looking for solutions.

CONCLUDING COMMENTS

The middle class is concerned about financial security, about protecting its standard of living. In essence, that group wants, if not a better lifestyle, at least a stable one; and it fears that, in the absence of federal assistance and protection, it will slip down the economic ladder. In recent years, the hold of some middle-class families on that ladder has grown precarious. The hopes of those new to the labor force and those long in it have been dashed. Young adults can no longer count on a dream home; the elderly can no longer expect a comfortable retirement on a fixed income.

We can expect young and old to clash over the issue of Social Security. Young workers doubt the system will be functioning when they retire, and, faced with escalating housing costs, higher fuel bills, and across-the-board inflation, want to minimize their contribution to the program. Retirees want larger benefits and oppose any postponement of their receipt.

Despite age-related disagreements on Social Security, age should not divide the middle class on health care cost containment and home financing. The costs of a serious, protracted illness can ruin the budget of anyone, of any age. High-priced or unavailable mortgage money also hurts people of all ages, making it difficult for both buyers and sellers to enter the market.

The climate of the Reagan administration is not encouraging for middle-class policy goals. With President Reagan and his congressional followers reducing the federal budget by tens of billions of dollars, it is unlikely that funds will be earmarked for national health insurance. Moreover, the president's penchant for reducing federal regulations leads us to doubt that attempts will be made to restore low interest rates or to cap hospital costs through fiat. Instead, at least in the short run, the middle class will be increasingly dependent on the outcome of competition to determine the prices it pays for health care and home loans. It may also be increasingly left to its own devices to prepare for an adequate retirement income through pensions and annuities.

NOTES

1. Margaret C. Thompson, ed., *Health Policy: The Legislative Agenda* (Washington, D.C.: Congressional Quarterly, 1980), pp. 19–23.
2. Louise B. Russell, "Medical Care," in *Setting National Priorities: Agenda for the 1980s*, ed. Joseph A. Peckman (Washington, D.C.: Brookings Institution, 1980), p. 178.
3. CBS News–*New York Times* Poll, May 2, 1981.

4. Thompson, *Health Policy,* p. 22.

5. Russell, "Medical Care," p. 185.

6. Linda E. Demkovich, "Reagan's Cure for Health Care Ills—Keep the Government's Hands Off," *National Journal* 12 (December 13, 1980): 2124.

7. Quoted in Thompson, *Health Policy,* p. 68.

8. Ibid., p. 67.

9. Linda E. Demkovich, "No Regulation Here," *National Journal* 13 (August 1, 1981): 1389.

10. Louise B. Russell, "Medical Care," in *Setting National Priorities: The 1984 Budget* (Washington, D.C.: Brookings Institution, 1983), pp. 125–126.

11. Elizabeth Wehr, "Competition in Health Care: Would It Bring Costs Down?" *Congressional Quarterly Weekly Report* 37 (August 4, 1979): 1590.

12. Robert J. Samuelson, "Shelter Squeeze," *National Journal* 13 (September 5, 1981): 1595.

13. Rochelle M. Stanfield, "High Interest Rates Are Sparking a Revolution in Home Financing," *National Journal* 13 (January 31, 1981): 172.

14. "Home Tax Breaks Up Prices, Study Says," *Atlanta Journal-Constitution,* October 10, 1981, p. 3A.

15. John C. Weicher, *Housing: Federal Policies and Programs* (Washington, D.C.: American Enterprise Institute for Public Policy Research, 1980), pp. 138–143.

16. The staff director of the Senate Banking, Housing, and Urban Affairs Committee quoted in Timothy B. Clark, "The American Housing Industry—From 'Sacred Cow' to 'Sacrificial Lamb,'" *National Journal* 13 (December 5, 1981): 2157.

17. George Steinlieb and James W. Hughes, "Housing: Past and Futures," in *Housing Finance in the Eighties: Issues and Options* (Washington, D.C.: Federal National Mortgage Association, 1981), p. 23. Also see Amitai Etzioni, "Housing: An Early Reagan Reindustrialization Test," *National Journal* 12 (December 20, 1980): 2196–2197.

18. Samuelson, "Shelter Squeeze," p. 1595.

19. Colleen Teasley, "Latest Figures Price 97% of Nation Out of Market to Buy a New Home," *Atlanta Journal,* October 6, 1981, p. 8D. Of course, these estimates do not take into account that one may already own a home. Large equity in an existing home, which translates into a large down payment, would allow a family to purchase a home for which their monthly income would not qualify them. Also, remember that these figures are based on the average national cost of a home; larger proportions of the public can afford less expensive dwellings.

20. Steinlieb and Hughes, "Housing," p. 35.

21. Timothy B. Clark, "Saving Social Security—Reagan and Congress Face Some Unpleasant Choices," *National Journal* 13 (June 13, 1981): 1054.

22. Ibid., p. 1052.

23. "Social Security Crisis: Demographics Tell the Tale," *National Journal* 13 (July 11, 1981): 1262.

24. Pamela Fessler, "Threat of Bankruptcy Spurs Action on Social Security Bill; Long-Term Changes Studied," *Congressional Quarterly Weekly Report* 39 (September 19, 1981): 1776.

25. Unless otherwise noted, figures in the next two paragraphs are from the CBS News–*New York Times* Poll, July 16, 1981.

26. CBS News–*New York Times* Poll, January 24, 1983.

27. Stanford G. Ross, "Income Security: A Framework for Reform," *National Journal* 12 (October 18, 1980): 1774–1775.

28. Martin Donsky, "Congress Opens New Debate on Private Pension System," *Congressional Quarterly Weekly Report* 37 (March 17, 1979): 450.

29. Pamela Fessler and Harrison Donnelly, "Congress Seeking to Assure Retirement Income Security," *Congressional Quarterly Weekly Report* 39 (November 28, 1981): 2334.

30. Donsky, "Congress Opens New Debate," p. 453.

31. Pamela Fessler, "Tax Incentives for Savings," *Congressional Quarterly Weekly Report* 39 (November 28, 1981): 2336.

SUGGESTED READINGS

Housing Finance in the Eighties: Issues and Options. Washington, D.C.: Federal National Mortgage Association, 1981.

Thompson, Margaret C., ed. *Health Policy: The Legislative Agenda.* Washington, D.C.: Congressional Quarterly, 1980.

Weicher, John C. *Housing: Federal Policies and Programs.* Washington, D.C.: American Enterprise Institute for Public Policy Research, 1980.

SEVEN

Education Politics

Educational policies, after years of being almost exclusively the responsibility of state and local governments, have increasingly come to be shaped by the actions of the national government. Although the role of the federal government as financier of elementary, secondary, and higher education has grown over the last two decades, the bulk of the revenue for schools still comes from state and local governments.

The debate over whether and to what extent the federal government should foot the bill for public education has often been overshadowed by another question: Under what conditions is it appropriate for federal decision makers to dictate policy to local school officials? Over the last few decades, federal authorities have sought to prescribe behavior in an increasing number of educational policy areas. And those prescriptions, instead of resolving the issues, have set off bitter, prolonged debate. Some opponents of federal intervention in schools have withdrawn from the struggle, transferring their children to private schools; others have kept their youngsters in public schools but have become increasingly critical of the quality of education there. They point accusatory fingers at Uncle Sam, blaming his interference for what they perceive to be a decline in the quality of education.

There are others in society who applaud federal intervention in educational policy. These groups, many of which were unable to secure the policies they wanted from state and local officials, turned to federal judges, the Congress, and Department of Education bureaucrats in their search for powerful allies.

Our purpose here is to describe the federal government's education policy, so we do not focus on state and local education issues—questions of parental control or the rights of teachers to organize and strike. Instead, we examine three major areas where the federal government is affecting public schools and colleges: (1) federal aid to education (whether and to what extent should the national government finance the facilities and programs of public elementary and secondary schools and universities?); (2) the inequities in present school-financing procedures (should the federal government produce more equitable funding among school districts?); and (3) the kinds of obligations imposed on local schools by federal policymakers. We end with a look at the impact of federal obligations on support for public education.

FEDERAL AID TO EDUCATION

Historically, the local school district has been the principal unit for administration of local school systems, and today there are still more than 15,000 school districts in the several states. (This figure represents a major decline from the more than 127,000 districts existing in 1932.) In the twentieth century, the states, on whom the local school districts have always depended for legal authority, have come to exert increasing control over the public schools on such matters as curricula, textbooks, teacher training, and attendance and periods of operation. State financial support for the schools has also grown, now accounting for around 40 percent of their revenues, and is often the lever by which state controls are made effective. Each state has a state department of education (or, perhaps, public instruction), headed by a chief state school officer, who supervises the state's public school system. Education, then, is the major area of governmental activity assigned primarily to the state and local governments in our federal system.

Although most children at the elementary and secondary levels attend public schools, private and parochial schools enroll several million pupils annually, most in schools operated by the Catholic church. The existence of parochial schools complicates the issue of federal aid to education because aid to parochial schools raises questions about the separation of church and state, a subject we return to in a later section.

The tradition of state and local control of education and the attitudes that support that tradition have been reinforced by the belief that control of education is reserved to the states (and their local subdivisions) by the Tenth Amendment. State control of education, consequently, has become an aspect of states' rights (and, of course, decentralization and local self-government). The proponents of state control and support of education—or, to put it negatively, the opponents of federal aid and control—often proclaim that the Founding Fathers "clearly" intended this to be the case. This is probably a better argument than a description of historical reality because, when the Constitution and the Tenth Amendment were adopted, there was no real state government responsibility for public education.[1] Most elementary and secondary education was privately provided, and what little public education there *was* was handled by towns and local communities. Still, the states' rights contention has been both politically appealing and useful for those who oppose federal aid.

Federal Aid before World War II

The tradition of state and local control of education notwithstanding, there is a long history of federal aid to education in the United States, dating back at least to 1785 and the Northwest Ordinance. That statute provided that one section of land in each township in the Northwest Territory be set aside for the support of education. Since that time, there have been a great many programs of aid for education started by the national government.[2]

The Morrill Acts of 1862 and 1890 provided first for land and later for cash grants to help the states maintain colleges offering instruction in the agricultural and mechanical arts. The Smith-Hughes Act of 1917 and later legislation have given financial support to high school vocational education. Since the late 1930s, food and money have been made available for school lunch programs. Under the Lanham Act of 1940, Congress has provided financial aid for the construction, maintenance, and operation of public schools in "federally impacted areas." This program, which has been especially popular in Congress (there is a bit of pork-barrel aura about it), helps schools in areas where enrollments have been increased by the presence of large numbers of federal personnel, or where school revenues are reduced by large amounts of tax-exempt federal property (e.g., at military installations). The National Defense Education Act of 1958, which was the product of public and congressional concern over Soviet space exploits, authorizes expenditures for the improvement of teaching in science, mathematics, and foreign languages at all educational levels, and makes funds available for loans to various categories of college students. Other federal postwar legislation has provided funds for veterans' education (including the famous "GI bill"); loans and grants for the construction of college dormitories, libraries, and academic buildings; and grants and contractual arrangements for college research activities (e.g., grants from the National Science Foundation). Over half the research conducted in American colleges and universities today is federally financed. And the Department of Education administers a wide range of research, advisory, and grant-in-aid programs for all levels of education.

The Controversy over Increased Federal Aid: 1945–1965

It is fair to say that until 1965 federal aid to primary and secondary education was essentially peripheral or indirect. It clearly did not satisfy the demands of the proponents of general federal aid for elementary and secondary education in the form of funds for school construction, or teachers' salaries, or both. Their general contention was that both existing school facilities and current levels of state and local support for education were inadequate, and that a major federal effort was needed to improve the quality of the schools, to broaden educational opportunities, and to provide classrooms and teachers for a growing school population. From 1945 to 1965, some sort of federal aid legislation was before Congress almost continuously.

In their efforts to secure federal aid, proponents used a variety of arguments over the years.[3] Following World War I, they argued federal aid was necessary to combat illiteracy and to help Americanize immigrants, many of whom could not speak English. There were also some who, interestingly enough, saw federal aid to education as a bulwark against communism, which they claimed would not be appealing to the educated. During the 1930s federal aid was advocated to solve the acute financial problems that the depression had created for the schools. After World War II, federal aid proponents stressed the need to alleviate the shortage of teachers and to close the "classroom gap," which stemmed in part from insufficient school construction during the war years and rising enrollments. With the Soviet space exploits in the late 1950s, the federal aid argument focused on the needs of national security and "keeping up with the Russians." In the mid-1960s, attention centered on improving educational facilities and opportunities as a means of combating poverty. More recently, there have been demands that federal funds help pay for expenses incurred by schools when complying with programs mandated under federal law. Although a belief in the need for federal aid to education has remained constant, the substance of the argument for that aid has changed with the existing conception of the needs and problems of the educational system.

Various opinion surveys during the 1950s and early 1960s revealed widespread popular support for federal aid to education.[4] But it also appeared that interest in federal aid was not intense. Consequently, very few members of Congress believed their chances for reelection would be hurt by the failure to enact a general federal aid law.

Over this period, coalitions of interests supporting and opposing federal aid to education developed. The proponents of federal aid included the National Education Association, the American Federation of Teachers, the Council of Chief State School Officers, the AFL-CIO, and various black, liberal, and women's service organizations. In opposition were the U.S. Chamber of Commerce, the National Association of Manufacturers, the American Farm Bureau Federation, "patriotic" organizations (among them the Daughters of the American Revolution), and other business associations. Resistance stemmed from opposition to increased federal spending and taxes, and from the belief that federal aid would inevitably lead to federal control of education, which was considered both intrinsically bad and a contradiction of states' rights. Fears of federal control were probably stronger when funds were earmarked for teachers' salaries; the "threat" was less immediate when funds were targeted for school construction. To mollify those fears, school aid bills usually contained provisions prohibiting "federal controls."

The coalition supporting federal aid was unsuccessful until 1965, in part because it was split by a number of controversial issues at times when success seemed imminent. Questions always arose over the way in which federal funds, once available, should be allocated among the states. Representatives from the poorer states favored formulas that would channel larger shares of the funds to them, to help equalize educational opportunities among the states. The wealthier states objected to paying federal taxes that would go for educational benefits in other states, and favored flat per pupil grants rather than equalization formulas.

This issue was not so troublesome as were two others—the questions of aid to segregated schools and to parochial schools. Here, differences of principle were involved, "moral issues" that made it much more difficult to secure compromise. Liberal and black groups asked for provisions in federal aid bills to prohibit the funding of segregated school systems, which in turn made these bills objectionable to southern Democrats. Conservative interests manipulated this issue to divide the supporters of federal aid. For example, in 1956 a combination of Republicans and northern Democrats in the House attached an antidiscrimination clause (the Powell Amendment) to a federal aid bill. Then, on final passage, most of the Republicans joined with southern Democrats to defeat the entire bill.

Protestant and other groups opposed aid to parochial schools as a violation of the constitutional principle of separation of church and state. At the same time, Catholic groups opposed federal aid to education that would not go to parochial as well as public schools. The Kennedy administration's 1961 school aid bill, which provided funds for school construction and teachers' salaries for public schools only, was killed in the House for just this reason. Two members of the House Rules Committee—both Catholics—who normally supported the administration joined with the conservatives on the committee to prevent floor consideration of the bill.[5]

Why was federal aid to education legislation finally enacted in 1965? There were a number of contributory factors. First, President Johnson was a much stronger supporter of that legislation than either of his two immediate predecessors, Eisenhower and Kennedy. Second, the large Democratic majorities in the 89th Congress, especially northern Democrats, provided votes that were not available earlier. Third, by emphasizing assistance to schools with children from low-income families and antipoverty action, the supporters of the act were able to avoid much of the controversy over the aid-to-parochial-schools issue that had been a stumbling block in the past. Aid was provided for children in parochial schools, which satisfied Catholic groups, while the fiction that the aid was going to the children, and not to the schools as such, made it less unacceptable to opponents of that aid. Fourth, by getting the Senate to pass the House bill without amendment, the Johnson administration and its congressional allies were able to avoid some of the roadblocks that had impeded federal aid in past years. Normally, on their way to becoming laws, major bills must receive favorable action at eight points: appropriate House committee, House Rules Committee, House floor action, appropriate Senate committee, Senate floor action, conference committee (where differences in House and Senate versions are resolved), and House and Senate floors (where compromises reached by the conference committee are approved). The strategy employed by the administration eliminated the last three steps, much to the displeasure of many congressional Republicans who opposed the legislation. Finally, the Civil Rights Act of 1964, which generally prohibited federal funds from being used for programs that discriminated against blacks, made the dispute over aid to segregated schools a nullity.

The Elementary and Secondary Education Act, 1965

In April 1965 the opposition to greater federal aid to education was finally overcome, and Congress passed the Elementary and Secondary Education Act (ESEA). Although the act was put forward as an antipoverty measure—and in fact most of the money went to schools with substantial numbers of children from low-income families—it provided funds to about 95 percent of the nation's school districts. Those funds were intended to give educational aid to students from low-income families whose achievement levels were substantially below those generally found in the district. ESEA funds were not to be used in place of, but in addition to, state or local aid so that special compensatory programs could be provided for low-income pupils. The authors of the legislation hoped these programs would raise the scholastic achievement of low-income students to a level comparable with that of their more affluent peers.

According to the provisions of the 1965 act, each state received ESEA funds equal to the sum of half its annual educational expenditure per child times the number of children from low-income families. The larger a state's education expenditure, the more federal money it received per child—a formula that worked to the advantage of the wealthier states. (Since 1965, Congress has changed that formula. The current weighting system, which uses the number of poor children and the relative level of state and local aid to education vis-a-vis the national mean, tends to benefit rural and southern states.) Under Title I, federal funds could be used for a variety of special services: remedial education, educational television, mobile education units, guidance and counseling, and speech therapy. These programs were made available to low-income children attending either public or parochial schools. Money was also made available to both public and parochial schools for purchase of nonsectarian textbooks and library materials. (Legal title to materials placed in parochial schools is retained by the state.)

The impact of ESEA.   With passage of ESEA came a fundamental change in American educational policy: the federal government made a direct commitment to improve elementary and secondary education in the United States. The change in dollar amounts spent by the federal government for education is impressive: $8.7 million in the 1957–1958 school year, $2.2 billion in 1965–1966, $4.3 billion in 1971–1972, and $9.1 billion in 1979–1980.

Perhaps the most important change in the federal role in education was in the administration of the Elementary and Secondary Education Act. Before the act was passed, the U.S. Office of Education (forerunner of the Department of Education) was the "kept" agent of a few education lobbies, and as such provided assistance and some information. The landmark ESEA was innovative, daring legislation, and the USOE was not prepared to administer it. Instead, the agency chose to deal directly with the local school districts, bypassing state boards of education (except for approving and monitoring local funds) and—more important—state and local governments.

The problem was that, under the provisions of Title I, monies were to be concentrated in the areas of greatest need. In New York City, for example, money should go to Harlem and not to middle-class Queens. The USOE was responsible for monitoring the spending of ESEA funds, for ensuring that the goals of the act were met. What happened? Audits of Title I funds showed that some local schools were misusing the money, purchasing football jerseys, swimming pools, bedroom suites, and carpeting. In 1968, HEW auditors estimated that $150 million had been misused. It was apparent that some local school districts were treating ESEA not as a categorical aid program (poverty package), but as a general aid program to be used as the locals determined. The Office of Education was not effective in getting these monies back, nor in administering and monitoring other aspects of ESEA.

Why was the USOE hesitant to administer ESEA programs aggressively and effectively? First, the Office of Education had a limited staff, and the staff that it did have was service oriented, not program oriented. Second, there was great pressure in the early days of ESEA to get the program off the ground and running. Therefore, USOE was not inclined to alienate its clientele by claiming misuse of funds. Third, the Johnson administration's eagerness to prove the program was a success obligated the USOE to generate figures showing that a large number of schools was involved. Fourth, a sizable number of USOE bureaucrats felt that Congress had really meant the bill to be a general aid bill. Finally, the USOE felt that if it pushed too hard on categorical aid, Congress would pass a general aid bill that would leave the agency with no control over education for the disadvantaged.

Eventually, bowing to pressure from civil rights groups and other organizations, the Office of Education did act to enforce Title I objectives.[6] In September 1976 the USOE issued new program guidelines intended to prevent school districts from using Title I funds for students who did not have educational disabilities. Hand in hand with these detailed regulations came an open commitment to their enforcement. In that same year, the USOE held up payment of more than $150 million in Title I funds to the state of California.[7] The agency demanded and received specific assurances that ESEA money would not be used for children who did not meet eligibility standards for participation in the program. This was the first time the USOE invoked its authority to withhold funds to secure compliance with program objectives.

Apparently, both the guidelines and the payment holdup have been effective. Title I money is being used increasingly to upgrade the educational opportunities of low-income children, and with real success. In a five-year study of more than three million students from forty states, the Stanford Research Institute determined that students in Title I reading programs experienced an average increase in reading skills of one month for each month in the program.[8] By being in the special reading program, students progressed at a rate comparable to that of the typical student in the nation. Because program participants come primarily from low-income families, and because children from families of this economic level generally progress at rates below the national mean, a program that lifts their achievement to the national average is a significant accomplishment. The importance of the Title I reading program is further supported by evidence that during the summer, when it does not operate, its enrollees make no progress, and may actually slip backward—in contrast with nondisadvantaged students, whose reading achievement continues to rise, although at a slower pace than during the school year.

Federal Aid and Higher Education

The federal government has been sharing its resources with higher education since the 1860s, when the Land Grant Colleges Act was passed. After World War II, the GI bill involved the national government in large-scale efforts to educate veterans. And in 1958, the post-Sputnik National Defense Education Act created a system of federal loans and grants (distributed through the schools) for college students.

As part of President Johnson's War on Poverty, some federal aid was earmarked for students from low-income families who wanted to attend college. The Guaranteed Student Loan Program encouraged banks to lend money to students from families whose income was less than $15,000 by promising to repay defaulted loans. The national government pays the interest on the loan while students are in school. When interest rates go above the amount specified by the legislation (7 percent from 1968 until 1981), the government pays the difference. Pell Grants, which were approved in 1972, were also designed initially to help students from poor families by paying up to half their college costs.

During the 1970s, the requirements for these programs were relaxed to allow students from more affluent families to participate. After the Middle Income Assistance Act was passed in 1978, 40 percent of the Pell Grants for freshmen went to students who were not from low-income families.[9] This legislation eliminated income restrictions from the Guaranteed Student Loan program and allowed undergraduates to borrow up to $12,500, graduate students up to $25,000. These more liberal requirements resulted in rapid growth as middle-income families rushed to obtain grants and low-interest loans. By 1981, a third of all university students in the country were tapping into $7.7 billion in loans.

The runaway growth in aid programs, coupled with stories of former students, now successful, who had failed to pay back federally guaranteed loans, made these programs prime candidates for President Reagan's budget cuts. The administration instituted a "needs test" (applied to applicants for guaranteed loans whose annual family income exceeds $30,000) and an origination fee of 5 percent. The result? An estimated drop in the value of guaranteed loans by more than one-quarter between fiscal years 1981 and 1982.[10] At the same time, funding cutbacks slightly reduced the average size of the grants going to 2.5 million Pell Grant recipients.

This first round of cuts denied eligibility to some middle- and upper-class students, most of whom could still afford college without federal aid. Although low-income students still had access to the programs, there is speculation that uncertainties over the availability and amount of aid may have dissuaded some of them from going on to school. For others, changes in the federal aid picture, along with the deteriorating economy, were instrumental in their choosing to attend less expensive schools in 1982. This economic-based change in college choice, although it swelled enrollments at junior colleges, hurt private colleges with their higher tuitions. In fact, with the size of the college-age cohort shrinking, declining enrollments due to a lack of federal aid may contribute to the death of some of those schools. Where expensive colleges survive, the lack of federal funds may well cost the student bodies the economic diversity they acquired over the last two decades.

In a second round of proposed budget cuts, President Reagan recommended the elimination of middle-class participants from the grant program; the removal of the interest subsidy from loans to graduate students; and the institution of a needs test for all of the almost 4 million applicants. The president also firmly opposed efforts to increase available funds so that assistance could keep pace with costs. But, as of late 1982, Congress, responding to the needs of middle-class constituents, had not approved the administration's proposals.

EQUALIZING EDUCATIONAL RESOURCES

Although the role of the federal government has increased substantially since passage of the Elementary and Secondary Education Act in 1965, the financing of public education remains primarily a responsibility of local government. State government is the second-largest contributor in most states; the federal government, a distant third.

Table 7-1 shows the wide differences in financing practices among the states. Hawaii has the most centralized system of financing; in 1979–1980, the state paid 85 percent of the costs of schooling, while local government contributed nothing. At the other extreme, in New Hampshire the local government provided 85 percent of the revenue, while the state contributed less than 10 percent. Generally, the state pays a larger share of the costs of education in the South; the role of the local community is largest in the Northeast and the Midwest. Thus, in the South the median contribution of state governments was 54 percent of the educational budget in 1979–1980, while the median contribution of local governments was 32 percent. In the rest of the country, the median state contribution was 43 percent; and the median local share, 51 percent.

Each state has a "foundation" program, which was originally designed to guarantee a minimally acceptable level of education throughout the state.[11] States usually specify that local districts must demonstrate a minimal effort, defined in terms of rate of taxation. Districts that cannot fund an acceptable program from locally raised revenue receive supplementary money from the state. In contrast to the foundation program, which seeks to redistribute wealth in order to equalize educational resources, other state aid is distributed, on the basis of average daily attendance, to all districts regardless of need. A third type of state aid, variable nonequalizing grants, actually favors wealthier districts by offering matching state funds to school districts. Affluent districts are more likely than poor ones to qualify for that money.

TABLE 7-1   Patterns of public school financing, 1979–1980

	High	*Low*	*Mean*
Percent from state government	85	8	47
Percent from local government	85	0	43
Percent from federal government	25	6	10
Annual per student expenditures	$5,146	$1,741	$2,494

SOURCE: Data from W. Vance Grant and Leo J. Eiden, *Digest of Education Statistics, 1982* (Washington, D.C.: U.S. Government Printing Office, 1982), pp. 74, 81.

The modest role of the federal government has generally been to help equalize school resources by making larger contributions to poorer districts. Not surprisingly, therefore, the South usually gets a larger share of its educational budget from the federal government than do other regions. The very poor state of Mississippi relies most heavily on federal aid, drawing almost a fourth of its school revenue from that source.

Despite the efforts of state and federal aid programs to offset the disparity in the capacity of local communities to finance schools, great differences persist. In 1979–1980, Alabama spent the least per student—$1,741 per student in average daily attendance—about a third of the $5,146 Alaska lavished on each student. Poorer states, and the South as a region, paid less for educating each child than did wealthier states. The average figure nationwide for public education was $2,494 per student, a figure reached by no southern state.

The disparities left by redistributive programs are also striking within states. School districts having some industry or commercial establishments or very expensive residential developments usually spend more per student than do districts having low-income housing or poor farmland.

The extent to which expenditure levels relate to the educational achievement of a district's children remains a question on which researchers disagree. It is beyond dispute, however, that districts with higher per pupil expenditures pay higher salaries, have more modern and better-equipped facilities, and offer more varied educational programs. Thus, children in poor districts clearly have fewer opportunities than do children in wealthier ones. Moreover, although nonschool factors (socioeconomic level, home environment) account for much of the difference in achievement, it is generally believed that graduates of poorly financed schools do less well in later life—have lower incomes and less prestigious jobs—than do graduates of schools with greater resources. Furthermore, children in poorer schools often have more learning disabilities. Consequently, schools in these districts need more money per student for their graduates to be on an equal plane with those of wealthier districts. For example, in poor systems there may be a greater need for remedial programs, counseling, and other services—yet the local community may lack the revenue needed to finance these services.

The belief that school resources do affect life chances has led parents of children attending underfinanced schools to file suits asking for more equitable allocation of state funds. Their claims that disparities constitute a denial of equal protection received strong support in August 1971, when the California Supreme Court dropped a bombshell on traditional methods of school financing. In *Serrano* v. *Priest*, the court ruled that the gap between the per pupil expenditures in Baldwin Park ($577) and Beverly Hills ($1,232) was so great that it violated both the federal and state constitutions.[12] The court ruled that whatever the cause of the disparity—in this case, vast differences in local revenue sources—redistribution of local educational resources was essential to reduce variations in school districts.

Although several lower federal courts followed the lead of the California court, momentum slowed in 1973. In that year the U.S. Supreme Court ruled on the obligation of the state to equalize school district revenues. In *San Antonio Independent School District* v. *Rodriguez,* the Court held that the disparity between two districts (one spent $356 per student, the other $594) did not violate the equal protection clause of the Fourteenth Amendment.[13] The Court concluded that the disparity in San Antonio was not so arbitrary that it was irrational for a state to tolerate differences of this size in financing a public school system. The majority reached this conclusion despite evidence that the poor district was taxing its residents at a much higher rate than was the affluent district. A dissenting opinion pointed out the impossible situation faced by the poor district:

> Both the Edgewood and Alamo Heights districts are located in Bexar County, Texas. Student enrollment in Alamo Heights is 5,432, in Edgewood 22,862. The per-pupil market value of the taxable property in Alamo Heights is $49,078, in Edgewood $5,960. . . . In order to equal the highest yield in any other Bexar County district, Alamo Heights would be required to tax at the rate of 68¢ per $100 of assessed evaluation. Edgewood would be required to tax at the prohibitive rate of $5.76 per $100. But state law places a $1.50 per $100 ceiling on the maintenance tax rate, a limit that would surely be reached long before Edgewood attained an equal yield.[14]

The 1973 decision foreclosed attempts to use the Constitution to equalize school revenues. Only where a state's constitution or statute is violated by heavy reliance on local property taxes can parents in poor districts use the courts to obtain more money for their schools. Thus far courts in more than half the states have ordered that school financing be based less on local property taxes, and that greater steps toward equalization be taken.

In California, which has been at the forefront of the equalization movement, efforts are under way to comply with a state court order that per pupil expenditures vary by less than $100 in all the state's school districts. One observer concludes of those efforts to date that "the result was more money for all schools—and a larger share of it from the state—but little change in the ability of the wealthier districts to outspend the poorer ones in terms of dollars per pupil." Similar results have occurred in other states, with court orders producing somewhat greater state aid but doing little to close the gap between poor and affluent districts.

In addition to holding the potential for eliminating intrastate differences, increased state financing of public education has other benefits. State funds would come from income or sales taxes, not property taxes. Because other sources of revenue generally increase faster than do property taxes, this means that during periods of inflation revenues would not fall behind expenses as much as they do when tax receipts are tied to property values. Another advantage of relying more on state taxes is that it eliminates the need for the local electorate's approval of additional revenue raising. In recent years, some local districts have failed repeatedly to get bond levies passed and have had to cease operations until new money became available. National figures indicate that the proportion of school bond proposals approved by the public dropped from more than 70 percent in the early 1960s to about 50 percent in the 1970s.[15]

An alternative, attractive to school officials, especially in states experiencing budget problems of their own, is to seek additional funding for education from the federal government. Repeatedly in our history we have seen demands shift to the national level when state and local resources have proved unable to meet needs. Of course, the reception those demands receive changes over time. Today, during the Reagan administration, the likelihood of getting additional federal aid for education does not appear to be good, as we discuss shortly.

THE TRADE-OFF: FEDERAL AID VERSUS FEDERAL OBLIGATIONS

The financial difficulties being experienced by many school systems are due, in part, to policies adopted by federal officials. These policies have generally been of two types: the first requires public schools to undertake activities fiercely opposed by some segments of the public; the second obligates local schools to institute new programs for which federal funds pay no more than a fraction of the cost. The latter, of course, may merge with the former when federal law mandates a costly new program without providing sufficient financial aid. Having to abide by controversial federal directives disadvantages public schools to the extent that it undermines support among important elements of the population, a point we return to later.

Here we look at three areas where federal interpretation of what constitutes acceptable behavior in local school districts is causing controversy: prayer in the schools, bilingual education, and education for the handicapped. (School desegregation and busing to promote racial balance are two other requirements that have reduced public support for the schools. We examine these subjects in chapter 8.)

Prayer in Schools

The separation of church and state has largely been defined in the context of schools. In recent years, much of the debate over what this constitutional principle means has centered on whether religious observances can be incorporated into the school day. In a series of cases beginning in the late 1940s, the Supreme Court has held that anything approximating worship is inappropriate if it involves use of tax-supported facilities and occurs during school hours.

The Court has held that voluntary religious instruction provided by privately hired teachers cannot be conducted in school facilities during school hours.[16] It has also found unconstitutional a requirement that a nondenominational prayer be read aloud daily,[17] and a state requirement that at least ten verses from the Bible be read at the beginning of every school day.[18] In contrast, the Court has approved released-time programs for off-campus religious instruction. It rationalized this provision of voluntary religious training during school hours, but not in tax-supported facilities, on the basis that "we are a religious people whose institutions presuppose a Supreme Being."[19]

The important element here seems to be where the religious activity takes place—on or off school property. Whether participation is compulsory or optional has no bearing on the Court's decisions. Because the Constitution's terminology has been interpreted as a prohibition on promoting religion, not simply on advancing a specific doctrine or faith, it is not acceptable to grant equal time to various beliefs or to use bland language when praying in the hope that no one will be offended.

Many Americans object to the prohibitions on school prayer. Numerous school districts, especially in the South, have continued classroom devotionals despite their unconstitutionality.[20] Since the 1960s, several proposals to amend the Constitution—to "put God back in the classroom" as proponents like to say—have been introduced in Congress. These efforts were particularly intense during the early 1980s, when conservatives' hopes were raised by the election of President Reagan and a Republican majority in the Senate. In 1982, Sen. Jesse Helms (R.–N.C.), a legislative leader of the New Right, proposed a constitutional amendment that would have prohibited courts from hearing cases challenging school prayer. Although the proposal was not approved, the desire to combine religious training with education continues to swell enrollments at a growing number of fundamentalist schools.

Bilingual Education

One of the long-accepted functions of public education has been the socialization of future generations of good citizens. In the American melting pot, that socialization translated into teaching English to immigrant children. In some schools, the imperative to learn English was reinforced by punishing children who used their native language in the classroom or on the playground. In others, although non-English speaking students were not punished, no special efforts were made to help them overcome the language barrier.

All of this changed with the black civil rights movement and its emphasis on ethnic pride and broadened interpretation of educational equity. In the late 1960s, Congress appropriated a small sum for educating children whose home language was not English, and the Office for Civil Rights informed schools of their obligations to teach these children. Not much happened until 1974, when the Supreme Court ordered schools in San Francisco to offer instruction for some Chinese-speaking students in their native language.[21] In carrying out this mandate, schools have had first to determine the native language of their students and then to establish programs for teaching those not fluent in English.

Educators and the parents of the students involved have disagreed on how this should be done. Should schools continue to help stir the melting pot? Or should

TABLE 7-2 Languages of selected bilingual education programs

Aleut	French Canadian	Lakota	Punjabi
Apache	Greek	Miccosukee-Seminole	Russian
Arabic	Gwichin	Mohawk	Samoan
Cambodian	Haitian French	Navajo	Seminole-Creek
Central Yupik	Havasupai	Northern Cheyenne	Spanish
Cherokee	Hebrew	Paiute	Tagalog
Chinese	Ilocano	Papago	Tewa
Choctaw	Italian	Passamaquoddy	Ute
Cree	Japanese	Pennsylvania Dutch	Vietnamese
Crow	Keresan	Polish	Walapai
Eelaponke	Korean	Portuguese	Yiddish

SOURCE: Merrill Sheils et al., "Teaching in English—Plus," *Newsweek*, February 7, 1977, p. 65.

they promote cultural identity? A number of local Hispanic leaders insist on bilingual-bicultural programs, designed to *maintain* students' fluency in Spanish and awareness of Hispanic culture, while at the same time developing their competence in English. Some would like to have social sciences and other classes taught in the students' native tongue. Oriental parents, on the other hand, are not as interested in having the schools help maintain skills in their native tongue; they want their children to master English as quickly as possible.

To understand what is at issue here, consider that the porous Mexican-American border has allowed millions of Spanish-speaking people to enter the United States. Add to those numbers the more than 100,000 Cubans who came to Florida via the Freedom Flotilla in 1980. Then think about the thousands of refugees from Indochina and Haiti.

Refugees and legal and illegal aliens combine to produce several hundred thousand children whose primary language is not English. To teach them, some urban school systems have had to offer instruction in a dozen or more language groups. Overall, seventy language groups are being served in one or more schools, although almost four of every five bilingual class participants are Spanish speaking.[22] To meet this responsibility, schools have had to hire additional staff and purchase materials in the students' native languages. These costs are no more than partially offset by federal bilingual education funds, which have become scarcer in recent years. It is not surprising, then, that schools generally choose to provide rapid transition to English, so that these students can be moved as quickly as possible into regular classes. And this rapid transition has been supported by the traditional view that people who want to be in this country should speak English. In a recent survey, only 43 percent of a national sample approved of conducting classes in the language of non-English speaking pupils.[23] So we could expect that an even smaller share of the public willingly countenances bilingual maintenance programs.

Not surprisingly, there has been strong opposition in Congress and in many school districts to proposals that would allow the Department of Education's Office for Civil Rights to cut off federal funds to school systems that provide only a transition to English, rather than a maintenance program. Early in 1981, the Reagan administration responded to this pressure and withdrew regulations for bilingual education that had been proposed in the waning days of the Carter presidency. Schools with at least twenty-five students in the same language group in two consecutive grades would have had to teach math, science, and social studies in the children's native language. In withdrawing the proposal, Secretary of Education Terrel Bell called the requirements "harsh, inflexible, burdensome, unworkable, and incredibly costly," estimating the expense at $1 billion over five years.[24]

Educating the Handicapped

The handicapped have long been provided special services at public expense, but in the past these services related more to health than to education. As it did with bilingual education, federal involvement in educating the handicapped began in 1967, with amendments to the Elementary and Secondary Education Act. That involvement was enlarged on by the Rehabilitation Act of 1973 and the Education for All Handicapped Children Act of 1974.

These statutes obligated school systems to provide appropriate education to the mentally and physically handicapped. They mandate the development of individualized programs for each handicapped child, annual progress reviews, and, to the extent possible, a mainstreaming program, in which handicapped children are taught in classes along with nonhandicapped students.

In effect the legislation has created a whole new clientele, with very specific needs, for the public schools, and it has placed an enormous financial burden on local school districts. Specially trained teachers have had to be hired; existing facilities have had to be modified, or new ones have had to be built, to accommodate handicapped students; and separate means of transportation have had to be found and paid for.

What we are seeing, then, is the adoption of expensive new programs by federal mandate, with little federal financial aid. At the very least, it costs twice as much to educate the handicapped as it does other children.[25] And in those instances where a school district is unable to meet the needs of a handicapped child in the school setting, and must pay for external training, costs run from four to eight times greater. Those costs aren't limited to a twelve-year span: the statutes require that the handicapped be educated from age 3 to 21. Although the federal government by the end of fiscal year 1982 began to shoulder 40 percent of the costs of educating special-needs students, appropriations come nowhere close to equaling the additional costs incurred by school districts. In fiscal year 1981, with the federal contribution still at 12 percent of the extra costs, many school districts were complaining bitterly.[26]

Of course, costs are only one part of the school districts' concerns. Many schools question their obligations once individualized education plans have been prepared.[27]

One of their fears, which the Bureau of Education for the Handicapped (the federal agency responsible for enforcement in this area) has sought to allay, is that the parents of handicapped students could sue the schools if the goals of the plans are not achieved.

Opposition to the mainstreaming of handicapped children comes from both teachers and the parents of the nonhandicapped. Teachers who are not trained in educating the handicapped often feel ill prepared to cope with special-needs children in addition to their other students; while some parents worry that their children's educations will suffer if teachers concentrate on handicapped students. This opposition does not extend to the concept of educating the handicapped. Almost 90 percent of a national sample taken in 1981 believe special-education efforts are worth their cost.[28]

Yet to be settled is whether public schools must provide a year-round curriculum for some or all special-needs students, rather than the nine- to ten-month programs provided for the nonhandicapped. Suits demanding twelve-month services have been filed by parents of handicapped children in several states. The basis for these actions is a claim that without training during the summer, the gains registered during the school year are lost. Typically, the response of school systems has been that the school year for the handicapped and the nonhandicapped should be equal. Of course, if additional state or federal funds were made available for educating the handicapped, local school districts would probably be less reluctant to create full-year programs.

PUBLIC EDUCATION: THE PROBLEMS TODAY

Public dissatisfaction has risen with the perception that the schools' new duties (bilingual education and educating the handicapped) have affected the quality of public education. Parents of exceptionally bright children complain that their kids are not being challenged; parents of children of average ability worry that their kids benefit from neither the enrichment programs designed for the academically gifted nor the special education programs aimed at disabled pupils. Educators point to the long, slow drop in average Scholastic Aptitude Test (SAT) scores, which declined every year from 1963 through 1981 before rising slightly in 1982. Middle-class parents, particularly in urban areas, worry about the safety of their children, and place much of the blame on federal desegregation efforts that have disrupted neighborhood school patterns. At bottom, then, much of what bothers parents about public education is change that the federal government has forced on the schools.

These dissatisfactions have had several consequences. First, they have contributed to the continued middle-class exodus from the schools of the central city and older suburbs. Second, in some communities there has been an upswing in private school enrollments as parents give up on public education. Third, perceptions that public schools are failing have combined with the inflation-induced financial pinch to reduce support for school taxes. And fourth, there is a sizable share of the population that is critical of the job being done by local schools. For example, a 1981 Gallup Poll found that although 60 percent of the respondents believed their children were getting better educations than they themselves had received, the sample split evenly between those who rated their local schools as excellent or good, and those who considered them fair or poor.[29]

The culmination of this dissatisfaction has been a back-to-basics movement. In a growing number of school districts, parents are demanding a renewed emphasis on the basics—reading, writing, and arithmetic (in today's jargon, language arts and analytical skills). Along with this emphasis comes support for tightened discipline and formal schedules—a move away from the open classrooms, new math, myriad electives, and self-motivated study of the 1960s.

The Issues in 1984

Those calling for educational reform had new emphasis given their efforts when a federal study panel announced in 1983 that the overall quality of American public education was so poor that it endangered the economic and military welfare of the country. In the months that followed, President Reagan and leading Democratic challengers jockeyed for positions on the issue of educational improvement.

President Reagan, true to his precepts of limited federal involvement, placed the problem squarely in the laps of state and local governments. Not so the Democratic presidential contenders, who almost unanimously agreed that the problem requires a national solution. In fact, former vice president Walter Mondale, a longtime favorite of education groups, proposed new federal efforts with a price tag of $11 billion.

One proposal endorsed by President Reagan that enjoys widespread public support would provide merit pay increases for outstanding teachers, a dramatic change from the traditional seniority- and education-based step increases. The National Education Association and the American Federation of Teachers, the two leading teachers' organizations, oppose merit pay, insisting it would open the door to favoritism. The organizations are less opposed to the development of corps of master teachers—teachers who are exceptionally well trained, experienced, and talented—who would receive pay supplements.

Testing the competence of teachers is another popular proposal for upgrading the quality of education. Some states require that new teachers undergo a probationary period during which they are observed and tested. Others would like to extend that evaluation to experienced teachers, a proposal that is not popular with teachers' groups.

Most observers agree that we cannot improve the quality of teachers without spending more money. The issue, they claim, is not competence testing; it is to attract and retain talented, dedicated educators. In the past, schools could draw on a large pool of qualified teachers, most of them women. Today, with the many alternatives open to women, it's not surprising that they are turning to those that are more lucrative than teaching.

Although the vast majority of Americans want better education, there is a less than universal commitment to paying taxes to support it. Editorial writer Jim Fain, commenting on a *Newsweek* Poll, writes that "45 percent of the respondents favor more funds for public education, even if it takes more taxes. Another 35 percent want more money for schools but without tax increases, proving that Santa Claus remains popular."[30]

The Alternatives to Public Education

The widespread discontent with public education has been translated into demands that the federal government help finance alternatives to public schools. One proposal, strongly supported by Catholic educators, is to amend the Internal Revenue Code, to make some or all of the costs of private school tuition tax deductible. Proponents of a tax break for parents of students in private schools were encouraged in 1983 when the U.S. Supreme Court upheld a Minnesota law that allowed deductions from state taxes for private school expenses. The push for a federal tax deduction has not succeeded although it is supported by President Reagan.

Representatives of the thousands of private schools, many of them linked with Fundamentalist churches, that have been established in recent years are split on the issue. Although they recognize that the tax concession is a means of attracting new students, some fear it is just the start of federal intervention in their schools. And in fact, tax-exempt status for private schools is conditioned on adherence to nondiscriminatory admission policies.

An alternative to a tax deduction is a voucher system. Parents could redeem vouchers at the school of their choice, public or private. All vouchers would have the same value, covering the full cost of a public school education but only a portion of the tuition at a private school. Advocates of this plan argue that if public schools have to compete for vouchers, they will have an incentive to improve.

Supporters of public education feel both proposals are dangerous. They worry that reducing the financial incentive to keep kids in the public schools would shrink middle-class enrollments to the point that public education would become a "charity ward [that] must take the students no one can handle."[31]

A Gallup Poll of parents sending their children to public schools indicates that these fears are not entirely baseless. If a tax credit of $500 or less were available, 15 percent of those surveyed in 1981 said it was very likely they would send their children to private schools. Another 12 percent said it was fairly likely their children would leave the public schools.[32]

Many public school backers believe that the educational experiences in schools where children come from varied economic, ethnic, and religious backgrounds are a more realistic preparation for life than the homogeneous experiences in private schools. Joining forces with those who support a strong system of public education are those who oppose federal aid to parochial schools because they see it as a violation of the First Amendment's separation of church and state doctrine.

Reagan's Proposals

Fiscal changes that might harm public education were put on the back burner during the 97th Congress. At the very least, this delayed President Reagan's proposal to allow families with annual incomes below $60,000 to claim a tax credit of $300 per child enrolled in a parochial school. Liberals claimed the president's plan primarily helped the affluent; some conservatives claimed the tax credit would produce rising budget deficits if increasing numbers of parents claimed the deduction.[33] In fact, a Senate committee projected that the revenue loss resulting from a $500 tax credit would zoom up from $40 million in fiscal year 1982 to $2.25 billion in fiscal year 1986, in the face of a mass exodus from the public schools. Timing was also working against the president's plan. It seemed anomalous to approve tax credits for private school tuition at a time when the president was proposing to cut federal aid to elementary and secondary schools by 25 percent.

Those proposed budget cuts came in conjunction with the resurrection of a Nixon proposal of a block grant approach to federal aid to education. As put forward by President Reagan, education revenue sharing would replace more than forty categoric grant-in-aid programs with two types of funds: one for the state department of education, the other for local school systems. Unlike the current grants, which earmark funds for specific needs (e.g., educating the handicapped), block grants would come with few strings attached, leaving the decision about how to use the money up to state or local school officials. Block grants would be a major step toward the general aid that many educators had been seeking at the time that the Elementary and Secondary Education Act was adopted in 1965.

Groups whose needs have been served by specific categoric grants, particularly parents and teachers of the handicapped, are loath to give up the direct claims they have on the federal treasury. They fear they will fare less well if they must compete for funds before each of the nation's thousands of school boards. Minority groups that have typically found federal officials to be more responsive than state or local officials are also leery of turning over chunks of money to school boards without federal guidelines. They remember some of the inappropriate uses of Title I money and fear that the needs of poor children would be even further shortchanged if there were no federal regulations on fund usage. And these groups are worried that unlike ESEA, the Reagan proposal does not prevent states or local governments from using federal funds in place of state and local revenues. This would permit still further reductions in total education funding, and the termination of special compensatory programs where school districts substitute federal funds for local revenues in order to reduce property taxes. House Democrats, led by Education and Labor Committee Chairman Carl Perkins (D.-Ky.), who has played a central role in creating several categoric programs, are strongly opposed to block grants.

Supporters of education block grants contend that local decisions on how best to use federal dollars will promote more efficient use of those funds than will Washington-directed policy. And they argue that the move away from categoric programs will reduce the influence—some would say interference—of federal rules and regulations. Secretary of Education Terrel Bell articulated this position when he told the American Association of School Administrators that he supported a first-class educational system, but one with less detail in the federal rules and with a few "less insulting demands in the regulations that emerge from our federal desks in Washington and end up on your desk in Pocatello or Portland or Pensacola."[34]

By the end of his first congress, President Reagan had succeeded in getting about half of what he had hoped to achieve through block grants. A number of the smaller categoric programs were replaced by a block grant. The funding was about a quarter less than had been given these programs before consolidation. For programs that remained outside the block grants, the president sought fewer funds. If approved by Congress, poorer school districts, which had been most dependent on federal funds, would be hardest hit.

CONCLUDING COMMENTS

There are a number of thorny problems confronting America's public schools. The breadth of responsibilities assigned to the schools is staggering, and continues to grow. A 1981 article in *Newsweek* characterized public expectations vis-a-vis the schools as follows: "They are expected to feed, inoculate, integrate, baby-sit, and counsel the young. They are expected to teach driver ed, sex ed, phys ed and special ed, and still have time for regular ed besides."[35] All of these are of value to society, but can we expect our schools to teach them all well?

Adding to the burdens of public education is the realization—often arrived at only when incorporated into federal law—that a share of the student-age population has traditionally been ignored. The Education for All Handicapped Children Act brings an entire new population into the schoolhouse. Bilingual programs, by making classroom activities comprehensible to the non-English speaking, give them a reason to go to school.[36] Various regulations have circumscribed the authority of schools to expel rulebreakers, establishing due process protections and requiring that even those excluded from regular classrooms be taught in alternative schools or through some other arrangement.

Providing services to students who used to be ignored because they were hard to educate is more expensive than educating the average student. Further contributing to rising costs are the demands of well-organized teachers' unions that are willing to strike for higher salaries and better working conditions. And, as with everything else, the cost of education in public schools and colleges has been sucked up into the inflation cyclone.

While paying more taxes for education, many citizens are dissatisfied with what they see happening in the schools. Often that dissatisfaction stems from a policy established by federal mandate. Whatever the source of that unhappiness—the quality of education or policy decisions—ultimately it leads to the defeat of school bonds and weakened public education, which triggers yet another round in this cycle of dissatisfaction. In the past, when local school performance sank to unacceptable levels, the federal government often came to the rescue. Not so today. It is unlikely that public education can hope for large amounts of additional federal aid during the Reagan presidency; concessions, if they come, will be in the way of loosening federal program standards and funding requirements.

Although it is conceivable that the 25 percent cut in federal aid to public schools could be offset by the savings produced by fewer regulations, it is clear that no such trade-off exists at the college level. If, as the budget cutters argue, federal aid is being denied only to those who can afford to pay for college without it, the consequence may be no more than a short-term dislocation. But if the reduction in federal aid to college students goes deeper, excluding people from college, we are denying them all the opportunities a college education brings.

NOTES

1. Homer Bobbidge and Robert Rosensweig, *The Federal Interest in Higher Education* (New York: McGraw-Hill, 1962), chap. 1.
2. See Charles A. Quattlebaum, "Federal Policies and Practices in Higher Education," in *The Federal Government and Higher Education*, ed. Douglas Knight (Englewood Cliffs, N.J.: Prentice-Hall, 1960).
3. Frank Munger and Richard Fenno, *National Politics and Federal Aid to Education* (Syracuse, N.Y.: Syracuse University Press, 1962), p. 176.
4. V. O. Key, Jr., *Public Opinion and American Democracy* (New York: Knopf, 1961), p. 88.
5. For an excellent discussion of the struggle during the Kennedy years, see H. Douglas Price, "Schools, Scholarships, and Congressmen," in *The Center of Power*, ed. Alan Westin (New York: Harcourt Brace Jovanovich, 1969), pp. 53–105.
6. *Title I of ESEA: Is It Helping Poor Children?* 2nd ed. rev. (Washington, D.C.: Washington Research Project and NAACP Legal Defense and Education Fund, 1969).
7. "USOE Holds Up California Title I Funds," *Federal Education Project Newsletter*, September 1976, pp. 1–2.
8. Thomas C. Thomas and Sol H. Pelavin, "Patterns in ESEA Title I Reading Achievement," mimeographed (Menlo Park, Calif.: Stanford Research Institute, 1976). Also see June A. O'Neill and Margaret C. Simms, "Education," in *The Reagan Experiment*, eds. John L. Palmer and Isabel V. Sawhill (Washington, D.C.: Urban Institute, 1982), p. 334.
9. Dennis A. Williams et al., "Why Public Schools Fail," *Newsweek*, April 20, 1981, p. 63.
10. O'Neill and Simms, "Education," p. 354.
11. This section is drawn from Arthur E. Wise, *Rich Schools, Poor Schools: The Promise of Equal Educational Opportunity* (Chicago: University of Chicago Press, 1972), pp. 130–133.
12. *Serrano v. Priest*, 487 P.2d 1241 (1971).
13. *San Antonio Independent School District v. Rodriguez*, 411 U.S. 1 (1973).
14. Ibid., pp. 65, 67.
15. W. Vance Grant and Leo J. Eiden, *Digest of Education Statistics, 1980* (Washington, D.C.: U.S. Government Printing Office, 1980), p. 72.
16. *McCollum v. Board of Education*, 303 U.S. 203 (1948).
17. *Engle v. Vitale*, 370 U.S. 421 (1962).
18. *Abington School District v. Schempp*, 374 U.S. 203 (1963).
19. *Zorach v. Clawson*, 343 U.S. 306 (1952).

20. Kenneth M. Dolbeare and Phillip E. Hammond, *The School Prayer Decisions: From Court Policy to Local Practice* (Chicago: University of Chicago Press, 1971), chap. 3.

21. *Lau* v. *Nichols*, 414 U.S. 563 (1974).

22. Abigail M. Thernstrom, "E Pluribus Plura—Congress and Bilingual Education," *Public Interest* 60 (Summer 1980): 15, 21.

23. *Newsweek*, April 20, 1981, p. 64.

24. Press release, Department of Education, February 2, 1981.

25. This draws on Erwin L. Levine and Elizabeth M. Wexler, *PL 94-142: An Act of Congress* (New York: Macmillan, 1981), p. 189. Also see *Congressional Record*, 96th Congress, 1st Session (1979), p. E 2804.

26. Levine and Wexler, *PL 94-142*, p. 189.

27. In response to a Gallup Poll asking about classes for gifted children and slow learners, 89 percent of the respondents supported both the classes and their cost. Another 7 percent approved the classes, but did not feel they were worth the money. The remainder of the sample was evenly divided between those who disapproved and those who had no opinion. See *Newsweek*, April 20, 1981, p. 64.

28. Ibid.

29. Albert Shanker, president of the American Federation of Teachers, quoted in *National Journal* 13 (June 13, 1981): 1066.

30. *Atlanta Journal,* June 29, 1983, p. 20-A.

31. *Newsweek*, April 20, 1981, p. 68.

32. Rochelle L. Stanfield, "The Public School Lobby Fends Off Tuition Tax Credits—At Least for Now," *National Journal* 13 (June 13, 1981): 1063–1066.

33. O'Neill and Simms, "Education," p. 343.

34. Susan Milstein, "Schools Preoccupied with Underachievers, Education Chief Says," *Atlanta Journal,* February 17, 1981, p. 2-A.

35. *Newsweek*, April 20, 1981, p. 63.

36. In addition to educating legal aliens in their native language, a federal district court judge has held that schools in Texas must provide a free education to illegal aliens. The state of Texas, which appealed this decision, estimated that the additional cost could run as high as $200 million. Warren Brown, "Texas Will Appeal U.S. Court Ruling on Alien Schooling," *Washington Post,* July 23, 1980, p. A-5.

SUGGESTED READINGS

Eidenberg, Eugene, and Morey, Roy D. *An Act of Congress.* New York: Norton, 1969.

Levine, Erwin L., and Wexler, Elizabeth M. *PL 94-142: An Act of Congress.* New York: Macmillan, 1981.

Munger, Frank, and Fenno, Richard. *National Politics and Federal Aid to Education.* Syracuse, N.Y.: Syracuse University Press, 1962.

Thomas, Norman. *Education in National Politics.* New York: McKay, 1975.

Wise, Arthur E. *Rich Schools, Poor Schools: The Promise of Equal Educational Opportunity.* Chicago: University of Chicago Press, 1972.

EIGHT

Civil Rights

A major element that separates democracies from totalitarian regimes is the concern for civil rights. In our nation's two-hundred-year history, an extensive list of rights has developed. Many of those rights are new, recognized by the courts or written into law by Congress within the last generation or two. Typically, these new rights expand on incipient guarantees included in the Constitution and the Bill of Rights.

As with most other significant policy changes, the broadening of our civil rights has not been without controversy. Each time the umbrella of guaranteed rights has expanded to cover new groups in society, there have been those in opposition. Consequently, the bold declaration of a newly protected right has often been only grudgingly implemented. As you go through this chapter, then, remember that the rights described here are ideals: they define protections American citizens *should* have. But for many individuals, those protections demand constant vigilance, a willingness to do battle in court, and more. People have risked their lives and fortunes first to define and then to enforce these basic rights. It is their sacrifices that prove how important these rights are.

The main item of contention in civil rights policy has been whether to extend rights and protections enjoyed by some groups in our society to groups that have been excluded. Although we examine many aspects of the civil rights struggle in this chapter, there is a pattern that recurs again and again: those who have been denied certain opportunities have petitioned the courts and Congress to recognize their right to equal treatment. Most of these claims have rested on the equal protection clause of the Fourteenth Amendment. The issue brought to bear by that clause is whether there is an acceptable basis for not treating different groups alike. The grounds for the distinction must be reasonable; where they are not, the distinction is unconstitutional. Of course, the definition of *reasonable* can be, and has, changed over time. For example, the separation of blacks and whites in schools and public facilities, once commonplace, is now indefensible. In other areas, the definition is still being refined. The rights of women is a case in point. Although many jobs once denied women are now available to them, in 1980 Congress rejected President Carter's proposal to make women as well as men subject to military draft registration. That decision was approved by the Supreme Court in 1981. The story of the expansion of civil rights, then, is one in which the discretion of states and private enterprise to treat some groups differently from others has been reduced.

Some of the issues we discuss in this chapter—voting, education, employment, housing, and public accommodations—are heavily, although not exclusively, oriented toward blacks. But we also examine the rights of other minorities, of women, and of the handicapped.[1]

VOTING

The right to vote is particularly important in a democracy because a democracy derives its authority to govern from the public. If some component of the population is not allowed to participate in the selection of its leaders, we must question the legitimacy of that government. Aside from the issue of legitimacy, there is also the practical consideration that disfranchised groups have no influence on public policymaking. Those who cannot vote can neither reward elected officials who look out for their interest nor turn out of office those who prove unresponsive.

During attempts to get Congress to protect blacks' right to vote, civil rights leaders and public officials prophesied that black suffrage would help eliminate racism from other aspects of American life. In the words of Martin Luther King, Jr.:

> Voting is the foundation stone for political action. With it the Negro can eventually vote out of office public officials who bar the doorway to decent housing, public safety, jobs, and decent integrated education. It is now obvious that the basic elements so vital to Negro advancement can only be achieved by seeking redress from government at local, state and Federal levels. To do this the vote is essential.[2]

Black Disfranchisement

Black Americans have had to fight for their enfranchisement twice. The voting rights they won after the Civil War were lost again at the turn of the century. In fact, the various civil rights acts passed between 1957 and 1982 were designed, to a large extent, to undo the mischief of that disfranchisement.

Black political activity declined in the 1890s as southern states, led by Mississippi, instituted obstacles to black voter registration. Prospective voters were required to demonstrate their literacy and/or an ability to interpret sections of the state constitution to the satisfaction of local white registrars. To protect illiterate whites, some states adopted a grandfather clause that exempted from literacy tests anyone whose ancestors had been registered before 1861. The requirements that applicants demonstrate a comprehension of the state constitution or prove their good character were often manipulated by county registrars so that most blacks were prevented from registering. Literate blacks were turned away for small mistakes on their applications, while registrars filled out the applications for illiterate whites. Other potential registrants were dissuaded by threats or violence.

Even blacks who withstood discriminatory procedures and harassment, and managed to get their names on the voting lists, often found they had won a hollow victory. In the South (i.e., the eleven states of the Confederacy), election laws stated that only whites could vote in Democratic primaries. Because Democratic nominees rarely faced Republican opponents, blacks were excluded from a critical decision point. Yes, they were allowed to participate in the general election, but in the absence of partisan competition, that election was a meaningless referendum.

Yet another limit on black suffrage was the poll tax. In fact, this tax, often due months before the election, eliminated the poor of both races from the electorate.

The combination of techniques designed to remove blacks as a political influence was very effective. In Louisiana, for example, the number of black voters registered dropped from 130,334 in 1896 to 1,342 in 1904.[3] And, as black officeholders at the state and local level were replaced by whites, more than half a century of virtually unchallenged white political hegemony began.

It is estimated that in 1940 only 5 percent of the South's voting-age blacks were registered. That registration was particularly low in areas where blacks made up a large share of the population, and in rural areas.[4] Whites had greater incentive to disfranchise the blacks in communities where, if they were registered, blacks could control local government. Black participation was somewhat higher in urban areas, where there was a more tolerant attitude.

The Legislative Turnaround

Steps to extend suffrage to southern blacks began in 1944, when primaries in which blacks could not vote were judged to be unconstitutional.[5] Although black voter registration increased once it became possible to participate in Democratic primaries (in most of the region Republican candidates were rare), a number of obstacles remained. In 1957 the chief impetus for change shifted from the courts to Congress, which, during the next eight years, enacted several laws designed to open the way to the ballot box. The 1965 Voting Rights Act did away with literacy and good-character tests in seven states (Alabama, Georgia, Louisiana, Mississippi, South Carolina, Virginia, and part of North Carolina), where discrimination in voter registration had been particularly widespread; the tests were banned nationwide a decade later. The Twenty-fourth Amendment (1964) and litigation brought an end to the poll tax. The 1965 law authorized the Justice Department to challenge local practices that discriminated against blacks who sought to register or vote. And finally, to reduce the impact of fear, federal registrars were sent into selected southern counties to sign up qualified applicants; and federal poll watchers were present on election day to see that blacks were not kept from voting.[6]

The most controversial part of the Voting Rights Act is the requirement that areas in which minority group participation is disproportionately low refer all changes in election procedures to the attorney general or to the Federal District Court of the District of Columbia for approval. An objection by the attorney general or the court blocks the proposed change. This preclearance requirement applies to redistricting, annexation, changes in election laws, and relocation of polling places. Although the attorney general has objected to less than 5 percent of the proposed changes referred to him (none has been referred to the court), the affected states have been trying, unsuccessfully, to have the requirement applied nationwide or eliminated. Civil rights groups believe that without mandatory federal review, recalcitrant whites would once again disfranchise blacks—especially poor blacks in rural areas.

The preclearance requirement was used in 1982 to invalidate portions of a number of redistricting plans brought about by population shifts recorded in the 1980 census. The Justice Department objected to congressional, state legislative, and local districting plans where it felt a different configuration would enhance the likelihood of a black or Hispanic being elected.

The implementation process. The many rallies staged by the Southern Christian Leadership Conference and the Student Non-Violent Coordinating Committee, the hundreds of programs run by the Voter Education Project, and the concentrated efforts of hundreds of young adults who participated in the Mississippi Freedom Summer encouraged blacks to get out and register. The proportion of southern voting-age blacks registered to vote rose from 25 percent in 1958 to more

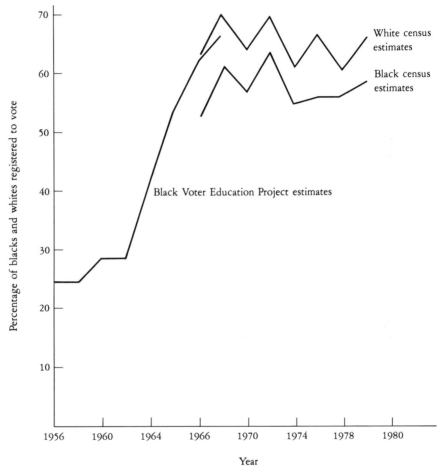

FIGURE 8-1 Southern registration rates, 1956–1980. Figures are estimates of the proportion of black and white Southerners of voting age who were registered to vote. Since 1966, figures have been available from the Census Bureau; from 1956 through 1966, the Voter Education Project estimated figures for blacks. The VEP estimates are based on the eleven-state old Confederacy, whereas Census figures use fifteen states and the District of Columbia. (*Sources: Harrell R. Rodgers, Jr., and Charles S. Bullock III*, Law and Social Change. *New York: McGraw-Hill, 1972, p. 25. Appropriate issues of U.S. Bureau of the Census,* Voting and Registration in the Election of ———. *Washington, D.C.: U.S. Government Printing Office.*)

than 40 percent in the mid-1960s, climbing above 60 percent in the early 1970s. In 1980, approximately 59 percent of the voting-age blacks in the South were registered, compared with 66 percent of the whites (figure 8–1). Clearly, race has become a less important factor in southern voter registration.

Increased black political involvement has changed southern politics. Although not wholly eliminated, racist campaign rhetoric has become less common;[7] black communities have obtained a larger share of public works projects,[8] new and better facilities and services, and more government jobs; white legislators have become more responsive to black interests;[9] and blacks have been chosen for various elected and appointive public offices.[10] In 1982 there were 3,140 black elected officials in the South, including 2 members of Congress and 148 state legislators. That blacks are holding political office not only has great symbolic importance, but also ensures that black policy preferences are brought to the attention of decision makers. True, those preferences may ultimately be rejected, but at least they are getting a hearing.

It is because they recognize the changes that have been produced by black political activity that Jesse Jackson and other black leaders have been so interested in registering additional black voters. The mayoral campaigns of Harold Washington in Chicago and Wilson Goode in Philadelphia confirmed for the North what the campaign of former Atlanta mayor Maynard Jackson had shown the South: A strong black candidate can stimulate additional black registration and voting. In a number of states and many communities, blacks already hold the balance of power. If Jesse Jackson mounts a serious campaign for the presidency, we can expect more blacks to enter the political system, enlarging the number of political units in which blacks can either bargain successfully for a larger share of the pie or cut the pie themselves. A successful voter registration drive would probably have its greatest effect in southern majority-black cities and counties that currently have no black elected officials.

Language Minorities

In 1975 the Voting Rights Act was expanded to protect linguistic minorities. The act applies to areas in which more than 5 percent of the population belongs to a single language group, where election materials were exclusively in English in 1972, and where less than half of the voting-age population actually votes. These areas are subject to preclearance requirements, and may have federal poll watchers sent in to monitor elections. If a large proportion of the population is below the national English literacy level, election materials must be available in the language of the minority group. Most areas affected have high concentrations of Hispanics and American Indians (see table 8–1).

EDUCATION

America has been called the land of opportunity, but most people would agree that that opportunity is a by-product of education. Parents who want their children to

TABLE 8-1 States covered by the 1975 Voting Rights Act

Covered by racial provisions	*Covered by language provisions*
Alabama[a]	Alaska[a]
Alaska[b]	Arizona[a]
Arizona[b]	California[a, b]
California[b]	Colorado[a, b]
Connecticut[a, b]	Connecticut[a, b]
Georgia[a]	Florida[a, b]
Hawaii[b]	Hawaii[a, b]
Idaho[a, b]	Idaho[a, b]
Louisiana[a]	Kansas[b]
Maine[b]	Louisiana[b]
Massachusetts[a, b]	Minnesota[b]
Mississippi[a]	Mississippi[b]
New Hampshire[a, b]	Nevada[b]
New York[a, b]	New Mexico
North Carolina[a, b]	New York[b]
South Carolina[a]	North Carolina[b]
Virginia[a]	Oklahoma[b]
Wyoming[b]	Oregon[b]
	South Dakota[a, b]
	Texas[a]
	Utah[b]
	Virginia[b]
	Washington[b]
	Wyoming[a, b]

[a]Election law changes must be precleared by the Justice Department before taking effect.

[b]Some but not all parts of the state are covered.

have a better life see quality education as the key to that life. As society becomes increasingly complex, it is imperative that young children receive a sound basic education on which to build more specialized training. During the last thirty years, two groups have challenged the fairness of existing educational policy. These are blacks and women.

Racial Desegregation

Just before the turn of the century, the Supreme Court decided a public accommodations case that legitimized state and local legislation requiring segregated schools. In *Plessy* v. *Ferguson*, by a vote of 8 to 1, the Court ruled that the equal protection clause of the Fourteenth Amendment did *not* require that blacks have access to the same public facilities as whites.[11] Instead, the majority interpreted the clause to mean that racially segregated facilities were constitutional so long as those for blacks were equal to those for whites. This decision opened the way for what is known as de jure segregation—segregation that is the product of public officials' actions.

The segregated schools that developed in southern and border states were anything but equal. White schools were better maintained and most had indoor plumbing; white students had newer texts and most rode buses to school; and white teachers and administrators were paid more than blacks with comparable training.

Judicial and legislative action.   Beginning in the late 1930s, the courts began to chip away at the separate-but-equal structure built on the foundation of *Plessy*. The first successful challenges involved higher education in states that made no pretense of providing separate, much less equal, facilities for blacks. These seventeen states, all of which prohibited integrated education, offered no graduate or professional training at public black colleges; instead, they paid to send black residents who wanted that training to out-of-state institutions.[12]

In 1938 the Supreme Court ruled that Missouri's offer to pay out-of-state tuition for a black who wanted to attend law school did not conform with requirements of the equal protection clause.[13] Twelve years later, a black plaintiff was ordered admitted to the University of Texas Law School, despite the availability of a recently established, state-supported black law school.[14] In the Texas case, the Court noted that the black law school was inferior to the University of Texas facility in several quantitative dimensions—size of the library, range of courses, and number of faculty members. The Court went beyond these readily measurable items, however, and cited criteria on which conditions at the black school could not be equalized—"the reputation of the faculty, experience of the administration, position and influence of the alumni, standing in the community, traditions and prestige."

Not until the mid-1950s did black plaintiffs succeed in getting court orders directed at elementary and secondary school segregation. The unanimous *Brown* v. *Board of Education* decision specifically overturned *Plessy:* "We conclude that in the field of public education the doctrine of 'separate but equal' has no place. Separate educational facilities are inherently unequal."[15]

Communities in some border states quickly implemented *Brown* and desegregated their schools. The response in the Deep South, however, took the form of massive resistance. Not one school board voluntarily came into compliance, and the state legislatures went on a rampage, passing laws to make desegregation more difficult. Some states threatened to close all public schools should even one be ordered to desegregate; others tried to interpose their authority between the federal government and local school systems. Ultimately, these efforts failed, but they did slow the integration process.

From 1954 to 1964, schools in the South desegregated one at a time, when ordered to do so by federal courts. Because the resources of private litigants, primarily the NAACP Legal Defense Fund, were limited and southern school systems numerous and adamant, very few black children were enrolled in white schools. A full

TABLE 8-2   Percentage of black students in public schools with whites in the South, by state

	1954–1955	*1959–1960*	*1964–1965*	*1965–1966*	*1966–1967*
Alabama	0.0	0.0	0.0[a]	0.4	4.4
Arkansas	0.0[a]	0.1	0.8	6.0	15.1
Florida	0.0	0.3	2.7	9.8	22.3
Georgia	0.0	0.0	0.4	2.8	8.8
Louisiana	0.0	0.0	1.1	0.9	3.4
Mississippi	0.0	0.0	0.0[a]	0.6	2.5
North Carolina	0.0	0.0[a]	1.4	5.2	15.4
South Carolina	0.0	0.0	0.1	1.7	5.6
Tennessee	0.0	0.1	5.4	16.3	28.6
Texas	0.0[a]	1.2	7.8	17.4	44.9
Virginia	0.0	0.1	5.2	11.0	25.3
South	0.0	0.2	2.3	6.1	16.9

SOURCE: Various issues of *Statistical Summary* (Nashville: Southern Education Reporting Service, annual).

[a]Some desegregation had occurred, but it involved less than 0.05 percent of the state's black student population.

decade after the Supreme Court struck down separate-but-equal schools, 97 percent of the South's black students still attended all-black schools (see table 8–2).

This halting pace accelerated once Congress approved the Civil Rights Act of 1964. That legislation authorized the attorney general to sue officials of segregated schools on behalf of black students (Title IV) and prohibited payment of federal aid to segregated facilities (Title VI). This dual attack on separate and unequal schooling was significantly advanced when the Supreme Court ordered a school board to "fashion steps which promise realistically to convert promptly to a system without a 'white' school and a 'Negro' school, but just schools."[16] Armed with this directive, and with court decisions that grade-a-year plans and freedom of choice plans were dilatory, Justice Department lawyers and HEW negotiators won court orders or agreements for school districts to desegregate by the fall of 1970.[17]

When the Nixon administration, which came into office with the electoral votes of five southern states, sought additional delays for some Mississippi schools, the Supreme Court quickly rejected the proposal.[18] The defendants, and the South in general, were warned that further delays would not be tolerated and that full desegregation must be achieved immediately.

When schools opened in the fall of 1970, after sixteen years of delay and obstinacy, almost every school system in the South was desegregated. In fact, statistics gathered that fall showed the South had the nation's least segregated schools. Only two years earlier, more than two-thirds of the region's black pupils attended all-black schools. By 1970, that figure had dropped to 14 percent. Between 1968 and

1972, as shown in table 8-3, the proportion of southern blacks in majority-white schools more than doubled, to 44.7 percent—over 8 percentage points higher than in the schools nationwide.

These dramatic changes did not come easily. Over two hundred school districts had federal education funds cut off before agreeing to desegregate, and many others came into compliance only after federal judges threatened to enjoin payment of state aid. And hundreds of other districts delayed desegregation while they battled the issue in court, in some cases all the way to the Supreme Court.

Desegregation in the North.   As the schools of the South began educating black and white children in the same classrooms, attention gradually shifted to the widespread racial separation in nonsouthern schools. Challenging segregation in the North and West—table 8-3 shows segregation has been greater there than in the South for more than a decade—proved difficult. In the South, six other states, and the District of Columbia, it was easy to demonstrate that segregation was de jure, because it was required by state or local statute. In the absence of laws of this type, plaintiffs had to prove that racial separation had been caused or promoted by official action.[19] Racial separation that cannot be linked to actions by public officials is called *de facto* segregation and does not violate the Fourteenth Amendment.

In states where segregation was not required by law in 1954, proof that segregation is de jure (and therefore illegal) is sometimes based on evidence that school

TABLE 8-3   Proportion of black students in schools with varying racial compositions, 1968-1980

	1968	1972	1976	1980
0-49.9% minority				
National	23.4	36.4	37.6	37.1
South	19.1	44.7	45.1	42.9
Border	28.4	32.8	39.9	40.8
Northeast	33.2	30.1	27.5	20.1
Midwest	22.7	24.7	29.7	30.5
West	27.8	31.9	32.6	33.2
90-100% minority				
National	64.3	38.7	35.9	33.2
South	77.8	24.7	22.4	23.0
Border	60.2	54.7	42.5	37.0
Northeast	42.7	46.9	51.4	48.7
Midwest	58.0	57.4	51.1	43.6
West	50.8	42.7	36.3	33.7

SOURCE: Gary Orfield, *Desegregation of Black and Hispanic Students from 1968 to 1980* (Washington, D.C.: Joint Center for Political Studies, 1982), p. 11.

boards locate new facilities, draw attendance zones, or design feeder patterns for elementary to junior high to high schools with the intent of separating the races. The evidentiary base needed to win this type of case demands painstaking research through decades of board minutes and careful reconstruction of attendance maps.

Despite the heavy burden of proof, there have been successful challenges to segregation in the North and West. Boston, Denver, Detroit, Indianapolis, and Milwaukee are among the major nonsouthern cities that have been ordered to desegregate. Still, figures in table 8–3 show that schools outside the South continue to have higher levels of racial isolation.

To some extent, the racial isolation in the North stems from the fact that blacks tend to live and go to school in the central city, where the logistics of desegregation are complex. To bring black students from the heart of these cities to the periphery means studying traffic patterns and travel times. In fact, some cities that once relied on neighborhood schools have had to develop entire transportation systems to implement desegregation plans. In rural southern districts, on the other hand, where most students had been bused for years, desegregation was a simple matter of rerouting.

Contributing to the persistent racial isolation in the North have been the positions taken by recent presidents and by Congress. Beginning with the Nixon administration, the Justice Department has been less aggressive in prosecuting school systems, and has often sided with school districts against black plaintiffs suing for desegregation. This shift is, in large part, the product of policy directives from the White House.[20] More recently, President Reagan's assistant attorney general for civil rights has opposed the use of busing to reduce racial isolation—again a shift that reflects the administration's conservative stance.

For its part, Congress in 1977 passed a bill that eliminated forced busing as an administrative corrective for racial isolation. Four years later, the Senate passed legislation that would have barred the Justice Department from seeking court-ordered busing, and would have prohibited federal judges from imposing that remedy. This action occurred after all but a few southern schools had desegregated, but could have had a retroactive effect on earlier court orders since it permitted reconsideration of earlier court orders. The House refused to approve the proposal.

Although recent presidents and a majority in Congress have opposed busing, they continue to pledge support for desegregation. They suggest voluntary remedies, like magnet schools and majority-to-minority transfers. Magnet schools offer special programs (say in the arts or computer training) that are not available elsewhere in the school system. The schools attract a heterogeneous student body from throughout the system. Majority-to-minority arrangements allow students to transfer from schools in which their race is the majority to schools in which they would be in the minority.

During much of the last decade, while the executive and legislative branches have moved away from the issue, the courts have continued to press for additional desegregation. But even the judicial branch has circumscribed what it is willing to do. By making a remedy contingent on proof that segregation was an objective of public officials, federal judges have largely precluded the possibility of demanding desegregation plans that would bring together the children of more than one district.[21] This creates a vicious circle: whites move to the suburbs to avoid schools with heavy minority enrollments, which results in higher percentages of blacks in the city schools, which causes more whites to flee. Although white flight is just a part of the post–World War II exodus to the larger lots and newer facilities of suburbia, some observers believe that the outmigration is helped along by court-ordered desegregation. The upshot in some cities has been futile efforts to apportion a shrinking number of white children across an increasingly black school system. For example, between 1970 and 1978, white enrollment in Boston's city schools declined from 62,014 (64 percent of the total) to 32,477 (40 percent). Even in Chicago, which did not have a desegregation plan approved until 1983, the proportion of white students had gone from 35 percent to 17 percent between 1970 and 1982.

What can cities do to curb white flight? In Atlanta and some other communities, blacks are questioning the utility of seeking racial balance among the schools of a system with few whites. Instead, they are demanding a share of top administrative positions and better funding for ghetto schools. Another factor that could reduce the white exodus from city schools is a Supreme Court ruling that once a school district desegregates, it does not have to continue to adjust its attendance zones to maintain racial balance among its schools.[22] The likely consequence of this decision is that urban systems will have racially balanced schools for a few years before shifting housing patterns once again make some schools all black. In the absence of periodic adjustment of attendance zones, whites in predominantly white neighborhoods may be more apt to stay in central-city schools.

Reagan administration policy.   Led by the Justice Department, which used to side consistently with black parents demanding desegregation, the Reagan administration has allied itself with critics of programs intended to desegregate schools. This opposition has taken two forms. The assistant attorney general for civil rights indicated in 1982 that the Justice Department might join school systems in attacking court-ordered busing plans. He explained that "if you have a [court] decree that is tearing apart the community, that is eroding the tax base, impeding public school education and causing resegregation rather than desegregation, we are not going to sit by and blink at that result simply because somebody, at some point, said busing is supposed to be a good thing."[23] Civil rights groups question the degree to which busing is responsible for the consequences attributed to it by administration officials, and fear that a willingness to side with school districts will cause a stampede to undo busing plans that are working.

The Justice Department was also instrumental in trying to reverse federal policy that disallowed tax exemptions for contributions made to private schools that discriminated against blacks. In 1982, department lawyers argued that the Internal

Revenue Service's denial of tax-exempt status to segregated private schools was without congressional authority. Bob Jones University and a Christian school justified their racial policies on Biblical interpretations, which they claimed were protected by the First Amendment. The Supreme Court did not agree: the justices rejected the pleas of the Fundamentalist schools and their Justice Department allies.

Postdesegregation problems.   There is relatively little pressure now on school systems to make further changes to achieve greater racial balance, even though some racial isolation persists. The desegregation that has occurred in many cases has been followed by subtle efforts to reduce cross-racial student contact. Some systems instituted special education programs for slow learners at the same time as they implemented their final desegregation plan; then used biased procedures to fill these programs with blacks. In other schools, tracking or grouping policies separated the races: college preparatory classes were disproportionately white; lower-track and special education classes, disproportionately black. (Perhaps the saddest outcome of tracking is that teachers assume students in "slow" classes *cannot* learn, and therefore expect little of them.)

We still find discrimination in punishment policies as well. In some schools, blacks are more harshly punished than whites for comparable offenses. In others, suspensions are dealt out to blacks in disproportionate numbers.[24] A study by the Children's Defense Fund concluded that suspensions are one technique through which blacks are induced to drop out of school.[25]

A final component of postdesegregation discrimination involves the treatment accorded black educators. When forced to eliminate all-black schools, many districts demoted black principals or failed to renew their contracts, and let go hundreds of black teachers. Through these discriminatory personnel practices, black children lost valuable role models and a sympathetic ear. White children also missed out on a valuable lesson—seeing black administrators and teachers making decisions and interacting in a biracial environment.[26]

Despite federal efforts to check discriminatory treatment in desegregated schools, the practices persist. Indeed, because they are more subtle than was de jure segregation in the South, it is sometimes impossible to determine conclusively whether the observed practices are motivated by an intent to discriminate. White teachers and administrators assert that blacks are suspended more than whites because they constitute a larger share of the discipline problems. Activist groups and Department of Education personnel disagree; they attribute the higher rates at which blacks are punished to cultural differences and white insensitivity. There is also conflict over the causes of black underrepresentation on faculties. Many school officials profess an eagerness to hire qualified blacks, but claim they are unavailable. Certainly equal employment opportunity legislation has opened a wide range of job opportunities, many of which pay more than teaching, to college-educated blacks. But whether that is the real reason black teachers are underrepresented is a valid question. It seems in some school systems that desegregation has not eradicated racism; it has simply made it more subtle, and more difficult to prove in court.

Equal Education for Women

Title IX of the 1972 Education Amendments was modeled on Title VI of the 1964 Civil Rights Act, and sought to do for women what the earlier section had done for blacks. In a sense, this is not surprising. Many of the discriminatory practices in schools denied both blacks and women the same opportunities.

Employment practices in schools have been one area of almost identical discrimination. Both women and blacks were, and still are, largely excluded from higher-paying positions with real decision-making responsibilities. Very few of either group serve as school superintendents or high school principals. One explanation for the underrepresentation of women in the administrative ranks is that administrators are recruited through the "Old Boy" network. Because it is believed in some quarters that male coaches are good disciplinarians, they have an inside track for principal or assistant principal vacancies. Systemwide administrators, in turn, are recruited from the principals.

A second area where women and blacks have long felt discrimination is in their disproportionately small share of school revenue. Home economics teachers were often paid less than their male counterparts teaching shop. Women's athletic teams often had a smaller share of school sports funding than did comparable men's teams. There are instances in which women's basketball teams had to make do with equipment discarded by the men's teams, and where women team members received less per diem when away from home than did male players.

There was discrimination, too, in course availability. Many school systems did not allow girls to take vocational training in areas that had been traditionally dominated by men. So, girls were excluded from classes in auto mechanics and heating and air-conditioning—fields that pay much better than secretarial work, the area in which girls were encouraged to get training.

All of these practices are now illegal. What impact has Title IX had? Figures show that schools have greatly expanded the opportunities in interscholastic athletic competition for female students—the number of girls involved in interscholastic high school athletics has doubled and redoubled. Steps are being taken to place more women in administrative positions, and to allow girls to have the same options in course work as boys.

One problem legislation has not solved, however, is the retention of sexual stereotypes by some school counselors. Those counselors do not encourage girls to pursue nontraditional vocations or to study math and sciences. To the extent that women are not pushed to take advanced math courses, they are handicapped on standardized exams (among them, the Scholastic Aptitude Test) because of the weight assigned to quantitative skills in those instruments. A weak performance on the math component can limit both the choice of college and the chance of a scholarship.

EQUAL EMPLOYMENT OPPORTUNITY

Discrimination in hiring and in the terms and conditions of employment is a problem that has long confronted many groups in American society. Blacks have long been the last hired and first fired; women have long been paid less than men for the same work. And the list goes on.

In an early effort to combat discrimination in employment, the Roosevelt administration established the Fair Employment Practices Commission in 1941. The commission's impact was limited to the defense industry and lasted only until the end of World War II, when southerners in Congress choked off its funding. Later calls for the creation of a new FEPC by the Truman administration were met with legislative inaction.

Although some study commissions were created over the next decade, no governmental action was forthcoming until the 1960s, when growing concern with civil rights helped produce change. Presidents Kennedy and Johnson issued executive orders prohibiting discrimination by firms receiving government contracts and establishing an equal employment opportunity program for federal administrative agencies.

In a somewhat different vein, Congress in 1963 passed the Equal Pay Act, which provides that employers covered by the federal wage and hour law could not discriminate on the basis of sex in compensation for jobs requiring equal skill, effort, and responsibility. (Wage differences based on seniority, merit, and piecework were still permitted.) In a 1981 decision, the Supreme Court interpreted the act to require that salary inequities resulting from sex discrimination be corrected even when the jobs performed by males and females are not identical. First considered in Congress in 1946, this legislation was supported by labor unions as a means of preventing employers from undermining wages by hiring lower-paid women workers. Support also came from women's organizations. Business groups, such as the National Association of Manufacturers and the U.S. Chamber of Commerce, opposed the law, claiming it would add to bureaucratic control of business.

As proposed by the Kennedy and Johnson administrations, the bill that became the Civil Rights Act of 1964 did not touch on the issue of employment. Title VII, the part of the law that prohibits unfair employment practices, was added to the legislation in the House. Title VII makes it illegal for an employer "to fail or to refuse to hire or discharge any individual, or otherwise to discriminate against any individual with respect to his or her compensation, terms, conditions, or privileges of employment, because of such individual's race, color, religion, sex, or national origin." The five-member Equal Employment Opportunity Commission (EEOC) was created to help enforce the act, which is the major legislation aimed against discrimination in private employment.

The prohibition on sex discrimination included in the act was an accidental breakthrough in public policy.[27] The opponents of Title VII, in an effort to defeat it, decided to load it up with controversial features. So, they proposed and adopted, over the opposition of most liberal spokespersons and women's groups, an amendment to prohibit sex discrimination in employment. The ploy backfired, and the conservative southerners who authored the amendment found themselves unwilling supporters of women's rights. "Today's male airline stewards and female telephone linemen and steelworkers owe their jobs directly to this amendment, the accidental result of the tactical maneuverings of a policy battle in Congress."[28]

The 1964 statute covered employers or unions having twenty-five or more employees (about 75 percent of the labor force). The EEOC was authorized to receive complaints and to seek settlements by means of "conference, conciliation, and persuasion." Where legal action was necessary, cases could be referred to the Justice Department for action, or complainants could initiate private suit. Where a state had an antidiscrimination agency, complaints had to be referred to that agency for sixty days before the EEOC could act. The EEOC, in short, was given limited enforcement authority.

Those who wanted to strengthen the agency urged that it be given the power to issue cease and desist orders to alleged offenders and to seek their enforcement through the federal courts—a proposal that encountered strong opposition from conservatives, especially those from the South. A compromise was reached in 1972, whereby the EEOC was empowered to initiate legal proceedings, but not to issue cease and desist orders, when conciliation and persuasion could not produce settlements. The jurisdiction of the agency was also expanded to reach unions and employers with at least fifteen workers, and state and local government employees.

Enforcement

Pursuit of the broad goals of equal employment opportunity has been along several tracks. In the first, its enforcement activities, the EEOC places primary reliance on the receipt and processing of complaints, the largest share of which involve charges of racial discrimination by employers in hiring and firing practices. Although the EEOC receives a large number of complaints (between thirty thousand and forty thousand a year), only a small proportion of them are settled to the benefit of the complainant. For the period 1966–1972, only 2 percent of the total complaints filed resulted in settlements in favor of the worker.[29]

A second approach has the EEOC initiating comprehensive reviews of employers' practices as they pertain to all workers, not just those who have filed individual grievances. The advantage of compliance reviews is their cost-effectiveness—a larger number of people benefit from agency efforts. Some of the large employers that have undergone these reviews are Western Electric, nine major steel producers, and the United Steelworkers of America. When reviews turn up industrywide discriminatory practices, an agreement may be negotiated, as was the case in the airline, trucking, and shipping industries. Firms that fail to come into compliance can be, although they rarely are, cut off from federal contracts.

Litigation is a third approach, one open to individuals as well as the EEOC. Where the agency is unable to negotiate a settlement of either a complaint or problems unearthed in a compliance review, the EEOC can file suit against the offending employer. And individuals, weary of efforts to negotiate a settlement, have the same right.

Although there are a great number of potential bases for alleging a denial of equal employment opportunity, several problems are fairly common. These include the maintenance of separate seniority rosters for blacks and women. Separate rosters—which have been declared illegal—perpetuate past discrimination by denying minority members and women access to good jobs and job security. Another issue involves recruitment and promotion practices that rely heavily on whom one knows, practices that keep women and minority members out of jobs. Remedies have been directed at breaking the established pattern, getting personnel officers to consider the merits of applicants from groups that in the past have been ignored.

Tests and prerequisites for employment raise questions of discrimination too. Employers may require a certain level of education or training, or they may have strength or size standards. Employers, when challenged, must demonstrate that tests and prerequisites that exclude more black than white applicants or more females than males are, in fact, job related.[30]

On-the-job harassment also constitutes an equal employment violation. Some minority members and women who have made the break into jobs traditionally denied them have been subject to slurs from other workers and unfair treatment by supervisors. Women—and occasionally men—have had to handle demands for sexual favors in exchange for career advancement.

Where discrimination in hiring practices is found, the employer may be forced to hire the plaintiff or even to develop and implement an affirmative action plan. *Affirmative action plans* set goals and timetables for achieving a labor force that is representative of the work force in the community. The terms may be worked out through negotiations between employer and the EEOC, or between management and union. A plan may involve advertising job openings in black or Hispanic publications, or sending recruiters into minority neighborhoods. In the construction industry, "hometown plans" were developed in thirty-one cities, creating hiring goals and timetables for building trades within entire urban areas. In 1980, hometown plans were replaced by new requirements that federal contractors must have a proportion of minority workers in each craft equal to the percent minority in the area's labor force. These new regulations apply nationwide.

Another source of hiring goals, and one that has been used frequently when dealing with public agencies, is the federal judiciary. Federal judges have established ratios at which police departments, city transit systems, fire departments, and prisons must hire minorities. For example, a police department may be told that a third or half of all new officers hired must be black, until the racial composition of its labor force approximates that of the community it serves.

Job opportunities for minorities have also been promoted through contracts for public works. The 1977 Public Works Employment Act stipulated that 10 percent of the funds provided under that legislation were to go to minority contractors. Some cities have adopted similar provisions. In Atlanta, for example, a share of the contracts for construction of the airport and the rapid transit system was earmarked for minority firms. These kinds of arrangements have the potential not only to increase job opportunities for minority workers, but also to help black and other minority entrepreneurs gain experience and become competitive. A criticism of these efforts has been that, at times, contracts are awarded to firms created by whites with a minority race member as figurehead leader, rather than to firms in which minority members make the decisions and reap the profits.

President Reagan's Justice Department has opposed a number of affirmative action plans, preferring voluntarism instead. It has joined white public employees in arguing against quotas that require a specific share of an agency's promotions be given to blacks. Administration officials have also objected to layoffs made on something other than a seniority basis—layoffs that protect the jobs of recently hired minorities, following affirmative action guidelines. The administration contends that those guidelines are often too broad: rather than simply restoring the rights of workers who have been discriminated against, they give those workers an advantage in competing with whites. Supporters of affirmative action argue that the problems are so extensive only specific standards that require hiring a certain percentage of minority workers can correct the long history of discrimination.

Reverse Discrimination

Pressures to have greater representation of minorities and women in job categories traditionally filled by white males have induced some employers to apply lower standards to minority or female applicants than to white male applicants. This practice has led to charges of reverse discrimination. That is, white males who have been passed over for promotions or for selection for special training programs in favor of minority members or women who seem to be less qualified have charged that they are being discriminated against because they are white males.

The best-known reverse discrimination case to date involved not a job applicant but a candidate for admission to medical school. Still, the decision in *University of California Regents* v. *Bakke* has had tremendous impact on equal employment opportunity guidelines.[31] Bakke, a white male, was refused admission to the University of California (Davis) Medical School. He challenged that decision because several minority members who were accepted had poorer records than he did. In its decision, the U.S. Supreme Court ruled it a violation of Title VI of the 1964 Civil Rights Act to set aside a certain number of slots in an entering medical school class for minority applicants. The Court, however, did not prohibit all consideration of an applicant's race; instead it implied that a candidate's race or sex could be a factor in making a selection, much like military service is a factor in civil service situations.

The implications of *Bakke* were restricted in 1979. In *United Steelworkers of America* v. *Weber,* the plaintiff challenged an agreement made between his union and

Kaiser Aluminum that reserved half of all slots in a training program for blacks.[32] Selection was based on seniority, and Weber, a white, was not selected even though he had greater seniority than some of the blacks who were accepted into the program. The Supreme Court decided that a training program entered into *voluntarily* by a union and an employer, which reserved at least half the slots for blacks, was permissible. Although the Civil Rights Act did not require that type of program, it certainly did not prohibit it as a short-term method of bringing the proportion of blacks in craft jobs up to the proportion of blacks in the area's labor force.

Impact

Certainly at a superficial level changes have been produced by equal employment opportunity programs. Just as almost every television commercial that features a group scene has its token black, so almost every business has its token black or Hispanic or woman. Although these changes are significant because they demonstrate that minorities and women can hold some of the better jobs in the workplace, they do not constitute full compliance with the spirit of equal employment policy decisions. Women and minorities have greater representation in high-paying fields (law, medicine, science), but most continue to find jobs in traditional areas. Table 8–4 shows changes in the distributions of nonwhites and women across occupational categories. Ratios below 1.00 indicate that women and nonwhites constitute a smaller

TABLE 8-4   Ratio of nonwhite and female workers to expected distributions if evenly distributed across occupations

	Nonwhite		Women	
	1960	1981	1960	1981
White collar	.37	.77	1.27	1.25
Professional and technical	.42	.82	1.08	1.04
Managers, officials, and proprietors	.24	.48	.46	.64
Clerical	.49	1.00	2.02	1.88
Sales	.23	.45	1.19	1.06
Blue collar	1.10	1.13	.45	.43
Craftspeople and supervisors	.47	.72	.08	.15
Operatives	1.12	1.38	.83	.93
Nonfarm laborers	2.55	1.43	.07	.27
Service	2.60	1.70	1.92	1.45
Private household	4.74	2.85	2.94	2.25
Other	1.91	1.60	1.60	1.38
Farm	1.54	.58	.55	.42
Farmers and farm managers	.75	.20	.12	.26
Laborers	2.47	1.04	1.05	.60
Proportion of labor force	10.5	11.2	33.5	42.9

SOURCE: Data compiled from U.S. Department of Labor, *Employment and Training Report of the President* (Washington: U.S. Government Printing Office, 1978), pp. 205–207; and *Employment and Earnings* 29 (January 1982): 165–166.

share of an occupational group than of the total labor force; ratios above 1.00 show that women and nonwhites are overrepresented in an occupational category.

From 1960 to 1981, nonwhites have obtained a larger share of white-collar and craft jobs. These are positions that provide greater pay and prestige, and from which blacks have traditionally been excluded. Jobs to which minorities were relegated for generations—laborers and private household workers—still have disproportionate numbers of nonwhites, although greater balance is being achieved, especially among farm laborers, who include tenant farmers and migrant workers. Despite the gains of the last two decades, nonwhites continue to be underrepresented in the ranks of professionals, managers, salespersons, and craftspeople and foremen.

Changes in the kinds of jobs held by women are much less striking. The number of women in managerial or craft jobs increased only modestly. Women continue to be overrepresented in the relatively poor-paying categories of clerical workers and private household workers (maids).

The figures in the table mask some significant occupational differences between white males, and women and blacks. For example, in the professional category, blacks are more likely to be represented among poorer-paying professions (social work, vocational counseling) than in law or medicine. Women, too, are concentrated in the poorer-paying professions (teaching, nursing). Even with recent in-

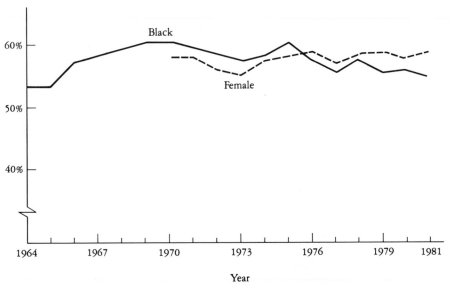

FIGURE 8-2 Ratio of black to white median family income and female to male income for year-round full-time workers. (*Sources: U.S. Department of Commerce,* The Social and Economic Status of the Black Population in the United States: An Historical View, 1790–1978. *Washington, D.C.: U.S. Government Printing Office, 1979, pp. 31, 195, and 250. U.S. Department of Commerce,* Money, Income and Poverty Status of Families and Persons in the United States: 1981. *Washington, D.C.: U.S. Government Printing Office, 1982, p. 10.*)

creases, in 1981 women constituted only 14 percent of the attorneys, 4 percent of the engineers, and 22 percent of the doctors.[33]

Given the persistence in patterns of job holding by minorities and women, we would expect little change in income patterns. As figure 8–2 shows, the disparities in pay that were evident for minorities in 1964 still exist. Black family incomes continue to be about 60 percent of the amount earned by white families; women continue to earn about 60 percent as much as men do.

There are some factors to consider in evaluating these statistics. First, even among those in better-paying jobs, women and minorities average less seniority than similarly placed males, and therefore earn less. For many women, their level of pay also reflects a work hiatus to raise families. For minorities, lower earnings are, in part, attributable to their schooling, which failed to prepare them for high-skill jobs. Also, for many, early entry into the job market to help support their families cut short education necessary for better-paying jobs. Thus, the inequities faced by one generation affect the life chances of the next.

HOUSING

Desegregating the Neighborhood

Residential patterns show the United States at its most segregated. Within urban areas, North as well as South, the population of central cities is disproportionately black (and, in some areas, Hispanic), while the suburbs tend to be overwhelmingly white. This is not because minorities necessarily prefer the central city. In a number of urban areas the population of the core city continues to decline as those blacks who can afford to do so follow whites out to suburbia.

The movement of blacks to the suburbs does not, however, seem to be a step toward racially heterogeneous neighborhoods. First, the suburbs blacks move into are often adjacent to central-city black ghettos.[34] Second, the same pattern of racial succession seen in the cities characterizes population change in the suburbs. As the black population rises, whites withdraw at an increasing rate. The distribution of population, then, continues to be homogeneous despite civil rights laws and litigation.

Federal limitations on housing discrimination began in 1948. Before that time, whites in some neighborhoods could go to court to prevent a neighbor from selling or leasing to a black. The first major step toward creating greater housing options for blacks came when the Supreme Court ruled that restrictive covenants entered into by residents of a neighborhood to forbid selling or renting to blacks were not enforceable.[35]

Over the next twenty years, the federal government did little to promote open housing. Indeed, officials responsible for approving home loan guarantees for the Veterans' Administration and the Federal Housing Administration considered racially mixed neighborhoods risky investments, and frowned on making loans to blacks who wanted to move into white communities.[36] Other federal officials located federally subsidized low-income housing where it reinforced existing racial patterns, rather than using it to integrate neighborhoods.

Legislative and judicial tolerance of residential segregation ended abruptly in 1968. Following the assassination of Martin Luther King, Jr., Congress reversed an earlier decision and approved a fair-housing statute. That legislation made it illegal for realtors to consider the race of prospective buyers or renters, forcing them to show homes in white neighborhoods to minority clients. The legislation also sought to curb another practice that retarded the evolution of biracial communities—blockbusting. Realtors who used the threat of black entry into a neighborhood to panic white homeowners into selling their property could be punished.

The Open Housing Act took into account the determinant role played by financial institutions (banks, savings and loan associations, and mortgage companies) in the housing market. Regulating realtors would have had little effect on that market if mortgage money were not available to blacks and whites wanting to buy homes in changing neighborhoods. The legislation outlawed redlining, where whole sections of a city would be ruled ineligible for loans, regardless of the financial characteristics of the loan applicant or the condition of the property in question. Lenders were warned not to consider the race of applicants or the racial composition of neighborhoods when considering loan applications.

Shortly after Congress acted, the Supreme Court rediscovered the Civil Rights Act of 1866, which it interpreted as guaranteeing blacks the same rights to purchase or rent housing as were enjoyed by whites.[37] The decision in *Jones* v. *Mayer* went a step further than the Open Housing Act. Where Congress had excluded from the legislation rentals and sales handled by owners, the Court made it illegal for individuals to refuse to sell to minority members.

The problems today.   Since 1968, when Congress and the Supreme Court embraced the goal of open housing, there have been only modest changes. Granted, there are now more subdivisions and apartment complexes in which black families reside, and there are more blacks applying for and receiving housing loans. Nonetheless, there remain a number of obstacles that contribute to racially segregated housing. Indeed, it has been estimated that black renters face a 75 percent chance of encountering discrimination; black home buyers, a 62 percent chance.[38]

What we are seeing is lingering fear and prejudice. Many whites still believe that a large-scale movement of blacks into their neighborhoods will depress property values and endanger the security of their families and homes. Prejudice and fear still lead some whites to move and others to harass their new neighbors.

There are economic limitations that prevent some blacks from moving into white neighborhoods. With median black income at less than 60 percent of what it is for whites, many blacks are simply unable to afford homes in the middle or upper price ranges. Until those economic differences shrink, blacks will be disproportionately concentrated in less expensive housing, while whites cluster in more expensive homes. Of course, the federal government could step in to equalize the situation by offering subsidies for suburban low-income housing. Federal authorities have been reluctant to tangle with suburbanites, to force them to accept subsidized housing projects, even though the Supreme Court has indicated that the decentralization of public housing might be necessary.[39]

Still another obstacle to real desegregation in the housing market is the Supreme Court's approval of local large-lot zoning ordinances.[40] If a suburban town zones all residential land for low-density development, it becomes economically unfeasible for low-income housing to be built in that town. Then too, builders are not eager to develop communities with housing for a range of incomes. They believe that by mixing prices, they will pull down the prices of more expensive units.

Finally, there is the issue of enforcement—the job the federal government is doing in enforcing housing statutes. There is practically no effort being made to determine whether realtors are guilty of steering (showing whites homes in white neighborhoods and blacks homes in black neighborhoods), whether lending institutions practice redlining, or whether landlords discriminate. Instead, enforcement relies heavily on lawsuits filed by minority members and complaints registered with the Department of Housing and Urban Development. HUD's authority here is limited to seeking negotiated settlements. It cannot bring suit even when it believes discrimination has occurred. Although HUD can refer cases to the Department of Justice, plaintiffs rarely obtain relief:

> In 1977, for instance, when officials estimated that 2.5 million acts of real-estate discrimination took place, about 3,400 complaints reached HUD. The Agency worked out compromises in 277 cases; 70 people actually obtained the housing they were originally denied.[41]

Data for 1982 indicate that of 5,112 complaints of housing discrimination, attempts to resolve disputes through negotiation occurred in 697 instances, of which 427 were successful.[42]

In 1983 President Reagan proposed legislation to strengthen federal fair-housing enforcement. Under the president's proposal, the Justice Department would be able to file suits on behalf of isolated individuals who have been discriminated against by realtors or landlords. (The 1968 Open Housing Act authorized federal suits only when the attorney general found a pattern of discrimination.) The president also asked that a penalty of $50,000 be set for people in the real estate industry who were found guilty of discrimination. Some civil rights leaders felt the proposal did not go far enough. They wanted a set of administrative judges created to hear housing-discrimination suits. This would allow for faster, less expensive resolution than is available through the courts.

Discriminatory housing practices do more than segregate our neighborhoods; they have a critical impact on other aspects of American race relations as well. Integrated neighborhoods lead automatically to integrated schools. When those neighborhoods are in suburbia they make it possible for blacks and other minority members to live closer to the growing job opportunities in suburban industrial parks, office buildings, and shopping malls.

Women and the Housing Market

The issue for women was not the availability of housing, but the availability of financing for housing. Lending institutions have long discriminated against women. They treated single women as poorer credit risks than men with comparable financial profiles—an obstacle that took on added significance as the number of female-headed households grew during the last twenty years. Mortgagees have long discriminated against married women too, a discrimination that affected the ability of two-breadwinner families to purchase a home. In assessing the size of a loan an applicant family could afford, the lending institution considered only the husband's earnings. By excluding the wife's salary from their computations, mortgagees reduced the size of the loan for which a family was eligible and, in some cases, made it impossible for that family to buy a home at all. Both of these aspects of discrimination were prohibited by Congress in 1974.

PUBLIC ACCOMMODATIONS

The major efforts to eliminate barriers impeding access to public accommodations came in 1964 and 1973. The earlier legislative debate questioned whether private entrepreneurs had a right to deny service to blacks; in 1973, debate focused on making facilities more accessible to the handicapped. The issue of racial access raised a good deal of controversy before being resolved, although it was implemented with less resistance than most programs designed to attain equal treatment for blacks. In contrast, relatively little controversy accompanied the requirement that public buildings and conveyances be accessible to the handicapped.

Racial Access

In the wake of *Plessy* v. *Ferguson*,[43] a whole range of segregated public services developed. Blacks were confined to the backs of buses and to separate railroad cars. They were restricted to specific seating areas in courthouses, theaters, and sports arenas. They were denied access to public golf courses, libraries, hospitals, parks, and swimming pools, even where no separate facilities were provided for them.

In the South, restaurants and motels universally rejected black customers, although sometimes they served them on a carry-out basis through the back door. Some filling stations had segregated restroom facilities and water fountains, but many offered no services at all to blacks. This made automobile travel in the South by blacks difficult. They had to know the locations of black hotels and restaurants and hope that filling stations would have a restroom for them.

During the early 1960s, equal access to public accommodations, along with school desegregation and suffrage, was a major objective of the civil rights movement. Demands for public accommodations were dramatized by the lunch counter sit-ins that began in Greensboro, North Carolina, and the Freedom Riders whose bus was burned in Anniston, Alabama. There were marches and protests aimed at desegregating public facilities as well as private businesses. Ultimately, though, it was economic pressure that gave blacks equal access. The first skirmish in the civil rights campaign, the Montgomery bus boycott led by Martin Luther King, Jr., forced the local transit system to end its Jim Crow (segregationist) practices and allow blacks to sit anywhere on the buses.

After *Brown* v. *Board of Education*,[44] the weight of the Constitution tilted to the side of blacks demanding equal access to facilities supported by public taxes. In a series of cases, the Supreme Court found the separate-but-equal doctrine inappropriate for public golf courses, parks, beaches, prisons, and other facilities.

For privately owned businesses catering to the public, the major blow against discrimination came in Title II of the 1964 Civil Rights Act. The legal theory on which that legislation rested was the Constitution's commerce clause.[45] Congress treated denial of services to blacks as an impediment to the free flow of commerce among the states. Therefore, it forbade discrimination against blacks by private businesses that catered to interstate travelers or that moved a substantial proportion of their goods in interstate commerce. The first provision covered operators of hotels, motels, restaurants, and theaters in the convention areas of central cities and along major highways; the second, thanks to America's extensive transportation network, encompassed almost every business in the country.[46]

Initial reluctance to comply with the public accommodations provision gave way when the courts upheld its constitutionality. Then too, desegregation made economic sense, opening up white businesses to a whole new market. Within a short time, blacks were sitting wherever they liked at sporting events, movies, and concerts, and were being served in hotels, motels, and restaurants. Soon black access to services and entertainment was limited only by personal taste and money.

The racial segregation that once characterized virtually every aspect of southern life is now legal only in private clubs. There continue to be country clubs and private organizations, including some fraternities and sororities, that limit membership to whites. Although social pressures are occasionally brought to bear on these clubs and their members—particularly members nominated for high public office—the membership restrictions are legal.

Access for the Handicapped

The Rehabilitation Act of 1973 required that public facilities be made accessible to the handicapped—that "no otherwise qualified handicapped individual . . . shall . . . be excluded from participation in . . . any program or activity receiving federal financial assistance."

The guidelines for implementing the statute set off public debate over the cost-effectiveness of required changes. City transit systems have been especially vocal in their opposition. They claim that very few wheelchair users patronize city buses even when those buses are adapted for wheelchair loading. They insist it would be much cheaper to convey these handicapped people in specially equipped vans that could take them wherever they wanted to go. The costs of adapting buses are high; the costs of adapting existing subway systems are even higher. It was estimated in 1976 that it would cost between $1.5 and $2.5 billion to bring the New York City system into compliance by installing elevators.[47] Critics questioned that expenditure, noting that the Metro in Washington, which was built to be accessible to wheelchair users, averaged only a dozen wheelchair-bound riders a day.[48]

The handicapped, on the other hand, contend that it is inappropriate to attach a price tag to rights. Moreover, they insist they are not the only beneficiaries of easier access to public transit and buildings: the elderly, pregnant women, and people with temporary disabilities would all use the ramps and elevators.

Should the federal government pay adaptation costs, the furor would end. The taxpayers' revolt and general disenchantment with federal programs make this unlikely. Indeed, the Reagan administration's opposition to costly regulations has been directed, in part, at access-for-the-handicapped requirements. The president's objection to standards for making federal buildings more accessible led him to try to close the agency responsible for enforcement.

ABORTION

In the last decade, the question of abortion has been one of the most heated issues on the nation's policy agenda. Debate started in 1973, with a Supreme Court ruling restricting the authority of states to regulate abortions. That ruling gave the states no control over first-trimester abortions and limited control during the second trimester; it did not affect third-trimester abortions, which can be prohibited by state law.[49] Since 1973, the Court generally has struck down state and local statutes that made it difficult to obtain abortions. In 1983, requirements that abortions in the second trimester be performed in hospitals and that doctors discuss alternatives to abortion with their patients were invalidated.

Leaders of the Catholic church, some Fundamentalist sects, and other pro-lifers define abortion as murder. They have lobbied Congress to approve a constitutional amendment restricting the availability of the procedure. One proposal, by specifying that life begins at the moment of conception (the Supreme Court has refused to tackle the issue of when life begins), would ban all abortions. A second proposal allows therapeutic abortions under very specific conditions—to protect the life of the mother or to terminate pregnancies caused by rape or incest.

Their inability to secure congressional approval of a constitutional limitation has led right-to-life advocates to try to limit abortions through legislation blocking the use of federal funds for abortions for welfare mothers, and restricting the availability of abortions to more affluent women. They have been successful in meeting the first objective. Since the late 1970s, appropriations bills have prohibited the use of federal funds to pay for abortions for low-income women who receive Medicaid. This restriction had popular support by 1980: most Americans opposed using tax dollars to pay for abortions for the poor.[50] Denial of federal funding—which in 1975 paid for 300,000 abortions[51]—has made the procedure less readily available to the poor in most states. In 1979, with federal assistance available only in extreme situations, federal funds paid for just 2,000 abortions. (A few states use public funds to pay for abortions for the needy.)

Turning to abortions in general, opponents introduced legislation in 1981 to declare that life begins at conception, that states can outlaw abortions, and that state laws banning abortions are not subject to review in federal courts. Sponsors of the legislation believed it would bring a fetus under the right to life that the Fourteenth Amendment guarantees all "persons." Opponents speculated the law would be unconstitutional (a moot point, since the law did not pass).

Those who support Supreme Court decisions limiting state control over abortions claim that women should be able to choose whether to carry a fetus to term; that this choice is derived from the Fourteenth Amendment; and that life begins, not at conception, but when existence outside the womb is possible. Although they were successful in defeating the 1981 pro-life legislation, the pro-choice groups have not been able to overcome prohibitions on federal funding of abortions. The courts have rejected their argument that the legislation discriminates against the poor.[52] Claims that unwanted children may be abused and run a higher risk of being a drain on society, either by being dependent on welfare programs or by going to jail, have fallen on deaf ears.

CONCLUDING COMMENTS

The conservative wind that swept across America in the fall of 1980 stopped, at least temporarily, efforts to expand the definition of civil rights. Indeed, some feared the Republican landslide would leave the guarantees of certain rights seriously eroded.

Certainly, the Reagan administration has opted for less federal involvement in protecting civil rights, a preference in line with its broader commitment to deregulation. Although most recent presidents have been critical of the extent of federal influence over American life, Ronald Reagan has gone further toward eliminating federal civil rights protections than did any of his predecessors.

Leaders in the Reagan Justice Department have opposed the involvement of department lawyers in efforts to desegregate schools through busing, and they have indicated a willingness to join school districts in having existing busing orders reexamined by the courts. Secretary of Labor Raymond Donovan has proposed a change in reporting requirements for federal contractors. Now contractors who employ fifty workers and have federal contracts in excess of $50,000 must file affirmative action plans; the administration would require reports only from those with one hundred workers and $100,000 in contracts. That suggested reduction in coverage goes hand in hand with the president's opposition to the use of enforceable hiring goals for increasing the number of women and minority members in the labor force.

The president was a late supporter of the 1982 Voting Rights Act extension. At first, he was sympathetic with conservative opponents of the legislation, among them Judiciary Committee chairman Sen. Strom Thurmond (R.–S.C.), who wanted to make the legislation applicable nationwide or allow it to lapse. Civil rights groups opposed both alternatives. Making the provision applicable nationwide was rejected when, in the course of congressional hearings, evidence showed continued obstacles to black participation in the South. A second rebuff to the president and his supporters came when Congress refused to require that plaintiffs demonstrate discrimination was intentional in order to secure a judicial remedy. Instead, the 1982 extension of the Voting Rights Act requires only that plaintiffs prove a law or practice has a discriminatory effect on minorities.

Other civil rights are being jeopardized by threats from a different quarter—budget cuts. Less money for personnel and investigations means weaker enforcement of civil rights protections. And it means a new federal role, a move from action to reaction, that is frustrating black leaders. "We cannot turn to the judiciary, the executive or the legislature. Washington has turned its back on us."[53]

In some other areas, we are seeing efforts to undo civil rights policy—to reinstate voluntary prayer in the public schools, to end court-ordered busing, and to ban abortions. Although these efforts have not succeeded, it is important to realize that they reflect a national trend. Many white Americans feel that federal civil rights protections are adequate. Surveys indicate most whites believe that the federal government has done enough to promote racial equality, that blacks are better off now than they were a decade ago, and that whites are more tolerant of blacks than in the past. Not surprisingly, blacks are significantly less positive on all of these dimensions.[54]

The worst examples of discrimination were largely eliminated during the 1960s and 1970s. The inequities that persist seem likely to remain for the present.

NOTES

1. We discuss a primary concern of Hispanics, bilingual education, in chapter 7. There we also examine education policy as it affects the handicapped, a topic some would consider a civil rights issue.
2. Martin Luther King, Jr., quoted in David J. Garrow, *Protest at Selma* (New Haven: Yale University Press, 1978), p. 238.
3. Charles Silberman, *Crisis in Black and White* (New York: Vintage, 1964), p. 23.

4. V. O. Key, Jr., *Southern Politics* (New York: Random House–Vintage, 1949), pp. 652–653, 666.

5. *Smith* v. *Allright*, 321 U.S. 649 (1944).

6. Some civil rights activists criticized the passivity of federal poll watchers. The poll watchers report actions that might dissuade black participation, but do not step in to prevent them.

7. Earl Black, *Southern Governors and Civil Rights* (Cambridge, Mass.: Harvard University Press, 1976).

8. William R. Keech, *The Impact of Negro Voting* (Chicago: Rand McNally, 1968).

9. Charles S. Bullock, III, and Susan A. MacManus, "Policy Responsiveness to the Black Electorate," *American Politics Quarterly* 9 (July 1981): 357–368; and Charles S. Bullock, III, "Congressional Voting and the Mobilization of a Black Electorate in the South," *Journal of Politics* 43 (August 1981): 662–682.

10. Charles S. Bullock, III, "The Election of Blacks in the South," *American Journal of Political Science* 19 (November 1975): 727–739; and David Campbell and Joe R. Feagin, "Black Politics in the South," *Journal of Politics* 37 (February 1975): 129–162.

11. *Plessy* v. *Ferguson*, 163 U.S. 537 (1896).

12. Richard Kluger, *Simple Justice* (New York: Knopf, 1976), p. 169.

13. *Missouri ex rel. Gaines* v. *Canada*, 305 U.S. 337 (1938).

14. *Sweatt* v. *Painter*, 339 U.S. 629 (1950).

15. *Brown* v. *Board of Education*, 347 U.S. 483 (1954).

16. *Green* v. *County School Board*, 391 U.S. 430 (1968).

17. Grade-a-year and freedom of choice plans were tactics adopted by many southern school systems once it was no longer possible to avoid desegregation. Systems adopting the former implemented desegregation at the rate of one additional grade each year, usually beginning with the twelfth grade. Freedom of choice plans resulted in desegregation only when a black student requested a transfer to a white school; otherwise students continued to attend their segregated schools.

18. *Alexander* v. *Holmes*, 396 U.S. 19 (1969).

19. *Dayton Board of Education* v. *Brinkman*, 433 U.S. 406 (1977).

20. Leon E. Panetta and Peter Gall, *Bring Us Together* (Philadelphia: Lippincott, 1971).

21. *Milliken* v. *Bradley*, 418 U.S. 717 (1974).

22. *Pasadena* v. *Spangler*, 427 U.S. 424 (1976).

23. Robert Pear, "Reagan Busing Stand," *New York Times*, September 29, 1982, p. 13.

24. Joseph Stewart, Jr., and Charles S. Bullock, III, "Implementing Equal Education Opportunity Policy: A Comparison of the Outcomes of HEW and Justice Department Efforts," *Administration and Society* 12 (February 1981): 427–446.

25. *Children out of School* (Washington, D.C.: Children's Defense Fund, 1974).

26. *Columbus Board of Education* v. *Penick*, 439 U.S. 1348 (1979).

27. Gary Orfield, *Congressional Power: Congress and Social Change* (New York: Harcourt Brace Jovanovich, 1975), pp. 299–300.

28. Ibid., p. 300.

29. Charles S. Bullock, III, "Expanding Black Economic Rights," in *Racism and Inequality*, ed. Harrell R. Rodgers, Jr. (San Francisco: Freeman, 1975), p. 82.

30. *Griggs* v. *Duke Power Co.*, 401 U.S. 424 (1971).

31. *University of California Regents* v. *Bakke*, 438 U.S. 265 (1978).

32. *United Steelworkers of America* v. *Weber*, 443 U.S. 193 (1979).

33. Frank J. Prial, "More Women Work at Traditional Male Jobs," *New York Times*, November 15, 1982, pp. 1, 22.

34. William P. O'Hare, Jane-yu Li, Roy Chatterjee, and Margaret Shukur, *Blacks on the Move: A Decade of Demographic Change* (Washington, D.C.: Joint Center for Political Studies, 1982), pp. 49–66.

35. *Shelley* v. *Kramer*, 334 U.S. 1 (1948).

36. Harrell R. Rodgers, Jr., and Charles S. Bullock, III, *Law and Social Change* (New York: McGraw-Hill, 1972), chap. 6.

37. *Jones v. Mayer*, 392 U.S. 409 (1968).

38. "Anti-Black Housing Bias Still Alive, Study Shows," *Atlanta Journal*, August 22, 1978, p. 3-A.

39. *Hills v. Gautreaux*, 425 U.S. 284 (1976).

40. *Belle Terre v. Boraas*, 416 U.S. 1 (1974).

41. Aric Press et al., "Fairer Fair Housing," *Newsweek*, November 17, 1980, p. 108.

42. Robert Pear, "President Asking Expanded Powers for Fair Housing," *New York Times*, July 13, 1983, pp. 1, 9.

43. *Plessy v. Ferguson*, 163 U.S. 537 (1896).

44. *Brown v. Board of Education*, 347 U.S. 483 (1954).

45. Congress chose the commerce clause rather than the equal protection clause as the constitutional basis for the public accommodations legislation because many years earlier the Supreme Court had ruled that the equal protection clause did not apply to private business [*Civil Rights Cases*, 109 U.S. 3 (1883)].

46. *Katzenbach v. McClung*, 379 U.S. 294 (1964).

47. Timothy B. Clark, "Access for the Handicapped—A Test of Carter's War on Inflation," *National Journal* 10 (October 21, 1978): 1674.

48. Ibid., p. 1672.

49. *Roe v. Wade*, 410 U.S. 113 (1973).

50. A November 1980 poll by CBS–*New York Times* found that public funding of abortions for the poor was opposed by a margin of 55 to 38 percent; opposition had increased from the 50 to 42 percent registered in a January 1978 survey. Press release, November 15, 1980, p. 13.

51. Sandra Stencel, "Abortion Politics," in *National Health Issues*, ed. Hoyt Gimlin (Washington, D.C.: Congressional Quarterly, 1977), p. 23.

52. *Beal v. Doe*, 432 U.S. 438 (1977).

53. Jesse Jackson, quoted in Peter Goldman et al., "Reagan and the Blacks," *Newsweek*, July 13, 1981, p. 20.

54. For a compendium of a number of recent polls, see Everett Carll Ladd, "The State of Race Relations—1981," *Public Opinion* 4 (April–May 1981): 32–40.

SUGGESTED READINGS

Bullock, Charles S., III, and Lamb, Charles. *Implementation of Civil Rights Policy*. Monterey, Calif.: Brooks/Cole, 1984.

Keech, William R. *The Impact of Negro Voting*. Chicago: Rand McNally, 1968.

Kluger, Richard. *Simple Justice*. New York: Knopf, 1976.

Orfield, Gary. *Must We Bus?* Washington, D.C.: Brookings Institution, 1978.

Rodgers, Harrell R., Jr., and Bullock, Charles S., III. *Coercion to Compliance*. Lexington, Mass.: Lexington Books, 1976.

St. John, Nancy H. *School Desegregation Outcomes for Children*. New York: Wiley, 1975.

NINE

Business Policies

American legislative bodies spend much of their time and energy on the problems and needs of the business community. Over the years, a vast collection of economic policies—complex, diverse, and sometimes inconsistent—has developed. Government, at times, has been promoter, regulator, mediator, even owner and operator of various industries. Although the extent and nature of its involvement in the business community has changed over the last two centuries, government has always intervened in the economy. Laissez faire has been more a dream than a reality.

We do not attempt to deal here with the total spectrum of business policies. Instead, we focus on three general areas: promoting business activities, antitrust policies, and the deregulation movement of recent years. Other policies that affect the business community—general economic policies, environmental pollution, and labor relations—are discussed in other chapters.

THE BUSINESS COMMUNITY

Diversity

The term *businessperson* encompasses a wide assortment of people: corporation executives, investment bankers, Wall Street brokers, chain-store managers, general-store owners, real estate agents, service station operators, barbers, florists, motion picture makers, textile manufacturers, poolroom owners, corner drugstore operators, and many others. This diversity of people and trades is matched by the diversity of organizations and associations that protect and promote their interests. Practically every line of industrial or commercial activity has its national trade association—for instance, the American Iron and Steel Institute, the Tobacco Institute, the American Bankers Association, the Automobile Manufacturers Association, the American Meat Institute, the National Association of Retail Grocers, the National Association of Retail Druggists, the American Federation of Retail Kosher Butchers, the National Fertilizer Association, the Portland Cement Association, and the Institute of Makers of Explosives. There are also such well-known general business organizations, or "peak associations," as the National Association of Manufacturers and the Chamber of Commerce of the United States. Organizations claiming to speak generally for "small business" include the National Small Business Association and the Conference of American Small Business Organizations.

The numerous spokespeople for the business community tend to expound a traditional ideology, one that stresses individualism, free enterprise, free competition, and government nonintervention. But though businesspeople may describe the operation of the economy in terms of laissez faire concepts, they often call for government to come to their aid when they are confronted with the pain of excessive competition or the possibility of business failure. The fact that their actions are inconsistent with their ideology seems not especially troubling to the business community and its supporters. Whether they advocate or oppose government action often depends more on calculations of economic advantage than on consistency with ideological precepts.

Business organizations and associations have been established to perform a variety of functions—promotion, research, education, and others—but nearly all of them, at one time or another, engage in efforts to influence the direction and substance of public economic policy. Some business organizations—the Business Roundtable and the U.S. Chamber of Commerce are examples—are continually involved in political activities; others, whose interests are narrower, are involved only occasionally. The recourse of business groups to government "results both from the need of these groups for help in furthering their aims and from the closely related need of protection from their economic and political rivals."[1] In the first instance, they want such things from government as subsidies, research and technical services, aid in controlling intragroup competition, and other forms of direct assistance. In the second instance, they may oppose demands for regulation or insist that the activities of rival economic groups be regulated. In either case, the basic motivational force behind the political activity is protection, security from disruptive economic changes, the "unfair" practices of rival economic groups, unwanted regulation, and so on.

Because of the complexity and diversity of our economy, there are many conflicts of interest and purpose among the different segments of the business community. Conflict and competition occur within and between industries: small businesses compete for advantage with big businesses; depressed industries with prosperous competing ones; importers with domestic manufacturers; railroads with motor carriers and other transportation providers; regional economic interests with national ones; "responsible" stockbrokers with less responsible members of the industry. Whatever the specific issue—government subsidies, tariff protection, wage and transportation rate differentials—a considerable portion of the legislation relating to business in the statute books is the product of conflict between business groups. Much support for the Interstate Commerce Act and the Sherman Antitrust Act, for example, came from small businesspeople and others arrayed against "big business."

Unity

Notwithstanding the conflicts among business interests, there does appear to be a measure of unity within the broad business community.

Conflicts among business groups are commonplace, yet a network of common interest pulls the business community together on major issues when its security is threatened. Party lines, sectional lines, religious lines rarely divide businessmen when their common interests are in peril. Within the business community powerful factors operate to bring conformity to the predominant views. Unanimity is rare, but a predominant business sentiment usually crystallizes and makes itself heard on major issues affecting the group as a whole.[2]

Most businesspeople would probably take a common position on opposing business tax increases, restricting "big labor," protecting business against foreign competition, and promoting general business activity. And when it is united, the business community is a potent political force.

What are some of the factors that help unite the diverse business community, and thus enhance its political influence? Business organizations, like other human groups, develop norms of conduct and common interests to which their members are expected to adhere. Group social pressures operate to encourage individual adherence to those interests, or at least to discourage open deviation from them. Financial relationships among business units are another basis for unity. Manufacturers who express "unbusinesslike" views may find their customers taking their business elsewhere. Newspapers may hesitate to editorialize against business interests for fear of losing advertising revenues. Then too, business associations, interlocking and overlapping corporate directorates, corporate hierarchies, and the dominance of many industries by a few large firms operate to help tie the business community together through a web of relationships. These, coupled with modern means of transportation and communication, permit the ready transmission of the views of business leaders throughout the community, and facilitate the mobilization of business for unified political action on broad policy questions.

Political Strategies

In attempting to influence public economic policies, business groups use several strategies. One is persuasion, which can involve activities ranging from threats of injury or retaliation for unwanted conduct, to lobbying before legislative and administrative bodies, to efforts to shape public opinion. The old "public be damned" attitude expressed by William K. Vanderbilt is largely a thing of the past. Today, using the mass media and other means of communication, business groups try to convince the public of the virtues, achievements, and benefits of private business and a free-enterprise economy. Business advertising is concerned with the merchandising of ideas as well as products, and, together with other public relations activities, is used to win support for some policy proposals and to create opposition to others. But, as V. O. Key has observed:

> Of more fundamental importance is the continuing propaganda calculated to shape public attitudes favorably toward the business system as a whole or toward particular types of business. The assiduous dedication of effort to the capture of public favor lays a foundation of good will on which business groups may build in their efforts to obtain particular legislation or to obstruct undesired governmental actions.[3]

A second method is to secure the selection of administrative officials who are sympathetic to business interests and viewpoints. In certain instances, as with some occupational licensing boards, officials are actually chosen by the regulated groups. In other cases, business influence is less direct but very much there. During the Eisenhower administration, one responsive to business interests, changes in labor-management relations policy favorable to business were secured through the appointment of business-oriented members to the National Labor Relations Board.[4] In still other cases, continued association by regulatory officials with businesspeople, and limited contacts with other groups, can flavor the attitudes of those officials. That is one reason why business groups (and other economic groups, for that matter) want separate agencies to handle programs with which they are concerned. "Probably the most effective way to make a public official act as an interest wishes him to do is to insure by institutional means that he will become thoroughly acquainted with its problems as the adherents of the interest see them."[5]

If business groups are unable to prevent the enactment of unwanted legislation, they may follow a third strategy—attempting to discredit, delay, or otherwise frustrate its implementation. Litigation has sometimes been used for this purpose. In the late nineteenth and early twentieth centuries, public utility concerns often resorted to the courts to combat administrative regulation of their rates. Until 1906, the Interstate Commerce Commission's effectiveness was greatly reduced by railroad-instigated judicial limitations. During the 1930s, business groups launched an all-out judicial attack on New Deal legislation and succeeded, prior to 1937, in getting a considerable portion of it declared unconstitutional. In recent years occupational safety and health rules have been subjected to a variety of judicial challenges. Although there is nothing improper about challenging the constitutionality or legality of government actions, at times those challenges are so numerous (and their obstructional intent so obvious) as to constitute a form of not-so-covert warfare against government action. Actual or threatened noncooperation by those affected by legislation can also slow down or prevent its implementation. Businesses affected by economic policies retain much discretion, which can be used to evade or frustrate unwanted rules and requirements. Witness, for example, the difficulties in getting companies to comply with environmental pollution control standards (see chapter 4).

In recent years, in order to secure the election of "friendly" public officials, business groups have relied on another strategy—direct participation in party and electoral politics. Literally hundreds of business political action committees (PACs) have been created in the last several years.[6] In some instances, these groups have overstepped the bounds of legality; for example, testimony during the Watergate scandals revealed that several companies had made direct contributions of corporate funds to certain candidates and officials. How typical such action is remains a matter for speculation. But, clearly, business groups and corporations are much more involved in electoral politics than they were in the past.

There is no precise way to determine the impact of business groups and the business community on the substance and implementation of public economic policy. Their effectiveness in this endeavor will be affected, at any given time, by such factors as the amount of cohesiveness and consensus among business groups, the strength and cohesiveness of opposing groups, the prestige of the business community, the degree of public acceptance of business ideas and viewpoints, the administration in power (e.g., Republican or Democratic), and the nature of the issues in question. With respect to the last factor, business groups would seemingly have more influence on a matter related directly to business, say a particular subsidy program, than on an issue involving society generally, civil rights or Medicare legislation, for example. But whatever the conditions, as long as the business community and its component groups retain control over the economic assets of the nation, they represent a force, or set of forces, of tremendous political strength.[7]

PROMOTING BUSINESS ACTIVITY

Government promotion of business involves the provision of positive aid, assistance, and encouragement to particular business groups, industries, or segments of the economy. It is intended to help recipients meet their goals, which would certainly include survival and enhanced profits, by protecting them from or helping them overcome some of the risks and uncertainties of economic life.

The business community has always depended on government for the performance of certain functions: maintaining law and order, protecting property rights, enforcing contracts, providing a monetary system, granting corporate charters, issuing patents and copyrights, and creating legislation to ease the pain of bankruptcy. Without this core of government activities, our system of private enterprise would be unable to exist. Although these activities could fairly be considered a form of business promotion, they are indivisible and indiscriminate in nature; they benefit workers, farmers, consumers, and citizens generally, as well as businesses. Our discussion will be centered on more direct and specific forms of assistance to the business community, such as subsidies and loans.

Governmental promotional activity involves minimal control of business behavior. Businesspeople typically are not required to make use of available assistance or benefits; no sanctions are imposed for their failure to do so, except as they may perceive the loss of an available benefit as a deprivation. However, to say that promotion involves minimal control is not to say that it involves no control. Businesspeople may be required to assume certain duties or obligations, to demonstrate the meeting of certain conditions, or to modify their behavior in specified ways in order to qualify for assistance or benefits. This is the case if they want to secure tax credits for industrial plant modernization, a loan from the Small Business Administration, or a subsidy for construction of a merchant ship. Government assistance frequently has "strings" attached.

Promotion and regulation of business activity are also intermingled in another way. Some measures undertaken to assist one group in the attainment of its goals involve regulation or restriction of the activity of other groups. The regulation of entry into the banking business benefits existing banks by reducing the likelihood of competition from potential entrants into the business. Tariffs and import quotas benefit the makers of competitive products but disadvantage the importers, sellers, and users of the foreign products involved. Whether a given policy is considered promotional or regulatory depends in some instances on whose ox is being gored.

The Politics of Promotion

Businesspeople and business groups, despite numerous protestations against government intervention in the economy, have long sought and obtained governmental aid and encouragement for their economic endeavors. It is often remarked that the second statute enacted by the government under the Constitution provided for a protective tariff. Under the nurture and guidance of Alexander Hamilton and the Federalists, business promotionalism became a firmly established national policy by the end of the eighteenth century. Throughout the nineteenth century, moreover, the dominant policy of the national government toward business was promotionalism, not regulation. Although business interests in the latter part of the nineteenth century proclaimed the virtues of laissez faire in their efforts to ward off regulation of their activities demanded by agrarian and other groups, they found such government policies as protective tariffs, cash subsidies and land grants for railroad construction, and lax incorporation laws much to their liking. However inconsistent this situation may appear from an ideological viewpoint, it is not inconsistent when viewed from the perspective of the (at least short-run) self-interest of the business community, especially "big" business. The business community, in its political activities, was motivated and guided by practical considerations, by the desire to secure positive advantages and to avoid disadvantages, and not by the desire to be ideologically consistent or pure. A similar situation prevails today, as American automobile and steel producers clamor for protection against the Japanese.

Businesses, especially large businesses encountering financial difficulties, have often sought government assistance in recent years. A list of favorable responses by the government to such pleas include financial assistance to the Chrysler Corporation and the Penn Central railroad; legislation to permit "failing" newspapers to use joint facilities otherwise prohibited under the antitrust laws; and the Regional Rail Organization Act of 1973, which was designed to alleviate the problems of a number of bankrupt northeastern railroads. These actions reflect a sort of "fail-safe" syndrome: large businesses should not be permitted to fail because of the disastrous economic consequences of their failure. Whether they represent a major new thrust in public policy rather than a series of particular actions remains to be seen.

The claims of business groups for governmental aid and assistance are advanced and supported in a number of ways. For instance, business representatives may point out that a particular action not only will contribute to business but also will promote the public interest. "Throughout American history particular sections or groups, . . . hoping to validate the claims of their interests, have capitalized on the popular acceptance accorded to the public interest."[8] Another tactic is to stress the benefits that will flow to groups other than the one directly aided. Protective tariffs have been defended on the ground that they support the interests not only of manufacturers but of farmers and workers as well. Construction subsidies to railroads in the nineteenth century were defended in terms of the economic benefits and advantages that would accrue to the regions served by those trains. Assistance to a particular industry may also be defended as necessary or vital to national security. Thus, some contend that subsidies for the construction and operation of American merchant ships are needed to ensure the existence of an adequate American merchant fleet in the event of war. This argument (and belief) has been important in gaining congressional support for these subsidy programs. Finally, promotional programs may be advocated as means of securing the "economic growth" necessary, for instance, to "keep up with the Russians" (as was the case in the 1960s), to expand employment, or to reduce poverty. Tax concessions for industrial plant modernization and programs for industries in economically depressed areas have all been justified as necessary for economic growth.

Patterns of Promotion

Because of the great number and variety of promotional programs, we cannot discuss all of them. Rather, we examine a number of categories under which promotional programs can be grouped. These include cash and in-kind payments, tax expenditures, credit programs, construction and maintenance of facilities, and technical and information services.

Cash and in-kind payments.   Cash and in-kind payments are commonly referred to as subsidies, although the term *subsidy* can be applied to any program that is provided at no cost or less than cost. Railroad construction was subsidized in the nineteenth century by both land grants and cash contributions. According to one estimate, national and state grants of land to railroads amounted to 183 million acres.[9] Operating subsidies have been paid to commercial airlines since 1926, although in recent years these have been limited to local-service airlines. The construction and operation of American merchant ships are subsidized by the government at a current rate of about 500 million dollars annually. These payments are designed to make up the differences between foreign and domestic construction and operating costs. American merchant shipping also benefits from cabotage legislation, which requires that coastal shipping be done in American-made or -registered ships.

Subsidies may also be indirect or hidden, as when the government sells services or products to private businesses below cost or when it buys products at more than market price. Newspaper and periodical publishers are subsidized by below-cost postal rates; this practice was initially justified as necessary to encourage the dissemination of information. The silver-mining industry has been subsidized by government purchases of silver at higher than market prices, while silver for industrial purposes is imported at lower prices from abroad.

Tax expenditures.   A great many activities are subsidized through the mechanics of the federal income tax system.[10] Exclusions from income, exemptions, deductions, credits against tax, preferential tax rates, and tax deferrals allow favored individuals or corporations to retain funds that otherwise would be paid as taxes. The effect is the same as if the government were making a direct payment to the favored party. Tax provisions that have a direct expenditure effect include the investment credit for industrial plant modernization, partial exemption of income from export business, and lower rates of taxation for capital gains. Such provisions are likely to be called tax incentives by their proponents, whereas critics tend to designate them as loopholes.

The use of tax expenditures to promote business activity has become extensive and costly. In 1984 tax expenditures for corporations were probably over $50 billion.[11] (Tax expenditures for individuals in the same year were three times that amount, many of them, though, were business related.) The use of tax expenditures, or favorable tax provisions, to promote business activity is probably preferred to more direct support because they are less open and obvious. They also capitalize on our general aversion to paying taxes and the notion that a tax break does not cost anyone anything. Tax expenditures for businesses were substantially increased during the Reagan administration.

Credit programs.   Although government credit and loan programs have been around for a long time, most current programs were established after 1930.[12] One of the best-known examples of government lending to business involves the activities of the Reconstruction Finance Corporation. Set up by the Hoover administration in 1930, the RFC made loans to businesses. By 1954, when the agency was liquidated by the Eisenhower administration pursuant to its pledge to reduce government business operations, RFC loans totaled nearly $50 billion. To help fill the gap left by the RFC, and at the insistence of small business groups, the Small Business Administration was established in 1953. The SBA administers loans and other programs for the benefit of small businesses. Interestingly, the economic difficulties experienced by some businesses during the recession of the mid-1970s led some members of Congress to unsuccessfully advocate that the RFC be restored.

Also in the category of credit programs are government loan guarantee operations. Such agencies as the Federal Housing Administration, the Veterans' Administration, and the Federal National Mortgage Association underwrite private loans and mortgages for residential housing. By assuming a large share of the risk in housing credit, the government has helped large numbers of home owners and, more to the point here, has contributed to the prosperity of home builders, realtors, and mortgage lenders (see chapter 6). In another area, the Synthetic Fuels Corporation, established by Congress in 1980, has extensive loan and loan guarantee authority to foster the development of synthetic fuels by private companies.

The subsidy element in credit programs comes into play when borrowers are able to obtain loans at lower interest rates than would have to be paid for similar loans from private lenders. A government study estimated that subsidies of this sort totaled around \$24 billion in 1980.[13]

Construction and maintenance of facilities.   Various types of physical facilities built and maintained by the government are of value to private business. To the extent that the users or beneficiaries of these facilities do not pay their cost, they can be said to be subsidized by the government. The transportation industries in particular have been served by this form of assistance. Shipping on inland waters has benefited from the billions of dollars that national, state, and local governments have spent on the construction of canals, the improvement of harbors, the dredging of rivers, and the construction of shipping terminals, locks, and lighthouses.[14] (User charge legislation covering part of the cost of these facilities was enacted by Congress after much struggle in 1978.) Commercial aviation has benefited from the public construction of airports. Although airlines are assessed operating costs, the capital costs of airports are met by taxpayers. The national government also spends several hundred million dollars a year on traffic control equipment, instrument landing systems, radio beams, and weather-reporting services—which are largely free of cost to the airlines. Public construction of roads and highways has greatly contributed to the growth of the motor carrier industry (although truckers claim their taxes are so high that no net subsidy is involved).

Technical and information services.   The primary purpose of the Department of Commerce is promotion of American business interests at home and abroad. One of the three major "clientele" departments (the other two are Labor and Agriculture), the Commerce Department is largely a service agency for business, and does little in the way of business regulation. Within the department, the Office of Industrial Economics and the Bureau of Foreign Trade provide information on domestic and foreign business activities and opportunities. The Bureau of the Census, through its decennial census and special agricultural and business censuses, provides businesspeople with data on economic and agricultural activity, income, employment, housing, business trends, and other matters. The National Weather Service issues weather forecasts, which are of importance to shipping, aviation, and other businesses as well as to agriculture. The National Bureau of Standards engages in physical research, conducts tests of materials and products, and develops commercial and industrial product standards. And the list goes on.

Outside the Department of Commerce, numerous other government agencies provide informational and technical services for business. Economic trends and forecasts are reported in the *Federal Reserve Bulletin* and the *Monthly Labor Review,* put out by the Federal Reserve Board and the Department of Labor, respectively. The Bureau of Mines, the Forest Service, and the Fish and Wildlife Service carry out research and informational activities, including development of new products and resource uses, of benefit to the mining, lumbering, and fishing industries. Generally, these and other technical and information services help businesspeople make informed decisions and plan their operations in a more rational manner.

The Persistence of Promotional Programs

Whether the benefits of promotional programs are great or small, few groups willingly agree to their termination, even when the conditions that gave rise to those programs have disappeared. Industries that benefit from protective tariffs continue to want them long after they have passed the stage of infancy. The case for protection is now stated in terms of the need to offset the low labor costs of foreign producers and maintain employment or of their relationship to the nation's defense needs. As prevailing conceptions of the proper objectives of public policy change, the justifications for particular programs will be altered to fit them.

Thus, promotional programs clearly tend to persist once established. As time passes and new programs are added in response to new or expanded demands, the programs proliferate and their costs increase. A government study has estimated the cost of all subsidy programs, for businesses and other groups and individuals, as $95 billion in 1975.[15] A third to half of this cost could fairly be assigned to the business community. The subsidy figure does not include, moreover, the costs of other programs, such as protective tariffs and import quotas. What these programs cost consumers can be translated into benefits for businesses.

ANTITRUST POLICY

Maintaining Competition

The maintenance of competition by preventing private restrictions on competition and the development of monopoly is a cardinal feature of public policy in the United States. But public policy is concerned with more than maintaining competition as such. A closely related policy goal is the prevention of unfair or unethical competitive practices. What is desired is "fair competition, competition that fights fair."[16] These policies can be collectively designated as antitrust policy.

Why is maintaining competition a major goal of public policy? What advantages or benefits does it confer? One way to answer these questions is in terms of the ideology of competition. (The term *ideology* is used here to indicate that some of the following statements lack solid empirical verification.) Competition, it is said, leads to the efficient allocation of resources. In a competitive economy, the production of goods is more responsive to consumer desires than it is under monopoly conditions. Further, competition operates to keep prices reasonable and quality high as producers compete for the consumer's favor; in addition, the consumer has greater choice among types and qualities of goods and services. For producers, competition means freedom of entry into lines of production that offer greater profits or other advantages. Those who sell their labor or services benefit from competition by having greater freedom of choice in the selection of occupations and employers. Competition stimulates economic growth by providing businesspeople with an incentive to adopt more efficient modes of production and to develop new or improved products. Politically, competition is identified with the diffusion of economic power, and consequently political power, throughout the society. A major line of thought holds that the best social setting for democracy is one in which the electorate consists of people relatively similar in economic position, wealth, and power. Finally, competition is alleged to foster such "desirable" personal traits as independence, initiative, and self-reliance.

Taken at face value, the ideology depicted here is highly congruent with many of the basic values and beliefs of the American political culture. Clearly, competition appears to be instrumental in the attainment of such values as equality of opportunity, freedom, democracy, individualism, and efficiency. It accords with beliefs in the desirability of private property, private enterprise, and economic growth. Competition is thus regarded as one of the basic rules of the game of American society. The burden of proof tends to rest with those who would deviate from it and not with its supporters.

But there is a lack of agreement, sometimes sharp conflict, on what constitutes competition or monopoly. Under what conditions is a situation competitive or monopolistic? We can define *competition* as a situation in which many buyers and sellers are engaged in rivalry in the sale and purchase of goods and services, and in which prices are determined by the interaction of supply and demand. But what number of buyers or sellers comprises "many"? And what kind of "rivalry" constitutes competition—rivalry in prices, product, design, advertising, supplementary services, or what? Economists have developed a concept of "workable competition" as a goal for public policy: "Workable competition is considered to require, principally, a fairly large number of buyers and sellers, no one of whom occupies a large share of the market, the absence of collusion among either group, and the possibility of market entry by new firms."[17] A lawyer, however, might define as competitive those situations in which the actions of competitors are not restrained in ways defined as illegal. What might be considered competitive in this sense would not necessarily be so regarded if "workable competition" were used as a standard of judgment.

Nor is there agreement about the meaning of *monopoly*. In one sense, monopoly means the control of an industry by a single firm. Such situations, however, are rare; more common are those designated by the term *oligopoly*—domination of a market by a few firms with control over prices or production. The automobile industry is an example. A policy definition of monopoly, as "the power to raise prices or exclude competitors if it is desired to do so," seems applicable to many oligopolistic situations. In other definitions monopoly is equated with "bigness" in business. That notion, however, produces much confusion and will not be discussed here.

The lack of agreed-upon definitions opens the way for conflicting groups or persons to employ definitions of competition and monopoly favorable to their interests when urging or opposing the need for government action to maintain competition. Thus, one group may call a particular situation competitive because no competitors are illegally restrained (a lawyer's definition), whereas another group might call the same situation noncompetitive because the market is dominated by a few firms with control over prices. Whichever definition and viewpoint decision makers accept, their decision will favor some interests over others. As an alternative possibility, the lack of clear standards (definitions) to guide decision making may cause delay, indecisiveness, or inaction by decision makers. If, as some assert, antitrust policy has not "lived up to its promise," its shortcomings may stem largely from the lack of agreement over which conditions are to be maintained as competitive and which are to be prevented as monopolistic. This lack of agreement is produced, in turn, by the conflict of group interests—small business versus big business, suppliers versus buyers—in our society. Conflict over material interests may be obscured by its transformation into symbolic conflict over the choice and meaning of definitions.

In the following discussion the term *competition* will be used to mean something akin to "workable competition," and the term *monopoly* to indicate power to raise prices or exclude competitors and, generally, any device to eliminate competition. This does not resolve the problem of definitions, but it does permit the discussion to proceed.

The Development of "Trusts"

With the expansion of industrialism in the latter part of the nineteenth century, control of many sectors of the economy came to be concentrated in a limited number of large concerns. Competition among these large firms, as well as between them and their smaller rivals, was often cutthroat and predatory. Moreover, competitive pressures were intensified by the development of nationwide markets that threw more businesses into direct competition with one another. Concerns with large investments were often compelled to slash prices, sometimes below total costs, in their quest for sales and at least a partial return on their investment. Under these and similar conditions, competition seemed to threaten mutual destruction. Businesspeople began to seek ways to lessen competitive pressures, and they found many. Monopolistic agreements to fix prices, to limit production, to allocate markets, and to share profits were entered into. Through purchase, merger, and other means, previously independent and competing companies were welded together to form huge combinations. These combinations—or "trusts,"[18] as they were popularly called—dominated many industries: sugar, meat packing, steel, tobacco, petroleum refining, whisky, matches, fruit preserving, lead, coal, gunpowder, and linseed oil, to cite some prominent examples.

The use of monopolistic agreements and combinations enabled business groups to become somewhat immune from control by competitive forces and the "unseen hand" envisaged by the classical economist Adam Smith. Some business groups benefited, but many others felt disadvantaged by the effects of these economic changes. Farmers complained of having to pay high railway rates, interest rates, and prices for the products they purchased while receiving low prices for the commodities they sold. Independent and small businesspeople were hard put to survive, or were driven out of business by what many considered to be vicious or antisocial practices on the part of large firms and combinations. The sellers of raw materials were at a disadvantage when dealing with combinations able to dominate the market and manipulate prices. Workers had to contend with large companies that controlled (or nearly controlled) particular labor markets. Many people feared that "big business" was destroying economic opportunity, competition, and the independence of the common man. The political power emanating from the trusts' control of economic resources was seen as a threat to "traditional American democracy."

The development of big business and the resort to monopolistic agreements and combinations thus altered or disrupted existing relationships among various economic groups and challenged existing political and economic beliefs and aspirations. The new economic order brought with it new group relationships and new "rules of the game," which many groups viewed as inadequate, undesirable, or unacceptable. Because "a major function of politics is the mediation of relations among groups of people,"[19] it seems only natural that farmers, owners of small businesses, workers, reformist elements, and others who felt in some way aggrieved or threatened by the new economic conditions should call for government control of big business and the trusts. They demanded laws and policies that, from the perspective of their economic and ideological interests, would be more satisfactorily geared to the changed economic order. In response to their demands and pressures, some of the states enacted antimonopoly laws in the late 1880s. But these state laws, and the common law applied by state courts, proved inadequate to prevent the abuses complained of, in part because of the interstate character of the operations of many large businesses and combinations.

The Sherman Antitrust Act

National action on the matter of monopoly and competition came in 1890, in the form of the Sherman Antitrust Act. Although there is conjecture about the motives of Congress in passing the act, there appeared to be much support among aggrieved economic groups and the public for national action to control monopolistic "abuses" and to "bust the trusts."[20] One crude indicator is the fact that by 1890 all of the political parties considered it expedient (at the least) to have antitrust planks in their platforms.

Provisions and enforcement.   The Sherman Act, which was passed by Congress without intensive deliberation or committee consideration, has as its broad policy goal the maintenance of competition.[21] The statute is a short, simple, general piece of legislation. The substance of its policy is embodied in the first two sections:

Section 1. Every contract, combination in the form of trust or otherwise, or conspiracy, in restraint of trade or commerce among the several states, or with foreign nations, is hereby declared to be illegal. Every person who shall make any such contract, or engage in any such combination or conspiracy, shall be deemed guilty of a misdemeanor.

Section 2. Every person who shall monopolize, or attempt to monopolize, or combine or conspire with any other person or persons to monopolize any part of the trade or commerce among the several states, or with foreign nations, shall be deemed guilty of a misdemeanor.

Taken at its word, Section 1 prohibits every formal arrangement between two or more persons or firms designed to limit independent economic action. This section is concerned with market conduct, with the activity of persons in the market. Section 2 is directed at market structures involving situations of monopoly. (Market structure involves the number of companies in a given market, the share controlled by each, etc.) Or so it would seem. However, because of its briefness and generality, the meaning of the Sherman Act is vague. No definitions are provided for such terms as *restraint of trade, combination . . . or otherwise, monopolize,* and *monopoly.*

Primary responsibility for the enforcement of the Sherman Act now rests with the Antitrust Division of the Department of Justice. Techniques available to the Antitrust Division include civil and criminal proceedings in the federal courts and the consent decree, which is an informal procedure. Criminal proceedings are punitive in nature and if successful can result in the imposition of fines and jail sentences on violators, up to a maximum of $1,000,000 for corporations and $100,000 for individuals and five years' imprisonment, on the basis of legislation enacted in 1974. Historically, jail sentences were largely symbolic because they were rarely imposed. In the last few years, however, jail sentences have been sought by the Antitrust Division and levied by the courts in a growing number of cases involving "cartel behavior." (This includes such actions as price fixing, bid rigging, and market allocation.)

An antitrust case usually arises out of complaints from citizens, businesspeople, government agencies, or even reports in the business press (of proposed mergers, for instance). An investigation is then conducted by lawyers in the lower levels of the Antitrust Division. Most investigations never go beyond preliminary probings, usually because there is not sufficient evidence to support a case. But in some instances, a draft complaint alleging violations is drawn up, supporting materials are prepared, and consultations are held among division personnel. If a recommendation for action is approved by the assistant attorney general in charge of the Antitrust Division, a case is filed in a federal district court for trial or settlement. At this point, the courts become the arena for action. District court decisions can be appealed to the federal courts of appeals and, in some instances, to the Supreme

Court. In all, several years may lapse between the initiation and conclusion of an important antitrust case. (The enforcement process is depicted in figure 9–1.)

Criminal suits are often used in the case of price fixing, predatory practices, and other flagrant violations. Whatever their deterrent value, criminal penalties do little to correct noncompetitive situations. More effective for this purpose are civil proceedings, which are remedial in character. A successful civil suit results in a court injunction or a decree. An *injunction* orders the defendants not to take some illegal action they had planned or to discontinue illegal activities engaged in in the past. Future violation of an injunction could involve punishment for contempt of court; but, when issued, it is simply an order to go forth and sin no more. A *decree* is more positive in form, requiring that some action be taken—for instance, the abolition of a trade association, the sale of illegally acquired stock, the separation of the units of a combination, or the breakup of a business unit into several parts. Decrees of this nature were used in 1911 to split both the Standard Oil and American Tobacco combinations into several parts. The courts, however, are reluctant to issue orders breaking up corporations or combinations, apparently because of "judicial reluctance to disturb rights such as those of stockholders, other investors, and workers in the interest of promoting nebulous public goals."[22] Old-fashioned trust-busting has been rare in recent decades.

Most civil antitrust proceedings are settled through the use of consent decrees. Negotiated by the Antitrust Division and the offending party before the completion of formal proceedings, or sometimes even before the start of those proceedings, consent decrees are the outcome of bilateral bargaining and compromise. Differences between the two parties are narrowed as proposals are advanced and counterproposals made, until a mutually acceptable agreement is reached. The consent decree, then, is an agreement concerning the particular actions the offending party will take or cease doing. For example, in 1958 the United Fruit Company, which had been accused of monopolizing the banana trade with Latin America, and the Antitrust Division negotiated a consent decree whereby the company agreed to create, out of its assets and by 1970, a competition capable of handling 35 percent of the banana import business. This was done, and in 1971 the new company was bought by Del Monte, the nation's largest producer of canned fruits and vegetables. When accepted by a federal district court, and they usually have been without question, consent decrees have the same legal standing as any other court decree.

Consent decrees have become an important and widely used means of settling antitrust cases because of the possible advantages each side—government and defendants—may gain from their use. Advantages gained by defendants include avoidance of the high cost of legal defense, which is especially important to small businesses, and the adverse publicity that may flow from litigation. Also, consent decrees cannot be used as evidence against them in private antitrust suits (discussed below). The consent decree procedure is of advantage to the Antitrust Division because it is less time consuming and expensive than litigation and thus permits the division to make wider use of its personnel and financial resources, which are

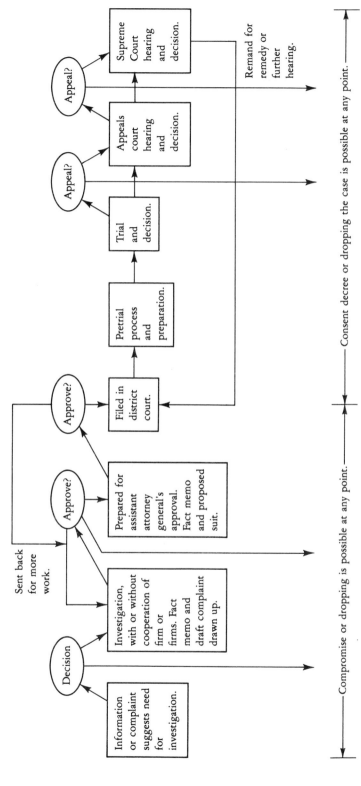

FIGURE 9-1 The process of antitrust decisions and litigation. (*Source: William C. Shepard and Clair Wilcox, Public Policies toward Business. Homewood, Ill.: Irwin, 1979, p. 103.*)

271

limited. This, in turn, may enable the division to bring and settle more cases and thereby build a more impressive enforcement record for itself. The consent procedure is also more flexible and permits decrees to be shaped to the peculiarities of particular industries; and it may enable the division to secure broader reforms than would be required by a court—although in its eagerness to settle cases, the division sometimes may accept less than a court would. Indeed, the division has been frequently criticized for doing just that, which would constitute another advantage of the procedure for defendants.

Until 1974, the negotiation of consent decrees was a closed affair, limited to the Antitrust Division and the offending party. Legislation enacted in that year requires publication of a proposed decree sixty days before its effective date and gives interested third parties an opportunity to make their views known. Moreover, the Antitrust Division must provide a justification for the proposed decree. A judge, before accepting a proposed decree, must make a finding that it is in the public interest. Whether these procedural requirements produce stronger decrees cannot readily be determined. They do, at the least, help open this segment of the governmental process to public scrutiny.

The Sherman Act also authorized private suits for triple damages by persons injured by violators of the law. The possible award of triple damages was intended to encourage private suits (thereby augmenting public enforcement activities) and to punish violators. Fewer then 200 private suits were started during the first fifty years of the Sherman Act, although the number has greatly increased in recent years. For several reasons, however, private plaintiffs have won redress in less than one-third of the cases filed.[23] First of all, private plaintiffs often lack the resources to secure evidence and establish proof of violations. Moreover, successful government proceedings usually end in a consent decree or, for criminal cases, a plea of nolo contendere, which involves no admission or finding of guilt and therefore cannot be used in support of private suits. Finally, lower federal court judges are often unsympathetic toward private suits. "The extraordinary remedy of triple damages," stated the judge in one case, "requires the closest scrutiny of the transaction . . . and . . . should be allowed only in the rarest of cases."[24]

An illustrative chain of events was triggered by the conviction of twenty-nine electrical equipment companies in 1960 for engaging in price fixing and market rigging during the preceding eight years. Over two thousand private triple-damage suits were filed against the companies by private utility companies and municipal agencies. By the summer of 1965, most of those private suits had been settled, largely by out-of-court negotiations. An Associated Press Poll revealed that the final settlement costs would total $400 million, most of which would be paid for by four companies (General Electric, Westinghouse, Allis-Chalmers, and McGraw-Edison). However, the financial and punitive impact of the settlements was greatly reduced by an Internal Revenue Service ruling that the settlement costs were tax deductible as "ordinary and necessary" business expenses. One government official said that the ruling may have resulted from concern about the ability of the less prosperous companies to survive the settlement payments. "General Electric can survive a blow like this but what about the smaller companies?" he stated. "Do you want to clobber an antitrust violator or do you want to clobber him and then stomp on him?" The official's remarks illustrate a continuing problem in antitrust activity: How severe should the sanctions be that are imposed on violators? Are factors other than punishment to be considered in shaping penalties and remedies?

Court interpretations.   In this section a few of the major aspects and developments in judicial interpretation of the Sherman Act will be outlined. Because of its generality, the Sherman Act permits different interpretations. The meaning given to the act has shifted from one time to another, Supreme Court professions of consistency in interpretation notwithstanding, as changes have occurred in judicial attitudes, executive enforcement activity, economic circumstances, and interest group configurations and conflicts.

Let us first look at the scope of the Sherman Act—the range of economic enterprises to which it has been held to apply. The first Sherman Act case to reach the Supreme Court was *U.S. v. E. C. Knight Company* in 1895.[25] Involved was the American Sugar Refining Company (the "sugar trust"), which controlled 98 percent of the country's sugar-refining industry. In its suit the government sought to compel the company to dispose of some of its recently acquired firms. The Court agreed that the company had a monopoly on sugar refining but went on to state that the Sherman Act, as an exercise of Congress's power to regulate commerce, applied only to commerce and not to manufacturing. The company had a monopoly in manufacturing but was beyond regulation by the national government because control of manufacturing was left to the states by the Constitution. Under this restrictive interpretation—an interpretation based on a narrow view of the commerce power—the Sherman Act applied mainly, if not exclusively, to monopolies in transportation.

A few years after the *Knight* case, however, the Sherman Act was held to apply to manufacturing activities that had a "direct effect" on interstate commerce. Since then, the scope of the commerce power has been greatly broadened, and, consequently, so has that of the act. The law has been applied to such diverse groups as railroads; manufacturing companies; trade associations; the American Medical Association; the Associated Press; newspaper publishers; insurance companies; realtors; the legitimate theater; motion picture companies; professional boxing, wrestling, and football; and the legal, engineering, and accounting professions. Even groups that have been exempted from the act by Congress—labor unions, agricultural cooperatives, and export trade associations—have been prosecuted under the act when they joined with other groups to restrain trade. As it now stands, any group or organization whose activities can be shown to have an "actual or threatened substantial effect" on interstate commerce can be prosecuted.

Although the words of the Sherman Act prohibit *every* contract, combination, or conspiracy in restraint of trade, conflict soon developed over the meaning of the phrase. Did it prohibit all restraints of trade or only all *unreasonable* restraints of trade? Those who favored strong government action to maintain competition and prevent monopoly tended to take the former position; business groups and others favoring broader scope for private action were inclined toward the latter view. In the *Trans-Missouri Freight Association* case, which involved a railroad rate-fixing agreement, the Supreme Court held that the act prohibited *every* restraint of trade, whether reasonable or unreasonable.[26]

In 1911, in the *Standard Oil* case, however, the Court reversed its position.[27] Standard, which controlled about 91 percent of the oil-refining industry, was convicted of violating Sections 1 and 2 of the Sherman Act. In his opinion for the Court, Chief Justice Edward D. White held that the act prohibited only *unreasonable* restraints of trade. Standard was guilty of violating the act, not merely because it had restrained trade, but because it had done so unreasonably. The opinion emphasized the vicious and predatory practices used by Standard to eliminate competitors. Thus, the Sherman Act was judicially amended to include the "rule of reason," something that Congress a few years earlier had refused to do.

During the next three decades, the Court used the rule of reason to develop differential applications of the law to close and loose combinations. The rule of reason was used in deciding the legality of close combinations (a number of previously independent business units integrated by common ownership and control). If a company, however large, had not achieved its size and market position by the use of unreasonable methods, it was held not to violate the law. This application of the Sherman Act can be illustrated by the famous *U.S. Steel* case in 1920.[28] When created in 1901, U.S. Steel controlled 60 percent of the steel capacity in the United States; in 1920 it still controlled 50 percent. Although U.S. Steel seemed to represent the very type of large combination against which the Sherman Act was directed, the Court held that the company had not broken the law. It had not coerced its competitors or, since 1911, conspired to fix prices. The contention that the company was so large as to constitute an illegal monopoly was rejected on the ground that "the law does not make mere size an offense. It . . . requires overt acts and trusts to its prohibition of them and its power to repress or punish them. It does not compel competition nor require all that is possible." Thus, the steel company, although big, had not acted unreasonably, and therefore was not bad. To use Theodore Roosevelt's terminology, the Court had drawn the line against "misconduct, not wealth," and had found the company to be a "good trust." In the light of the rule of reason, only "monopolizing," and not "monopoly," was an offense. (If a monopoly position were "thrust" on a company through no action of its own, it would have a monopoly, but it would not have "monopolized"; that is, it would not have acted to control the market.) As a consequence of this interpretation, Section 2 of the Sherman Act was largely a dead letter until the 1940s.

Although the law was applied with leniency in close-combination cases, its application was much more severe to loose combinations (agreements or arrangements among independent companies for the purpose of eliminating competition). Agreements among competitors to fix prices, divide markets, or limit production were held to be per se violations of Section 1 of the act. The rule of reason was not used, and no effort was made to determine whether the objectives or results of such agreements were reasonable or unreasonable. The mere existence of an agreement constituted a violation of the law. As the Supreme Court stated in a price-fixing case: "It does not follow that agreements to fix or restrain prices are reasonable restraints and therefore permitted by the statute, merely because the prices themselves are reasonable. . . . The aim and result of every price-fixing agreement, if effective, is the elimination of one form of competition."[29]

Only when a loose combination took the form of a trade association did the Court use the rule of reason in applying the Sherman Act to such combinations. Trade associations perform a variety of useful functions—research, industry promotion, cost studies, commercial arbitration—that may improve industry performance. Some, however, may engage in activities, such as price fixing and reporting schemes, that restrict competition. In passing on the legality of trade association activities, the Court attempted to balance the interests opposing restrictions on competition against those in favor of improved industry performance. Only those activities that unreasonably restrained competition, such as efforts to eliminate price competition, were banned.

A double standard thus existed in the application of the Sherman Act because of the courts' use of the rule of reason. The differential application of the law to close and loose combinations can be accounted for in terms of a "law-economic conflict."

> The antithesis of the legal conception of monopoly is *free* competition, understood to be a situation in which the freedom of any individual or firm to engage in legitimate economic activity is not restrained by the state, by agreements between competitors, or by the predatory practices of a rival. But free competition thus understood is quite compatible with the presence of monopoly elements in the *economic* sense of the word *monopoly*. For the antithesis of the economic conception of monopoly is not *free* but *pure* competition, understood to be a situation in which no seller or buyer has any control over the price of his product. Restriction of competition is the legal content of monopoly; control of the market is its economic substance. And these realities are by no means equivalent.[30]

Judges, because of their legal training and familiarity with the legal conceptions of competition and monopoly, accepted the legal attitude. They tended to regard the intent of the Sherman Act as prohibition of restrictions on competitors and, through use of the rule of reason, so interpreted and applied it. The legal attitude was undoubtedly reinforced by the nature of judicial antitrust proceedings. It was much easier for judges to examine and weigh evidence concerning collusive or predatory practices than it was to devise standards for measuring corporate (or monopolistic) power over output or prices. Further, although "competitors aggrieved by predatory practices" could bring cases into court, an abstraction such as competition could not. Consequently, the courts were inclined to concern themselves with protecting private interests against predatory practices rather than with limiting monopolistic power in the "public interest."[31] Also, the general conservative orientation of most judges, including a majority of the Supreme Court justices, made them reluctant to interfere with private property interests. Their use of the rule of reason was in harmony with this reluctance.

In the late 1930s, however, following two decades of relative inactivity, antitrust enforcement activities were revitalized. Strong administration support for antitrust enforcement resulted in larger congressional appropriations for the division. The courts, in turn, were persuaded to provide broader, more effective interpretations of the Sherman Act. Since the late 1930s, the act's prohibitions against collusive and predatory practices have been strengthened. Moreover, the courts' position concerning the rule of reason and close combinations has shifted.

A major interpretive change began with the decision of a federal circuit court, acting as the highest appellate court, in 1945 in the *Alcoa* case.[32] The government charged Alcoa with monopolizing the production of virgin aluminum in violation of Section 2 of the Sherman Act, and the court agreed. The appeals judge, Learned Hand, held that monopolization is illegal per se and that the Sherman Act makes no distinction between "good trusts" and "bad trusts." Alcoa controlled 90 percent of the production of virgin aluminum, and this, said Judge Hand, "is enough to constitute monopoly; it is doubtful whether sixty or sixty-four percent [is] enough; and certainly thirty percent is not." But what about the fact that the act prohibits monopolization and not monopoly as such? Alcoa, stated Hand, had not had monopoly "thrust" upon it. It had worked effectively to exclude would-be competitors by acting "progressively to embrace each new opportunity as it opened, and to face each newcomer with new capacity already geared into a great organization, having the advantage of experience, trade connections, and the elite of personnel." A monopoly position could thus be gained and held by means other than predatory practices and the destruction of competitors. In short, Alcoa had violated the law because of its excessive size, as measured by its share of the market. Since no use was made of the rule of reason in determining the violation, the distinction between close and loose combinations was apparently eliminated.

The Supreme Court endorsed the *Alcoa* decision in 1946 in the second *American Tobacco Company* case.[33] In a criminal proceeding, the three leading cigarette manufacturers (American, Reynolds, and Liggett and Myers) were found guilty of monopolization. The evidence presented by the government did not show open collusion, but demonstrated through economic and statistical evidence that the three companies had apparently pursued common pricing and purchasing policies in an effort to squeeze out some of their smaller competitors. They had not succeeded, and their share of the market had declined from over 90 percent in 1931 to 68 percent in 1938. Affirming the condemnation of monopoly power per se in the *Alcoa* case, the Court held that actual exclusion was not necessary to sustain the charge of monopolization. "The material consideration in determining whether a monopoly exists is not that prices are raised and competitors excluded, but that power exists to raise prices or exclude competitors when it is desired to do so."

The decisions in *Alcoa* and *American Tobacco* produced a new interpretation. By condemning "the power to abuse rather than the abuse of power,"[34] they largely eliminated the rule of reason as a standard for determining the legality of monopoly and monopoly power.

But problems do remain. It still must be determined in particular cases how much market power a company must have before its possession becomes illegal as monopoly power. Is it control of 90 percent of the market, or 68 percent, or what? No precise answer has been provided. A second problem relates to defining the market allegedly being monopolized. Depending on whether the relevant market is narrowly or broadly defined, a company may or may not be guilty of monopolization. For example, in a 1956 case DuPont was accused of monopolizing the cellophane market: The company produced over 80 percent of the supply; its licensee, the remainder.[35] The Supreme Court defined the relevant market to include all flexible wrapping materials—glassine, waxed paper, and aluminum foil, as well as cellophane. Because DuPont produced only 18 percent of all flexible wrapping materials, it was exonerated on the monopolization charge. Had the market been narrowly defined to include only cellophane, the decision could well have gone against the firm. One year later, in another case, DuPont's 23 percent stock interest in General Motors was held to violate Section 7 of the Clayton Act (see below) by causing a substantial lessening of competition in the market for automotive fabrics and finishes.[36] Had the relevant market been defined as *industrial* fabrics and finishes, the portion accounted for by GM's purchases would have been only a few percentage points, and the decision would likely have been in favor of DuPont. In short, whether a company has monopoly power depends significantly on the standards of measurement used, and the selection of those standards is a matter for judicial determination in particular cases.

To summarize, judicial interpretation has made the meaning of the Sherman Act more specific and, in recent decades, has made it a potentially more effective legal tool for maintaining a competitive economy. The double standard once employed in the interpretation of the law has largely disappeared, and the rule of reason no longer provides large close combinations with a shield against prosecution. How the law is enforced, however, can still make a substantial difference, as will now be seen.

The proponents of vigorous antitrust policy were encouraged when the government filed a monopolization case against International Business Machines in January 1969. IBM, a huge multinational corporation, was charged with using a variety of unfair, anticompetitive practices to monopolize the computer industry. Then, in 1974, the Antitrust Division brought suit to break up American Telephone and Telegraph by separating ownership of AT&T's local telephone companies, its long-lines department, and its equipment-making subsidiary, Western Electric. It was contended, for example, that AT&T's operating subsidiaries were required to buy equipment from Western Electric even though other companies offered better equipment at lower prices. During this time, the Federal Trade Commission also launched several major antimonopoly cases (see page 284).

The IBM case finally came to trial in May 1975. The trial dragged on and on, until finally, in January 1983, the Antitrust Division announced it was dropping the case. In the view of the Reagan administration's antitrust officials, IBM had acquired its strong market position by legal means. William Baxter, the assistant attorney general in charge of the Antitrust Division, said that the suit was "without merit" and that the government's contentions were "flimsy." The IBM case, he added, may have been an example of previous antitrust enforcers "trying to push the boundaries of antitrust prosecution beyond what the law provides."[37]

The AT&T case was also resolved in 1982, through negotiation of a consent decree that provided for a major restructuring of the company. AT&T acceded to the government's chief demand that it divest itself of its twenty-two Bell System operating companies.[38] In return, AT&T got to keep Western Electric, Bell Laboratory, and its long-lines long-distance network. Intrastate long-distance service and the Yellow Pages directories were given to the Bell companies. (It was subsequently decided that the twenty-two Bell companies would be grouped under seven regional holding companies.) Importantly, AT&T was given free rein to move into the "promised land" of high technology—computer and information-processing services. Perhaps the most important antitrust case ever settled, it will be years before the consequences of the AT&T decree can be fully assessed.

No major antitrust cases have been filed since 1974. Nor do any appear likely to be filed so long as the Reagan administration, an administration very tolerant of most business behavior, is in office. However, the Reagan administration, like the Carter administration, has brought scores of cases against highway construction companies for rigging bids on contracts.

Other Antitrust Legislation

Dissatisfaction with the enforcement and accomplishments of the Sherman Act during its first two decades of existence produced a variety of pressures and demands for additional legislation. Critics of the Supreme Court's inclusion of the rule of reason in the Sherman Act wanted legislation to reduce the discretion that this ruling conferred on the courts. Small-business interests wanted additional protection against their larger competitors. Many businesspeople wanted the law to be more specific, so that they could know with greater certainty whether their actions were legal; others wanted elimination of practices that disrupted stable trade relationships. Organized labor and some wholesale and retail groups wanted exemption from the Sherman Act. Generally, those supporting the policy of maintaining competition wanted legislation against various predatory competitive practices, in order to prevent the development of monopolies.

By 1914, two general patterns of thought concerning additional antitrust legislation had crystallized out of this welter of interests and demands. Some contended that specific legislation that would enumerate and prohibit a list of unfair practices was needed, so as to make the law more definite and eliminate some of the uncertainty generated by the rule of reason and the general language of the Sherman Act. Others contended that specific legislation would not be effective because new unfair practices that were not prohibited would be developed. What was needed, in their view, was a general prohibition of unfair competition enforced by an administrative commission with authority to determine what was fair or unfair in particular cases. The first pattern of thought is reflected in the Clayton Act; the second, in the Federal Trade Commission Act. Both of these acts were passed in 1914.

The Clayton Act.   Four specific sets of practices are prohibited by the Clayton Act: price discrimination, exclusive dealing and tying contracts, intercorporate stockholding, and interlocking corporate directorates. The first three, however, are banned only if their effect "may be to substantially lessen competition or tend to create a monopoly." Enforcement of the act is entrusted jointly to the Antitrust Division and the Federal Trade Commission.

Section 2 of the act prohibits sellers from discriminating in prices among buyers unless that discrimination is based on "differences in grade, quality, or quantity," makes only "due allowance for differences in the cost of selling or transportation," or is done "in good faith to meet competition." This section was directed primarily at local price cutting by large companies to eliminate small competitors while maintaining their prices elsewhere. The Standard Oil Company and other trusts had often engaged in such predatory activity. Section 2 was rarely applied to local price cutting and was in general not effective, both because of exceptions in the law and because of unfavorable judicial interpretations. It was amended by the Robinson-Patman Act of 1936, which sought to strengthen its prohibitions.

Section 3 prohibits exclusive dealing and tying contracts, which are devices for excluding competitors from the market. Under an exclusive dealing arrangement, a seller agrees to give a buyer access to goods only if the buyer does not handle goods from any of the seller's competitors. Under a *tying contract,* a seller gives a buyer access to certain goods only if the buyer takes others as well. One tying contract declared illegal under this section was the International Salt Company's requirement that lessees of its salt-dispensing machines also purchase the salt they dispensed from International, thereby foreclosing this market to other sellers of salt.[39] Exclusive dealing and tying contracts, when challenged, usually have been held illegal where the concern using them has "dominant" or "substantial" control of the market.

Section 8 declares illegal interlocking directorates among banks with over $5 million in capital, or competing corporations with over $1 million, "where elimination of competition . . . would constitute a violation of any provision of the antitrust laws." This provision reflects, inter alia, concern over the possible development of a "combination of combinations," one of the spectres of the era. The antitrust agencies have shown little interest in enforcing this section, although recently some proceedings have been initiated under it. For example, Alcoa was charged by the FTC with having an illegal interlock with two other metal companies.

Section 7 forbids any corporation engaged in commerce to acquire stock in a competing company, or in two or more companies that are themselves competitors, where the effect "may be to substantially lessen competition or tend to create a monopoly in any line of commerce." This section, intended to combat corporate mergers, had little real significance until the 1950s. In 1926, the Supreme Court held that it prohibited only mergers through stock acquisitions, not mergers achieved by a corporation's purchasing the physical assets of a competitor, even if the acquisition (or merger) of physical assets was brought about through the use of illegally acquired voting stock, as long as action was completed before the government filed suit.[40] This created a large loophole, because competitors wanting to merge could easily and legally do so by transferring their physical assets.

Although the Federal Trade Commission and other antitrust supporters continually urged Congress to close this loophole, no action was taken until the adoption of the Celler Anti-Merger Act in 1950. That statute, which amends Section 7 of the Clayton Act, prohibits mergers by either stock or physical-assets acquisitions where the effect may substantially lessen competition or tend to create a monopoly "in any line of commerce in any section of the country." The Celler Anti-Merger Act, it should be noted, is future oriented, directed toward "probabilistic" behavior—toward what *may* happen, not what has actually happened or what will indeed happen. As one would guess, this has contributed to conflict over enforcement of the act.

The Supreme Court has acted to broaden the scope of Section 7 in cases coming before it. In the 1957 *DuPont–General Motors* case, the Court held that the Clayton Act bans combinations by vertical stock acquisition (when a manufacturer gains control of a supplier of raw materials) as well as horizontal merger (involving companies in the same stage of production).[41] DuPont was held to have illegally used its 23 percent stock ownership in General Motors, which it had acquired in 1919, to gain preference over its competitors in the sale of automotive fabrics and finishes to General Motors. DuPont was subsequently ordered to divest itself of its GM stock.

In 1963, the Supreme Court ruled that bank mergers could be proceeded against under the Clayton Act, even though the Bank Merger Act of 1960 gave the various federal banking agencies (Comptroller of the Currency, Federal Reserve Board, Federal Deposit Insurance Corporation) authority to control bank mergers, and even though those agencies might have approved bank mergers subsequently moved against by the Antitrust Division. Experience has revealed that the banking agencies are more sympathetic toward bank mergers than is the Antitrust Division, with its procompetitive orientation. Banking interests succeeded in getting Congress to pass the Bank Merger Act of 1966 to overcome, at least in part, the Court's action. But the Court's interpretation of the new legislation continues to leave the Antitrust Division ample scope to challenge bank mergers as anticompetitive.[42]

Three great merger movements have occurred in American history. The first took place between 1898 and 1903; the second, between 1923 and 1930. The third began in the middle 1950s and lasted through the 1960s. In 1968 alone, the Federal Trade Commission reported 4,003 mergers. Many of these were of the conglomerate variety, horizontal and vertical mergers having been somewhat discouraged by antitrust action. A *conglomerate merger* involves companies that are neither direct competitors nor related by supplier-producer ties. Conglomerate mergers occur when a company acquires a second concern to move into a new geographic market (market extension), a concern producing a related product (product extension), or a concern that has no apparent relationship to the acquirer (pure).

During the Kennedy-Johnson years, the antitrust agencies moved against a few conglomerate mergers (among them, the Procter & Gamble acquisition of Clorox). However, Antitrust Division officials generally took the position that the Celler Anti-Merger Act did not reach conglomerate mergers and that new legislation was necessary. Enter the Nixon administration in 1969. Nixon administration officials contended that the Celler Act could indeed be used against conglomerate mergers. The administration seems to have been motivated by the reasoning that it might get unwanted antitrust legislation from the Democratic-controlled Congress if it did not file and win some conglomerate merger cases. Five significant cases were filed, including three against International Telephone and Telegraph's acquisitions of the Hartford Fire Insurance Company, the Grinnell Corporation, and the Canteen Food Vending Corporation. All three cases were settled informally by consent decrees, which do not provide any authoritative interpretation of the law. The administrations in office since then have not been inclined to act against conglomerate mergers. Two huge conglomerate mergers that took place in 1981 and 1982—DuPont's acquisition of Conoco and U.S. Steel's acquisition of Marathon Oil—went unopposed by the Reagan administration.

In 1982, in order to reduce uncertainty about the kinds of corporate mergers it would allow, the Department of Justice published a new set of merger guidelines.[43] (They replaced a more rigorous set issued by the Johnson administration in 1968.) Especially concerned with horizontal mergers, the new guidelines feature a mathematical measure of market concentration known as the Herfingdahl Index. Once the market is defined for a horizontal merger, the index is calculated by squaring the market share percentages of each company in a market, and then summing the squares. For example, the Herfingdahl Index for a market with five firms having shares of 40 percent, 20 percent, 20 percent, 15 percent, and 5 percent, would be $40^2 + 20^2 + 20^2 + 15^2 + 5^2 = 1,600 + 400 + 400 + 225 + 25 = 2,650$. Squaring is intended to give greater weight to large market shares and better reflect their anticompetitive impact. The guidelines indicate that a merger is unlikely to be challenged in a market with a postmerger Herfingdahl Index of 1,000; that a merger would come under scrutiny if the index is in the 1,000–1,800 range, especially if it added more than 100 points to the index; and that it is likely to be challenged if the index is above 1,800, particularly if the merger adds more than 100 points to the index. Other factors would also be considered in evaluation mergers. The guidelines reflect a lessening of concern about vertical and conglomerate mergers.

On the same day the new merger guidelines were issued, the Justice Department announced it was taking action to block a merger of two drapery hardware producers. Newell Companies, the second largest producer of drapery hardware, in 1980 had sales of approximately $32 million and a market share of approximately 14.8 percent. It wanted to acquire Stanley Works, the sixth largest producer, which had sales of approximately $17 million and a market share of approximately 7.8 percent. The acquisition "increased the Herfingdahl Index for the industry from 2,368 to 2,600—increasing the concentration in an already highly concentrated industry."[44] A person may wonder why the department found this merger of two small companies objectionable while it found the huge DuPont–Conoco merger acceptable. (The two companies had combined sales of $31.9 billion in 1980.) The answer is that the department is not concerned about the aggregate size of a merger and the economic and political power that this may entail but with its impact on a particular market, even when that market is quite small in relation to the rest of the economy. "Bigness is not necessarily badness" is the view of the Reagan administration officials, and they have acted accordingly. Most mergers, however, involve small companies that have little competitive impact, however measured, and little consequence for the aggregation of economic and political power.

The Federal Trade Commission Act.   The 1914 Federal Trade Commission Act created an administrative commission, headed by a five-member board, with executive, rule-making, and adjudicatory functions. The commissioners are appointed by the president for seven-year terms, and no more than three of them can come from the same political party. They are subject to presidential removal from office only for "inefficiency, neglect of duties or malfeasance in office." The commission chair is designated by the president and serves at the president's discretion in that capacity. Section 5 of the act empowered the commission to prevent "unfair methods of competition in commerce" through the issuance, after formal complaint, notice, and hearing, of cease and desist orders to those found engaging in such practices. The commission was given jurisdiction jointly with the Department of Justice to enforce the Clayton Act. The FTC was also authorized to conduct studies or investigations and issue reports on business organizations and practices; to investigate alleged violations of the antitrust laws at the request of the president or Congress; to investigate the effectiveness of antitrust decrees when requested by the attorney general; and to assist the courts in formulating antitrust decrees when called upon to do so. The commission's investigational or information-gathering authority was partly a product of the belief, widely shared at the time, that "pitiless publicity" would prevent many antitrust violations.

Legislation enacted since 1914 has considerably enlarged the jurisdiction of the FTC. It shares responsibility with the Department of Justice for enforcing the various amendments to the Clayton Act, especially the Robinson-Patman Act and the Celler Anti-Merger Act. The Wheeler-Lea Act of 1938 amended Section 5 of the original FTC act to prohibit "unfair or deceptive acts or practices" in commerce as well as unfair methods of competition. Deceptive acts or practices include activities—false or misleading advertising, for example—that may deceive or injure consumers without necessarily harming competitors of those engaged in deception. The Wheeler-Lea Act was passed by Congress to overcome a judicial ruling that, under the original Section 5, competitive practices could be prohibited as unfair only if they hurt competitors, regardless of the harmful or deceptive effects they might have on consumers. The act gives the commission clear power to protect consumers, as well as to move against anticompetitive behavior.

The FTC also enforces a number of statutes that require honest, accurate labeling of fur, wool, and textile products. Although these statutes protect consumers, they were enacted primarily at the behest of producer groups concerned with promoting the sale of their products. The Wool Products Act of 1940, for example, was passed mainly at the insistence of sheep raisers and wool weavers who wanted to protect wool products (especially those made from virgin wool) from "unfair" competition by other fibers that, in the absence of accurate labels, might be passed off, or unwittingly purchased, as wool. More recently, the FTC has been given jurisdiction over the Fair Packaging and Labeling Act of 1966 and the Consumer Credit Protection Act of 1968.

In enforcing the laws under its jurisdiction, the FTC employs a number of formal and informal techniques. The commission's current emphasis is on securing voluntary compliance with policy. Methods used for this purpose include advisory opinions and trade regulation rules, both of which were adopted in 1963, and trade practices conferences. The commission gives advisory opinions to businesspeople seeking counsel about the legality of a proposed action—for instance, whether a proposed quantity discount would violate the Robinson-Patman Act. Advisory opinions are considered binding on the commission unless under changed economic circumstances their reconsideration would be "in the public interest." Trade regulation rules, issued after all interested parties have had an opportunity to be heard, express the judgment of the commission, based on its knowledge and experience, as to the substantive requirements of the laws it administers. A rule may cover all possible applications of a statutory provision and be nationwide in effect, or it may be limited to a particular area, industry, or product. One notable example is the rule issued by the commission in 1964, which required health warnings on cigarette packages and advertising. This rule touched off a major political controversy, and was rescinded following the enactment of congressional legislation. Congress took jurisdiction of warnings on cigarette packages and delayed FTC action on cigarette advertising until 1971. Under the trade practices conference procedure, which was first used in 1919, the commission meets with the members of an industry to draw up a code of fair trade practices. The code includes Group I rules, which condemn practices found illegal by the FTC and the courts, and Group II rules, directed against practices considered unfair by industry members, although the practices are not illegal. Generally, the procedures summarized in this paragraph are designed to guide businesses away from illegal actions and to encourage voluntary compliance by informing them of the meaning and requirements of the law.

The commission also uses several techniques in proceeding against those accused of violating the law. A complaint against an alleged offender may be dropped upon the receipt of a letter of assurance in which the offender states that the practice complained against has been discontinued. When a complaint issued by the FTC is contested, the case may be formally tried (adjudicated); if the action in question is found to violate the law, an order is issued directing the offender to "cease and desist." These orders, which become effective after sixty days unless appealed to a federal appeals court, are enforceable through judicial action. At any time during a formal proceeding, or even before it actually begins, a case may be settled by a consent order negotiated by the commission and the offender. Under the consent order, the offender agrees to stop the practices objected to without necessarily admitting their illegality. In line with its stress on voluntary compliance, the commission over the years has made extensive use of consent orders in settling cases.

The substantive work of the Federal Trade Commission falls into two categories: deceptive-practices cases and antimonopoly cases. Deceptive-practices cases involve actions that mislead or deceive consumers and that also unfairly divert trade from competitors. False advertising claims are a common form of deception. Antimonopoly cases involve restraints of trade coming under the FTC and Clayton Acts, as amended. These cases can involve price fixing, mergers, exclusion from markets, and discriminatory pricing.

In the early 1970s, the commission acted to give greater emphasis to its antimonopoly activities. It initiated several major cases, including one charging four large cereal companies with monopolizing the breakfast market, another alleging that eight major oil companies had conspired to monopolize the refinery industry, and yet another charging Xerox with monopolizing the photocopy machine industry. The first two cases were eventually dismissed; the Xerox case was terminated in 1975 by a consent order under which Xerox agreed to license its patents for reasonable fees, supply know-how to competitors, and sell as well as lease copying machines. Although criticized by some as ineffective, the order may have helped open the industry to new competitors.

These cases and others like them are costly, time consuming, and controversial. The FTC has not begun any new major cases since the mid-1970s. In fact, right after President Reagan took office, administration officials discussed whether the FTC should continue to have antimonopoly jurisdiction. With the appointment of conservative James C. Miller III as commission chairman, the issue became moot. Miller and his supporters on the commission, believing that more matters should be left to the operation of market forces, took steps to moderate commission action in both the consumer protection and antimonopoly areas, to make the agency less active than it had been during the 1970s.

One area in which Miller has acted to restore the jurisdiction and vigor of the FTC is professional services (e.g., medical and dental care, and legal services). It is his view that many of the markets for professional services "are not free, when professionals and their trade associations can join in cartel-like activities that drive up prices, inhibit competition, and stifle innovation."[45] In 1982, medical and other professional groups made a major effort to secure legislation exempting their organizations from the jurisdiction of the FTC.[46] Although the commission and its supporters were able to prevent the adoption of that legislation, controversy promises to continue.

The Politics of Enforcement

Here we deal with some of the conditions, traditions, arrangements, and pressures that affect the implementation of antitrust laws and, consequently, the substance of antitrust policy.

The role of the president.   A major factor in shaping antitrust enforcement has been the policy positions and attitudes of the various presidential administrations in office since 1890. The conservatively oriented Harrison, Cleveland, and McKinley administrations manifested little enthusiasm for the Sherman Act. They initiated a total of eighteen antitrust cases. During the Progressive era, there was comparatively vigorous antitrust enforcement by the Roosevelt, Taft, and Wilson administrations, in response to strong pressures for the control of monopoly and private economic power. Theodore Roosevelt, indeed, acquired a historical reputation (somewhat undeserved) as a trustbuster. After 1917, a period of lax enforcement lasting two decades set in: the Wilson administration and the nation were preoccupied with winning the Great War and "making the world safe for democracy." Then, during the 1920s and the return to "normalcy," the business-oriented Republican administrations were disinclined to disturb business—the dominant source of their political support—by active antitrust enforcement. Nor, in an era in which business values were predominant, did there appear much public support for antitrust activity. The early New Deal, using the National Industrial Recovery Act as a means of helping combat the depression, was more concerned with limiting competition (through "industry" codes of fair competition) than with promoting it. Since the late 1930s, however, with the exception of the war years, there has been more active antitrust enforcement by both Democratic and Republican administrations. Indeed, as measured by case activity, Republican administrations have been more active than Democratic administrations. One explanation for this seeming paradox is political: the Republicans are more active in order to counter the notion that they are "the party of business"; while the Democrats ease up somewhat in enforcement to offset their antibusiness image.

Political pressure and enforcement.   Antitrust enforcement is often shaped by current political pressures. In 1969, for example, the Justice Department filed three suits against ITT, charging that it had violated the Clayton Act (see page 281). The government lost the cases at the federal district court level, and Richard McLaren, then head of the Antitrust Division, was considering an appeal to the Supreme Court. ITT officials were distressed by this and communicated their feelings to the Nixon administration, complaining that McLaren was objecting to their mergers because of a "bigness is bad" viewpoint. White House officials responded that that was not Nixon administration policy. When the president heard about it, he joined in the attack on McLaren. On April 19, 1971, he telephoned Richard Kleindienst, deputy attorney general and McLaren's superior, and ordered the case dropped. As Nixon told Kleindienst in rather earthy language:

> I want something clearly understood, and if it is not understood, McLaren's ass is to be out within one hour. The ITT thing—stay the hell out of it. Is that clear? That's an order. . . .
>
> The order is to leave the goddamned thing alone. Now, I've said this, Dick, a number of times, and you fellows apparently don't get the message over there. I do not want McLaren to run around prosecuting people, raising hell about conglomerates, stirring things up at this point. Now you keep him the hell out of that. Is that clear?[47]

As a consequence of the president's phone call, the Antitrust Division did not file its planned appeal. A couple of days later, Nixon had cooled down and, responding to Attorney General Mitchell's warning that abandoning the appeal would be "political dynamite," permitted the appeal of the ITT cases to proceed. While the appeal was pending, the cases were settled informally in the summer of 1971 by consent decrees, and ITT was permitted to keep the profitable Hartford Fire Insurance Company. Shortly afterward, McLaren was appointed to a federal district judgeship. The decision to settle the cases informally and the terms of the settlement were roundly criticized.[48] McLaren, however, denied there was any pressure from administration officials during the settlement negotiations.

Budgetary influences.   The amount of funds made available by Congress to antitrust agencies, especially the Antitrust Division, also has a significant effect on enforcement activity. Until 1935, the annual appropriation for the Antitrust Division was less than $300,000, an amount sufficient to finance the prosecution of only a few cases a year. This led one observer to remark that, until the late 1930s, antitrust enforcement was "merely symbolic in nature. In any one year, from half a dozen to a dozen cases were selected for investigation and trial. . . . With all available resources committed . . . the prosecution of a few lawbreakers became in effect a guarantee of immunity to the rest."[49]

Since the late 1930s, the appropriations for the division have gradually increased, reaching a level of $10 million annually in the mid-1960s, then moving upward to $45 million for fiscal year 1984. Although the costs of handling cases have also risen, the larger appropriations have facilitated the initiation of an increasing number of cases. More than three times as many cases have been started since 1940 than during the preceding fifty years. Other things being equal, whether antitrust enforcement is lax or vigorous depends upon available funds.

Even with the larger appropriations of recent years, the Antitrust Division is still limited in the number of cases it can mount. A major case, like the monopolization proceeding against IBM, can cost the division a couple of million dollars or more a year. A really intensive enforcement program, then, would require substantially more funds to hire personnel and to finance investigations and litigation. But Congress seems unwilling to make additional funds available. Why? There are several reasons: the belief that antitrust violations are not as serious, or "morally wrong," as other law violations; ideological opposition to "excessive" government interference with private economic activity; uncertainty among both officials and citizens on the difference between monopoly and bigness, and on the amount of competition needed in the economy; and the lack of strong, consistent, organized group support for a strong enforcement program.

Selection biases.   Setting aside the matter of financial support, it appears that the Antitrust Division has been and still is somewhat haphazard in its selection of cases for legal action. There is a continuing tendency to choose cases largely on the basis of complaints received from competitors of, or buyers from, alleged offenders, or from members of Congress who represent or reflect the opinion of those interests. In short, most antitrust cases stem from the mail bag; relatively few originate from the division's own economic analyses and investigations. This haphazard selection procedure may mean that important violations are overlooked or not presented in the absence of specific outside complaints. To the extent that private complaints are relied on, private interests help shape the division's enforcement program and the impact of antitrust; and their actions may be motivated more by the desire to gain an advantage over their rivals or to "even up the score" than by an interest in maintaining a broadly competitive economy.

About two-thirds of the antitrust cases filed since 1890 have dealt with collusive practices (or restraints of trade) in violation of Section 1 of the Sherman Act, with particular emphasis on price-fixing agreements. Not only has antitrust enforcement focused on Section 1, but its application has centered on three broadly defined sectors of the economy: food processing and distribution, production and distribution of building materials, and the service trades.[50] About half of the antitrust cases since 1890 have involved these industrial groupings, although they are characterized by far lower economic concentration than metals production, chemicals, and electrical goods and machinery, areas that have been more lightly dealt with. Only a few monopolization (Section 2) cases have been started annually. Moreover, most of the monopolization cases have not been structural in nature—that is, cases seeking to break up existing monopoly power. If the double standard has disappeared from the interpretation of the Sherman Act, it certainly has not disappeared from the enforcement process.

Why do we find these trends or biases in the enforcement process? First, under present procedures, many antitrust cases originate out of private complaints. A large proportion of the complaints received by the Antitrust Division concern industrial groupings that deal mainly with many small customers. Second, these industrial groupings deal with the "necessities" of life (like food) or come into contact with large numbers of buyers (building materials). The focus of the Antitrust Division on these industries may be politically expedient insofar as it is seeking congressional and public support. And the Antitrust Division, like any government agency, needs that support if it is to survive and prosper. Third, companies in industries with many firms and low concentration may be more inclined to engage in formal agreements or collusion than companies in more concentrated industries, who can gain "monopoly" profits or shield themselves against economic risks without formal restraint of competition. Fourth, Section 2 monopolization cases are more costly—in terms of time, money, and personnel—to prosecute and more difficult to win than are cases involving collusion; the more obvious and easily provable violations tend to occur in low-concentration industries. It is reasonable to assume that in allocating its scarce resources of money and personnel, the Antitrust Division will be motivated, at least in part, by the desire to produce the best record possible—a winning one in terms of both total numbers and percentages of cases won. This will provide personal satisfaction for agency personnel as well perhaps as political support for the division. The House appropriations subcommittee that handles the Antitrust Division's budget request has shown considerable interest in the number of antitrust cases begun and won by the division, taking these as measures of its effectiveness. Fifth, antitrust lawyers prefer collusive-practices cases because they can be handled in a fairly short period of time. This enables them to build a good prosecutorial record, which enhances their opportunities for private employment. In actuality, there is considerable movement of attorneys from the agencies to private law firms, which prefer to hire those with the best records in winning cases.[51]

A point we should make here is that antitrust officials have discretion in the enforcement of the law. What they do or do not do is influenced by how they interpret the laws they enforce, their policy biases, and the like. A case in point involves the Robinson-Patman Act of 1936. Ostensibly intended to strengthen the Clayton Act's prohibition against price discrimination, it has had the effect of discouraging price competition and making prices "sticky." Critics contend the act was designed to protect competitors rather than competition; and, indeed, its enactment was part of a general effort during the 1930s to protect small businesses against their larger competitors, such as chain stores, discount houses.[52] The Antitrust Division and the Federal Trade Commission both have enforcement jurisdiction under the Robinson-Patman Act. In forty years, the Antitrust Division has never completed a proceeding based on the act. Agency officials offer as an explanation their lack of resources. A better explanation, however, probably is that the division, given its procompetitive orientation, finds enforcement of the Robinson-Patman Act distasteful and has chosen to neglect it. In contrast, the Federal Trade Commission, which has often depicted itself as a defender of small business, has completed several hundred Robinson-Patman cases. In the mid-1970s, however, the FTC almost entirely stopped bringing cases under the Robinson-Patman Act, an action that is in accord with the recommendations of various antitrust study commissions and is pleasing to the statute's critics. What these enforcement patterns do, in effect, is to administratively repeal the statute. However agreeable one might find this result, should agencies be permitted to so act? Is this a proper exercise of administrative discretion? What becomes of the principle of the rule of law?

Conflict among agencies.   The enforcement of antitrust policy is complicated and further opened to political struggle by the fact that jurisdiction under antitrust law is shared by some twenty agencies. Because the various agencies have different institutional and policy orientations, and because they respond to different interests and values, they can differ in their interpretation and application of the law. Whether lawyers for potential antitrust defendants seek to have their problems handled by the Antitrust Division or the Federal Trade Commission (the two major antitrust agencies) depends on which agency they believe will give their clients easier treatment. Bank mergers approved by the Comptroller of the Currency and the Federal Reserve Board, who have authority over these mergers under the banking laws, have later been successfully attacked in antitrust proceedings launched by the Antitrust Division. Although there has been conflict between the division and some of the regulatory commissions, the Federal Trade Commission–Antitrust Division relationship has usually been harmonious. They have developed coordinating procedures and traditional areas of jurisdiction. Thus, the steel industry "belongs" to the Antitrust Department, whereas the milk industry falls into the FTC's bailiwick.

The Antitrust Improvements Act, 1976.   Those who favor stronger antitrust action have frequently sought legislation to strengthen antitrust enforcement procedures. These efforts have met with considerable opposition from various business and conservative interests. But in 1976, following an intense legislative struggle, Congress adopted the Antitrust Improvements Act. The act contains three major elements: (1) an expansion of the power of the Antitrust Division to investigate potential violations; (2) a requirement that the FTC be given thirty days' notice of major mergers; and (3) authorization for state attorneys general to sue violators in federal court for triple damages on behalf of injured consumers. No new offenses were added to existing laws.

Business groups, while proclaiming their belief in competition, insisted the new law conferred too much power on government officials and was unnecessary. Opposition to the merger notification provision was especially strong among investment bankers, who contended that many mergers are economically desirable.[53] It is worth noting, however, that investment bankers are often the agents who put mergers together and that they earn substantial fees for finding companies that may be available for acquisition by companies that are eager to expand. Notice is now provided on several hundred mergers a year to the FTC. Few are acted against.

Antitrust: Is It Effective?

How effective have the antitrust laws been in maintaining a competitive economy? We have no simple or definitive answer. An evaluator's conclusions depend upon the criteria of evaluation utilized.[54] Those who contend that antitrust has been ineffectual and of little or no use in maintaining competition frequently point to the general absence of trust-busting to support their position. But antitrust policy involves more than trust-busting. Although large concerns have only rarely been broken up, those entrusted with antitrust enforcement have acted to prevent their use of predatory and restrictive practices and to discourage their growth through mergers. Collusive agreements among independent firms have been consistently, if not always thoroughly and vigorously, moved against. Undoubtedly, many who would have acted to restrain competition, alone or severally, have been deterred by the prospect of discovery and legal action. It seems reasonable to argue that the economy today is more competitive than it would have been in the absence of antitrust policy, although we cannot say with any precision how much more competitive.

On the other hand, antitrust policy has not been as effective as its more avid supporters would prefer. There is a considerable concentration of economic power in certain industries—automobiles, aluminum, steel, breakfast cereals, and computers, for example. Many violations of the laws in all likelihood go either undetected or unprosecuted. The effectiveness of antitrust has also been reduced by exemptions (to labor unions, agricultural cooperatives, insurance companies, soft drink bottlers); by the adoption of laws or policies inconsistent with antitrust (state laws permitting holding companies and restricting entry into occupations); and by the suspension of antitrust activity during crisis periods. Inadequate congressional support, public indifference, uncertainty and conflict over policy goals, and unfavorable judicial action have all, at various times, operated to diminish the effectiveness of antitrust enforcement. Collectively, these conditions have prevented the development of a really systematic, comprehensive, vigorous program for the maintenance of competition. Still, antitrust policy seems to have played a significant role in ensuring the existence of competition in the American economy.

REGULATION, REGULATORY REFORM, AND DEREGULATION

In the twentieth century, the national government has established a large number and variety of economic regulatory programs. The bulk of these programs are directed in some way at business activities; others have as their targets labor or agriculture. We examine the programs that focus on environmental pollution and on labor-management relations and terms of employment in other chapters of this book. Here we take a general look at the development of business regulation, the problems associated with that development, and the regulatory reform movement in recent years, especially as it involves deregulation.

The Growth and Expansion of Regulation

The United States has seen three major periods of regulatory expansion. The first came during the Progressive era, in the first two decades of the twentieth century. Major developments at that time included the expansion of antitrust and railroad regulation, passage of the Federal Reserve Act, and the beginning of consumer protection activity with the adoption of meat inspection and pure food and drug legislation. Regulation was seen as a moderate way of dealing with the problems of an industrial society; it avoided the unacceptable extremes of laissez faire and socialism.

The second major expansion of business regulation came during the New Deal years, in the 1930s. Major regulatory legislation was enacted on securities and securities exchanges, banks, motor carriers, commercial airlines, communications, consumer protection, labor-management relations, wages and hours of work, and price discrimination. Much of this legislation, as the list shows, focused on particular industries, and often restricted competition among industry members. Competition generally was not held in high regard in the 1930s. The New Deal firmly established the national government in the role of regulator of the economy.

The third major period of regulatory expansion dates from the mid-1960s through the 1970s. During this period, a large amount of legislation was adopted, especially on consumer protection, environmental protection, and health and safety. (Table 9–1 lists the various regulatory laws adopted during the 1970s.) Much of this legislation was intended to protect and improve the quality of life. Often quite detailed in nature, these statutes usually had a functional rather than particular industry focus. They also conferred much discretion upon administrative agencies for their implementation.

Regulatory Problems

As we would expect, regulatory programs have generated many problems, complaints, and allegations of "regulatory failure." Coming from both critics and supporters of various programs, complaints have focused on both the economic and administrative aspects of regulation.[55]

• Regulation often involves rate or price control, which can distort the operation of the market and interfere with prices as an allocator of resources. For example, some critics contend that regulation of airline passenger rates by the Civil Aeronautics Board (CAB) kept rates too high, thus discouraging air travel while at the

TABLE 9-1   Federal economic regulatory legislation, 1970–1979

Year enacted	Title of statute
1970	Clean Air Act Amendments
	Egg Products Inspection Act
	Occupational Safety and Health Act
	Poison Prevention Packaging Act
	Securities Investor Protection Act
	Economic Stabilization Act
	Fair Credit Reporting Act
1971	Economic Stabilization Act Amendments
	Federal Boat Safety Act
	Lead-Based Paint Poisoning Prevention Act
	Wholesome Fish and Fisheries Products Act
1972	Consumer Product Safety Act
	Motor Vehicle Information and Cost Savings Act
	Noise Control Act
	Equal Employment Opportunity Act
	Federal Environmental Pesticide Control Act
	Federal Water Pollution Control Act Amendments
	Ports and Waterways Safety Act
1973	Agriculture and Consumer Protection Act
	Emergency Petroleum Allocation Act
	Flood Disaster Protection Act
1974	Atomic Energy Act
	Commodity Futures Trading Commission Act
	Magnuson-Moss Warranty/FTC Improvement Act
	Council on Wage and Price Stability Act
	Employee Retirement Income Security Act
	Federal Energy Administration Act
	Transportation Safety Act
	Fair Labor Standards Act Amendments
	Safe Drinking Water Act
	Equal Credit Opportunity Act
	National Mobile Home Construction and Safety Standards Act
1975	Energy Policy Conservation Act
	Securities Act Amendments
1976	Railroad Revitalization and Regulatory Reform Act
	Consumer Leasing Act
	Medical Devices Act
	Antitrust Improvements Act
	Consumer Product Safety Commission Improvement Act
	U.S. Grain Standards Act
	Toxic Substances Control Act
1977	Surface Mining Control and Reclamation Act
	Clean Air Act Amendments
	Food and Agriculture Act
	Clean Water Act
	Fair Labor Standards Act Amendments

TABLE 9-1   *(continued)*

Year enacted	Title of statute
1978	Petroleum Marketing Practices Act
	Federal Pesticide Act
	Airline Deregulation Act
	Public Utility Regulatory Policies Act
	Futures Trading Act
	Natural Gas Policy Act
1979	Aviation Safety and Noise Abatement Act
	Pipeline Safety Act
	Trade Agreements Act
	Staggers Rail Act
	Regulatory Institutions Deregulation and Monetary Control Act
	Federal Trade Commission Improvement Act
	Motor Carrier Reform Act
	Solid Waste Disposal Act Amendments

SOURCE: Stuart S. Nagel, ed., *Encyclopedia of Policy Studies* (New York: Marcel Dekker, 1983), pp. 425–426.

same time encouraging competition among the airlines in terms of excess services and "frills."

• Regulation can reduce competition, especially when it controls entry into a particular industry. Examples include control of airline entry by the CAB, banking entry by the Comptroller of the Currency, and motor carrier entry by the Interstate Commerce Commission. Then, too, as we saw earlier in this chapter, the Robinson-Patman Act reduces price competition.

• Regulation can reduce or delay scientific and technological progress. For example, the requirement that new drugs be proven both safe and effective, which is administered by the Food and Drug Administration, is presented as a cause of delay in the introduction of new and desirable drugs.

• A frequent complaint in recent years has been that the dollar costs of regulations often exceed their benefits, thus producing inefficiency. Such complaints have been levied at air pollution standards adopted by the Environmental Protection Agency, health standards adopted by the Occupational Safety and Health Administration, and automobile safety requirements (such as air bags) proposed or adopted by the National Highway Traffic Safety Administration. These charges assume that the costs and benefits of regulations can be quantified with reasonable accuracy and that economic efficiency should be the basis on which judgments of the desirability of regulation are based.

• A familiar feature of regulatory lore is the contention that regulatory agencies are often "captured" by the groups they regulate and then become protectors of business interests rather than the "public" interest. Thus, the CAB, the ICC, and the Federal Maritime Commission (FMC) have been depicted as captives of the airlines, railroads, and shipping companies, respectively. Although it is not always clear what "capture" involves or how it occurs, the conclusion is that regulation does not serve its intended public purposes.

• When regulatory agencies have overlapping or competing jurisdictions, the result can be a lack of coordination. In the transportation field, for example, the CAB, the ICC, the FMC, and the Department of Transportation all have operating authority. Again, conflicts or divergences may occur when both national and state regulatory agencies operate in the same area, as they do in environmental protection and banking regulation.

• Business regulation in the twentieth century is handled predominantly by administrative agencies operating under broad, general statutory mandates. (Table 9–2 lists the various independent regulatory commissions and their jurisdictions.) Administrative regulation is often characterized by such problems as complex and cumbersome procedures, delay, and slowness in proceedings, inadequate information, and a lack of qualified personnel. Better personnel, for instance, would produce better regulation. Or so it is contended.

• Agencies are often accused of making bad decisions on regulatory issues—decisions that are unwise, unnecessary, or ill considered. In some cases, these judgments come from people who find given agency actions inconvenient, inexpedient, or contrary to their economic or ideological interests; in other instances, these judgments are more impartial, perhaps based on rigorous analysis of their effect on business or society. People who believe strongly in the desirability and efficacy of free markets are likely to find many regulatory programs unnecessary and undesirable.

Complaints about regulation come from those who believe there is too much regulation of business and from those who believe that either more or better regulation is needed to effectively protect the interests of the public. Consequently, proposals for reform may either involve reducing the amount of regulation, strengthening regulatory programs and agencies, or simply improving regulatory procedures to increase administrative efficiency.

Regulatory Reform

Regulatory reform is probably as old as regulation. However, since the early 1970s, perhaps because of the large amount of regulatory activity that had developed, regulatory reform has attracted both much attention and a permanent place on the political agenda. Many proposals for change in regulatory policy and procedure have been made. Presidents Ford, Carter, and Reagan have each given consid-

TABLE 9-2 Independent regulatory commissions

Name	Year established	Jurisdiction
Interstate Commerce Commission	1887	Railroads, motor carriers (trucks and buses), express companies; shipping by coastal and inland waterways.
Federal Reserve Board	1913	Monetary policy; banks in the Federal Reserve System.
Federal Trade Commission	1914	Unfair methods of competition; unfair or deceptive acts and practices; some antitrust statutes.
Federal Home Loan Bank Board	1933	Savings and loan associations.
Securities and Exchange Commission	1934	Securities markets; gas and electric utility holding companies.
Federal Communications Commission	1934	Radio, television, telephone, cable, and satellite communications.
National Labor Relations Board	1935	Unfair labor and employer practices; union certification procedures.
Civil Aeronautics Board[a]	1936	Commercial airlines (economic aspects).
Federal Maritime Commission[b]	1961	Shipping in domestic and foreign commerce.
Consumer Product Safety Commission	1972	Safety of consumer products.
Nuclear Regulatory Commission	1975	Civilian use of nuclear energy (construction, safety, export, etc.).
Commodity Futures Trading Commission	1975	Futures trading on commodity exchanges; commodity options.
Federal Energy Regulatory Commission[c]	1977	Natural gas; electric power; oil pipelines; hydroelectric power sites.

[a]To be phased out by 1985.

[b]Dates back to the Shipping Board of 1916.

[c]Replaced the Federal Power Commission, which was set up in 1920.

erable attention and support to regulatory improvement, although they differed with regard to what should be done.

According to David Welborn, there are three general orientations toward that reform: traditionalist, populist, and restrictivist.[56] The *traditionalist* orientation has long dominated thinking about regulation. Traditionalists view business regulation as essentially sound and necessary to control the exercise of private economic power. They are comfortable with the regulatory state, although they do see a need to improve the performance of regulatory agencies. To this end, they recommend such correctives as better personnel, larger budgets, improved procedures, clearer statutory authority, and improved internal agency organization and management. Many traditionalists also favor stronger presidential control of regulatory agencies to ensure responsibility and coordination.

Those holding the *populist* orientation also accept the need for business regulation. However, they are suspicious of corporate power and want to strengthen governmental control of business, especially big business. In their view, business has often used its political power to bend regulation to its own interests. The populists propose two routes of reform: one involves reducing the influence of business interests in regulation by such means as limiting ex parte (off the record) contacts with agencies, by enacting strong conflict of interest rules, and by restricting the employment of regulatory officials by regulated companies. The other involves enhancement of public influence in agency proceedings, as by open meeting ("sunshine") requirements, the subsidization of public participation in agency proceedings, and the creation of offices of consumer counsel within agencies. Populists also favor the elimination of those regulatory programs that they believe unduly serve the interests of business to the disadvantage of the public. Some transportation regulatory programs fall into this category.

People with a *restrictivist* orientation have a general dislike for regulation, viewing much of it as a burdensome and unnecessary interference with the operation of the market—a cause of inefficiency, resource misallocation, and reduction of economic freedom. A favored reform of restrictivists is the elimination of regulatory programs that limit competition. Another is the use of economic incentives (among them, a tax on environmental pollution) rather than administrative regulation to achieve regulatory goals. A third is the use of cost-benefit analysis to appraise the impact of and desirability of regulatory programs.

Almost everyone believes in regulatory reform. But as these three orientations indicate, everyone does not agree on the direction that reform should take. And even those who fall into a general orientation may advocate changes that fit into still another of these categories.

Deregulation

The facet of regulatory reform that has attracted the most attention in the last decade is deregulation. As Alan Stone states, "The term 'deregulation' is usually confined to explicitly economic matters such as rates, routes, or entry barriers, particularly in connection with transportation, communications, or infrastructural services such as banking."[57] *Deregulation*, then, usually means a reduction in the amount of regulation of an industry and not the complete elimination of regulation. Stone suggests that the term should be distinguished from *overregulation* (or *excessive regulation*), which is directed toward environmental, health, safety, and consumer protection regulatory programs. "The cry against overregulation is not an attack on safety, health, and consumer protection regulation *per se* but on the alleged excesses of such programs."[58]

The deregulation campaign has had its greatest success in the area of transportation. Launched during the Ford administration, the deregulation movement experienced considerable success through the Carter presidency and on into the Reagan administration. Strong presidential support obviously helps account for the program's success. Other contributing factors include support from the regulated industries (except in the case of commercial airlines, most of which opposed deregulation) and growing public dissatisfaction with the performance of many regulatory programs. Economists provided a rationale for action with their theories stressing the effectiveness and beneficence of competition as a regulatory mechanism.[59]

Transportation deregulation legislation includes the following statutes:

- *Airline Deregulation Act (1978)*. This law provides for a phasing out of economic regulation of the airlines over a seven-year period. CAB authority over domestic airline routes ended in 1981. Its authority over domestic rates, fares, mergers, and acquisitions expired on January 1, 1983. The agency itself is slated to go out of existence on January 1, 1985. With that, domestic air transportation will become a competitive industry, free of economic regulation. Safety regulation by the Federal Aviation Agency will continue.

- *Staggers Rail Act (1980)*. This statute gives the railroads greater flexibility in raising and lowering freight rates, and makes it easier for them to abandon unprofitable routes. Also, the law eliminates most of the authority the railroads have had to set rates collectively through rate bureaus.

- *Motor Carrier Reform Act (1980)*. This act reduces regulation of trucking. It gives truckers greater flexibility in setting rates, makes it easier for new companies to enter the industry, and ends some of the industry's antitrust immunity in making rate agreements. The law also removes some restrictions on "piggyback" freight traffic and trucking route authorizations.

- *Bus Regulatory Reform Act (1982)*. Applying to intercity buses, this statute makes it easier for new bus companies to enter the industry, facilitates the expansion or abandonment of service by existing companies, and gives companies greater flexibility in raising and lowering rates. As in the case of railroad and trucking companies, the law limits the ability of companies to set rates jointly.

Collectively, these laws comprise a major change in transportation regulatory policy. Although economic regulation will be eliminated only for airlines, in all four industries greater room is now provided for the play of competitive forces. In air transportation, for instance, dozens of new companies have entered the industry in the last few years. Who will benefit from transportation deregulation, and in what ways, are questions we cannot answer now. Neither the suppliers nor users of transportation services have had time to adapt to this new policy and economic environment. Change is taking place, though, in the air, on the rails, and along our highways.

CONCLUDING COMMENTS

To some it might appear that everything is regulated by the government and that nothing much remains for private choice. Such is not the case. Much discretion remains with private businesses and their personnel. The antitrust laws, for example, set forth some rules—essentially prohibitions—to govern competitive relationships. Within that framework of rules, businesses are left free to compete or not compete or to compete as vigorously as they choose. To use a sports analogy, government provides some rules for the competitive game, but it does not call the individual plays or specify the vigor with which they are executed. In some other areas, though, such as occupational safety and health and public utility regulation, the rules may become more extensive and detailed and leave less discretion in private hands.

As the economy has become larger and more complex, government has been called on to deal with more problems and conflicts; consequently, the volume of public policies, often regulatory in nature, has increased. Many people have become convinced, as a consequence, that there is too much regulation and that at least some of it should be deregulated. The Ford, Carter, and Reagan administrations all made regulatory reform and deregulation important goals. As we have seen, a number of important deregulation statutes were enacted during the Carter administration. The Reagan administration, in contrast, focused its attention on eliminating "unnecessary" administrative rules and regulations and established a Task Force on Regulatory Relief to oversee its efforts in this regard. When the task force was disbanded in mid-1983, the administration claimed that its efforts had saved businesses and consumers over $150 billion over the next decade. Such figures should be treated with a measure of skepticism.

Promotional programs also involve governmental intervention in the economy. They involve elements of control in that they are intended to help induce businesses to take actions or to continue doing things that they otherwise would not do—modernizing industrial plants, providing barge transportation, selling goods abroad, and the like. Promotional programs also have the effect of reducing the risks inherent in private enterprise. Although the possibility of business failure is sometimes depicted as the "right to fail," most people are not eager to exercise that right. The large number of promotional programs in existence are testimony to that fact.

In recent years, concern has arisen over the ability of businesses in the United States to compete successfully in the international economic arena with the Japanese and others. This has produced contentions that we need an "industrial policy" to stimulate, coordinate, and focus our efforts in the world economy. An industrial policy would substitute a substantial amount of government–business cooperation and partnership for the present dominant pattern of adversarial relationships. Such is the situation in Japan and to a lesser extent in some of the western European countries. Should cooperation replace regulation? Should government be more actively involved in guiding the activities of American industries? Questions of this nature will draw the attention of policymakers in the future. They are far different from the dominant business issue of a century ago—namely, should government control the "trusts"? Yet they all relate to the same central, continuing issue: What is the appropriate relationship between government and business? Each generation has to struggle to answer this question.

NOTES

1. David B. Truman, *The Governmental Process* (New York: Knopf, 1951), p. 79.
2. V. O. Key, Jr., *Politics, Parties, and Pressure Groups*, 4th ed. (New York: Crowell, 1958), p. 83.
3. Ibid., p. 103.
4. Seymour Scher, "Regulatory Agency Control through Appointment: The Case of the Eisenhower Administration and the NLRB," *Journal of Politics* 23 (November 1961): 667–688.
5. Murray Edleman, "Governmental Organization and Public Policy," *Public Administration Review* 12 (Autumn 1952): 279.
6. See, generally, Edwin M. Epstein, *The Corporation in American Politics* (Englewood Cliffs, N.J.: Prentice-Hall, 1969).
7. Charles E. Lindblom, *Politics and Markets* (New York: Basic Books, 1978).
8. Frank J. Sorauf, "The Public Interest Reconsidered," *Journal of Politics* 19 (November 1957): 620.
9. See Joint Economic Committee, *Federal Subsidy Programs* (Staff Study), 93rd Congress, 2nd Session (1974).
10. The definitive work here is Stanley S. Surrey, *Pathways to Tax Reform: The Concept of Tax Expenditures* (Cambridge, Mass.: Harvard University Press, 1973).
11. See *Special Analyses, Budget of the United States Government, Fiscal Year 1984* (Washington, D.C.: U.S. Government Printing Office, 1983), Special Analysis G, especially table G-2.
12. Clifford M. Hardin and Arthur T. Denzan, *The Unrestrained Growth of Federal Credit Programs* (St. Louis: Center for the Study of American Business, Washington University, 1981).
13. *Special Year Analyses, Budget of the United States, Fiscal Year 1982* (Washington, D.C.: U.S. Government Printing Office, 1981), table F11.
14. Some fees were finally imposed on inland-waterway users in 1978. For a good account of the struggle, see T. R. Reid, *Congressional Odyssey: The Saga of a Senate Bill* (San Francisco: Freeman, 1980).
15. Joint Economic Committee, *Federal Subsidy Programs*.
16. Woodrow Wilson, *The New Freedom* (Garden City, N.Y.: Doubleday, 1914), p. 17.
17. Edward S. Mason, *Economic Concentration and the Monopoly Problem* (Cambridge, Mass.: Harvard University Press, 1957), p. 354.
18. The trust form of organization, which gave its name to antimonopoly policy, was a device for combining independent firms under common control. A trust was formed when the majority stockholders of a number of independent firms were persuaded by an organizer to give control of their shares, and voting rights, to a single group of trustees. The trustees would then run the previously independent companies as a single enterprise. The stockholders, in turn, received trust certificates for their shares, which entitled them to receive dividends from the trust's profits.
19. Key, *Politics, Parties, and Pressure Groups*, p. 83.
20. Compare John A. Garraty, *The New Commonwealth 1877-1890* (New York: Harper and Row, 1968), pp. 121–127.
21. See William Letwin, *Law and Economic Policy in America* (New York: Random House, 1954), for an excellent discussion of the passage of the Sherman Act.

22. Donald Dewey, "Romance and Realism in Antitrust Policy," *Journal of Political Economy* 63 (April 1955): 102.

23. Senate Select Committee on Small Business, *The Role of Private Antitrust Enforcement in Protecting Small Business—1958* (Senate Report 1955), 85th Congress, 2nd Session (1958), p. v.

24. Ibid., pp. 9–10.

25. *U.S.* v. *E. C. Knight Co.*, 156 U.S. 1 (1895).

26. *U.S.* v. *Trans-Missouri Freight Assn.*, 166 U.S. 290 (1897).

27. *U.S.* v. *Standard Oil Co.*, 211 U.S. 1 (1911).

28. *U.S.* v. *U.S. Steel Corp.*, 251 U.S. 417 (1920).

29. *U.S.* v. *Trenton Potteries Co.*, 273 U.S. 392 (1927).

30. Mason, *Economic Concentration*, p. 334.

31. Merle Fainsod, Lincoln Gordon, and Joseph Palamountain, *Government and the American Economy* (New York: Norton, 1959), pp. 458–459.

32. *U.S.* v. *Aluminum Co. of America*, 148 F. 2d 416 (1945). Several Supreme Court justices disqualified themselves from hearing the *Alcoa* case because of previous involvement in its prosecution. Because a quorum of six was not available to hear the case, the judicial code was amended to permit a circuit court to make the final decision in this and other such' instances.

33. *American Tobacco Co.* v. *U.S.*, 328 U.S. 781 (1946).

34. Harold Koontz and Richard W. Gable, *Public Control of Economic Enterprise* (New York: McGraw-Hill, 1956), p. 340.

35. *U.S.* v. *E. I. DuPont de Nemours and Co.*, 351 U.S. 377 (1956).

36. *U.S.* v. *DuPont*, 353 U.S. 586 (1957).

37. *Wall Street Journal*, January 11, 1982, p. 6; and *New York Times*, January 9, 1982, p. 27.

38. *Wall Street Journal*, January 19, 1982, pp. 1, 14. Also see Martin Schnitzer, *Contemporary Government and Business Relations*, 2nd ed. (Boston: Houghton Mifflin, 1983), pp. 171–173.

39. *International Salt Co.* v. *U.S.*, 332 U.S. 392 (1947).

40. *FTC* v. *Western Meat Co.*, 272 U.S. 554 (1926).

41. *U.S.* v. *DuPont*, 353 U.S. 586 (1957).

42. See William Jenkins, Jr., "The Supreme Court and National Bank Merger Policy," in *Economic Regulatory Policies*, ed. James E. Anderson (Lexington, Mass.: Heath, 1976), pp. 105–124.

43. *U.S. Department of Justice Merger Guidelines* (Washington, D.C.: U.S. Government Printing Office, 1982).

44. News release, Department of Justice, June 14, 1982.

45. *Wall Street Journal*, August 19, 1982, p. 16.

46. Michael Wines, "Doctors, Dairymen Join in Effort to Clip the Talons of the FTC," *National Journal* 14 (September 18, 1982): 1589–1594.

47. Quoted in *Statement of Information, Hearings before the Committee on the Judiciary* (House of Representatives), 93rd Congress, 2nd Session (1974), v, p. 316. (These are the Watergate Hearings.) Also see *Wall Street Journal*, July 22, 1974, p. 3.

48. See, for example, Harlan M. Blake, "Beyond the ITT Case," *Harper's*, June 1972, pp. 74–78.

49. Corwin D. Edwards, *Maintaining Competition* (New York: McGraw-Hill, 1949), p. 293.

50. Joe S. Bain, *Industrial Organization* (New York: Wiley, 1959), p. 612.

51. See James Q. Wilson, ed., *The Politics of Regulation* (New York: Basic Books, 1980), chaps. 4–5.

52. See, generally, Joseph C. Palamountain, Jr., *The Politics of Distribution* (Cambridge, Mass.: Harvard University Press, 1955).

53. *New York Times*, February 20, 1976, p. 45.

54. See the viewpoints expressed in *Hearings on Planning, Regulation and Competition* (Subcommittee on Monopoly, Senate Small Business Committee), 90th Congress, 1st Session (1967).

55. This discussion draws on James E. Anderson, "Economic Regulation," in *Encyclopedia of Policy Studies*, ed. Stuart S. Nagel (New York: Marcel Dekker, 1983), chap. 17.

56. David M. Welborn, "Taking Stock of Regulatory Reform" (Paper delivered at the annual meeting of the American Political Science Association, Washington, D.C., September 1, 1977).

57. Alan Stone, *Regulation and Its Alternatives* (Washington, D.C.: Congressional Quarterly, 1982), p. 250.

58. Ibid., p. 254.

59. Compare *Regulation: Process and Politics* (Washington, D.C.: Congressional Quarterly, 1982), pp. 61–76, 89–98.

SUGGESTED READINGS

Bernstein, Marver. *Regulating Business by Independent Commission.* Princeton, N.J.: Princeton University Press, 1955.

Hughes, Jonathan R. *The Governmental Habit.* New York: Basic Books, 1977.

Lowi, Theodore J. *The End of Liberalism.* 2nd ed. New York: Norton, 1979.

Reagan, Michael D. *The Managed Economy.* New York: Oxford University Press, 1963.

Redford, Emmette S. *The Regulatory Process.* Austin: University of Texas Press, 1969.

Reid, Samuel Richardson. *The New Industrial Order.* New York: McGraw-Hill, 1976.

Stone, Alan. *Economic Regulation and the Public Interest.* Ithaca, N.Y.: Cornell University Press, 1977.

———. *Regulation and Its Alternatives.* Washington, D.C.: Congressional Quarterly, 1982.

TEN

Government and Labor

The transformation of the United States from an agrarian to an urban industrial society has produced an economic system characterized by big labor as well as big business. The masses of workers in an industrial society face many problems: the necessity of bargaining for jobs and wages with large corporate employers, insecurity in employment because of fluctuations in the business cycle, industrial accidents and sickness, and the loss of creative job satisfactions because of the routinization of work tasks. In dealing with these problems, workers may act individually, through private collective organizations (unions), or through government. In the twentieth century, American workers have come to rely heavily on the last two methods to protect and promote their interests. They have formed unions for economic bargaining with employers, and they have sought legislation, both to protect their right to organize and bargain collectively and to promote their interests directly (for instance, through minimum wage laws). Indeed, most labor legislation in this country is a twentieth-century phenomenon, as is the development of labor as a significant political force along with agriculture and business.

A HISTORY OF THE LABOR MOVEMENT

The Labor Force

In 1981, the total civilian labor force of the United States, which includes all persons over the age of 14 who are working or looking for work, numbered 108.6 million (see also table 10–1). Of these, 2.7 million were engaged in agricultural work and 8.3 million were unemployed. Although a portion of the labor force is

TABLE 10-1   Composition of the civilian labor force, 1950–1979 (in millions)

	1950	*1960*	*1970*	*1975*	*1979*
White-collar workers	22,373	28,522	37,997	42,227	49,342
Professional and technical	4,490	7,469	11,140	12,748	15,050
Managers and administrators	6,429	7,067	8,289	8,891	10,516
Sales workers	3,822	4,224	4,854	5,460	6,163
Clerical workers	7,632	9,762	13,714	15,128	17,613
Blue-collar workers	23,336	24,057	27,791	27,962	32,066
Craft and kindred workers	7,670	8,554	10,158	10,972	12,880
Operatives	12,146	11,950	13,909	12,856	10,909
Nonfarm laborers	3,520	3,553	3,724	4,134	4,665
Service workers	6,535	8,023	9,712	11,657	12,834
Farm workers	7,408	5,176	3,126	2,936	2,703
Total employed	59,652	65,778	78,626	84,782	97,511
Unemployed		3,852	4,088	7,830	5,963

SOURCE: U.S. Bureau of the Census, *Statistical Abstract of the United States, 1980* (Washington, D.C.: U.S. Government Printing Office, 1981).

made up of the self-employed, proprietors, unpaid family workers, and the like, most people now earn their livelihood by working for someone else—or depend upon those who do.

In this century, some significant changes have occurred in the composition of the labor force. In 1900, when it numbered 28 million, some 37.5 percent of the country's workers were employed in agriculture; in 1976, that proportion had dropped to 3.4 percent. The percentage of white-collar workers has been increasing, so that white-collar workers now constitute slightly more than half the labor force. The number of women who work has also been increasing, and now accounts for one-third of the labor force.

The Rise of Labor Unions

Labor unions—organizations formed by wage-earners to maintain or improve their terms and conditions of work by bargaining with employers—have existed in the United States, at least at the local level, since the 1790s. Until the 1930s, however, only a small proportion of workers belonged to unions; in 1933, union membership totaled 2.3 million members. Since then, there has been substantial growth in union membership, particularly during the 1930s and 1940s. In 1981, there were 20.5 million American members of over 150 national and international unions (these also have Canadian members).[1] In recent years, however, the proportion of the labor force that is unionized has been declining.

Union membership.   Currently, about one in five gainfully employed persons belongs to a union. Figures of this sort are somewhat deceptive, however, because there is much diversity in union strength among different industries and geographic areas. Four sectors of the economy—manufacturing, mining, transportation, and construction—account for four-fifths of union membership. Substantial majorities of the wage-earners in each of these industrial groupings are unionized. Only small percentages of the workers in service industries, wholesale and retail trade, and finance and insurance are organized. These sectors include large numbers of white-collar workers, who have traditionally been difficult to organize. Until recently, agricultural workers have been almost completely unorganized.

Geographically, union membership as a percentage of nonagricultural employment is highest in the Middle Atlantic, East North Central (Ohio, Illinois, etc.), and Pacific Coast regions; workers in the Mountain, South, Southwest, and West North Central (Kansas, North Dakota, etc.) regions are comparatively poorly organized. On a state basis, high rates of union membership (30 to 40 percent) are found in West Virginia, New York, California, Michigan, Illinois, Ohio, and Pennsylvania; low rates (less than 15 percent), in North Carolina, South Carolina, South Dakota, Texas, Mississippi, and New Mexico. This situation results, in part, because industries with high rates of union membership tend to be concentrated in certain states and regions. But other factors are operative too. In the South, for example, strong resistance by business interests and an unfavorable political climate contribute to low rates of unionization.

Great disparity also exists in the membership size of various unions. The Teamsters, Steelworkers, Automobile Workers, Electrical Workers, Food and Commercial Workers, and State, County, and Municipal Employees Unions each count more than a million members. A number of other unions have several hundred thousand members each (see table 10–2). In contrast, there are nearly a hundred unions—from the Amalgamated Lace Operatives of America to the International Broom and Whisk Makers Union—with fewer than 25,000 members each. Collectively, these groups constitute more than half the total number of national unions, but have only around 5 percent of the membership. Many unions, in short, are small, poorly organized or financed, and possessed of little economic or political power. The Steelworkers, Teamsters, and Machinists are not typical unions, as some people believe.

The AFL-CIO.   In the two decades prior to 1955, the labor movement was divided between two rival and often sharply antagonistic national labor federations. The American Federation of Labor, created in 1886 and long the dominant force in American unionism, was composed largely of unions of skilled craftspeople—machinists, carpenters, electricians, plumbers, musicians. The Congress of Industrial

TABLE 10–2   Union membership, large unions, 1964–1980 (in millions)

Union	1964	1972	1980
Teamsters	1,507	1,885	1,891
Steelworkers	1,250	1,400	1,238
Auto Workers	1,168	1,394	1,357
Electrical	806	957	1,041
Carpenters	760	820	832
Machinists	808	758	745
Retail Clerks[a]	428	633	1,300
Laborers	432	600	608
Meat Cutters[a]	486	529	—
State, County, and Municipal Employees	235	529	1,098
Service Employees	320	484	650
Hotel and Restaurant	445	458	400
Communications Workers	294	443	551
Ladies Garment	442	428	323
Operating Engineers	311	402	423
Paperworkers	309	389	219

SOURCE: U.S. Bureau of the Census, *Statistical Abstract of the United States, 1980* (Washington, D.C.: U.S. Government Printing Office, 1981), p. 411.

[a]In 1979, Retail Clerks merged with Meat Cutters to form the Food and Commercial Workers.

Organizations, which began as a faction within the AFL in 1935 and became a separate federation in 1938, was essentially made up of industrial unions formed to include all of the workers in particular industries—steelworkers, automobile workers, rubber workers. The CIO represented a response to the development of mass-production and other industries employing large numbers of unskilled and semi-skilled workers. Such industries could be only partially and ineffectively organized along skilled-craft lines. In the late 1940s and early 1950s, the pressures created by declining union membership, political reverses (for example, enactment of the Taft-Hartley Act), and the presence of a Republican administration in Washington caused many leaders in both federations to adopt the position that unity in the labor movement was necessary if organized labor was to preserve its economic gains and be able to fend off political attacks. In December 1955, and after the failure of various previous attempts, the two federations were merged to form the American Federation of Labor and Congress of Industrial Organizations (AFL-CIO).

The AFL-CIO in 1978 included over a hundred unions having a total membership of over 15.5 million workers. Prominent among the unions outside the AFL-CIO are the Teamsters, the United Automobile Workers, the United Mine Workers, and some of the railroad brotherhoods. The AFL-CIO can be described as a loose federation of national unions that are largely autonomous in the conduct of their internal affairs and in bargaining with employers. Each of the constituent unions also maintains its own headquarters and lobbyists in Washington, D.C.

Unions and Politics

Labor unions use two general methods to promote and protect their interests: collective bargaining (including strikes, picketing, and boycotts) and political activity. Our concern is with the latter. Political action by unions has been and is necessary because they exist in a socioeconomic environment that has generally been critical of them, and sometimes hostile toward them, and has often produced unfavorable governmental attitudes and actions. Although work enjoys high regard in this country ("hard work never hurt anyone," "idle fingers are the devil's playthings"), the same is not true for organized labor. At the least, then, labor has had to defend itself in the political arena against labor injunctions, right-to-work laws and other legislative restrictions, and executive intervention in strikes on behalf of management. To this extent, labor's political activity has appeared to be a necessary condition for its survival and the opportunity to bargain collectively. But, and especially in recent decades, the political objectives of labor have been more than merely defensive. Unions now rely on political action, in addition to collective bargaining, to promote the economic interests of their members (and often those of other workers as well).[2]

Objectives.   The present-day objectives of labor's political activity, beyond its desire to protect its rights to organize and bargain collectively, can be categorized in this manner.

First, there are general goals that labor seeks and that cannot be obtained through collective bargaining—goals such as unemployment compensation, other social security programs, policies to maintain full or maximum employment, job retraining programs, and employment services.

Second, there are general objectives that could possibly be attained by collective bargaining but that may be more readily secured through government legislation. Illustrative are minimum wages, maximum hours, the prevention of child labor, and improved standards relating to industrial health and safety.

Third, particular objectives are sought by particular unions relating to their respective industries and their positions therein. The railroad brotherhoods have advocated legislation to protect or improve the competitive position of the railroads vis-a-vis other forms of transportation. The Bricklayers and other unions in the building trades typically support public housing programs. The Seafarers International Union has been a strong advocate of construction and operating subsidies for the maritime industry. In taking policy positions of this sort, unions are obviously motivated by the desire to protect or increase job opportunities for their members.

Fourth, organized labor takes policy positions on and works for the enactment or defeat of proposed legislation that is of general social concern but not directly related to its economic interests. Thus, in recent years the AFL-CIO supported the repeal of both the oil depletion allowance and the antitrust exemption for state fair trade laws; advocated legislation to create a consumer protection agency, impose strip-mining controls, reform income taxes, and extend the Voting Rights Act; and opposed the deregulation of natural gas and legislation to restrict busing for school desegregation. Labor, because of its increasing social and political consciousness, no longer confines its legislative attention to the traditional job-centered issues, as it customarily did before the New Deal.

Methods.   In seeking the adoption of its legislative goals, organized labor has chosen the course of pressure politics, striving first to influence the election or appointment of public officials favorably inclined toward its interests and, second, to persuade them to adopt policies supported by labor once they are in office. Labor has rejected the alternative, favored by some intellectuals and minor labor leaders, of establishing an independent political party. Attempts to establish labor parties were unsuccessful in the nineteenth century, and there is little prospect for their success today. In many states, election laws make it difficult for new parties to get on the ballot; in other states a labor party probably would be weak because of the paucity of union members. "Fears of electoral failure, of antagonizing employers, of rupturing labor unity, 'of taking a risk in a hostile environment' impel pragmatic union leaders to resist efforts to form a new party."[3]

In its political activities, organized labor still holds, at least formally, to the traditional policy first enunciated by Samuel Gompers, of promoting its interests by rewarding its friends and punishing its enemies, without regard to their party affiliation. However, in actuality, and especially since the New Deal years, labor has become increasingly committed to the Democratic party. Most of the candidates for office endorsed by labor are Democrats, and organized labor is often the most important element within the Democratic party. Except for Republican-inclined unions, as in the building trades, the Republicans get little support from labor. (The Teamsters were one of a handful of unions that supported Ronald Reagan in 1980.)

Organized labor also maintains a considerable number of lobbyists, or legislative representatives, in Washington on a permanent basis to look after labor's legislative interests. In addition to those lobbyists on the staff of the AFL-CIO, many of the larger national unions have their own legislative representatives. In contrast, at the state legislative level, lobbying is a part-time activity of officials of individual unions and state labor federations. The lobbying techniques used by labor groups include testifying before committees, help in bill drafting, personal contacts with members of Congress, logrolling and alliance building, and the stimulation of grass-roots pressure on legislators. AFL-CIO personnel coordinate the overall effort.

Effectiveness. How successful is labor at winning its political objectives? There is no denying that labor is a significant political force. However, it seems to be most effective when it is operating as part of the liberal-labor coalition on civil rights, welfare, tax reform, and other matters of broad public concern. When it comes to legislation on strictly labor issues, the unions have not had much success in the post-World War II era. Both the Taft-Hartley and the Landrum-Griffin Acts were enacted over the strong opposition of labor. On two narrower matters on which labor has expended much effort—the repeal of the authorization for state right-to-work laws and legislation to permit common situs picketing—it has also failed.[4] As one union president remarked: "On straight labor legislation we can't get out of the box. We've been fighting a defensive battle since 1950."[5]

A number of factors affect the political success of labor and help explain its legislative difficulties:

• Although labor unions by and large have accepted the capitalist system and have worked within its framework to improve the position and well-being of workers, they have tried to limit employers' ability to control and use their property. As a consequence, the labor movement has been interpreted historically as an attack on private property and the right to run a business as the owner sees fit. This interpretation, in turn, has lowered the status of labor unions in American society, reduced support for them in the middle class, and strengthened business interests in their efforts to resist unionism by enabling them to pose as the defenders of private property against "radical" attack.

• Labor's political activity evokes strong opposition from conservative business groups and, at times, similarly oriented farm and professional groups. The National Association of Manufacturers is usually at the head of the opposition. Depending on the issue in question, it may draw allies from the U.S. Chamber of Commerce, the American Farm Bureau Federation, the American Medical Association, or the

American Bar Association. Business alliances, such as the National Right to Work Committee and the National Action Committee, also oppose prounion labor legislation. And in recent years, many well-financed political action committees (PACs) have entered the political fray against labor. In competing with these groups, labor is disadvantaged by its lower social status and fewer political resources (e.g., money and propaganda skills).

• Within Congress, a conservative coalition of Republicans and southern Democrats often opposes labor-supported measures. Moreover, certain legislative procedures may be utilized by the coalition to thwart labor—such procedures as the filibuster rule in the Senate, which led to the defeat of right-to-work repeal (see below), and the two-thirds vote needed to override presidential vetoes, which resulted in the upholding in 1976 of President Ford's veto of the common situs picketing bill. Although the power of southern Democrats, who tend to be conservative on economic issues, is waning, they still occupy many positions of power in Congress.

• The Republican party has controlled the presidency half of the time since World War II. Although a Republican president cannot be totally unresponsive to labor, the influence of labor in Washington is diminished during Republican years. Thus, labor leaders have expressed much dissatisfaction with the policies of the Reagan administration.

• Organized labor is handicapped, at least sometimes, by a lack of unity in its political efforts: "Today the lobbying of the AFL-CIO is hampered by the contradictory political pressures exerted by the jurisdictional groups within it. The bitterest complaints about labor lobbying often come from labor-supported legislators faced with the conflicting demands made upon them by different unions or groups of unions."[6] In fact, disunity within the labor movement about the form that labor reform legislation should take was an important factor in labor's inability to prevent the passage in 1959 of the Landrum-Griffin Act.[7] In addition, the Teamsters' crude lobbying techniques, which included "threats of certain election defeat for voting 'wrong,'" antagonized many members of Congress, and probably lost votes for labor and contributed to passage of the act.[8] Currently, union leaders sometimes disagree about their general objectives—that is, whether lobbying efforts should be confined primarily to trade union issues or whether unions should continue to work for the enactment of liberal legislation generally.

AN OVERVIEW OF LABOR LEGISLATION

Jurisdiction in the area of labor legislation is divided constitutionally between the national government and the states. Although federal legislation is limited to businesses engaged in or affecting interstate commerce, the concept of interstate commerce has been greatly broadened, especially since 1937. No longer, for example, do the courts hold that labor matters are an aspect of production and thus primarily for the states to regulate. If a labor matter has some substantial effect on interstate commerce, it can be dealt with by the national government.

Since the early decades of the nineteenth century, American legislative bodies—national, state, and occasionally local—have enacted a considerable amount of labor legislation. Most nineteenth-century legislation was at the state level, and was concerned with child labor, hours of work for women (and sometimes men), industrial safety, methods of wage payments, and mediation of labor disputes. State laws on minimum wages, workmen's compensation, and unemployment compensation were twentieth-century developments, as were laws relating to hours of work for men (for the most part), labor relations, and fair employment practices.

In the nineteenth century, the national government did enact a few statutes affecting labor—for instance, laws concerning the hours of work of government employees and the mediation of railway labor disputes (the Erdman Act). Between 1900 and 1930, federal activity increased but was largely confined to efforts to prevent child labor (which were declared unconstitutional) and to regulate the hours, working conditions, and labor relations of railroad workers. The predominant view during this period was that labor problems, except when the employees of interstate railroads were involved, were essentially under state government jurisdiction. Since 1950, as a consequence of changing economic, political, and constitutional conditions, the national government has legislated on wages and hours, child labor, unemployment compensation, labor relations, employment services, job training, employee pensions, internal union affairs, and fair employment practices. Today, labor looks primarily to the national government to protect and promote its interests.

We can classify existing labor legislation by the subjects with which it deals, such as wages and hours or collective bargaining. Or, we can categorize that legislation by its objectives, a system that focuses our attention on the problems at which the laws are directed. If we use purpose as our organizing criterion, we can group labor policies under the following nonexclusive categories.

First, numerous laws have been enacted by the national and state governments to prevent the exploitation or mistreatment of workers and to help guarantee a minimum standard of living. Because of the usually weaker bargaining power of workers—particularly women, children, and migrant workers—the terms and conditions of work in most instances would be unilaterally determined by employers in the absence of governmental controls (and, it should be added, labor unions). Consequently—through legislation on minimum wages and maximum hours, methods of wage payment (e.g., outlawing payment in scrip redeemable only at company stores, a practice that seems archaic now), child labor, workmen's compensation, unemployment compensation, and industrial health and safety—government has acted to protect the interests of employees in their relationships with employers. Such policy action is supported by the middle-class ideal of protecting the weak against the strong, by humanitarian motives, and by the practical desire to enhance the economic well-being of workers.

The Fair Labor Standards Act is an example of legislation in this category.

Adopted over strong business and conservative opposition in 1938, the statute mandated a minimum wage of $.25 an hour and a forty-four-hour workweek (with compensation at time and a half for excess hours), and prohibited most child labor. Since then the act has been amended several times. The most recent amendments, made in 1977, raised the minimum wage in a series of step increases, from $2.30 an hour to $3.35 an hour as of January 1, 1981. The law applies to about 55 million workers nationwide—employees engaged in interstate commerce or the production of goods for interstate commerce unless specifically exempt from coverage (executive, administrative, and professional employees); employees of small retail or service businesses; and agricultural workers on small farms. Efforts in 1974 to extend coverage to state and local government employees were declared unconstitutional by the Supreme Court. Under certain circumstances, apprentices, handicapped workers, and full-time students can be paid less than minimum wage, but attempts to amend the law to allow payment of a subminimum wage to encourage youth employment have failed.

Second, some labor laws are designed to promote greater equality of opportunity for workers. Child labor laws, together with compulsory school attendance laws, contribute to future employment opportunities and earning capacities. It is statistically demonstrable that people's incomes generally increase with their level of education; the average high school graduate, for example, earns more money during his or her working career than the average person with an eighth-grade education or less. More job opportunities will also typically be available for better-educated people. Some states have adopted fair employment practices acts, which prohibit discrimination against workers on the basis of race, religion, sex, or national origin. (The state of New York also bans discrimination on the basis of age.) At the national level, the Civil Rights Act of 1964 set up a national Equal Employment Opportunity Commission to prevent such discrimination. Legislation providing for employment services, public works programs, and employment training is also designed to improve employment opportunities for unemployed or underemployed workers.

Third, legislation has been enacted to protect and promote the right of workers to organize and bargain collectively through unions of their own choosing. Fourth, there are both national and state laws that regulate unions to lessen or prevent the abuse of their economic power, to prohibit unfair union activities, and to ensure the meaningful participation of members in union governance. Fifth, legislation has established agencies and procedures for the resolution of labor-management disputes. These three types of legislation are discussed in later sections of this chapter.

Legislation falling into each of these categories, in support of each of these objectives, has been enacted at both the national and state levels. This does not mean, however, that the national government and the various state governments have been equally vigorous in enacting each type of legislation. Much diversity exists among the states in terms of the nature, scope, and effectiveness of the laws they have passed, and in their enforcement activities. For example, different states give different emphasis to the objectives. Northern industrial states focus greater attention on providing more equal opportunities for workers, including the prevention of job discrimination, than do southern states. The latter, in turn, along with some of the North Central states, are more active in regulating and restricting unions. Even where there is general agreement on a particular objective, say the resolution of labor-management disputes, there is often considerable disagreement as to the form government action should take. That disagreement manifests itself in diverse policies.

In broadest terms, the function of labor legislation is the establishment of socially approved norms of behavior to be followed by labor and management in their relationships. Another function of labor legislation is the distribution of advantages and disadvantages among labor and management groups. Because it performs these functions, the substance of labor legislation is affected, at any given time and place, by economic circumstances, public attitudes and beliefs, and the balance of power among contending interest groups. Whether the resulting policy is "good" or "bad" depends on the interests and values of those passing judgment on it.

COLLECTIVE BARGAINING: 1789–1947

Collective bargaining is the process by which a contract or agreement governing terms of work, fringe benefits, and working conditions is negotiated by an employer and a union representing that employer's workers. An agreement at least minimally acceptable to each party is reached through give and take, proposal and counterproposal, bargaining and compromise. Most labor agreements are arrived at without actual resort to the economic weapons available to each side—strikes, boycotts, slowdowns, lockouts, and the like.

Collective bargaining in the United States is conducted within a framework of public law—both statutory and common (judge-made) law, with the former being most important now—that sets forth various rules concerning the rights, duties, and limitations of labor and management. This framework of legal rules has been developed and modified in response to changing social, economic, and political circumstances. First one party and then the other in the bargaining relationship has been favored. Since 1789, public policy has moved from a period in which labor unions were of doubtful legality, to an era in which unions were legal but often treated hostilely, to an era of positive support and encouragement, to the present situation of detailed regulation of labor-management relationships.

Until 1842: The Question of Legality

Although little legislation relating to labor unions was enacted in the nineteenth century, or indeed until the 1930s, labor unions have been subjected to judicial controls from the time they first appeared in this country. In the early nineteenth century employers confronted with unions turned to the courts for assistance. In a number of cases, beginning in 1806, the courts held that any sort of union activity constituted an illegal conspiracy in restraint of trade under the common law. Such activity was consequently subject to punishment by fine or imprisonment. In other cases, the courts were less harsh in their attitudes toward unions, but there was substantial doubt about the legality of unions until 1842. In that year, in the famous case of *Commonwealth* v. *Hunt*, the highest court of Massachusetts ruled that union activities were not illegal per se but, rather, that their legality depended on the objectives they were seeking to attain. Other state courts followed this ruling, and the doctrine that unions were illegal criminal conspiracies fell from grace; the legality of unions was thus established.

Judicial acceptance, of course, did not necessarily mean judicial approval of unions as economic organizations. Throughout the nineteenth century, and to a lesser extent the twentieth, most judges tended to be hostile toward unions. This judicial hostility stemmed partly from the judges' legal training and partly from their personal beliefs and group affiliations. The common law, in which the judges were trained, was conservative in nature and strongly directed to the protection of property rights. Unions, as mentioned earlier, were historically viewed as an attack on property rights; consequently, they appeared in conflict with the spirit of the common law. This aroused judicial dislike of unions—a dislike strengthened by most judges' political predilections. "[The judges] were drawn mainly from the property class, mingled more frequently with employers than with workers, and tended naturally to sympathize with the propertied interests. Their political thinking was influenced also by the classical economics, which could find no useful place for joint action by wage earners."[9]

1842–1932: Legality, Hostility, Neutrality

During this span of ninety years, unions existed as lawful organizations, but there was very little governmental protection of their rights to organize and bargain collectively. Employers were required neither to recognize nor to bargain with unions representing their workers. Rather, they were legally free to interfere with, obstruct, or combat the development and activities of unions as they saw fit, within the broad confines of criminal law. This meant that individual employers or associations of employers resorted to such methods as discharging or discriminating against union members; blacklisting union members to prevent them from obtaining other jobs; using labor spies and strikebreakers and lockouts; and requiring that, as a condition of employment, workers sign "yellow-dog" contracts forbidding union membership. Violence on the part of both sides often accompanied labor disputes.[10]

Government, particularly executive and judicial officials at the state and local levels, not only left management unrestricted but often intervened in its behalf in labor matters. Local law enforcement officials, the state militia, and occasionally federal troops were employed against strikers. Local authorities prohibited union meetings, helped drive organizers out of town, clothed company police or guards with legal authority, and in other ways helped employers harass the unions. Moreover, employers usually enjoyed the sympathy and support of middle-class elements and the owners of newspapers and other opinion-shaping communications media.

In the 1880s, the courts developed the labor injunction as a means of limiting union activity. Employers who believed that a strike or some other type of concerted worker activity threatened their property interests could go to court and seek an injunction against that activity on the ground that it would cause irreparable harm or injury to their property. Judges had wide discretion in issuing injunctions, and were usually sympathetic to the pleas of employers. Injunctions against union activity were often issued without any notice or hearing to the union. They were frequently both sweeping and vague, prohibiting "all persons whomsoever" from aiding a strike. Violators could be tried without a jury for contempt of court and, if found guilty, punished by fine or imprisonment. If an injunction was broadly drawn and strongly enforced by the police, it was an almost infallible method of breaking strikes. Even if it was not well enforced, an injunction stigmatized the union before the public, interfered with union activities, and generally helped demoralize the union and its supporters. Of course, unions bitterly opposed the use of labor injunctions, and worked long and hard for legislation restricting that use. They did not succeed until the Norris–La Guardia Act was passed in 1932.

Another tool used against the unions was the Sherman Antitrust Act (see chapter 9). Although it was generally thought that the act applied only to restraints of trade and monopolistic activities by business organizations, in 1908 the Supreme Court held that it was applicable to labor unions if their activities had the effect of restraining trade. The Sherman Act was thus transformed into a legislative obstacle for labor unions. Amendment of the act to exempt labor unions joined the elimination of government by injunction on labor's list of legislative objectives.

At the urging of labor groups, and under the leadership of the Wilson administration, Congress included some labor provisions in the Clayton Act (1914). Section 6 of the act stated that the antitrust laws should not be construed to prohibit the existence of labor unions or to forbid "members of such organizations from lawfully carrying out the legitimate objects thereof." Section 20 was designed to prevent the issuance of labor injunctions against strikes, boycotts, and picketing, except to prevent irreparable damage to property or a property right. These provisions were hailed by Samuel Gompers and other labor leaders as "labor's Magna Carta." Labor's victory, however, was of short duration: hostile judicial interpretations soon deprived the Clayton Act provisions of most of their intended meaning. Antitrust laws continued to be applied to unions, and injunctions continued to be issued against union activities held by the courts to be neither "lawful" nor "peaceable." By the early 1920s, the courts had largely frustrated the congressional effort to protect unions against unfavorable judicial action.

In 1932, labor won its greatest legislative victory to that time, when Congress passed the Norris–La Guardia Act, which prohibited the enforcement of yellow-dog contracts in the federal courts. It also deprived the federal courts of jurisdiction to issue labor injunctions against strikes, union membership, payment of strike benefits, peaceful picketing, or publicizing a labor dispute by any persons, singly or in concert, participating or interested in a labor dispute. The act set down procedural rules governing the issuance of injunctions and making them more difficult to obtain. The effect of the Norris–La Guardia Act was to neutralize the courts in labor disputes, and to give labor as much freedom from injunctions as management had long enjoyed. The act reflected a new philosophy: "The law should intervene [in labor disputes] only to prevent damage to tangible property and to preserve public order; otherwise, the disputants should be left to their own resources to work out their own problems. Both labor and business would now be free to promote their own interests in the field of labor policy through self-help without interference of the courts."[11]

A "liberalized" Supreme Court later interpreted the statute to provide labor unions with almost complete freedom from judicial action in labor disputes. Most of labor's grievances against government by injunction were finally remedied.

Throughout this period, then, labor unions were handicapped by hostile executive and judicial action. With the exception of the Norris–La Guardia Act, most legislation favorable to unions usually was rendered ineffective by the courts. Although unfavorable community attitudes and periodically depressed economic conditions also worked to the disadvantage of organized labor, the legal environment created by a hostile judiciary was certainly an important obstacle to the growth of unionization and collective bargaining. Between 1900 and 1933, union membership was usually below 10 percent of nonagricultural employment. Outside of the railroad industry and the skilled crafts, unions were largely nonexistent.

1933–1947: Protection and Promotion

From 1933 until 1947 the policy of the national government toward unions can be described as one of protection and positive support for unionization and collective bargaining. During this period, the New Deal–Fair Deal administrations provided a favorable politico-legal environment for organized labor.

The National Industrial Recovery Act.   The first New Deal measure to directly aid unionism was the National Industrial Recovery Act of 1933. This act attempted to alleviate the problems of unemployment, economic insecurity, and declining production by encouraging business self-regulation through industry codes of fair competition. Section 7a of the NIRA provided that each code should contain a guarantee of the rights of workers to organize and bargain collectively through unions of their own choosing. This effort to help unions proved ineffective because of employer resistance and because the administrative boards later created to enforce Section 7a had no meaningful sanctions to use against employers who refused to bargain collectively. Indeed, the only sanction available to those boards was withdrawal of the Blue Eagle emblem—which was used to symbolize compliance with the law—from noncompliers.

The Wagner Act. When the NIRA was declared unconstitutional in 1935, Congress quickly replaced Section 7a with the National Labor Relations Act, better known as the Wagner Act after its leading sponsor, Senator Robert Wagner (D.-N.Y.). The general purpose of the Wagner Act was to guarantee the right of workers to organize and bargain collectively through unions of their own choosing, free from employer interference. To make this guarantee effective, the act prohibited a number of unfair employer practices:

- It forbade employers to "interfere with, restrain, or coerce" employees in exercising their rights to organize and bargain collectively.
- It prohibited employers from dominating or interfering with labor organizations or giving them financial or other support; that is, it banned "company unions"— unions set up and controlled by management.
- It barred employers from discriminating against workers in hiring, firing, or conditions of employment because of union membership.
- It prohibited employers from discharging or discriminating against workers who filed charges under the act. This was intended to prevent employer retaliation.
- It prohibited employers from refusing to bargain collectively with unions representing their employees. This placed on employers the obligation to bargain with unions, but not necessarily to agree with them.

To enforce these prohibitions, the act established the National Labor Relations Board (NLRB), an independent regulatory commission headed by a three-member board (its size was later increased to five by the Taft-Hartley Act). The board was authorized to investigate and hold hearings on complaints of unfair employer practices, and to issue cease and desist orders to employers found guilty of specified unfair practices. The board's orders were enforceable through the federal courts of appeals. In addition, the board was given the duty of determining the appropriate unit for collective bargaining—craft, plant, company, or other unit. Where there was controversy over which union should represent employees in a particular bargaining unit, the NLRB was to determine by secret election or other suitable methods which union (if any) the majority of employees wanted to represent them. That union was then certified the sole bargaining agent for the unit.

In general, then, the Wagner Act created a procedure for selecting the employees' bargaining representative, required employers to bargain, and placed some restraints on employers in their dealing with unions. As far as the results of the bargaining process were concerned, unions and management were left free to agree or disagree on terms of work, working conditions, fringe benefits, and union security arrangements. The NLRB was given no authority to directly intervene in the bargaining process. The act, however, did place the weight of government on the side of the unions, offering support and protection they previously had not enjoyed. In contrast, under the Norris–La Guardia Act, the government had taken an essentially laissez faire position on labor relations.

The twelve years following passage of the Wagner Act saw collective bargaining established as an accepted method of conducting labor-management relations. At the same time, although the act did not require union membership, unions prospered during this period; their membership rose from 4 million in 1935 to about 15.5 million in 1947. Although favorable economic conditions (especially after 1940), vigorous union leadership during the 1930s, and the strong organizing efforts of the newly established CIO in mass-production industries played a part in that growth, certainly the favorable politico-legal environment created by the Wagner Act was an important factor. The act clearly achieved its purpose of promoting unionization and collective bargaining. On the other hand, the act did not generally reduce the causes or numbers of labor disputes. In this respect the act was intended only to reduce strikes by unions to gain recognition and the opportunity to bargain, and here it was apparently successful. The proportion of strikes over recognition declined sharply between 1939 and 1947. Disputes over wages, hours, and other conditions of work were outside the scope of the Wagner Act.

A variety of criticisms were directed at the Wagner Act, involving both the content of the law itself and the way in which it was administered by the NLRB. Because the act embodied a sharp shift in national policy to the advantage of unions, most of the criticism came from business and conservative sources. The National Association of Manufacturers, the Liberty League (a conservative lawyers' organization), and other conservative groups initially contended that the law was unconstitutional because it exceeded the scope of the commerce clause. This contention was rejected by the Supreme Court in 1937, when it upheld the act as a legitimate means of preventing obstructions to interstate commerce in the form of work stoppages.[12]

Business interests called the act one-sided, claiming it restricted the activities of employers but not those of unions. Employers, for example, were required to bargain in good faith; not so the unions. The act did favor unions, of course, because its essential purpose was to promote collective bargaining by unions. Most, if not all, legislation is partial (or "one-sided") in the sense that it favors some groups over others. But partiality is not the equivalent of unreasonableness here. Whether a law is reasonable or unreasonable depends upon the criteria (values) of judgment used. Consequently, those opposed to unions tended to view the act as one-sided (i.e., unreasonable).

Another criticism of the Wagner Act was that it violated minority and individual rights because some employees in a bargaining unit might not want the union selected by the majority to bargain for them. Furthermore, if a closed shop or union shop was established, those not favoring the union would have to join it or give up their jobs. In reply, it was said that majority rule is not an alien principle in a democracy. Senator Wagner and other proponents of the law believed that democracy in industrial relations, which they saw as an objective of the Wagner Act, went hand in hand with political democracy.

Professor Robert Lane offered an insightful analysis of this controversy:

The proponents of regulation clearly select symbolic references which have the weight of cultural approval. . . . The National Labor Relations Act was commonly supported on the ground that it would extend the accepted right of freedom of association to the employee and substitute democratic electoral processes for violence. In this society businessmen writing for a closed circle of other businessmen did not challenge these objectives, but, accepting their validity, said that the law was confused because it would "foment strikes," "cause trouble," "shackle labor," and put labor under John L. Lewis, who sought "to become the virtual dictator of labor policies." That is, at the deeper level of basic objectives, symbols, and myths, there is a remarkable consensus. Ideologically we are a high-consensus society. Hence, manufacturers will say that measure will not achieve these objectives, or better will destroy them, which is the way businessmen most frequently express "contrary to the public interest."[13]

Questions of democracy aside, it is probably true that collective bargaining would not be very effective if small groups or individuals in the bargaining unit were allowed to bargain on their own. By protecting dissenting groups, then, the act would have weakened the union in the bargaining process. Opposition to strong unions, more than a concern for minority rights, was probably the motivation behind complaints that the Wagner Act was "undemocratic."

Finally, it was charged that the NLRB, in its administration of the law, was biased in favor of unions. Many of these criticisms applied directly to the law itself, because the board, in administering the law as written, could not avoid helping or protecting unions. "By their inherent nature . . . [NLRB] decisions either favored union growth or permitted the status quo to continue. Under the Wagner Act they could not place the company in a stronger bargaining position than it already enjoyed, for there were no union unfair labor practices."[14] In some instances, NLRB officials did directly involve themselves in union organizing activities and otherwise act beyond the agency's proper concern, but those actions were not representative of the board as a whole.

Charges of bias against the NLRB also came from unions, especially those in the AFL, as an outgrowth of the board's responsibility for determining bargaining units. The AFL alleged that the board favored the CIO by selecting plant and company rather than craft units for bargaining purposes; the CIO responded that the board went out of its way to be fair to the AFL. The board was never able to fully satisfy either of the two. In 1940, the AFL was sufficiently dissatisfied to join forces with a conservative coalition in the House of Representatives that wanted to amend the Wagner Act to weaken the board's position and restrict unions. Included in the package were amendments protecting AFL craft unions. The product of this strange alliance passed the House by a 2-to-1 majority, but failed in the Senate, where support for the Wagner Act was strong.

Business and conservative groups, dissatisfied with the Wagner Act and with the growth and activities of unions, devoted much time and energy to seeking amendments to the law, in order to curb unions and strengthen the position of employers.

The attitude of business groups can be generally illustrated by brief reference to the National Association of Manufacturers.[15] The NAM had opposed the enactment of the Wagner Act, claiming it was both unconstitutional and undesirable. But, after 1939, following the Court's upholding of the act and the development of greater acceptance of the principle of government intervention in labor relations, the NAM changed its position. It ceased its efforts to disprove the validity of labor's rights to organize and bargain collectively; instead, it gave limited approval to these rights but criticized the law guaranteeing them, because it promoted injustices. Specifically, the NAM charged, the law violated the rights of employees and employers and was destructive of the welfare of employers. Government legislation favorable to employers' interests rather than a policy of laissez faire now became the NAM's goal. It set out to use lobbying, public relations, and electoral activities to secure its new objective.

UNIONS AND REGULATION: 1947–1980s

In the late 1930s, a political reaction against labor unions set in, and the states began to enact restrictive labor legislation. By 1947, three-fourths of the states had passed legislation prohibiting union shops and closed shops and restricting strikes, picketing, secondary boycotts, jurisdictional and sympathetic strikes, and the use of coercion and violence. At the national level the movement to place restraints on unions moved more slowly. Many bills amending the Wagner Act in ways unfavorable to labor were introduced in Congress, but opposition by the administration and Democratic congressional leaders was strong enough to prevent their adoption. The efforts of those seeking restrictive legislation intensified after the end of World War II, and in 1947 they bore fruit when the Taft-Hartley Act was passed by large majorities in both houses of Congress. Composed primarily of Republicans and conservative southern Democrats, they were sufficient to override President Truman's veto, which was strongly urged by labor groups and their allies.

A number of factors contributed to the enactment of the Taft-Hartley law. By 1947, labor had lost considerable public support because of jurisdictional disputes between AFL and CIO unions and occasional misuses of power by unions, such as failure to bargain in good faith and coercion of employers to recognize unions despite the wishes of employees. Internal conflict also lessened labor's political power and effectiveness. Serious strikes in the steel, automobile, meat-packing, railroad, and other industries after World War II cost labor more public favor, as did the resentment created by John L. Lewis and the United Mine Workers when they defied a government order against a coal strike in the fall of 1946. For many people, an "arrogant and malevolent" John L. Lewis became the stereotype of all union leaders. While labor was losing prestige, that of business groups was rising because of their contributions to "winning the war," the return of prosperity, and their many "image-building" activities. The Republican party, which had little support among unions, gained control of Congress in the 1946 elections; its leadership believed that it had a mandate to enact legislation curbing unions. Conservative southern Democrats supported the Republicans in this endeavor. Neither organized labor nor the Truman administration could agree on proposals for moderate labor reform legislation, which might have prevented or softened the sweeping changes embodied in the Taft-Hartley Act.[16]

The Taft-Hartley Act

The Taft-Hartley Act, formally entitled the Labor-Management Relations Act, marked a major change in national labor relations policy. It replaced union promotionalism with a policy of detailed regulation intended to restrict unions and "equalize" the power of labor and management. Although the act was not as harsh as some of the more extreme antilabor spokespeople in and out of Congress would have liked, in no way did it enhance the status or power of unions.

Provisions.   First, the act attempted to strengthen the prerogatives of management and to reduce those of unions. The series of unfair employer practices in the Wagner Act were retained, but their impact on employers was partially reduced. Employers were accorded greater freedom of speech in opposing unions and more freedom to discharge employees who engaged in the unfair union practices listed below. Employers were given more opportunity to secure NLRB elections on union demands for recognition and on petitions for decertification of unions. To supplement the Wagner Act's unfair employer practices, such union activities as the following were declared unfair:

- Restraining or coercing employees in their right to join or not join a union.
- Charging, under a union shop agreement, "excessive or discriminatory" initiation fees.
- Causing or attempting to cause an employer to pay for services not actually performed ("featherbedding").
- Engaging in secondary boycotts and jurisdictional strikes.
- Refusing to bargain collectively in good faith with the employer.

Second, the Taft-Hartley Act regulated certain internal and political union practices. The law required that unions file annual reports with the Secretary of Labor on their finances, compensation of principal officers, internal rules and procedures, and initiation fees and dues. Unions that failed to comply with this requirement were not allowed to use NLRB machinery for certification and handling of unfair employer practices complaints. In addition, as the act was originally framed, union officers were required to file affidavits stating they were not members of the Communist party or other organizations advocating overthrow of the government by violence or unconstitutional methods. The unions were vigorously opposed to this requirement, arguing it was both unnecessary and unfair, because it was not applied to employers. It was repealed by Congress in 1959.

Third, the act dealt with various aspects of collective-bargaining procedure. Existing labor contracts could be legally modified or terminated only if the party wanting change gave sixty days' written notice to the other party and, after thirty days, to the Federal Mediation and Conciliation Service and any state agency with jurisdiction. During the sixty-day period, the parties were bound by the existing contract. Any workers who went out on strike during that period lost their status as employees unless their employers decided to retain them. Unions have come to give strike notices as a matter of routine, so this provision has not proved overly restrictive.

Fourth, the act outlined a special procedure for dealing with "emergency disputes" involving the "national health or safety." We discuss this aspect of the law in a later section.

Fifth, the act prohibited employees of the federal government from striking, although they were allowed to join unions and bargain with the government. The penalty for striking was immediate discharge, loss of civil service status, and ineligibility for reemployment for three years. Strikes against the government are unpopular in the United States, and are often viewed as something akin to "insurrection."

Sixth, the law abolished the Conciliation Service in the Department of Labor, and gave its mediation and conciliation activities to a new, independent agency, the Federal Mediation and Conciliation Service. The old Conciliation Service had helped settle a large majority of the cases referred to it. But employer groups believed that its location within the labor-oriented Department of Labor prevented it from being fully impartial. Supposedly, an independent agency would not have this shortcoming.

Finally, in contrast to the Wagner Act, the 1947 legislation regulated what could be included in agreements reached by collective bargaining. Limitations were placed on union security arrangements negotiated by labor and management. The closed shop, which requires employers to hire only union members, was prohibited. Union shop agreements, under which workers must join the union within a certain amount of time after being hired, were allowed, as were membership agreements, in which workers are free to join or not to join a union, but those who join must retain their membership for the length of the agreement. Originally, the Taft-Hartley Act permitted these two union agreements only if they were approved by a majority of the workers affected in an NLRB election. That requirement was removed in 1951, because up to that time workers had approved those agreements in 97 percent of the elections held.

Effect on right-to-work laws.   The Taft-Hartley Act also provided that state laws concerning union security arrangements should take precedence over federal law. In other words, in this particular area of policy, national supremacy was replaced by state supremacy. This provision left the way open for the states to enact right-to-work laws, which, by stating that union membership or nonmembership cannot be a condition of employment, outlaw all of the union security arrangements listed above. What remains permissible is the "open shop," where the worker is legally free to join or not join a union as he or she sees fit. Twenty states now have "right-to-work" laws. The proponents of right-to-work legislation have been successful primarily in the more rural states, and particularly in the South, where unions are weakest. Among the major industrial states, only Indiana enacted a right-to-work law. However, in the 1964 elections, the Democrats gained control of both houses of the Indiana legislature; and early in 1965, in accordance with the desires of labor groups, the state's right-to-work law was repealed. Voters in Missouri rejected a right-to-work law in a 1978 referendum.

Strong support for right-to-work legislation has come from employer groups seeking to increase (or retain) their power in relation to unions by eliminating union shops and compulsory unions. Their arguments, however, are usually phrased in terms of voluntarism and workers' right to freedom from coercion by unions and "labor bosses." Even the phrase *right-to-work law* is a misnomer, since these laws guarantee no one the right to work—that is, a job. But, like *fair trade* and *states' rights,* the term has strong emotional and ideological appeal because of its seeming congruency with widely shared values and beliefs in American society. Unions have outspokenly opposed right-to-work legislation as being a form of "union busting" and because it permits "free riders" to gain the benefits of collective bargaining without sharing the costs (dues) or risks (strikes) involved. (The union is required to serve all workers in the bargaining unit it represents.) Repeal or prevention of right-to-work legislation has been a major objective of organized labor.

The effect of right-to-work laws is difficult to determine. Studies of those laws in Texas and Virginia in the 1950s revealed that closed shops did exist where they were acceptable to both employers and unions, especially in the building trades.[17] The enactment of a right-to-work law probably both reflects and helps create an unfavorable political environment for unions. There is, however, some evidence that right-to-work laws may adversely affect union membership and union strength, since workers who would have to join the union under a union shop arrangement may not do so when membership is made nonmandatory by right-to-work laws. While social pressures generated by fellow workers may "compel" some to join the union, they are not always operative or effective. But whatever the actual impact of right-to-work laws on unions, the controversy over them continues.

Having had little success in obtaining the repeal of right-to-work laws in the states, the AFL-CIO decided to seek congressional action to repeal Section 14b of the Taft-Hartley Act, the provision that allows right-to-work laws. With the sweeping Democratic presidential and congressional victories in the 1964 elections, the AFL-CIO believed it had enough support to obtain favorable action during the 89th Congress. Repeal of Section 14b was given top priority on the AFL-CIO's legislative agenda, and, in the spring of 1965, President Johnson sent a message to Congress supporting repeal. Most unions, especially the large industrial ones, actively supported repeal. Opposition came from business and conservative groups, among them the National Association of Manufacturers and the National Right to Work Committee.

The repeal legislation was considered first in the House of Representatives, where it passed by a 221 to 203 vote. This was made possible by a farm-labor coalition formed by the Democratic leadership, in which Democrats from northern industrial areas agreed to support the 1965 farm bill in return for support of Section 14b repeal by farm state Democrats. The votes of some Republicans from industrial areas were also vital to its passage. In the Senate, although a majority of members appeared to favor repeal, a coalition of Republicans and southern Democrats conducted a filibuster that led to the bill's defeat. A second effort to secure repeal was made in 1966, but it too was defeated by a Senate filibuster. Since then, labor has made no significant efforts to eliminate Section 14b, although it has not abandoned its dislike of the provision.

Impact and administration.   The Taft-Hartley Act has been a focal point of labor politics since its enactment. Organized labor denounced it as a "slave-labor law," and made its repeal or substantial modification a major legislative objective. President Truman promised to work for its repeal during the 1948 presidential campaign, and made various efforts to redeem his pledge. In 1954, President Eisenhower proposed a series of amendments to the act, some of which favored labor. However, there have been no substantial legislative modifications of the statute (although several changes were made by the Landrum-Griffin Act of 1959, discussed below). The absence of major changes has resulted in part because those who favor change disagree over the specific form it should take. Moreover, the act has become a symbolic issue on which both supporters and opponents have tended to take extreme, intransigent positions. This has made it difficult to get proposed amendments considered on their merits, and has reduced the possibility of compromise solutions. With the passing of time, labor has learned to live with the act, even though it has not stopped seeking favorable changes in the law.

It should be clear, on the basis of the preceding discussion, that the Taft-Hartley Act restrained unions in a variety of ways to the advantage of management. This was the intent of the limitations placed on the bargaining process, the content of agreements, and union organizing and bargaining practices. However, it seems agreed that the law has probably affected new or weaker unions more seriously than it has such strong, well-established unions as the Teamsters, the Steelworkers, and the Automobile Workers. Moreover, its impact on existing unions has been softened by the fact that generally prosperous economic conditions have existed since 1947. Consequently, employers have usually found it more profitable to get along with unions than to provoke them.

The operational meaning and the impact of the Taft-Hartley Act are conditioned by the way in which the law is administered by the NLRB. Although the board does not have a free hand in applying the law, it does have considerable discretion in interpreting the general provisions. Supporters of the act included provisions for revamping the NLRB—its membership was increased from three to five, and a separate office of General Counsel was created to handle case prosecution—to ensure the statute would be administered as they intended. The unexpected election of President Harry Truman in 1948, however, resulted in the appointment of board members between 1947 and 1953 who were favorably inclined toward unions. Consequently, the impact of Taft-Hartley on labor during its first five years was eased by board decisions, this despite management groups who complained that the board's bias was perverting the meaning of the act. In early 1953, a U.S. Chamber of Commerce spokesman contended: "A dispassionate review of the decisions of the board seems to disclose a studied attempt to evade the clear-cut intent of Congress, as expressed in the Taft-Hartley Act, and to revert to the principles established under the Wagner Act."[18]

When the Eisenhower administration took office in 1953, it was urged by business groups to "do something" about the NLRB. The course of action decided on was the appointment of persons to the board favorable to business interests; and this the administration did as vacancies appeared. The "Eisenhower Board," as it was dubbed by labor, proceeded to reverse many of the pre-1954 decisions that were favorable to labor. The shift created unhappiness among labor groups and satisfaction in the business community. As a representative of the National Association of Manufacturers commented in late 1954:

> Though the language of Taft-Hartley has remained unchanged, its interpretation by the Labor Board has not. On numerous and important issues, a new board, a majority of whose members have been appointed by President Eisenhower, has overturned long-established rulings, and given the act a new, and almost antilabor, meaning. Indeed, the Eisenhower appointees seem to have taken office with that end consciously in mind. . . . They have proceeded to imbue the board with the employer-oriented interests of the new administration.[19]

After 1961, the pendulum swung back in the direction of labor. Responsive to labor interests, the Kennedy administration appointed people to the NLRB who were sympathetic toward unions and collective bargaining. As a consequence, the board reversed or modified many of the decisions made by the "Eisenhower Board." The impact of this labor-oriented swing was to blunt restrictions on union tactical weapons (picketing, boycotts), to restrict employers' counterweapons (speeches opposing unions), and to define the bargaining unit so as to facilitate union organizing. For example, the board held that a single store in a retail chain was an appropriate bargaining unit; the "Eisenhower Board" had held that the appropriate unit for bargaining should embrace all the employees in all the stores located in an employer's administrative division or geographic area.[20] Obviously, this decision made it easier for unions to organize stores in a chain on a one-by-one basis. Once again, employer groups began to criticize the NLRB for being biased toward labor, while organized labor expressed satisfaction with the board's decisions.

Changes in the general thrust of NLRB decision making have continued to occur with changes in presidential administrations, but this does not mean that the board has simply engaged in case-by-case decision making, responding only to immediate pressures and neglecting to develop any coherent and overriding policies. For example, Friendly has characterized the NLRB as an agency "that has done much to translate the general words of its charter into more specific guides for behavior by the regulated and decisions by the regulators."[21] Two factors seem especially important in explaining the board's behavior as a systematic policymaker.

First, the NLRB deals with two strong, well-organized groups with differing economic interests. In making decisions in labor relations cases, it is hard to avoid antagonizing the loser, who is likely to appeal the case in either a political or a judicial manner. In order to avoid reversal of its decisions, the board needs to follow correct legal procedures and to make each decision appear as part of a pattern of previous decisions. Such behavior makes it more difficult to successfully challenge particular decisions. Second, the NLRB's decisions do not involve the direct distribution of material awards or benefits (such as higher rates or television broadcast licenses). Instead, the NLRB helps shape the rules that parties in collective-bargaining decisions must abide by. Although this helps determine the outcome of a dispute, the board does not determine the content of the final agreement. Rather "it bases its decisions on principles of democratic representation, the integrity of contracts, bargaining ethics. . . . These lend themselves to general policymaking far more than purely economic matters which have less ethical content."[22]

The criticism most frequently directed at the NLRB is that it is too legalistic and formal in its decision-making activities. This style of operation has led to the development of a long, complex set of rules to govern bargaining behavior, which in turn has made the task of resolving bargaining disputes more difficult, costly, and time consuming. This, in turn, has caused the parties to a dispute to rely increasingly on the agency to adjust their differences, rather than do this on their own.[23]

The Landrum-Griffin Act

In the late 1950s, there were continuing and increasing complaints about corruption, abuses of power, and undemocratic procedures in unions. From 1957 to 1959, the McClellan Committee (officially, the Senate Select Committee on Improper Activities in Labor-Management Affairs) conducted investigations and held hearings on alleged corruption and racketeering by union officials.[24] Attention was especially focused on the Teamsters (particularly its president, Jimmy Hoffa, and his predecessor, David Beck) and a few other unions, such as the Carpenters. The committee's charges and findings were widely reported by the news media, and many people came to believe that the unsavory practices of these few unions were typical of all unions. Specific actions—among them, the indictment and conviction of Beck for misuse of Teamsters' funds and the expulsion of the Teamsters and a few other unions from the AFL-CIO for unethical practices—seemed to confirm the committee's allegations of union wrongdoing.

By 1959, there was widespread agreement that union reform legislation was needed. Antiunion and management groups wanted tough legislation to restrict unions. The Democratic leadership in Congress, perceiving that the public favored union reform, believed that some kind of reform legislation was a political necessity. The AFL-CIO also saw a need for that legislation. Although the AFL-CIO had tried to clean its own house, it recognized that reform legislation was necessary to rebuild the waning prestige of labor as a law-abiding group deserving of public respect. The unions were questing for what sociologists would call a new identity.

A reform bill fairly acceptable to labor (the Kennedy-Ervin Bill) was passed by the Senate. In the House, however, things were different. Antiunion sentiment was stronger, and labor and its supporters were in disarray. The House Committee on Education and Labor, which was controlled by liberal Democrats, supported the Elliott Bill, which was more lenient than the Kennedy-Ervin Bill. The AFL-CIO, however, refused to support the Elliott Bill, favoring instead the even more lenient Shelley Bill. Some unions, such as the Teamsters and the United Mine Workers, were opposed to any legislation. Some railroad and building trades unions lobbied in favor of items of particular benefit to them, such as amendments to the Taft-Hartley Act and neglected everything else. Finally, Rep. Phil Landrum (D.–Ga.) and Rep. Robert Griffin (R.–Mich.) introduced a stringent bill that included provisions on internal union affairs and some amendments to the Taft-Hartley Act. Its adoption was strongly supported by President Eisenhower. Although the Landrum-Griffin Bill was opposed by labor, a conservative coalition of Republicans and southern Democrats pushed it through the House. The conference committee which met to resolve the differences between the two houses did reduce some of the bill's economic restrictions. Nonetheless, the bill remained objectionable to the AFL-CIO, and its enactment was regarded as a political defeat for labor. Labor's disunity certainly contributed to this result.

The Landrum-Griffin Act, officially titled the Labor-Management Reporting and Disclosure Act of 1959, injected the government even more deeply into internal union affairs than did the Taft-Hartley Act. It was also much more specific and detailed than the earlier act. Section 1 of the Landrum-Griffin Act contains a "bill of rights" which is intended to guarantee union members equal rights to participate in union meetings and vote in union elections, to protect their rights to sue the union, and to be free from unfair disciplinary action. Procedures for increasing union dues and initiation fees are regulated. A later section provides that officers of national or international unions be elected at least every five years by secret ballot of the members or by a convention of delegates chosen by secret ballot. Local labor organizations must choose their officers at least every three years by secret ballot. Detailed procedures governing union elections are also set forth. These provisions were intended to increase member control of union affairs (or at least make it possible), and they rested on the assumption that the interests of union leaders and members may often be divergent.

Other sections of the act require unions to file with the Secretary of Labor detailed reports on their financial practices and condition, operating procedures, and loans to officers, members, or employers; regulate the administration of trusteeships (local unions taken over and directly managed by the national union); require the bonding of union officials; and prohibit persons convicted of felonies or persons belonging to the Communist party from serving as union officials until five years after their release from prison or the termination of their party membership, respectively. Criminal penalties are provided for most violations of the act, and the Secretary of Labor is given broad investigatory power to uncover violations.

The last section of the act, Title VII, contains a number of amendments to the Taft-Hartley Act. This part of the legislation caused the most controversy during its enactment because it directly affected the balance of union-management power. Restrictions on secondary boycotts and organizational picketing were strengthened; and the use of "hot cargo" contracts, whose legality under Taft-Hartley had been unclear, was outlawed. (A "hot cargo" contract is an agreement between a union and an employer whereby the employer agrees not to require workers to handle materials coming from another employer with whom the union has a dispute. It is a form of secondary boycott that was much used by the Teamsters Union.) The no-man's-land created by the NLRB under Taft-Hartley was also eliminated. That is, the board had declined to take jurisdiction over some disputes because of the small size or nature of the industry involved; and the Supreme Court had held that, because the board *could* take jurisdiction, the states were excluded from doing so even in the absence of board action. Consequently, no agency regulated labor-management relations in these instances. Landrum-Griffin dealt with this situation by authorizing the states to act in this area. The relevant state laws usually provide less protection for labor than does Taft-Hartley. Title VII also contains a number of sweeteners for labor. Something approaching the closed shop was legalized in the building industry; this provision lessened the opposition of the building trade unions to the new legislation and helped create disunity in the ranks of labor. Unions in the building and clothing industries were also exempted from the restrictions on secondary boycotts when attempting to control subcontracting in their respective industries.

The impact of the Landrum-Griffin Act appears to have been beneficial, although it has produced no major changes in union power. The use of union trusteeships has greatly lessened, many union constitutions have been changed to bring them into harmony with the electoral provisions of the statute, and a number of union officials have been indicted and/or convicted each year, mostly for misuse of union funds. Generally, the act seems to have contributed to more openness in the conduct of union affairs; at the same time, there is not much solid evidence to suggest that rank-and-file participation in internal union affairs has increased appreciably.[25]

Labor Law Reform

Faced with a steady decline in the unionized portion of the nation's labor force, in 1977 the AFL-CIO sought the enactment of legislation to make it easier for unions to recruit members and negotiate collective-bargaining agreements with employers.[26] The proposed Labor Reform Act was designed to make a number of procedural changes in existing labor laws. For example, the bill would have required that union representation elections be held within forty-five days after a petition for an election was filed with the NLRB. This would give employers less time to campaign against unionization. And an election would not be necessary if 55 percent of the affected employees signed cards saying they wanted to be represented by a given union. (Under existing law, a union representation election cannot be avoided if an employer demands one.) Where an employer refused to bargain with a certified union, the bill would have empowered the NLRB to write the collective-bargaining contract it determined the parties would have signed had the employer bargained in good faith. Also, the NLRB would have been empowered to bar an employer found to have engaged in flagrant or repeated unfair labor practices from receiving government contracts for three years.

The AFL-CIO launched a massive lobbying campaign to secure enactment of the reform bill, which it made its top legislative priority. Business groups, who believed the bill would give too much power to organized labor, established the National Action Committee on Labor Law Reform to coordinate their efforts to defeat the legislation. A titanic legislative struggle followed. The bill, which had the support of the Carter administration, passed the House in October 1977 by a vote of 257 to 163. It ran into difficulty in the Senate, however. Conservatives conducted a filibuster, which the Democratic Senate leadership was unable to defeat by cloture motions to cut off debate. (Two such motions received 58 of the 60 votes needed to end debate.)[27] The labor reform bill was referred back to committee, from which it never reemerged. Once again, organized labor had failed to secure the enactment of priority legislation of direct benefit to itself.

SETTLEMENT OF LABOR DISPUTES

One of the basic issues raised for public policy by collective bargaining is the problem of work stoppages (or strikes) that interfere with production considered essential to the general welfare. The strike, or the threat thereof, is an effective means by which a union can influence employer behavior in the bargaining process primarily because it interferes with production. But, because it does this, a strike will also affect the goals or desires of others in the community—persons who are neither strikers nor struck employers—by depriving them of desired services, products, or commodities, by interfering with national defense activities, or by indirectly putting them out of work. Consequently, there are demands for government action to prevent or aid in the resolution of strikes and disputes. Such demands have been especially strong when work stoppages disrupt wartime or national defense industries or when they involve activities considered essential to community well-being, such as hospitals, police protection, government agencies, and, often, public utilities. Governments have sometimes acted to prohibit strikes in these areas. Recall Taft-Hartley's prohibition of strikes by federal employees.

Generally, however, government action has not taken the form of prohibition of strikes. Rather, government policymakers have focused their efforts on developing means for settling labor-management disputes that keep government intervention at a minimum and preserve freedom of action for the private bargainers. Nonetheless, the trend has been toward greater government intervention in disputes. But although government action can lessen the possibility of work stoppages that affect important public or group goals, it cannot do so entirely without eliminating collective bargaining by prohibiting strikes and providing for government determination of the terms and conditions of work. In short, strikes and the resulting inconveniences are part of the costs of collective bargaining and economic freedom. Those who value the latter must be prepared to accept the former.

There are a number of reasons why bargaining parties may be unwilling or unable to reach agreement on a particular issue or set of issues. First, one of the parties may want a strike. An employer may see a strike as an opportunity to eliminate a union; union leaders may believe a strike is necessary to demonstrate that the union has not "gone soft." Second, the parties may be unable to reach an acceptable compromise. The employer may insist on a change in work rules that the union perceives as a threat to its security and survival; or the union may insist on a wage increase that the employer cannot or will not pay. Third, external factors may prevent agreement even when the negotiators themselves are willing to compromise. Union leaders may believe that concessions will weaken their position within the union; or a plant manager may be directed by an absentee board of directors to take a position that leads to a strike. Fourth, on the basis of past behavior, one party may underestimate the other's strength and willingness to resist. An employer who has made concessions to the union in the past may decide that he or she can no longer afford to do so. The issues themselves are not always the problem, then. Often the conditions of bargaining play a role in the settlement process too.

Methods of Settlement

There are several ways in which government can deal with labor-management disputes and work stoppages. In addition to those discussed below—mediation and conciliation, emergency procedures, and arbitration—are the use of fact-finding boards, compulsory delay of strikes to permit settlement efforts, and government seizure and operation of struck plants (this last alternative was used frequently during World War II).

Mediation and conciliation.   Governments in the United States have relied primarily on mediation and conciliation in trying to settle labor-management disputes. Mediation agencies at the national level include the Federal Mediation and Conciliation Service and the National Mediation Board (the NMB has jurisdiction over railroad and airline disputes). Many of the states and some large cities also have mediator services. Mediation is a voluntary approach under which the government does not compel a settlement or the acceptance of its services. Nor is the right to strike denied. In general, mediation involves working with the parties to a dispute to get them to discuss their differences, to help define the essence of the dispute, and to suggest possible solutions. Much depends on the skill and experience of the mediator, who must fashion that role to fit the particular dispute situation. A good mediator may be able to devise, and persuade the parties to accept, a previously unthought of solution, or may be able to employ the threat of adverse public opinion in promoting a settlement. There is no way of determining how many disputes have been settled through government mediation, but most observers believe the number is high. They also agree that the process is more effective in the earlier stages of a dispute, before the positions of the parties have hardened.

The existence of mediation agencies at the national, state, and local levels, together with the absence of clear jurisdictional lines among them, has produced many situations in which two or more agencies intervene in the same dispute. What results is conflict and competition among the mediators in an effort to have their services accepted by the parties to a particular dispute. Instances have been reported in which a mediator "urged one party to withdraw the dispute from a rival agency on the promise that a shift would assure a better settlement."[28] Because alternative mediators are available, disputants may pick and choose among them, each favoring the mediator thought most agreeable to its interests. Thus, the selection of a mediator can become a new issue for labor and management to struggle over. Conflict and competition among different mediators for "business" may actually hinder the resolution of disputes.

Why do these situations occur when the use of mediators is voluntary and when government mediators typically receive the same salary regardless of the number of cases they handle? Mediators are human; they want opportunities to display their talents, both to enhance their self-esteem and to gain the respect and approval of others. Moreover, large case loads justify the mediation agency's existence and its budgetary requests. In a move to eliminate jurisdictional friction, and to improve the effectiveness of mediation, federal and state mediators in 1964 adopted a code of professional conduct to govern their relationships and to promote cooperation among themselves. In effect, the mediators mediated their own "jurisdictional dispute."

Not all mediation is handled by permanent government agencies. Mediation of disputes, particularly serious ones, may also be undertaken on an ad hoc, "extralegal" basis by top-level executive officials or others at the direction of the president. In 1964, for example, President Lyndon Johnson, his Secretary of Labor

(Willard Wirtz), and other executive officials, together with some nationally known mediators appointed by the president, brought about a settlement of the five-year-old dispute over work rules in the railroad industry. Because of their status and the political pressure they can exert, the parties to a dispute find it difficult to reject efforts by the president or top-level executive officials to gain a settlement. Since the Johnson administration, however, presidents have been less inclined to intervene in labor-management conflicts.

Settling of emergency disputes.   The framers of the Taft-Hartley Act set up a special procedure for dealing with "emergency disputes" that "imperil the national health or safety." If the president believes that a dispute fits into this category, he first appoints a board of inquiry to investigate and report the facts. With that report in hand, the president may direct the attorney general to seek an injunction from a federal district court, postponing the strike or lockout for an eighty-day period. The courts have always issued these injunctions when requested. The Federal Mediation and Conciliation Service is then brought in to help the disputants reach agreement. If the dispute is unsettled after sixty of the eighty days have elapsed, the NLRB enters the scene and polls employees to determine whether they would accept "the employer's last offer of settlement." The employees have always upheld the union, overwhelmingly rejecting the employer's last offer. When the eighty-day period is over, the injunction is dissolved, and a strike or lockout becomes legal. The president then submits a report on the dispute to Congress, together with any recommendations for legislative action he may care to make.

This procedure has been employed about thirty times since 1947, primarily in longshore, atomic energy, and coal industry disputes. Most observers agree that it has not been very effective. Most recent presidents have preferred to use extralegal forms of action rather than the emergency dispute procedure.

Arbitration.   Another alternative open to government in resolving labor disputes is arbitration. Under arbitration, the terms of a settlement are determined by a third party after a formal or informal hearing. Arbitration may be voluntary (agreed to by the contending parties) or compulsory (mandatory by law). Voluntary arbitration is widely accepted and used by labor and management as the final step in settling grievances arising under labor contracts. Under the Railway Labor Act of 1926, as amended, public boards are provided for voluntary arbitration of disputes in the railroad and airline industries. Neither industry has used the procedure much in recent years, preferring instead mediation and other means of settlement.

Compulsory arbitration has not been used extensively in the United States. Both labor and management generally oppose the process, in part because its effect is to substitute government action for collective bargaining. Some use of compulsory arbitration to settle disputes has been made by the national government during wartime (when national emergency serves as a justification) and by a few states in labor disputes affecting public utilities. Experience in those states indicates that the laws encourage weak bargainers to avoid private bargaining in the hope of better promoting their interests through government arbitration. The first peacetime use of compulsory arbitration by the national government in a major labor dispute came in 1963. In order to prevent a nationwide rail strike, Congress passed a law providing for compulsory arbitration of the conflict between the major railroads and five railway unions on two issues: the employment of fire fighters in diesel locomotives and the makeup of train crews. The AFL-CIO and the railway unions strongly opposed this legislation, and, although they were not successful in preventing it, succeeded in having the arbitration handled by a special board rather than the Interstate Commerce Commission as proposed by the Kennedy administration. The unions contended that the ICC was biased in favor of the railroads. Congress also acted to prevent nationwide railway strikes in 1967 and 1971. Because of their vital relationship to the operation of the economy, railroads have come to represent a special case. Since World War II, Congress and the president, by various means, have not allowed a major railroad strike to last more than a few days. In other areas of the economy, intervention has usually been confined to less severe forms.

A notable exception was the Reagan administration's handling in 1981 of the illegal strike by the Professional Air Traffic Controllers Organization (PATCO). The controllers had signed a waiver of their right to strike when they took jobs as Federal Aviation Administration employees at the nation's airports. All of those who refused to return to work were fired by the Secretary of Transportation. Moreover, PATCO was later decertified, and subsequently ceased to exist. Illegal strikes by public employees are nothing new—there were several hundred in 1980, for instance. What was new was the tough stance taken by the Reagan administration; although it was not repeated during the next two years, it stands as a chilling symbol for public employee unions.

THE OCCUPATIONAL SAFETY AND HEALTH ACT

The federal, state, and local governments have adopted a substantial volume and variety of protective labor legislation. Two comparatively new areas of protective activity involve efforts to guarantee equal employment opportunities and to ensure safe and healthful work environments. Public policy in both areas has been, and remains, controversial. We examined equal employment opportunity in chapter 8 because of its civil rights content; here we turn to occupational safety.

Until Congress passed the Occupational Safety and Health Act in 1970, the regulation of safety and health conditions in the workplace was left primarily to the state governments. There were, however, some exceptions: railway safety legislation (such as that requiring the use of automatic couplers on trains) was first passed in the 1890s. Coal mine safety was another area of early federal involvement, although the legislation, including the 1969 Coal Mine and Safety Act, has never been especially effective because of inadequate enforcement. An early occupational disease statute was the White Phosphorus Match Act of 1912, which taxed those matches out of existence. (These matches were cheaper than other matches, but workers engaged in their manufacture frequently developed a disease known as "phossy jaw," which caused the destruction of their jawbones.)

On the whole, the record of the states in protecting workers against job hazards was not impressive, and pressure for general federal legislation began to grow. In 1970, the House Committee on Education and Labor cited the following data from the Bureau of Labor Statistics in support of federal action: "15,500 workers killed, 2,700,000 workers injured, 390,000 cases of occupation disease (lung cancer, asbestosis, etc.). 250,000 man-days of work lost (ten times as many as by strikes). More than $1.5 billion in lost wages. More than $8 billion loss to GNP."[29]

A three-year legislative campaign, which featured a bitter struggle between labor and business lobbyists, culminated in the enactment of the Occupational Safety and Health Act in late 1970. Organized labor and liberals wanted the Department of Labor to be authorized both to establish and to enforce health and safety standards. Business groups and conservatives wanted program administration to be handled by two independent boards—one to set standards, the other to handle enforcement. They contended that the Department of Labor would be too responsive to labor's interests, and that due process would be violated if the same agency both set and enforced standards. Labor groups, in response, argued that the independent boards were likely to become "captives" of the regulated businesses. The bill passed by the Senate followed the labor recommendation; the House bill took the independent-boards approach. In the end, a compromise was struck.

The Occupational Safety and Health Administration (OSHA) was established in the Department of Labor with authority to set safety and health standards "reasonably necessary or appropriate to provide safe or healthful employment and places of employment." For toxic substances, the law is a bit more specific, stating that OSHA "shall set the standard which most adequately assures, to the extent feasible, on the basis of the best available evidence, that no employee shall suffer material impairment of health or functional capacity even if such employee has regular exposure to the hazard dealt with by such standard for the period of his working life." The law left OSHA with considerable discretion in adopting health and safety standards.

The enforcement of the health and safety standards is also handled by OSHA, through the inspection of workplaces. However, its decisions on violations can be appealed to the independent Occupational Safety and Health Review Commission (OSHRC), which consists of three presidentially appointed members. The National Institute for Occupational Safety and Health, an agency charged with conducting research on health and safety and recommending standards to OSHA, was placed in the Department of Health, Education, and Welfare (now Health and Human Services).

To get the health and safety effort under way quickly, Congress directed OSHA to adopt existing "national consensus standards," voluntary standards that had been developed by various industrial and private organizations. Unfortunately for OSHA, many of the thousands of consensus standards which it quickly adopted turned out to be obsolete, unnecessary, or ridiculous. For example, one of the standards specified that fire extinguishers be hung precisely 39 inches high; another banned the use of ice in drinking water; still another required clothes hooks on restroom walls; and there was one that specified the shape of toilet seats. These rules generated a lot of criticism of OSHA, which still colors attitudes toward the agency. In 1978, OSHA acted to repeal over nine hundred consensus rules.

The Occupational Safety and Health Act covers over 4 million workplaces (ranging from large factories to small retail stores), approximately 65 million workers. Penalties of up to $1,000 may be assessed for serious violations of health and safety standards and up to $10,000 for willful or repeated violations. A provision that would have allowed the agency to shut down plants presenting an "imminent danger" to the lives of workers was deleted from the act before its adoption. In 1979, OSHA had about fifteen hundred health and safety inspectors. They inspected 59,937 workplaces and issued 128,544 citations for violations, with proposed penalties totaling over $30 million.[30] The penalties assessed for violations have usually been modest, and some have been reduced or eliminated by appeals to OSHRC.

In its operations, OSHA has been variously viewed as too punitive by business groups (notwithstanding its limited enforcement capabilities), as rather ineffectual by labor, as poorly administered by some members of Congress, and as too little concerned about the financial costs of compliance with its standards by business and conservative spokespersons. Here we can deal briefly with only a few of the issues that have developed concerning the act and its administration by OSHA.

1. Operators of small businesses and their congressional advocates have contended that the costs of compliance are especially burdensome for small businesses, and could drive many of them out of existence. Most efforts to exempt small businesses from the act's coverage have not been successful, although farms with ten or fewer employees were excluded. In 1977, OSHA announced it would focus its enforcement efforts on "high-risk" industries. Because most small businesses are not in this category, their chances of being inspected dropped to 1 in 1,300.

2. Under present law, inspectors must issue citations when violations are found in a workplace. Industry spokespeople argue that, in order to ease the costs of compliance and to encourage voluntary compliance, inspectors should be able to enter workplaces and consult with employers without issuing citations. Opponents contend this would dilute the enforcement effort and delay needed corrections (many employers would not try to bring their plants into compliance until after OSHA visitation).

3. Although dissatisfaction with state action contributed to the enactment of the national statute, the law contains a provision that allows the states to take over

enforcement of health and safety standards within their boundaries. And by mid-1983, twenty-two states had done just that. State plans are subject to OSHA approval, and must have standards "at least as effective" as those in the federal program. The states can, and some have, set standards beyond the federal requirements. Criticism here is that variations in standards can and do create compliance problems for companies with plants in several states; also, there is skepticism, based on past performance, as to how well the states will enforce standards.[31]

4. Undoubtedly, the major source of controversy has been the safety and health standards themselves. Employers contend that in many instances they are too complex, too stringent, and too costly—impossible to comply with. Others argue that the standards are often too lax to adequately protect workers, and that the agency acts too slowly in setting standards. And there are other issues. To what extent should feasibility—the technological and economic capabilities of industry to comply—be taken into account in setting standards? How can one accurately assess the impact of health hazards in the face of such problems as misdiagnosis, latency (a long time lapse before appearance), and second-generation effects? More specifically, what is an acceptable level of noise in a workplace? Should the problem of noise be dealt with by reducing its level or by having workers wear protective devices? On the whole, OSHA's setting of health standards has probably been more productive of controversy than the setting of standards for physical safety, although until 1977 the agency devoted most of its efforts to safety activities. Less is known about the health effects of many industrial chemicals and substances, and that uncertainty provides a basis for resistance by those who find proposed standards objectionable. In some instances, opposition does not rise much above the level of "what we don't know won't hurt us."

5. OSHA's insistence on the use of engineering controls rather than personal protective equipment to reduce health hazards has appeared irrational to many businesspeople and others. Reducing noise levels in factories by engineering practices is often very expensive, whereas ear plugs or muffs would cost very little. Each protects the hearing of workers. Health and safety professionals prefer engineering controls because, once installed, the problem is essentially solved. Moreover, they dislike the personal protection alternative because it places the burden of compliance on workers, not employers.[32]

6. Industry has argued that health standard rules should be put into effect only when their benefits exceed costs. This argument is based on the inclusion of the phrase "to the extent feasible" in OSHA's authorization to issue health rules. This issue was addressed in a 1981 Supreme Court case involving a rule on cotton dust (which can cause byssinosis, or "brown lung," in exposed workers). In the Court's view, the word *feasible* in the act means "capable of being done"; Congress did not intend to require cost-benefit analysis before a rule could be issued.[33]

There is no question that the maintenance of safe and healthful workplaces is a costly undertaking. The U.S. Chamber of Commerce estimates that, during the 1970s, businesses spent $116 billion on health and safety measures. On the other hand, the costs of worker illnesses and injuries are also high. The National Safety Council estimated that work accidents cost the nation $25 billion in 1979, including lost wages, medical expenses, administrative costs of insurance, and production losses to employers.[34] These, of course, are estimates, not firm figures; and given their gross nature, they tell nothing about the necessity or desirability of particular health or safety measures. Still, they do convey some notion of the financial costs involved in industrial health and safety.

The values of safe, healthful workplaces are unlikely to be yielded solely by the operation of market forces. One can argue that it is good business to maintain safe workplaces. However, such factors as the urge to hold down operating costs and the inability of workers to adequately assess the risks in given jobs will likely interfere. Regulation is thus necessary to control and improve the operation of the marketplace. Whether health and safety regulation should take the form of the standard setting and enforcement used by OSHA is another issue.

CONCLUDING COMMENTS

National labor policy, which is largely a twentieth-century development, has made organized labor a part of the American establishment. The legitimacy of unions and collective bargaining, despite the dissatisfaction of some people, has become firmly grounded in the economic structure of the country.

As it pertains to unions, labor policy is mostly concerned with the process of collective bargaining. Only infrequently does it deal directly with the outcome of labor-management bargaining. Or, to put it differently, *how* labor and management bargain is regulated, but most of *what* they bargain over is left to their discretion.

In recent decades, labor policy issues have become more technical and complex. The broad, easily understood issues—Are unions legal? What kinds of unions can exist? Must employers bargain with unions?—have been settled. Current policy questions are more detailed, more difficult to comprehend. What criteria, for example, can the NLRB use to decide when an employer is bargaining in good faith? There is no easy answer to this question.

Public policies on labor unions and collective bargaining do not create the intense, bitter conflicts they once did. The Wagner Act, in a sense, was redistributive legislation—it was intended to transfer economic and political power from management to labor. The ideological struggles generated by such legislation are usually productive of intense political conflicts based on a sharp divergence of interest. Today organized labor is a widely accepted participant in the economic and political systems. Disagreements over labor policy now take the form of pressure group politics focused on limited changes in policy.

NOTES

1. Most of the data on the labor force and unions are drawn from U.S. Bureau of the Census, *Statistical Abstract of the United States, 1981* (Washington, D.C.: U.S. Government Printing Office, 1982).
2. Gus Tyler, *A New Philosophy for Labor* (New York: Fund for the Republic, 1959), p. 11.
3. William J. Keefe and Morris S. Ogul, *The American Legislative Process* (Englewood Cliffs, N.J.: Prentice-Hall, 1964), p. 317.
4. Right-to-work laws are discussed later in this chapter. The common situs picketing bill would have allowed a construction union to picket, and close down, an entire project in a dispute with the employer. Under existing law, the union is limited to picketing only one or two entrances to a project.
5. *Houston Chronicle*, April 16, 1972, sect. 1, p. 14.
6. Paul Jacobs, *Old before Its Time: Collective Bargaining at 28* (Santa Barbara, Calif.: Center for the Study of Democratic Institutions, 1963), p. 35.
7. Alan K. McAdam, *Power and Politics in Labor Legislation* (New York: Columbia University Press, 1964), pp. 270–271.
8. Ibid., pp. 199, 210–211.
9. Lloyd G. Reynolds, *Labor Economics and Labor Relations*, 4th ed. (Englewood Cliffs, N.J.: Prentice-Hall, 1964), p. 112.
10. See Foster R. Dulles, *Labor in America*, rev. ed. (New York: Crowell, 1966); Samuel Yellen, *American Labor Struggles* (New York: Harcourt Brace Jovanovich, 1936); and Sidney Lens, *The Labor Wars* (New York: Anchor, 1974).
11. Herbert R. Northrup and Gordon F. Bloom, *Government and Labor* (Homewood, Ill.: Irwin, 1963), p. 22.
12. *NLRB* v. *Jones and Laughlin Steel Corp.*, 301 U.S. 1 (1937).
13. Robert E. Lane, *The Regulation of Businessmen* (New Haven: Yale University Press, 1954), pp. 42–43.
14. Murray Edleman, "New Deal Sensitivity to Labor Interests," in *Labor and the New Deal*, eds. Milton Derber and Edwin Young (Madison: University of Wisconsin Press, 1957), p. 171.
15. This discussion rests substantially on Richard W. Gable, "NAM: Influential Lobby or Kiss of Death?" *Journal of Politics* 15 (May 1953): 254–273.
16. For a detailed discussion of this topic, see Seymour Z. Mann, "Policy Formulation in the Executive Branch: The Taft-Hartley Experience," *Western Political Quarterly* 13 (September 1960): 597–608.
17. Frederic Myers, *"Right to Work" in Practice* (New York: Fund for the Republic, 1959); and J. M. Kuhlman, "Right to Work Laws: The Virginia Experience," *Labor Law Journal* 6 (July 1955): 453–461.
18. Quoted in Seymour Scher, "Regulatory Agency Control through Appointment: The Case of the Eisenhower Administration and the NLRB," *Journal of Politics* 23 (November 1961): 669.
19. Quoted in ibid., p. 687.
20. Sav-on-Drugs, Inc., 138 NLRB 1032 (1962).
21. Henry J. Friendly, *The Federal Administrative Agencies* (Cambridge, Mass.: Harvard University Press, 1962), p. 36.
22. Roger Noll, *Reforming Regulation* (Washington, D.C.: Brookings Institution, 1971), pp. 47–52.
23. See Charles O. Gregory and Harold A. Katz, *Labor and the Law*, 3rd ed. (New York: Norton, 1979), chaps. 12–16.
24. For one view of the committee's work, see Robert Kennedy, *The Enemy Within* (New York: Harper & Row, 1960).
25. John Hutchinson, *The Imperfect Union: A History of Corruption in American Trade Unions* (New York: Dutton, 1970), chap. 23.

26. James W. Singer, "Labor Is Giving Labor Law Reform the Old College Try," *National Journal* 9 (May 28, 1977): 818–822.

27. *Congressional Quarterly Weekly Report* 36 (June 24, 1978): 1599.

28. Edward J. Silverfarb, "Who Will Mediate the Mediators," *Reporter* 28 (March 14, 1963): 25.

29. Cited in *Congressional Quarterly Almanac* 26 (1970): 675.

30. Senate Committee on Labor and Human Resources, *Hearings on Oversight on the Administration of the Occupational Safety and Health Act,* 96th Congress, 2nd Session (1980), pp. 286–287.

31. Compare Frank J. Thompson, *Health Policy and the Bureaucracy* (Boston: MIT Press, 1981), pp. 240–242.

32. This is based on Steven Kelman, "Occupational Safety and Health Administration," in *The Politics of Regulation,* ed. James Q. Wilson (New York: Basic Books, 1980), pp. 251–252.

33. *American Textile Manufacturers Institute* v. *Donovan,* 101 S.Ct. 2478 (1981).

34. Michael Wines, "They're Still Telling OSHA Horror Stories, But the Victims Are New," *National Journal* 13 (November 7, 1981): 1989.

SUGGESTED READINGS

Derber, Milton. *The American Idea of Industrial Democracy, 1865-1965.* Champaign, Ill.: University of Illinois Press, 1970.

Dulles, Foster R. *Labor in America.* Rev. ed. New York: Crowell, 1966.

Greenstone, J. David. *Labor in American Politics.* New York: Knopf, 1969.

Gregory, Charles O., and Katz, Harold A. *Labor and the Law.* 3rd ed. New York: Norton, 1979.

Lens, Sidney. *The Labor Wars.* Garden City, N.Y.: Doubleday, 1973.

McAdam, Alan K. *Power and Politics in Labor Legislation.* New York: Columbia University Press, 1964.

Wykstra, Ronald A., and Stephens, Eleanor V. *American Labor and Manpower Policy.* New York: Odyssey, 1970.

ELEVEN

Agricultural Policy

Though often characterized as a rugged individualist who wants nothing more than to be left alone by the government to "hoe his own row," the American farmer has not hesitated during the past century to turn to the government for political redress of his economic grievances. Whatever the specific cause of dissatisfaction—low market prices, high railroad rates, insects and pests—economic insecurity, in the form of low or unstable income, has been behind most agrarian political demands. And, agrarian political discontent and agitation have tended to wax and wane with decline and improvement in the economic fortunes of the farmer.[1]

The farmers' success in invoking the aid of government is attested to by the substantial volume of legislation enacted to deal directly with farm needs and problems, and by the favorable treatment accorded agricultural interests in much nonfarm legislation. In the first instance, we can cite a multitude of programs involving agricultural price supports; agricultural education, research, and extension; the marketing of farm commodities; soil conservation, land reclamation, and irrigation; farm credit; crop insurance; and animal and plant pest control. During the 1970s, the total cost of the farm programs administered by the Department of Agriculture was about $7 billion annually.

Additionally, it seems to have long been a rule of American politics that farm interests should receive actual or symbolic preferential treatment when they are affected by nonfarm legislation. Thus, agricultural cooperatives are exempted from antitrust laws, and vehicles transporting agricultural commodities are largely exempted from national motor carrier legislation. In the interests of farm operators, farm workers are excluded from unemployment compensation and workmen's compensation, and were not covered by minimum wage laws until 1966. The federal tax code contains a variety of pro-farming provisions. Even in immigration legislation the farmer has received preference, as in the law that long permitted the importation of *bracero* (cheap) labor from Mexico to work on farms in the West and Southwest. All of this simply indicates that farmers have frequently mixed agriculture and politics to their advantage.

In this chapter, our primary focus is on agricultural price supports, the most important area of farm policy over the last three decades. It has cost the most money and generated the most conflict, both within and outside of the farm community, and, in short, it epitomizes the politics of agriculture. We also examine a number of other farm programs to show the variety and scope of government aid to agriculture.

THE TECHNOLOGICAL REVOLUTION

In the early decades of the nineteenth century, farmers produced most of their own food, clothing, and tools, and depended very little on the market for the sale of their products or the purchase of goods. After the Civil War, however, profound changes took place in the agricultural sector of the economy. Mechanized farming methods and specialized production processes led to the commercialization of agriculture. Farmers increasingly concentrated on the production of one or a few crops for sale in the market. This made farmers *interdependent* with other groups in the economy—meat packers, grain merchants, elevator operators, railroads, manufacturers of farm equipment—and dependent on the market conditions of supply and demand and prices for their income. Farming became a business, as well as a way of life.

In the twentieth century, especially since the 1930s, a vast, far-reaching technological revolution has been in progress in American agriculture. This revolution has manifested itself in mechanical, chemical, biological, and managerial forms.[2]

- Tractors and trucks have almost entirely replaced horses and mules as the sources of farm power. Along with them have come grain combines, mechanical corn and cotton pickers, gang plows, and a host of other machines. Rural electrification has permitted the use of a wide range of equipment—milking machines, feed mills, and grain dryers.
- Commercial fertilizers have led to great improvements in soil productivity. Insecticides, pesticides, fungicides, and herbicides have been developed to combat insects, pests, and plant and animal diseases that adversely affect agricultural production.
- New and improved plant varieties and livestock breeds have been developed. Hybrid seed corn has greatly increased the production of corn per acre, while in the poultry world hybrid hens lay more eggs, more often, and hybrid broilers grow drumsticks faster than their nonhybrid compatriots or ancestors. Advances have also come in animal nutrition, disease control, and sanitation.
- Farm operators (at least the more successful ones) are giving more attention to cost and output data in planning their operations and to organized production and marketing methods. Some farmers have begun to use home computers or computerized advising services to help them manage their operations.

The broad consequences of this technological revolution have been a sharp increase in agricultural productivity (per acre, farm worker, etc.), a decline in the number of farms and the farm population, and a trend toward concentration of farming operations in fewer and larger units capable of using the new technological developments to best advantage.

Increased Productivity

We can see a significant increase in agricultural production since the early 1930s. The farm output index, which is a measure of the annual volume of farm production (1967 = 100), was 60 in 1940, 91 in 1960, and 110 in 1972. In other words, in a little over three decades agricultural output nearly doubled. Because agricultural productivity has increased so greatly, only a small proportion of the population is needed to produce food for the nation. Where one farmer supplied five people in 1850 and ten people in 1940, today he or she supplies seventy-eight people.

Expanding farm output made possible by increased productivity will not bring greater farm income, however, unless the demand for farm products increases at a similar rate. Despite increases in population and in living standards, there were frequently years in which farm prices were close to or even below the cost of production because supply exceeded demand in the primary markets. Meanwhile, the costs of farm production went up (especially if we exclude the cost of farmers' own labor) because of the expense involved in using the new technology. This set of conditions produced a cost-price squeeze that had an adverse impact on farmers' income.

Concentrated Operations

The cost-price squeeze, together with the possibility of higher incomes in industrial and other nonagricultural employment, has caused a farm-to-city population movement. Both the number of farms and the farm population have declined markedly in recent decades, while the average size of farms has increased (see table 11–1).

The total amount of land under cultivation has not changed significantly in the last three decades. As the poorer and smaller farmers (they are often synonymous) have left agriculture, their land has usually been taken over by larger and better farmers. Consequently, farm production has tended to become concentrated in the hands of larger, wealthier, more efficient farmers, though many low-income farm units still remain. In 1978, the top 32 percent of farm units accounted for 78 percent of farm production, as measured by cash receipts. Many farms are either part-time or part-retirement farms, with their operators drawing most of their income

TABLE 11-1 The farm population, 1920–1980

Year	Number of farms	Average size (acres)	Farm population	Percent of U.S. total
1920	6,518,000	147	31,974,000	30.1
1930	6,546,000	143	30,529,000	24.9
1940	6,350,000	167	30,547,000	23.2
1950	5,648,000	213	23,048,000	15.3
1960	3,962,000	297	15,635,000	8.7
1965	3,356,000	340	12,363,000	6.4
1970	2,954,000	378	9,712,000	4.8
1975[a]	2,621,000	420	8,864,000	4.2
1980	2,428,000	429	6,051,000	2.1

SOURCE: U.S. Bureau of the Census, *Statistical Abstract of the United States, 1981* (Washington, D.C.: U.S. Government Printing Office, 1982), pp. 600, 657.

[a]A more restrictive definition of *farm* was adopted in 1974, which excluded some units previously counted.

from nonagricultural sources. However, the operators of about half of the farms in this category draw the major portion of their income from farming. They represent the core of farm poverty, and contrast sharply with those at the top of the agricultural income pyramid.

Competition and Prices

Agriculture is the principal sector of the economy in which conditions approaching pure competition would prevail in the absence of government price support. In any given area of farming there are typically a large number of producers, no one of whom can affect prices by controlling his production or sales. If the largest wheat farmer in Kansas were to disappear, he might be missed by some relatives and a couple of creditors but he would not be missed by the market. Further, whether because of their geographical dispersion, traits of independence, or whatever, farmers have been unable in most instances to voluntarily cooperate to reduce supply or otherwise act to increase prices. Nor can individual farmers afford to withhold their commodities from the market until they consider prices to be satisfactory. Therefore, farmers sell their products for whatever the prices may be in a highly competitive market.

Farm prices have frequently fluctuated widely from season to season. It is characteristic of agriculture that a small increase in the supply of a commodity usually produces a relatively large decrease in price. As a result, a larger quantity of a commodity may result in a smaller total return for the farmer. An example may help here. During 1951–1955, there was a steady high-level consumer demand for pork. Pork prices, however, fluctuated between $10 and $25 per hundredweight during this period as high prices brought increased production, which drove prices down, which led to cutbacks in production, which led to a price increase, and so on. Price instability of this sort obviously is detrimental to farmers (and is of little real benefit to customers). It causes farm income to be unstable, especially as farmers become more specialized and concentrate on the production of one or two commodities.

The "Farm Problem"

Out of this unstable economic situation emerged the "farm problem." How the "farm problem" is defined will help shape the solutions proposed for it. Some describe the farm problem as a price problem—farm prices are unstable and too low. The solution, then, is to raise farm prices, make them more stable, or both. The emphasis is usually on raising prices.

Others contend that the farm problem is an income rather than a price problem and cite low average farm incomes to substantiate their position. Farm per capita income is customarily less than nonfarm per capita income (see table 11–2). Farm income may be improved by raising farm prices, making direct payments to supplement farm income, or increasing the efficiency of farm operations.

TABLE 11-2   Farm income situation, 1950–1980

Year	Total net income (000,000s)	Average income per farm	Per capita farm income	Farm income as a percent of nonfarm per capita income	Parity ratio[a]
1950	$13,648	NA	$ 840	57.6	101
1955	11,305	NA	847	47.8	84
1960	11,518	$ 2,907	1,073	53.1	80
1965	12,852	3,830	1,675	67.4	77
1970	13,787	4,667	2,460	71.9	72
1971	14,194	4,879	2,643	72.4	70
1972	18,171	6,332	3,133	80.8	74
1973	33,099	11,639	4,572	106.8	88
1974	26,072	9,211	4,258	91.8	81
1975	24,475	8,845	4,520	88.4	76
1976	18,662	6,824	4,316	77.7	71
1977	18,391	7,489	5,328	89.7	70
1978	26,458	10,861	6,324	96.1	71
1979	32,697	13,456	7,475	102.5	65
1980	19,860	8,180	6,553	81.5	61

SOURCE: U.S. Bureau of the Census, *Statistical Abstract of the United States, 1981* (Washington, D.C.: U.S. Government Printing Office, 1982).

[a]Parity is a ratio of prices received by farmers to prices paid. The higher the ratio the better off farmers are likely to be.

A third view is that low farm prices and per capita farm incomes are only symptoms of the basic problem: overproduction. When supply exceeds demand, prices and income must fall. Their solution: fewer farmers. They cite the need for programs to facilitate the migration of persons off farms and into other employment—a solution not too popular with farm groups.[3]

Finally, a fourth group diagnoses the farm problem as a combination price and income problem—low farm prices produce low farm incomes. This is the definition we find used for public policy purposes, and it is the reason the government has enacted a wide variety of price support programs over the past four decades. These programs have tried to raise prices by restricting production, and directly to raise incomes by subsidizing farm operations.

For a time in the late 1970s, it seemed that the farm problem was no more. There were major changes in the marketplace: world demand for U.S. agricultural commodities increased and surpluses disappeared. Farmers were urged to plant from "fence row to fence row." However, demand fell off in the early 1980s, bringing a return of surplus production and low prices to the American market. (We can see this fluctuation in the total net income column in table 11-2.) Price support policies, once again, are being shaped in response to the traditional concept of the farm problem.

THE POLITICS OF AGRICULTURE

Historical Aspects

In the last four decades of the nineteenth century, agrarian discontent manifested itself in third-party movements that sought control of the centers of political decision making. The Greenback party, the Farmers' Alliances of the late 1880s, and the Populist party of the early 1890s were directed against the "traditional enemies" of the farmer: railroads, monopolists, bankers, and "middlemen" generally. Their political programs called for regulation of railroads and grain storage facilities, antimonopoly laws, and currency reform (this often involved proposals to enlarge the currency supply to enable farmers to pay their debts more easily). These third-party movements initially enjoyed some electoral success but were short-lived, dwindling into insignificance with the return of agricultural prosperity. They were not totally unsuccessful or without impact, however. The Granger movement, which did not take the form of a political party, gave rise to laws regulating railroads and grain warehouses in several midwestern states. Agrarian discontent was also an important factor in the adoption of the Interstate Commerce Act and the Sherman Antitrust Act (see chapter 9).

In the early 1920s, the agricultural depression, which was touched off by the decline of wartime demand for farm products, led to the development of a new strategy by farm groups for the exertion of political influence. That strategy was to elect members of Congress who were sympathetic to agricultural interests, whatever their party affiliation, and then to organize them into a disciplined, unified "farm bloc" that would support farm legislation. The American Farm Bureau Federation had much to do with the creation of the "farm bloc" and was joined by most other farm groups. The farm bloc in Congress—composed primarily of midwestern Republicans and southern Democrats—operated with considerable vigor and effectiveness. By 1926, it had secured the enactment of legislation on agricultural tariffs, farm credit, supervision of packers and stockyards, regulation of the sale of grain futures, and cooperative marketing. Although conflicts among farm groups and interests led to the decline of the farm bloc as a formal grouping during the 1930s and 1940s, a bipartisan alliance of legislators in Congress was sufficiently strong and unified to pass price support and other legislation wanted by farm interests and to prevent the enactment of unwanted legislation.

Farm organizations came into their own during the New Deal years, and agricultural politics since that time have been characterized by continuous pressure group activity intended to influence the formation and administration of agricultural policies. As the technological revolution in agriculture has increased the economic pressures on farmers, and as farm production has become more specialized, conflicts and divergencies have either developed, or become manifest, among farm groups and interests. To understand farm politics and policy issues today, we must understand the nature of those groups and interests.

Agricultural Groups

It is elementary but nevertheless highly important to recognize that there is no single farm interest. While we sometimes speak of "farmers" as if they all came out of the same mold, or hay field, they differ greatly in such factors as size of farms, amount of investments, efficiency of operations, income, education and background, political loyalties and involvement, and commodities grown.

Dairy farmers, tobacco growers, sheep and cattle raisers, feed grain producers, vegetable farmers, and wheat growers have more or less separate and distinct problems and interests, "which induce commodity consciousness rather than broad agrarian consciousness."[4] Dairy farmers and fruit growers would have little or no interest in a price support program that is considered vital by tobacco growers and that stirs them to political action to secure and maintain it. Tobacco growers, in turn, would not be much concerned with the problems of rice farmers. But, what is more pertinent here, the interests of different commodity groups may directly conflict rather than merely diverge. A price support program that will raise the price of feed grains may draw the opposition of poultry farmers and dairy farmers who use that grain to feed their stock. Dairy farmers producing butter engaged in a long struggle with the growers of soybeans and cottonseed, which yield oil used in making oleomargarine, over the issue of oleomargarine taxation. Conflict may also occur within the ranks of the growers of a particular commodity. Cotton growers in the Southeast compete with the producers of cotton on large, modern, irrigated farms in California and the Southwest, and each of the two groups seeks cotton support policies favorable to itself. Here the conflict is a regional one, as is conflict between southern livestock raisers and midwestern feed grain producers over the level of price supports for corn and feed grains.

General organizations.   The differences among farmers are reflected in the variety of organizations that represent their interests. There are several large farm organizations—the American Farm Bureau Federation, the National Farmers Union, and the National Grange—that claim to represent general farm interests. These organizations are politically important, and, in their programs and actions, reflect some of the broad ideological and economic differences that exist within the agricultural population.

The American Farm Bureau Federation, organized in 1919, is the largest and most conservative of the general farm organizations. Although it has members in every state, most come from the Midwest (especially the Corn Belt) and the South. The federation has been described as a coalition of corn, hog, and cotton farmers. It tends to speak primarily for large, prosperous commercial farmers, and has been a rather constant opponent or critic of programs designed to benefit tenant farmers, farm laborers, migratory workers, and other marginal farm groups.

The Farm Bureau was an active and vigorous defender of agricultural price support programs during the New Deal years. In the 1940s, however, in a policy position shift, the organization began to advocate a "free market" for agriculture, and allied itself closely with Republican administrations. Sometimes the Farm Bureau leadership has had to temper its free-market advocacy because of contrary positions taken by some of its membership. During the consideration of the 1977 farm bill, for example, it explained its endorsement of price supports as necessary until free-market conditions actually exist.

A second general agricultural organization is the Farmers Educational and Co-operative Union of America, more commonly known as the National Farmers Union, which began in 1902. Its members are located primarily in the wheat states of the Great Plains, and in Wisconsin, Minnesota, and Montana. The most liberal of the farm groups, the NFU advocates an active, expanded role for government in agriculture, and stresses that "farm prices are made in Washington." Especially concerned with promoting the interests of the family farms and low-income farm groups, the NFU favors high price supports, strict production controls, limitation of the government benefits available to any one farmer, rural relief programs, more agricultural credit facilities, and expanded federal crop insurance programs. To some extent, the liberal economic position of the NFU is explainable by the fact that its main strength lies in an area where the weather is especially hazardous for farming. This increases the economic insecurity of farming, a condition the NFU wants to remedy through extensive government action.

The National Farmers Union has been closely identified with the Democratic party in recent decades, and has enjoyed considerable influence in the Department of Agriculture during Democratic administrations. The NFU generally takes a liberal position on nonagricultural matters and, in contrast to the Farm Bureau, often is effectively allied with organized labor.

The National Grange is the oldest of the general farm organizations, dating back to 1867. Its membership is concentrated in New England, New York, Pennsylvania, Ohio, and the Pacific Coast states. Fruit and vegetable growers and poultry and dairy farmers predominate among its members. The Grange is deeply committed to maintaining the family farm and stresses the virtues and benefits of farming as a way of life. (It has, incidentally, been a longtime foe of drinking, smoking, and gambling.) Once the prime symbol of agrarian discontent and radicalism, since the 1920s the Grange has been the least politically aggressive of the general farm organizations. During the New Deal years, it was the most conservative, but by the late 1940s, its position shifted again. Today, the Grange favors high price supports and production controls—but not as enthusiastically as the National Farmers Union. In recent years its political significance has diminished.

A fourth farm organization, the National Farmers Organization, contrasts sharply with the "big three" in style and mode of action. Originating in Iowa in 1955, the NFO now has around 200,000 members, located primarily in the Midwest and drawn mostly from small and medium-sized farms. These are the farmers who feel squeezed the hardest by the agricultural revolution. Dissatisfied with government efforts to support farm prices and with the Farm Bureau's position, the NFO initially advocated direct action and "farm bargaining power" to improve the farmers' economic situation. By concerted action to withhold farm products from the market, the NFO hoped both to raise prices and to induce food processors to sign contracts for the purchase of farm commodities at high prices. The NFO tried withholding actions during the 1960s, but had little success in part because too few farmers participated and in part because many farmers (including some NFO members) hastened to sell their products when market prices went up a little. Today, the NFO engages in more conventional pressure group politics and advocates government action to maintain farm prices at high levels.

Dissatisfaction with the moderate positions taken by these organizations led disgruntled farmers to establish a more radical organization, the American Agricultural Movement, in the fall of 1977.[5] Many of AAM's members came from the ranks of farmers experiencing financial distress as a consequence of overexpansion during the boom of the early 1970s. The group advocated price supports at 100 percent of parity (which would set a high price level for farm products) and a ban on beef imports, and, in 1978, threatened a general agricultural strike. A massive "tractorcade" demonstration in Washington, D.C., that year brought public attention. Public officials were also responsive. The Secretary of Agriculture set higher target prices (see below), as he was authorized to do by existing law. Also, an emergency farm credit bill was passed by Congress.

In 1979, still unhappy with the farm situation, AAM held another demonstration in Washington. This one caused considerable inconvenience and damage to public property, and in the end hurt the group's image. Today, the organization relies on more conventional lobbying activities. "The AAM serves as a continued reminder to all of the other farm interest groups that many farmers will actually and at some personal expense promote positions that are inconsistent with the moderate and conservative policy positions of many farm organizations."[6]

Commodity organizations.   In addition to the general farm organizations, a large number and variety of specialized commodity organizations have arisen to represent the interests of particular commodity producers. Some of them are listed in table 11–3. They reflect the increasing specialization of American agriculture, and now have a greater impact on the nuts and bolts of farm commodity policies than do the general farm organizations. This is partly because they are able to focus on a narrower set of issues than can those general organizations. More important, they have also been able to work closely with legislators on the commodity subcommittees of the House and Senate agriculture committees.

Disagreements can and do occur among the commodity organizations when the interests of their members overlap or conflict. All is not always harmonious with the National Cattlemen's Association, which represents range cattlemen, and the National Livestock Feeders Association, which represents feedlot operators who fatten cattle for a few months prior to marketing. In the sugar industry, producers of beet, cane, and corn sweeteners at times have very different objectives. In contrast, some

TABLE 11-3 Farm commodity organizations

American Beekeeping Association
American Poultry and Hatchery Association
American Soybean Association
American Sugar Cane League
Catfish Farmers of America
National Association of Wheat Growers
National Cattlemen's Association
National Corn Growers Association
National Cotton Council
National Livestock Feeders Association
National Milk Producers Association
National Pork Producers Council
National Turkey Federation
Tobacco Institute
United Fruit and Vegetable Association
United States Beet Sugar Association
United States Feed Grains Council
Vegetable Growers Association of America

---

commodity groups have quite limited, distinct interests. The American Beekeeping Association, for example, is concerned with a single program, one that pays indemnities when honeybees are killed by pesticides.

Agribusiness organizations. These are a third type of organization involved in agricultural politics. Some are suppliers of farm inputs—fertilizers, herbicides, farm equipment, feed and feed supplements, and so on. Others are involved with commodity sales, the storage, transportation, and processing of commodities, export sales, and other output aspects of agriculture. These organizations have been especially active in the last couple of decades. Although their members are not farmers, farm policies can have tremendous impact on their economic well-being. The Carter administration's embargo in 1980 on grain sales to the Soviet Union quickly drew the attention of transport, shipping, and export firms, as well as grain producers. On price supports, input firms tend to favor higher supports, whereas output firms tend to favor lower supports. The political emergence of agribusiness groups has clearly contributed more uncertainty and complexity to the agricultural policymaking process.

Ideology and Representation

There appears to be a broad if somewhat ill-defined belief and expectation in the United States that government is obligated to help people in difficulty. As Boulding has remarked, in a quite applicable statement: "Agricultural policy is frequently sold politically, even in countries with predominantly urban populations, by an appeal to social justice; farmers are poor, the argument goes, and should, therefore, be aided."[7] Are not farm incomes, on the average, lower than nonfarm incomes? Are there not many low-income farmers? The proponents of price support programs often urge or defend them as necessary to protect small and low-income farmers. And does not the concept of parity, which measures "fairness" in the relationship between farm and nonfarm prices, indicate that the former are too low and need raising? Parity tends to be equated with social justice, a highly valued goal and symbol in American politics.

Beyond this matter there is the "myth of agricultural fundamentalism," which is manifested in a number of ways in our society and culture. It is expressed in the belief that agriculture is the basic industry of a people, that it provides the food that all need for survival. Farming is thus indispensable to the welfare of all, and so the material benefits accruing to farmers should at least be on a par ("parity") with those of other economic groups. Again, the myth was given form in the old slogan "Depressions are farm led and farm fed." The obvious implication is that general prosperity—an argument often used to justify farm price support legislation—is dependent on agricultural prosperity. In recent years, however, this argument has fallen into disuse, probably because there is little empirical support for it.

The myth of agricultural fundamentalism also appears in the notion that farm or rural people are better, more virtuous, more suited to govern than are urban dwellers. Moreover, out in the country the air is fresh, the water is pure, beauty abounds, and life is pleasant and tranquil—a sharp contrast with the hustle and bustle, the noise and dirt, the vices and sins of urban life. So many appear to believe. Thus, a Cornell University study based on a broad sample of the population found that nearly every group surveyed believed a rural environment to be the best place in which to raise children, presumably because of the values of rural living.[8] Beliefs of this sort contribute to the status of agriculture and the existence of favorable attitudes toward it in our society. They also served in the past to justify overrepresentation of rural areas in American legislative bodies.

Until the "reapportionment revolution" of the 1960s, the relative and absolute numerical decline of the agricultural population was not accompanied by a proportionate decline in the representation of rural areas in Congress. A *Congressional Quarterly* study in 1962 concluded that rural areas had twenty-seven more members of Congress than they were entitled to on the basis of the population (the "one-man–one-vote" criterion). Equal representation in the Senate meant that rural states such as Mississippi and South Dakota had (and still have, of course) the same voting strength as such populous urban states as New York and Pennsylvania. In short, farm interests maintained a fairly strong, though diminishing, power base in Congress through the early 1960s. Barton comments on its implications for policymaking:

Within that environment, policymaking tended to revolve around how best to structure governmental assistance programs for producers (rigid versus flexible commodity price supports, for example), rather than whether to support assistance programs per se. Conflict tended to be resolved within what might be termed the "commercial agricultural establishment"—that is, by the formation of coalitions among cotton, wheat, and other commodity interests, and including agribusiness interests such as farm implement dealers, seed companies, and fertilizer manufacturers—and generally did not evoke critical urban-rural confrontation.[9]

Since the 1960s, there has been a substantial decline in rural representation in the House. By the mid-1970s, only 130 representatives came from rural districts (i.e., those in which 50 percent or more of the population lived outside a standard metropolitan statistical area). If we define farm districts as areas in which 20 percent or more of the population lives on farms, the number of those districts fell to 12 in the mid-1970s. This is reflective of the declining farm population. Clearly, the support of urban legislators is now a necessity for farm legislation to be enacted.

Congress and Agricultural Policy

In agricultural policy, as in many other areas of public policy, the initiative in proposing new legislation or modifying existing legislation usually rests with the executive branch. Congress, however, has maintained and exercised substantial control over farm policy, and has not hesitated to modify, reject, or even substitute its own policy proposals for those emanating from the executive and the Department of Agriculture. There are times, moreover, when the initiative comes from Congress, as in the case of the 1975 bill intended to raise the target prices for wheat, cotton, and feed grains. It passed Congress only to be vetoed by the president on the grounds that it would be too costly and inflationary in impact.

Within Congress, the major centers of decision making are the Agriculture Committees. These committees have been constituted almost entirely of representatives and senators from farm districts and states in the South, Midwest, and Great Plains regions. One study of congressional committee assignments reported that, in making assignments to the House Agriculture Committee, "both parties take it for granted that wheat, cotton, and tobacco interests should have the majority of representation on the committee."[10] Since the 1930s, most of the Agriculture Committee and subcommittee chairpersons have come from the South. This situation, a function of the committee selection process plus the safe district–seniority syndrome that has importantly shaped the distribution of power within Congress, has given southern farm interests a large voice in agricultural policy formation. It is no accident that four of the six commodities (wheat, corn and feed grains, cotton, rice, tobacco, and peanuts) designated as basic for price support purposes are produced mainly in the South.

The Agriculture Committees are organized along commodity lines for handling price support legislation. The House committee has a number of permanent subcommittees on cotton, tobacco, wheat, livestock and feed grains, and so on, each of which is dominated by representatives from districts producing the commodity in question. In the Senate committee the chairperson, under an informal arrangement, tends to rely on committee members whose states have substantial farm interests in particular commodities for decisions thereon. On the whole, committee structure and action have contributed to the decline of general farm legislation and the substitution of a series of commodity programs acceptable to legislators and groups from the areas in which each commodity is important.[11] This, in turn, is both a response to and a reflection of the fact that commodity groups have different interests, problems, and desires.

Given the domination of the Agriculture Committees by farm-oriented members of Congress, it has been almost impossible to obtain farm legislation that is unacceptable to the major interests represented on the committees, since they must approve such legislation. (What is "acceptable" is not necessarily what the affected interests would ideally prefer.) On the other hand, the decline in rural representation noted above means that farm-area legislators are no longer sufficiently numerous or powerful to secure the enactment of farm legislation without the support of many of their urban colleagues. Most farm legislation reported to the floor by the committees in recent years has passed, but this is probably due, in considerable part, to the skill of the committee leadership in judging what kind of legislation will be accepted by a majority of the House or Senate and later by the president, especially if he is from the opposition party. During the 1950s, the Eisenhower administration was able to shape farm policy through actual or threatened use of the veto power. "The major commodity blocs often needed to have their programs renewed or revised; the Eisenhower programs were better than no new programs at all."[12]

In writing federal farm legislation, the usual pattern is for the Senate to act first, passing a bill that pleases both farm groups and rural constituencies.[13] Farm bills usually pass the Senate without much difficulty. As one close observer comments, "Almost every Senator has some substantial crop that is raised in his state. No Senator can afford to turn his back upon an economic bloc of voters no matter how relatively small, since dedicated single interest groups often decide closely contested elections."[14]

The House customarily passes a bill that is less liberal than the Senate's position. Here, the law-making procedure begins in the Agriculture Committee, which must design a farm bill that will, at least minimally, satisfy producers of the major agricultural commodities—wheat, feed grains, cotton, tobacco, peanuts, and dairy products—in order to hold a farm coalition together. Then, the committee must devise a strategy to pick up enough urban votes to get the bill through the House. This form of coalition building usually takes place within the Democratic congressional party.

To find support from nonfarm legislators, farm groups use one of two strategies, or a combination of both. The first is to seek to trade votes with nonfarm groups. This was the case in 1964, when the rural bloc supported an expanded food stamp program (see chapter 5) in trade for urban votes on a cotton and wheat act. A year later, the Food and Agriculture Act received urban votes in return for rural votes to repeal the authorization of state right-to-work legislation (see chapter 10). The Agriculture Act of 1970, which contained both price supports and an expanded food stamp program, was a rural-urban package. Although urban legislators were somewhat less reliable in 1973, urban votes in favor of price supports were swapped for rural votes in support of increasing the federal minimum wage.[15] This logrolling helps explain not only the enactment of farm legislation, but also the substantial unity among Democrats on farm bills.

The second strategy involves nonfarm groups in the drafting of bills that can be supported on their merits. For example, provisions were included in the 1977 farm bill on commodity and other programs that made the bill attractive to progressive and liberal members of Congress.[16] As a consequence, the bill passed the House by a substantial margin (despite the fact that usually farm bills just squeak through the House).

Farm legislation was once thought to be of concern only to the agricultural community. This is no longer true. Farm policy has been shifted from the subsystem to the macropolitical arena, and nonfarm groups have become important participants in the development of agricultural policy.

TYPES OF AGRICULTURAL PROGRAMS

Although government had provided some assistance before 1862, that year marked the beginning of important government involvement in agriculture. Three significant statutes were enacted that year. One created the Department of Agriculture, which was given cabinet status in 1889. The Morrill Act provided public land grants to the states to assist them in establishing colleges that would offer instruction in the agricultural and mechanical arts (the "land-grant" colleges). The third statute, the Homestead Act, offered free public land (160 acres per family) to settlers who wanted to live on and cultivate it for five years.

The year 1933 marked the beginning of a major change in the government's involvement in agriculture. Until then, farm programs were limited in number and were essentially promotional in nature, providing aid and assistance to the farmer in increasing farm productivity. The Department of Agriculture was largely a skilled scientific and statistical agency. In 1933 came a major change: the regulation of agricultural production as an adjunct to price support operations was instituted. In the following years, many other action programs—rural electrification, soil conservation, market development, crop insurance, and rural development—were added. Table 11–4, which lists the major administrative units in the Department of Agriculture, conveys a notion of the wide range of programs now handled by the department. In the pages that follow we will comment only on a few aspects of these programs.

Research and Education

Many government programs are intended to increase farm productivity and efficiency (and, hence, farm income), or, as is often said, "to make two blades of grass grow where one grew before." Included here are research, education, and extension programs. The primary burden for agricultural research rests with the Agricultural Research Service and the Agricultural Experiment Stations (a joint federal-state venture). The results of research are disseminated by such means as the Extension Service. Government-sponsored research has been a major force for change in agriculture.[17]

Regulations

Regulation of those with whom the farmer deals is another form of government assistance. Farm groups supported railroad and warehouse regulation in the nineteenth century, with the National Grange a leading force at that time. Concern over alleged manipulation of livestock markets by large meat-packing companies led to the enactment of the Packers and Stockyards Act in 1921. Other regulatory programs deal with markets for perishable commodities, commodity exchanges, plant and animal diseases, and the quality of plant seeds. The meat and poultry inspection programs have the dual purpose of protecting consumers and facilitating the sale of products.

Credit Terms

Agrarian complaints that private sources of credit were undependable, that interest rates were too high, and that the terms of loans were too short culminated in the adoption of the Federal Farm Loan Act in 1916. This statute created a system of twelve federal land banks to provide long-term loans to farmers for the purchase of land, buildings, and other property. The Agricultural Credit Act of 1923 provided for intermediate credit banks (which make loans to production credit associations and agricultural loan corporations, which then in turn lend money to farmers). The Farm Credit Act of 1933 set up a series of banks to make loans to farm marketing, purchasing, and service cooperatives. These various banks now collectively comprise the Farm Credit System, which operates under the supervision of an independent agency, the Farm Credit Administration. The funds lent by these banks are now obtained primarily from private sources. Other farm credit agencies include the Farmers Home Administration and the Rural Electrification Administration (REA). Today, low-income farmers derive little benefit from these agencies.

Soil Conservation

Abuse of the soil was commonplace in the nineteenth and early twentieth centuries. Despite growing concern about soil wastage, not much was done until the New Deal, when soil conservation became a major item on the agricultural policy

TABLE 11–4 The U.S. Department of Agriculture organizational structure

---

Small community and rural development
    Farmers Home Administration
    Federal Crop Insurance Corporation
    Office of Rural Development Policy
    Rural Electrification Administration
Marketing and inspection services
    Agricultural Cooperative Service
    Agricultural Marketing Service
    Animal and Plant Health Inspection Service
    Federal Grain Inspection Service
    Food Safety and Inspection Service
    Office of Transportation
    Packers and Stockyards Administration
Food and consumer services
    Food and Nutrition Service (includes Food Stamp Program)
    Human Nutrition Information Service
    Office of Consumer Adviser
International affairs and commodity programs
    Agricultural Stabilization and Conservation Service
    Commodity Credit Corporation
    Foreign Agricultural Service
    Office of International Cooperation and Development
Science and education
    Agricultural Research Service
    Cooperative State Research Service
    Extension Service
Natural resources and environment
    Forest Service
    Soil Conservation Service
Economics
    Economic Research Service
    Economic Analysis Staff
    Office of Energy
    Statistical Report Service

SOURCE: *U.S. Government Manual, 1982–1983* (Washington, D.C.: U.S. Government Printing Office, 1982).

agenda. The Soil Conservation Service (SCS) was organized in 1935 to provide technical assistance to farmers organized in soil conservation districts. These districts are established, under state enabling legislation, as units of local government, and are controlled and administered by farmer-elected committees. They have banded together in the National Association of Soil Conservation Districts to support continuation and expansion of the program.

A considerably different approach to soil conservation is represented by the Rural Environmental Assistance Program (REAP), formerly the Agricultural Conservation Program. Where SCS provides technical assistance, REAP offers financial assistance to farmers for soil-conserving and building practices—the construction of erosion control structures, the planting of cover crops, and the application of fertilizers (especially limestone) to the land. This program has been criticized as an unnecessary subsidy for farmers in that, the argument runs, they are paid for doing things they ought to undertake on their own as good farming practices. The Johnson administration sought to greatly reduce expenditures for the program, and the Nixon administration tried to eliminate it entirely. Neither succeeded, because the program is politically popular and has strong support in Congress. (The limestone companies, who find the program good for business, are staunch supporters too.)

Despite conservation programs, soil erosion has increased in recent years as a result of efforts to increase farm production. The continuous growing of soybeans, fall plowing of land in the Midwest, and the cultivation of hilly and marginal land have all contributed to the problem. Existing soil conservation programs, which were developed during an era of excess production, are not really adequate to meet the conservation problems created by all-out production. In the future, soil conservation may again become an active item on the policy agenda.

Marketing Assistance

There are many programs to assist the marketing of farm commodities. The Department of Agriculture carries on marketing research, looking for better methods, facilities, and equipment for the handling, processing, storage, transportation, and retail sale of farm products. Market information is available to farmers, processors, and others on the supply, demand, quality, and prices of farm commodities, all to help them conduct their buying and selling activities. Standard grades have been established for agricultural products, and inspection and classifying services are also performed. All of these activities contribute to what economists call "allocative efficiency."

The Agricultural Marketing Act of 1937 created a more direct source of marketing assistance. The statute authorizes the Secretary of Agriculture to enter into marketing agreements and to issue marketing orders to ensure the "orderly" marketing of such commodities as milk, fruits, nuts, and vegetables. Both orders (which are mandatory) and agreements (which are voluntary) regulate the actions of processors and distributors of farm products for the benefit of the producers (farmers). Marketing orders for milk are currently in effect in seventy or so milkshed areas; they prescribe the prices handlers must pay producers. Agreements and orders for fruits, vegetables, and other products do not directly establish commodity prices. However, prices may be affected (raised) by rules relating to quality, rates of shipment, and surplus control. "Orderly" marketing, in practice, can involve efforts to raise commodity prices as well as to reduce fluctuations in those prices.

Farm Security

In the 1930s, the government made a substantial effort to combat farm poverty. The Resettlement Administration was created by executive order in 1935 to aid the rehabilitation of low-income rural families, to retire land unsuited for farming, and to resettle impoverished families on good land. In 1937, the Bankhead-Jones Tenant Act was passed to combat the problems of tenant farming by furnishing poor farmers with federal credit when they were unable to obtain low-interest loans elsewhere. The act authorized long-term (ownership) loans for the purchase of land and buildings and short-term (operating) loans for the acquisition of equipment, fertilizer, and other materials. The Farm Security Administration was established to handle these loan programs and to take over the various activities of the Resettlement Administration.

The Farm Security Administration thus had responsibility for both loan programs and other activities to assist low-income farm groups. These included farm-purchasing cooperatives, cooperative land-leasing associations and farm communities, camps for migrant workers, and subsistence homesteads. These projects generated considerable political controversy, and were denounced by businesspeople, well-to-do commercial farmers, landlords, and others as "communistic," "socialistic," "collectivistic," and the like. The assault on the Farm Security Administration was led by the Farm Bureau (the voice of well-to-do farm interests), which saw the FSA as both radical and a threat to its dominant position in farm politics. Further, in the South, the FSA was perceived as a force for racial integration. In 1946, the conservative campaign against the FSA succeeded: the agency was abolished. In its stead was created a stripped-down Farmers Home Administration that restricted aid to low-income farmers to more conventional loan programs. The first war on rural poverty was at an end.[18]

Price Supports

Many proposals for direct governmental support of farm commodity prices have been advanced since the early 1920s; and beginning with the Agricultural Adjustment Act of 1933, a large volume of price support legislation has been enacted. Here we briefly survey, then evaluate, price support programs and the issues surrounding them.

The evolution of price support.   Demands for government action to support farm prices began in response to the agricultural depression that followed World War I and the disappearance of wartime markets. Depressed agricultural conditions persisted throughout the 1920s and went from bad to worse when the Great Depression set in during the early 1930s. Disequilibrium in the marketplace stimulated the quest for political solutions for depressed farm prices and income.

Under the spur of the farm bloc, the first attempt to raise farm prices utilized a traditional instrument—the protective tariff. Tariffs on farm commodities were raised in 1921 and again in 1922. In most cases, though, their impact was only symbolic: domestic production exceeded domestic consumption of practically all farm products; thus, the tariff worked to keep out commodities that had never come in. Attention soon shifted to making the tariff effective through the use of a two-price plan for export crops. Most important of the proposals along this line were the McNary–Haugen Bills. Essentially, they provided that the federal government should purchase sufficient quantities of farm commodities to raise their domestic prices to suitable levels. The accumulated stocks would be sold abroad at presumably lower world prices, with the losses recouped by a tax on domestic sales. Strongly supported by the Grange and the Farm Bureau, the McNary–Haugen Bills were defeated in Congress in 1924 and 1926 because of opposition from the South and Northeast. In 1927 and 1929, versions of the bills were passed only to be vetoed each time by President Coolidge, who took the position that not much could be done to help the farmer.

In the course of these struggles, Coolidge and his administration became deeply involved in the formulation of farm policy. This set a pattern for the executive branch that has continued to the present time. Before Coolidge came into office, the president and the Secretary of Agriculture had little involvement in the development of economic policy for agriculture.

In 1933, Congress passed the first Agricultural Adjustment Act (AAA). That legislation, mutually agreed to by farm group leaders and the Roosevelt administration, provided for production controls to reduce the supply of commodities and thereby raise commodity prices. Farmers who agreed to restrict production were eligible for cash benefit payments (financed by a tax levied on the processors of agricultural commodities). Also, commodity loans were made available to farmers, to encourage the withholding of commodities from the market until prices improved; and direct purchases were made of surplus commodities. The goal of the act was *parity,* which was defined as the establishment of "prices to farmers at a level that will give agricultural commodities a purchasing power with respect to articles farmers buy equivalent to the purchasing power of agricultural commodities in the base period—August 1909–July 1914." Or, as one farmer put it, parity means that "if a man could take a bushel of corn to town in 1912 and sell it and buy a shirt, he should be able to take a bushel of corn to town today and buy a shirt."[19] The focus, then, was on maintaining farmers' purchasing power (or real income).

The first AAA came to an end in 1936, when the Supreme Court declared it unconstitutional. The Court ruled that agricultural production was a matter for state control, and that the tax on processors was for the benefit of "special interests," not the general welfare.[20] Congress responded by quickly passing the Soil Conservation and Domestic Allotment Act of 1936, to help maintain farm income. The act provided payments to farmers for taking "soil-depleting" crops out of production and for various other soil conservation practices. The soil-depleting crops happened to be those in excess supply, such as corn and wheat. The real purpose of the act was to provide income assistance for farmers in the guise of payments for soil conservation.

The 1936 measure did not reduce surpluses enough to raise prices; so in 1938, Congress adopted the second Agricultural Adjustment Act, which restored the policy of direct price supports and production controls to raise farm income.[21] Price supports were authorized at rates ranging from 52 to 75 percent of parity. Farmers who reduced their production and stayed within their allotted acreage were eligible for commodity loans, parity payments, and/or soil conservation payments. When necessary to reduce excess production of wheat, cotton, corn, tobacco, or rice (and, later, peanuts), the Secretary of Agriculture—with the approval of two-thirds of the growers in a referendum—could impose mandatory marketing quotas. Penalties were provided for producers who exceeded their marketing quotas. The act also included a number of surplus disposal programs, including a food stamp plan to help families on relief, free distribution of food to needy families, provision of food for school lunch programs, and subsidization of the export of cotton and wheat. In decisions in 1939 and 1942, the Supreme Court held that the act was a legitimate exercise of the commerce power.[22]

World War II began before the effectiveness of the second AAA in controlling surpluses and raising prices could be assessed. During the war years, the prices of many farm commodities were supported at 90 percent of parity, to encourage production adequate for wartime needs. The supports were mandatory for the basic commodities—corn, wheat, cotton, tobacco, rice, and peanuts—and were eventually applied to a dozen or so other commodities (e.g., hogs, eggs, soybeans, and potatoes). Farm groups were also able to secure amendments to the Emergency Price Control Act of 1942—amendments prohibiting price ceilings on farm products until they reached 110 percent of parity. Needless to say, most farmers prospered during the war years.

In 1948, with the wartime legislation due to expire at the end of the year, new legislation was required. Although farm interests generally agreed on the need for some kind of price support protection, they disagreed on the particular form that protection should take: high, fixed price supports or lower, flexible supports. High supports were favored by southern Democrats, some western Democrats, and a number of farm-area Republicans; lower supports, by President Truman and many Democrats, and most Republicans. The Agriculture Act of 1948 was a compromise. It extended high supports (90 percent of parity) for the basic commodities plus hogs, chickens, eggs, and milk products through May 1950, after which time a system of flexible supports would go into effect.

In the 1948 fall election, President Truman won a presidential term in his own right, and Democratic majorities regained control of Congress. Because of the party's apparent success in farm areas, the president and many Democratic legislators perceived the election as a mandate to help farmers through high price supports.

Consequently, legislation was adopted continuing price supports for the basic commodities at 90 percent of parity through 1954. Support for high, fixed support prices became a traditional Democratic party position.

When the Republicans returned to office in 1953, agricultural policy changed direction. President Eisenhower and his Secretary of Agriculture, Ezra Taft Benson, advocated lower, flexible price supports as a means of reducing both the cost of farm programs and the amount of government control of agriculture. The Agriculture Act of 1954 represented a moderate victory for the proponents of flexible supports. With the exception of tobacco (whose supports were maintained at 90 percent of parity), the prices of basic commodities were to be supported at between 82.5 and 90 percent of parity in 1955, and between 75 and 90 percent thereafter. Support for other commodities was continued on an optional basis.

There was considerable criticism of the Eisenhower–Benson farm policies by some groups, especially the Farmers Union, and by Democrats and some farm-area Republicans in Congress. In 1956 and 1958, Congress passed bills designed to halt the administration's efforts to reduce price supports. Both bills were vetoed by President Eisenhower on the ground that they would contribute to overproduction. The Eisenhower administration was subsequently able to secure the enactment of legislation permitting a reduction of price supports on rice, cotton, and corn to 65 percent of parity over a period of years. Following the 1958 congressional elections, which returned heavy Democratic majorities, Congress passed bills to increase or maintain support prices for wheat and tobacco. Both of these were also vetoed by President Eisenhower. In short, during the 1955–1960 period, agricultural policy-making was characterized by a stalemate between a Republican president and a Democrat-controlled Congress. Each was largely able to prevent or deny what the other wanted in the way of price support policy—higher price supports in the case of the Democrats and further movement toward a "free market" for the Eisenhower administration.

The Kennedy administration came into office in 1961 espousing a policy of "supply management" (or adjustment) for agriculture. That is, through rigorous production controls and higher price supports, agricultural surpluses would be controlled and supply brought into better balance with demand, while farm income increased. Congress, however, was unwilling generally to provide stringent controls on production because of farmers' resistance to them. Although price support levels were increased somewhat, controls on agricultural production and surpluses were only mildly strengthened. Congress did provide strong controls on wheat production, but these were rejected by wheat growers in 1963 in a nationwide referendum.

The next major legislation was the four-year Food and Agriculture Act of 1965. (It was later extended for another year.) The programs for wheat, feed grains, cotton, and wool, which comprised the major substance of the act, contained two significant features. First, price supports close to world prices were authorized, to reduce both the incentive to increase production and the need for export subsidies to allow American commodities to compete in world markets. Second, income supplements were provided, in the form of cash subsidy payments or their equivalent, for cooperating farmers who voluntarily reduced their crop acreage. Under this program, farm income increased and government holdings of surplus commodities diminished. Direct payments to farmers ranged from $2.5 billion in 1965 to $3.7 billion in 1970. Complaints about the high cost of the farm program were common.

One of the goals of the Nixon administration was to reduce government controls and make farming more market oriented. The Agriculture Act of 1970 eliminated the traditional commodity-by-commodity production controls for several commodities. It also required that producers set aside minimum acreage to qualify for program benefits. Once this was done, they were free to grow whatever they wanted on the remaining acreage. (Under earlier programs, farmers were limited to a set number of acres of corn, or wheat, or cotton. For some crops, such as rice and tobacco, traditional controls were retained.) Cash payments were provided for participants, but were limited to $55,000 per commodity program. This was the first time a limitation was put on payments, which under previous programs had run into hundreds of thousands of dollars for some producers. Public criticism of these high payments was rather extensive.

Further changes were made in farm programs by the four-year Agriculture and Consumer Protection Act of 1973, which dealt primarily with wheat, cotton, and corn and feed grains.[23] The principal innovation was the substitution of target prices for traditional price supports. Under the target price system, farmers are guaranteed a particular price for their commodity (e.g., $2.05 a bushel for wheat in 1974 and 1975). If average market prices during a specified part of the production year do not equal the target price, producers are given deficiency payments equal to the difference between the target price and the market price on their crops. A major difference between the target price system and previous price support programs is that payments are tied to market prices. When market prices are above the target prices, farmers receive no payments, as was the case in 1974–1975. In 1976, rice was the first crop to receive deficiency payments. The target price was $8.25 per hundredweight; the average market price, $6.55. Consequently, $146 million was paid to rice growers to make up the difference. Generally, however, government payments to farmers declined from a level of almost $4 billion in 1972 to around $500 million dollars annually from 1974 through 1976.

The 1973 legislation also authorized acreage set-asides to qualify for benefits. However, with the increased demand for farm commodities, no set-asides were required, and farmers were left free to plant "from fence row to fence row." The 1973 legislation also limited payments to $20,000, which applied to all commodity programs combined, not to each separately, as was the case with the 1970 limitation. Farm groups and their congressional supporters fought hard to secure a more lenient limitation, but urban and consumer interests prevailed.

The 1973 farm legislation came up for renewal in 1977. It was generally agreed that the target price system should be retained; however, the level at which target prices should be set became a major issue. Congress, responding to pressures from farmers faced with falling prices in the mid-1970s, favored higher target prices, to provide more support for farm incomes. The Carter administration, in contrast, favored lower target prices than did Congress in order to hold down the cost of the farm program and overall government spending. A Senate-passed measure providing higher target prices was subsequently rejected by the House. The result was the enactment of legislation providing for only modest increases in target prices, but raising the overall limitation on payments to individual farmers to $50,000.

Unexpectedly large wheat crops in the Soviet Union and other wheat-importing countries were produced in 1976–1977, while bumper wheat crops were harvested in the United States. Farmers were faced with falling wheat prices and inflationary production costs. Demands for action brought the imposition of set-aside requirements by the Carter administration to reduce wheat production. A bumper corn crop in 1978 led to the use of set-asides for corn also. The set-asides, of course, were intended to reduce production and raise market prices, thereby reducing government costs in the form of deficiency payments. A "free market" was still only a future prospect for agriculture.

The Reagan administration and farm policy today.   The farm program came up for renewal again in 1981. In line with its free-market orientation, the Reagan administration called for the elimination of target prices and deficiency payments.[24] (Loan rates act as floor prices for basic grains. Farmers can borrow from the government on their crops at the loan rate. Although they must pay interest, when loans come due they can simply default and allow the government to take title to the grain if the market price is below the loan rate.)

The Republican-controlled Senate acted first. Its bill retained the target price system and specified loan rates, but generally provided a level of price supports that was agreeable to the administration. The usually conservative House, however, produced a bill that was far more costly than the Senate version. Bargaining in conference committee and pressure from the administration finally produced legislation fairly close to what the Senate had initially approved. The statute included a new sugar price support program and retained the peanut program, both of which the administration had initially opposed. However, the president changed his stand on those programs in order to pick up southern conservative votes for his 1981 tax-cut legislation.

In 1981, the farm coalition in the House was in disarray. Commodity groups, for the first time, were faced with an overall budget limit on farm programs, imposed as part of the Omnibus Reconciliation Act of 1981. This forced them to compete with one another for price support funding. At times, some farm-state members abandoned their usual logrolling and voted against programs—such as those for peanuts, dairy, and sugar—that were of little interest to their constituents.[25] The conference committee bill passed the House by the narrow margin of 205 to 203. Some predicted that the 1981 law would be "the last farm bill."

Depressed export markets and bumper grain crops in 1981–1982 left the United States with huge surpluses of all major commodities. These surpluses drove market prices below farmers' production costs, and greatly increased their reliance on the government's price support programs. Those programs cost the Treasury an unprecedented $12 billion in fiscal year 1982. To relieve this situation, the Reagan administration asked Congress to authorize a payment-in-kind (PIK) program, to cut production and hold down the cost of the farm program. When Congress refused, the administration took executive action on the basis of existing statutory authority to institute the program.[26]

The payment-in-kind program took the following shape: producers of wheat, corn and feed grains, cotton, and rice who set aside 20 percent of their normal crop acreage (for which they received cash payments) were eligible to participate in the program. Those farmers could withdraw another 10 to 30 percent of their land from production. For doing this, they would receive surplus commodities worth 80 percent (95 percent in the case of wheat) of the value of their normal production on that acreage. In some instances, entire farms could be taken out of production. The commodities farmers received could be used for feed or sold on the market.

Initially, there was some skepticism about the viability of the PIK program. However, the farmers' reaction to it turned out to be quite positive.[27] By the end of the sign-up period in March 1983, farmers had agreed to take over 83 million acres of land out of production (overall, the U.S. base acreage for the affected crops was 230 million acres). The administration predicted that the program would increase farm prices above their 1982 levels, and would reduce surpluses and the cost of the price support program. In actuality, the cost of price supports soared to a record high of around $21 billion in 1983. The production controls in the program marked quite a turnaround for the Reagan administration, given its earlier preference for a free market for agriculture. Except for wheat, the PIK program was discontinued in 1984.

An evaluation.   First of all, we should note that only some farm commodities—about 20 out of 300—have been subject to price support operations in the post–World War II period. These include wheat, cotton (both upland and extra-long staple), corn, peanuts, rice, tobacco, milk and milk products, wool, mohair, tung nuts, barley, oats, rye, soybeans, grain sorghum, honey, flaxseed, dry edible beans, and gum naval stores. Measured by dollar value, these commodities account for 40 to 50 percent of agricultural production, with by far the largest portion coming from wheat, cotton, and corn and feed grains. Most farm commodities, then, move in the market free from price support operations. Their prices, however, can be affected by price supports on other commodities. If prices on corn and feed grains are kept up by support operations, the price of meat and poultry products must rise too.

Under the price support programs, the government has used two primary methods to increase farm income: (1) production limitations to increase the market prices of commodities, and (2) direct payments to farmers to enhance their income. Initially, more emphasis was put on production controls in the form of acreage allotments and marketing quotas. Acreage allotments were voluntary, but farmers were not eligible for price support benefits if they did not comply; marketing quotas, in comparison, were mandatory, but were imposed only if approved by a two-thirds vote of the producers of the commodity in a referendum. Production controls were not popular among the producers of most commodities (tobacco and rice are exceptions). Consequently, from the mid-1960s, greater emphasis was placed on the use of direct payments to enlarge farm income. This caused the cost of farm programs to go up, which in turn led to more criticism of them and greater political opposition to them.

What has been the effect of price supports on farm prices and incomes? A study published in 1968 estimated that net farm income in 1970 would be $15.6 billion if the major commodity programs then in effect were continued; conversely, in a free market, net farm income would be about $11.3 billion.[28] Another careful estimate holds that in recent years, the net effect of both production controls and support payments for cotton, wheat, and corn and feed grains has been to increase net farm income between $1 billion and $2 billion annually—an increase that probably costs consumers and taxpayers $3 billion to $4 billion annually.[29] Both of these studies indicate that the programs had a positive effect on farm income. Whether they were worth the cost is another question.

It has frequently been contended that price support programs, by holding farm prices above normal market levels, have caused a misallocation of economic resources. That is, resources that could have been used more efficiently elsewhere in the economy have been retained in or attracted to agriculture. So runs the argument, although data to support it are scarce. In response, others argue that price support programs have not prevented a shift of many workers from agricultural to industrial and other employment, as is indicated by the declining size, both absolutely and relatively, of the farm labor force. Put differently, farm prices and incomes have not been supported at levels sufficient to keep farm workers "down on the farm."

In fact, most of the direct benefits of price support programs have gone to a fairly small segment of the farm population.[30] Thus, in 1980, approximately 80 percent of total government payments to farmers (including some conservation payments) went to 39 percent of the farmers (about 1 million). (See table 11–5.) Low-income farmers have benefited comparatively little from price support programs—although the programs have often been advocated or defended as necessary to help low-income farmers—because of the small quantities of commodities they sell. In reality, within the agricultural sector, price support operations have enlarged the disparities between higher- and lower-income groups by channeling most of the benefits to larger, well-to-do commercial farmers. The operative principle here was set forth by the prophet Isaiah: "To those who hath, shall be given." If the policy goal

TABLE 11-5 Government payments to farmers, 1980

Farms with sales of	Total payments (000,000s)	Percent of total payments	Average payment per farm	Percent of farms
Less than $2,500	$ 25	1.9	$ 49	21.0
$ 2,500–4,999	54	4.1	153	14.5
$ 5,000–9,999	78	6.0	235	13.7
$ 10,000–19,999	103	8.0	356	11.8
$ 20,000–39,999	222	17.2	787	11.6
$ 40,000–99,999	418	32.5	1,091	15.8
$100,000–199,999	235	18.3	1,327	7.3
$200,000 and over	151	11.7	1,438	4.3

SOURCE: *Statistical Abstract of the United States, 1981* (Washington, D.C.: U.S. Government Printing Office, 1982), p. 673.

one wants to pursue is the elimination of farm poverty, a vehicle other than the conventional price support program is needed.

Since the early 1970s, farm price programs have become more market oriented. For a time, they worked reasonably well. Increased demand, especially from abroad, kept the market prices of farm commodities at acceptable levels above the target prices. It looked as though we might well see the end of conventional price support programs, although some action to prevent wide fluctuations in price levels might be called for. But in 1976–1977, and again in 1981–1982, when reduced demand drove prices down, there came an immediate outcry for increased government price and income assistance.

CONCLUDING COMMENTS

Although the farm population represents a declining segment of the nation's population, agriculture remains the largest single industry in the country. Moreover, everyone is affected by it. Just so, everyone is affected by agricultural policy, especially where it influences farm production or controls the prices of farm commodities.

Until recently, agricultural policies were shaped largely within a subsystem (or a series of subsystems) dominated by agricultural groups and representatives without much opposition or participation by other groups or interests. That situation has changed as "farm politics" has become "food politics." Farm groups can no longer control the agricultural policy agenda as successfully as they once did. In a much-noted speech delivered in September 1975, Don Paarlberg, a top-level Department of Agriculture official during the Eisenhower and Nixon administrations, concluded that "the agricultural establishment has, in large measure, lost control of the farm policy agenda." According to Paarlberg, new items appearing on the agenda over the protests of the agricultural establishment include food prices, food programs (e.g., food stamps) handled by the Department of Agriculture, rural development, ecological issues, and collective bargaining for hired farm workers. In short, the technological revolution in agriculture has broadened the scope of that policy and the interests in it.

How will this change affect the government's role in agriculture? Although we are likely to see a continuing moderation of price support activity (how long will price supports on milk remain acceptable?), we are also likely to see an increasing concern with conservation, land-use controls, ecological issues, food and nutrition programs, and concentration of control in farm production. In the area of ecology, for example, the use of various pesticides has already been banned on environmental grounds, and the Environmental Protection Agency has replaced the Department of Agriculture as the dominant agency in this arena (see chapter 4). No longer are farmers free to wage war on insect pests as they see fit. The coyote and the bald eagle have become focal points of other policy controversies. Public policies will continue to be an important element in the agricultural environment, but they will be less agreeable to traditional agricultural groups.

NOTES

1. V. O. Key, Jr., *Politics, Parties, and Pressure Groups,* 4th ed. (New York: Crowell, 1958), pp. 27–36.
2. Don Paarlberg, *American Farm Policy: A Case of Centralized Decision-Making* (New York: Wiley, 1964), chap. 4. See also Wayne D. Rassmussen, "The Mechanization of Agriculture," *Scientific American* 247 (September 1982): 76–89.
3. This discussion is drawn from Geoffrey Shepard, *Farm Policy: New Directions* (Ames, Iowa: Iowa State University Press, 1965).
4. Merle Fainsod, Lincoln Gordon, and Joseph Palamountain, *Government and the American Economy* (New York: Norton, 1959), p. 40.
5. William P. Browne, "Farm Organizations and Agribusiness," *Proceedings of the Academy of Political Science* 34 (1982): 209–210.
6. Ibid., p. 210.
7. Kenneth Boulding, *Conflict and Defense* (New York: Harper & Row, 1965), p. 205.
8. W. A. Anderson, *A Study of the Values of Rural Living, Part VIII, Summary of Findings,* Rural Sociology Publication, no. 34 (Ithaca, N.Y.: Agricultural Experiment Station, Cornell University, 1952).
9. Weldon V. Barton, "Food, Agriculture, and Administrative Adaptation to Change," *Public Administration Review* 27 (March–April 1976): 149.
10. Nicholas A. Masters, "Committee Assignments in the House of Representatives," *American Political Science Review* 55 (June 1961): 354.
11. Willard W. Cochrane and Mary E. Ryan, *American Farm Policy 1948–1973* (Minneapolis: University of Minnesota Press, 1976), pp. 104–121.
12. David R. Mayhew, *Party Loyalty among Congressmen* (Cambridge, Mass.: Harvard University Press, 1966), p. 32.
13. John G. Peters, "The 1981 Farm Bill," *Proceedings of the Academy of Political Science* 34 (1982): 157–170.
14. John Kramer, "Agriculture's Role in Government Decisions," in *Consensus and Conflict in U.S. Agriculture,* eds. Bruce L. Gardner and James W. Richardson (College Station, Tex.: Texas A&M University Press, 1979), p. 209.

15. Barton, "Food, Agriculture, and Administrative Adaptation," pp. 149–150. See also "Coalition Building in the United States House of Representatives: Agricultural Legislation," in *Cases in Public Policy-Making*, 2nd ed., ed. James E. Anderson (New York: Holt, Rinehart and Winston, 1982), pp. 99–115.

16. Don F. Hadwiger, "Agricultural Policy," in *Encyclopedia of Policy Studies*, ed. Stuart S. Nagel (New York: Marcel Dekker, 1983), p. 511.

17. Compare Don F. Hadwiger, *The Politics of Agricultural Research* (Lincoln, Neb.: University of Nebraska Press, 1982).

18. The story of the Farm Security Administration is well told in Sidney Baldwin, *Poverty and Politics: The Rise and Decline of the Farm Security Administration* (Chapel Hill: University of North Carolina Press, 1968).

19. Quoted in Clair Wilcox, *Public Policies toward Business* (Homewood, Ill.: Irwin, 1960), p. 471.

20. *United States* v. *Butler*, 297 U.S. 1 (1936).

21. The 1938 legislation is permanent. The effect of the various farm bills passed since then has been to temporarily suspend or replace certain of its provisions. In the absence of such legislation, the programs authorized by the original act would go into effect.

22. *Mulford* v. *Smith*, 307 U.S. 38 (1939); and *Wickard* v. *Filburn*, 317 U.S. 111 (1942).

23. Garth Youngberg, "U.S. Agriculture in the 1970's: Policy and Politics," in *Economic Regulatory Policies*, ed. James E. Anderson (Lexington, Mass.: Heath, 1976), pp. 51–68.

24. Robert J. Samuelson, "U.S. Farms: More Acres, More Exports, and Less Federal Aid on the Horizon," *National Journal* 13 (May 23, 1981): 916–919.

25. *Congressional Quarterly Weekly Report* 39 (December 19, 1981): 2481.

26. *Congressional Quarterly Weekly Report* 41 (January 15, 1983): 87; and *New York Times*, January 22, 1983, pp. 1, 6.

27. *Houston Chronicle*, March 23, 1982, sect. 3, p. 1.

28. Leo V. Meyer, Earl O. Heady, and Howard C. Madsen, *Farm Programs for the 1970's* (Ames, Iowa: Center for Agriculture and Economic Development, Iowa State University, 1968).

29. D. Gale Johnson, *Farm Commodity Programs* (Washington, D.C.: American Enterprise Institute for Policy Research, 1973), pp. 48–49.

30. Charles L. Schultze, *The Distribution of Farm Subsidies* (Washington, D.C.: Brookings Institution, 1971).

SUGGESTED READINGS

Borgstrom, Georg. *The Food and People Dilemma*. North Scituate, Mass.: Duxbury, 1973.

Brown, Lester R. *By Bread Alone*. New York: Praeger, 1974.

Cochrane, Willard W., and Ryan, Mary E. *American Farm Policy 1948–1973*. Minneapolis: University of Minnesota Press, 1976.

Hadwiger, Don F. *The Politics of Agricultural Research*. Lincoln, Neb.: University of Nebraska Press, 1982.

Hardin, Charles M. *Food and Fiber in the Nation's Politics*. Washington, D.C.: U.S. Government Printing Office, 1967.

Talbot, Ross B., and Hadwiger, Don F. *The Policy Process in American Agriculture*. San Francisco: Chandler, 1968.

TWELVE

Foreign Policy

Foreign policy is the course of action designed to pursue the nation's interests in the international environment. Since the establishment of the first cabinet agency—the Department of State, in 1789—foreign policy has been a critical area of U.S. governmental activity. And over this time, the process of making that policy has grown increasingly complex. Today, the United States maintains diplomatic relations with scores of other independent nations in the world, and participates in the activities of numerous international organizations. It spends large sums of money to help other countries both economically and militarily. And, it maintains a military presence around the globe. Adding to this complexity is the growth of "intermestic" (*inter*national and do*mestic*) policies. In the highly interdependent world in which we live, the United States is no longer insulated from foreign events. We can see this clearly in terms of energy, with U.S. dependence on foreign oil sources and the impact of oil price increases on various facets of life in this country. "Most issues on the new international agenda have an immediate and profound impact upon domestic interests in the United States."[1]

In this chapter, we trace the evolution of American foreign policy. Then we consider the roles of the different actors in the policy process—the president, the bureaucracy, Congress, political parties and interest groups, public opinion and the mass media—and how they differ from those played in domestic policymaking. Next, we outline the instruments those actors use to shape foreign policy. Then, we review the interdependence of foreign policy and defense policy, and examine a case study that shows the interrelationship between foreign policy and what seems to be exclusively a domestic policy area—agriculture. Finally, we conclude with a discussion of the dilemmas of foreign policymaking in a democratic system.

ALTERNATING PHASES IN U.S. FOREIGN POLICY

One way of studying U.S. foreign policy is to think of it in terms of the amount of activity going on at any given time.[2] This approach has often led people to discuss U.S. foreign policy in terms of "isolationism" and "interventionism." In "isolationist" periods, U.S. involvement in international matters is minimal; the policy reflects a reluctance or refusal to intervene in the international arena. In "interventionist" periods, the government takes direct action in the international arena to pursue its interests through the use of foreign policy tools.

Obviously, these two terms represent ends of a continuum, not mutually exclusive behaviors. U.S. foreign policy is never totally isolationist or totally interventionist. The country simply cannot afford to bury its head in the sand; nor can it strike out at anything that moves about it. The foreign policy pendulum swings back and forth between these two extremes; and during any period, there are forces pushing it both ways. If we know, then, toward which end of the continuum the pendulum is moving, we should know the general slant of foreign policy at that time. But what the pendulum cannot tell us is tomorrow's policy. Even as we watch, the pendulum may be swinging back toward the other end. Table 12–1 lists the approximate dates in U.S. history when the pendulum has been closer to each extreme.[3]

An Historical Perspective: 1789–1940[4]

During the first period, 1789–1798, the primary concern of the new nation was to establish an infrastructure. George Washington and his successor, John Adams, pursued a policy of noninvolvement at almost any cost. Washington formalized this policy with his Proclamation of Neutrality in 1793, which prohibited U.S. citizens from assisting warring European nations. And Congress followed by including enforcement powers in the Neutrality Act of 1794.

But foreign entanglements proved unavoidable. By 1798, the United States and France were joined in an undeclared naval war. This new activist phase was furthered by Jefferson and subsequent presidents. Most notably, under James Madison, the country fought the War of 1812 with Great Britain. At the end of this period, President James Monroe issued his now-famous Monroe Doctrine, which promised U.S. noninterference in European affairs but warned European powers to stay out of Latin America. The statement was largely symbolic, and was grounded in the idea of self-defense. In the short term, it foreshadowed a period of isolationism; in the long run, it offered an excuse for U.S. intervention in Latin America.

Only when John Quincy Adams entered the White House, in 1825, did the country again shift toward isolationism. We can see the totality of that shift in Andrew Jackson's inaugural address: not once did the new president refer to foreign policy in his speech. The United States remained officially neutral during the war for Texas's independence, and refused to annex Texas in 1838. Even the succession of a more interventionist president, John Tyler, was not enough to break the country out of its isolationist stance. Tyler's renewed efforts to annex Texas were rejected in the Senate by a 2 to 1 margin in 1844.

TABLE 12–1 Years of isolationism and interventionism in U.S. foreign policy, 1789–?

Isolationism	Interventionism
1789–1798	1798–1825
1825–1844	1844–1871
1871–1891	1891–1918
1918–1940	1940–1967
1967–?	

SOURCE: Adapted from Frank L. Klingberg, "Cyclical Trends in American Foreign Policy Moods and Their Policy Implications," in *Challenges to America: United States Foreign Policy in the 1980s,* eds. Charles W. Kegley, Jr., and Patrick J. McGowan (Beverly Hills: Sage, 1979), p. 38.

With the election of James Polk to the White House, the pendulum swung back. Texas was admitted to the Union, and a war with Mexico was fought. Interventionism was so popular during this period that Franklin Pierce, in his inaugural address (1853), declared territorial expansionism a goal of his administration. Even the Civil War did not halt the policy of interventionism. In the years following that conflict, the United States forced the French out of Mexico, purchased Alaska, and occupied Midway Island in the Pacific.

But by 1871, expansionist fervor had waned. In many ways, this period was like the 1825–1844 era. First, all boundary disputes with Great Britain, a major source of tension until this time, had been settled. Second, domestic activities were very absorbing. Post-Civil War Reconstruction, westward expansion, centennial celebrations, political scandals in Washington, and the changes produced by the Industrial Revolution, all demanded attention. Third, during this time, there were no major wars in the world that might have embroiled the United States in international conflict. The apathy toward foreign policy was so deep that some major newspapers called for the abolition of the diplomatic corps.

In the early 1890s, change was in the air. A renewed willingness to be involved in world affairs was manifested in 1895–1896, when the United States almost went to war with Great Britain over a Venezuela–British Guiana boundary dispute. The U.S. rationale for intervening in that dispute was a reinterpretation of the Monroe Doctrine. In this instance, the United States held that any European interference in New World affairs was an unfriendly act toward the United States. The country gained tremendous prestige when Great Britain backed down on its claims. It was clear to most observers that the United States had joined the circle of great powers.

Any doubts about American stature in the world were erased when the United States intervened in the Cuban revolution and fought the brief Spanish–American War (1898). The country was clearly launched on its way to playing a primary role in world affairs. In less than three years, as a result of negotiations and the war, the United States acquired (in various statuses) Cuba, Hawaii, American Samoa, Puerto Rico, the Philippines, Guam, and Wake. Some saw these acquisitions as the first parts of what would become an American empire. Certainly, the acquisitions in the Pacific, particularly the Philippines, extended U.S. power in the Far East. American troops were used to quell rebellions in both the Philippines and China. In addition, Britain's reduction of its naval activities left the United States the naval guardian of the Western Hemisphere. Never before and seldom since was there a period of such activity in U.S. foreign policy. This activist phase lasted through World War I, and, with Woodrow Wilson's plans for the League of Nations, seemed destined to continue. But the pendulum was swinging back toward isolationism. The Senate rejected U.S. participation in the League, and the country turned inward.

The period 1918–1940 witnessed the most intense political and economic isolationism in the country's history. The American public was simply unwilling to spend money on anything that might lead to foreign entanglement. For instance, when the nation signed a treaty with the other major naval powers limiting the building of warships, the United States could not raise enough tax money to build the ships it was permitted by treaty. Symbolic of this period was the Kellogg-Briand Pact of 1928, which "outlawed war." It seemed the American people, along with people worldwide, were ready to ignore reality, to pretend that aggression could be dispensed with by treaty.

This mood was further strengthened by the Great Depression. People could not afford to worry about foreign affairs when they were struggling for survival at home. Isolationism was codified in the Neutrality Act of 1935, which was strengthened in 1936 and again in 1937. In these acts, Congress attempted to mandate "permanent neutrality" for the country, to wrap the nation in a cocoon to protect it from the surrounding, and increasingly dangerous, environment. But international events soon proved that the defense offered by the neutrality cocoon was illusory. World War II forced the country to change its policy.

Recent Interventionism: 1940–1967[5]

The expansion of World War II, especially the fall of France to Nazi Germany in 1940, led to U.S. interventionism even before the Japanese attack on Pearl Harbor. Although many Americans wanted to remain neutral, at the same time they did not want to risk fighting Germany and Japan without allies. With the threatened collapse of the British, Russians, and Chinese, the costs of interventionism paled by comparison to the potential costs of continued isolationism. In 1940, then, the United States began to provide assistance to Great Britain, began to expand its naval and air forces, and instituted the first peacetime military draft in the nation's history. U.S. policy was firmly set on an interventionist course that was escalated by the Japanese attack on Pearl Harbor in December 1941.

That attack set the stage for continuing U.S. involvement in world affairs. On January 1, 1942, President Roosevelt signed an executive agreement—an agreement between heads of state that is not subject to ratification by the Senate—that bound the United States in a military alliance with twenty-six other countries. This agreement provided for unity in the war effort, and served as the basis for the postwar establishment of the United Nations. The United States had never before committed itself to international involvement on such a scale. "Entangling alliances" became common.

After World War II, unlike the post–World War I experience, the pendulum did not immediately swing back toward isolationism. There was rapid demobilization of the military, but the United States did not and could not withdraw from involvement in world affairs. Even if the country had wanted to withdraw from the international arena, two technological innovations made it impossible for it to do so. First, the airplane had become a demonstrably powerful weapon of long-range warfare. Second, the atomic bomb had ushered in the Age of Extermination, the time of a very real threat to the world's population. Quite simply, with the inevitable spread of these two developments, no country could isolate itself within secure borders.

And, something else contributed to continued U.S. activity in international affairs: postwar conflict with a wartime ally, the Soviet Union. With the common enemies defeated, the communist regime in the USSR rekindled its efforts to spread its doctrine. It began by buffering itself against invasion, by incorporating its neighbors inside an "iron curtain." The United States assumed the lead in the cold war—a nonshooting war—with its former ally. The first expression of this leadership was the Truman Doctrine (1947), which committed the United States to a policy of containment—the restriction of Soviet communism to fixed territorial limits. At first, this entailed aid only to two countries directly threatened by communism, Greece and Turkey. Very quickly, however, that commitment was followed by the promise of massive aid to the rest of Europe for economic redevelopment. This aid—the Marshall Plan—was enormously successful in helping Europe recover from the war, and in stopping the westward expansion of communism. President Truman followed the Marshall Plan with his "Bold New Program," which offered technical assistance to "backward" countries throughout the world. The idea was to spend money to prevent people from becoming communists, rather than to spend it later to fight communists. This program, too, was a success.

American postwar involvement was not limited to financial aid. From 1947 through 1954, the United States entered interlocking defense pacts with the other republics on the American continents, the other nations of the North Atlantic, Japan, Nationalist China (Taiwan), Australia, New Zealand, the Philippines, Thailand, and Pakistan. Each of these alliances had anticommunism as a central goal.

Nor was postwar involvement limited to nonviolent anticommunism. By both overt and covert means, the United States reacted to almost any perceived communist threat throughout the world. The most dramatic of the early postwar conflicts was fought to a stalemate with communist forces in Korea.

Frustration with the Korean stalemate and the need to garner votes in the 1952 presidential election led Republicans to argue that the United States should not simply contain communism; it should work to eliminate it. When their candidate, Dwight Eisenhower, was successful in that election, he proclaimed a "New Look" diplomacy that promised "instant" and "massive" retaliation—nuclear retaliation—to communist aggression.

The obvious problem with a policy of massive retaliation was deciding at what point provocation warranted using the awesome nuclear threat. The clear answer during this era was never. Communist aggression was manifest in various forms—guerilla warfare, supported coups d'etat, internal subversion, and extended alliances—but never in such a way as to prompt a U.S. nuclear attack on the Soviet Union or Communist China. America continued to combat communism through nonnuclear means. The Central Intelligence Agency (CIA) helped install the Shah of Iran, and engineered the overthrow of Guatemala's "communist-tinged" government in 1954. In 1958, the Eisenhower Doctrine, which promised economic and military aid to any Middle East nation threatened either internally or externally by communism, was used to send U.S. marines to Lebanon. And once the Soviets developed their own nuclear weapons, massive retaliation was little more than a hollow policy statement.

If any event could have triggered the use of massive retaliation, it would have been the Cuban missile crisis in 1962. The United States discovered that the Soviet Union was building missile launching bases in Cuba only 90 miles off U.S. shores. Fortunately, President Kennedy realized the pitfalls of nuclear attack, and resorted to conventional means of dealing with the crisis. A naval "quarantine" was imposed on Cuba, and the Soviet Union withdrew its threat. Clearly massive retaliation was not a workable policy: it did not deter Soviet piecemeal aggression; and it was not credible if the Soviets thought they could survive a first strike and retaliate.

With massive retaliation largely symbolic, the United States continued its policy of containment. To do this, America chose to protect far-flung interests, to present an image of strength, and to support anticommunist regimes throughout the world. The sum of these approaches led to Vietnam.

U.S. involvement in Vietnam was a classic instance of containment policy at work. Communists were threatening the frontier in an area where American allies could not stem their incursion. Enter the "policeman of the world": the United States was enmeshed in the Vietnam War. It was a guerilla war—a war of hit-and-run raids fought over the "hearts and minds" of people. It was a war the United States did not understand and could not wage effectively. Despite the limited scope of many of the battles, the total effort was massive. U.S. troop strength in South Vietnam reached 550,000 at one point; over 50,000 U.S. military personnel were killed and many thousands more were wounded. Even with this commitment of military might, the war effort came to be seen as increasingly futile.

Renewed Isolationism: 1967–?

As the United States escalated its military involvement in Vietnam, protests against the war began to be heard. By 1967, the pendulum was clearly, if at times haltingly, swinging back toward isolationism. The inability of the U.S. military to understand or counteract guerilla warfare, which was highlighted by the North Vietnamese Tet Offensive (1968), raised challenges to the policy of containment. The public was tired of the war and disillusioned with leaders who promised a victory that, as was apparent to anyone who watched the evening news, was not forthcoming. Demands rose for the withdrawal of U.S. troops, and in 1968 peace talks began in Paris. "Vietnamization"—the process of turning more of the fighting over to South Vietnamese troops—began the following year. By 1973, a peace agreement was signed.

On other fronts, too, President Nixon was disengaging the United States from conflict. Anticommunism was no longer an acceptable rationale on which to base U.S. foreign policy; instead, administration officials spoke of *detente*—of pursuing U.S. interests without constantly confronting other countries. Early in 1972, Nixon visited Communist China and began the process of establishing regular diplomatic relations. Later that year, he participated in the Moscow summit conference and signed the Strategic Arms Limitation Talks (SALT) I and Anti-Ballistic Missiles (ABM) treaties, which were further strengthened in 1974. And, in 1973, he reduced U.S. troop strength in Europe under the U.S.–Soviet Mutual and Balanced Force Reductions agreement (1973).

In broader terms, renewed isolationism was manifest in other ways. There was renewed interest in domestic policies—in urban riots and oil spills—matters far closer to home than communists in Southeast Asia.

Congress tried to limit U.S. involvement in world affairs by limiting the president's power as commander-in-chief and as chief foreign policymaker. It began by demanding that executive agreements be reported to the legislative branch. If the subject of the agreements was of major significance, Congress suggested they be submitted as treaties for ratification by the Senate, not as executive agreements.

Second, Congress placed a number of restrictions on the president's ability to conclude military transfers. For example, Congress asserted the right to cancel large arms sales to other nations in 1974, and specifically blocked arms sales to Turkey in 1975.

Third, Congress attempted to rein in U.S. intelligence operations. Specifically, several congressional committees required they be kept informed of CIA covert operations and attempted subversions of foreign governments.

Fourth, and most important, Congress passed, over President Nixon's veto, the War Powers Resolution of 1973. This resolution requires the president to consult with Congress before using U.S. military forces except in three carefully defined situations: (1) when the United States has been attacked; (2) when U.S. forces outside the country have been attacked; or (3) when it is necessary to rescue U.S. citizens in certain dangerous situations. When a president finds it necessary to deploy forces under these circumstances, he must make an immediate report to Congress and obtain approval for extension of the action beyond sixty days (ninety days if U.S. forces are in danger). Congress can terminate the action by refusing to approve it within sixty days or by passing a concurrent resolution of termination that is not subject to presidential veto.

The War Powers Resolution was a clear attempt to hold presidents more accountable for their actions and to ensure that the United States would not again aimlessly, blindly, and incrementally be sucked into a war without congressional concurrence. Although the act may infringe on the president's expressed constitutional power as commander-in-chief—no decision has been made on this point—it still gives the president a not inconsiderable amount of freedom of action. In fact, the War Powers Resolution has never been invoked. No president has seen fit to notify Congress under the provisions of the resolution whenever he has committed U.S. troops.

The isolationist pattern continued in subsequent years. President Carter in 1977 announced his intention to withdraw U.S. troops from South Korea (a decision that was later reversed) and halted planned production of the B-1 bomber, and in 1978 delayed production of the neutron bomb. In 1979, the mutual defense treaty with Nationalist China was terminated and the SALT II treaty was signed.

The New Interventionism: Reagan and Foreign Policy

President Reagan entered office with open antagonism toward communism in general and the Soviet Union in particular. He chose as his first Secretary of State a retired army general, Alexander Haig, a signal of his intention to move U.S. foreign policy away from detente toward a pattern reminiscent of the cold war. He planned to drastically increase military spending and delayed arms control negotiations—both clear deviations from the recent past. He raised the specter of communism on the U.S. doorstep as a rationale for supplying arms and advisors to El Salvador and cutting off economic aid to Nicaragua, an alleged conduit for Soviet–Cuban aid in Central America. In aiding El Salvador, Reagan pointedly rejected arguments about the ruling regime's violations of human rights, which had been a major issue in Carter's foreign policy. He justified the action as necessary to counteract "international terrorism," a term apparently used to refer to violent efforts for political change presumably backed by the Soviet Union.

In the Middle East, Reagan also pursued a more interventionist policy. He sold military equipment to the closest Arab ally in the area, Saudi Arabia. He agreed to sell the Saudis fuel tanks and air-to-air missiles for planes they already owned, five airborne warning and control system (AWACS) planes, and air refueling planes. His goal was to solidify opposition to what he perceived to be the major threat to the rest of the world, the Soviet Union.

But in each of these areas, the president was unable to fully swing the pendulum. In El Salvador, no broad support for an expanded U.S. presence emerged, and Congress agreed to continue aid only if El Salvador's human rights performance improved. Comparisons of El Salvador and Vietnam were too easily made to allow Reagan to push further.

In the Middle East, Reagan was unable to convince anyone else that the Soviet Union was the major enemy; the Arab–Israeli conflict maintained center stage. Instead of directing hostilities at the Soviet Union, Israel and Syria became involved in the Lebanese civil war. Israel also bombed an almost-completed Iraqi nuclear reactor, annexed the West Bank, and invaded Lebanon to annihilate the Palestinian Liberation Organization there. It seemed U.S. involvement was not producing the results Reagan had wanted.

Now that we have discussed various phases in U.S. foreign policy, we need to discuss the identity of the leaders and opponents in these trends—the foreign policymakers—and how each works to push the foreign policy pendulum in one or the other direction. Who are the foreign policymakers? How do they interact to produce the patterns we have talked about? How do they influence the policymaking process?

THE FOREIGN POLICYMAKERS

Many of the people who are instrumental in domestic policymaking are also important in foreign policymaking. The difference lies in the roles they play and their interaction. Here we look at their various roles and at how the sum of these parts produces foreign policy outputs.

The President

The president clearly plays the starring role in U.S. foreign policymaking. The reasons for this are varied. First, the Constitution gives the president the power to negotiate treaties, to enter into executive agreements, to appoint the officials who implement foreign policy (ambassadors, other public ministers, and consuls), and to receive diplomatic representatives from other nations. In addition, the Constitution makes the president the commander-in-chief of the military and the nation's chief executive officer. These powers have been further strengthened by court decisions. In *Missouri* v. *Holland*[6] (1920), the Supreme Court ruled that treaties and executive agreements with other nations have the same status as the Constitution: they are the supreme law of the land. And in *U.S.* v. *Curtiss-Wright Export Corporation*[7] (1936), the Court held that the national government has inherent power in the area of foreign policy, and that the president is the "sole organ" of the national government in that area.

Beyond these formal powers, the president has other sources of power. As the single executive in a system of government where power is diffused, the president is better able than other policymakers to act quickly and decisively when a crisis arises. He can amass information and make a decision, for better or worse, without having to go through the time-consuming process of majority building that is an integral part of group decision making.

Second, after he has amassed this information, the president can, because of his position, use the mass media to explain, justify, or rationalize his policies; to plead for understanding, sympathy, or time; or to argue against opponents of his policy.[8] As any semialert citizen knows, when the president does anything, it is news.

Finally, there is a long tradition of presidential predominance in foreign policymaking. Even though presidents have become more involved in foreign policymaking in this century than in previous times, we have merely to review U.S. history to see presidential influence. The various doctrines that have guided U.S. foreign policy from Monroe to Carter have been named after presidents. U.S. foreign policy is what the president says it is.

But despite the Supreme Court's declaration that the president is the "sole organ" of the national government in foreign policymaking, presidents clearly do not have a totally free hand in the area. They are constrained in at least three ways. First, they are unable to devote their full attention to foreign policy. As one observer has noted, there are "two presidencies; one . . . for domestic affairs, and the other is concerned with defense and foreign policy."[9] No president can totally ignore one or the other of these policy areas. Second, and related, is human limitation. There are only a certain number of hours in the day and only a certain amount of information that the president can receive and process. This means some policymaking responsibilities must devolve to others. The president must rely on others to screen and interpret information for him, even though he maintains the ultimate responsibility in this nuclear age. Third, there are other actors who have their own roles to play in foreign policymaking, and they limit the president's powers.

The Bureaucracy

Although the president is highly involved in decision making in crisis situations and in determining the general direction of U.S. foreign policy, day-to-day foreign policymaking, like domestic policymaking, is a function of the bureaucracy. At the level closest to the president, this bureaucracy includes personal advisors and political appointees. At another, lower level are the career bureaucrats in the executive branch departments and agencies (e.g., the State Department or the Arms Control and Disarmament Agency).[10] Together, these offices employ thousands of employees who are nominally under the president's control. But, as Richard Neustadt concluded several years ago, the president can seldom command; he more often has to exercise his "power to persuade."[11]

Personal advisors and political appointees. Within this "innermost circle" of foreign policymakers are the president's staff, the Secretaries of State and Defense, and the director of the CIA, among others. Exactly how these officials interact and affect foreign policymaking depends on their personalities and the president's inclinations. Presidents Truman and Eisenhower relied on strong Secretaries of State, and President Kennedy had an assertive Secretary of Defense. But in recent years, most presidents have turned to their personal advisors for foreign policy direction. The most notable example is Nixon's use of Henry Kissinger as his national security advisor, a position Kissinger retained for a time even after he became Secretary of State.

The tension between these various officials and the apparent trend toward presidential reliance on personal advisors is easy to understand. First, each individual has his or her own interests and vision of how foreign policy should proceed. Thus, each is pushing for the adoption of that particular view by the president.

Second, each participant has different loyalties. The cabinet secretaries are not only presidential appointees, but department heads as well. To be effective in a larger sense, they must please the president and protect their departments. The president's personal staff does not suffer from divided loyalties. Its members are selected by the president without scrutiny or confirmation by the Senate, and answer only to the president. Thus, whatever the official powers of the cabinet officials, personal staff members often wield more influence. They are closer to the president, and do not have to consider the bureaucratic implications of their advice.

Executive departments and agencies.   The career bureaucrats with the primary responsibility for foreign policymaking are in the State Department. They do the actual work of negotiating international agreements, representing the United States in international organizations, providing information for and advising the "innermost circle," and implementing chosen policies. Important positions are held by the foreign service officers (FSOs), traditionally an elite group of men.[12] That sense of elitism has often led the State Department to assume its preeminence in the foreign policy arena, not to fight for it. This lack of assertiveness, in combination with the disadvantages the Secretary of State has as a cabinet officer, has worked to undercut State Department leadership in the foreign policymaking process.

Of course, members of other departments have been quite willing to step in where the FSOs are shy. In the Department of Defense (DOD), the Office of International Security Affairs (OISA) houses the personnel who are involved in overseeing foreign policy interests in that department. These interests are obviously not small. The DOD, as the civilian branch that includes the military, has a vital interest in U.S. foreign policy. Indeed, much of U.S. foreign policy, particularly in the post–World War II era, has been focused on defense policy. It is in OISA that the intersection of foreign and defense policies occurs.

OISA has an advantage over the more isolated FSOs in that DOD has more clout in the political system. That strength arises from several sources. First, national defense is recognized as a primary need without which other needs cannot be addressed. If the nation is not secure from external threats, the condition of the nation's roads and sewers, for example, matters little. Second, DOD is a larger bureaucracy. Table 12–2 shows the recent budgetary figures for both DOD and the State Department, with DOD's civilian and military budget separated. The contrast is striking. For 1984, for example, the State Department was allotted a little more than 1 percent of DOD's total budget.

Third, DOD has a noticeable effect on the economy through the massive amounts of money it spends each year. Although there is some evidence that defense spending actually results in a net loss of jobs in the economy,[13] it is widely perceived that

TABLE 12–2   Budget authority[a] for Defense and
State Departments, 1982–1984 (in thousands of dollars)

	1982	*1983[b]*	*1984[b]*
DOD–military	213,751,284	239,407,108	273,400,146
DOD–civilian	2,996,182	2,987,452	2,136,354
State Department	2,585,826	2,725,445	2,907,170

SOURCE: *Budget of the United States Government, Fiscal Year 1984*, pp. 8–70, 8–74, 8–132.

[a]Budget authority is the legal authority provided by Congress to spend money.

[b]Estimated.

defense spending creates work opportunities. Certainly, that is the case in congressional districts where large defense contractors (Lockheed, Boeing) have plants.

Fourth, since Vietnam, the nation's top military leaders, embodied in the Joint Chiefs of Staff (JCS), a part of DOD, have been noticeably voicing their opinions of how U.S. foreign policy should operate. Unlike other participants in the policymaking process, the military generally has alternatives ready to be presented to policymakers. Despite the fact that "Vietnam itself stands as a monument to military thinking about foreign policy problems,"[14] the military's influence with both Congress and the public remains strong. The United States would rather have too much national defense than not enough; the same cannot be said for diplomacy. Thus, it is not uncommon for career bureaucrats in DOD to have a greater say in U.S. foreign policymaking than the FSOs in the State Department. DOD effectively presents the image of an agency providing something to the American electorate; the State Department has trouble portraying itself as anything but an agency serving "faceless foreigners."

Like other career bureaucrats, members of the intelligence-gathering community are also willing to play an active role in the policymaking process. The CIA and a host of lesser-known agencies collect, screen, and interpret the information on which policy decisions are made. Through the screening and interpretation steps of that information gathering, these agencies, like the military, can structure the decision-making process. Again, much of this activity is conducted under the aegis of DOD; a lesser amount is directed by the State Department.

Finally, there are career bureaucrats in other departments who contribute to foreign policymaking but often go unrecognized. For instance, the Treasury Department, by representing the United States in the International Monetary Fund and the World Bank, and by enforcing tariff and tax laws, is instrumental in foreign policymaking. And the Department of Agriculture has personnel who promote international sales of U.S. agricultural products, regulate foreign agricultural imports, and collect information on international agricultural trends and developments.

In sum, the bureaucracy plays a significant role in the foreign policymaking process. Although these actors are part of the executive branch, and so nominally are under the control of the president, the reality is not quite that simple. The president can play his leading role effectively only if he can manage some of the obvious problems. He must rely on the bureaucracy for information and for possible alternatives. At the same time, he must be aware that bureaucrats are pursuing their own interests, interests molded by their personal beliefs and their positions within their bureaucracies. The result is a foreign policy that is shaped by both the president and his nominal subordinates. But even this is an oversimplification. Other participants act to further modify U.S. foreign policy, and it is to these actors that we now turn.

Congress

Reading the Constitution, it seems that Congress is more powerful than the president in foreign policymaking. Congress has the authority to regulate international commerce, punish those who commit crimes on the high seas, declare war, and raise and spend money for defense and other purposes. In addition, the Senate must approve certain key appointments and ratify treaties negotiated by the president. These powers taken together appear to give Congress a strong role in foreign policymaking. But in fact, presidential leadership in the foreign policy arena is only occasionally affected by Congress. Perhaps the best analogy is that of a bobsled team: the president is the driver, directing the vehicle; Congress is the brakeman, at times slowing the vehicle to make sure it stays on course.

The reasons Congress takes the back seat are varied. First, many members of Congress (MCs) think foreign policy is irrelevant. Yes, a representative with a large Jewish constituency will closely follow U.S. policy toward Israel, and a senator from a state that has a large number of military bases within its borders will pay close attention to defense policy. But unless they believe foreign policy issues are relevant to their interests, most MCs simply ignore them.

Reinforcing this tendency to ignore foreign policy is the congressional committee system. That system forces legislators to specialize in certain policy areas. Members who are not on a committee or subcommittee that deals with foreign policy have even less reason to be aware of what is going on in that policy area. And even if an MC happens to draw a foreign policy-related committee or subcommittee assignment, there is no comprehensive foreign policymaking committee. Although there are the Senate Foreign Relations Committee and the House Foreign Affairs Committee, foreign policy matters are also decided in the Appropriations, Armed Services, and Budget Committees in each chamber.

This fragmented policymaking process means that Congress as an institution generally fails to develop the expertise, unity, and capacity to make foreign policy decisions. There are exceptions, to be sure. For instance, President Reagan found his efforts to sell the AWACS aircraft to Saudi Arabia in 1981 complicated by the Arms Export Control Act of 1976. That act allows Congress to block proposed arms sales if both chambers pass an identical concurrent resolution within thirty days of being notified of the intended sale by the president. In this case, the Senate refused to go along with the House-passed rejection of the deal, and the sale went ahead. The fact that this was considered a foreign policy victory for Reagan indicates that Congress does have at least the potential power to limit the president's foreign policymaking prerogatives. But, more generally, Congress must rely on the bureaucracy or the president for information; it requires time to have the various members consider matters in each chamber; and its expertise is affected when key members leave for whatever reason. It is difficult to sort out exactly how much Congress affects foreign policymaking. What appears to be a lack of congressional assertiveness may in fact be simple agreement with presidential actions.

Certainly, it seems unlikely that Congress will ever replace the president as the dominant policymaker. The advantages the president has over Congress, of being able to act quickly and decisively while maintaining flexibility, are just too great. Congress can, however, be a more cautious brakeman. Through careful scrutiny of the various foreign policymakers who rely on the legislative branch for authority and money, Congress can ensure that the president does not drive the foreign policy bobsled recklessly. In addition, Congress can act as a conduit for public input into the foreign policymaking process.

Political Parties and Interest Groups

Political parties and interest groups are the organizations most citizens use to have input into public policymaking in the United States. By aggregating demands and supports, these organizations amplify the feelings of individuals.

Political parties generally present competing points of view, but in foreign policy this competition is minimal. Foreign policy is usually bipartisan—agreed to by the major political parties. Indeed, Clausen has argued that, within Congress, "party is not an important factor in the policy decisions."[15]

Bipartisanship is a key element in foreign policy because it allows the country to project an image of solidarity throughout the world. And presidents since Franklin Roosevelt have emphasized this theme. The underlying argument has been that foreign policy is too important to the welfare of the nation to be undermined by partisan differences. To ensure at least a semblance of bipartisanship, presidents have generally appointed some officials of the other party to key foreign policymaking positions.

On a more practical level, the bipartisanship has probably been necessitated by the fact that often party control of the White House and at least one chamber of Congress has been split. Until very recently, the best examples of bipartisan foreign policymaking have occurred during those times of split partisan control of the executive and legislative branches. For instance, the Marshall Plan and the formation of NATO were products of a time when Democrats held the White House and Republicans controlled Congress.

Recent changes in this pattern have resulted more from increased intraparty tension than from interparty conflict over foreign policy. Some Democrats have begun to argue for isolationism; on the other hand, some Republicans have come to push for interventionism. The result is that, although foreign policy is likely to have supporters from both major parties, it is not bipartisan in the traditional sense. Current bipartisan policies do not enjoy the broad support common in earlier years.

Perhaps a major reason for the change in the role of political parties in foreign policymaking is the increasing complexity of the process. What is making that process more complex is the growing interrelationship between foreign and domestic policy issues. For example, the continuing debate over increases in the defense budget in the face of growing budget deficits and high levels of unemployment is, of necessity, about the nature of an intermestic policy. Whatever policy is pursued will have both foreign and domestic implications. With the growth of intermestic problems, foreign policy issues have lost their separate identity, and with that their pressure for bipartisanship. Today, participants, particularly within Congress, can legitimately focus on other aspects of proposed policies to inform their vote. And because MCs are generally more interested in domestic issues, it is not surprising that they focus on the domestic aspects of intermestic policies. The traditional pattern of bipartisan support for foreign policy, then, seems to be giving way to a partisan pattern based on the issues' domestic implications. If this is the case, political parties may become more important constraints on presidential leadership in foreign policymaking, but in a less predictable way.

The other type of political organizations—interest groups—has traditionally played a very minor role in the foreign policymaking process. These groups are weak for two reasons. First, unlike domestic policy interest groups, they seldom serve as significant sources of information for policymakers. The intelligence-gathering capability of the government is clearly superior to what any interest group is likely to achieve. Second, there is seldom a broad constituency for foreign policy programs. The direct beneficiaries of those programs are not likely to help vote anyone into or out of office, so interest group representatives have trouble getting access to elected policymakers. When interest groups have become influential in foreign policymaking, they have, in some way, overcome these handicaps.

One group that has done just that is the American Israel Public Affairs Committee (AIPAC). AIPAC and other Jewish groups are able to influence policies because they can, in some areas, offer independent sources of information (e.g., from Soviet Jews), and because, in other areas, they represent a large constituency. But this group's, or any interest group's, power is not unbridled. Jets were sold to Egypt and Saudi Arabia in 1978 over AIPAC objections. And, other groups, among them the Association of Arab-Americans and, at times, black organizations, have opposed AIPAC, countering its influence on foreign policymaking.

The most influential group in the foreign policymaking arena is the Council on Foreign Relations.[16] The CFR is hardly a traditional interest group, however. It does not articulate mass public opinion; instead it aggregates elite opinion. Its members are fourteen hundred of the most prestigious leaders of business, academia, the media, and the government. The council generally works by supporting scholarly research on foreign policy issues and disseminating the results of that work. The CFR is able to gain wide notice for its work through its publication, *Foreign Affairs*, which is widely recognized as a forum for unofficial statements of U.S. foreign policy. In fact, policies like containment and human rights were either developed under CFR auspices or first announced in *Foreign Affairs*. The interrelationship between the CFR and the federal government on foreign policy matters is so great that one observer has asserted that the CFR, "while not financed by the government, works so closely with it that it is difficult to distinguish Council actions stimulated by government from autonomous actions."[17] The international extension of the CFR is the Trilateral Commission, so named because it is composed of the top officials in multinational corporations and governments in the United States, Western Europe, and Japan. The focus of the Trilateral Commission is on coordinating economic policy.

In sum, interest groups begin with a greater disadvantage in foreign policymaking than do political parties. Only in rare circumstances do they have the proper levers to significantly influence the process. Perhaps, with the continuing evolution toward intermestic policies, they will be able to tie their interests to domestic issues that are of concern to a broader range of decision makers. But, until this happens, interest groups, except for the CFR, are unlikely to be powerful on a broad range of issues. And the public is likely to remain unorganized on foreign policy matters.

Public Opinion and the Mass Media

If American citizens are unlikely to affect foreign policymaking through their actions in traditional political organizations, how can they have an impact? There should be some line beyond which "wrong" foreign policy actions mobilize the public to rein in and redirect the policymakers. Thus, it seems important to consider what citizens know and think about foreign policy.

The adjectives that best describe the public stance in foreign affairs are *uninformed* and *apathetic*. Public opinion polls consistently show that the public knows very little about world affairs and is unwilling to exert the effort to learn. Just because people know very little, however, does not mean they do not have opinions. The phases of U.S. foreign policy are essentially reflections of different moods, or periods of dominant opinions. In essence, public opinion serves to set boundaries within which foreign policy can be pursued. And over time, these boundaries shift.

Shifts in those boundaries are anchored by some general rules. The first is, of course, nationalism. U.S. citizens value loyalty to the country (as do citizens of most countries) and see other nations as competitors. Thus, to be acceptable, U.S. foreign policy must seem to pursue U.S. interests. To the extent that leaders pursue those interests, they are allowed to exercise their judgment about exactly what should or should not be done. It is when questions arise about the compatibility of actions with U.S. interests that leaders' discretion is narrowed. For example, as casualty rates in a war rise, as the public begins to weigh those casualties against the objectives of the struggle, support for the war declines.[18] But, as long as questions of conflict with the public concept of national interests do not arise, foreign policymakers have wide latitude in decision making.

That latitude is particularly important for the president acting as the chief foreign policymaker; it is an important base of power, a means of boosting his support. A study of changes in presidential popularity from Franklin Roosevelt to Ford shows that in over three-fourths of the cases where the president took some kind of action in international affairs, successful or not, his popularity rating rose.[19] For example, the rescue of the crew of the *Mayaguez* during the Ford administration was only accidentally successful. Almost in spite of the operation, the crew members were saved. Yet, President Ford's popularity rating shot up immediately afterward. This suggests that the president can benefit from action in the foreign policy arena, at least in the short term, regardless of what he does. The president can then shape public opinion, particularly in times of crisis, to enhance his power. Nationalism, exhibited as a "rally 'round the flag" attitude, interacts with presidential flexibility, not to constrain foreign policymaking, but to allow the president a virtually free hand.

Playing a part in this phenomenon is the president's access to both information and the mass media, particularly in times of crisis, which allows him to mold public opinion. But this power, like other presidential powers, is not absolute. The mass media are only partially effective in communicating with the public about foreign affairs for at least two reasons. First, a general lack of concern has many citizens tuning out foreign policy matters reported by the media. Second, and related to the first, that public lack of concern makes it good business for the commercial media to deemphasize foreign policy matters. This is obviously not true for national television networks, but certainly can be true elsewhere. For instance, the *New York Times* has a general policy of not devoting over half of its front page to foreign affairs. In short, the mass media can be a valuable tool for foreign policymakers, but they are not without limitations.

But the media are not only instruments of foreign policymakers; they also have tremendous impact on those officials. First, the media inform policymakers as well as the masses. In this way, the media affect how policymakers think much as they affect how the masses think. Second, to the extent that the media do structure public opinion about foreign policy matters, they structure the environment in which foreign policymakers must work. Finally, the media's penchant for the dramatic can create foreign policy problems that policymakers have to deal with whether they want to or not. Presumably, foreign policymakers would just as soon not have had to deal with "Koreagate"—the charges published by the *Washington Post* in late October 1976, that South Korean agents, principally Tongsun Park, dispensed cash and gifts to MCs to maintain a "favorable legislative climate"—but exposure by the mass media put the matter on the policy agenda.

THE POLICYMAKING INSTRUMENTS[20]

Even though the foreign policymaking process is more direct than the domestic process, it is by no means self-executing. Various tools or instruments must be used by the actors to implement that policy.

Diplomacy

The most common instrument in foreign policymaking is diplomacy, which covers a wide range of responsibilities:

- Communicating with representatives from other countries and international institutions about goals

- Gathering information
- Spelling out reasons for policies
- Making threats and promises
- Negotiating international differences
- Protecting the country's citizens and property abroad
- Representing the government at ceremonial occasions
- Advising and assisting in the making of foreign policy

Diplomacy has evolved from a relatively simple pattern of communication between two countries on a few issues to a highly complex pattern of interaction between countries and multinational organizations over a broad range of issues. Most dramatically, there has been a sharp increase in the amount of direct communication between heads of state through hot lines and summit meetings.

Propaganda

As the communications media have reached more and more people throughout the world, countries have invested greater resources in projecting a favorable image to the peoples of other countries. Often this means using propaganda. (When other nations disseminate information, we generally call it *propaganda;* when we do the same thing, we call it an *external information* or *educational program.* There is a negative connotation in the common usage of the word *propaganda* that is not part of its definition.) Propaganda involves (1) a communicator who deliberately attempts to change the attitudes and opinions of others with the presumption that that change will produce a change in behavior; (2) the symbol or message being communicated; (3) the communication media; and (4) the target audience.

Economic Rewards and Sanctions

As the economies of the world's nations have become more dependent on one another, the potential for offering economic rewards or imposing economic sanctions has grown. These rewards and sanctions take various forms:

- *Tariffs*—taxes on the importation of foreign-made goods—can be used to promote or constrict the markets for foreign economies. If tariffs are raised high enough, they can price goods out of the market.
- *Quotas*—restrictions on the amount of foreign goods that can be sold—may be imposed. Voluntary standards have limited imports to the United States of Japanese automobiles since 1981.
- *Boycotts*—refusals to buy certain foreign-made products—may be imposed. Boycotts can be enforced on private importers by requiring a license to buy products from the country being boycotted.
- *Embargoes*—refusals to sell certain goods to a foreign country—are sometimes used. The United States has a list of thousands of items (about seventy pages

long in 1983) that cannot be exported without a license because of their military value.

- *Loans* (at favorable rates) and *credits* can be used to reward countries that support U.S. foreign policy goals.

Foreign Aid

Closely akin to economic rewards, but distinct from them, is foreign aid. *Foreign aid*—the transfer of funds, goods, technology or expertise from one country or international organization to another—like economic rewards and sanctions can take a variety of forms. The first and oldest is military aid. It has been common through history for one country to provide military support to an ally in times of war. The second is technical assistance, the least costly type of foreign aid. This involves the transfer of technologies and skills (sanitation, agricultural production methods, education, and public administration). Perhaps the best-known example of this type of U.S. foreign aid is the Peace Corps. The third is grants and commodity export programs. The United States often makes direct grants of military equipment when a nation is threatened by what are perceived to be communist-backed forces. And when a natural disaster, say an earthquake or flood, strikes a foreign country, the United States is often there with direct aid in the form of money, food, and medical supplies. And, under the Food for Peace program, the United States distributes large amounts of surplus agricultural products to foreign countries.

Intervention

Intervention—an act that constitutes a sharp break in the pattern of a relationship, directed at changing or preserving the existing regime in the target nation without the consent of the commonly recognized government—has become almost commonplace in the twentieth century. It, too, takes a variety of forms. First, intervention can mean diplomatic interference in internal affairs. For example, an ambassador may make a public statement indicating which political party his or her government would prefer to win an election. Second, there is covert political intervention. Bribes may be offered, propaganda released, or leaders assassinated. Third, demonstrations of force can effectively influence other nations' internal affairs. For example, when a coup was threatened in the Dominican Republic in 1961, the United States sent twenty-two warships on maneuvers off that country's coast. The would-be rebels took this as a sign of U.S. support for the existing regime, and fled the country. Fourth, intervention can mean subversion—organizing, supporting, or directing dissident factions in another country. The United States commonly charges that communists are engaged in subversion if there is any linkage between them and a rebel movement, say the Sandinistas in El Salvador. Fifth, a country can intervene by supporting guerilla warfare. And sixth, a nation can intervene directly with military force, as the United States did in the Dominican Republic in 1965 or as the Soviets and their allies did in Czechoslovakia in 1968.

Weapons

Weapons are considered separate instruments of foreign policy because they have political value beyond their military value. Nothing makes this point more clearly than today's nuclear weaponry. Even though it has been four decades since a nation has actually used a nuclear weapon against another nation, those weapons are very much bargaining chips in modern diplomacy. The simple threat of nuclear attack is a potent foreign policy tool.

FOREIGN POLICY AND DEFENSE POLICY[21]

Many different policies are interrelated with foreign policy, but national defense has the greatest interdependence. Defense policy is a subset of foreign policy that addresses problems specifically related to the defense of the nation in a potentially hostile world. It is important if for no other reason than its magnitude. In fiscal year 1984, approximately $.29 of every dollar spent by the United States went for national defense. Table 12–2 shows vast differences in the budgets of the State Department and the Department of Defense; Table 12–3 shows a different breakdown of the budget but a similar picture. In Table 12–3, the budget is divided by use rather than department. That is, all foreign policy expenditures regardless of the department in which they occur are brought together; the same is done for defense expenditures. Again, we see that defense spending far outstrips spending for foreign policy matters.

Despite this spending gap, defense policy deals with a narrower set of concerns than does foreign policy. The most basic of these concerns is a question: Is there

TABLE 12-3 Outlays for national defense and international affairs, fiscal years 1977–1984 (in millions of dollars)

	National defense—Military	*International affairs*
1977	97,501	4,813
1978	105,186	5,922
1979	117,681	6,091
1980	135,856	10,733
1981	159,765	11,130
1982	187,418	9,982
1983[a]	214,769	11,939
1984[a]	245,305	13,250

SOURCE: *Budget of the United States Government, Fiscal Year 1982*, p. 600; and *Budget of the United States Government, Fiscal Year 1984*, pp. 9–42.

[a]Estimated.

a defense? Because the United States maintains its sovereignty and territorial integrity, the obvious response must be yes, but a more meaningful response is not quite so simple. The basic fact is we live in a nuclear age, where a number of countries have the potential to seriously disrupt life as we know it. The full implications of nuclear war are unknown. Beyond the immediate impact of explosion there would be the widespread effects of radiation on both people and the food chain on which they depend.

In today's world, then, the question changes: Is there a defense against nuclear weapons? Antinuclear weapons strategies can be divided into three types. First, there is the passive policy, which emphasizes survival and retaliatory capability. Programs like hardening missile silos and civil defense fall into this category. Second, there is the active policy, which would have the government concentrate on developing the capability to counteract or in some way stop a nuclear attack. Third, there is a first-strike policy, which assumes that the best defense is a good offense. This policy would have the United States preempt an attack by attacking first. Each of these policies has been advocated by different people at different times (although seldom do we find serious advocates of using the third policy to start a nuclear war). The result is a defense policy that reflects components of each strategy.

Exactly which combination of strategies we choose depends on how we answer four other questions: What deters other nations? What is the intent of the Soviet Union? What is the current state of arms and technology development, and what is likely to be developed in the future? How do we achieve international stability?

The Nuclear Threat

What deters other nations? There are three variables that interact in answering this question: the threshold of provocation at which nuclear weapons will be used; the amount of destruction these weapons could cause; and the chance that this destruction will occur. These are analytically separate considerations, but in reality they are inseparable. The product of these variables should yield some insight into the basis of a nation's defense policy. At one extreme, if a nation must be highly provoked before it uses its nuclear weapons, can only do so in a way that is designed to produce widespread destruction, and perceives that its target's defenses might be effective in minimizing damage or allowing retaliation, it would seem unwise to use nuclear weapons. At the other extreme, where a nation has a low threshold of provocation, can respond in a limited way (and therefore believes that a limited nuclear war is possible), and believes that it can penetrate its enemy's defenses, nuclear attack seems viable. Here again, U.S. defense policy has varied. At times, massive retaliation with a high threshold has been the dominant policy; at others, a more flexible response has held sway.

Soviet Intent

The question "What deters?" has been most often addressed toward the Soviet Union. Since shortly after World War II, the Soviet Union has been the major U.S.

rival for primacy in world affairs. Exactly what are the Soviet goals? Are they bent on destroying the United States? Are they out to dominate the world? While these two possibilities are not mutually exclusive, they have different implications for how we interpret Soviet actions and construct U.S. defense and foreign policies.

Consider, for example, the Soviet invasion of Afghanistan in late December 1979. The Soviets amassed troops on the border with their southern neighbor; airlifted soldiers and military equipment into Afghanistan's capital, Kabul; and then "supported" a military coup that overthrew the regime of President Hafizullah Amin. If we believe that the Soviet objective is to bury the United States, how do we explain the situation in Afghanistan? It is very unlikely that the Russians hoped to embroil the United States in yet another conflict far from U.S. borders. In fact, if the Soviets' primary goal is U.S. destruction, the invasion of Afghanistan must be either unfathomable or a mistake—a "Russian Vietnam." But, if we accept that the USSR is intent on dominating the world, we have a more plausible explanation. The invasion of Afghanistan becomes just another stepping-stone in the Soviets' path to world conquest.

How we interpret Soviet intent shapes the response we make to their actions. If in fact the Soviets were hoping to lure the United States into another long-distance war, U.S. noninvolvement would be a sensible response; but if the Soviets were using Afghanistan as a stepping-stone toward world domination, the United States might well want to lend support to the anti-Soviet elements in the country. Of course, there is little way of knowing the Soviets' real intentions. So, U.S. defense and foreign policy changes depending on which motive is perceived to be in operation at any given time.

Arms and Technology Development

Much of the U.S. reading of Soviet intentions comes from intelligence about the current types and numbers of arms in Soviet stockpiles and estimates about the path of future Soviet arms development and deployment. These data, in combination with comparable facts about U.S. status, are important determinants of U.S. strategies for the development, manufacture, and deployment of weapons and delivery systems. Both in the USSR and in the United States, the pressure for new arms can come from two potent sources: First, the internal actors (the military–industrial complex) may push for continuous arms production as a way of guaranteeing continuous business. Second, there is an action-reaction sequence, in which for every reported Soviet development or buildup, there is a U.S. response, which precipitates a Soviet response, which precipitates a U.S. response, in a never-ending cycle.

Although these two factors may appear obvious to even a casual observer of the policymaking process, there is another element at work here: arms and the technology necessary to use them can wear out periodically or become obsolete. As a result, the arms race is punctuated with periodic spurts in spending for weapons, whatever the intentions of the participants. That is, even if the United States and the Soviet Union could agree not to develop any new weapons, we would still see periodic jumps in defense expenditures as old weapons wore out and had to be replaced by new editions of the same thing. As it is, with the next generation of weapons on the drawing board while we are manufacturing this generation, the rapid pace of technological development condenses the space between the periods of greater expenditure.

International Stability

How do we achieve international stability? The options fall into three general categories. First, some would argue that the United States can promote stability unilaterally by taking actions that reduce international tensions or by outpacing the Soviet Union in the arms race, becoming the clearly predominant world power. In practice, this would mean following one of two opposite strategies: (1) reducing arms production and not building certain types of weapons, whatever the actions of the Soviet Union; or, (2) more in line with the policy preferences of President Reagan, increasing arms production and developing new weapons, again whatever the actions of the Soviet Union.

Second, others would argue that stability can be promoted through coordinated behavior with the Soviet Union. This means taking an action, articulating its rationale, and communicating to the Soviet Union how a like action on its part would benefit all concerned. This would not, however, be formalized through negotiation or written agreement. The objective here is to turn the action-reaction cycle into a force for disarmament, not rearmament.

Third, others insist that world stability depends on the cooperation, through formal negotiation, of the major powers. The SALT I treaty is an obvious example of how this has worked, if only temporarily, in the past.

While it is clear that U.S. defense policy is at the heart of U.S. foreign policy and that we cannot discuss the latter without considering the former, in other policy areas the connections with foreign policy are not so obvious but may still be very important. It is to one of those areas—agriculture—that we now turn.

GRAIN SALES AND EMBARGOES: A CASE STUDY OF INTERMESTIC POLICY

Many would think that U.S. foreign policy and U.S. agricultural policy are literally worlds apart. After all, what does the wheat farmer in Kansas have to do with U.S. activity in world affairs? But the simple fact that one-fourth (about $40 billion in 1982) of U.S. agricultural production is exported belies this assumption. These two policy areas are drawn together along with many others in a complex web of policymaking.

The interface between U.S. foreign policy and U.S. agricultural policy revolves around two questions: How can the United States use its agricultural production to influence the behavior of other nations? And, can an international system of agricultural producers and consumers help stabilize world tensions?[22] Although some dispute whether the United States should use its agricultural production to influence other nations' behavior, there have been efforts to develop positive answers to both of these questions. Those answers center around governmental restrictions on or promotions of agricultural exports.

The saga of U.S.–Soviet grain dealings is long and complicated. Beginning in 1971, the Nixon administration moved to promote trade with the Soviet Union by withdrawing restrictions on grain exports to that country and offering credit for grain purchases. For the first time since 1963, U.S. grain companies could sell directly to the Soviet Union. The magnitude of the response was unexpected. In 1972, the Soviets purchased almost half of America's stored wheat and over a fourth of the current crop. This tremendous sale and Department of Agriculture subsidization of the exports drove up the price of wheat on the world market and contributed to the inflationary spiral at home. In an attempt to improve relations with the Soviet Union, domestic problems were worsened.

The 1972 grain deal set the stage for subsequent grain decisions. In 1973, in response to an anticipated shortage of soybeans, the Nixon administration announced (through the Secretary of Commerce) an embargo on the export of soybeans and soybean by-products. There were several implications of this move. First, because the United States was the world's major exporter of soybeans, importing countries were severely affected. Second, because the United States took the action unilaterally, allies, particularly in Western Europe and Japan, were snubbed. Third, the embargo decision signaled our allies that in times of crisis the country would take action without apparent regard to their needs. Although the embargo was eased just over a month later, and lifted in just over two months, the damage in foreign policy had been done. Unlike the 1972 situation, and probably in reaction to that, domestic economic considerations had dominated in foreign policymaking. Concerns about relations with importing countries were either ignored or overridden.

At about this same time, there were calls throughout the world for the establishment of a system of grain reserves to ensure against world hunger and price fluctuations. In the United States, this issue pitted those most concerned with domestic agricultural policy against foreign policymakers. U.S. farmers insisted the plan would depress prices; others argued that storage and administrative costs would drain the Treasury. But those interested primarily in foreign policy saw an international grain reserve as a way to stabilize international relations and to make a breakthrough in international cooperation. The foreign policy interests were able to mobilize enough support so that, by early 1974, there was a general feeling that something along these lines should be done. Then, several key staff members left the executive branch. Without their support, and in the face of domestic opposition, the United States was left to take only symbolic action at the World Food Conference. Foreign policy was forced to bow to domestic interests. Only where an issue is clearly a foreign policy matter, then, can foreign policymakers expect to hold sway. Where domestic interests are too obvious to be ignored, foreign policy may be made by those interests.

Also in 1974, the Soviets reentered the U.S. grain market. In October, they made large purchases of corn and wheat (though small compared to the amounts purchased in 1972). But, before the grains were shipped, the president interceded and, citing domestic pressures and a fear of congressional intervention, temporarily suspended the sales. The sales were later made after renegotiation with the Soviets by Secretary of the Treasury William Simon, taking into account U.S. supplies. Reaction to the 1974 Soviet grain purchases gave the U.S. Department of Agriculture the responsibility for monitoring grain exports. USDA required prior approval of exports of some grains until March 1975, after which it merely required notification after the act of sale. But, when the Soviets entered the market in July, again with relatively large purchases, Secretary of Agriculture Earl Butz once more suspended sales.

At this point, organized labor entered the picture. Union leader George Meany announced that longshoremen would not load grain being exported to the Soviet Union. Although Meany's public reason for the work stoppage was solidarity with U.S. consumers, he was clearly maneuvering in preparation for negotiations on the U.S.–Soviet maritime agreement that expired at the end of 1975.

In September, President Ford brought the various interests together and negotiated a settlement. The unions agreed to delay their boycott for a month; the government agreed to continue the suspension of grain sales through mid-October, and to negotiate a long-range agreement with the Soviets concerning grain purchases. A similar suspension of sales and efforts for a long-term agreement were directed toward Poland. Finally, in October, five-year agreements were negotiated with both countries and trade was restored. Minimum Soviet grain purchases were set at 6 million to 8 million tons per year. The goal of the agreement for the United States was to stabilize Soviet grain buying, to prevent market problems like those that had arisen with the 1972 purchases.

Trade proceeded smoothly until President Carter placed an embargo on grain sales to the Soviet Union in 1980, to protest the Soviet invasion of Afghanistan. Never before had the United States tried to use food as a foreign policy weapon on such a scale. Yet, even during this "embargo," the minimum quantity of grain agreed on in the 1975 arrangement was sold. And other countries, notably Argentina, were quite willing to increase their exports to the Soviet Union to negate the effect of the U.S. action. In the end, the embargo did not work.[23] President Reagan stopped the action in April 1981, and extended the 1975 agreement twice for one-year terms.

FOREIGN POLICY AND DEMOCRACY

Although interest groups and political parties do occasionally take an interest in foreign policymaking (when that policymaking has domestic implications that affect their members' interests), the public at large knows and cares little about the process. What does this mean about foreign policymaking in a democratic system? To what extent is the foreign policymaking process democratic?

These are difficult questions to answer because they bring to mind several conflicting demands of foreign policymaking and democracy.[24] First, foreign policymaking, more than domestic policymaking, demands secrecy; democracy calls for open, public decisions. We can reconcile the need for secrecy in foreign policymaking for two reasons: strategy and national security. Obviously, secrecy is an important bargaining tactic, one that the United States must be able to use if it is going to compete effectively with the other nations of the world. You don't win card games by showing your hand too early. As to the matter of national security, revelations of defense matters could threaten the very existence of the nation. Secrecy, then, becomes a tool for saving the democracy. Of course, the danger lies in the potential abuse of the secrecy privilege. That is, proponents of a particular policy would invoke the need for secrecy as a way to avoid opposition or publicity, not because that need is valid.

A second conflict arises between the need for speed in foreign policymaking and the slow deliberation inherent in the democratic process. In the extreme, should missiles be detected coming toward the United States, there would simply not be time to convene Congress and debate the proper response. But somewhere between this immediacy and endless deliberation, foreign policy has to be made.

A third conflict is between the united front foreign policy traditionally demands and the right to open dissent on which democracy rests. If other countries detect a lack of unity in a U.S. position, they may be less inclined to negotiate or may decide to stall negotiations, hoping that dissent will create policy more favorable to them. However, by insisting on a united front, we may stifle legitimate dissent and allow the country to continue on an erroneous course.

CONCLUDING COMMENTS

The progression of phases in U.S. foreign policy, especially the last isolationist and interventionist periods, clearly demonstrates the changed nature of U.S. foreign policy. First, the United States can no longer isolate itself from international affairs. Even in the "we don't want another Vietnam" era, the level of foreign policy activity remained high, as U.S. officials worked to support Middle East peace negotiations and to arm the combatants. President Carter deployed cruise missiles on B-52 bombers when he canceled the B-1, ordered a military rescue of U.S. hostages in Iran, put an embargo on Soviet-bound shipments of high technology, declared a U.S. boycott of the 1980 summer Olympics in Moscow, and issued the Carter Doctrine (1980), committing the United States to the defense of Persian Gulf oil-producing nations against external threats. The intensity of earlier isolationist periods was simply unattainable.

The second, and related, point is that the level of U.S. foreign policy activity is less a matter of official discretion than it was in earlier times. Increased international interdependence and the evolution of an international economy mean that the United States at times must react to events in other nations. For example, when the Organization of Petroleum Exporting Countries (OPEC) quadrupled oil prices in 1973, U.S. policymakers were forced to consider the issue whether they wanted to or not. Similarly, in 1975, when the Cambodians seized a U.S. merchant ship, the *Mayaguez*, a decision, for either action or inaction, was required. Obviously, these types of events have occurred in the past also; what has changed today is their frequency.

The third point is that it has become increasingly difficult to exhibit leadership in U.S. foreign policy. We have cited several instances where isolationist pressures have been felt during interventionist periods, and vice versa.

The picture that emerges from the review of the various participants in foreign policymaking is one of different and clearly defined statuses. The president is at the center of the picture, and much of the exact nature of the rest of that picture is at his discretion. In general, his personal advisors stand closest to him; the relevant cabinet officers, slightly farther away. Congress is in the next tier of participants, and political parties and interest groups compose the background. Public opinion and the mass media help determine the shape of the picture.

But in foreign policy, as in no other policy area, the president commands center stage. U.S. foreign policy is virtually made—that is, adopted and implemented—whenever the president makes a statement. His primacy is reinforced by the difficulty of evaluating foreign policy. Only when the nature of foreign policy blends with domestic policies do the other actors play a consistently significant role.

The foreign policymakers have a variety of tools, the most important of which we have outlined briefly, to ply their trade. Exactly which instruments are used, and how they are used, like the mix of relevant actors, depends on circumstances.

We can see, even in the highly nontechnical presentation offered in this chapter, that U.S. defense policy involves a very complicated set of calculations that are colored by the equality of intelligence information available to policymakers and by their perceptions of what other countries, particularly the Soviet Union, plan to do. The picture is even more complicated in this nuclear age by uncertainty about exactly what the use of nuclear weapons would mean.

The case study of intermestic policymaking illustrates much of what has been stated earlier about foreign policymaking. First, the only clearly defined role in foreign policymaking is played by the president, and he is unable to devote his full attention to this policy area. Even when the president is concerned, he often has to delegate responsibilities to other officials, who, on the face of it, have few foreign policymaking duties. In these various grain dealings, the Secretaries of Commerce, Treasury, and Agriculture were most evident, not the Secretary of State. And their enlarged roles were at the president's choosing.

Another factor that affects the roles these actors play is the extent to which an issue is defined as a foreign policy problem or as an intermestic problem. The greater the role of domestic issues in the area, the more likely we are to find other actors involved in the policymaking process. In the grain dealings, the Secretary of Agriculture, for instance, could legitimately argue that his voice should be heard in attempting to solve the problem at hand. By the same token, the greater the involvement of domestic issues, the more likely we are to see interest groups and partisan politics involved in the process. The entry of labor unions into policymaking in this example is a case in point. Where there is a clear domestic link, then, foreign policymaking takes on new players and creates new roles, in a more complex production.

In short, foreign policymaking in the United States is like domestic policymaking in its complexity. It is further complicated by the fact that the nature of the problems with which foreign policymakers deal is fundamentally different from domestic problems. And, increasingly, those who have the responsibility for making foreign policy are having to consider domestic matters too. The evolution of intermestic policymaking has added a new dimension to an already complex process.

NOTES

1. Bayless Manning, "The Congress, the Executive and Intermestic Affairs: Three Proposals," *Foreign Affairs* 55 (January 1977): 308.
2. Another way of classifying foreign policies is by their objectives. For a discussion along these lines, see Thomas A. Bailey, *A Diplomatic History of the American People*, 8th ed. (New York: Appleton-Century-Crofts, 1969).
3. Statistical evidence for these alternative periods is presented in Frank L. Klingberg, "The Historical Alternation of Moods in American Foreign Policy," *World Politics* 4 (January 1952): 239–273. For an updated presentation, see "Cyclical Trends in American Foreign Policy Moods and Their Policy Implications," in *Challenges to America: United States Foreign Policy in the 1980s*, eds. Charles W. Kegley, Jr., and Patrick J. McGowan (Beverly Hills: Sage, 1979), pp. 37–55.
4. The historical matters presented here are drawn from Klingberg, "Historical Alternation of Moods," pp. 242–249; and Bailey, *Diplomatic History of the American People*, pp. 66–725.
5. In addition to the works in note 4, this section draws on John Spanier and Eric M. Uslaner, *Foreign Policy and the Democratic Dilemmas*, 3rd ed. (New York: Holt, Rinehart and Winston, 1982); and John Spanier, *American Foreign Policy since World War II*, 9th ed. (New York: Holt, Rinehart and Winston, 1983). The examples used in the text are meant to be illustrative; for other examples, refer to these works.
6. 252 U.S. 416 (1920).
7. 299 U.S. 304 (1936).
8. Terry F. Buss and C. Richard Hofstetter, "The President and the News Media," in *The Presidency: Studies in Policy Making*, eds. Steven A. Shull and Lance T. LeLoup (Brunswick, Ohio: King's Court Communications, 1979), p. 24.
9. Aaron Wildavsky, "The Two Presidencies," *Trans-Action* 4 (December 1966): 7.
10. This conceptualization is suggested in Roger Hillsman, *To Move a Nation* (New York: Doubleday, 1967), pp. 541–544.
11. Richard E. Neustadt, *Presidential Power* (New York: Wiley, 1960).
12. The tradition of recruiting only men from Ivy League schools has changed somewhat over the past few years. At the end of 1979, 11.5 percent of the FSOs were female. And the geographic and social distributions of FSOs have become more representative of the U.S.

population than they used to be. As one FSO commented, "Never again will 3 eastern universities each provide 10 percent of entering Foreign Service classes year after year." See Barbara J. Good, "Women in the Foreign Service: A Quiet Revolution," *Foreign Service Journal* 58 (January 1981): 47–50; and Libbie S. Mathes, "Is the Foreign Service in Decline?" *Foreign Service Journal* 58 (May 1981): 20–22.

13. A recent UPI story cites a study by Employment Research Associates of Lansing, Michigan. The study reportedly shows that for every $1 billion spent by the Pentagon, there is a net loss of eighteen thousand jobs over what would have been generated by the same expenditure of money by consumers for goods and services (food, housing, clothes, automobiles, and medical care). See "Study: Jobs to Be Lost If Defense Budget Ok'd," *New Orleans Times-Picayune/States-Item,* February 7, 1983, p. 2. Professor Monte Piliawsky, Dillard University, New Orleans, brought this to our attention.

14. Charles W. Kegley, Jr., and Eugene R. Wittkopf, *American Foreign Policy: Pattern and Process* (New York: St. Martin's, 1979), p. 280. This point is reiterated, though not in exactly the same words, in the second edition of this book (1982, p. 367).

15. Aage R. Clausen, *How Congressmen Decide: A Policy Focus* (New York: St. Martin's, 1973), p. 99.

16. For a fuller discussion of the CFR and a list of its board of directors, see Thomas R. Dye, *Who's Running America? The Reagan Years,* 3rd ed. (Englewood Cliffs, N.J.: Prentice-Hall, 1983), pp. 151–154, 244–247.

17. Lester Milbrath, "Interest Groups in Foreign Policy," in *Domestic Sources of Foreign Policy,* ed. James Rosenau (New York: Free Press, 1967), p. 247.

18. John E. Mueller, "Trends in Popular Support for the Wars in Korea and in Vietnam," *American Political Science Review* 65 (June 1971): 358–375.

19. Jong R. Lee, "Rallying around the Flag: Foreign Policy Events and Presidential Popularity," *Presidential Studies Quarterly* 7 (Fall 1977): 252–256.

20. This section draws on K. J. Holsti, *International Politics: A Framework for Analysis,* 3rd ed. (Englewood Cliffs, N.J.: Prentice-Hall, 1977), pp. 183–356.

21. This section draws heavily on discussions with Professor Richard J. Stoll, Rice University. He may or may not recognize the interpretations of some of his arguments as presented here.

22. This section draws on I. M. Destler, *Making Foreign Economic Policy* (Washington, D.C.: Brookings Institution, 1980), pp. 36–64, 88–120.

23. Robert L. Paarlberg, "Lessons of the Grain Embargo," *Foreign Affairs* 59 (Fall 1980): 144–162.

24. These conflicts are suggested in William O. Chittick, *State Department, Press, and Pressure Groups: A Role Analysis* (New York: Wiley-Interscience, 1970), p. 292.

SUGGESTED READINGS

Destler, I. M. *Making Foreign Economic Policy.* Washington, D.C.: Brookings Institution, 1980.

Kegley, Charles W., Jr., and Wittkopf, Eugene R. *American Foreign Policy: Pattern and Process.* 2nd ed. New York: St. Martin's Press, 1982.

Spanier, John. *American Foreign Policy Since World War II.* 9th ed. New York: Holt, Rinehart and Winston, 1983.

———— and Nogee, Joseph, eds. *Congress, the Presidency and American Foreign Policy.* New York: Pergamon Press, 1981.

———— and Uslaner, Eric M. *Foreign Policy and the Democratic Dilemmas.* 3rd ed. New York: Holt, Rinehart and Winston, 1982.

Speed, Roger D. *Strategic Deterrence in the 1980s.* Stanford, Calif.: Hoover Institution Press, 1979.

Some Final Considerations

We begin with two aspects of the policy process that deserve more explicit treatment than they received in earlier chapters: the characteristics of policy change and the impact of policy. We conclude with a brief look at the Reagan administration and its effort to effect a major change in the role of government.

POLICY CHANGE

By policy change we mean both the adoption of new policies and the modification or repeal of existing ones. Here we contend that policy change can take three forms: (1) incremental changes in existing policies, (2) the enactment of basic statutes in particular policy areas, and (3) major shifts in public policy as a consequence of realigning elections.

Incrementalism

Most change in the American political system takes the form of limited or marginal changes in or additions to existing public policies;[1] others are basic or fundamental. Whether a particular policy change is incremental or basic is open to argument, especially in close cases. It is a little like determining whether a particular animal is a large pony or a small horse. (The Interstate Commerce Commission, incidentally, once put itself in just that position by creating different truck rates for the transportation of horses and ponies.) To some, every or almost every policy is incremental, but that view makes the concept meaningless because it neither describes nor explains any particular category of things. If all people are tall, the concept of tallness has no real meaning; it distinguishes no one.

To clarify the distinction we are making, consider the Fair Labor Standards Act of 1938 and subsequent amendments. The 1938 law marked a basic change in public policy: for the first time, the national government became involved in the general regulation of wages and hours of work. Where previously there had been no regulation, a substantial portion of the labor force was now covered by federal labor standards. (There are a few antecedents, among them the Adamson Act of 1916, which provided an eight-hour day for railroad workers; but in no meaningful sense can the Fair Labor Standards Act be regarded as merely a limited or marginal addition to existing national policy.) Since 1938, many incremental changes have been made in the law—increasing or sometimes decreasing its coverage, hiking the minimum wage, and the like. Over the years, the minimum wage has been increased from the initial requirement of $.25 an hour to the 1984 standard of $3.35 an hour. These, in the best sense of the word, represent policy increments.

Why is incremental change the most common kind of policy change in the American political system? In our discussion of the reasons, we again make use of the sequential policy model we talk about in chapter 1.

At any given time, there are numerous public problems on the policy agenda, many of them quite technical or complex. Policymakers have neither the time, the information, nor the ability to fashion complete once-and-for-all solutions to these problems. And uncertainty adds to the complexity. Which alternative is the right one? What are the consequences of each alternative? In the end, a limited or piecemeal approach may seem the safest way to alleviate or partially resolve many problems.

Second, power is fragmented and dispersed along many points in the American political system—national, state, and local governments; legislative, executive, and judicial branches; upper and lower legislative houses; a variety of administrative departments, agencies, and commissions; organized lobbies; and a multitude of political interest groups. Majority building, or otherwise winning the approval necessary to secure the adoption of policy alternatives, is a major task confronting those who formulate and adopt policy. Negotiation, bargaining, and compromise become necessary to win the support or reduce the opposition of those who could block adoption. On its way to enactment, then, a statute may be reduced in scope, shorn of some of its provisions, and otherwise modified in strength and impact.

Third, political expedience contributes to incremental policy change. It is easier to secure agreement on limited policy changes than on those of a sweeping or drastic nature. An incremental policy may well satisfy the need or demand for action, the notion that "we have got to have a bill," that often motivates policymakers to act. The search for a policy alternative often ends when any plan is found that will work, even though that plan is not the ideal solution.

Fourth, the beneficiaries of existing programs, the agencies and officials who administer them, and those who regard them as wise and proper public policy can be counted on to resist sweeping changes, or perhaps any changes, in them. Comprehensive deregulation of business is unlikely to result because of the interests of the regulated and those who regulate them. Both have a stake in the status quo. Limited or piecemeal deregulation is more likely to win approval because it will create less opposition. For example, the Nixon administration's proposal for a guaranteed annual income, which would have constituted a basic change in welfare policy, failed, in part, because many persons would receive higher benefits from the existing welfare programs than they would have received under the administration's proposal.

Finally, governmental bodies and officials are often reluctant to take action or, once moved to action, are not inclined to act in a radical fashion. Action, or change, may be unsettling, disruptive of established routines, productive of conflict. Subtle or incremental change is less disturbing and thus preferred over something more jarring or far-reaching.

Basic Change

Basic change in particular policy areas is not a well-studied phenomenon, so generalizations are hard to come by. Therefore, we begin by giving some examples of basic change and commenting briefly on them.

One example is the Atomic Energy Act of 1946. Until World War II, atomic energy was only a theoretical possibility. After Enrico Fermi, Albert Einstein, and others in the Manhattan Project had successfully split the atom, and President Truman had ordered the use of atomic bombs on the Japanese, theory became reality. In the cold war atmosphere after 1945, it became necessary to develop an explicit policy on atomic energy. Who should be in control? What form should control take? The Atomic Energy Act made nuclear energy a government monopoly and vested control in the Atomic Energy Commission, a civilian agency. In Congress, the Joint Committee on Atomic Energy was given jurisdiction over such legislation. In 1946, a basic, nonincremental policy change was necessitated by a technological innovation and national security considerations.

Another striking example of basic policy change is federal air pollution policy under the 1970 amendments to the 1963 Clean Air Act.[2] Until 1970, changes in this policy area were essentially incremental. In 1955, a subcommittee of the Public Works Committee devoted less than a day's hearing to air pollution. In 1963, growing interest in the problems of pollution led the Senate to form a subcommittee on air and water pollution, chaired by Sen. Edmund Muskie (D.–Me.). Consideration of the Clean Air Act in that year focused on the question of whether or not the government should set standards for air quality. The Air Quality Act of 1967 demanded that state and local air pollution programs be established. Yet, by the time of the 1970 legislation, there was no federal agency with either the expertise or the resources to oversee state and regional programs. With regard to moving sources of air pollution (cars, trucks, buses), the picture for the 1955–1970 period is much the same. Both the Air Pollution Control Act of 1955 and the Schenck Act of 1960 emphasized research and problem definition. The Clean Air Act of 1963 and the Motor Vehicles Air Pollution Control Act of 1965 set weak federal emission standards. From 1955 to 1970, then, the politics of air pollution showed "a reasonably close fit" to incrementalism.[3] In sum, from 1955 to 1970 pollution control policy was characterized by multidimensional complexity and many special interest groups seeking to shape action; the result was incremental public policy produced by the need to build congressional majorities for legislation.

What happened in 1970 to change air pollution policy from incremental to innovative? The answer lies in the magnitude of public response in 1969–1970. Public opinion about the environment was intense, and that opinion seemed to be in strong support of clean air and water. Congress and the president responded quickly and dramatically. The National Environmental Protection Act was passed, the Environmental Protection Agency was created to enforce federal standards, and the 1970 amendments to the Clean Air Act established stringent federal emission standards. For example, by 1975 automobiles were to have reduced pollutant emissions by 90 percent from the 1970 emission levels. This was done even though the federal government lacked knowledge of the trade-offs between the economy and the environment, and automobile manufacturers lacked the expertise to reduce emissions to the specified standard. Instead of the normal incremental policy process, where majority support has to be built for a policy, "in 1970 air pollution policymakers had to find a policy for [the] coalition."[4] In sum, public pressure created a mandate for clean air and water, and the political system responded with a nonincremental policy change. (It has yet to be fully implemented.)

It would be foolish to try to generalize about basic policy changes in particular areas from these examples. We can see, however, that different types of conditions can give rise to basic policy developments. In the case of atomic energy, policy was nonincremental and decisive because atomic energy did not exist before World War II. So technological innovation and national security considerations led to the Atomic Energy Act. The 1970 amendments to the Clean Air Act were a consequence of intense public pressure for strong action to protect the environment. A real or perceived crisis or dissatisfaction with state action and strong pressure from an interest group can also lead to major policy changes.

Realigning Elections

Although the configuration of interests and institutions in the United States is such that limited adjustments in public policy are often all that are possible, during certain periods in American history major policy shifts have occurred. In 1876, policies were adopted that helped institutionalize industrialism, and, in 1896, the Populist threats to industry were deflected.[5] In 1933, the federal government's role in the economy shifted dramatically. Franklin Roosevelt's New Deal helped convert the United States into a modern welfare state. Thus, during certain periods policy is innovative rather than incremental. In this section we describe the conditions under which major policy "revolutions" can take place.

Over time, in any given society, social crises arise.[6] These crises may be the product of fundamental imbalances in the social order; and if the government cannot solve the problems, either a new regime or a new type of government results. Such crises are timeless. When, in the fifteenth and sixteenth centuries, the middle class in England grew in economic strength and number, the old feudal order gave way to a stronger monarchy, and ultimately to parliamentary government. In the nineteenth and twentieth centuries, as the laboring classes grew in number, governments shifted to welfare policies, away from laissez faire. Every industrial society has experienced a crisis of the old order with the shift from an agricultural to an industrial economy. During these periods of crisis, the various issues involved are translated into a major pressing issue, and the government must resolve the crisis by dealing satisfactorily with that issue, or suffer defeat at the polls.

Over the last century, the United States has experienced at least two such crises. The first was the threat to the industrial order from agricultural interests during the 1890s; the second was the crisis created by the Great Depression in the 1930s. In both cases there was an overriding question. The first: What future is in store for America—industrial or agricultural? The second: What should the government do to combat the effects of the depression? In the American political system, these kinds of questions are resolved in critical elections that bring to power a new set of party leaders who are believed able to act across a number of policy areas to combat the crisis. Perhaps the best way to illustrate how critical elections bring about major changes is to look at the elections of 1932 and 1936.

In the early twentieth century, business and business values reigned supreme in the United States. Government actors were firm believers in this American way of life; President Calvin Coolidge once put it, "The business of America is business." As a result, social welfare was largely a private concern, and government intervention in the economy was minimal. The market economy was in its heyday. There were, of course, protests from farmers and other groups who were especially subject to the ups and downs of the marketplace. Nevertheless, it is accurate to say that the role of government in everyday life was minimal. The consensus that had formed around these business values was shaken when the stock market crashed in 1929. The effects of the Great Depression steadily worsened, and by 1932, in any given three-month period over half of the American people suffered some unemployment. On a single day in 1932 in Mississippi, one-quarter of the farmland in the state was up for sheriffs' auctions; and in Davenport, Iowa, irate farmers took over the town to prevent tax sales of their land. The American dream of unlimited progress and prosperity seemed to be turning into a nightmare.

The great question of the era became: What should the government do to combat the effects of the depression? On one side were those who argued that the national government must actively pursue policies to alleviate the effects of the depression—loans to farmers and businesses; programs to guarantee that banks would not collapse and leave depositors without money; provisions for feeding and clothing people until they could go back to work; and improved distribution of economic goods and services. The other side took the traditional hands-off position. President Hoover, for instance, contended that "economic depression cannot be cured by legislative action or executive pronouncement. Economic wounds must be healed by . . . the producers and consumers themselves." In this great debate, the two major political parties took distinct positions. The Republicans, who were in power, argued that the government could not and should not enact programs to combat the effects of the depression. The Democrats by 1932 had formulated activist programs such as a $900 million federal works program, a billion-dollar Reconstruction Finance Corporation loan fund, and a $100 million mercy fund. The Republican and Democratic platforms in 1932 differed markedly on the aggregation of wealth, on control of the distribution of wealth, and on the exercise of governmental power. In sum, the parties differed fundamentally over the government's role in curing the depression.

The election of 1932 became a referendum over this question. The election results gave Franklin Roosevelt and the Democrats an overwhelming victory. Democratic candidates swept to power in unprecedented numbers in both the House and Senate. The newly elected president and Congress believed they had a mandate to act, and act they did. In the first four years of the Roosevelt era, more social welfare and economic regulatory legislation was passed than in the previous century and a half. Social Security, labor legislation, public works, and economic stimulation programs abounded. American public policy shifted sharply from laissez faire to welfare statism. And these policy changes occurred across all policy areas, not just in isolated ones. From consumerism to social welfare, the New Deal groundswell changed the face of American government and public policy.

The elections of 1932 and 1936 provided support for these policy changes. Northern urban ethnics and blacks, who had traditionally voted Republican, changed parties and became Democrats. Those voters who had been hard hit by the depression favored the Democratic programs to combat the depression. Attempts by Republicans and others to eliminate the economic management and social welfare programs of the New Deal were turned back because those who favored the policies could and did continue to elect majorities to Congress who supported the New Deal. It was not until the Republicans accepted the main outlines of New Deal policies that they elected a president—Dwight Eisenhower in 1952.

The crisis of the depression, then, produced a policy question that was comprehensible to the average voter. The major parties adopted profoundly different policy stands on the central question—the role of government in the economy. The Republicans defended the old order; the Democratic platform advocated an activist government. The election results in both 1932 and 1936 affirmed and reaffirmed the people's preference for the latter. The newly elected (1932) president and Congress formulated and adopted sweeping policy changes, and they created a bureaucracy capable of implementing those changes. What we had, then, was a crisis that raised a central question; a distinct set of answers to that question; the election of a new majority; and the enactment of fundamental changes. The crucial elements in such realigning elections are the nature of the questions generated by the crisis and the fact that the election results in a massive turnover of elected officials. The newly elected officials, chosen on the basis of their stand on the critical question, enact policy changes consistent with their party's stand.

In this century, only the New Deal period clearly involves a realigning election with the attendant major policy changes. However, both Woodrow Wilson's and Lyndon Johnson's elections were characterized by high electoral turnover of members of Congress because of special circumstances surrounding the election. (We look at Ronald Reagan's election in a later section.) Wilson's election in 1912 was the result, in part, of Theodore Roosevelt's break with the Republican party over Progressive policy. In one sense, then, the 1912 election can be interpreted as a mandate for Progressivism. Johnson's landslide victory in 1964 followed the death of John Kennedy and the subsequent nomination of a very conservative Republican candidate for president. In both the 1912 and 1964 elections, a large number of new representatives were elected, and they were strong supporters of the new policies associated with Wilson and Johnson. Under such electoral conditions the adoption of policies that are nonincremental is far easier than in "normal" times. In sum, major policy changes are much more likely to occur during periods of rapid electoral turnover associated with crisis periods.

In terms of our sequential policy model, a social or economic crisis generates policy demands for a solution to the problem. The policy formulation stage is dominated by the need to resolve the crisis. Under these conditions, policy formulation and the political agenda merge. That is, during a crisis the government must formulate policies to deal with the socioeconomic problems on everyone's mind; so the problem becomes the agenda. The party in control of the government and the opposition develop alternative policies to deal with the crisis, and the realigning election determines which party controls policymaking. In the newly elected Congress, the majority party and its president readily adopt their stated policies and formulate new ones. This is in distinct contrast to normal elections, in which representatives, senators, and the president run on different issues, and policies adopted in these Congresses are a matter of compromise. Policy adoption in Congress is usually a bargaining process, in which the many interests that must be accommodated water down the policy (incrementalism). The politics of policy adoption in true election realignments is different because the legislators and the president are elected specifically to deal with the problems causing the realignment.

Most policies, incremental or basic, are implemented by the bureaucracy. Meier and Kraemer argue that election realignments (especially in 1932) cause high turnover of personnel in established agencies as well as the creation of new agencies and bureaus to implement new policies.[7] Moreover, the newly created agencies and bureaus are, initially at least, very serious about their jobs. Although we do not know much about implementation during realignments, it seems plausible that the combination of new agencies and new personnel is sufficient to see that new policies are implemented more effectively than they would be if they were handled by old-line agencies with their commitments to older policies. At each stage of the policy sequence, policymaking during realignments differs from what it is at other times.

THE IMPACT OF POLICY

What impact does public policy have? Does policy really solve anything? People often express concern that while government action persists and expands, so do public problems; hence, nothing ever seems finally resolved. Why, people ask, cannot government solve "problem X" once and for all and be done with it?

Part of the answer lies in the very nature of public problems. They involve ongoing conditions or situations and therefore require continuing governmental action. Such problems as monopolistic business conditions, deception of consumers, pollution of the environment, income insecurity, inadequate transportation services, or unemployment do not admit of easy, once-and-for-all solutions. Unemployment cannot, for example, be wiped out by an inoculation program as was done with smallpox. And even in the case of smallpox continued vigilance is necessary lest it recur.

Part of the answer also lies in differing perspectives on public policies. From one perspective, policies obviously do make a difference—roads are built, welfare benefits paid, price-fixing agreements broken up, and sewage treatment plants constructed. We can point to many public policies and programs that have been successful, that have greatly lessened or ameliorated the conditions at which they were directed. Social Security, labor union rights, public school desegregation, rural electrification, conservation of forest resources, and the elimination of child labor are cases in point. On the other hand, of course, one can also point to some public policies and programs which have had less success. Examples include some facets of the War on Poverty, urban renewal, coal mine safety, and the Nixon administration's wage and price controls. An example of an abortive public policy was the swine flu vaccination program launched in 1976 by the Ford administration. Although the predicted swine flu epidemic did not occur in the winter of 1976–1977, the vaccination program can be given little credit. Chalk up the absence of an epidemic to either environmental conditions or incorrect prediction.

From another viewpoint, however, public policies solve few problems totally, because few if any public policies satisfy everyone. Although some would say that policy was successful if most air pollution was eliminated, others would deny its success as long as *any* air pollution existed. Most policies, moreover, are the products of bargaining and compromise and thus satisfy no one fully. If they indeed accomplished all that they were intended to accomplish, some people still would contend that more needed to be done about the matters at hand. We could totally eliminate environmental pollution (or any other problem) if we could reach complete agreement on the nature of the problem, what sort of future environmental conditions we wanted to exist, and what sort of actions were necessary to bring them into existence, and if we were willing to pay whatever costs were necessary to achieve those goals. But this kind of consensus is impossible. So, controversy will continue—with some claiming that policy is ineffective and others insisting that it tries to do too much.

Why Policies Fail

Leaving broad issues aside, we now turn our attention to a more specific question: do public policies have their intended impact? That is, even though they are not designed to do all that some persons want, do they achieve what was intended? In recent years, numerous public agencies and private scholars have studied and evaluated the impact of public policies. A major conclusion emerging from their research is that policy often fails to have its intended effect, to accomplish fully its stated goals. Many factors contribute to this result.[8]

A policy cannot be implemented without adequate resources. For example, the War on Poverty started by the Johnson administration was not wholly successful because only limited resources were provided for its various programs. Some say that antitrust policy would be much more effective in eliminating monopolistic activity if more dollars and personnel were devoted to its enforcement. Opposition to these two policies continued after their adoption, and critics have been able to restrict their impact by limiting the resources available to them and otherwise impeding their administration.

New problems and policies distract attention from older problems and policies. The war in Vietnam shifted attention from the War on Poverty, and it was argued (especially by opponents of the War on Poverty) that we "couldn't have both guns and butter." During the 1930s, opponents of vigorous antitrust action contended it would interfere with economic recovery; during the 1940s, they said that it would impede the war effort; today, in the age of the energy crisis, they say that it would hamper the development of energy sources. Those who favor competition, in contrast, have a rather weak lobby, however popular the notion of competition might be in economic theory.

Policies may be inadequately administered. This has been the case, for example, with equal employment opportunity programs. The Office of Federal Contract Compliance has been reluctant to crack down on discrimination by government contractors. The Equal Employment Opportunity Commission has been hampered by internal strife and desultory enforcement processes. The Bureau of Mines, another example, never displayed much enthusiasm for the enforcement of mine safety legislation.

People affected by policies can react to them in such a way that they lessen or nullify their impact. Much discretion usually remains with those subject to given policies. Thus, farmers confronted with crop control programs take their poorest acres out of production and use more fertilizer on the remaining acreage. The consequence is greater production from fewer acres and more surpluses for the government. Until 1978, price controls on natural gas sold in interstate commerce were avoided, in part, by increased sales in the unregulated intrastate market. The result: less gas in the interstate market. There was nothing illegal about these actions (unlike the black market that developed during World War II to evade price and rationing controls), but they certainly reduced the effectiveness of the programs.

Policies adopted at different times in response to different problems and pressures may conflict with one another. Thus, while some units within the Department of Agriculture in the 1960s and 1970s were trying to control farm production, other units, through research and conservation programs, were working to expand production. In the same vein, the government has acted to discourage smoking at the same time that it has supported prices for tobacco farmers. And fiscal and monetary policies have sometimes been used in contradictory fashion to control inflation or recession, as was seen in chapter 2.

Public problems are often very complex, the product of a number of factors or conditions. This is the case with poverty. A policy that focuses on only one cause of poverty—say job training to eliminate the lack of job skills—can have only limited impact on the overall problem. Moreover, we cannot be certain what causes a particular problem, such as inflation or juvenile delinquency; as a result, the policies formulated to deal with that problem are necessarily tentative, modest, or restricted in scope and strength. They may even miss the target completely.

The solutions for some problems may involve greater costs than society, or important segments thereof, finds acceptable. It is estimated, for example, that hundreds of billions of dollars would be required to totally eliminate environmental pollution. Moreover, extensive pollution control activity may substantially increase energy usage at a time when there is growing concern about scarce energy resources. Improved mass transit systems would reduce traffic congestion in many metropolitan areas, but the great cost involved is a barrier to their installation. Consequently, we institute minor palliatives—one-way streets, bus lanes on freeways, and car-pooling plans—and traffic congestion continues.

Some problems simply are not totally soluble. Many jobs will continue to be dull, tedious, or intellectually unsatisfying unless, as a society, we can eliminate such tasks as garbage collection, housework, retailing, and meat packing, which seems unlikely. No matter what we do, some children are probably not going to learn much in school. And crime has been with us since Cain slew Abel.

Finally, the adoption of policies marks the end of just one phase of the policy process. Many groups and individuals do their level best to ensure that a statute enacted by Congress has the least possible impact. Judicial challenges, efforts to limit administration, procrastination, noncompliance, attempts to secure amendments or repeal, all limit the impact of policy. We saw this kind of massive resistance to school desegregation in the South after 1954. We saw it, too, in the railroad industry's attack on the Interstate Commerce Act of 1887, in the courts and elsewhere, which greatly weakened that act by the end of the century.[9]

The foregoing discussion should not be taken as a counsel of despair, or as an argument that policy is mostly ineffective. As policy analysts, we need to be concerned about factors that can limit the impact of policy, along with other facets of the policy process. As policy advocates, that knowledge can make our advocacy more realistic and more successful.

THE REAGAN REVOLUTION

In his first year in office President Ronald Reagan initiated a number of major changes in American public policy:

- The largest tax cut in U.S. history
- A significant increase in national defense spending
- The consolidation of many categorical grant-in-aid programs into a few block grants

- A reduction in the growth of domestic program spending
- A major campaign to reduce government regulation of the economy

Initially, there was speculation that the 1980 election might have been a realigning election. Certainly, the election and the policy shifts that followed met many of the criteria for realigning elections. The state of the economy in 1980 raised critical questions that the two major presidential candidates (Reagan and Carter) answered in markedly different ways. In the election, the Republicans won control of the Senate for the first time since 1952 and gained thirty-three seats in the House of Representatives. In 1981, the Republicans in Congress acted as though the 1980 election had been, in fact, a mandate for significant policy changes. They voted unanimously in support of the administration's major policy initiatives.

In 1982, however, the Reagan administration began to encounter difficulties. A budget deficit of over $100 billion in fiscal year 1982 and a predicted deficit of twice that amount in 1983 worked against the administration. So did the economic recession and the increase in unemployment. The upsurge in business activity predicted by administration economists failed to materialize until the spring of 1983. High interest rates, low federal revenues, and general apprehension about the state of the economy kept the economy slack, even though there was a significant decline in inflation. Many Republicans in Congress began to disassociate themselves from Reaganomics, and opinion polls showed a decline in the president's popularity. The 1982 session of Congress was characterized more by legislative deadlock than by success for the administration.

In the 1982 congressional elections, the Republicans lost twenty-six seats in the House while breaking even in the Senate. The Democratic victory clearly demonstrated that the 1980 election was not a realigning election and that it would not lead to a major, *permanent* shift in public policy. Although the Republicans still controlled the Senate, in 1983 Reagan found it necessary to bargain and compromise, to settle for incremental changes in policy. The Reagan revolution, for the moment at least, was over.

NOTES

1. See Charles E. Lindblom, *The Intelligence of Democracy* (New York: Free Press, 1965).
2. The following discussion is based on Charles O. Jones, "Speculative Augmentation in Federal Air Pollution Policy-Making," *Journal of Politics* 36 (May 1974): 438–464.
3. Ibid., pp. 439–440.
4. Ibid., p. 453.
5. Benjamin Ginsberg, "Elections and Public Policy," *American Political Science Review* 70 (1976): 65.
6. The best interpretations of such crises can be found in V. O. Key, Jr., "A Theory of Critical Elections," *Journal of Politics* 17 (1955): 3–18; V. O. Key, Jr., "Secular Realignment and the Party System," *Journal of Politics* 21 (1959): 198–210; Walter D. Burnham, *Critical Elections and the Mainsprings of American Politics* (New York: Norton, 1970); and James R. Sundquist,

Dynamics of the Party System: Alignment and Realignment of Political Parties in the United States (Washington, D.C.: Brookings Institution, 1972).

7. Kenneth Meier and Kenneth Kraemer, "The Effects of Realigning Elections on Bureaucratic Politics" (Unpublished paper, Rice University, 1976).

8. This discussion draws on James E. Anderson, *Public Policy-Making,* 2nd ed. (New York: Holt, Rinehart and Winston, 1979), pp. 171–173.

9. Ari Hoogenboom and Olive Hoogenboom, *A History of the ICC* (New York: Norton, 1976), chap. 1.

INDEX

CREDITS

p.   1, UPI
p.   26, UPI
p.   69, © Mark Godfrey, Archive Pictures, Inc.
p. 107, Peter Tartsanyi, EKM-Nepenthe
p. 135, © Mimi Forsyth, Monkmeyer Press Photo Service
p. 175, © Hays, Monkmeyer Press Photo Service
p. 201, © Elihu Blotnick, Omni Photo Communications, Inc.
p. 225, Martin A. Levick, Black Star
p. 255, Hugh Rogers, Monkmeyer Press Photo Service
p. 303, Bob Eckert, EKM-Nepenthe
p. 341, Coerett Johnson, PHOTRI
p. 371, PHOTRI
p. 401, Coerett Johnson, PHOTRI